FLORIDA GULF COAST

JOSHUA LAWRENCE KINSER

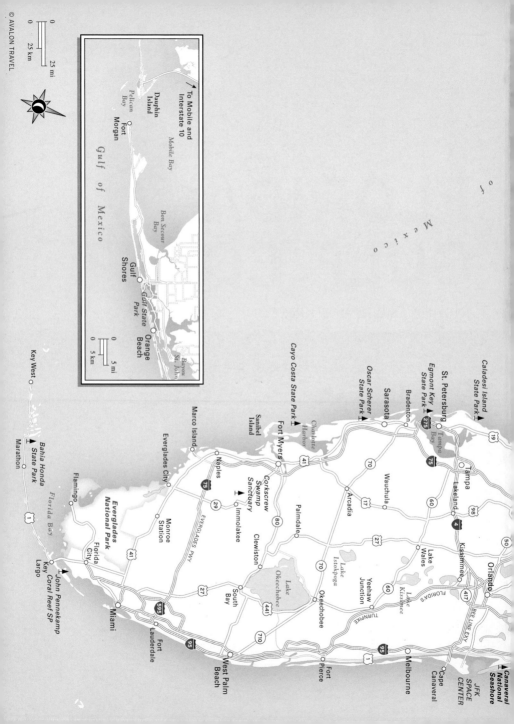

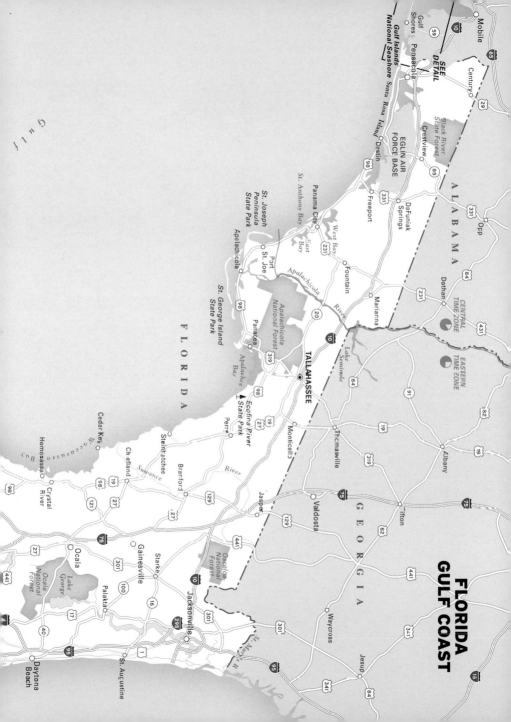

FLORIDA GULF COAST

Contents

DISCOVER

the Florida Gulf Coast

Crystal quartz beaches fade into the emerald waters of the Gulf of Mexico, luring millions each year to Florida's Gulf Coast. There isn't anywhere else in Florida where the name "sunshine state" feels truer than on the Gulf Coast, where sandals, shorts, and sunglasses are the local attire.

Beyond the sandy beaches and tropical bungalows, cities like Tampa, Pensacola, Sarasota, and Naples provide all the excitement and amenities you could ask for—and they are about as similar to each other as the Westminster dog show and a rodeo. In Tampa you'll find a modern skyline of glass skyscrapers gleaming in the sun, while in Pensacola, Old-Florida charm and Southern hospitality still exist. And what would a trip on the Gulf Coast be if you didn't spend the day screaming down 100-foot drops on a Busch Gardens roller coaster?

Clockwise from top left: skimboarding on Holmes Beach; a dolphin at the Clearwater Marine Aquarium; Florida oranges; fishing nets; a palm tree; an egret on the beach.

But the best place to be on the Gulf Coast is out on the water. Sunbathe on Pensacola Beach with a piña colada in your hand. Body surf alongside a giant winged manta ray. Collect fresh scallops in the spring-fed waters of Apalachicola Bay. Explore the winding maze of mangrove islands in Everglades National Park. Sail a yacht through the canals of Tampa. Sit down to a dinner of fresh crab cakes, raw oysters, and a bowl of seafood gumbo.

Experience the life that so many have come to love, enjoy, and return to year after year: a life with sand between your toes and sunshine on your shoulders, in a state whose true borders extend deep into the dark blue waters of the Gulf.

Clockwise from top left: Big Cypress National Preserve in the Everglades; sunset on Sanibel Island; an egret in the Everglades; canoes ready for launch near Pensacola.

Planning Your Trip

Where to Go

Naples, the Everglades, and the Paradise Coast

At the southwestern tip of Florida's Gulf Coast, **Naples** is full of upscale resorts, high-end restaurants, cultural amenities, and more **golf courses** per capita than anywhere else on the Gulf Coast. **Marco Island,** just south, similarly boasts resort hotels and condos rising up on a long crescent of **white-sand beach.** **Everglades City** provides a paddler's and outdoors enthusiast's paradise at one end of the Everglades backcountry, the famous **Wilderness Waterway** route linking Everglades City to Flamingo.

Fort Myers, Sanibel, and Captiva

Fort Myers is the largest and oldest city in southwest Florida, set on the banks of the Caloosahatchee River. **Sanibel Island** is a casual, low-rise beach town with just enough to do (visit the **J. N. "Ding" Darling National Wildlife Refuge** and the **Bailey-Matthews Shell Museum**) to keep the whole family entertained. There's less to do on neighboring **Captiva Island,** and that's just the way residents and visitors like it. The superlatives heaped upon it include "exclusive," "romantic," and "tranquil."

Sarasota County

Sarasota has been recognized as **Florida's cultural capital,** home to a professional symphony, ballet, and opera. There are theaters, art galleries, the **John and Mable Ringling Museum of Art,** and the **Van Wezel Performing Arts Hall.** A chain of narrow barrier islands sits offshore to the west. Lido and St. Armands Keys are fairly urban extensions of downtown Sarasota, connected by a causeway. **Longboat Key** to the north and **Siesta Key** to the south are destinations in their own right, the former lined with upscale resort hotels and condominiums, the latter a more casual and fun, low-rise beach getaway.

Tampa

Busch Gardens, Ybor City, the Florida Aquarium, Tampa Bay Buccaneers, Tampa Bay Rays, and Tampa Bay Lightning—notice I didn't mention the beach? Tampa fronts **Tampa Bay,** not the Gulf of Mexico. A huge **port city**—the largest pleasure and industrial port in the Southeast—it doesn't have any beaches to speak of. Before you fret, though, it's an excellent **family vacation destination.** There's a perfect convergence of warm weather, affordable accommodations, professional sports, kids' attractions, and upscale shopping that seems to suit every taste.

St. Petersburg and Pinellas County

Easygoing and relaxed, the city of **St. Petersburg** exerts its pull with a vibrant downtown of pastel art deco buildings and cultural attractions like the **Salvador Dalí Museum,** the symphony at Ruth Eckerd Hall, and theater at American Stage. But on the Gulf side of the peninsula, **Clearwater Beach** and **St. Pete Beach** are welcoming shores of Gulf water lapping at white sand, backed by restaurants, souvenir shops, and boogie-board-and-bikini stores. Caladesi Island, Honeymoon Island, and Fort De Soto Park are all favored Pinellas beaches.

The Nature Coast

The Nature Coast includes Homosassa and Crystal River in the south, both famous for their **tarpon fishing** and **manatee habitat.** South of that, and worth a day's excursion, is **Weeki Wachee Springs** with its historic mermaid show and incredible high-magnitude spring.

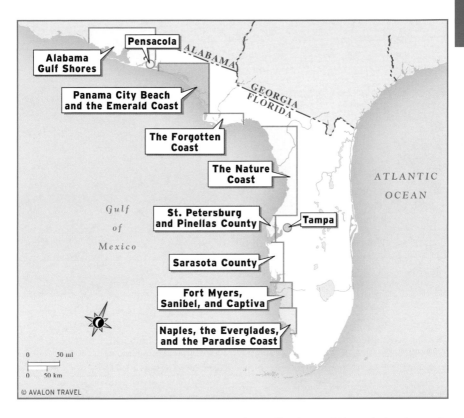

ATLANTIC
OCEAN

Gulf
of
Mexico

Pensacola
Alabama
Gulf Shores
ALABAMA
GEORGIA
FLORIDA

Panama City Beach
and the Emerald Coast

The Forgotten
Coast

The Nature
Coast

St. Petersburg
and Pinellas County
Tampa

Sarasota County

Fort Myers,
Sanibel, and Captiva

Naples, the Everglades,
and the Paradise Coast

0   50 mi
0   50 km

© AVALON TRAVEL

To the north, the small fishing communities of Cedar Key and Steinhatchee require a little extra effort to get to, but the payoff is big. Each is like a look back into Florida's past, populated by anglers, some great bars, relaxed motels, and plenty of guides eager to take you out into the beauty of the Nature Coast.

The Forgotten Coast

With 200 historic homes and buildings on the National Register, and a downtown of repurposed 1850s brick cotton warehouses, Apalachicola has antebellum charm to burn. The **Apalachicola National Estuarine Research Reserve,** historic **Grady Market,** and the very "cool" **John Gorrie State Museum,** which celebrates the inventor of modern refrigeration—there's enough here to occupy visitors for at least a couple of days.

Top it off with incredible nearby beaches on **St. George Island** and **St. Joseph Peninsula** or a view into Franklin County's **oystering business** in Eastpoint.

Panama City Beach and the Emerald Coast

The Emerald Coast—Fort Walton Beach and Destin, Beaches of South Walton, Panama City Beach—got its name from the deep green color of its water that laps against its glinting white-sand beaches. But this is basically all that these coastal communities have in common. Its easternmost section, **Panama City Beach,** is a densely populated beachside playground, especially favored by college kids on spring break. Farther west, the **Beaches of South Walton** feature quieter, more luxurious beachside enjoyments. And still farther

Panama City Beach

west, fishing is what put **Destin** on the map, and that continues today with anglers arriving from all over the planet to get a crack at the local marlin, sailfish, and spearfish.

Pensacola

If you're looking for a relaxed, fun, and casual place to explore beautiful beaches where you will be welcomed with Southern hospitality, then Pensacola is the place to go. Its long stretches of white beaches are a popular summer destination for Floridians and tourists from across the country. It's known as the **City of Five Flags,** having been occupied at different times by Spain, France, England, the Confederacy, and the United States; and as the Cradle of Naval Aviation, being home to the **Naval Air Station Pensacola;** or

even "America's first European settlement" (the Spanish attempted to colonize Pensacola in 1559).

Alabama Gulf Shores

Considered a natural extension of the Florida Gulf Coast, the **Orange Beach** and **Gulf Shores** coastline offers 32 miles of sugar-white beaches pretty enough to rival the more popular vacation destinations of Pensacola and Destin to the east. Known as **"Pleasure Island,"** this stretch of Alabama coastline is booming with newly developed vacation properties and classic Gulf Coast hangouts that are remarkably family-friendly. For something more low-key, take the ferry across Mobile Bay to **Dauphin Island** and explore this easygoing Gulf Coast community teeming with history and Southern charm.

When to Go

Florida is a year-round destination, but each broad geographical area along the Gulf Coast has its own peak season, off-season, and in-the-know in-between times.

Southwest Florida sees a huge influx of "snowbirds" in the **winter months.** These northerners come after Thanksgiving and stay just through Easter, generally speaking, bumping up the populations in Naples and Fort Myers up through Sarasota and Bradenton. The timing isn't arbitrary—**March and April** along much of the Gulf Coast are magical: temperatures in the high 70s, a little breeze, low humidity, little rain, and Gulf water just warm enough for swimming. That said, if you visit before the snowbirds arrive in the fall or after they depart in the spring, you'll find plenty of accommodations, unoccupied tables in restaurants, and room to roam the beaches.

The **Central West** region encompasses the southern portion of Florida's Nature Coast, as well as the popular vacation destinations of Tampa, St. Petersburg, and Clearwater. Again, **Thanksgiving to Easter** is the peak visitor time, but it's less clear-cut here. A huge family draw, partly because of its proximity to Orlando and Walt Disney World, the area is at its busiest during school vacations, including the hot, steamy summer one.

On the **Panhandle,** which has colder winters and more moderate summers than elsewhere on the Gulf Coast, it's busiest during the **summer.** Many of the summer-season tourists here are Florida residents from elsewhere hoping to improve upon the high temperatures and humidity of their hometowns.

For college kids, the time to visit the Gulf Coast, and specifically Panama City Beach, is **spring break,** which falls during the months of March and April.

The Best of the Florida Gulf Coast

The entire length of the Florida Gulf Coast covered in this guide is just under 700 miles long. If you were to drive from Pensacola to Everglades City and never stopped for a break, you could go the length in just under 11 hours. Divided between ten days, you can explore the entire Gulf Coast and hit many of the best attractions with about three hours of driving a day (it's quite a bit of time on the road, but it's possible). It's also possible to pick any of the three regions mentioned for a shorter trip.

Mid Coast

DAY 1

If you're flying into **Tampa,** spend the day riding roller coasters, exploring re-created African savannahs, and splashing down log flume rides at **Busch Gardens.** Cross the bridge to **St. Pete** for an evening baseball game with the **Tampa Bay Rays** at **Tropicana Field,** with the required

dinner of ballpark hot dogs and cold beers. For something a little more fancy, stay in Tampa and have a nice seafood dinner at an outdoor fireside table at **Oystercatchers** alongside Tampa Bay at the Grand Hyatt, or head to **Shula's Steak House** at the InterContinental if you want a sizzling-good steak. Finish off the evening with wine and dessert at **Armani's** rooftop bar, also in the Hyatt, with the best views of Tampa all lit up at night. Spend the night in Tampa at the **InterContinental Tampa** downtown or the **Grand Hyatt Tampa Bay.**

DAY 2

Get on I-75 and take the hour-long drive south to **Sarasota.** Spend the morning shopping at the luxurious **St. Armands Circle** before popping over to **Marie Selby Botanical Gardens** for a short tour through their fabulous orchid exhibit and gardens. Take the John Ringling Causeway,

downtown Sarasota

Highway 789, over Sarasota Bay. Pass through Longboat Key, stopping for a walk on **Coquina Beach.** Continue on Highway 789 until you arrive on **Anna Maria Island.** Enjoy dinner at the **Beach Bistro,** one of Florida's most award-winning restaurants. Make sure to have the lobster tail and seafood bouillabaisse and then the decadent chocolate truffle for dessert. Spend the night on Holmes Beach at the **Mainsail Beach Inn** and enjoy the rest of the evening relaxing on Holmes Beach or by the inn's pool and hot tub surrounded by palm trees.

South Coast

DAY 3

Drive south on I-75 for a little more than an hour to **Fort Myers.** Eat breakfast at **First Watch Restaurant** downtown, and then spend the morning walking the grounds and exploring the museums at the **Edison Estate.** Drive out to the barrier islands of **Sanibel and Captiva** and spend the rest of the day enjoying the beautiful beaches and driving down the mansion-lined roads. Have lunch at the **Island Cow** and make sure to be on the beach at the **Mucky Duck** on

Captiva to watch the sunset and have dinner. Spend the night on Captiva at the **South Seas Island Resort** or at **'Tween Waters Inn Beach Resort.**

DAY 4

Drive south on I-75 for two hours to **Naples Municipal Beach and Fishing Pier** and spend a few hours in the sun. Walk down Second Street to Fifth Avenue and admire the spectacular homes along the stroll that leads to one of the Gulf Coast's most upscale shopping districts. Spend the afternoon exploring the shops, cafés, and gelato along **5th Avenue South.** Have dinner at **Trulucks** for steak and seafood within walking distance of the Inn on Fifth, or at **Pazzo Cucina Italiana** on Fifth Avenue for Italian fare in a more intimate setting. If posh Naples isn't really your style, drive farther down to **Everglades City** and enjoy the eco-centric atmosphere at the **Ivey House Inn Bed and Breakfast.** Spend the night in Naples at **The Inn on Fifth** for some truly fancy accommodations or the **Lemon Tree Inn** for a more laid-back experience.

Gulf Islands National Seashore

DAY 5

Enjoy the scenic drive through **The Everglades** on your way to **Chokoloskee Island** for breakfast on the delightful back porch of the **Havana Cafe.** Get Cubano sandwiches and fresh fruit to go before taking an airboat ride with **Wooten's** through the swamps for a high-adrenaline adventure. Spend the day spotting wildlife and spectacular scenery as you drive down Turner River Road in **Big Cypress National Preserve.** It's a place where you can venture into the true heart of Florida's wild lands yet remain in the safety of your own car. Take a sunset paddle in the **Ten Thousand Islands** of **Everglades National Park** and then have dinner at the **Oyster House Restaurant.** Spend the night in **Everglades City** at the **Ivey House Bed and Breakfast** and relax for the the evening by their impressive indoor pool. Enjoy their first-class breakfast in the morning.

North Coast

DAY 6

Drive north on I-75 for three hours to **Crystal River** and spend a few hours swimming and snorkeling with the manatees. Have lunch at the **Plantation on Crystal River** and then take the very scenic hour-long drive to **Cedar Key.** Spend the evening exploring **Dock Street** and eating fresh seafood at the **Island Hotel and Restaurant.** Stay the night at the charming **Cedar Key Bed and Breakfast.**

DAY 7

Continue west on U.S. 98 for about three hours and pass through the town of **Carrabelle,** and the oystering town of **Eastpoint.** Continue west to **Apalachicola** and try a dozen oysters on the half shell. Then take the historic home walk around downtown Apalachicola for a tour of antebellum, Greek Revival, and Victorian homes on wide, tree-lined streets. Head over the St. George Island Bridge to **St. George Island.** Word of its first-class fishing and fabulous beaches has not been disseminated widely, which means much of the year you'll be walking alone in the 1,900-acre

beachfront **St. George Island State Park.** Spend the night renting a small cottage on St. George Island or camping at St. George Island State Park.

DAY 8

Stay on U.S. 98 and follow the coastline for three hours west to Highway 30A and take the short and scenic drive past the picturesque towns of **Santa Rosa Beach, Seaside, Blue Mountain Beach,** and **WaterColor.** Explore the quaint town squares and superb beaches tucked away along the Emerald Coast. Have a drink or a small plate at the rooftop bar at **Bud and Alley's Restaurant** in Seaside. Spend the day at the public beach in Seaside and then drive to **Destin** for a dinner of peel-and-eat shrimp and fresh oysters at **AJ's Seafood and Oyster Bar.** Sit on the back deck, watch the sunset, and enjoy the excellent view of Choctawhatchee Bay, East Pass, and the Gulf of Mexico. Spend the night at the phenomenal **Henderson Park Inn Bed & Breakfast** in Destin, and don't miss their delectable complimentary breakfast in the morning.

DAY 9

Drive west for an hour on U.S. 98 and cross the Beach Causeway Bridge to **Navarre.** Follow Gulf Boulevard west to the pristine stretch of beach at **Gulf Islands National Seashore,** between Pensacola and Navarre Beach. Stop at one of the public beach accesses along the way and spend a few hours hiking through the impressive dunes on the **Florida Trail.** Grab a grouper sandwich for lunch at **Peg Leg Pete's** in Pensacola Beach, and then cross the Pensacola Bay Bridge to historic downtown **Pensacola,** the westernmost city on the Florida Gulf Coast. Tour the historic homes surrounding **Seville Square,** and then watch the sun go down and have dinner at the back deck of **The Fish House** on Pensacola Bay. Finish the night with cocktails at historical **Seville Quarter** in downtown Pensacola. Spend the night at the **Margaritaville Beach Hotel** on Pensacola Beach so you can watch the

From sea bass to billfish, stone crabs to blue crabs, and redfish to red snapper, there are many popular species of fish to hook in the Gulf and surrounding waters. You can fish for some species year-round in Florida, but most fish generally run during specific months, and the peak fishing season shifts out of the summer months and into the spring, fall, and winter the farther south you go. In north Florida from Pensacola to Cedar Key, the best season for fishing runs April-October. Once you reach the Everglades, the peak season runs October-March.

PENSACOLA

Fish offshore for snapper, grouper, triggerfish, and amberjack or head into deeper waters in search of blue marlin, white marlin, tuna, wahoo, and mahimahi. For exceptional **pier fishing,** try your luck at the **Pensacola Beach Fishing Pier.**

DESTIN

Offshore **deep-sea fishing** dominates the Destin area. Known as the **"World's Luckiest Fishing Village,"** Destin is lucky indeed— its position on the Gulf Coast places it closest to the **100-Fathom Curve,** where the sea shelf abruptly drops and provides habitat for deep-sea fish species. Red snapper, grouper, amberjack, king mackerel, sailfish, and blue marlin are the favorite target species from Destin.

APALACHICOLA

The **oyster** is king in the Apalachicola area. A combination of nutrient-rich and spring-fed waters has made Apalachicola Florida's capital for harvesting oysters. Charter services, primarily embarking from downtown Apalachicola, offer oyster harvesting trips as well as exceptional **flats fishing** in Apalachicola Bay and **offshore fishing** in the Gulf of Mexico. Speckled trout, flounder, tarpon, and redfish are popular catches in the flats and bays. Cobia, mahimahi, and snapper are easy to hook in the Gulf of Mexico, and **scallops** are harvested around Apalachicola July-September.

CEDAR KEY

Redfish and **speckled trout** are abundant in the shallow waters surrounding **Cedar Key.** The island-dotted bay is not very well marked and can

red snapper on ice

be hard to navigate without a guide, but the fishing in this area is legendary. **Cobia, mackerel, grouper,** and **snapper** are the usual suspects when fishing offshore in the Gulf.

SARASOTA

There's not much need to go offshore when the inshore fishing for **snook,** redfish, trout, pompano, and bluefish around **Siesta Key, Longboat Key,** and **Sarasota** is so good. The narrow and winding mangrove channels in this area give inshore **fly-fishing** and light-tackle trips a wilderness backcountry feel. Offshore trips mostly target grouper, amberjack, and snapper.

THE EVERGLADES

Fishing the sheltered waters and mangrove islands throughout **Everglades National Park** and surrounding **Everglades City** is one of the most rewarding and unique fishing experiences to be had in the entire state of Florida. Snook, redfish, trout, and tarpon are popular targets in the Everglades, and Everglades City is regarded as the capital for harvesting **stone crabs.** The season for collecting the juicy clawed crabs runs October-May.

sunrise from your balcony overlooking the Gulf of Mexico.

DAY 10

If you're flying back home from Tampa, the drive back will take you about seven hours. Take I-110 North from Pensacola for 5.6 miles, and then take exit 6 to merge onto I-10 East toward Tallahassee. Follow I-10 East for 283 miles to exit 296A, and merge onto I-75 South. Follow I-75 South toward Tampa and follow for 161.4 miles. Merge onto I-275 South and follow for 21.1 miles, and then take exit 39 onto FL-589 to **Tampa International Airport.**

Best Beaches

Some people say "You see one beach, you've seen 'em all." Well, not here—most Gulf Coast beaches are entirely unique. There is a diverse amount of sand types, sealife, and natural settings and an equally wide range of waterside activity. You'll also find an extremely large number of barrier islands off the coast of the mainland. Many times these barrier islands are very thin, and in a few minutes time you can walk from the beaches of the Gulf Coast to the beaches on the bayside, two very different and equally interesting and beautiful environments. Here's a list of the Florida Gulf Coast's most "sandsational" top picks.

Naples, the Everglades, and the Paradise Coast

- **Naples Municipal Beach and Fishing Pier:** Take a break from the shopping on Fifth Avenue and walk a few blocks toward the sound of waves to find yourself sitting on one of the most beautiful beaches on the Florida Gulf Coast. Nestled amid an upscale neighborhood, this beach and pier is known for its superb people-watching, excellent swimming, and close proximity to some of the best fine dining and fancy boutique shops in the city (page 30).

Venice Beach

Fort Myers, Sanibel, and Captiva

- **Fort Myers Beach:** Head to Bowditch Point Regional Park on the northern tip of Estero Island and enjoy the excellent beaches that border both the Gulf and Hurricane Bay (page 71).

- **Lovers Key State Park:** This very secluded beach park is spread out among four stunning barrier islands. The state park's pet-friendly policy brings beach-loving pet owners to the 2.5 miles of shore (page 72).

- **Captiva Beach:** Hands down the best beach for sunsets on the Gulf Coast. Search for shells or just enjoy the rolling dunes and clear water of the Gulf that is perfect for swimming (page 95).

Sarasota County

- **Turtle Beach:** Tucked among villas and a residential district, this family-oriented beach has excellent picnic facilities and is much less crowded than the more popular Siesta Key Beach to the north on the island, yet it still

has that special sugar-white sand that makes this barrier island a big draw for beach hunters (page 139).

- **Siesta Key Beach:** This beach is always drawing praise for its superiorly white sand. It gets crowded in the summer, but the exceptional size of this beach leaves sun seekers with plenty of spots to spike a shade-supplying umbrella or spread out a supersize beach towel (page 137).

- **Venice Beach:** This beach is famously regarded as the place to go to hunt for fossilized sharks' teeth. The super-convenient location close to the heart of Venice makes this beach just a bike ride from most of the popular inns and villas. A great beach for families, it has nice picnic pavilions and shower facilities (page 139).

St. Petersburg and Pinellas County

- **Clearwater Beach:** Go to this urban beach surrounded by seaside hangouts and hotels during the day to find the epicenter of oceanfront activity around Tampa. Sunsets from the

Clearwater Beach

It's an exciting time for birders in Florida. The **Great Florida Birding Trail** (GFBT, www.floridabirdingtrail.com) is a 2,000-mile trail through the state, its numerous sites selected for their excellent bird-watching or bird-education opportunities. The trail is split into four sections—the east, the west, the Panhandle, and South Florida—and trail maps can be downloaded from the GFBT website. Even if you focus your energies on the western or the Panhandle sections of the trail, there's too much area to cover in a single trip. Pick a smaller section of either one, or play it fast and loose and hit a few spots in each, like these.

LOWER SUWANNEE NATIONAL WILDLIFE REFUGE

The Lower Suwannee National Wildlife Refuge extends north and south along the Gulf Coast from the Nature Coast town of Suwannee and is one of the largest undeveloped river delta-estuarine systems in the United States. The refuge headquarters is on Highway 347, 16 miles west of U.S. 19, with a nearby river trail and boardwalk from which to see migratory songbirds. Citrus County is home to 250 bird species, with red-cockaded woodpeckers, Bachman's sparrows, American white pelicans, and Florida scrub jays among the more rare. The county has its own birding website at www.citrus-birdingtrail.com.

CEDAR KEY SCRUB STATE RESERVE

You can see a more dense concentration of Florida scrub jays at Cedar Key Scrub State Reserve, which protects one of the fastest-disappearing habitats in Florida. The park has 12 miles of marked walking trails. Also in Cedar Key, the **Cedar Keys National Wildlife Refuge** is accessible only by boat but is worth the effort—you're likely to see egrets, white ibis, cormorants, herons, pelicans, and anhingas.

SANIBEL ISLAND

Once on this island in Lee County, you can do a little

egrets in the Everglades

birding warm-up, looking for some of the many resident bird species. You'll find rare white pelicans hanging out in Pine Island Sound and ospreys and eagles nesting on telephone poles above the bike paths and along Sanibel-Captiva Road. The lighthouse area of Sanibel is a good place to see birds, as are the mangrove islands off Pine Island Sound, as is Tarpon Bay.

You're going to hit paydirt at **J. N. "Ding" Darling National Wildlife Refuge,** which takes up half of Sanibel Island. It's serious birder territory—everyone is equipped with high-powered binoculars and huge camera lenses. There's a naturalist-led tram ride on which you're bound to see rare species, colorful species, and important life-list species. There are more than 238 species in the refuge, among them tricolored and little blue herons, black-crowned night herons, ibis, wood storks, peregrine falcons, roseate spoonbills, and anhingas. The best time to go is early morning, about an hour before or after low tide.

beach pier are phenomenal, and by night the beach transforms into a fun spot with a nice mix of family fun and beach bar nightlife (page 189).

- **Fort De Soto Park:** Take a break from the city and explore the seven miles of pristine, preserved beaches at this beautiful park. You can also camp, hike, fish, launch a boat, and explore the historic fort on the southwest tip if you get tired of lounging and swimming (page 189).

The Forgotten Coast

- **St. Joseph Peninsula State Park:** Do you love long, quiet walks on the beach? White sand and exceptionally tall sand dunes stretch down this preserved peninsula for more than seven miles. Combine that with one of the best oceanfront campgrounds in the state of Florida and you've found a special slice of paradise. If you only go to one beach in Florida, go here (page 252).

The Emerald Coast

- **Panama City Beach:** Known as the headquarters for spring break mania, this town also has pretty beaches if you can look past the short-sighted development. The oceanfront has the same wonderfully white sand as the more upscale destinations like Destin to the west, and the rock-bottom hotel and motel prices draw a large portion of tourists each year. It's the place to party, with more beach bars, dance clubs, and all-day-breakfast diners than anywhere else on the Gulf Coast (page 290).

- **Grayton Beach State Park:** It's a favorite beach for those visiting the idyllic, affluent beach communities like Seaside and

WaterColor found along Highway 30A. The tranquil vibe of this preserved beach makes it a perfect spot to camp or find yourself in beautiful beach-bliss (page 315).

Pensacola

- **Pensacola Beach and Fishing Pier:** Just follow the three-mile bridge to the iconic beach-ball water tower and you'll find yourself at the center of Pensacola's beach activity. Surrounded by beach bars and restaurants, the beach and fishing pier is a favorite among surfers, sun seekers, and swimmers (page 329).

- **Gulf Islands National Seashore:** This preserved beach is managed by the National Park Service and a wonderful choice for beach lovers looking to shore fish, swim, or just lounge on the beach in an undeveloped setting away from all the hubbub found on Pensacola Beach. Hikers can also explore a section of the Florida Trail that traverses through the large, rolling dunes on the sound side of the park (page 330).

Alabama Gulf Shores

- **Gulf Shores Public Beach:** Surrounded by beach hangouts, restaurants, and beach shops, this beautiful beach with excellent picnic pavilions is popular among tourists and young folks looking for a beach party (page 362).

- **Bon Secour National Wildlife Refuge:** Whether you drive or hike in to the preserved beaches at the refuge, you'll find miles of secluded rolling dunes and white-sand beaches. Enjoy hiking the inland trails around Little Lagoon for some excellent fishing and birdwatching in this beautiful sanctuary for wildlife (page 365).

Coastal Camping

Florida has some of the best campgrounds in the country, and a few of them are right on the Gulf. So whether you're a tent-staking, fire-making, s'mores-eating, backcountry-camping purist or a modern-day road warrior coasting in a 40-foot RV with a hot tub and gourmet kitchen, these campgrounds will accommodate and appease you with their range of amenities, natural beauty, and proximity to some of the best beaches on the Gulf Coast.

Grayton Beach State Park

This beautiful campground puts you right in the heart of the incredible beaches of Walton County. You won't have to rough it out here, though, because the idyllic New Urbanist villages of **Seaside** and **WaterColor** are right down the road. After spending the day **sunbathing and relaxing** on the perfect, bright white beaches of the state park, you can meander over to Seaside for an escape to a casual pedestrian wonderland of upscale seafood restaurants, high-fashion shopping, and a little bit

of coastal nightlife fun. If you're not into including all that comfort and city life in your camping trip, the park has miles of **hiking trails** and **beaches** to explore. The campground has 34 sites that can accommodate tents or RVs.

St. Joseph Peninsula State Park

This is one of my favorite parks in the state. The two campgrounds at the park are located right on the Gulf. The extensive **boardwalk** that connects the two campgrounds gives you an opportunity to explore all of the ecosystems represented in the park, and the **miles of beach** that stretch to the tip of the peninsula can keep you intrigued for days. The park has some of the largest **sand dunes** anywhere on the Gulf Coast, and the **fishing, crabbing,** and **scalloping** in Apalachicola Bay are out of this world. The park has backcountry camping throughout the peninsula and 119 campsites. I recommend camping in the **Shady Pine Campground,** which offers private campsites surrounded by stands of pine

camping at Fort De Soto Park

trees and separated by strips of thick shrubs and palmetto ferns.

Turtle Beach Campground

The golden rule of real estate is location, location, location, and the same should be said for campgrounds on the Gulf Coast. And for location, Turtle Beach Campground has all the competition beat. It is right on the Gulf in incredibly beautiful **Siesta Key**. What more could you ask for? The campground may be small, but the 40 campsites are **well designed** with fences providing a bit of privacy and noise reduction between the sites. About a block away is the **public beach** access point, and the campground is a short drive to the city center, with plenty of fun restaurants, bars, and shops to keep you entertained. The park even has Wi-Fi for all the sites.

Fort De Soto Park

As you get past Tampa, finding a decent place to camp becomes increasingly difficult. There are quite a few places you can get to by ferry or boat, but this isn't going to help RV campers very much. One exceptional anomaly is Fort De Soto Park, run by Pinellas County. Fort De Soto Park has a whopping 236 campsites, with 86 reserved for tent, van, or pop-up campers only. The park is over 1,136 acres and is made up of five interconnected islands. It has miles of **beautiful white-sand beaches** and **hiking trails,** a sprawling fort area to explore, 13 artificial reefs to dive and snorkel, and a large network of **paddling trails.** The park is just off the coast of **St. Petersburg,** if you find yourself in need of an escape to the city, and just south of all the urban beach excitement of **St. Pete Beach.**

Everglades National Park

The Everglades is the granddaddy of camping on the Gulf Coast. The **Flamingo Campground** is a little isolated from anything else on the coast, being 38 miles from the entrance to the park in Everglades City, but it is the best choice for RV and tent camping in the area. It gives you access to the surrounding national park from its 234 drive-in sites and 64 walk-in sites. The campground is open all year, but I recommend visiting between October and March. The other parts of the year are too hot and buggy. Park ranger-guided **canoe and kayak tours** launch from the campground, which is equipped with showers and restrooms, a marina store and gas station, bike rentals, and a visitors center with a museum.

Kid Stuff

A family vacation on the Gulf Coast should start in Tampa—first, because it boasts a big, easy airport with lots of flights; second, because it's only an hour away from Walt Disney World and all the other excitement in Orlando; and third, because it's where Busch Gardens is!

Day 1

Tampa really has family fun dialed. First stop must be a day at **Busch Gardens** for a ride on the new Cheetah Hunt, or the Montu, the SheiKra, the Kumba, the Python, and the tooth-rattling Gwazi, in descending order of priority. It's a park for all ages, with a mix of big, scary coasters and cool animal attractions.

Day 2

Right across the street from Busch Gardens is Tampa's **Museum of Science & Industry** **(MOSI)**, probably the best science museum on the Gulf Coast. It's nearly impossible to see this the same day as Busch Gardens, so visit MOSI on your second day, and spend the other half of the day wandering at either the **Florida Aquarium** (with a stop-off for lunch across the street at the portside dining/entertainment complex of **Channelside Bay Plaza**) or the **Lowry Park Zoo.** Both of these attractions are midsize, thus very walkable and requiring less than four hours to fully explore. Before you get out of Tampa, take one of the aquarium's **Wild Dolphin Cruise** out

West Indian manatee

into the bay to eagle-eye dolphins, manatees, and migratory birds.

Day 3

Start heading north along the coast on U.S. 19. Stop and visit the mermaids at **Weeki Wachee Springs** (about an hour north of Tampa on U.S. 19). The show is brief, and afterward the family can cool off at the attached **Buccaneer Bay Waterpark,** fed by a natural spring. This is a warm-up for the manatees, about another 30 miles north on U.S. 19.

Day 4

You may need to stay overnight in **Homosassa** or **Crystal River** to get a jump on the day. From October 15 to March 31, you'll find hundreds of the endangered **West Indian manatee** swimming in the warm waters of Kings Bay in the Crystal River and the Blue Waters area of the Homosassa River. They are herbivores, huge and playful. **Manatee Tour & Dive** or **Bird's Underwater** will take whole families out for snorkel trips with the manatees. If you find yourself and your family along the Nature Coast when manatees aren't in season, there are still good reasons to get wet. From July 1 to September 10, **scalloping in Steinhatchee** is lots of fun.

Day 5 and Beyond

So far this family vacation has been action-packed. You'll need a couple of extra days to cool down—keep driving north up and around the Big Bend for 300 miles on U.S. 19/98. Head over the St. George Island Bridge for a few days of fishing, beachcombing, and relaxing on **St. George Island.** It's very family-focused, with comfortable beach houses (many with bunk-bed rooms and private pools), biking paths the length of the island, and a tremendous 1,900-acre state park that encompasses the whole eastern end of the island.

Naples, the Everglades, and the Paradise Coast

Look for ★ to find recommended
sights, activities, dining, and lodging.

Highlights

★ **Naples Municipal Beach and Fishing Pier:** This urban beach features a 1,000-foot fishing pier considered the heart of the city, flanked on either side by a wide swath of beach and the length of upscale houses known as Millionaires' Row (page 30).

★ **Corkscrew Swamp Sanctuary:** Head north out of Naples to see wood storks with faces only a mother could love and a strange plant called a resurrection fern that comes back from the botanically dead (page 34).

★ **The Baker Museum:** This museum featuring 15 galleries is itself a work of art, with spectacular chandeliers by acclaimed glass artist Dale Chihuly (page 38).

★ **Naples Zoo:** Kids will enjoy the gator-feeding show, the Panther Glade, the big cats show, and the boat ride out to see the antic monkeys on their little islands. Parents will appreciate the park's incredible native and exotic plants (page 40).

★ **3rd Street South:** Some of Florida's most upscale boutiques, antiques shops, and galleries line Naples's main drag. There's even a street concierge to help get you oriented (page 42).

★ **Tigertail Beach:** Against a backdrop of resort hotels, this beach draws a fun-seeking crowd. For some, fun is Jet Ski rentals and water sports; for others it's a cutthroat game of beach volleyball (page 49).

★ **Boat Tour to Calusa Shell Mounds:** Motor around tiny mangrove islands near Marco Island, stopping to search for remnants of this Native American culture (page 51).

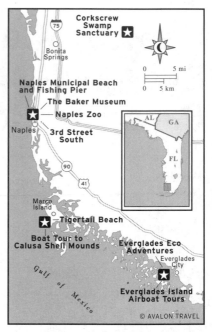

★ **Everglades Eco Adventures:** Take an adventurous canoe tour, gliding through mangrove tunnels and drifting by wading birds, rare orchids, and gators of all sizes (page 58).

★ **Everglades Island Airboat Tours:** Get out and explore the area's exotic "walking trees" by hopping aboard an airboat tour of the mangrove islands (page 58).

This breathtaking region is called the Paradise Coast, but one person's paradise is another person's episode of *Survivor.* And the three cities that make up the paradise in question couldn't be more different.

Naples satisfies more worldly tastes with upscale shopping, fine dining, and first-rate golf courses. A little farther south you find Marco Island, a relaxed barrier island that's a favorite beach vacation spot for families. Everglades City is the gateway to Everglades National Park and the surrounding wilderness areas.

Even after the Spanish had evicted the indigenous residents, the land lay virtually empty until the late 1800s when the Naples Town Improvement Company was formed, purchasing 3,712 acres between the Gulf of Mexico and what is now known as Naples Bay. The group had big plans. The name alone says quite a bit: These founders were modeling the new Naples on the cultured and thriving Italian seaport. They built a pier, blocked out plans for a city, built their own homes on the beach—and then the Naples Town Improvement Company ran out of money. The Napes Town Improvement Company was

sold at a public auction in 1890 to the only bidder, Walter Haldeman.

The city chugged on with minimal growth until rail service came to Naples in 1927 and the Tamiami Trail was completed the next year. New growth was quashed by the Great Depression, followed swiftly by World War II. Since then, Naples has experienced an enormous population boom, mostly among midwestern and northern retirees. Now it's got the look of many monied, sunny American cities (Santa Barbara, Palm Springs).

As for Marco Island and Everglades City, differences go deeper. Much of Marco Island has modest, ranch-style homes built a couple of decades ago. On the beach you'll find tall resort hotels and condos stretching for two miles along Collier Boulevard. Vacationers may never see much of the island, their eyes focused continuously on the gorgeous water of the Gulf and the maze of mangrove islands to the south.

Previous: Wooten's Everglades Airboat Tours; the pier in Naples. **Above:** an egret in the Everglades.

Everglades City and the little town to the south called Chokoloskee are the end of civilization before you run into Everglades National Park. Some of the mystery and wildness of that park has rubbed off on these little towns. Hang out at the Rod and Gun Club or paddle through the quiet tunnels of mangroves, and you'll feel like you've entered the Wild West—only with gators.

PLANNING YOUR TIME

How do you pack for this type of place? If you threw open the suitcase of someone about to travel the entire length of the Paradise Coast, you would know it right away from the sheer variety of clothes. There would be smart slacks, polo shirts, and dress shoes or little black dresses and heels for Naples; swimsuits and sandals for Marco Island; and an old pair of sneakers, durable zip-off outdoors pants, vented long-sleeve shirts, and bug spray for Everglades City and the surrounding wilderness. To travel down the Paradise Coast and comfortably enjoy it all, you'll need exceptionally diverse attire.

Where you should stay depends on what you're looking to do. Most of Naples's accommodations are considered upscale and expensive, and the ones that are not are generally overpriced for what you get compared to the surrounding areas, as are those on Marco Island. Regardless, most visitors choose to stay in the Naples area, the preferred fancy 5th Avenue where they are close to the upscale shopping, fine dining, and entertainment, and where the best beaches are within walking distance. Everglades City attracts more outdoors enthusiasts, and therefore most of the accommodations are simple, less expensive places. Family travelers are welcomed most on Marco Island, with many of the large hotels offering programs for kids.

Peak season in and around Naples is roughly December through March. Rates for hotels reflect this, and you may save a bundle visiting instead in the late spring or early fall (when the weather in Naples and on Marco Island is really nice). Everglades City, on the other hand, is best to visit November-February. During the hotter months in the Everglades, the heat, humidity, and mosquitoes keep most visitors away. There is plenty of tent and RV camping in and around the Everglades and Big Cypress National Preserve. Many of these campgrounds are fairly primitive, but several have electricity, running water, showers, and restrooms. Paddling and boating are popular in the Everglades area. If you rent a kayak or canoe, prepare to paddle against strong winds and dramatic tides. For something less strenuous, plant your umbrella at one of stunning beaches along the Paradise Coast. The best beaches are found around Naples.

If you plan to explore everything the Paradise Coast has to offer, you will definitely want a car, especially down in the Everglades where there is no real form of community transportation and the attractions and outdoor destinations that you may want to visit are often separated by long miles of backcountry roads. I-75 is the main artery into the region, with Davis Boulevard as the connector to Naples and U.S. 41 primarily servicing the coastline. Collier Boulevard gets you out to Marco Island while U.S. 41, the Tamiami Trail, leads down south to the Everglades. Highway 29 ventures to Everglades City, the Everglades National Park Gulf Coast Visitor Center, and Chokoloskee Island.

By air, the closest large airport is **Southwest Florida International Airport** (11000 Terminal Access Rd., 239/590-4800, www.flylcpa.com), 40 minutes to the north in Fort Myers. There is a little commuter airport in Naples, the **Naples Municipal Airport** (160 Aviation Dr., 239/643-0733, www.fly-naples.com).

Naples, the Everglades, and the Paradise Coast

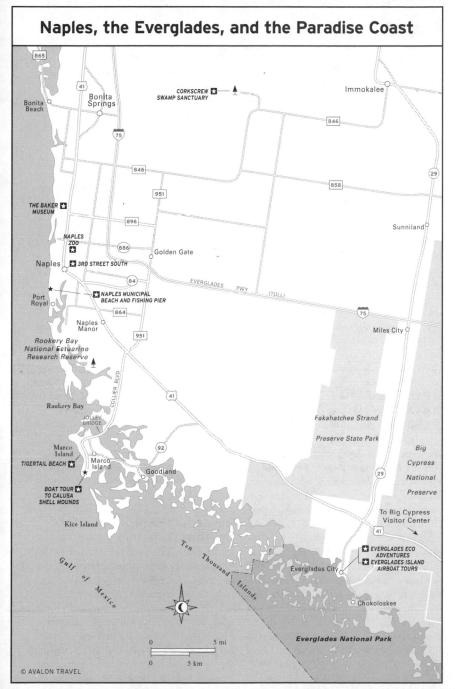

865

41
Bonita
Springs

CORKSCREW ✚
SWAMP SANCTUARY

Immokalee

Bonita
Beach

846

75

846

951

858

29

THE BAKER ✚
MUSEUM

896

Sunniland

NAPLES
ZOO
✚

886

Golden Gate

Naples ✚ 3RD STREET SOUTH

84

EVERGLADES   PWY   (TOLL)

Port
Royal

✚ NAPLES MUNICIPAL
BEACH AND FISHING PIER

75

864

Naples
Manor

951

Miles City

Rookery Bay
National Estuarine
Research Reserve

COLLIER BLVD

41

Rookery Bay

JOLLEY
BRIDGE

Fakahatchee Strand

Preserve State Park

Marco
Island

92

Big

TIGERTAIL BEACH ✚

Marco
Island

Goodland

Cypress

National

29

BOAT TOUR ✚
TO CALUSA
SHELL MOUNDS

Preserve

To Big Cypress
Visitor Center

Kice Island

41

Ten Thousand Islands

✚ EVERGLADES ECO
ADVENTURES
✚ EVERGLADES ISLAND
AIRBOAT TOURS

Gulf

of

Mexico

Everglades City

Chokoloskee

Everglades National Park

0   5 mi

0   5 km

© AVALON TRAVEL

Naples

Naples has been dubbed the "Palm Beach" of Florida's Gulf Coast. With nearly 90 golf courses, Naples has one of the highest ratios of greens to golfers in the United States. Beyond the links, the city is known for world-class shopping, dining, and a preponderance of beautiful people. Although a stroll of trendy 5th Avenue is certainly reminiscent of the posh Atlantic Coast resort, the analogy breaks down at Naples's tranquil beauty which begins just five miles out of town: the Rookery Bay National Estuarine Research Reserve (with sprawling mangroves and a high diversity of rare birds) to the south, Big Cypress National Preserve to the east, and the untamed mystery of Everglades National Park.

And then there are the nine miles of sun-soaked, white-sand beaches. Boosters often describe Naples as the crown jewel of southwest Florida. The jewel that sparkles brightest may just be the downtown beach, arguably the finest city beach in Florida.

SPORTS AND RECREATION
★ Naples Municipal Beach and Fishing Pier

For an urban beach experience, stroll along **Naples Municipal Beach and Fishing Pier** (access the pier at 12th St. and Gulf Shore Blvd., just south of downtown, 239/213-3062, open 24 hours, no fee, metered parking near entrance). Known locally as The Pier, the 1,000-foot structure that juts into the Gulf attracts anglers, new and old (best fishing months: May-July and Sept.-Oct.). There's a bait house, fish-cleaning tables, chickee shelter, restrooms, and concessions on the pier, which was originally built in 1888 as a freight and passenger dock. The pier is a symbol of the locals' tenacity and civic pride, having been damaged repeatedly by fire and hurricanes and rebuilt in 1910, 1926, and 1960. It's perhaps the most photographed spot in

Naples, the emerald-green Gulf water and wide swath of beach flanking it on either side.

The beach's proximity to downtown (and the stretch of fancy houses known as Millionaires' Row) makes it ideal for a moonlit stroll after dinner or even a sandy escape after an afternoon in the city. The beach can be accessed at the Gulf end of each avenue—the downtown is a grid, with streets running north and south, avenues east and west—with ample metered parking. Many of the parking meters on the roads near the beach are $1.50 per hour and take quarters only; if you don't mind walking five blocks or more, you can park downtown for free and walk to one of the beach access points. New parking meter stations that take credit and debit cards have also been installed at several of the beach parking areas, so now you don't always have to bring a roll of quarters to spend the day at the most popular stretch of beach in the city. Parking passes at these metered stations are up to $8 per vehicle per day. With the high price of daily parking in the area, it often makes better sense to buy a 12-month parking pass ($50, available at most parks in the area). While spending a day at the beach you may find a loggerhead sea turtle nest, a swirl of prehistoric-looking pelicans, or any of the other lures that have made Naples a top vacation spot for the past 150 years.

Conservancy of Southwest Florida

In the center of town, the 13 acres of the **Conservancy of Southwest Florida** (1450 Merrihue Dr., 239/262-0304, 9:30am-4:30pm daily, $12.95 adults, $8.95 children 3-12) provide opportunities for canoe tours and nature hikes, as well as aviaries and a serpentarium (that's a snake house). Its Discovery Center has undergone extensive renovations, replacing the aquatic touch tank and constructing a new Florida panther exhibit, which shows

Naples

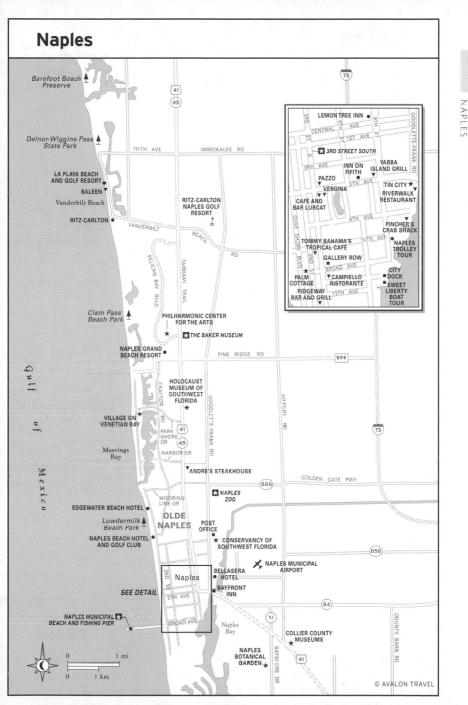

Barefoot Beach Preserve

Delnor-Wiggins Pass State Park

111TH AVE   IMMOKALEE RD

LA PLAYA BEACH AND GOLF RESORT

BALEEN

Vanderbilt Beach

RITZ-CARLTON

VANDERBILT

RITZ-CARLTON NAPLES GOLF RESORT

PELICAN BAY BLVD

TAMIAMI TRAIL

BEACH RD

Clam Pass Beach Park

PHILHARMONIC CENTER FOR THE ARTS

THE BAKER MUSEUM

NAPLES GRAND BEACH RESORT

PINE RIDGE RD   996

HOLOCAUST MUSEUM OF SOUTHWEST FLORIDA

CRAYTON RD

GOODLETTE-FRANK RD

AIRPORT RD

75

VILLAGE ON VENETIAN BAY

PARK SHORE DR

Moorings Bay

HARBOUR DR

ANDRE'S STEAKHOUSE

GOLDEN GATE PWY   886

MOORING LINE DR

NAPLES ZOO

EDGEWATER BEACH HOTEL

Lowdermilk Beach Park

OLDE NAPLES

POST OFFICE

CONSERVANCY OF SOUTHWEST FLORIDA

NAPLES BEACH HOTEL AND GOLF CLUB

856

BELLASERA HOTEL

NAPLES MUNICIPAL AIRPORT

SEE DETAIL

3RD ST

Naples

5TH AVE

BAYFRONT INN

84

31

NAPLES MUNICIPAL BEACH AND FISHING PIER

BROAD AVE

Naples Bay

COLLIER COUNTY MUSEUMS

BAYSHORE DR

41

COUNTY BARN RD

NAPLES BOTANICAL GARDEN

Gulf of Mexico

0   1 mi
0   1 km

© AVALON TRAVEL

Detail

41
45

3RD ST

CENTRAL AVE

6TH AVE   8TH AVE   9TH ST   1ST AVE

GOODLETTE-FRANK RD

LEMON TREE INN

3RD STREET SOUTH

3RD AVE

PAZZO

YABBA ISLAND GRILL

INN ON FIFTH

5TH AVE

VERGINA

CAFÉ AND BAR LURCAT

GULF SHORE BLVD

TIN CITY

RIVERWALK RESTAURANT

6TH AVE

PINCHER'S CRAB SHACK

TOMMY BAHAMA'S TROPICAL CAFÉ

10TH AVE

NAPLES TROLLEY TOUR

GALLERY ROW

BROAD AVE

CITY DOCK

PALM COTTAGE

CAMPIELLO RISTORANTE

SWEET LIBERTY BOAT TOUR

RIDGEWAY BAR AND GRILL

13TH AVE

Tee Time

Naples isn't called the golf capital of the world for nothing. Here are the courses available to visitors, plus the driving ranges and pro shops. All of the greens fees quoted fluctuate seasonally and according to the time of day. Call ahead.

THE COURSES

Arrowhead Golf Course
2205 Heritage Greens Dr., 239/596-1000
Semiprivate, 18 holes, 6,832 yards, par 72, course rating 73.1, slope 130
Greens fees: $105 7am-11:52am, $95 noon-2:22pm, $59 2:30-3:52, $39 after 4pm

Cypress Woods Golf and Country Club
3525 Northbrook Dr., 239/592-7860
Semiprivate, 18 holes, 6,330 yards, par 72, course rating 71.7, slope 136
Greens fees: $35-70 7am-11:59am, $28-79 noon-2pm, 2pm-close $28-52, cart included

Eagle Lakes Golf Club
18100 Royal Tree Pkwy., 239/732-0034
Public, 18 holes, 7,150 yards, par 71, course rating 71.1, slope 122
Greens fees: $39-89 for 18 holes

Hibiscus Golf Club
5375 Hibiscus Dr., 239/774-0088
Public, 18 holes, 6,476 yards, par 72, course rating 71.7, slope 128
Greens fees: $45-95

Lely Flamingo Island Club
8004 Lely Resort Blvd., 239/793-2223
Classics Course: private, 18 holes, 6,805 yards, par 72, course rating 72.4, slope 128
Flamingo Course: resort, 18 holes, 7,171 yards, par 72, course rating 73.9, slope 135
Mustang Course: resort, 18 holes, 7,217 yards, par 72, course rating 75.3, slope 141
Greens fees: $49-162 depending on the month for both Flamingo and Mustang courses, cart included

Marco Island Marriott Beach Resort, Golf Club, and Spa
400 Collier Blvd. S., Marco Island, 239/389-6600
Resort, 18 holes, 7,152 yards, par 72, course rating 75.2, slope 145
Greens fees: $99-205

Naples Beach Hotel & Golf Club
851 Gulf Shore Blvd. N., 239/435-2475
Resort, 18 holes, 6,488 yards, par 72, course rating 71.2, slope 129
Greens fees: $55-95, cart included.

Naples Grande Golf Club
7760 Golden Gate Pkwy., 239/659-3700
Resort, 18 holes, 7,102 yards, par 72, course rating 75.1, slope 143
Greens fees: $39-99

---

the endangered Florida panther in its natural environment.

Clam Pass Beach Park

At the south end of Naples, you'll find **Clam Pass Beach Park** (465 Seagate Dr., at the end of Seagate Dr., 239/353-0404, 8am-sunset daily, $8 parking fee or beach parking pass required). Clam Pass consists of 35 acres of mangrove forest, rolling dunes, and 3,200 feet of white-sand beach. There's a three-quarter-mile boardwalk from a

Quality Inn and Suites Golf Resort
4100 Golden Gate Pkwy., 239/455-1010
Resort, 18 holes, 6,564 yards, par 72, course rating 70.8, slope 125
Greens fees: $25-75, cart included

Riviera Golf Club of Naples
48 Marseille Dr., 239/774-2011
Public, 18 holes, 4,090 yards, par 62, course rating 60.4, slope 95
Greens fees: $45-60, cart included

Tiburon Golf Club
2620 Tiburon Dr., 239/594-2040
North Course: resort, 9 holes, 3,693 yards, par 36, course rating N/A, slope N/A
South Course: resort, 9 holes, 3,477 yards, par 36, course rating N/A, slope N/A
West Course: resort, 9 holes, 3,500 yards, par 36, course rating N/A, slope N/A
Greens fees: $60-225 depending on the time of year

Valencia Golf Course
1725 Double Eagle Trail, 239/352-0777
Public, 18 holes, 7,145 yards, par 72, course rating 74.3, slope 130
Greens fees: $55-90, cart included

DRIVING RANGES

Coral Isle Golf Center
4748 Championship Dr., 239/732-6900

Ferguson Golf Center
9100 Immokalee Rd., 239/732-6900

PRO SHOPS

Fix Up Stix
1101 Sun Century Rd., 239/591-3743

For the Love of Golf
9765 Tamiami Trail N., 239/566-3395

Golf Balls Galore & More
2181 J&C Blvd., 239/597-6528

Golfsmith
6428 Hollywood Dr., 239/254-0483

Naples Discount Golf Co.
5091 Tamiami Trail E., 239/643-5577

PGA Tour Superstore
2135 Tamiami Trail N., 239/384-6380

high-rise development through the mangroves and out to the beach. It's easily walkable (and you're likely to see eagles, ospreys, and waddling armadillos along the way), but you can also take a fun, free tram that runs continuously throughout the day. Once at the beach, there are kayak, canoe, sailboard, and catamaran rentals. The water is shallow and the surf mild, a perfect combination for a family day at the beach. Clam Pass also contains a concession area and picnic pavilions.

Delnor-Wiggins Pass State Park

To the north end of the city, **Delnor-Wiggins Pass State Park** (11135 Gulfshore Dr., 5 miles west of I-75, exit 17, 239/597-6196, 8am-sunset daily, $6 parking, 5 parking areas) regularly makes Dr. Beach's (aka Dr. Stephen Leatherman of the University of Maryland) top 20 list of America's best beaches. On Delnor-Wiggins you'll find the white-sand swath framed by picturesque sea oats, sea grapes, and cabbage palms. Delnor-Wiggins is on a narrow barrier island separated by a maze of mangrove swamp and tidal creek, and it boasts a nature trail and observation tower from which to spy on the abundant wildlife. It's a superior shelling beach, and Wiggins Pass generates much enthusiasm among anglers. Again, the water is shallow, with a gentle slope and calm surf suitable for swimming. There are picnic facilities, a lifeguard on duty, and a boat ramp. (Caution: Stay out of the dunes and don't pick the sea grass, which is protected due to its important role as a sand stabilizer.)

Other Beaches

Other beaches in the area would be star attractions anywhere but here, but the wealth of possibilities make **Lowdermilk Beach Park** (Gulf Shore Blvd. S., 239/213-3029), **Vanderbilt Beach Park** (near the Ritz-Carlton at the end of Vanderbilt Dr., 239/252-4000), and **Barefoot Beach Preserve,** also known as **Lely Barefoot Beach** (take U.S. 41 to Bonita Beach Rd. and head west, 239/591-8596), less popular here in Naples. All of them have restrooms and picnic facilities, are open sunrise-sunset daily, and charge for parking. In addition, Lowdermilk has lively sand volleyball courts, and Vanderbilt offers exceptional bird-watching. Barefoot boasts a learning center with exhibits on sea turtles and shorebirds, as well as a nature trail; it was ranked No. 10 among American beaches by Dr. Beach in 2006.

★ Corkscrew Swamp Sanctuary

The greater Naples area offers several outstanding opportunities to explore the exotic and wild natural world of the Gulf Coast—easily accessible to those with disabilities, seniors, or the stroller-bound.

In Collier County, huge swaths of bald cypress forest stood until right around World War II. Logging quickly decimated most of it, with just one virgin stand of cypress left

Corkscrew Swamp Sanctuary

in southwest Florida—the Corkscrew Swamp near Immokalee, now **Corkscrew Swamp Sanctuary** (375 Sanctuary Rd. W., 239/348-9151, 7am-5:30pm daily, $14 adults, $6 college students, $10 Audubon Society members, $4 children 6-18, children under 6 free). It provides visitors with a 2.25-mile raised boardwalk—there's also a 1-mile trail if the longer one sounds daunting, and benches and rain shelters along the way—through four distinct local environments: a pine upland, a wet prairie, a cypress forest, and a marsh. Interpretive signs along the boardwalk give you the basics, but the guide-led tours are tremendous, and there's a field guide and a kids' activity book that you can pick up at the admissions desk. There's a birders' checklist and a white board for birders to jot down what they've seen for the benefit of those who've just arrived. It's also a great place to spot gators, wood storks, resurrection ferns, and rare orchids. To get there, take I-75 to exit 111, go approximately 15 miles, and turn left onto Sanctuary Road.

Rookery Bay National Estuarine Research Reserve

Another worthwhile day trip is to be had about 13 miles south of Naples at **Rookery Bay National Estuarine Research Reserve** (300 Tower Rd., 239/530-5940, 9am-4pm Mon.-Fri., and Sat. Nov.-Apr., $5 adults, $3 children 6-12, children under 6 free). The Rookery Bay and Ten Thousand Islands estuarine ecosystem is one of the few pristine mangrove estuaries in North America, with 110,000 acres of forest, islands, bays, interconnected tidal embayments, lagoons, and tidal streams that are home to bald eagles, pink roseate spoonbills, and lots of other birdlife. You can explore the estuary on your own by kayak or with a guided kayak excursion through Rookery Bay's mangrove estuary (offered twice per month). There are also daily naturalist-led 45-minute walks (11am and 2pm) that take a closer look at the plants and animals you can find in the park and some of the problems and issues they face, on which visitors learn about the mighty

Calusas and the pioneering families of the Little Marco Settlement. A 16,500-square-foot Environmental Learning Center opened in 2004, with 5,000 square feet of interactive exhibits and a visitors center, four marine research laboratories, a coastal training center, and five aquariums; an authentic Seminole chickee was added in 2007, and an observation bridge over Henderson Creek opened in 2009. (The big fish at the entrance, by the way, is a polka-dot batfish.) The coolest part of the center is the climb-in "bubble" that allows visitors to observe the many creatures that live among the roots of a 14-foot mangrove in the center aquarium, including the recent unwelcomed and highly invasive lionfish that is decimating native aquatic life. An aggressive eradication program has begun in the park, and classes on how to catch and handle the fish are frequently held. Do your part to protect Florida's aquatic environment and learn how to remove these fish from Florida's waterways.

Big Cypress National Preserve

This part of Florida also boasts the first national preserve in the national park system, the **Big Cypress National Preserve** (Oasis Visitor Center, 52105 Tamiami Trail E., Ochopee, midway between Naples and Miami on U.S. 41, 239/695-1201, www.nps.gov/bicy, welcome center 9am-4:30pm daily, preserve 24 hours daily, free), contiguous with Everglades National Park and just about as big. The preserve encompasses 720,000 acres of the Big Cypress Swamp of southwest Florida—terrain is varied, with swamp, freshwater marshes, forests of slash pine and palmetto, and wet prairies containing abundant wildlife. What's the best way to investigate this vast area? There are two terrific choices.

Hike it. There's a public boardwalk located at the **Kirby Storter roadside pullout** that allows you to walk into a cypress dome without getting your feet wet. If this sounds too training-wheels, the **Florida Trail** stretches across the state from Gulf Islands National Seashore through the Big Cypress National Preserve. It's wonderful hiking, which the park rangers divide into three logical sections. Part 1, **Loop Road to U.S. 41** (7.8 miles one-way) begins at Loop Road about 13 miles from its east end on U.S. 41. The other end is across from the **Big Cypress Visitors Center** (53 miles east of Naples on U.S. 41). The easy path meanders through dwarf cypress and prairies and crosses through Robert's Lake Strand (can be very wet during rainy months). Part 2, more for the seasoned backpacker, **U.S. 41 to I-75** (30 miles one-way) has trailheads on U.S. 41 near Big Cypress Visitors Center and on I-75 at the rest area at mile marker 63. A harder hike (for which you'll need to pack in all your own water), it takes you through hardwood hammocks, pinelands, prairies, and cypress. There is high-ground camping at the 13-mile mark. Part 3, **I-75 to Preserve North Boundary** (7.6 miles one-way) follows an old oil road through hardwood, prairie, and pine forest.

Canoe it. The park's main canoe trail begins at U.S. 41 and follows the **Turner River** until it ends in Chokoloskee Bay (about a 5-hour paddle). You can also put in at the Everglades National Park Gulf Coast Visitor Center. There's another trail called the **Halfway Creek Canoe Trail,** for which you

can put in at Seagrape Drive and paddle south past Plantation Island.

Big Cypress also accommodates camping, hunting, biking, and sightseeing by car. There are eight campgrounds that accommodate tent and RV camping across the preserve, the most popular being the Midway campground. The Gator Head and Pink Jeep campgrounds cater exclusively to tent campers for those of you looking for a more authentic wilderness experience and who would prefer to get away from the hum of generators that frequently power behemoth RV air-conditioners in the other more developed campgrounds. The best camping season is between December and January when the weather is cooler and the mosquito population is tolerable. Before camping in the reserve you'll need to go to a visitors center (or visit the National Park Service website at www.nps.gov/bicy) to see an informative 15-minute movie about the preserve, view a small wildlife exhibit, and pick up a permit ($10-30, depending on location) and literature about the preserve.

Naples Botanical Garden

If you would like to experience all of the incredible plantlife that the Big Cypress Preserve has to offer in a less wild and more cultivated

a gator at Big Cypress National Preserve

Walking Trees

This area owes much of its landmass to the **mangrove tree.** They are often called walking trees because they hover above the water, their arching prop roots resembling so many spindly legs. The mangrove is one of only a handful of tree species on planet Earth that can withstand having its roots sitting in ocean water, immersed daily by rising tides, and that thrives in little soil and high levels of sulfides. The mangrove's hardiness is just one of its many idiosyncrasies, however.

Mangroves are natural land builders. Seed tubules about the heft and length of an excellent Cuban cigar sprout on the parent tree, drop off, and bob in the brackish water until they lodge on an oyster bar or a snag in the shallows. There the seed begins to grow into a tree, its leaves dropping and getting trapped along with seaweed and other plant debris. This organic slurry is the bottom of the food chain, supplying food, breeding areas, and sanctuary to countless tiny marine creatures. In addition, it is the foundation upon which a little island—or "key"—begins to take shape, this buildup of sediment and debris creating a thick layer of organic peat upon which other plant species start to grow. This first tree drops more seed tubules, which get stuck in the soft mud around the base of the parent tree and send up shoots. Soon, there's an impenetrable tangle of trees and roots extravagant enough to support birdlife and other animals.

Three types predominate in the Everglades and Ten Thousand Islands: The red mangrove forms a wide band of trees on the outermost part of each island, facing the open sea. The red mangrove encircles the black mangrove, which in turn encircles the white mangrove at the highest, driest part of each mangrove island (they are the least tolerant of having their roots sitting in saltwater). The mangroves' leathery evergreen leaves fall and stain the water a tobacco-colored tannic brown, but in fact mangroves and all the species dependent upon them do much to keep the waters clean and pure.

For all these reasons, mangrove trees are protected by federal, state, and local laws. Do not injure, spindle, mutilate, or even taunt a mangrove or face steep penalties.

---

setting, the **Naples Botanical Garden** (4820 Bayshore Dr., 239/643-7275, 9am-5pm daily, $14.95 adults, $9.95 children 4-12, children 3 and under free) won't disappoint. It's a living botanical museum within minutes of downtown. The garden expanded in June 2008, dramatically growing from a meager 1.5 acres to a 170-acre tropical garden. And in the fall of 2010 the garden added another 50 acres of cultivated garden, 2.5 miles of walking trails, and 90 acres of native preserve where you'll spot gopher tortoises and bald eagles among other native plants and wildlife. Also don't miss the butterfly house, history exhibitions, the wonderful lecture series, and the exceptional garden store.

Boat Tours

There are many ways to get out on the Gulf and Naples Bay, to wind through the Ten Thousand Islands, and idle along one of the area's many rivers. Here's just a sampling

of the tours to be had. The **Sweet Liberty** (Naples City Dock, 880 12th Ave. S., 239/793-3525) is a 53-foot sailing catamaran available for public tours and private charters. Departing from Crayton Cove in Naples Historic District, the boat offers a variety of tours (each around $29.50 adults, $20 children): shelling tours (9:30am-12:30pm), sightseeing tours (1:30pm-3:30pm), and two-hour sunset tours. On all the cruises, the boat is usually trailed by a playful pod of dolphins, and you'll have an opportunity to see the large homes of Port Royal.

The **Lady Brett** (departing from Tin City, 1146 6th Ave. S., 239/263-4949, departure times vary, $89 adults, $59 children under 12) offers deep sea fishing tours for up to 20 people, and the double-decker **Double Sunshine** (departing from Tin City, 1200 5th Ave. S., 239/263-4949, 10am, noon, 2pm, 4pm, and 1 hour before sunset daily, $35 adults, $17.50 children under 12) takes folks out on sunset and sightseeing cruises aboard a 45-foot vessel equipped with bathrooms. If you want to wet a line in the Ten Thousand Islands (think snook, sheepshead, redfish, snapper, and trout), **Captain Paul** (departing from Tin City, 1200 5th Ave. S., 239/263-4949, $79 adults, $49 children under 12) takes people on half-day bay fishing trips on a comfortable pontoon boat.

A fancier experience, the *Naples Princess* (departing from Port-O-Call Marina, 550 Port-O-Call Way, 239/649-2275, www.naplesprincesscruises.com, $16-62) has narrated lunch cruises and sunset buffet dinner cruises on a 93-foot, air-conditioned luxury yacht that can accommodate 149 passengers.

Or make yourself useful: The *Dolphin Explorer* (Marco River Marina, 951 Bald Eagle Dr., Marco Island, 239/642-6899, www.dolphin-study.com, departures at 9am and 1am, $59) is a 30-foot catamaran that takes up to 28 passengers out for a laid-back dolphin-watching cruise that is actually part of the Ten Thousand Islands Dolphin Project, an ongoing scientific dolphin research study, the only one in the country that involves the public on a daily basis. Passengers work with a naturalist on board to identify the resident dolphin population and catalog their activities. Dolphins are identified by their dorsal fins, as unique as human fingerprints, and if a passenger spots a dolphin not already cataloged in the study, he or she gets to name it. Cruises include a stop at a barrier island for shelling and beach walking.

SIGHTS
Trolley Tours

A good place to start and orient yourself in Naples is with a long ride aboard a **Naples Trolley Tour** (1010 6th Ave. S., 239/262-7300, hourly 8:30am-5:30pm, $27 adults, $12.50 children). The open-air trolley has a narrated tour of more than 100 local places of note, including historic Naples Pier and Tin City. The tour itself lasts about two hours, but you can embark and disembark to explore, catching the next trolley when it suits

you. Tickets are available at all boarding stops, but to get oriented you might want to begin at the Experience Naples depot, the welcome center for the Naples Trolley, and Segway and Everglades van tours offered by Naples Transportation, Tours, and Event Planning.

There are two guided Segway tours available in downtown Naples. One departs from the Charter Club Resort on Naples Bay and the other from the Experience Naples store, which is also the Naples Trolley depot. Both offer insight into the history of downtown Naples and are a fun way to get your bearings.

Galleries

Collier County had nearly 200 commercial art galleries at last count, wedged in among the shops of downtown, largely congregated along the length of **3rd Street South,** on what is called "Gallery Row" on Broad Avenue off 3rd Street South, and along **5th Avenue** (many between the 600 and 800 blocks).

Naples was selected as the No. 1 small art town in America by author John Villani in his fourth edition of *The 100 Best Art Towns in America.* He cited the area's "amazing range of natural splendor," along with its "sophistication and serious art galleries," art fairs, community arts centers and theaters, and the Philharmonic Center complex. *American Style Magazine* also named Naples in the top 25 arts destinations in the United States, with good reason. Most of the galleries are found downtown, and to see the work of many local artists, stop in at the **von Liebig Art Center** (585 Park St., next to Cambier Park, 239/262-6517, 10am-4pm Mon.-Sat., free). It houses the Naples Art Association and features changing exhibitions in five galleries.

★ The Baker Museum

The Baker Museum (formerly the Naples Museum of Art, 5833 Pelican Bay Blvd., 239/597-1900, www.artisnaples.org, 10am-4pm Tues.-Sat., noon-4pm Sun., $10 adults, $5 students and military, free for children under 17, higher admission may be charged for special exhibitions) is the crown jewel of Naples's cultural attractions, located at the incredible $19.5 million **Artis—Naples campus**. The visual arts center, opened in 2000, is a three-story, 30,000-square-foot museum with 15 galleries. Exhibits are varied and expertly curated, from a small antique walking stick show to the underwater-phantasmagorical blown glasswork of Dale Chihuly, from an Andy Warhol print show to one of the largest collections of Mexican art in the Southeast. Beyond the permanent collection and visiting shows, the space itself is a work of art with a huge glass-domed conservatory, interesting entrance gates by metal artist Albert Paley, and an impressively cool Chihuly chandelier. There are also educational programs and art lectures held at the museum—many of them sell out, so buy tickets early on the museum's website.

Collier County Museums

Five minutes east of downtown Naples, history enthusiasts flock to the Naples site of the **Collier County Museums** (3331 Tamiami Trail E. in the Collier County Government Center, 239/252-8476, 9am-4pm Mon.-Sat., free). There are three other locations of the museum—the Museum of the Everglades in Everglades City, the Immokalee Pioneer

Museum at the home of the Robert Roberts family, and the newly renovated Naples Depot historic train station on 5th Avenue South—but it's the Naples main museum that's worth the most time. Established in 1978, the museum offers interpretive exhibits that illuminate the history, archaeology, and development of this part of Florida, as well as a five-acre botanical park with a native plant garden, orchid house, two early Naples cottages, a logging locomotive, swamp buggies, and a World War II Sherman tank. The museum holds the **Old Florida Festival** ($10 adults, $5 children 10-18, children under 10 free, free parking) every year in March—a good time for people who like historical reenactments.

Palm Cottage

Another walk through Naples history can be had at **Palm Cottage** (137 12th Ave. S., 239/261-8164, 1pm-4pm Tues.-Sat., $10, children under 10 free). On the National Register of Historic Places, it's the second-oldest house in Collier County, built for Henry Watterson, the editor of the *Louisville Courier-Journal*. It reopened recently after a significant facelift that included new woodwork, a new roof, and improved landscaping. The house is one of the few remaining "tabbie mortar" structures in

Palm Cottage

the area—a mortar goo made from burned seashells mixed with lime and seawater. The Palm Cottage is now home to the Naples Historical Society.

Holocaust Museum of Southwest Florida

Growing out of an exhibit created by Golden Gate Middle School students in Naples, the **Holocaust Museum of Southwest Florida** (4760 Tamiami Trail N., 239/263-9500, www. holocaustmuseumswfl.org, 1pm-4pm Tues.-Sun., $10 adults, $5 children 12-18, children under 12 and museum members free) is another small history museum. The students collected more than 300 death camp and Holocaust artifacts, which constitute the bulk of the exhibit. Docents lead tours for individuals as well as local school groups. The museum has also embarked on an oral history project with local survivors, liberators, and others, and it installs traveling Holocaust exhibits in local schools as well.

★ Naples Zoo

Adults will be able to while away days in Naples with the sophisticated pleasures of dining, shopping, the arts, and so forth. But as every parent knows, the kids must be entertained with regularity, or mutiny is assured. The single most mutually agreeable family attraction in Naples is **Naples Zoo at Caribbean Gardens** (1590 Goodlette-Frank Rd., 239/262-5409, www.napleszoo.com, 9am-5pm daily, $19.95 adults, $18.95 seniors 65 and up, $14.95 children 3-12 and military, children 2 and under free).

It began as a botanical garden, founded by botanist Henry Nehrling in 1919. The original garden was expanded in the 1950s by Julius Fleischmann, and the Tetzlaff family introduced the rare animals in 1969. In 2004 the zoo acquired nonprofit status after local taxpayers opted to tax themselves to save the zoo land from being sold to a developer. Since then this quickly expanding zoo has been able to add a new exhibit every year.

The zoo has greatly increased the number of species in the presentations and now includes raptors and dozens of native and exotic venomous reptiles, from diamondback rattlesnakes and Gila monsters to an African puff adder and Komodo dragon, as well as South American poison dart frogs and bushmaster snakes. Other notable exhibits are the Panther Glade and Leopard Rock, which separate you from the big cats by a thrillingly thin sheet of glass, and the three rare and beautiful Malayan tigers, the only such cats in Florida. Two new male tigers were born at the zoo in 2009.

Kids will prefer the baby alligator-feeding shows and the fossa exhibit (which the kids will instantly recognize from the movie *Madagascar*). The zoo recently shifted the alligator-feeding area from an elevated deck to a beach area, where zookeepers hand-feed the alligators, which has added more excitement and up close action to the feedings. Be sure to catch the Planet Predator and Meet the Keeper live animal shows. Seeing these animals up close inspires a certain amount of awe, and the keepers' banter keeps the shows entertaining. There's also a wonderful short boat ride that takes you past a bunch of tiny islands, from which you can view various species of primates. In 2012 the zoo welcomed seven young giraffes; for a $5 fee you can hand-feed the giraffes from an elevated deck.

Family-Friendly Attractions

If the weather is nice during your visit, which it doubtless will be, kids enjoy a round of mini golf at **Coral Cay Adventure Golf** (2205 Tamiami Trail E., 1 mile east of Tin City, 239/793-4999, 10am-11pm daily, $9.50 adults, $8.50 children 5-11, $3.50 children 4 and under), with its exotic tropical setting featuring caves, reefs, and a waterfall. There's a snack bar, slushies, and ice cream, and a game room as well.

North Collier Regional Park (15000 Livingston Rd., 239/252-4000, 6am-10pm daily, free) is a great destination for families, with eight tournament soccer fields, five tournament softball fields, an interactive playground and Calusa fossil dig play area for children, an exhibit hall with ranger-led tours, and a recreation center. For visitors, the more salient part is the **Sun-N-Fun Lagoon Water Park** (239/252-4021, 10am-5pm daily during summer, weekends only spring and fall, $13 for those taller than 48 inches, $9 seniors 60 and up, $6 children less than 48 inches tall, children 3 and under free), with one million gallons of good times for children and their handlers. Opened in 2006, the center features water-dumping buckets, water pistols, four pools (a family pool, a "tadpole" pool for kids 6 and under, Turtle Cove for kids 7 and up, and a lap/diving pool), and Sunny's River, a lazy river attraction with three waterslides.

Also worth a couple of hours of investigation is the Conservancy of Southwest Florida's **Naples Nature Center** (1450 Merrihue Dr., 239/262-0304, www.conservancy.org/nature-center, 9:30am-4:30pm daily Nov.-Apr., Mon.-Sat. May-Oct., $12.95 adults, $8.95 children 3-12), just a few blocks from the Naples Zoo. There are education programs and lectures on the common area's deck (11am-3pm Mon.-Sat.), talks about the aquatic life found in the area's bays and the Gulf at the touch tank (every half hour 10:30am-3:30pm Mon.-Sat.), and electric boat cruises through the mangrove habitat on the Gordon River (hourly 10am-noon Mon.-Sat.); make sure to check the Nature Center's website for up-to-date schedules for talks and programs. The Nature Center reopened in 2013 after the first phase of a $20 million expansion was completed. Newly added to the center is the Dalton Discovery Center, where visitors can view 125 animals in their natural habitat, and the von Arx Wildlife Clinic, where animals are cared for and often released back into the wild. In 2014, the Nature Center completed the expansion with the addition of the Ferguson Learning Lab, where state-of-the-art classrooms provide hands-on learning experiences for science students, and the Eaton Conservation Hall, which hosts environmental conferences and lectures. The center also completed environmental restoration work on several filter marshes on the property that will enhance Gordon River and Naples Bay water quality. Kudos to the Naples Nature Center!

ENTERTAINMENT AND EVENTS

The **Philharmonic Center for the Arts** (5833 Pelican Bay Blvd., 239/597-1900, www.thephil.org, box office hours 10am-5pm Mon.-Fri., 10am-4pm Sat., noon-4pm Sun., ticket prices and showtimes vary) is an outstanding venue hosting more than 400 events a year, including world-class dance, opera, classical and popular music, and traveling Broadway musicals. The center contains a 1,425-seat main hall and a 283-seat black box theater. The **Naples Philharmonic Orchestra** (239/597-1111) performs here with more than 120 concerts per year including classics, pops, chamber orchestras, and numerous educational performances.

There isn't any professional theater company in Naples, although the **Sugden Community Theatre** (701 5th Ave. S., 239/434-7340) is home to the 40-year-old **Naples Players,** a community theater troupe that stages around 14 musicals, comedies, dramas, and children's productions annually (it also hosts a program called KidzAct, with musical theater workshops for kids). The Sugden also screens a "Films on Fifth" series, mostly independent and art house films.

And for mainstream movies, head to the 20-plex **Regal Hollywood 20** (6006 Hollywood Dr., 844/462-7342), the **Towne Centre 6 Theater** (3855 Tamiami Trail E., 239/774-4800), **Pavilion Cinemas** (833 Vanderbilt Beach Rd., 239/596-0008), or **Marco Movies** (599 S. Collier Blvd., Marco Island, 239/642-1111), where you can dine on Greek salad, beer, or wine with your movie popcorn.

SHOPPING

Of anyplace along the Gulf Coast of Florida, Naples stands out as a top-notch shopping destination. Comparisons are often made to

Rodeo Drive and some of the United States' other prime shopping spots, but Naples may win for sheer diversity.

★ 3rd Street South

Start at **3rd Street South,** with exquisite clothing and giftware shops, chic restaurants, and dozens of galleries. Just a couple of blocks from the beach and Naples Pier, the street was Naples's real core at the turn of the last century. Don't know where to begin? Consult the **street concierge** (1203 3rd St. S., 239/434-6533, 10am-6pm Mon.-Sat., noon-5pm Sun.), just opposite the Fleischmann Fountain, for help navigating the area's shops and restaurants.

5th Avenue South

Not far from there, **5th Avenue South** (239/692-8436) is another huge draw. Seminoles once sold their crafts from a stand on 5th, and before that Calusas used this area as a canal connecting Naples Bay with the Gulf. The Ed Frank Garage was the first commercial building—erected in 1923—and growth puttered along organically for decades (maybe a hardware store, then a gas station). Then, as in so many cities around the country, the birth of the mall heralded the death of downtown.

In 1996, savvy civic planners had 5th Avenue South join the Florida Main Street Program, and a master plan was created with the help of Miami urban planner Andrés Duany. The upshot was that dilapidated one-story storefronts were razed and replaced with sleek Mediterranean two- and three-story buildings (with room for people to live above). Today, 5th Avenue encompasses 12 blocks and 50 buildings (including the Bayfront and Tin City shopping and dining complexes), with such a crafty mix of shops, dining, and nightlife possibilities (as well as a strange preponderance of brokerages and realties) that the length of it is busy at most hours. There is free street entertainment the second Thursday of the month during Evenings on Fifth, tucked at intervals

the upscale shopping district of 5th Avenue South

along the banyan- and flowering poinciana-bedecked avenue.

Village on Venetian Bay

Equally fancy-pants is the **Village on Venetian Bay** (4200 Gulf Shore Blvd., 239/261-6100), with a kind of Venetian canal-side vibe. You'll find lots of independent clothing boutiques (plus familiar faces like Tommy Bahama and Chico's), a couple of high-end shoe stores, a handful of restaurants (plus Ben & Jerry's), and some home interior shops.

Tin City

More overtly touristy, but fun, **Tin City** (U.S. 41 E. at Goodlette Rd., 239/262-4200, www.tin-city.com), at the eastern end of downtown, was built in 1976 on the site of a 1920s clam- and oyster-processing plant. It incorporated the crusty waterfront buildings, with oodles of rustic maritime charm, into a shopping emporium (surf shop, bikini shop, and plenty of Jimmy Buffett-themed items) with a few restaurants (Riverwalk Restaurant at Tin City, Pincher's) worthy of your money. The Naples Trolley drops you right here, and it's an easy walk from 5th Avenue South.

Waterside Shops

The **Waterside Shops** (5415 Tamiami Trail N., in Pelican Bay, 239/598-1605, www.watersideshops.com) are anchored by huge draws such as Saks Fifth Avenue, Nordstrom, Tiffany & Co., Gucci, Coach, Polo Ralph Lauren, MaxMara, Pottery Barn, Banana Republic, and the like. It's a classic, high-end mall with covered walkways and restaurants like California Pizza Kitchen.

Other Shopping Areas

Before you start getting fatigued by all this shopping, let me put in a word for the boutiques along the **Dockside Boardwalk** (1100 6th Ave., corner of 11th St. and 6th Ave. S) and **Crayton Cove** (at the historic City Dock, off 10th St.). If you need a good old-fashioned JCPenney or Sears to offset all the glitz, there's the **Coastland Center Mall** (1900 Tamiami Trail N., 239/262-2323), with Macy's, Dillard's, and restaurants including Moe's Southwest Grill and the Cheesecake Factory.

FOOD

Naples has an extremely active restaurant scene that is continually evolving. It is one of those few cities that takes dining extremely seriously. It's a place where top chefs open up another branch of their namesake kitchen and green chefs fresh out of culinary college come to cut their teeth. There are lots of restaurants competing for the diner's dollar, and when there is competition as stiff as you find in Naples, it means only great restaurants can stay open. Despite the abundance of great choices, in high season you will need to make a reservation at most of the spots that have become hip for the moment.

At the beginning of May, make sure not to miss the annual **Taste of Collier** in Naples. Here you can sample all the top restaurants in the area as they showcase their best flavors in a one-day, family-friendly festival.

5th Avenue South

There are a few exceptionally dense concentrations of wonderful restaurants in downtown Naples; 5th Avenue has the greatest embarrassment of riches, assembled between 9th Street and 3rd Street. The gamut is impressive, from trendy to fancy continental, covering a range of prices and ethnicities.

Naples has a thriving culinary scene.

The best ones are listed here from east at 9th Ave. S. (the beginning of downtown) to the west as it reaches the Gulf.

Pazzo Cucina Italiana (853 5th Ave. S., 239/434-8494, 5pm-10pm daily, $15-28) presents diners with an instant conundrum—sit in the lovely modern dining room with its open bar and kitchen, or settle into one of the sidewalk tables through open French doors and watch the world stroll by? Pazzo makes a mean Bellini—champagne and peach nectar cocktails that are the height of festivity—and lots of elegant spins on familiar Italian dishes. Worth trying are the grouper piccata and the house made gelato.

Practically next door is one of downtown's most happening places, **Chops City Grill** (837 5th Ave. S., 239/262-4677, 5pm-10pm daily, $15-34). The menu possibilities might sound a bit schizophrenic, but it all works. Try the pan-seared black grouper served with wild mushroom risotto and a spicy rock shrimp sauce, or an order of addictive roasted candy cane beets drizzled in oil infused with Indian River orange juice and aged balsamic vinegar. Singles: Dine at the long food bar and you won't be alone long. Everyone's friendly, and the look of the place is hip.

A block down you'll find the other hippest, waitlist-for-miles place, **Yabba Island Grill** (711 5th Ave. S., 239/262-5787, noon-10pm daily, $15-30). It's no coincidence, really, as Pazzo, Chops, and Yabba are all owned and operated by the same folks. Yabba has a menu that's centered around seafood and steak entrées that have an Asian or island fusion spin to them. It's just plain good and inventive fusion in an upbeat and island-inspired atmosphere.

From here, take your appetite to the more upscale **Vergina** (700 5th Ave. S., 239/659-7008, 11am-11:30pm daily, $15-30). Again, there's wonderful outdoor seating in a sheltered plaza and a soaring indoor space with a long, inviting bar. The food is all familiar Italian, with a bold Caesar salad and hearty seafood pastas.

The ★ **Café and Bar Lurcat** (494 5th Ave. S., 239/213-3357, 4pm-11pm Sun.-Thurs., 4pm-midnight Fri.-Sat., $11-32) has been knocking people's socks off with its New American cuisine and über-stylish atmosphere. It's owned and managed by D'Amico & Partners, which also owns Campiello, on 3rd Street, and it was awarded a spot on the Top 10 Wine Lists by Food & Wine Magazine. The first floor is the bar, with live music and a small plate approach, and the upstairs is the more formal dining room. The wine program is quirky and thoughtful, with good suggestions on food and wine pairings. And what food it is: pot roast braised in cabernet sauvignon with roasted veggies; seared foie gras with kumquat; black grouper bouillabaisse.

There are plenty of other fine choices along 5th—walk and peer in, reading menus as you go. For ice cream, try **Regina's Ice Cream Pavilion** (824 5th Ave. S., 239/434-8181).

3rd Street South

Once the central business district of Old Naples, these days 3rd Street South is fairly overrun with galleries, high-end boutiques, and antiques shops. There aren't as many restaurant choices as on 5th, but a few of Naples's absolute best restaurants line up along 3rd.

★ **Campiello Ristorante** (1177 3rd St. S., 239/435-1166, 11am-3pm and 5pm-10pm Sun.-Thurs., 11am-3pm and 5pm-10:30pm Fri.-Sat., $17-38) is a favorite around town. It's got a healthy and fresh Cal-Ital bistro approach to the menu, but the atmosphere reminds you of power-lunch restaurants of the 1980s. Bite into a spit-roasted turkey sandwich with smoked bacon, red onion and avocado, or sample the crab linguini with heirloom tomatoes. The food is good, and presentations are simple. The produce is fresh and well selected, and the slow-roasted meats steal the show.

A totally different vibe, but equally popular, is **Tommy Bahama's Tropical Café** (1220 3rd St. S., 239/643-6889, 11am-10pm daily, $12-35). It's the same company as the clothing line, the "purveyor of island lifestyles," and as one might expect this means an upscale island cuisine—great macadamia encrusted grouper, tropical fruit cocktails—served under slowly rotating bamboo-blade fans and a palm frond-thatched roof. Tommy Bahama's also has live music most nights, so it's a good place to stop in and relax.

A longtime Naples institution, **Ridgway Bar & Grill** (1300 3rd St. S., 239/262-5500, 11:30am-9:30pm Mon.-Sat., 10am-9:30pm Sun., $16-30) actually closed up a while back and then was reborn. Owner Tony Ridgway is something of a legend in Naples, having brought one of the first restaurants using a traditional gourmet approach to Naples 30 years ago. He owns a small cooking school as well as **Tony's Off Third** (1300 3rd St. S., 239/262-7999), a gourmet deli and wine shop next door; the restaurant's wine offerings reflect this close proximity, with more than 600 bottles on the far-reaching list. The food is mostly American, with a bit of French flavor here and there.

Tin City

Tin City Waterfront Marketplace is a waterside indoor shopping center with about 40 mostly nautical-theme upscale shops and several good restaurants. The complex is on U.S. 41 at Goodlette Road. The most casual of the restaurants is **Cafe Europa Patisserie** (1200 5th Ave. S., #19, 239/262-5911, 10am-9pm daily, $5-12), where you'll find good coffee, breakfast, bakery items, and sandwiches. A little more upscale is the lively **Riverwalk Restaurant at Tin City** (1200 5th Ave. S., 239/263-2734, 11am-9pm Mon.-Sat., 10:30am-9pm Sun., $14-28), serving local seafood and classic American grill selections. And then there's **Pincher's Crab Shack** (1200 5th Ave. S., #8, 239/434-6616, 11am-10pm daily, $10-30), a part of the southwest Florida family of restaurants as famous for their fresh-caught Gulf grouper and snapper as for their cheesy crab dip. Right across from Tin City is a casual joint called **Kelly's Fish House Dining Room** (1302 5th Ave. S., 239/774-0494, 4:30pm-10pm daily, $15-25). It's one of the oldest restaurants around

here, and where you'll find the city's best stone crabs.

Downtown and Vicinity

The rest of the area's top restaurants are fairly spread out, although there's a dense concentration of fine eats north of downtown on the Tamiami Trail (U.S. 41) between about Golden Gate Parkway and Pine Ridge Road. **Andre's Steakhouse** (2800 Tamiami Trail N., 239/263-5851, 5pm-9pm daily, $20-40) falls squarely in the luxury American steak house idiom. Try the porterhouse for four people, like something from the *Flintstones*, with a bottle from the wine list that contains 4,000 bottlings.

If you love French food and the French way of life, visit chef Claudio Scaduto's **Cote D'Azur** (11224 Tamiami Trail N., 239/597-8867, 5pm-10pm Tues.-Sun., $18-36). At this intimate restaurant, you'll find what you're looking for with dishes like *loup de mer Antibois* (Mediterranean sea bass) and *noisettes d'agneau peillois* (roasted spring lamb loins).

Back downtown, next to Sugden Theater, **Trulucks** (698 4th Ave. S., 239/530-3131, 5pm-10pm daily, $15-35) is part of a small chain out of Texas, but the seafood is great. Especially the crab, and there's lots of it: northwest Dungeness crab, Florida stone crab, and red king crab.

Hotel Restaurants

These are all upscale and expensive restaurants, suggesting reservations and dress attire. Starting at the top, **The Grill** (Ritz-Carlton, 280 Vanderbilt Beach Rd., 239/598-6644, 6pm-10pm daily, $30-55), formerly Artisans in the Dining Room, features "aged prime meats, chops and fresh seafood paired with rare vintages." Nightly entertainment and a cozy fireplace are attractions.

Baleen at LaPlaya Beach & Golf Resort (9891 Gulf Shore Dr., 239/598-5707, 7am-10pm daily, $25-40) is also a favorite among visitors and locals livin' large. The dining room has wonderful indoor-outdoor seating that overlooks a perfect swath of beach and the Gulf of Mexico. The menu contains a variety of dishes: seared sea scallops, broiled lobster risotto, filet mignon with blue cheese polenta, ceviche, and lamb gnocchi.

ACCOMMODATIONS

$100-200

My favorite mid-priced hotel in Naples is the ★ **Lemon Tree Inn** (250 9th St. S., 239/262-1414, www.lemontreeinn.com, $89-199). In early 2013, the owner remodeled the 35 rooms, adding new furnishings, flat-screen televisions, and carpeting. Many rooms now include mahogany four-poster beds. There's a sweet little gazebo and swimming pool surrounded by lush tropical landscaping, where breakfast is served each morning. But the real draw is the people—the owner is incredibly warm, as are all the people he employs. It has an Old Florida charm married to a sophisticated Naples aesthetic and an ideal location in the heart of downtown. Just around the corner is the upscale dining and shopping district of 5th Avenue. A short walk past the galleries, boutiques, and beautiful homes will take you to the happening beach hangout surrounding the Naples Municipal Pier. There's even free lemonade in

the office, very thirst-quenching after a long day of beach-bumming.

The **Bayfront Inn on Fifth** (1221 5th Ave. S., 239/649-5800, $125-350) has spacious rooms, tropical decor, a central location, and a full-service marina; and **Hampton Inn** (2630 Northbrooke Plaza Dr., 239/596-1299, $95-175) is off exit 111, closer to I-75 and Corkscrew Swamp Sanctuary.

$200-300

Naples is lousy with luxury hotels—so much so, in fact, that the Ritz-Carlton boasts not one property, but two in town. Once you enter the luxury accommodation price point, where to stay depends largely on your priorities. If you want an urban experience, so you can roll out of bed and be wandering the downtown shops within minutes, consider ★ **The Inn on Fifth** (699 5th Ave. S., 239/403-8777, www.innonfifth.com, $175-400), a boutique hotel filled with Mediterranean charm. The 87 rooms are beautiful, with sliding French doors to a balcony or terrace. The common space features splashing fountains, courtyards, and nice gardens—all at the center of downtown. The inn features the Asian-influenced **Spa on Fifth.** An expansion in 2012 added 32 more club-level rooms at a new location

The Inn on Fifth

directly across the street in what used to be a swanky apartment complex. The club-level suites range 550-1,160 square feet and have sleek, modern furnishings, a separate private check-in, and access to a private rooftop hot tub with a sunbathing area and excellent views of 5th Avenue. Breakfast is served daily for club-level guests, as well as an assortment of fresh fruits, snacks, evening cocktails and appetizers. Also added during the expansion was a 750-square-foot conference and event center equipped with state-of-the-art technology.

On a residential street downtown, the **Trianon Old Naples** (955 7th Ave. S., 239/435-9600, www.trianon.com, $220-500) is another small luxury hotel with a pool, lounge, off-street parking, and complimentary continental breakfast served in the lobby (although there's no on-site restaurant, thus no room service). The 55 roomy guest rooms and three large one-bedroom suites have all the usual fine amenities with balconies and easy access to Tin City and 5th Avenue South.

The **Naples Grande Beach Resort** (475 Seagate Dr., 888/722-1267, www.waldorfastorianaples.com, $164-869), was previously known as the Waldorf Astoria Naples until it was purchased by Northwood Hospitality in 2013. Since then it has received a $13 million renovation. A sweeping granite lobby leads to the Aura restaurant and bar, complete with a South Beach-style, draped lounge. The Naples Grande is surrounded by 200 acres of tropical mangrove preserve, with beach access and three swimming pools. The newest additions are the Naples Grande Spa and The Catch of the Pelican seafood restaurant.

Over $300

The **Bellasera Hotel** (221 9th St. S., 888/205-7322, $300-600) was named one of the "top 10 hidden gems in the U.S." in the Travelers' Choice awards on TripAdvisor. It features 100 luxurious studios and one-, two-, and three-bedroom suites with kitchens and spacious living and dining areas, all with bold Tuscan-style architecture and decor. It's a AAA Four Diamond award winner just far enough

removed from the bustle of 5th Avenue to seem restful. A heated outdoor pool, fitness center, Zizi Restaurant & Lounge, meeting space, and business center round out the amenities.

If your favorite time is tee time, there are several golfy wonderlands. The **Naples Beach Hotel & Golf Club** (851 Gulf Shore Blvd. N., 239/261-2222, www.naplesbeachhotel.com, $430-600) is a 125-acre beachfront resort with 317 guest rooms and suites, on-site championship golf, an award-winning tennis center, large beachside swimming pool, fitness center and spa, complimentary kids' program, four restaurants, an open-air beach bar, and a handful of lovely boutiques. In early 2013, the hotel completed its $5 million beachfront pool complex, which includes a free-form pool as well as a secluded oval-shaped pool for adults. This all-new pool complex follows the completion of the resort's multimillion-dollar renovation in 2010.

LaPlaya Beach & Golf Resort (9891 Gulf Shore Blvd. N., 239/597-3123, $300-1,000) had a multimillion-dollar makeover in 2002 that turned an already incredible property into one of the best in the area. The 189 spacious guest rooms and suites offer goose-down pillows and Frette linens. There are marble bathrooms with jetted tubs, a tremendous spa, twice-daily maid service—and there's golf. You have to drive a little over three miles from the hotel, but enthusiasts say the Bob Cupp-designed course is worth it. It's an 18-hole, par 72, 6,907-yard championship layout with a driving range, practice area, and 12,000-square-foot clubhouse.

Not to be outdone, the **Ritz-Carlton Naples Golf Resort** (2600 Tiburon Dr., 239/593-2000, $350-1,000) has received kudos from *Golf Digest* as one of the best golf resorts in North America. And in fact all of the 295 guest rooms manage to look out on the sweeping vistas of the Greg Norman-designed Tiburon Golf Club. Guests can also enjoy the amenities at the sister Ritz-Carlton in town.

And if your aim is to have sand in your bed, or at least the beach within walking distance, there are several wonderful luxury hotels that fit the bill. The **Edgewater Beach Hotel** (1901 Gulf Shore Blvd. N., 239/403-2000, $300-700) is an intimate, 126-suite boutique hotel right on the beach. All suites, the lobby, and pool deck area had a hip redecoration in 2006. It's another AAA Four Diamond property, with a deliciously edgy lobby restaurant called Coast.

The other **Ritz-Carlton Naples** (280 Vanderbilt Beach Rd., 239/598-3300, $400-1,000) is a Mobil Five-Star, AAA Five Diamond resort, all 463 rooms with stunning views of the Gulf of Mexico. There are seven on-site restaurants, tennis courts, a 33-treatment-room spa with fitness center, two pools, championship golf nearby at Tiburon, and white sand as far as the eye can see.

Vacation Rentals

Reflecting the Naples demographic, most of the rental homes and condos in the area tend toward the upscale. The price you are going to pay largely depends on where you want to stay. A large majority of the rental homes are located on one of the many golf courses in the area, while the more expensive homes are the luxurious mansions in the beachfront districts. During the heat of summer you can find exceptional deals on vacation rentals in the area. Most of the year a spectacular five-bedroom, four-bath house on the beach will run upwards of $1,000 per night and around $6,000 per week; a more modest two- or three-bedroom home with a pool on a golf course $200-500 per night; and a one- or two-bedroom condo near the beach $150-400 per night. Renting in the area is a great choice for an extended stay or if you just want the added privacy and the private pool. The top rental agencies in the area are **Marco Naples Vacation Rentals** (239/774-1273, www.marconaplesvacationrentals.com) and **Naples Rentals** (www.naplesrentals.com). Both agencies have an extensive variety of homes available to rent and exceptional websites for browsing and finding the perfect getaway in the Naples area.

GETTING THERE AND AROUND
Car

From I-75, you can take exit 101 to Highway 84, which leads to downtown Naples (best if your aim is to do a little shopping or dining along 5th Avenue South or 3rd Street South, or if you want to amble along the Naples Pier). The new exit 105 is best to reach Naples Zoo and Naples Municipal Airport. Exit 107 (Pine Ridge Rd.) takes you directly to U.S. 41, otherwise known as the Tamiami Trail, and is the best exit for reaching Clam Pass and Vanderbilt Beach parks and beaches. The National Audubon Society's Corkscrew Swamp Sanctuary is easiest accessed by exit 111 (Immokalee Rd.), which also takes you to North Naples.

If you're coming from Miami, take U.S. 41 the whole way. The Tamiami Trail is a little slower than I-75, but it offers more sightseeing possibilities, as it has been designated a National Scenic Byway and Florida Scenic Highway. The route celebrated its 75th anniversary in 2003 and takes you right through the Everglades and Big Cypress National Preserve.

Air

There is a little commuter airport in Naples, the **Naples Municipal Airport** (160 Aviation Dr., 239/643-0733, www.flynaples. com), which offers charter jet service from several air charter airlines to Key West and other nearby destinations. Private jets constitute much of this airport's daily traffic. From the Naples Municipal Airport, there is a convenient **Naples Airport Shuttle** (888/569-2227).

Private planes can also fly into Marco Executive Airport, Immokalee Regional Airport, and Everglades Airpark in Everglades City.

Bus

Greyhound Bus Line (239/774-5660) provides regular service into Naples, and **Collier Area Transit** (239/252-7777, www.colliergov.

net) operates a reliable network of city buses ($4 for a daylong pass).

One of the most pleasant sightseeing opportunities in Naples is the **Naples Trolley** (1010 6th Ave. S., 800/592-0848, day passes $27 adults, $12.50 children 4-12, children under 4 free). The narrated tour covers over 100 local points of interest and offers a nice historical overview of the area. You can disembark whenever something captures your interest and then hop the next trolley that comes shuffling by.

Marco Island

Marco Island is a beach vacation spot that especially caters to families. It is the largest and northernmost of the Ten Thousand Islands, with an average annual high temperature of 85°F and an average low of 65°F, so most of the year it's enjoyable to be outside. Unfortunately, it doesn't have the best civic planning and development in the area; in some areas on the island the high-rise hotels block all view of the ocean for long stretches of the coast, and there is a lack of public beach access and parking. But, Marco Island has lots going for it—gorgeous sunsets, gentle Gulf breezes, a subtropical lushness, as well as easy access to Naples (to the north) and the Everglades National Park (to the south). Beyond the beaches, there are several fine private and semiprivate golf courses; lots of good snook, redfish, and pompano fishing; and access to more tiny, wonderful islands than you can count. Most of the residents who live on Marco reside in the low-rise, ranch-style homes on the bridge end of the island. The rest of the island is given over to a luxury-resort paradigm. During high season, the island becomes a retreat for more than 14,000 people.

Marco Island used to be two separate landmasses—one part of it a shell mound raised by generations of shellfish-eating Calusas. Their detritus, along with some more-recent swamp dredging, yielded the current-day 6,800-acre island with its rolling sand hills, beaches, and slash pine forests. The island was named La Isla de San Marco, the Island of St. Mark, by the Spaniards shortly after they landed on these shores in 1513 (around the time the Calusa disappeared). The island's history dates back much further, though—archaeology enthusiasts and history buffs flock to the island's historical markers and wealth of artifacts. A dozen markers around town chart Marco Island history, including one of the most significant excavations in North America—the priceless Key Marco Cat, the first known North American example of a half man-half animal figurine. The cat itself is now at the Smithsonian, but the small sculpture was unearthed here in 1896 and is thought to be more than 3,000 years old (there's a replica in the historical society museum).

SPORTS AND RECREATION
★ Tigertail Beach

Marco Island boasts a four-mile crescent of white sandy beach. Not too far from the long stand of tall condominiums and resort hotels, **Tigertail Beach** (entrance at Spinnaker Dr. and Hernando Dr., 8am-sunset daily, parking $8) is pretty much all things to all people. There's a rental stand for water sports and toys, umbrellas, and chairs; volleyball nets that see heavy action; a concession stand, showers, and restrooms; and a children's play area. You'll see little Sand Dollar Island out across the lagoon, which was Tigertail's sandbar only 10 years ago, a perfect place for shelling and sand castle-building at low tide. The 32-acre beach park is also a birder's favorite for watching shorebirds (but the bird sanctuary nearby is off-limits to visitors).

Marco South Beach

Marco South Beach (walkway access from

Collier Blvd. north of Cape Marco, sunrise-sunset daily, parking $8/day, $1.50/hour) is a residents' beach, which has public parking and access. This beach has no facilities but is a good place to beachcomb for Florida sand dollars, whelks, fighting conchs, lion's paws, calico scallops, and others of the more than 400 types of seashells found on the island. Be sure to leave all live shells on the beach. Pets are prohibited on Marco Island beaches.

Fishing

Island visitors and locals surf-cast for black drum and sheepshead; they take boats out in the backcountry mangrove flats to fish for tarpon, snook, and redfish; or they head into deeper water offshore for grouper, amberjack, snapper, and kingfish. A number of species in the area have game fish status, and are thus more exotic and often the most sought after. This means redfish, snook, tarpon, bonefish, and sailfish are illegal to buy or sell (that's why you don't ever see them on restaurant menus), and many of them have low catch limits and specific seasons. For instance, in the Gulf of Mexico and the Everglades, open season for snook (the period of time you are allowed to harvest a fish) is now limited to the months of March, April, September, October,

and November. Fish must be between 28 and 33 inches to keep, with one snook allowed per person. If you catch a snook during December-February or May-August, the fish must be released alive. Don't wet a line until you've studied up on what you can catch, how many, and when.

If you want to head out fishing with an expert, Marco Island, as with much of the Gulf Coast, has many specialists willing to show you the way. Specializing in light tackle and fly-fishing, **Captain Gary Eichler** (239/642-9779, www.doublersfishingandtours.com, $400-800, depending on the boat and location) has a number of boats from which to choose and lots of experience in the area. He does individual private charters (no split charters) with six passengers at the most.

Captain Bill Walsh takes visitors out with his company, **Dawn Patrol** (239/394-0608, www.dawnpatrolcharters.com, $350 half day for 4 people), known for fishing the nearshore artificial reefs and ledges. Dawn Patrol specializes in family trips and will tailor a fishing trip to include a mix of shelling, fishing, and sightseeing so even non-anglers in your group are entertained.

Specializing in fly-fishing and light tackle angling is **Naples Fishing Charters** (1500

Marco Island coastline

The Stingray Shuffle

It's not a dance, exactly.

It's strictly anecdotal, but Marco Island seems to have more than its share of flat, seafloor-living stingrays. Visitors occasionally step on these creatures, their winglike fins hidden in the sandy shallows. When trod upon, a stingray flips up its tail in self-defense and delivers a nasty stinging puncture with its barb. To avoid this, drag your feet along the sandy bottom (as opposed to stepping up and down). The "shuffle" may not look too swift, but it alerts stingrays to your approach. They are just hanging around the shallows to catch shellfish and crustaceans, and they'd rather not waste their time on stinging you.

If you are unlucky enough to be stung, it's important that you clean the wound with freshwater immediately (other bacteria in seawater can infect the area). As soon as you can, soak the wound in the hottest water you can stand for up to 90 minutes to neutralize the venom. The pain can be severe, often accompanied by weakness, vomiting, headache, fainting, shortness of breath, paralysis, and collapse in people who are allergic to the venom. You may want to see a doctor, who might add insult to injury with a tetanus shot.

Always report stingray injuries to the lifeguard on duty.

Danford, Naples, 239/450-9230, www.naplesfishingcharters.org, $400-750 depending on the length and type of trip). Captain Mike Ward used to run the Everglades Angler Fly Shop. He has lots of experience in the area, and is Orvis endorsed.

If you want to go it alone, **Marco River Marina** (951 Bald Eagle Dr., 239/394-2502) rents out the largest array of boats on the island including center consoles, deck boats, and pontoons. Boats at **Walker's Hideaway Marina** (705 E. Elkcam Cir., 239/394-9333, www.walkersmarine.com) all come equipped with a bimini (sun top), plastic cooler stocked with ice and drinks, VHF radio, USCG equipment, and an easy-to-navigate color chart of the local waters. They're endlessly patient with beginners, too. Deck boats are $200 for half day, $300 for full. The Marco River Marina is also the debarkation point for **Key West Express** (239/463-5733, departs 8:30am daily, no sailings Tues.-Wed. June-Dec., round-trip $154 adults, $144 seniors 62 and over, $91 junior, $60 children), a three-hour cruise to Key West; this is an affordable way to explore Key West without having to fly.

Golf

Guidebooks all bandy about the statistic that Naples has more golf courses per capita than anywhere else. Many of these are in East Naples, and many are private. On Marco Island there are several notable private courses—**Hideaway Beach Club** (250 Beach Dr. S., 239/394-5555), **Island Country Club** (500 Nassau Rd., 239/394-6661), and others—but only a couple of public possibilities. The Marco Island Marriott's **Rookery Golf Club** (3433 Club Center Blvd., 239/389-6600), designed by Joe Lee, is an 18-hole, par 72, Scottish links-style course built on 240 acres of rolling terrain and featuring several mounds coming into play around the greens. The signature hole is No. 16, a 165-yard par 3, requiring a tee shot over water to a peninsula green. Swing tune-ups for experienced players as well as beginners' lessons are available at the Marriott's Faldo Institute located at The Rookery at Marco.

Despite its name, the **Marco Shores Country Club** (1450 Mainsail Dr., Naples, 239/394-2581) is in Naples, but close by. The course has long, wide fairways and well-maintained greens blended seamlessly into the native mangroves and waterways of the Ten Thousand Islands. With four separate tees, Marco Shores accommodates all skill levels.

★ Boat Tour to Calusa Shell Mounds

The Calusa tribe lived on the coast and along the inner waterways in this area. They were tall and fierce and regularly battled with neighboring tribes. They did not farm, but rather fished and hunted for their sustenance from the bountiful bays, rivers, and Gulf (these were so bountiful, in fact, that as many as 50,000 Calusas may have been living here at a time). They controlled much of the south-west coast of Florida, and many other tribes justifiably feared their aggression. This is all ancient history, though, as the Spanish settlers ran them off or killed them off, either actively, or passively with the introduction of small-pox and other diseases, starting soon after the Spanish arrived in the 1500s. By the 1700s the tribe was wiped out, the remaining handful of Calusas purportedly lighting out for Cuba when the Spanish turned Florida over to the British in 1763.

The impact of the Calusas on the area and their unique way of life are still apparent today, however. They built homes on stilts with palmetto leaf roofs and no walls and fashioned nets from palm tree fiber to catch mullet, catfish, and pinfish. But their most ingenious work was with shells. Shellfish was a staple in the Calusa diet—once the succulent meat was removed, the shells were used to make jewelry, utensils, spearheads, other tools, and vast heaps upon which other things could be built. Little mangrove keys, uninhabitable on their own, became homes or sacred places with the addition of a few thousand carefully piled shells.

These shell mounds are literally the building blocks for Marco Island and many of the Ten Thousand Islands. If you want to spend a day exploring the remnants of Calusa mounds, **Florida Backcountry Adventures** (239/595-7495, $380 for a 3-hour trip for up to 6 people, $280 for 2 hours) offers wonderful ecotours. Captain Alex Saputo takes small groups out on his 24-foot boat, weaving in and out of the Ten Thousand Islands while pointing out wildlife and explaining in detail the horticultural and local history. He's extremely knowledgeable about the Calusa and Seminole peoples and history, and his enthusiasm is infectious as you tramp around a shell mound, crouching to see a fat whelk shell once used as

Chickees

What is a chickee, you ask? You'll see the term a lot around here. It's a Seminole word for an open, handmade structure made up of cypress poles and a roof of palm fronds. Historically, there was an art to erecting chickees, the cypress stripped in a process called "draw knife" and the fronds nailed in a particular pattern to keep out the area's heavy rains. A chickee is now more broadly defined as any open-air structure, but usually ones in which boozing and general merriment occur.

a hammerhead or other tool. And on the way back, watch for dolphins that leap in the wake of the boat—they're either playing or "drafting" off the boat's speed (even dolphin experts disagree about why they do it)—but it's about as close as you'll ever get to dolphins outside of Sea World.

SIGHTS

History enthusiasts have a couple of small yet illuminating museums on the island. Marco Island Historical Society operates the **Marco Island History Museum** (180 S. Heathwood Dr., 239/642-1440, www.themihs.org, 9am-4pm Tues.-Sat., free), which opened in 2010 and replaced the former Museum at Olde Marco. The focus is on archaeological finds of the area with an emphasis on Calusa culture. There's even a sweet life-sized diorama of a Calusa household, and the grounds of the museum are beautifully landscaped with native plants and ponds.

The second museum, the **Key Marco Museum** (in the lobby of the Board of Realtors office, Waterway Ct., 9am-4pm Mon.-Fri., free) covers some of the same ground, with Calusa treasures displayed prominently. But it moves forward in time to capture moments of pioneer history and early island industries into the 20th century. Both museums are unstaffed, but a guided tour can be arranged by calling ahead. There are also maps at the museums for a self-guided tour of Marco Island's 13 historical markers, including that of the Cushing Archaeological Site from 1895, said to be one of the most historically significant excavations in North America (it unearthed a renowned statue known as the Key Marco Cat). It doesn't take long to zip through the tour, either by car or bike, and it's a good orientation to the island.

SHOPPING

Marco doesn't have as many upscale shops as Naples to the north, but it certainly has more shopping than you'll find in Everglades City to the south. There are a few concentrated areas: The **Esplanade** (740-760 Collier Blvd. N., 239/394-6333) is a newer development with clothing and home decor stores, a few restaurants, and a nice day spa. It's also the only place on the island with a Starbucks (and a Cold Stone Creamery). Beyond that, there's a collection of shops at the **Marco Town Center Mall** (1017 N Collier Blvd., on Collier Blvd. N. at Bald Eagle Dr., 239/394-7549). Adjacent to the Olde Marco Island Inn at the northern tip of the island, the **Shops at Olde Marco** (100 Palm St., 239/475-3466) complex has a couple of boutiques, gourmet food shops, and the inn's spa and fitness center.

But for the big kahuna of shopping, you have to drive just north off the island. **Naples Outlet Center** (7222 Isle of Capri Rd., 239/775-8083, 10am-8pm Mon.-Sat., 11am-6pm Sun.) has more than 40 stores, most of them big names, with designer clothes and shoes, books, and housewares at up to 70 percent off retail prices.

FOOD

All the times listed below reflect peak season hours. If you're dining here during the off-season, it's best to call for hours of operation.

Casual

Originally called the Snook Hole for the wealth of snook you could catch right off the dock, the **Snook Inn** (1215 Bald Eagle Dr.,

239/394-3313, 11am-10pm daily, $10-25) was first a sprawling, casual restaurant that catered to construction workers in the 1960s. Right on the Marco River, the Snook Inn is a fun indoor-outdoor joint with live music and long lines. Locals and visitors seem to come for the grouper and the vast salad bar with a neat old-fashioned pickle barrel. The garden courtyard is a great locale to get creamy seafood chowder or tackle a pile of peel-and-eat shrimp (if you aren't wild about seafood, the jerk chicken quesadilla is quite good). There's docking available for more than 20 boats near the chickee.

Most of the island's other restaurants are lined up along Collier Boulevard. You'll see a lot of locals tucking into a thick-crust pizza at **Joey's Pizzeria and Pasta House** (257 Collier Blvd. N., 239/389-2433, 11am-10pm daily, $10-15).

Or browse the range of possibilities at the Marco Town Center Mall: **Crazy Flamingo** (1035 Collier Blvd. N., 239/642-6633, 11am-2am daily, $10-20) is a lively raw bar with good fish entrées, and **Susie's Diner** (1013 Collier Blvd. N., 239/642-6633, 7am-2pm Mon.-Sat., 7am-1pm Sun., $5-15) is a favorite for breakfast and lunch. Go early for fresh housemade biscuits, waffles, pancakes, and omelets in the morning. Lunches are a good deal, as the price includes beverage and dessert.

Upscale

Marek's Collier House (1121 Bald Eagle Dr., 239/642-9948, 5pm-10pm daily, $20-35) gets the nod from local publications nearly every year for upscale and romantic continental dining. It's partly due to the setting—the restaurant is nestled in Captain Bill Collier's beautiful historic home—and partly because of chef/owner Peter Marek's tasteful take on rich seafood dishes. This guy is a triple gold medalist at the World Culinary Olympics—yes, there is such a thing—and his lamb chops, swordfish in green peppercorn sauce, and veal scaloppini with blue crabmeat all score a solid 9.8.

The **Bistro Soleil** (100 Palm St.,

239/394-3131, 5pm-10pm daily, $25-35) restaurant at the Olde Marco Island Inn is another expensive favorite in the area for those looking for a nice bottle of wine and perfectly prepared steak, seafood, and more. There are five individual dining rooms, each with a slightly different feel, so try to wander through each before settling on a table (there's also an upper dining deck that looks out over the inn's gardens).

Arturo's Italian Restaurant (844 Bald Eagle Dr., 239/642-0550, 5pm-10pm daily, $15-25) opened in 1994 and serves a justifiably famous stuffed pork chop, a range of hearty pastas, and an extensive wine list.

Dining with a Twist

Dine one of several ways aboard the 74-foot *Marco Island Princess* (departs from the marina, 951 Bald Eagle Dr., 239/642-5415, www.themarcoislandprincess.com, $38-50), sister ship to the *Naples Princess*. There's the Sea Breeze lunch buffet cruise, a sunset hors d'oeuvres cruise, or a sunset dinner cruise. Head out on the luxury yacht as it glides along the scenic Marco River into the Gulf of Mexico with leaping dolphins in hot pursuit. The ship itself is beautiful, as is the scenery, either by day or with a sunset casting its warm glow. The food is pretty good, but the cash bar is expensive. The ship gets busy for holidays (Valentine's Day, Mother's Day, New Year's Eve) and is often rented out for private parties, so reserve early if you can.

Marco boasts another unusual dining experience. An evening at **Marco Movies** (599 S. Collier Blvd., Ste. 103, 239/642-1111, $8-15) is the oldest date-night one-two punch in the books: dinner and a movie, but both at the same time. A small, family-owned four-screen theater, it shows first-run movies (there's always at least one family-appropriate pick) and serves food and alcoholic beverages. A sampling of the menu includes Greek salad, good sweet-potato fries, several tortilla-wrapped sandwiches, pizzas, banana splits, beer, wine, cocktails, and, of course, popcorn.

Marek's Collier House

ACCOMMODATIONS
Under $100

There's not much on Marco Island for the budget traveler. However, satisfaction is just a couple of minutes away. Goodland is a little town adjacent to Marco Island that's about a mile square and boasts a few hundred residents, mostly fisherfolk, and a bunch of down-home bars. There has been a shift toward more upscale development in recent years, but you can still find casual and reasonably priced accommodations at the **Pink House Motel** (310 Pear Tree Ave., Goodland, 239/394-1313, $59-99), a historic family-owned waterfront motel with boat docking, efficiency kitchens, laundry facilities, and the Marker 7 Marina and Tackle Shop.

$100-200

On Marco Island, the **Boat House Motel** (1180 Edington Pl., 239/642-2400, www.theboathousemotel.com, $99-290) is a little more glamorous—two stories with a gazebo and boat docks—and a little pricier than Pink

House Motel, but still a straightforward low-rise motel.

Marco Island Lakeside Inn (155 1st Ave., 239/394-1161, $140-350) has 10 one-bedroom and 2 two-bedroom units and 7 studio efficiencies located on Marco Lake one mile from the beach. There is a pool area with a thatched-roof gazebo and gas grill overlooking the lake, an Italian steak house, and a full bar on-site.

Over $300

Maybe it's an "if you can't beat 'em, join 'em" mentality, but if you're going to stay on Marco Island you might as well pony up the dough and stay at one of the "Big Three." Three beachfront resorts dominate the most coveted piece of shoreline. Each has lots of amenities, good restaurants on-site, and a broad price range to accommodate different budgets.

Having experienced a $187 million renovation in 2007, the **Marco Island Marriott Beach Resort, Golf Club, and Spa** (400 Collier Blvd. S., 239/394-2511, www.marcoislandmarriott.com, $250-1,000) may be best suited to a romantic golf-and-pampering getaway, with more than 700 rooms and lavish resort activities and facilities, the 24,000-square-foot Balinese-themed spa, a tiki pool, and the Rookery at Marco—the resort's wonderful golf course.

The **Marco Beach Ocean Resort** (480 Collier Blvd. S., 239/393-1400, www.marcoresort.com, $400-1,000) opened in 2001 with 98 one- and two-bedroom suites, a spa, upscale Italian restaurants, and a stunning rooftop swimming pool with a panoramic view of the Gulf.

And the 25-year-old **Hilton Marco Island Beach Resort** (560 S. Collier Blvd., 239/394-5000, www.marcoisland.hilton.com, $199-1,000) is a luxury resort that consistently wins four-diamond status and so forth for its large guest rooms with Gulf-view private balconies, lighted Har-Tru tennis courts, vast amoeba-shaped pool, and other amenities. An incredible luxury spa opened in 2008 with spacious massage and relaxation rooms all designed in a stylish and bold Greco-Roman theme.

Right out the back door of all three hotels, you can rent aqua trikes and personal watercraft with **Marco Island Ski & Watersports** (239/642-3377), which also offers parasailing, shelling trips, WaveRunner tours, sunset cruises, and dolphin-watching tours on the Gulf.

For a more historic, small-inn experience, try **Olde Marco Island Inn & Suites** (100 Palm St., 239/394-3131, www.oldemarcoinn.com, $250-600), a 116-year-old Victorian in the historic district. It features one- and two-bedroom suites with roomy screened lanais. There are six luxurious penthouses and a much-lauded restaurant. It's a convenient location, near beaches, shopping, and golf, and guests enjoy complimentary use of the inn's 38-foot catamaran.

Vacation Rentals

There are hundreds of vacation rental homes and condominiums on Marco Island. Many of these rent only by the week, especially in high season, and most work out to less than $150 per night. Several rental companies have nice websites from which you can peruse properties: **Coldwell Banker** (239/394-6121, www.marcoislandvacations.net) seems to rent largely in high-rise condos, **Holiday Homes of Marco Island** (239/389-9940, www.marco-island.com) represents a number of single-family homes, and **Prudential Florida Realty** (239/642-5400, www.prudentialfloridarealty.com) offers a wide range, from fancy high-rise condos to individual homes right on a golf course.

GETTING THERE

To get to Marco Island, take exit 101 off I-75, then follow Collier Boulevard (Hwy. 951) west to the island, crossing Jolley Bridge on the way. From Naples, the drive is a little over 18 miles, which usually takes about 30 minutes. From Everglades City, drive north on County Road 29, then take U.S. 41 north to San Marco Road (County Road 92), and drive to Marco Island. The 30-mile drive will take you about 40 minutes.

Everglades City

Everglades City is a locus of ecotourism, with canoe tours, airboat rides, fishing guides, and other nature-based businesses capitalizing on the mystery and majesty of the million acres of mangrove jungle just to the south. It's significantly more rustic than swanky Naples to the north—there are no Ritz-Carltons, tux-clad waiters, or turndown service with mints on the pillow anywhere near, but Everglades City is a must for adventure seekers.

SIGHTS

Everglades National Park

Everglades National Park (mail: 40001 Hwy. 9336, Homestead, FL 33034-6733, 305/242-7700; in Everglades City: Gulf Coast Visitor Center, 815 Oyster Bar Ln., 239/695-3311, 8am-4:30pm daily mid-Nov.-mid-Apr., 9am-4:30pm mid-Apr.-mid-Nov., no entrance fee on this side of the park) is the third-largest park in the continental United States and has been designated a World Heritage Site, an International Biosphere Reserve, and a Wetland of International Importance. It's the only subtropical preserve in North America, containing both temperate and tropical plant communities. Really, it's the only everglade in the world.

The Seminoles called the park "grassy water," because it is essentially a wide, shallow river with no current, and no falls or rapids, that flows slowly southward along the subtle slope of the land, eventually meeting open water in Florida Bay 100 miles away. This river flows along sawgrass prairies, mangrove and cypress swamps, pinelands, and hardwood hammocks. Everywhere there are wading birds, alligators, and dense and exotic tropical plantlife.

Still, I don't think any of this conveys exactly what's so cool. A couple of days of paddling Everglades National Park will have you gliding past 12-foot gators, beautiful orchids and epiphytes (air plants) dotting the swamp

with color, and birds engaged in a strenuous call-and-response—it's an exceptionally wild and beautiful park, best explored by kayak or canoe, that is well worth extensive exploration.

The Everglades region is mild and pleasant December-April, rarely reaching freezing temperatures, and mostly without a drop

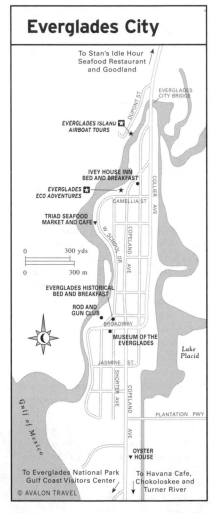

Everglades City

To Stan's Idle Hour
Seafood Restaurant
and Goodland

EVERGLADES
CITY BRIDGE

DUPONT ST

EVERGLADES ISLAND
AIRBOAT TOURS

IVEY HOUSE INN
BED AND BREAKFAST

EVERGLADES
ECO ADVENTURES

COLLIER AVE

CAMELLIA ST

TRIAD SEAFOOD
MARKET AND CAFE

W SCHOOL DR

COPELAND AVE

0   300 yds

0   300 m

EVERGLADES HISTORICAL
BED AND BREAKFAST

ROD AND
GUN CLUB

BROADWAY

MUSEUM OF THE
EVERGLADES

Lake
Placid

JASMINE ST

SHORTER AVE

COPELAND AVE

Gulf of Mexico

PLANTATION PWY

AVE

OYSTER
HOUSE

To Everglades National Park
Gulf Coast Visitors Center

To Havana Cafe,
Chokoloskee and
Turner River

© AVALON TRAVEL

Everglades City

Mosquitoes are surprisingly not a real problem until the summer, when you absolutely don't want to be paddling through the steamy swamp anyway due to the heat and humidity. Still, you'll need bug spray, water, sunglasses, a flotation device (required by law), shoes you don't mind getting wet or muddy, comfortable clothes, a hat—and a plan.

Check at the **Gulf Coast Visitor Center** (815 Oyster Bar Ln., 239/695-3311, 8am-4:30pm daily mid-Nov.-mid-Apr., 9am-4:30pm mid-Apr.-mid-Nov.) for maps and directions; you can rent canoes downstairs from the visitors center at **Everglades National Park Boat Tours** (239/695-2591, $38/day). It's fairly daunting to head off by yourself the first day, so the visitors center and Everglades National Park Boat Tours both offer guided tours on a first-come, first-served basis.

After that, if you want to push off on your own, put in at the canoe ramp next to the visitors center or the ramp next to Outdoor Resorts on Chokoloskee Island. As everyone

of rain. Summers are hot and humid, with temperatures hovering around 90°F and humidity at a fairly consistent, steamy 90 percent. And, as with most places along the Gulf Coast, there are tremendous afternoon thunderstorms in the summer.

CANOEING AND KAYAKING

Everglades National Park is America's only subtropical wilderness, a third of it given over to marine areas and shallow estuaries easily paddled by rookie or seasoned kayakers or canoers (in my experience, a kayak seems easier to navigate through these sometimes-tight quarters). The mangroves form canopied tunnels through the swamp, through which you pick in a peculiar way: Often the flat of your paddle is used to gently push off from the tangle of mangrove roots when it's too tight to actually dip the paddle into the water. In this way you pole through the tight spots, the nose of your craft sometimes hitching up in the roots, necessitating backward paddling to disengage.

will tell you: Don't overestimate your abilities, and time your trip with the tides (a falling tide flows toward the Gulf of Mexico; a rising tide flows toward the visitors center). If you want to pick up a nautical chart, No. 11430 covers the Chokoloskee Bay area. There are also detailed descriptions to be had at the visitors center and other local shops of how to traverse the **Wilderness Waterway,** a 99-mile canoe trail that winds from Everglades City over to the Flamingo Visitor Center at the southeast entrance to the national park. It's about an eight-day excursion, to be undertaken only after plenty of diligent preparation.

Collier County has completed Phase I of the **Paradise Coast Blueway,** a system of GPS-marked paddling trails in the Ten Thousand Islands region, which will eventually extend north to Bonita Springs. There is a main trail route from Everglades City to Goodland, as well as six day-trip routes ranging 2-10 hours of paddling time. If you only have time to do one section of the trail, I would highly recommend reserving a campsite at Rabbit Key through the Everglades National Park visitors center and camping out on the sandy, palm-lined, private beach for the night. The paddling trip embarks from the Outdoor Resorts center on Chokoloskee Island and is about five miles to Rabbit Key. It can easily take an entire day depending on your skill level, strength, and the speed and weight of your kayak or canoe. It is especially important to check the tides when paddling in the Ten Thousand Islands region of the Everglades, as they are dramatic and can leave you stranded in water too shallow to paddle in, with nowhere to camp. You should also bring a GPS and use the GPS waypoints posted on the Paradise Coast Blueway website for ease of navigation, as it is easy to get lost among the literally thousands of mangrove islands that look extremely similar. Visit www.paradisecoastblueway.com for more information and detailed downloadable route maps.

led by naturalist guides who have a clear passion for the abundant natural beauty of the area. You will stop occasionally to view unusual orchids, alligators sunning, and eagles overhead. Paradise, really, with the dense lushness and lack of human marks that make you feel as if you've somehow fallen into a prehistoric jungle. Substitute pterodactyl babies for the osprey fledglings you see peering from that huge nest above, and the illusion is complete.

One of the trips it offers launches into the water off U.S. 41 at the old Turner River, quickly passing into narrow mangrove tunnels, then out into lagoons and past sawgrass prairies and into Turner Lake. The company runs its tours November 1-April 30 and offers a range of specialty tours for small groups, from photography workshops to night paddles. It also rents equipment you can take out on your own.

★ EVERGLADES ECO ADVENTURES

Everglades Rentals & Eco Adventures (Ivey House Inn Bed and Breakfast, 107 Camellia St., 239/695-3299, $99-600) offers spectacular half-day, full-day, and overnight guided canoe, kayak, and boating adventures

★ EVERGLADES ISLAND AIRBOAT TOURS

Lots of airboat companies offer competent tours with nature-focused narration, but the most historically significant is **Everglades Island Airboat Tours** (929 Dupont St., just before the Everglades City Bridge,

a heron in the Everglades

One Day in the Everglades

an alligator in Everglades National Park

For this trip you'll definitely want strong bug spray, plenty of water, sunglasses, shoes you don't mind getting wet or muddy, comfortable clothes (preferably quick dry, lightweight pants and a long-sleeved shirt), and a hat to protect you from the sun.

Start the morning off with breakfast at **Havana Café** (191 Smallwood Dr., Chokoloskee, 239/695-2214, www.myhavanacafe.com, 7am-6pm daily, call for summer hours, $6-15), and then take a sunrise paddle through **Everglades National Park.** It's a wonderful place to observe birds, alligators, and other native wildlife. Then do something a bit more thrilling and take an airboat ride with **Everglades Island Airboat Tours** (239/695-2591, $38/day). The tours are offered on a first-come, first-served basis. Make sure to be cautious around wildlife when adventuring around the Everglades. And do not feed the alligators!

Have lunch in Everglades City at the **Oyster House Restaurant** (901 S. Copeland Ave., 239/695-2073, 11am-9pm Sun.-Thurs., 11am-11pm Fri.-Sat., $10-19) and then drive to Turner River Road in the **Big Cypress National Preserve** (3 miles east of the Big Cypress Welcome Center on Highway 41) and spend the rest of the day spotting wildlife and enjoying the scenery.

Stay the night at the **Ivey House Inn Bed and Breakfast** (107 Camellia St., 239/695-3299, $100-200), a relaxing inn built in 2001 that's beautifully landscaped, and has an excellent screened pool and waterfall area. A delicious breakfast accommodating all tastes is served in the morning, and complimentary coffee is available throughout the day.

239/695-2333, 30-minute, 1-hour, and 1.5-hour tours, $20-40).

Loren "Totch" Brown, author of *Totch: A Life in the Everglades* (a must-read if you are interested in the crusty, taciturn folks who've eked a living out of the Everglades over the past 100 years), grew up on an island near Chokoloskee during the Depression. As a young man he fought in World War II before going home to work variously as a pompano fisher and stone crabber (legally) and

an alligator poacher and marijuana smuggler (illegally). You can see a picture of the local legend in Smallwood Store, a tiny museum on Chokoloskee Island (150 acres made entirely of shells by the Seminoles), or catch a glimpse of him in the 1955 film *Wind Across the Everglades* with Christopher Plummer.

Totch died in 1996, but his tour company consists of his family members and a number of fourth- and fifth-generation Everglades residents. They'll take you out either in backcountry or open water to Totch's Island to see his rustic family cottage on a tiny mangrove island. Along the way, you'll be trailed by pelicans, catch glimpses of manatees lumbering along the brackish shallows beneath you, and see alligators (big ones), wild pigs, ospreys, and incredible plantlife.

OTHER BOAT TOURS

You've seen them. They're the embodiment of Newton's Third Law: Those tall boats propelled by air whooshing through their giant fans—with no outboard motor and rudder for propulsion and control, these boats can scoot through extreme shallows on their flat bottoms, perfect for swamp exploration. It's an Everglades cliché, and a loud one, but fun. (Although they're not allowed in Everglades National Park proper, they scoot around the edges in the Ten Thousand Islands.)

One successful airboat company is **Everglades City Airboat Tours** (907 Dupont St., 239/695-2400, www.evergladescity-airboattours.com, $39.62 adults, $20.75 children 10 and under). The airboat tour groups are small, and the tour is one hour of meandering through the mangrove forest backcountry and a sawgrass wetland.

My favorite place to take a thrilling airboat ride is definitely **Wooten's Everglades Airboat Tours** (32330 Tamiami Trail E., Ochopee, 5 miles south of Everglades City, 239/695-2781, www.wootenseverglades.com, 9am-4:30pm daily, $28 adults for either tour, $20 children 12-4, $2.50 kids under 4, $8 for the farm), also known as Wooten's. It's a little farther afield but famous in these parts, and their airboat rides explore a diverse section of wetland while their narrators and captains deliver an overview of the history of the Everglades with an overtly environmental and libertarian message. You may also want to take one of the 30-minute swamp tours on the swamp buggy ($24). You'll travel through spooky cypress swamp and spot alligators (as well as North American crocodiles—the Everglades being the only area you'll find these guys in the United States), deer, snakes, and tons of birds. Wooten's small zoo with native Florida wildlife (Florida panthers, bobcats) gives you an opportunity to get as close to a Florida panther as you will ever want to be.

A quieter ride can be found on the **Everglades National Park Boat Tour** (at the ranger station on the causeway between Everglades City and Chokoloskee Island, 239/695-2591, every 30 minutes

one of the airboats at Wooten's Everglades Airboat Tours

9:30am-4:30pm, $31.80 adults, $15.90 children), a wonderful 1.5-hour motorboat tour departing from the Gulf Coast Visitor Center. The cruise is slower, following a loop through a dizzying number of the Ten Thousand Islands. Along the way, tour-goers are likely to see manatees, frisky bottlenose dolphins, bald eagles, and loads of smirking alligators.

Everglades Area Tours (238 Mamie St., Chokoloskee Island, 239/695-3633, www.evergladesareatours.com, $99 and up) provides year-round, half-day, guided kayak ecotours assisted by a motorboat shuttle that carries kayaks and up to six passengers. Aptly named the Yak Attack, the tour strategy allows you to quickly get to the remotest and most beautiful paddling areas. All tours are guided by experienced naturalists. Motorboat ecotours, sea kayaking and camping trips, backcountry charter boat and kayak fishing trips, bicycle tours, and aerial tours in the winter season are also offered.

Museums

The dire economic climate of Reconstruction after the Civil War prompted some robust families to move to the southwest Florida frontier, a "grass is always greener" hopefulness that didn't necessarily pan out as planned. They came, cleared the land on little islands (many of them now named after the original family inhabiting them), built rough-hewn cabins of pine and cypress, and hunted, fished, and farmed. Stoically, they made do in the wilderness, many of them visiting their neighbors by boat only infrequently. Then Ted Smallwood opened Chokoloskee Island's first general store in 1906. There, settlers and the remaining Seminoles would bring in their hides, furs, and produce in exchange for sugar, coffee, ammunition, and other of life's essentials.

Today, **Smallwood Store** (3 miles south of Everglades City, 360 Mamie St., Chokoloskee, 239/695-2989, 10am-5pm daily, $4) is preserved as a 1920s-era general store with its original structure and its last stock of merchandise. The small museum provides stirring insight into the hard lives of the pioneers who settled at the edge of this vast wilderness, and the isolation born of living on tiny, remote mangrove islands. The store was placed on the National Register of Historic Places in 1974 and reopened as a museum by Ted Smallwood's granddaughter in 1989.

Just off the circle in the center of Everglades City, the little **Museum of the Everglades** (105 W. Broadway, 239/695-0008, 9am-4pm Mon.-Sat., $2 suggested donation) is in the town's Old Laundry, a building that dates to the 1920s when Everglades City was Barron Collier's "company town" during the construction of the Tamiami Trail. The focus is more on the area's Seminoles and other tribes who were here before settlers arrived. The building is of note for the history buff—listed on the National Register of Historic Places, it's the only unaltered original building in town. Don't just visit the museum, though, make sure to get a sense of the area's unique history by chatting with the locals or gliding through the mangroves in a canoe. And if it's a rainy day, put aside an hour or two for the museum.

Big Cypress Gallery

East of Everglades City, famous black-and-white landscape photographer Clyde Butcher has a photo gallery worth the drive. **Clyde Butcher's Big Cypress Gallery** (52338 Tamiami Trail, Ochopee, 239/695-2428, 10am-5pm daily) features Butcher's own work on local themes—he is to Big Cypress and the Everglades what Ansel Adams was to Yosemite—as well as the work of other nature-inspired photographers. If you happen to be in the area around Labor Day, the gallery sponsors a huge party with a naturalist-led swamp walk, music, and more.

EVENTS
Everglades Seafood Festival
The annual **Everglades Seafood Festival** (239/695-2277, www.evergladesseafoodfestival.org) in Everglades City draws thousands in February with the promise of stone crabs (they say Everglades City is the world's capital,

with more than 400,000 pounds of crab claws harvested Oct. 15-May 15), fish chowder, gator nuggets, fresh Gulf shrimp, grouper, and fish of all local vintage, along with live country music, rides, and arts and crafts.

SHOPPING

There's a squat nondescript building in the middle of nothing near where the road ends in the Everglades. You can buy ice, bait, gas, and a small assortment of groceries here. It's called the Chokoloskee Mall. I'm sure it's a joke the locals play on tourists, but that about sums up the shopping options in this edge-of-the-wilderness area. Head back up into Naples if the retail bug bites.

FOOD

Dining in Everglades City is unilaterally casual, but with no fast food and few ethnic restaurants. All the times listed below reflect peak season hours. If you're dining here during the off-season, it's best to call for hours of operation.

Several spots are outstanding, both for the food and the convivial ambience. ★ **Havana Cafe** (191 Smallwood Dr., Chokoloskee, 239/695-2214, www.myhavanacafe.com, 7am-6pm daily, call for summer hours, $6-15) has

the best breakfast and lunch in town. They specialize in Cuban cuisine and American eats with a bent toward fresh seafood and classic sweets. It's the best spot to grab an omelet and a cup of authentic Cuban-style *café con leche* as well as delicious Cuban sandwiches, fish platters, peel-and-eat shrimp, and key lime pie. There are a few tables inside, but the best seats are out on the back patio, which is surrounded by hibiscus and other tropicals. The place is as charming and upbeat as they come anywhere in the Everglades, and the owners are extremely friendly. Even if you're not hungry, stop in for a cup of Cuban coffee and some friendly banter with Carlos and Dulce Valdez, the owners of this excellent café.

The **Oyster House Restaurant** (901 S. Copeland Ave., 239/695-2073, 11am-9pm Sun.-Thurs., 11am-11pm Fri.-Sat., $10-19) is a fun and sprawling place with model boats, murals, and mounted largemouth bass and the like. They have fresh fried fish platters, and stone crabs are a house specialty—eat them like the locals, chilled with mustard sauce—as is fried gator tail. And here's a must after lunch or dinner: Take the walk up to the top of the Ernest Hamilton Observation Tower right behind the restaurant. This is a

Rod and Gun Club

75-foot-tall structure built in 1985, with a panoramic view of Chokoloskee and the Ten Thousand Islands.

At the **Rod and Gun Club** restaurant (200 Broadway, 239/695-2101, 11am-2:30pm and 5pm-9:30pm Mon.-Sat., $12-25, no credit cards), set your sights on the conch fritters, gator nuggets, hush puppies, or blue crab claws. At **Triad Seafood Market and Cafe** (401 School Dr., 239/695-0722, 10:30am-6pm daily, $7-15), try the crab cakes, grouper sandwiches, fried shrimp platters, and homemade peanut butter pie. If you've worked up an appetite after a day of Everglades adventure, order up the all-you-can-eat stone crab.

Anyplace that's known for a dance called the Buzzard Lope and that throws the biggest annual party around in honor of mullet is worth some investigation. ★ **Stan's Idle Hour Seafood Restaurant** (221 Goodland Dr. W., Goodland, 239/394-3041, 11am-10pm Tues.-Sat., 11am-7pm Sun., $14-25) is on the tiny island of Goodland, in between Marco Island and Everglades City, connected by causeways. Sunday afternoons are the time to go to Stan's—heck, anytime the place is actually open is a good time to go to Stan's—when a fair percentage of the island's 200 or so residents show up for some live music, pitchers of beer, peel-and-eat shrimp, and fried oysters. (For fisherfolk, Stan's also has a "you caught 'em, we cook 'em" policy.) The weekend after the Super Bowl every January brings the Mullet Festival to Stan's, with lots of rowdy fun and festivities to enjoy.

ACCOMMODATIONS
$100-200

There are three wonderful places to stay in Everglades City, and all are significant pieces of local history and legend. The white clapboard **Rod and Gun Club** (200 Broadway, 239/695-2101, www.evergladesrodandgun.com, $95-140, no credit cards) was built in 1850 on the site of the first homestead in Everglades City. It has hosted movie stars, U.S. presidents, and lots of other celebs needing to get away from it all. The Rod and Gun

Club was, for years, where local and visiting sportspeople gathered to tell big fish stories or share hunting information. A long, low lodge, it contains 17 comfortable rooms, a waterfront restaurant, and dock space.

The ★ **Ivey House Inn Bed and Breakfast** (107 Camellia St., 239/695-3299, $100-200) is my absolute favorite. The property consists of three accommodation options. There is the historic Ivey House, which was first built as a recreation hall for workers on the Tamiami Trail and then converted to a boardinghouse. Today it is a lodge with seven rooms and a great choice for anglers or large family and group gatherings. It has a welcoming and comfortable gathering room with a casual Old Florida style. Next door you'll find the Ivey House cottage. You can rent this two-bedroom, fully equipped cottage and have access to all of the inn's amenities and breakfast for $179-269 depending on the time of year. The inn part of the property was built in 2001 and added 17 spacious rooms all centered on a beautifully landscaped, screened pool and waterfall area. A delicious breakfast accommodating all tastes is served in the morning, and complimentary coffee is available throughout the day. The inn is committed to sustainable environmental practices that earned them Florida Green Lodge certification.

The inn's staff is knowledgable about the area; there's an Everglades library on-site; and the complimentary bikes make familiarizing yourself with the environs a snap (take a bike and ride all the way to Chokoloskee Island for a coffee at Big House). The Ivey House is also the headquarters for Everglades Rentals & Eco Adventures, with exemplary naturalist-led charter trips and canoe and kayak rentals. Staying at the Ivey House gets you 20 percent off kayak rentals and guided eco-adventures. You can paddle through the mangrove tunnels of the Big Cypress National Preserve during the day or take a sunset tour and paddle through the Everglades at night if you're feeling exceptionally bold and adventurous.

Just outside of Everglades City and closer to the expansive Fakahatchee Strand Preserve and Big Cypress National Preserve, you'll find the classic Old Florida **Port of the Islands Resort and Marina** (2500 Tamiami Trail E., 844/884-8567, $120-150). This beautiful, affordable two-story property offers 32 one-bedroom and studio suites. Some are fully equipped with kitchens. All include televisions, refrigerators, microwaves, a private balcony or patio; high-speed Internet is available in the lobby area. The pool area is landscaped with tropical plants, and the adjacent marina is convenient for boaters who would like to sail up to their accommodations. There is an on-site restaurant and bar with a friendly staff and a great breakfast buffet with omelet chef.

Camping

Camping opportunities are abundant around here but not recommended in the hot, wet season. According to the National Park Service, the rainy season runs June-October. The hot season is definitely a bit longer, with the temperature averaging 87 degrees in May. Temperatures can easily climb to above 90 degrees in April and May. For a sure bet to beat the heat and the bugs, the best time to visit the Everglades is November-February. The park and surrounding areas get pretty busy during the week between Christmas and the New Year. The slowest season to visit, when there is still cool weather and few bugs, is the last week in October or the first week in November and the last week in January before all the outdoorsy spring breakers come out for paddling trips.

If you do want to camp in **Everglades National Park,** stop off at the Gulf Coast Visitor Center for an overnight pass. There are two campgrounds accessible from the Homestead entrance of the park. The **Long Pine Key Campground** is six miles from the Ernest Coe Visitor Center in Everglades City, and the **Flamingo Campground** is near the Flamingo Visitor Center near the shores of Flamingo Bay. Both accommodate RV and tent campers and offer a limited number of group sites. They both cost $20 a site per night. Campsites are first come, first served.

The nearby **Big Cypress National Preserve** also offers many campgrounds that are generally closed during the wet season, June-October. More information on these sites and a listing of open campgrounds can be found through the **Oasis Visitor Center** (239/695-1201).

RV campers have an appealing option at **Outdoor Resorts of America** (at the entrance to Chokoloskee Island, 239/695-3788, $69-89). Tent camping is prohibited, but the RV campsites are nice. The campground offers canoe rentals ($35/day), 16-foot skiff rentals ($150/day), showers, laundry, and a small convenience store. It may be the quickest route from under the covers to steering through the magical Ten Thousand Islands. Pets are welcome.

GETTING THERE

To reach Everglades City from Naples, continue south on U.S. 41. The 36-mile drive takes about 50 minutes. From Miami, take I-95 North for 2.3 miles. Then take I-75 North for 117 miles to exit 105. The 125-mile drive takes about 2.5 hours.

Information and Services

Naples and environs are located within the **eastern time zone.** The telephone area code is **239,** but it used to be 941 (unfortunately, some guides and brochures still list the old area code, and the automatic call-forwarding expired in 2003).

TOURIST INFORMATION

The *Naples Daily News* (239/213-6000, www.naplesnews.com) may be the best way to find out about local events and entertainment (it also produces the *Bonita Daily News,* the *Marco Island Eagle,* and the *Bonita Banner*). Kiosks are pretty much everywhere. For visitor information, stop in at the **Chamber of Commerce Visitors & Information Center** (2390 Tamiami Trail N., Naples, 239/262-6141) to pick up brochures, maps (there's a good city one that's worth the couple of bucks it costs), and lots of coupons. The **Convention & Visitors Bureau** (800/688-3600) maintains a tremendous visitor information website at www.paradisecoast.com.

Marco Island events and information can be found easily in a copy of *Marco Island Sun Times* (239/394-4050, www.marcoislandflorida.com), the widely distributed free community paper. For Everglades City information, call the **Everglades Area Chamber of Commerce** (239/695-3941, www.evergladeschamber.org), or visit it at the junction of U.S. 41 and Highway 29, where there's a nice little gift shop and lots of good books on the area.

POLICE AND EMERGENCIES

As always, if you find yourself in a real emergency, pick up a phone and dial 911. For a nonemergency police need, call or visit the **Naples Police Department** (355 Riverside Cir., 239/213-4844, www.naplespolice.com). The **Marco Island Police Department** can be reached at 239/389-5050, and the sheriff in **Everglades City** can be reached at 239/252-9900. In the event of a medical emergency, stop into the **Naples Community Hospital** (350 7th Ave. N., 239/624-5000) or **Marco Urgent Care Center** (40 S. Heathwood Dr., Marco Island, 239/624-8540). To fill a prescription there are nine CVS pharmacies in the Naples area, with one most central to downtown (294 9th St. S., 239/261-8610). **Island Drug** (1089 Collier Blvd. N., #409, Marco Island, 239/394-3111) has met Marco Island's pharmaceutical needs for 30 years.

RADIO AND TELEVISION

For when you feel like cranking a little music around here, turn to **100.1 FM** for top 40, **96.1 FM** for classic rock, **101.1 FM** for smooth jazz and easy listening, or **102.9 FM** for an eclectic "we play anything" format. Turn to **770 AM** for Spanish radio, and **1270 AM** for news talk.

And on the television, **WBBH Channel 2** out of Fort Myers is the NBC affiliate, **WFTX Channel 4** is the FOX affiliate, **WGNASD Channel 11** is the WGN affiliate, **WZVN Channel 7** is the ABC affiliate, and **WINK Channel 5** is the CBS affiliate.

LAUNDRY SERVICES

If you're staying at one of the upscale hotels, condos, or inns on Marco Island or in Naples, most offer their own laundry services to guests. There's also the cool **24 Hour Laundromat** (4045 Golden Gate Pkwy., Naples, 239/352-2430) that doesn't use coins. You stick in bills and it issues you a card, which you then stick in the washer or dryer. In Everglades City it's a little trickier—the Ivey House and a few other accommodations have laundry services for their guests.

Fort Myers, Sanibel, and Captiva

The long stretches of beach in this area are spectacular for their sand, birds, sunsets, and, most strikingly, for their shells. Lightning whelks are abundant in the area, and shell hunters are commonly seen searching for perfect conchs along the water's edge.

The city of Fort Myers, in large measure due to its most famous residents, Thomas Edison and Henry Ford, is culturally rich, with attractions spread along the banks of the Caloosahatchee River. It is the oldest and largest city in southwest Florida and, as such, dense with history.

Nearby, the barrier islands offer tropical island getaways. The most well known of this group of islands are Sanibel and Captiva. The siblings bear a family resemblance but have vastly different personalities. Both cater to mostly wealthy winter visitors, but Sanibel is more accessible (financially and physically), with miles of bike paths and low-rise, independently owned inns and smaller hotels. A tremendous wildlife refuge takes up nearly half of the island, with white-sand beaches on the Gulf side and picturesque mangrove forests on the eastern side. Captiva, to the north

and connected by a causeway, is the playground of the even more affluent. Many people own homes on Captiva, most tucked down driveways shielded from prying eyes by lush foliage. There's less to do on Captiva; there are fewer places to stay, fewer tourist amenities. But that's how people on Captiva like it.

Then there are the other barrier islands, each with its own character. Fort Myers Beach is on the long strip of coast-hugging land known as Estero Island. It's the closest thing this area has to a spring break-type beach, with affordable motels and crowded, family-friendly beaches. Gasparilla Island has made a name for itself as the tarpon capital and host to American presidents and a wide array of fish-seeking celebrities. Its town of Boca Grande is worth the quick boat ride or slightly longer car ride (you've got to go north and then out a causeway) to see. Cabbage

Previous: Lighthouse Beach; McGregor Boulevard in Fort Myers. **Above:** a heron on Sanibel Island.

Look for ★ to find recommended
sights, activities, dining, and lodging.

Highlights

★ **Lovers Key State Park:** Lovers Key State Park has 2.5 miles of beautiful beach and 5 miles of bike trails. This a great place for recreation, shelling, and bird-watching (page 72).

★ **Edison & Ford Winter Estates:** Thomas Edison, who spent 46 winters in Fort Myers, is considered the most inventive man who ever lived. Henry Ford paid his buddy a visit one year and bought the house next door. The tour of their estates is fascinating (page 74).

★ **J. N. "Ding" Darling National Wildlife Refuge:** Occupying more than half of Sanibel Island, this refuge is home to a tremendous array of birdlife (page 86).

★ **Bailey-Matthews Shell Museum:** This museum is a crash course in Neptune's treasures—a must if you want to know which species you're unearthing along the shoreline (page 90).

★ **Palm Island:** A day or two on Palm Island is good for the soul. It's an unbridged barrier island paradise (page 103).

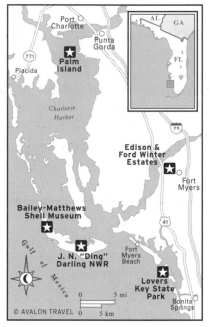

Fort Myers, Sanibel, and Captiva

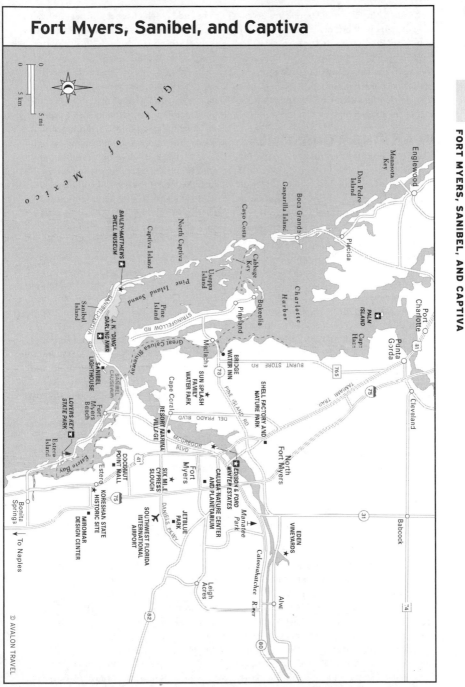

Gulf of Mexico

Englewood

Manasota Key

Don Pedro Island

Boca Grande

Gasparilla Island

Cayo Costa

Placida

Port Charlotte

BAILEY-MATTHEWS SHELL MUSEUM

North Captiva

Captiva Island

Cabbage Key

Useppa Island

Pine Island Sound

Pine Island

Charlotte Harbor

Bokeelia

Pineland

PALM ISLAND

Cape Haze

Punta Gorda

Sanibel Island

J.N. "DING" DARLING NWR

Great Calusa Blueway

STRINGFELLOW RD

Matlacha

BRIDGE WATER INN

78

BURNT STORE RD

Cleveland

75

SANIBEL CAUSEWAY

SANIBEL LIGHTHOUSE

SANIBEL-CAPTIVA RD

Cape Coral

SUN SPLASH FAMILY WATER PARK

RESORT MARINA VILLAGE

PINE ISLAND RD

SHELL FACTORY AND NATURE PARK

765

TAMIAMI TRAIL

North Fort Myers

Babcock

LOVERS KEY STATE PARK

Fort Myers Beach

Estero Island

Estero Bay

DEL PRADO BLVD

McGREGOR BLVD

COCONUT POINT MALL

Estero

41

EDISON & FORD WINTER ESTATES

Fort Myers

SIX MILE CYPRESS SLOUGH

CALUSA NATURE CENTER AND PLANETARIUM

Manatee Park

EDEN VINEYARDS

31

Bonita Springs

KORESHAN STATE HISTORIC SITE

75

JETBLUE PARK

DANIELS PKWY

SOUTHWEST FLORIDA INTERNATIONAL AIRPORT

MIROMAR DESIGN CENTER

Caloosahatchee River

Alva

80

To Naples

82

Leigh Acres

74

0 5 mi
0 5 km

© AVALON TRAVEL

Key, North Captiva, and Useppa are accessible only by boat but make a beautiful day trip. And Pine Island is the largest of the barrier islands in this area, mostly residential, with the charming maritime towns of Matlacha, Bokeelia, Pineland, and St. James City. Anglers know it for its "Fishingest Bridge in the United States."

PLANNING YOUR TIME

This area could entertain the troops for a week or more. The budget traveler will make his or her home base in Fort Myers or Fort Myers Beach, sliding over the causeway ($6/car, $4/motorcycle, free for bicycles) to Sanibel and Captiva for a day of rejuvenating beach therapy. The Edison and Ford estates in Fort Myers will occupy much of a day, as will the J. N. "Ding" Darling National Wildlife Refuge on Sanibel. The rest of the area's attractions are more fleetingly entertaining (although the beach never gets old). Families will spend a fair amount of time at the kids' water park and attractions to the north in Cape Coral; history buffs will likely occupy themselves at one of several Calusa museums; the outdoors enthusiast will choose fishing, canoeing, sailing, or all of the above. The Great Calusa Blueway Paddling Trail is a truly remarkable, newly charted route for beginning or advanced paddlers— well worth a half day's exploration for even the most timid boater.

The end of each October and beginning of November, the **Calusa Blueway Paddling Festival** (www.calusabluewaypaddlingfestival.com) is another event around which to plan an outdoors-oriented trip. Paddlers, competitors, families, and outdoors enthusiasts enjoy nine days of festivities including competitive canoe/kayak races, a pro-am kayak fishing tournament, paddling clinics and demonstrations, seminars, family activities, archaeological and environmental events, guided tours, a speakers' series, and more celebrations along the Great Calusa Blueway.

Fall is beautiful here, while summers are extremely hot and humid. If your aim is winter, it's cheaper to visit in the first two weeks of December. Rates generally increase for high season during the third week of December, and the large crowds arrive in February and March. In early December, you'll find lots of accommodations and nominal traffic (which can be frustrating on Sanibel and Captiva in March).

Lee County is along southwest Florida's Gulf Coast between Naples and Sarasota. The biggest north-south driving routes are I-75 and U.S. 41. East-west major arteries include Alligator Alley (I-75) and U.S. 41 (where it jogs east at around Naples). By air, the area is served by **Southwest Florida International Airport** (11000 Terminal Access Rd., Fort Myers, 239/590-4800, www. flylcpa.com).

Fort Myers

A hurricane in the 1840s drove the soldiers out of Seminole Wars Fort Dulaney at the mouth of the Caloosahatchee. The evacuation had an upside. First Lt. John Harvie found a safer, more sheltered place for a fort, which he named Fort Myers in honor of that war's Col. Abraham C. Myers. Retired soldiers came back to the area after the war, making use of the picturesque Caloosahatchee to ship cattle to Cuba. Fort

Myers was mostly a sleepy rural town, even on the beach, when Thomas Alva Edison visited and fell in love with it in 1885.

Fort Myers was incorporated that same year, and the banks of the Caloosahatchee Intercoastal Waterway started to be settled by mostly northerners. Edison talked his buddy Henry Ford into exploring the area, and Ford promptly bought the house next door on McGregor Boulevard. Because of Edison's

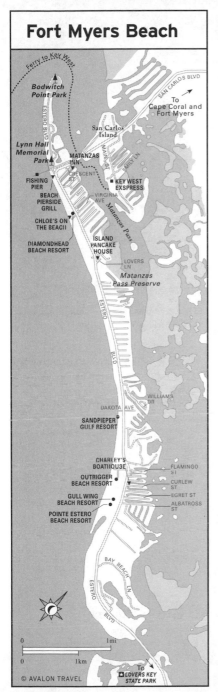

Fort Myers Beach

gift to the city of hundreds of royal palms, its nickname is City of Palms.

These days, Fort Myers is Lee County's working center, the biggest urban center in southwest Florida (well, nearby Cape Coral has greater landmass). There are attractions, restaurants, and hotels centered on the bustling downtown historic district and along the riverfront. A downtown city renovation designed by famous New Urbanist architect Andrés Duany was completed in 2015. The city spent $5.4 million to restore the riverfront shopping zone, add ponds with fountains, increased access to the water, and increase the amount of water views in the district.

Its easy access to nearby barrier islands (Sanibel, Captiva, Pine Island, and Gasparilla), combined with its wealth of family-friendly attractions, makes it an obvious home base for the dynamic traveler. There are full-service marinas connected to several of the hotels along the river, so boaters can pull right up.

The city of Fort Myers is beachless, but you can head down to Fort Myers Beach on Estero Island for fun in the sun and sand—its gentle slope and lack of steep drop-offs make it a safe beach for young swimmers or waders. At the north end of the island a casual beach village offers a cluster of restaurants and shops, and at Estero's southern end Lovers Key State Park is a huge draw, with a number of nearby resort hotels.

SPORTS AND RECREATION
Beaches

Fort Myers Beach is actually on the island of Estero, connected to Fort Myers by a causeway. There are several worthwhile beaches here. **Bowditch Point Regional Park** (50 Estero Blvd., 239/765-6794, parking $2/hour) is a 17-acre park that fronts both the Gulf and the bay at the northern tip of Estero Island, with a boardwalk over to a beach with beautiful views of nearby barrier islands. Ten boat slips that accommodate boats up to 28 feet in length are available for day use, and a paddle craft launch provides access to the Great Calusa Blueway Paddling Trail. Parking is available behind the bathhouse (nice showers and changing rooms). Just a bit to the south and on the Gulf side, **Lynn Hall Memorial Park** (950 Estero Blvd., 239/765-6794, parking $2/hour) is a great family beach and a teen hangout. There's also a fishing pier here, heavily frequented by opportunistic pelicans. (If you happen to hook a pelican or other bird while fishing, reel the bird in slowly, cover its head with a towel to calm it, cut the line close to the hook and remove all monofilament from wings and body, then call **Clinic for the Rehabilitation of Wildlife** (CROW, 239/472-3644), a local nonprofit bird rescue organization.

★ Lovers Key State Park

Lovers Key State Park (8700 Estero Blvd., Fort Myers Beach, 239/463-4588, 8am-sundown, $8/car up to 8 people, $4/car single occupancy car and motorcycles, $2 walkers and bicyclists) occupies four small barrier islands (Black Island, Long Key, Inner Key, and Lovers Key) between Fort Myers Beach and Bonita Beach to the south. The park contains a 2.5-mile stretch of beautiful beach and 5 miles of bike trails (bike, canoe, and kayak rentals available on-site), including the Black Island Trail through a maritime hammock. There are excellent picnic facilities at the New Lovers Key Bayside area on Estero Boulevard and free tram service to the beach (9am-5pm daily).

In addition to roseate spoonbills, snowy egrets, and American kestrels, birders will see active osprey nests and a couple of bald eagle nests. The park offers two-hour **sunset ecotours** (239/765-7788, $85-60) Friday and Saturday nights, and there is a **full moon tour** ($85-60) offered once or twice a month depending on weather and tides.

Six Mile Cypress Slough Preserve

The **Six Mile Cypress Slough Preserve** (7751 Penzance Crossing, 239/533-7550, www.leeparks.org, sunrise-sunset daily,

the picnic areas at Bowditch Point Regional Park

parking $1/hour maximum of $5) is a fabulous wild spot in south Fort Myers, easily accessible to those on the way to or from the airport. You'd never know you were in a county of a half million people. There are ongoing free guided **nature walks** (twice daily during high season at 9:30am and 1:30pm) along a 1.5-mile fully accessible boardwalk trail through a wooded wetland, as well as monthly nature programs in which children and adults learn to identify animal tracks, evening moon walks, summer camps for kids, and wilderness exploration camps for teens. In 2010, the Six Mile Cypress Interpretive Center, Lee County's first LEED-certified green building, opened on-site.

Manatee-Watching

Spend a little time on the Orange and Caloosahatchee Rivers, and chances are you'll see a West Indian manatee. Take a guided kayak tour with **Gaea Guides** (239/694-5513, www.gaeaguides.com, $40-95) and the odds get even better that you'll see a few of these mammals, related biologically to the elephant and, unlikely though it may seem, the aardvark. The narrated ecotour provides insight into the life of the area's most famous species, as well as information about how they are threatened by outboard motors and habitat destruction. Manatees seem to congregate in the Orange River in the winter, basking in the waters warmed by the outflow of the nearby power plant. This is a good family adventure, and if you are extremely interested by these gentle sea cows, you can head on over to **Manatee Park** (10901 Hwy. 80, 1.5 miles east of I-75, North Fort Myers, 239/690-5030, 8am-sunset daily, parking $2/hour Dec.-Apr., $1/hour May-Nov., maximum $5 parking fee year-round, kayak rentals $15/hour). There are three observation decks for viewing and hydrophones so you can listen in (I don't speak manatee, but even scientists are unsure how they make these chirps, whistles, and squeaks). A cow and her calf are especially talkative, vocalizing back and forth. The park rents kayaks in winter and on summer weekends, with kayak clinics the second Saturday of the month and free guided walks through the native plant habitats at 9am every Saturday.

Golf

The greater Fort Myers area has around 100 public and semiprivate golf courses, the egalitarian nature of which makes the city duly proud. The city of Fort Myers itself maintains two professionally designed golf courses. **Fort Myers Country Club** (3591 McGregor Blvd., 239/321-7488, public, 18 holes, 6,414 yards, par 71, course rating 70.5, slope 118, greens fee $25-70, depending on season and time of day) was designed by the great Donald Ross in 1916 and opened in 1917—one of the oldest courses on the Gulf Coast. It hosts the pro-am Coors Open tournament every year in January and is only a mile from downtown. **Eastwood Golf Course** (4600 Bruce Herd Ln., 239/321-7485, public, 18 holes, 6,772 yards, par 72, course rating 73.3, slope 130, greens fee $30-70) reopened in December 2007 after a $1.5 million renovation that included 84 new bunkers, 54 new tee grounds, new irrigation, resurfaced cart paths, and a new driving range. Golfers will also enjoy the recently added $2 million clubhouse.

Spring Training

When the regular season just isn't enough, Boston Red Sox fans can take in a **Boston Red Sox Spring Training** (JetBlue Park,

Six Mile Cypress Slough Preserve

11500 Fenway South Dr., 866/800-1275, www.boston.redsox.mlb.com, $10-46) game at the brand-new ballpark that opened in March 2012. The new ball field cost a whopping $77.9 million and is a near exact replica of the classic Fenway Park in Boston, complete with some of the ballpark's most classic features such as the famed Green Monster in the outfield, the triangle, Pesky's pole, and the lone red seat that marks the spot of the longest home run in the history of Fenway. However, here's the "catch": This outfield wall has seats carved into the middle and a net to protect fans from deep fly balls. The stadium also has a welcomed roof that shades spectators from the Florida sun. Go get a preview of what the Sox are capable of this season at this fantastic ballpark that is quickly becoming a favorite of Grapefruit League fans. Spring training games are the whole month of March at 1:05pm or 7:05pm.

Minnesota Twins Spring Training (Hammond Stadium, 14400 Six Mile Cypress Pkwy., 239/768-4210, www.fortmyers.miracle. milb.com, $16-18) also takes place locally at the Lee County Sports Complex, recognized widely as one of baseball's top five spring training facilities. Games are at 1:05pm during all of March, and after that, in April, fans can watch the Miracle League, a minor-league affiliate of the Minnesota Twins and member of the Florida State League.

SIGHTS
★ Edison & Ford Winter Estates

Thomas Edison arrived in Fort Myers on March 20, 1885. Not one to be indecisive, evidently, he purchased 13-plus acres along the Caloosahatchee River within 24 hours, with the aim of building his winter home.

Seminole Lodge was duly constructed in pieces in Maine from his designs and then sailed to Florida and assembled. The home served as the winter retreat and workplace for the prolific inventor until his death in 1931. It's encircled with large overhanging porches; grand French doors encourage a

a butterfly at the Edison & Ford Winter Estates garden

cross breeze. There are electric chandeliers— "electroliers"—designed by Edison. It's a fascinating house, deeded to the city for $1 by Edison's widow, Mina.

Edison's close buddy Henry Ford must also have fallen in love when he visited Fort Myers in 1915. He bought the house next door. Called The Mangoes, it became another top destination for the country's elite—Harvey Firestone, naturalist John Burroughs, Nobel Laureate Alexis Carrel, and Charles Lindbergh all made their way to this Florida paradise. For quite a while it was essentially Fort Myers's biggest tourist destination.

Edison & Ford Winter Estates (2350 McGregor Blvd., 239/334-7419, www.efwefla. org, 9am-5:30pm daily, combined estates tour: $20 adults, $11 children 6-12, children 5 and under free) raised $10 million in the past few years through a laudable public-private partnership, restoring the houses and grounds and repositioning the attraction as a community and cultural center.

The two estates encompass 14 acres of

botanical landscaping, the two titans' historic homes and guest cottages, Edison's laboratory, a museum containing his famous inventions and exhibits, a museum store, a garden shop, and an outdoor café. It's worth at least a couple of hours of wandering through the gorgeous environs, but the real draw is peeking into the lives of these fascinating men.

Poke your head into the laboratory and the museum of Edison's inventions and artifacts, spend a little time in Ford's garage, then walk through the tropical botanical garden. Edison planted it as an experimental garden with more than 1,000 species, focusing on the byproducts of plants (rubber for his buddy Firestone's tires, for instance). Later, Mina Edison prettied it up by adding roses, orchids, and bromeliads.

In the painstakingly restored houses, the year 1929 was chosen as the "period of interpretation," the interiors accurately reflecting the decor and accoutrements of that time. Also explore Edison's lab, which underwent a $1 million renovation that began in 2010, where the inventor discovered that the solidago plant produces an excellent material that can be used as an alternative to rubber. It's fun to mosey on your own with the electronic audio tour, but the staff-led tours are a must, giving the place context and depth.

You can dispel Edison myths (alas, the lightbulbs burning in the estate are not Edison's originals), hear funny stories (Henry Ford stuffed the seats of his first Model T imprudently with local Spanish moss, which prompted the first automotive recall when little chiggers started crawling out and biting drivers on the butts), or just learn a little about the quirks of these American legends (Edison hated paparazzi, so he disembarked from the train before the station and walked the rest of the way).

The very young may be underwhelmed by all the Edison-Ford-obilia, but everybody feels a sense of awe when navigating the huge banyan tree out front. Its circumference spans more than 400 feet, making it one of the largest in the country, a gift to Thomas Edison from Harvey Firestone.

A combined **tour of the estates** is available 9am-5:30pm daily, with the last tour leaving promptly at 4pm ($20 adults, $11 children 6-12, children 5 and under free). **Botanical tours** are offered at 10:30am on Wednesday ($30 adults, $16 children 6-12).

McGregor Boulevard

Fort Myers is sometimes called the City of Palms. Why? Edison and Ford's estates are poised just at the edge of **McGregor Boulevard,** which is lined on both sides by 60-foot-tall royal palms. The original 200 or so, from Cuba, were gifts from Thomas Edison to the city. The idea caught on, and now more than 2,000 palms flank the roadside of stately McGregor Boulevard. Drive the length of the 15-mile boulevard and the city's nickname seems fairly apt.

Museums

Southwest Florida Museum of History

(2031 Jackson St., 239/321-7430, www.cityftmyers.com, 10am-5pm Tues.-Sat., $9.50 adults, $8.50 seniors, $5 with student ID) is a quirky mix of stuff, but its wide net gathers a broad catch. The history of the Calusa and Seminole people, as well as this area's Spanish explorers, is a major focus of the museum, and more broadly the history of Fort Myers. Set in a restored Atlantic Coastline railroad depot built in 1924, the museum houses photographs and memorabilia; there's an 84-foot-long Pullman railcar built in 1929 and a replica of a late 1800s Cracker house.

A changing exhibit lends a different flavor to the museum every few months. The museum also runs 90-minute architectural and historical downtown walking tours in Fort Myers on Wednesday and Saturday at 10am ($12, reservations required).

Koreshan State Historical Site

Hands-down winner of Weirdest Attraction in the Area prize is the **Koreshan State Historical Site** (3800 Corkscrew Rd., Estero,

Excursion to Key West

Something to think about: If you have an extra day and nothing on the docket, why not pop off to Key West? Explore the country's southernmost city just for the day. There are high-speed shuttles from Fort Myers, a welcome alternative to driving (about 7 hours) or flying (usually several hundred clams).

Key West Express (1200 Main St., 239/463-5733, $154 adults, $144 seniors, $91 children 6-12, $60 children 5 and under, and there are sometimes coupons in local papers) has a couple of boats that head out of Fort Myers.

The company currently operates three vessels, the 140-foot *Atlanticat* catamaran, the 155-foot *Big Cat* catamaran, and the 170-foot *Key West Express* catamaran. The catamaran ferry zips over to Key West in 3.5 hours.

Most seating on the boat is contoured, airplane-like chairs, but there are also plush couches with tables. Although the floor-to-ceiling windows provide plenty of entertainment (and there's a full outdoor deck upstairs), there are six plasma-screen TVs showing movies, sports, and more. The *Key West Express* catamaran features two enclosed cabins, a sundeck, satellite TV, slot machines, and full galley and bar. The ships depart Fort Myers Beach at 8:30am, arrive Key West at noon; depart Key West at 6pm, arrive Fort Myers Beach at 9:30pm. That gives you five hours or so to noodle around town. Alternatively, you can find a hotel or inn, stay overnight, and come back on the next day's ferry for no additional ferry fee. This tiny 3- by 5-mile island, 100 miles from the coast, has the only living coral reef in the United States, not to mention great restaurants and nightlife.

239/992-0311, 8am-5pm, $5/car with 2-8 passengers, $4/car with one passenger, $2 walkers or bicyclists, $32.70 camping, $5/hour canoe rentals). It commemorates an eccentric religious sect begun by Dr. Cyrus Teed in 1894 after he had a spiritual "great illumination." It seems he and his followers believed the world is a hollow globe, with humankind residing on the inner surface, gazing into the universe below. The Koreshan followers (at its peak there were 250) gave their commune to the state on the condition it would be maintained as a historic site in perpetuity. Now the site is a compound of buildings and a theater, but visitors also avail themselves of the park's fishing, camping, nature study, and picnicking. There's a boat ramp and canoes for rent, and guided walks and campfire programs are offered seasonally.

Family-Friendly Attractions

Cape Coral, north of Fort Myers, isn't among the area's biggest draws for adults. As soon as children get a say, however, you may find yourself driving north with regularity. On a hot day, the kids will help navigate you to

Sun Splash Family Waterpark (400 Santa Barbara Blvd., 239/574-0557, www.sunsplashwaterpark.com, 10am-5pm Fri.-Sun. mid-Mar., 10am-5pm daily late Mar. and late May-early Aug., 10am-5pm Sat.-Sun. Apr.-late May and late Aug.-late Sept., $19.95 adults, $17.95 seniors, $17.95 children 12-2), on the shore of Lake Kennedy. It's not huge, but there are two new tall water flume rides, a big family pool, a tot playground, a "river" tube ride, a café, and a super-fast ride called the Electric Slide, which is an enclosed tube in which you twist and turn at high speed. Not far away is **Mike Greenwell's Family Fun Park** (35 NE Pine Island Rd., Cape Coral, 239/574-4386, 10am-10pm Sun.-Thurs., 10am-11pm Fri.-Sat., $3-6.50 for miniature golf, $2 for 24 pitches in batting cages plus $1 equipment rental, $5-8.50 for go-carts). It fills in the activity gaps with miniature golf, batting cages, four go-cart tracks, a maze, an arcade, and a sweet fish-feeding dock that's much more fun than it may sound.

Located in downtown Fort Myers, another bad-weather delight for little kids comes at the **Imaginarium Hands-On Museum** (2000

Cranford Ave., 239/321-7420, www.imaginariumfortmyers.com, 10am-5pm Tues.-Sat., noon-5pm Sun., $12 adults, $10 seniors, $8 children 3-12, children 2 and under free). It's a calm hands-on museum in which kids can fly and be free. A hurricane simulator, fossil dig, miniature TV weather studio—it's hard not to get engrossed. There's also a fairly nice aquarium here, with cool moray eels and a lively coral reef tank.

Bigger kids have a couple of similar options in Fort Myers, with science and nature centers more suited to school-age kids and adults. The **Calusa Nature Center & Planetarium** (3450 Ortiz Ave., 239/275-3435, www.calusanature.com, museum and trail 10am-4pm Mon.-Sat., 11am-4pm Sun., $10 adults, $5 children 3-12) enables people to learn about southwest Florida's natural history in a number of ways. There are nature trails on boardwalks through pine flatwoods and cypress wetlands, on which you'll pass a Seminole village replica, a live bobcat, and a native birds-of-prey aviary for permanently injured birds. Inside the nature center, there are live animals and exhibits about their habitats. The best parts of the center are the regularly scheduled guided walks and animal lectures (cool stuff about snakes, gators, and Florida's endangered species). The center also has a planetarium, in which you can learn about the Hubble telescope and the night sky or just chill out while watching a laser light show.

The kind of Old Florida tourist draw people get nostalgic for, the **Shell Factory & Nature Park** (2787 Tamiami Trail N., North Fort Myers, 239/995-2141, www.shellfactory.com, free admission, miniature golf $5 for adults and $3 for children and seniors, boat rides $5, rock climbing wall$3, trampolines $3) adopts a something-for-everyone approach (and has been doing so since the 1950s). There's a lot of kitschy shell themed merchandise to check out while kids get into the miniature golf, bumper boats, batting cages, and a video arcade. Supposedly it has the world's largest collection of rare shells and coral, but the glass-blowing artisans are more entertaining

to watch (there's also the funny little History of Glass Museum on-site). Outdoors you'll have to visit the nature park ($12 adults, $10 seniors, $8 children 4-12, children 3 and under free) with a petting zoo (camels, llamas, donkeys, potbellied pigs, goats), trails, and a botanical garden. Sounds like a lot under one roof, huh? This is the kind of place where you simply have to give in and consume a batter-dipped hot dog followed by a pound of fudge.

After the fudge, you may need to get the blood flowing at Fort Myers's **Skatium** (2250 Broadway, 239/321-7509, www.cityftmyers.com/Skatium, public skating 1pm-3pm and 7:30pm-9:30pm Sat.-Sun., $7 for all ages, $3 for skate rentals) a 72,000-square-foot facility with an ice-skating rink, an in-line rink, laser tag arena, and video arcade. Most of the time the rink is given over to local youth hockey and figure skating. If your kids are more into outdoor in-line skating or skateboarding, the **Brotherhood Skate Park** (2277 Grand Ave., downtown Fort Myers, 239/275-7787, skating 3pm-8pm Tues.-Sat., noon-5pm Sun., $5/day, helmets mandatory) is right next door, the area's premier street-style course with wood and galvanized steel ramps surfaced with Skatelite Pro sitting on a 15,000-square-foot base.

ENTERTAINMENT AND EVENTS
Music and Theater
The **Barbara B. Mann Performing Arts Hall** (on the campus of Edison College, 13350 FSW Pkwy., 239/481-4849, www.bbmannpah.com) is the center of arts activity for Fort Myers. The full-sized and fully equipped stage hosts traveling Broadway musicals, popular music, and **Southwest Florida Symphony** (8290 College Pkwy., 239/418-0996, www.swflso.org) concerts. The professional symphony orchestra offers classical and pops series annually (its chamber orchestra series takes place in Schein Hall at BIG Arts on Sanibel Island).

The **Florida Repertory Theatre** (Arcade Theater, 2268 Bay St., 239/332-4488, www.floridarep.org) is an 18-year-old ensemble-based company with a year-round season. Split between musicals, comedies, and serious dramas, the professional repertory's season features nine productions, staged in a great restored 1908 Victorian movie house.

Broadway musicals and family-friendly comedies are the mainstay at **Broadway Palm Dinner Theatre** (1380 Colonial Blvd., 239/278-4422, www.broadwaypalm.com), which has a main stage as well as a more intimate black box theater (in which Off Broadway Palm stages smaller-scale comedies and musical revues, as well as children's theater). Some of the performers are local, and they occasionally bring in talent from farther afield. Performances are accompanied by cocktails, salad bar, and a buffet.

Visual Arts

Lee County isn't the visual arts smorgasbord of Naples to the south. Still, there are several nice galleries and the local arts center. The Lee County **Alliance for the Arts** (10091 McGregor Blvd., 239/939-2787, www.artinlee. org, 9am-5pm Mon.-Fri., 9am-noon Sat., free) is a multipronged arts organization founded in 1975. On a 10-acre campus, the organization contains the Frizzell Cultural Center with galleries, classrooms, a 175-seat indoor theater, and an outdoor amphitheater. The adjacent Charles Edwards Building houses local artists and arts groups. Local, regional, and national art and crafts are displayed in the public galleries, and the theaters host live theatrical performances and festivals throughout the year. Locals use the facility for adult and youth art classes of all kinds, from glass fusing to acrylics.

The densest concentration of crafts and fine arts in the area is to be found on the main drag of Matlacha on Pine Island. Many of the galleries are in little houses painted in a variety of sunset colors. Leoma Lovegrove's work is on display at **Leoma Lovegrove Gallery & Gardens** (4637 Pine Island Rd., 239/283-6453), and you'll find the metal sculptures of Peggy McTeague next door at **Wild Child Art Gallery** (4625 Pine Island Rd., 239/283-6006,

9am-5pm daily), with a dozen or so other whimsical galleries within walking distance of the Matlacha drawbridge. So visitors can tour a number of these small galleries, Art Nights are held the second Friday of each month November-April, with the artists on hand to discuss their work.

SHOPPING

Downtown Fort Myers is the city's entertainment district, but east of **Centennial Park** there is a strip of nice shops, galleries, and cafés perfect for exploring on a walk. Strictly a driving route, the **Tamiami Trail,** or U.S. 41, is lined with the basic businesses that cater to locals. You'll also find chain restaurants of all stripes along the busy road.

Serious shoppers will head to **Tanger Outlets** (20350 Summerlin Rd., 239/454-1974), which has more than 60 shops stocking deeply discounted clothing, housewares, and gifts. It's nothing you haven't seen before, including Polo Ralph Lauren, Under Armour, Gap, Coach, Guess, Calvin Klein, Brook Brothers, and Banana Republic.

A more pleasant shopping experience, capitalizing on the area's glorious weather, is the **Bell Tower Shops** (13499 U.S. 41 SE, 239/489-1221). It's an outdoor mall anchored by Saks Fifth Avenue, with the usual upscale chains (Banana Republic, Williams-Sonoma) and a 20-screen movie theater.

Edison Mall (4125 Cleveland Ave., 239/939-5464) is more of a workhorse mall serving the local community, with Macy's, Dillard's, JCPenney, Sears, and lots of little mall stores. It's the biggest mall in southwest Florida.

Fleamaster's (4135 Dr. Martin Luther King Blvd., 239/334-7001, www.fleamall. com, 9am-5pm Fri.-Sun.) is a serious hoot. It's a vast, 400,000-square-foot indoor flea market with something like 900 vendors—perfect for a rainy day exploration. From hardware to bath soap, this place sells some of everything.

The **Miromar Design Center** (10800 Corkscrew Rd., Estero, 239/390-5111, www. miromardesigncenter.com) opened in 2007 as an interior design resource for fine furniture, accessories, fabrics, wall coverings, lighting, kitchen and bath products, flooring, and antiques. More than 80 internationally known showrooms (Ralph Lauren Home, Ligne Roset, Flexform, Poggenpohl, Casa Italia, Henredon, Francesco Molon, Jardin de Ville, and Paris Ceramics, for example) anchor the three-story center.

Another newcomer in Estero, **Coconut Point** (23106 Fashion Dr., intersection of U.S. 41 and Coconut Rd., 239/992-4259, www.simon.com/mall/coconut-point) is an open, Main Street-style shopping destination with Mediterranean architecture. The property includes 90,000 square feet of office space, residential units, and 1.2 million square feet of retail space. There you'll find Dillard's, GNC, Chico's, White House/Black Market, Pacsun, Hollywood Theatres, and restaurants like Bice Grand Café, Ruth's Chris Steakhouse, California Pizza Kitchen, and Blue Water Bistro.

And the **Gulf Coast Town Center** (9903 Gulf Coast Main Center Dr., 239/267-5107, www.gulfcoasttowncenter.com) is another new shopping center with some of the usual suspects, but its real calling card is the hugely buff **Bass Pro Shops Outdoor World** (www.basspro.com), a 75,000-square-foot retail center that includes the Islamorada Fish Company Restaurant and a boat showroom along with outdoor gear, clothing, and accessories for hiking, backpacking, wildlife-viewing, camping, outdoor cooking, and hooking those bass. Kids will be entertained by the indoor aquariums and water features stocked with native fish species.

FOOD

Fort Myers is awash in chains, from Carrabba's to Olive Garden to T.G.I. Friday's. You have to look a little to find the unique, independent gems.

Breakfast

For traditional American breakfast, **Mel's Diner** (4820 Cleveland Ave., 239/275-7850,

6:30am-10pm Mon.-Thurs., 6:30am-10:30pm Fri.-Sat., 6:30am-9pm Sun., $8-12) gives you all the diner staples. Mel's biscuits and sausage gravy will give you the get-up-and-go for a day at the beach, and kids love it here. It's a regional chain.

A delicious short stack of banana nut pancakes can be had for an affordable price at **The Island's Pancake House** (2801 Estero Blvd., Seagrapes Plaza off Estero Blvd., Fort Myers Beach, 239/463-0033, 7am-3pm daily, $4-10), along with a wide variety of essential pre-kayaking breakfast foods.

Fort Myers residents swear by the hangover special at **Oasis Restaurant** (2260 Martin Luther King Jr. Blvd., 239/334-1566, 7am-3pm Mon.-Fri., 8am-2pm Sat.-Sun., $8-12) of three fluffy eggs enfolding cheese, sausage, and sautéed veggies, instrumental in the post-booze, saturated-fat-induced flushing, topped off by 26 ounces of Gatorade in the car on the way back to the hotel to take a nap. It serves breakfast all day—very casual—and is near the Edison and Ford estates.

Casual

If you find yourself at the Bell Tower shopping center, you can't go wrong with a stop at **Blue Pointe Oyster Bar & Seafood Grill** (13499 S. Cleveland Ave., 239/433-0634, www.bluepointerestaurant.com, 11:30am-10pm Mon.-Thurs., 11:30am-11pm Fri.-Sat., noon-9pm Sun., $15-35). It's a New England-style fish restaurant with excellent grilled swordfish and Florida black grouper, a nice crab cake, and good but slightly pricey oysters on the half shell.

Also at the Bell Tower, **Bistro 41** (13499 S. Cleveland Ave., 239/466-4141, 11:30am-10pm Mon.-Fri., 11:30am-10:30pm Sat., 11:30-8pm Sun., $15-35) seems to be a local business favorite, upscale with an American seafood-and-steaks menu. Beware the daily specials' prices, which can run close to $40. Otherwise, it's a pleasant, something-for-everyone kind of place with a nice outdoor patio.

On Fort Myers Beach on Estero Island, lots of casual beachfront restaurants make great use of the location and purvey mostly seafood-centric cuisine. **Matanzas Inn Restaurant** (416 Crescent St., 239/463-3838, 11am-10pm daily, $15-25) has a great deck and a nice fried grouper plate. **Chloe's on the Beach** (2000 Estero Blvd., 239/765-0595, 7:30am-11am and 5pm-9pm daily, $15-30) is in the DiamondHead Beach Resort, with more upscale continental cuisine and gorgeous water views. Make sure to check out the daily frozen drink special. And **Beach Pierside Grill** (1000 Estero Blvd., next to the pier, 239/765-7800, 11am-11pm daily, $12-20) is more family-friendly, featuring ribs, fried seafood platters, and the fat beach burger.

Fine Dining

A favorite fancy restaurant in Fort Myers is ★ **Veranda** (2122 2nd St., 239/332-2065, 11am-9pm Mon.-Fri., 5:30pm-9pm Sat., $25-35), partly because it's set in two stately 100-year-old homes joined by publishing heir Peter Pulitzer in the 1970s for his buddy Fingers O'Bannon, who ran the restaurant then. So it's the history, but the Veranda also seems like a happening place. The menu at Veranda is traditional but with contemporary touches, meaning pan-seared local grouper with wilted spinach, New York steak covered

in gorgonzola, and artichoke fritters stuffed with blue crab.

The new Coconut Point Mall in Estero has introduced a number of upscale eateries to the local restaurant scene, the best of which are probably the hip **Blue Water Bistro** (23151 Village Shops Way, 239/949-2583, www.bluewaterbistro.net, 5pm-9:30pm daily, $10-25) and the ubiquitous **Ruth's Chris Steakhouse** (239/948-8888, 4:30pm-10pm Mon.-Sat., 4:30pm-9pm Sun., $15-30)—worth a visit, especially if you're planning on being at the mall anyway. Otherwise, check out a selection from the huge salad bar and then the slow-roasted prime rib at **Charley's Boat House Grill** (6241 Estero Blvd., Fort Myers Beach, 239/765-4700, 5pm-9:30pm daily, $15-30).

One of my personal favorites for seafood, located in the Bonita Springs Hyatt Regency Coconut Point Resort & Spa, is ★ **Tarpon Bay** (5001 Coconut Rd., Bonita Springs, 239/390-4295, 5:30pm-10pm daily, $15-35). Start with a sampler of the ceviche, or order a platter of oysters on ice. Don't miss out on the decadent lobster mac-and-cheese before treating yourself to the whole, fried snapper, their signature entrée. The wine list is geared toward seafood pairings. If you're

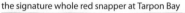

the signature whole red snapper at Tarpon Bay

throwing caution to the wind, try the chocolate lava cake. There are excellent views of Estero Bay from many tables, and on cooler nights the best seats in the house are out on the back deck, which juts out over the water. Reservations are recommended, and attire is nice-casual.

ACCOMMODATIONS
Under $100
For not a lot of money, you can get just about everything at **Rock Lake Resort** (2937 Palm Beach Blvd., 239/332-4080, www.bestlodgingswflorida.com, $69-145). The nine little cottages (18 units) encircling a small lake were built in 1946. Canoeing, lighted tennis courts, a nature trail, barbecue facilities, and comfortable porches overlooking the water—it all sits on Billy Creek, which allows direct access for small boats to the Caloosahatchee River. Rock Lake isn't fancy, but it's just a short drive to the beach and half a mile from downtown. Rooms are wheelchair accessible, and there are also rooms for the hearing-impaired. Pets are welcome.

$100-200
At Matlacha Pass right near the drawbridge on Pine Island, there is the funky **Bridge Water**

Inn (4331 Pine Island Rd., Matlacha, 239/283-2423, $140-200). Some multitasking enthusiasts have been known to throw a line right out their motel window into the water off the west deck below—fishing and catching the football game simultaneously. You can watch the late-night snook anglers battling catfish for their bait right out the window.

$200-300
The **Outrigger Beach Resort** (6200 Estero Blvd., Fort Myers Beach, 239/463-3131, www.outriggerfmb.com, $160-330) is a casual, tropical-themed, high-rise hotel. It is a great choice for families and couples, located on a wide stretch of beach where there is plenty of room to stretch out during the busy summer months. All of the rooms are efficiencies with a king or two double beds, an additional sleeper sofa, and a full kitchen with stove, oven, and microwave. A comfortable living room adjoins a dining room with a private balcony. Thatched-roof cabanas and a lively tiki bar surround the pool area.

On Fort Myers Beach, a natural family destination, there are lots of mid-priced hotels and motels that fit the bill. **Sandpiper Gulf Resort** (5550 Estero Blvd., 800/584-1449, www.sandpipergulfresort.com, $200-400) is

the Bridge Water Inn

a fairly big, fairly low-rise hotel set in a few buildings. Opened in 1969, the resort has 63 large guest suites, some of them recently remodeled. There's a big pool surrounded by tropical gardens and the beach just beyond.

Over $300

Gull Wing Beach Resort (6620 Estero Blvd., Fort Myers Beach, 239/873-5527, www.sunstream.com, $250-600) is a high-rise hotel on the quiet south end of Estero Island. There are 66 comfortable and spacious one-, two-, and three-bedroom family suites, with a lovely Gulf-side swimming pool, tennis courts, outdoor spa, barbecues, and a gazebo area. Its parent company, **SunStream Hotels & Resorts** (888/627-1595, www.sunstream.com), is headquartered in Fort Myers Beach and has a number of other luxury properties locally.

The **DiamondHead Beach Resort** (2000 Estero Blvd., Fort Myers Beach, 888/568-9330, $250-500) offers one-bedroom, one-bath suites with Gulf, island, or pool views. All suites are 700 square feet, and some have been recently upgraded with granite countertops, flat-screen TVs, new furnishings, flat stove cooktops, and an interactive computer in each room that allows communication to the front desk, room service, and multimedia concierge services. Each suite has free wireless Internet, private balcony, refrigerator and microwave, and an additional queen-size sofa sleeper. The resort has a large heated pool, two hot tubs, and a fitness facility on-site.

The **Pointe Estero Beach Resort** (6640 Estero Blvd., Fort Myers Beach, 855/923-8075, $250-550) is the best pick for families and groups. All of the two-bedroom suites offer wraparound balconies with nice views of the Gulf. One-bedroom units are available upon request only. The resort features spacious kitchens, dining room seating for six people, two full baths with a marble jetted tub in every master bathroom, and a spacious living room with a huge wraparound couch and 180-degree views of the Gulf of Mexico. The property also has tennis courts, a heated pool, a trolley service around town,

and water-sports activities on the beach. This family-oriented property offers a kids' program and playroom as well.

One of the most stylish and well-appointed resorts in the area is the **Resort at Marina Village** (5951 Silver King Blvd., Cape Coral, 259/541-5000, $250-500), built in 2009. The resort offers studio and one-, two-, and three-bedroom suites that range up to 2,225 square feet with views of the surrounding Caloosahatchee River, San Carlos Bay, and Gulf of Mexico. The on-site Tarpon Point Marina has a depth of 8-12 feet that can accommodate cruising boats of almost any size. The on-site restaurants and bars include lunch and dinner at the fun, outdoor tiki bar, with an exceptional happy hour menu and drink specials; fine dining at Marker 92, specializing in seafood; and delicious brick oven-fired pizza. The pool area, with surrounding fountains and hot tub, is not to be missed, nor is the exceptional spa and fitness center.

Sanibel Harbour Resort & Spa (17260 Harbour Pointe Dr., Fort Myers, 239/466-4000, www.sanibel-resort.com, $200-600) had a huge renovation and reopened in 2005 with updated guest rooms, lobby, meeting space, and restaurants (including a good Chicago-style steak house). This is a big place, with 240 hotel rooms, 107 more elite and private accommodations complete with concierge services at Grande Bay, and waterfront condominiums as well. It's just about the most luxurious resort-style spot in Fort Myers, with two gorgeous pools, restaurants and lounges to suit all needs, and a spa.

Bonita Springs is a nice residential area of Florida's Gulf Coast, and one of the draws for the visitor is ★ **Hyatt Regency Coconut Point Resort & Spa** (5001 Coconut Rd., Bonita Springs, 239/444-1234, $200-600), halfway between Fort Myers and Naples. It's a deluxe, destination-style hotel with 454 elegantly appointed guest rooms and lots of amenities on-site, including a Raymond Floyd-designed championship golf course, a day spa, poolside waterslides for the kids, and views of beautiful Estero Bay (a private water taxi transports guests to the resort's private beach not far away). There are several excellent restaurants on-site, and the resort's grounds are expertly landscaped and complete with stunning fountains and even a large, relaxing outdoor fire pit. Golf packages ($225-425 for a standard room) include accommodations, one round of golf at 18-hole Raptor Bay per night stay, a golf cart, unlimited range balls, a yardage book, and a golf club bag tag.

Vacation Rentals

In the Fort Myers area, there is more opportunity to find a relatively affordable beachfront home than in Naples farther to the south. The prices run the gamut, but a two- or three-bedroom house on the Gulf is generally $1,500-4,000 per week or $200-600 per night, a bargain compared to what you will pay around Naples. The prices go down from there for condos and homes outside of the beach area, which run about $800-3,000 per week or $150-400 per night. For an exceptional website where you can view a large number of photos of a large selection of vacation rentals, contact **Coldwell Banker Fort Myers Vacation Rentals** (7502 Estero Blvd., Fort Myers, 239/463-3151, www.ftmyersbeachvacations.net) or **VIP Vacation Rentals** (239/472-1613, www.vip-vacationrentals.com), which also serves Sanibel and Captiva.

GETTING THERE
Car

To get to Fort Myers, you can take either I-75 or U.S. 41. In town, McGregor Boulevard runs alongside the Caloosahatchee River and is also called Highway 867. Highway 865 (also known as Hickory Boulevard, Estero Boulevard, and San Carlos Boulevard, depending on where you are) is the route south to Fort Myers Beach on Estero Island.

Driving into Florida from the north via Jacksonville, take I-95 south to I-4 to I-75. The drive is 317 miles via I-75, and it will take about five hours.

Air

The area is served by **Southwest Florida International Airport** (11000 Terminal Access Rd., Fort Myers, 239/590-4800, www.flylcpa.com). The airport's Midfield Terminal Complex opened in 2005 with three concourses and 28 gates. The terminal is one of the first in the United States to be built with new security equipment and procedures incorporated into the design. The $438 million project focused on passenger convenience with a lovely subtropical look and a permanent photography collection of the work of Florida photographer Alan Maltz.

Most major domestic airlines serve the airport, and there are international flights from Germany and Canada. The airport, opened in 1983, currently serves Air Berlin, Air Canada, American, Delta, Frontier, JetBlue, Silver, Southwest, Spirit, Sun Country, United, and Westjet.

Alamo (800/327-9633), **Avis** (800/230-4898), **Budget** (800/227-5945), **Dollar** (800/800-3665), **Enterprise** (800/736-8222), **Hertz** (800/654-3131), **National** (800/227-7368), and **Thrifty** (800/847-4389) provide rental cars from Southwest Florida International Airport. Enterprise and Thrifty offices are directly across the street from baggage claim.

Bus and Train

LeeTran (239/275-8726, www.rideleetran.com, $1.50/ride, $0.60/ride seniors, $4 all-day pass) serves the Lee County area with most stops in the Fort Myers region. The south Fort Myers routes serve the beach areas. LeeTran has hourly service 6am-10pm to a transfer point at Daniels Parkway and U.S. 41, with connections to other routes.

Greyhound Bus Line (239/774-5660) offers bus service to the Fort Myers station, but from here you really need to rent a car. Public transportation to and between the islands is limited to taxis and limousines.

Sanibel Island

There are more than 100 small barrier islands that flank the coastline of the greater Fort Myers area. Of these, Sanibel stands out—literally, because it bucks the system and lies east-west in a gentle, shrimp-shaped curve, and figuratively, because it is so well known and widely trafficked. The island's biggest draw is nothing the chamber of commerce had any control over: The island's orientation, coupled with the fact that there are no offshore reefs, means that Sanibel is the recipient of the Gulf of Mexico's beneficence: More than 400 varieties of shells have been found along the 16 miles of white-sand beaches. Expect crown conch, lion's paw, angel wings, alphabet cones, and sand dollars to wash up whole at your feet.

Birders would take issue with the shellers, though, on top draw. The birding on Sanibel is impressive for breadth as well as sheer numbers. More than half the island is encompassed by the J. N. "Ding" Darling National Wildlife Refuge, 6,354 acres of preserved subtropical barrier island habitat for Florida's native wetland, part of the largest undeveloped mangrove ecosystem in the country. Whether on foot, biking, canoeing, or with a narrated tram ride, naturalists and sightseers can observe wading birds, wetland birds, and the array of other Sanibel wildlife.

Connected to the mainland by a three-mile-long scenic drive across a causeway, Sanibel is a comfortable island. It welcomes families and traveling couples with a friendly, easy charm and fairly reasonable prices. It isn't the kind of island on which you'll find gigantic resort hotels. Most accommodations are low-rise; in fact, buildings on the island can be only as tall as the tallest palm. There are no traffic lights, no street lamps, and no motorized water sports (such as Jet Skis or Ski-Doos).

Sanibel's main street is Periwinkle Way, a picturesque thoroughfare that, pre-Hurricane Charley, was canopied by a tall stand of Australian pines (not native) and palms. A massive replanting effort in recent years has made it fully leafed once again (but no pines). Shops, small inns, and casual restaurants punctuate the road from the Sanibel

Sanibel Island

Sea Turtles

From the beginning of May to the end of October, the beaches of Sanibel play host to a different kind of visitor. Loggerheads, the most common sea turtles in Florida, make their way out of the Gulf and up the beaches to lay their eggs. An estimated 14,000 females nest in the southeastern United States each year, many of them from the northern tip of Fort Myers Beach to the Lee-Collier border of Bonita Beach. Called loggerheads because of their big heads, they can reach 200-350 pounds and measure about three feet long.

Female loggerheads return to the beaches on which they were born to lay their own eggs. They painstakingly dig nest cavities with their rear flippers, deposit about 100 golf ball-sized eggs, cover them up, and head back out to sea. And two months later the two-inch hatchlings break out and flap their way toward the moonlit sea. Sanibel has a lights-out policy on beaches so the little turtles aren't confused in their mission, stumbling toward a brightly lit condo instead.

According to the Florida Fish and Wildlife Research Institute, the number of known nesting loggerheads between the years 1998 and 2010 declined by 25 percent. However, the most recent data shows a dramatic recovery in the loggerhead populations. The 2015 census data shows that between 2010 and 2015 the number of nests nearly doubled, from around 3,500 in 2010 to near 6,000 In 2015.

What you can do to help:

- Pack up your beach trash, monofilament fishing line, and especially plastic bags and plastic six-pack holders. Turtles mistake this stuff for tasty sea creatures undulating in the water, and they often get snarled in fishing line.

- Observe nesting turtles only from a distance. That goes for your curious pets, too. Dogs must be leashed on Sanibel, and do so even at night when no one's around to enforce the regulation.

- Stack up beach chairs or other items that might impede the baby loggerheads' progress toward the water.

- If you're staying in a beach house, close your drapes or blinds after dark. If you use exterior lights, make sure they are 25-watt yellow bug lights. Don't use flashlights, fishing lanterns, or flash photography on the beach.

- Leave nest identification markers in place. To report a wandering hatchling or a dead or injured turtle, call the **Florida Fish and Wildlife Conservation Commission** (888/404-3922) or the volunteer organization **Turtle Time** (239/481-5566).

Lighthouse to Tarpon Bay Road. Fort Myers is where to have your home base if you want museums, spectator sports, and attractions; Captiva is where to go for a slow pace and lots of quiet relaxation. Sanibel is like the middle child who likes to mix it up a little—there are things to do beyond beach walking, with friendly restaurants and a great shell museum.

SPORTS AND RECREATION
Beaches

Sanibel is unusual among barrier islands due to its east-west orientation. Because of this, the surf is gentle and the shells arrive whole and pristine. The beaches along East, Middle, and West Gulf Drive slope gradually, making the shallows vast and safe for young waders and beachcombers. There are some beach rules to follow: Pets must be on leashes and cleaned up after (no pets at all on Captiva beaches); no alcoholic beverages on the beaches November-May; no open fires; and no collecting live shells. All public beach access areas on the island have restrooms, some with concessions and picnic tables. Beach parking is $2 per hour.

If you have to pick two beaches to visit from among the 14 miles of sand, start with **Lighthouse Beach & Fishing Pier** (turn left on Periwinkle Way, the first stop sign as you enter the island, and follow Periwinkle Way, which terminates at the parking lot for the boardwalk) and **Bowman's Beach** (off Sanibel-Captiva Rd., turn left on Bowman's Beach Rd.). The heart of the former is the **Sanibel Lighthouse Boardwalk** (1 Periwinkle Way), the most frequently photographed landmark on the island. It's been here since 1884 on the eastern tip of the island, near the bay side. The beach has a lovely T-dock fishing pier and a boardwalk nature trail through native wetlands. Bowman's Beach is remoter and quieter. Park in the lot and walk over a bridge to the secluded white beach. It offers showers and barbecue grills.

Beyond these, **Gulfside City Park** (mid-island on Algiers Ln. off Casa Ybel Rd.), **Tarpon Bay Beach** (also mid-island at the south end of Tarpon Bay Rd. at W. Gulf Dr.), and the **Causeway Beaches** (adjacent to the causeway on both sides) are inviting.

★ J. N. "Ding" Darling National Wildlife Refuge

J. N. "Ding" Darling National Wildlife Refuge (1 Wildlife Dr., 239/472-1100, www.fws.gov/dingdarling, 7:30am-sunset Sat.-Thurs., $5/vehicle, $1 walkers or bicyclists)

takes up more than half of Sanibel Island. The refuge was named for Pulitzer Prize-winning cartoonist Jay Norwood Darling, the first environmentalist to hold a presidential cabinet post (during FDR's administration), and it is an absolute marvel. It contains a visitors center, a five-mile driving tour route, hiking trails, canoe and kayak rentals, and guided interpretive programs.

The 6,354-acre refuge is made up of a variety of estuarine and freshwater habitats. You'll see mudflats and mangrove islands, wide swaths of sea grass and open water, West Indian hardwood hammocks and ridges, and places poetically described as spartina swales. But the real draw is birds.

Ordinarily I'd advise walking or biking through a refuge like this, 2,825 acres of it designated as wilderness area—you know, go at your own pace, get a close-up look at things. But then you'd miss out on the naturalist-narrated tram ride full of competitive birders.

An up-close look at birders is half the fun of a day at "Ding" Darling. On the tram ride, listening to these birders, you can learn to recognize black-crowned night herons and immature ibis and see wood storks, peregrine falcons, and a wealth of the 238 bird species that hang out in the refuge. The best

the Sanibel Lighthouse

birding time is early morning, about an hour before or after low tide, when you'll see birders equipped with cameras set up on tripods. Watch what they're watching, and ask questions. You'll see things rare and magnificent. The wildlife observation tower is a superb place to hang out any time of the day, and the **education center** (9am-5pm daily Nov.-Apr., 9am-4pm the rest of the year) provides a little guidance to the rookie.

Tarpon Bay Explorers (900 Tarpon Bay Rd., 239/472-8900, www.tarponbayexplorers.com), which runs a tram tour through the refuge ($13 adults, $8 children), also offers a 90-minute kayak trail tour ($30 adults, $20 children) along the Commodore Creek water trail and a sunset paddle ($40 adults, $25 children) out to the rookery islands in the refuge. You'll see hundreds upon hundreds of egrets, herons, anhingas, and ibis, all bedded down in the treetops for the night.

Shelling

Beaches are the most magnetic draw on Sanibel, with wide lengths of white-sand beach and some of the best shelling in the world. Some say 400 species of seashells dot the beaches here, from polka-dotted junonia to lacy apple murex and fat lightning whelks.

The most fruitful time to shell is early morning, at low tide, and after a storm, especially after the big-wave coastal storms in January and February. Other experts say the peak season for shelling is May-September. Walk slowly and look for seashells hidden just beneath the surface of the sand where the surf breaks, about where the water comes up to your knee. Wear polarized sunglasses so you can see into the water, bring a bag or fanny pack for your treasure, and don't take any shell that's inhabited.

The south side of Sanibel has a wide shallow beach that seems to attract shells without battering them—they stay whole and perfect. You're more likely to find good ones where the competition isn't too fierce—the less populated the stretch of beach, the better. (The beaches of North Captiva and Cayo Costa Islands are known, among aficionados, for their lack of people and wealth of starfish, conchs, and sand dollars.) Generally, smaller shells are found closer to the Lighthouse Beach end, with larger shells the closer you get to Captiva. Common shells include lightning whelk, cockle, scallop, murex, tulip, olive, little coquina, and conch. If you find a junonia, hang on to it for the bragging rights.

If you're coming up empty-handed, turn it

J. N. "Ding" Darling National Wildlife Refuge

over to the professionals, with one of the local shelling charters. **Captain Mike Fuery's Shelling Charters** ('Tween Waters Marina, 239/466-3649, www.sanibel-online.com/fuery, $250 for a 3-hour private charter for up to 4 passengers) is a famous shelling outfit, its tours featured in *National Geographic, Southern Living, Martha Stewart,* and other magazines. Shelling trips for romantic couples seem to be a specialty.

Kayaking

The **Great Calusa Blueway Paddling Trail** (www.greatcalusablueway.com) is a 100-mile mapped-and-markered route for paddlers of all skill levels to explore. Following the trail of the area's early fishers, the Calusa people, it runs along Lee County's coastal waters from Cayo Costa and Charlotte Harbor south through Pine Island Sound and Matlacha Pass to Estero Bay and the Imperial River in Bonita Springs.

If you're not an outdoorsy type whose idea of fun is an Eskimo roll in fierce white water, you can enjoy a couple of days of nice, easy kayaking, with stops for lunch and birdwatching, and a comfy bed at the end of each day.

The website gives details on the routes, what you'll see along the way, where to launch or stop, maps, GPS coordinates, and more, but you will still need to pick up a kayak or canoe. Outfitters offer guided trips (even some moonlight excursions), and there are numerous rentals and launch areas if you want to head out on your own.

You start the first day on the Pine Island Sound-Matlacha Pass section of the paddling trail. Crunching over the gravel at the Fish House Marina, you find your way to **Gulf Coast Kayak** (4120 Pine Island Rd., Matlacha, 239/283-1125, www.gulfcoastkayak.com, 9am-5pm daily, single kayak $35 half day, $50 full day). You get paddles, life jackets, trail maps, and kayaks and put in just at the drawbridge at Matlacha Pass.

The second segment to be mapped, the Pine Island Sound trail is gentle and sheltered.

kayaking the Great Calusa Blueway Paddling Trail

You can see small black crabs scoot along red mangrove trunks and great blue herons wade in their shade as you meander through backwaters and mangrove tunnels from marker 84 to marker 89. A few hours later, you realize paddling makes you hungry.

From here you head back down through Buzzard Bay until you reemerge at the Old Fish House. Lunch here is local shrimp quesadillas, local smoked mullet, and a novelty food: fried mullet gizzard (it seems that the mullet, mostly vegetarian, is like a chicken in that it has no stomach but a crop and a gizzard). Order at the counter, eat at picnic tables, and watch the snook and needlenose gar churn the water down below.

On day two you put in at Fort Myers Beach, which is actually on the island of Estero, connected to Fort Myers by a causeway. There are several worthwhile beaches here (Bowditch Point Regional Park, Lynn Hall Memorial Park), but we set our sights on **Lovers Key State Park** (8700 Estero Blvd., 239/463-4588, 8am-sundown, $8/car up to 8 people, $4/car single occupancy, $2 walkers and bicyclists), another key embarkation point on the Great Calusa Blueway.

From here you head to the **Nature Recreation Management concessionaire** (8700 Estero Blvd., 239/765-7788, single kayak $38 half day), pick up paddles and gear, then head to the launch spot to put in your kayaks. Using a Blueway map, you can make your way from marker 8 to markers 13 and 22. In parts the water is shallow, maybe a foot deep, and you quietly make your way out to congregations of ibis, egrets, and herons. If you keep paddling you can make it to **Mound Key** (Estero Bay, 239/992-0311, daylight hours, free), a complex of Calusa mounds made of shells, fish bones, and pottery. Thought to be a sacred ceremonial center for the native people, in 1566 it was settled by the Spanish and became the site of the first Jesuit mission in the Spanish New World. That didn't last long, as the Calusa weren't thrilled with the settlers.

The shell construction contains mounded platforms, ceremonial mounds, ridges, substantial carved out canals, and open water courts—evidence of a fairly elaborate community some 2,000 years ago. There are not a lot of interpretive markers or signs here, but it's a nice place for a picnic.

Adventure Sea Kayak ("Tween Waters Marina, 15951 Captiva Dr., Captiva, 239/822-3337, www. captivaadventures.com, $40 adults, $30 children) conducts kayak tours, its specialty being interactive trips that focus on the wildlife, ecology, and history of the barrier islands. Also based in Captiva, **Captiva Kayak Company & Wildside Adventures** (11401 Andy Rosse Ln. at bayside McCarthy's Marina, Captiva, 239/395-2925, www.captivakayaks.com, 9am-5pm daily) offers rentals, instruction, and sunrise, sunset, and starlight tours. On Sanibel, **Tarpon Bay Explorers** (900 Tarpon Bay Rd., Sanibel, 239/472-8900, www.tarponbayexplorers.com, 8am-6pm daily, $15-180) has a range of services, from canoe, kayak, and bike rentals to guided tours. And if you just want to rent a kayak or canoe, try **Gulf Coast Kayak** (4120 Pine Island Rd., Matlacha, 239/283-1125, www.gulfcoastkayak.com, 9am-5pm daily, single kayak or canoe $35 half day, $50 full day) or farther south **Estero River Canoe & Tackle Outfitters** (20991 S. Tamiami Trail, Estero, 239/992-4050, www.esteroriveroutfitters.com), which offers a large variety of canoes, kayaks, stand-up paddleboards, and paddling accessories.

Sea School

Sanibel Sea School (414 Lagoon Dr., 239/472-8585, www.sanibelseaschool.org) is dedicated to teaching children and adults about marine ecosystems. It uses the setting of the barrier island habitats of Sanibel and Captiva as an opportunity to touch, feel, and understand. Adult classes might focus on bivalves, gastropods, local history, and natural history, with field trips to study mollusk distribution, fish seining, investigating the mangroves at Blind Pass, and exploring the island on Indigo Trail and the Bailey Tract hikes. Call for a schedule of classes and drop-in events.

Biking

It's an island pastime partly because it's relatively safe (there are 25 miles of wide, paved biking paths) and partly because you can cover serious ground on these pancake-flat islands. You can take an extremely enjoyable bike ride from the eastern tip of Sanibel to the northern tip of Captiva, stopping occasionally to take a swim in the Gulf. You can also bike on the main drags, Sanibel-Captiva Road and Periwinkle Way, or swing through a stretch of the J. N. "Ding" Darling National Wildlife Refuge, or skirt the water's edge along Gulf Drive. The **Sanibel-Captiva Islands Chamber of Commerce** (1159 Causeway Rd., Sanibel, 239/472-1080) has a free bike path map.

Many inns on Sanibel and Captiva offer complimentary bikes to their guests—ask before you set up a rental elsewhere. The oldest bike shop on Sanibel is **Billy's Rentals** (1470 Periwinkle Way, 239/472-5248, www.

billysrentals.com, 8:30am-5pm daily, $5-10 for 2-hour rental, also daily and weekly rentals). Billy's offers regular hybrids, but also a range of unique stuff from adult trikes to recumbent bikes, Segways, and these cool multiperson surreys. You can even rent jog strollers and motor scooters at Billy's. **Finnimores Cycle Shop** (2353 Periwinkle Way, 239/472-5577, www.finnimores.com, 9am-4pm daily, $9-11 for 4-hour rental) is another wonderful shop, with no charge for delivery and pickup for a multiday rental. It also has in-line skates (they come with free helmet and pad rentals), umbrellas, fishing equipment, boogie boards, and most other essential fun-in-the-sun beach gear.

Birding

Birds just like it here. Some live here year-round, while other migrating species choose this island as a stopover or a convenient flyway terminus. J. N. "Ding" Darling National Wildlife Refuge is a wealth of avian splendor, but the rest of the island is a birder's paradise, too. Sanibel boasts so many habitats—freshwater wetlands, brackish mangrove estuaries, beaches, woodlands—that 240 different species feel at home here.

The ornithologically inclined have websites and chat groups devoted entirely to bird trails and spots on Sanibel. One of the local papers even has a regular bird column, and traffic stops fairly regularly for the recalcitrant crossing heron or egret.

Part of the thrill is the chase, tramping around with your binoculars trained on the treetops or water's edge at low tide. Here's where to look: Rare white pelicans hang out in Pine Island Sound; ospreys and eagles nest on telephone poles above the bike paths and along Sanibel-Captiva Road; wood storks troll for snacks in roadside ditches in the winter; burrowing owls dig tunnels in shopping center parking lots; sandhill cranes walk gracefully across expanses of lawn in groups of three; great blue herons search the Gulf's shoreline for an easy meal. The lighthouse area of Sanibel

is a good place to see birds, as are the mangrove islands off Pine Island Sound and Tarpon Bay on Sanibel. The little clumps of island off the causeway area attract lots of species as well. For an absolute sure thing, you'll hit paydirt in Periwinkle Park, which has an aviary for lovebirds, toucans, flamingos, and talking birds.

SIGHTS
★ Bailey-Matthews Shell Museum

Slippersnail. White baby ear. Ponderous ark. All of these are the beautiful names of shells. The **Bailey-Matthews Shell Museum** (3075 Sanibel-Captiva Rd., 239/395-2233, www.shellmuseum.org, 10am-5pm daily, $11 adults, $5 children 5-16, children 4 and under free) will make a shell collector out of most people. It's not a vast museum—it will occupy a pleasant 90 minutes or so—but it equips you to go out there and get yourself some of Neptune's treasures. Shells are arranged in thematic groupings from around the world, with an emphasis on the local offerings, and there are anthropological exhibits on humanity's relationship to shells (did you know that Native Americans' use of conch shells as weapons was the origin of the expression "conk on the head"?). There's also a video called *Mollusks in Action* shown five times each day.

Sanibel Historical Village and Museum

Sanibel Historical Village and Museum (950 Dunlop Rd., 239/472-4648, 10am-4pm Tues.-Sat., $10 adults, children 17 and under free) is a celebration of the local history of the island. This little cluster of historic buildings dragged from all over the island includes pioneer Clarence Rutland's original island home from the early 1900s, the Burnap Cottage built in 1898, Miss Charlotta's Tea Room restored to its 1930s look, Bailey's General Store, the original Sanibel post office, an old schoolhouse, an antique Model T, a Sanibel Lighthouse display, archived newspaper articles, and photos. The on-site town historian is a wealth of information and a wonderful storyteller.

Old Town

For more historical sightseeing, the East End village of **Old Town** was originally a fish camp built by Cuban fishers in the 1860s, prior to construction of the lighthouse in 1884. The Sanibel Historical Society has a walking and biking tour map of 19 historic sites along a stretch of about 2.5 miles. You can pick up a copy of the map at the **chamber of commerce** (1159 Causeway Rd.) or at the Sanibel Historical Village and Museum.

ENTERTAINMENT AND EVENTS

Theater and Cinema

The **Big Arts Herb Strauss Theater** (2200 Periwinkle Way, 239/472-6862, www.bigarts. org, 8pm Mon.-Sat., $42-30 adults, $5 children 16 and under), an institution in town, moved in 2004 to a larger, 160-seat theater. The little community group puts on crowd-pleasing musical revues. With a grand piano on stage, the theater does all-music performances. The restored 1896 one-room schoolhouse that used to house the theater has been hauled over to the Sanibel Historical Village and Museum to add another element to the little cluster of historic sites.

If you're just itching to be entertained, catch a flick at the **Island Cinema** (535 Tarpon Bay Rd., in Bailey's shopping center, 239/472-1701). It shows first-run mainstream films.

Festivals

The biggest festival in the area takes place peak season, in March, but it's still worth considering. Sanibel hosts an annual **Sanibel Shell Festival** (www.sanibel-island.sanibel-captiva.org), usually held at the **Sanibel Community House** (2173 Periwinkle Way, 239/472-2155). The largest and longest-running shell festival in the country, it draws serious shell collectors from around the world.

Sanibel's shopping is as low-key as the island itself. **Periwinkle Place** (2075 Periwinkle Way, 239/395-1914, www.periwinkleplace. com) boasts 28 attractive shops, a wonderful restaurant called The Blue Giraffe, and the enjoyable Sanibel Day Spa, all connected by covered walkways and shaded by banyan trees. Its clothing shops are mostly geared to beach- and sportswear; there are nice toy and swimsuit shops. **Olde Sanibel Shoppes** (630 Tarpon Bay Rd., 239/472-2783) is another cluster of gift, clothing, and jewelry shops, with a couple of casual restaurants thrown into the mix. The **Village Shops** (2340 Periwinkle Way) has roughly a similar lineup, and the 15 shops arrayed in the low pink buildings of **Tahitian Gardens** (1975-2019 Periwinkle Way) sell artisan candles, bright cotton clothing, jewelry, bathing suits, T-shirts, and giftware. This center also contains one of the island's best breakfast spots, the Sanibel Café.

None of this will rock your world—for a real one-of-a-kind island shopping experience, browse awhile in **She Sells Sea Shells** (2422 Periwinkle Way, 239/472-8080, www. sanibelshellcrafts.com). The funky shop contains shells from all over the place, but many are the same species you'll see stooped enthusiasts mining for (some even wear lighted miners' hats in the early mornings) along Sanibel beaches.

And if you need a regular old grocery store, **Bailey's** (2477 Periwinkle Way, 239/472-1516, 7am-9pm daily) is the biggest local market.

Galleries

Sanibel has got some galleries worth investigating. It seems to attract residents of artistic temperament, many of them opening shops that feature their work. **Tower Gallery** (751 Tarpon Bay Rd., 239/472-4557, www.towergallery.com, 10am-9pm daily) is a good place to start, and it's hard to miss in an electric blue and green building. It's a cooperative of 23 local artists. Representing all media and a real mix of styles, the work in the gallery is all juried. Right nearby you'll find another small cooperative called the **Hirdie Girdie Gallery** (2490 Library Way, 239/395-0027, www.hirdiegirdiegallery.com, 10am-5pm Mon.-Sat.), and next door to it the **Tin Can Art Gallery** (2480 Library Way, 239/472-9002), with the eccentric work of artist Bryce McNamara.

Sanibel's **BIG Arts** (Barrier Island Group for the Arts, 900 Dunlop Rd., 239/395-0900) is a community cultural arts organization that has a center for island arts. It has two galleries open to the public (9am-4pm Mon.-Fri. Oct.-Apr., 9am-3pm Mon.-Fri. May-Sept., also open 9am-1pm Sat. Jan.-Mar.), a sculpture garden, and performance space. Exhibits change monthly, and there are frequent workshops, lectures, films, and concerts.

FOOD

The restaurants of Sanibel are mostly fun, casual locations that serve lots of delicious seafood. Expect menu prices on Sanibel to be slightly higher than most other areas along the Gulf Coast. You're mostly paying for the view and expensive location, but you can cut the cost by doing the early-bird special before 6pm offered at many restaurants and happy hour at the bars. Plus, there are a few great deals on the island.

Breakfast

Lighthouse Cafe (362 Periwinkle Way, 239/472-0303, 7am-3pm daily year-round, 5pm-9pm daily Dec.15-Apr. 30, $8-15) usually beats the early-morning competition, hands down, whether you're a fan of the seafood Benedict or the blueberry whole-wheat hotcakes.

Lunch

Novelist Randy Wayne White is about the biggest booster this area has. Although I know when he was young he was a light-tackle fishing guide right in this neighborhood, I'm not quite sure how often he's in residence at the restaurant named for the main character of many of his books set in these parts. Wayne White is actually purported to be a good cook, with a seafood cookbook to his name. Regardless of who's cooking, **Doc Ford's Sanibel Rum Bar & Grille** (975 Rabbit Rd., 239/312-4275, 11am-10pm daily, $12-25) is a blast, with lots of TVs blaring the game, good sandwiches, and great drinks. The food—panko-breaded fried shrimp, Cuban sandwiches, pulled pork—is better than you might expect for such a laid-back setting.

Sanibel Café (2007 Periwinkle Way, 239/472-5323, 7am-2:30pm daily, $8-17)

The Island Cow restaurant has a wonderful outdoor patio.

seems like a locals' hangout, unpretentious and friendly. Go for the fat blue-cheese hamburgers.

Dinner

The menus at the following two places seem cut from the same mold. The **Island Cow** (2163 Periwinkle Way, 239/472-0606, 7am-9pm daily, $8-16) occasionally has a mooing contest among the guests, the winner of which gets a T-shirt in addition to deep and abiding respect. There's also live music, a wonderful outdoor patio, generous seafood baskets with fries—and they serve a great breakfast, too. It's a wonderfully fun restaurant, with excellent food, where you can save a lot of "moooo-lah." And **Jacaranda** (1223 Periwinkle Way, 239/472-1771, 5pm-10pm daily, $15-30) has a funky bar and a screened patio (good for when the bugs are biting). The Jac has music nightly (reggae on the weekends), sweet oysters from the patio raw bar, and a fairly extensive late-night menu.

Matzaluna (1200 Periwinkle Way, 239/472-1998, 4:30pm-9:30pm daily, $10-20) is more traditional. The wood-fired pizzas get top honors, with hearty baked pasta dishes (lasagna, stuffed shells) placing a close

second. Like many island spots, it offers excellent drink specials during happy hour.

ACCOMMODATIONS

There's little on Sanibel Island that's dirt cheap. On the other hand, nothing is extremely upscale. It's the kind of place where you get a sweet apartment, hotel, or motel rental a few steps from the beach, and you don't worry about whether there are luxurious amenities because you have the Gulf of Mexico at your doorstep.

If you're thinking about staying for a whole week, it makes sense to rent a condo or cottage. **Cottages to Castles of Sanibel & Captiva** (2427 Periwinkle Way, 800/472-5385, www.cottages-to-castles.com) has a number of intimate and affordable one-week rentals; it also offers the enormous seven-bedroom pink house called Sandhurst that was featured as the 2004 MTV Summer Beach House. The rates on the condos are reasonable off-season ($700-1,750/week).

My two favorites on the island have a subtle Old Florida nostalgia to them. They not only have nice interiors and modern amenities like Wi-Fi, but they also have a historical feel—the kinds of places you could imagine visiting for decades. The ★ **Island Inn on Sanibel**

One of the cottages at the Island Inn on Sanibel Island

Island (3111 W. Gulf Dr., 800/851-5088, www. islandinnsanibel.com, $200-600) opened in 1895. Look at the scrapbook of clippings to get a sense of who has roamed this compound of lovely little cottages and larger lodges on 10 acres, with 550 feet of unobstructed beachfront. Draws include shuffleboard, table tennis, and bike rentals, but it's the warmth of the staff and other guests that seems anachronistic. The same can be said of ★ **West Wind Inn** (3345 W. Gulf Dr., 239/472-1541, www. westwindinn.com, $200-400), a beachfront place in the quiet part of the island. Rooms have kitchenettes, but don't skip breakfast at its Normandie Seaside Restaurant, which seems to be a locals' morning hangout. West Wind's 500-foot stretch of beach is a marvel for stargazing. The lush landscaping surrounding the large heated pool captures the essence of this tropical destination. The inn is casual and comfortable, with a touch of Old Florida styling in the rooms and a focus on traditional elegance in the dining room. The staff goes out of their way to ensure superb customer service and provide a unique level of attention to their guests' needs.

Shalimar Resort (2823 W. Gulf Dr., 239/472-1353, www.shalimar.com, $300-500) is another favorite getaway, with 33 one- and two-bedroom cottages, apartments, and motel efficiencies spread around a huge property right on the Gulf. All units have full kitchens, and the pool is beautiful.

Sundial Beach Resort (1451 Middle Gulf Dr., 239/472-4151, www.sundialresort.com, $200-700) has 270 one- and two-bedroom suites that all have a condo vibe, complete with full kitchens. It sits in 33 acres of tropical landscape right along the beach and has a tremendous weekday camp for children 4-11. **Sanibel Inn** (937 E. Gulf Dr., 239/472-3181, www.sanibelinn.com, $200-600) is smaller, with 94 hotel rooms and one-bedroom suites. Outside, the inn sits in the shade of more than 600 palms, with butterfly gardens all around and complimentary use of the inn's bikes. Inside, bamboo flooring and shades of green, blue, and light brown give the rooms a relaxed style. The Sanibel Inn also offers a wonderful children's educational/entertainment program. For adults, the Dunes Golf & Tennis Club is nearby.

GETTING THERE

To get to Sanibel from I-75, take new exit 131 or old exit 21 (Daniels Parkway) west to Summerlin Road, approximately seven miles. Turn left onto Summerlin Road and drive approximately 15 miles to the Sanibel Causeway ($6 toll). Drive across and onto Sanibel Island. At the four-way stop at Periwinkle Way, either a right or a left turn will lead you to beaches, shops, and accommodations. Sanibel Island has a couple of main roads that parallel each other: Periwinkle Way, the main business route, and Gulf Drive, segmented into East, Middle, and West Gulf Drive. Tarpon Bay Road connects Sanibel-Captiva Road with Periwinkle Way at its west end. And Sanibel-Captiva Road—most folks call it San-Cap—goes by most of Sanibel's attractions before crossing over a short bridge at Blind Pass, where it becomes Captiva Drive on Captiva Island.

Captiva Island

Sanibel's northern neighbor, Captiva Island, is smaller, only about a half-mile wide and five miles long. It is at once more laid-back and more exclusive, perfect for a solitary getaway or romantic escape. Captiva has less commerce, fewer hotels and inns, fewer people in general. A fair percentage of the island's houses, all recessed behind dense pines and thick foliage, are the beach retreats of wealthy and often absentee owners, contributing to the island being quieter than Sanibel.

Captiva, with Captiva Drive running its length, has a relaxed downtown area of beach bars, restaurants, and gift shops that draw their inspiration from the beaches of Key West and the lyrics of Jimmy Buffett tunes. Captiva Village uses colorful and upbeat pastels, and some of the restaurants (such as the Bubble Room) adopt a fun and eccentric approach to decorating. Things are casual without being run-down—which lets much more upscale accommodations seem proper on Captiva. The South Seas Island Resort dominates a whole section at the northern tip of Captiva, where it breaks before the island of North Captiva

(once attached). Its sprawling charm and incredible beach set a tone for the island.

There are few attractions on the island, although much to do. Walk, run, fish, canoe, sit and read, or just sit. Anne Morrow Lindbergh was so inspired by Captiva's tranquility that it's where she wrote her best-selling book, *A Gift from the Sea.*

SPORTS AND RECREATION
Beaches

Captiva's beaches are less populated than those on Sanibel, for a couple of reasons. First, there are more private homes on Captiva, visited sporadically by their affluent owners. Thus, there are just fewer feet to churn the sand and rustle the packs of waterbirds. Second, the shelling is better on Sanibel. But Captiva's waters are clearer and the swimming slightly better. **Captiva Beach** (at the end of Captiva Dr., parking $4/hour) is a case in point—beautiful sand, lovely clear water, and only a few people in sight. It's a great place from which to watch the sunset. Because of

Captiva's beaches are less populated than those on Sanibel Island.

fairly swift currents, don't count on swimming at **Turner Beach** (Sanibel-Captiva Rd. at Blind Pass Bridge), but it's still a favorite among fisherfolk and shellers.

Gulf-side beach erosion has been a problem in recent years, exacerbated by recent storms. Private and public funds have been raised to restore beaches by pumping in sand from offshore.

Fishing

The South Seas Island Resort hosts the annual **Caloosa Catch & Release Tournament** on Captiva each June. This one is known as the largest single-site public flats tournament in Florida. People here are serious about fishing, and not just about the seasonal giant tarpon.

What are you likely to catch? Redfish is a pretty steady catch in these parts, some over 10 pounds. The species has rebounded since the New Orleans blackening craze made them a hot commodity. They can be fished on the flats. Snook is best in the springtime, and the season is closed December 15-January 31 and June-August. You'll catch lots of speckled trout in the winter when they're especially large; they tend to hang out in three-five feet of water near the edges of the grass flats and sand holes. Tarpon are the area's biggest draw, huge fish that range 100-150 pounds with lots of fight in them. (Some say the very first tarpon ever taken on rod and reel was in southwest Florida, near Punta Rassa across San Carlos Bay from Sanibel in 1885.) Tarpon season (recently changed to catch-and-release only) runs from the latter part of April through August. Then there are cobia (here Feb.-July, but best Apr.-May), tripletail, and jacks for much of the year on the flats, and black grouper far out in the Gulf. Commercial catches of grouper have been limited recently, so sportfishers might benefit from increased numbers.

Fishing charters start at around $250 for a half-day trip, and the charter captain provides the boat, fishing license, fishing gear, equipment, and bait. Sometimes the client pays an additional fee for gas—ask about this. As a matter of etiquette, a tip of $25-50 is customary, as is buying your captain and crew a meal or drinks at the end of your fishing trip. Many guides will clean and fillet your edible catch—if you don't want all the fish, give it to whomever seems interested dockside. As for mounting and taxidermy: Big fish are largely catch-and-release, so have a picture taken of yourself with your catch before you release it. Then, one of the new breed of high-tech taxidermists will create a lifelike plastic model of your prize.

Figure out whether you want to do deep-water fishing, cast in the flats, or maybe take a fly-fishing lesson, then visit the marinas to ask around about charter captains, prices, what people are catching, and where. **Capt. Jim's Charters** ('Tween Waters Marina, 15951 Captiva Dr., 239/472-1779, www.sanibelcaptivafishing.com, $100/hour) does back-bay fishing; **Capt. Joe's Charters** (Castaways Marina, Sanibel-Captiva Rd., Sanibel, 239/472-8658, www.captjoescharters.com, $250-400) does back-bay and fly-fishing; **Soulmate Charters** (17544 Lebanon Rd., Fort Myers, 239/851-1242, www.soulmatecharters.com, $350-600) offers backcountry fishing with light spin tackle and fly-fishing. The list goes on, with more than 50 charter captains willing to help you wet a line.

Sailing

Take the three-day certification program with **Offshore Sailing School** (16731 McGregor Blvd., Fort Myers, 239/454-1700, www.offshoresailing.com, courses for beginners, racers, and cruisers, basic keelboating class tuition $895). It's a tremendous amount of fun—three days on the water with an instructor and three other students, plus hours of classroom time learning all the sailing jargon, parts of the boat, points of sail, etc. At the end of the class you take a fairly difficult 80-question test, then you get out and show your sailing chops to your teacher, complete with man-overboard demonstrations and doing a quick stop by "shooting" into the wind.

If you're a goal-oriented person, it's a great activity to build a vacation around. You learn on a midsize daysailer, a Colgate 26, designed specifically for training and chosen by the U.S. Naval Academy to replace its training fleet. From here, you can take any number of other courses designed for more advanced sailors—performance sailing, live-aboard cruising, or a camp for racing sailors. At the very least you'll be able to tie nautical knots as a party trick.

Classes are held at the Pink Shell Beach Resort & Spa in Fort Myers Beach and the South Seas Island Resort on Captiva. Call for information.

SHOPPING

Hand-painted souvenirs and shell trinkets can be found along Sanibel-Captiva Road and in the Captiva Village area along Andy Rosse Lane, at the only four-way stop on Captiva. A popular shop here is **Jungle Drums** (11532 Andy Rosse Ln., 239/395-2266), a collection of wildlife, island, and environmental art in a variety of media.

FOOD

Most of the restaurants here are casual and reasonably priced, set in pastel-colored

cottages with outdoor seating. There's a nice, fun, beachy style and a funky charm.

The ★ **Bubble Room** (15001 Captiva Dr., 239/472-5558, 11:30am-3pm and 4:30pm-9pm daily, $15-28) is definitely fun and entirely eccentric. The waiters and bartenders are in scouting uniforms, with patches of their own devising meticulously sewn on. They wear neckerchiefs and mischievous grins. The interior is like something out of Santa's workshop, with toy trains and elves and hobbyhorses, but then add in 2,000 movie stills and glossies, lots of Betty Boop memorabilia, and a long list of other stuff. The food is definitely good, from fried shrimp to grilled fish cooked with a pineapple/ginger marinade.

Andy Rosse Lane, the area often called Captiva Village, has a cluster of fun places. The **Keylime Bistro** (in the Captiva Island Inn, 11509 Andy Rosse Ln., 239/395-4000, 8am-10pm daily, lounge until 1am, $15-30) offers live entertainment daily—it's a great place to hear musicians performing island music like Jimmy Buffett covers. The kitchen serves an excellent grouper sandwich, as well as a delicious sausage sandwich with onions and peppers; at dinner, choose shrimp scampi or grouper piccata. Good margaritas, and there's a Bloody Mary bar for Sunday brunch.

the Bubble Room

Tropical Fruit

Jackfruit, carambola, mamey sapote, sapodilla, lychee, longans, pineapple, and papaya are the kinds of fruits you imagine eating on a far-flung tropical island. Fling a little closer, and you've got Pine Island. Just west of Cape Coral, it is the largest island along the southwest coast of Florida and the producer of some of the state's most exotic fruits. Not the usual Florida orange, Pine Island's king of fruits is the mango. Its reign is so celebrated that there is an annual two-day festival, the **Pine Island MangoMania Tropical Fruit Fair** (239/283-0888) in July with mango-inspired foods, entertainment, and lots of fragrant fruits and plants for sale.

From late May to about Labor Day, enthusiasts can also stop into the tent-covered **Pine Island Tropical Farmer's Market** in Bokeelia (10am-4pm daily June-Aug., 10am-4pm Mon.-Sat. Sept.-May) for a wide array of tropical fruits. The **Fort Myers Downtown Farmers' Market** in Centennial Park offers a fair sampling of the local exotic fruits (7am-1pm Thurs.). Even local winemakers applaud the local fruits by making wine from carambola.

But what is a carambola, exactly?

Carambola is another word for starfruit, a light-yellow, ribbed, ovoid fruit that, when sliced, has star-shaped cross sections. The flesh is yellow, crisp, juicy, and not fibrous, ranging from sour to mildly sweet.

Mamey sapote is a large, football-shaped fruit that grows on an ornamental evergreen. The brown skin has a rough texture—rougher than a kiwi. The flesh is either a creamy pink or salmon color, and it has a big avocado-like pit. The flavor is described as a combination of honey, avocado, and sweet potato. Closely related, the **sapodilla** has soft brown flesh that tastes a little like sweet root beer. The sapodilla tree is also the source of chicle, a chewing gum component.

Lychee are nubby red fruits with pearly white flesh and the texture of a grape. The flesh is sweet but tart, and with a strong scent. Experienced lychee eaters bite lightly through the skin of the top and then squeeze the fruit out. The **longan** is known as the little brother of the lychee. They look alike, only the longan is smaller. The flesh is whitish and translucent like the lychee, but less strong smelling and a little muskier.

Jackfruit is a fruit for the intrepid. It is the largest tree-borne fruit in the world, up to 80 pounds, and the unopened fruit has a strong, disagreeable smell. The exterior is spiky and green, and the inside has large edible bulbs that taste like a cross between banana and papaya. You may not want to bother with jackfruit, but do check out the rest of Lee County's tropical bounty.

RC Otter's Island Eats (11506 Andy Rosse Ln., 239/395-1142, 8am-10pm daily, $8-20) is right across the street, with a vast menu of accessible American staples, and care put into vegetarian options. It serves wine as well as a house-made beer. Depending on the weather, you can sit indoors, on the covered veranda, or out on the patio, where there's usually live island music. **Mucky Duck** (11546 Andy Rosse Ln., 239/472-3434, 11:30am-3pm and 5pm-9:30pm daily, $18-28) has more of an English pub vibe, only set right on the beach. The only thing on the menu that might be construed as English is fish-and-chips, but no matter when the seafood platter is so good. Every night at sunset, revelers convene on the beachside patio to watch the colorful sunset show.

The **'Tween Waters Inn Beach Resort** (15951 Captiva Rd., 239/472-5161) is something of an institution around here, going from the bay side to the Gulf side across the island, and with a couple of restaurants on-site. For my money, I'd skip the fine-dining at **Old Captiva House** (7:30am-10:30am and 5:30pm-9:30pm daily, $18-34) and head for the ★ **Crow's Nest Beach Bar and Grille** (5pm-midnight daily, cocktails until late, $8-15). Not that the former isn't good—it often wins Florida's Golden Spoon Award, with swordfish saltimbocca, jerk grouper, seafood jambalaya, and key lime pie served in an intimate, special-occasion kind of space (sit in the Sunset Room). It's more that the latter is so much fun, with good drink specials, fine bar staples, and a band on many nights. And you cannot miss the hermit crab races, 6pm for families, 9pm for adults. Pick your hermit crab, the one who looks most like Dale Earnhardt Jr. or Jeff Gordon, and line him up. The competition is an ESPN-worthy drama. For lunch at 'Tween Waters, opt for the **Oasis Pool Bar** (11am-6pm daily, $7-10) on-site, where you can eat a fat sandwich, a cold salad, or a fruity drink while watching the commotion around the resort's pool.

When you're looking for a cocktail and a place to watch the sun go down, the **Green Flash Bayside Bar & Grill** (15183 Captiva Dr., 239/472-3337, 11:30am-3:30pm and 5:30pm-9:30pm daily, $13-20) is another top choice. The two-story restaurant is situated on Roosevelt Channel and overlooks Buck Key and Pine Island. The menu offers a wide range of choices, including seafood, steak, and burgers. The barbecue shrimp and lobster bisque are favorites.

ACCOMMODATIONS
$100-200
Jensen's Twin Palm Cottages (15107 Captiva Dr., 239/472-5800, 1-bedroom $110-180, 2-bedroom $125-190) are spread out along the bayside marina and fishing action.

You can rent a boat right here, grab some bait, and be out on the water before your pajamas have had time to miss you. The 14 cheerful tin-roofed cottages have kitchens and screened porches.

$200-300
If you want to be where the action is, ★ **Captiva Island Inn** (11509 Andy Rosse Ln., 239/395-0882, www.captivaislandinn. com, $150-300) is a wonderful bed-and-breakfast right in the middle of teeny Captiva Village. There are traditional B&B rooms, one- and two-bedroom cottages, a loft, and a suite. The owners also have a four-bedroom house with 4.5 baths for big gatherings.

Jensen's on the Gulf (15300 Captiva Dr., 239/472-4684, www.gocaptiva.com, motel suites $150-300, apartments $175-400, houses $300-600) has nine units directly on the Gulf.

Over $300
The biggest game in town in recent years has been ★ **South Seas Island Resort** (5400 Plantation Rd., 239/472-5111, www.southseas. com, $329-1,200) at the northern tip of the island, which closed after Hurricane Charley in 2004 for a massive $140 million renovation. Set in 330 acres of mangroves, the resort,

'Tween Waters Inn Beach Resort

which has an ownership time-share complex too, is casual but spectacular, with beautiful rooms and added draws such as a popular children's program, world-renowned sailing, pools, kayaking, a fishing pier, 2,100 feet of dockage for boats up to 130 feet long, and Gulf-edge golf.

The main pool area at the resort offers sleek cabanas for rent with a private attendant and spa services. The Point restaurant overlooking the pool offers casual Caribbean fare, and an upscale bar upstairs provides grand views of Pine Island Sound. The renovation included 24,000 square feet of meeting space complete with video and data projectors, and new sound and lighting systems. Captiva Golf Club was redesigned by Chip Powell as one of the Top Five Short Courses in the world.

'Tween Waters Inn Beach Resort (15951 Captiva Dr., 239/472-5161, www.tween-waters.com, $200-650) is another heavy-hitter on the island, with a huge resort complex that stretches from the bay side to the Gulf side. The inn dates back to 1926, when the collection of cottages hosted Teddy Roosevelt, Charles and Anne Lindbergh, Roger Tory Peterson, and J. N. "Ding" Darling. There are 137 water-view rooms, suites, and cottages; Olympic-sized and children's pools; tennis courts (free to guests); a day spa; four restaurants; and a full-service marina. The rooms are attractive, and there's a nice complimentary breakfast for guests, but it's all the great amenities that make this a special experience. Rent a canoe or kayak and head out for the day.

GETTING THERE

You have to drive through Sanibel to reach Captiva. From Sanibel, turn right onto Periwinkle Way, drive two miles, turn right onto Tarpon Bay Road, and at the next left turn onto Sanibel-Captiva Road. Drive for approximately eight miles, cross Blind Pass Bridge, and you're there.

Charlotte Harbor and the Barrier Islands

From Charlotte Harbor south past Fort Myers, there is an incredible number of great little islands in the waters of Lee County and Charlotte County. A long line of curves and dots on the map between the Gulf waters and the Intracoastal Waterway, some of these islands are accessible by causeway, others just by boat. What unifies them is unbelievable natural beauty and romanticized, often pirate-related histories. Sailboating outfits, fishing charters, regularly scheduled ferries, and water taxis head out to these barrier islands. One of the area's first tourists was Spanish explorer Ponce de León, who ended up taking a Calusa arrow and dying in these waters. The natives are friendlier now.

CHARLOTTE HARBOR

Most people hadn't heard of Florida's Charlotte Harbor and Punta Gorda until Hurricane Charley blew through and over them on August 13, 2004. Punta Gorda took one of the category IV storm's worst beatings, with loads of people months later still trying to decide whether to renovate or rebuild.

The area not only rebounded, but went further and added an estimated 500 new hotel rooms, a $5.5 million new Bailey Airport Terminal at Charlotte County Airport, and the $46 million rebuilt and expanded sports arena, the **Charlotte Sports Park,** which now hosts the Tampa Bay Rays for spring training. The whole area is worth exploring, especially for the eco-traveler. Charlotte Harbor is the second-largest estuary in the state, encompassing 270 square miles. It has 365 miles of canals: 190 miles of them saltwater, 175 miles of freshwater. Most of the area bordering the harbor is preserved land, with parks, 57 blueway trails, and the largest undisturbed pine flatwoods in southwest Florida. To reach Charlotte Harbor from Fort Myers, follow U.S. 41 North for 24 miles, which will take about 30 minutes. Once you cross the Peace River, you're there.

The area has been featured on *Sail* magazine's list of the "10 Greatest Places to Sail in the United States" and was ranked by *Golf Digest* as the "Third Best Place to Live and Play Golf in America."

If you're visiting Lee County, don't skip **Punta Gorda.** It's worth the drive north from Fort Myers to visit **Babcock Wilderness Adventure** (8000 Hwy. 31, 800/500-5583, tours by reservation 9am-3pm, $24 adults, $23 seniors, $16 children 3-12, also special group and seasonal prices) for an exhilarating 90-minute tour through the Babcock Ranch, Telegraph Cypress Swamp, and the 90,000-acre Crescent B Ranch. Guides offer narration on birds, animals, plants, and the cattle and horses raised on the ranch. You'll see Florida panthers (okay, not wild, exactly), big gators, white-tailed deer, wild turkeys, and ornery-looking Florida Cracker cattle that are raised on the ranch. It's thrilling, especially for kids.

Out of Fisherman's Village in Punta Gorda, **King Fisher Fleet** (1200 W. Retta Esplanade, 941/639-0969, www.kingfisherfleet.com,

cruises range $12-23 adults, half price for children 3-11, children under 3 free, back-bay fishing $325-675/day, deep-water $850/day) pays equal attention to sightseers and anglers. It offers sightseeing cruises to the out islands, ecotours, full- and half-day cruises, sunset cruises, and harbor tours. After a day of fishing, you can visit one of Punta Gorda's two excellent day spas, **Spa One** (115 Taylor St., 941/506-6111) and **Bisous at the Spa** (321 Taylor St., 941/575-6363).

At Christmastime, all the houses and boats along the canals in Punta Gorda are decorated lavishly for the holidays. King Fisher offers a charming evening cruise along the canals to check out the lights and holiday festivities.

The little town of **Englewood,** west of Charlotte Harbor and north of Cape Haze, is definitely worth the drive. A great place for an evening barbecue is the covered pavilion on the downtown beachfront at **Chadwick Park.**

There's also the 135-acre **Oyster Creek Regional Park** in Englewood, located on the greenway waterway corridor known as the Oyster Creek-Lemon Bay Aquatic Preserve-Ainger Creek waterway.

Lemon Bay is at the north end of the Cape Haze peninsula, where evidence suggests early Floridians lived well from about 1000 BC to

Charlotte Sports Park

AD 1350. You can see their faint evidence at **Paulson's Point** (210 Winson Ave., 941/861-4000, dawn-dusk daily, free), also known as the Sarasota County Indian Mound Park. The tall shell-mound park features helpful interpretive markers and a beautiful, easy walkway around and through the Native American mound.

If you find yourself in the northern part of Lee County, I highly recommend a stay at **Turtle Bay Condos** (2375 N. Beach Rd., Manasota Key, 941/473-2335, www.myturtlebaycondos.com, $175-230/night, $770-1,395/week) on **Manasota Key** off the coast of Englewood. All of the eight two-bedroom condo units are fully furnished, exceptionally spacious, and have a fully equipped kitchen, which makes this property a top choice for families and extended stays. Each unit has its own stock of beach chairs, beach towels, a private back deck, and a washer and dryer. The heated pool is surrounded by palms and lush landscaping. Across the street is a public access point to the Gulf where you can hunt for sharks' teeth and shells. Behind the condos you can tie up a boat or fish from the wooden dock that offers visitors picturesque views of Lemon Bay and Englewood to the east. Each unit is uniquely furnished, so go to the website to view excellent pictures that will help you choose the one that best fits your style. Wi-Fi is free throughout the property, and the area restaurants are within walking distance, which makes this already competitively priced lodging one of the best deals in the area.

Food

The area has a number of worthwhile restaurants. There's **Amimoto Japanese Restaurant** (2705 Tamiami Trail, Punta Gorda, 941/505-1515, 5:30pm-9:30pm Mon.-Sat., $15-22), serving sushi presented artistically. It is a great lunch spot. Also popular in Punta Gorda are the restaurants of **Fisherman's Village** (1200 W. Retta Esplanade, www.fishville.com, 10am-6pm Mon.-Sat., noon-6pm Sun.), including **The Captain's Table** (941/637-1171, 11:30am-9pm Sun.-Thurs., 11:30am-10pm Fri.-Sat., $16-25), **Village Fish Market** (941/639 7959, 11am-9pm Mon.-Sat., 11:30am-8pm Sun., $10-25), and **Harpoon Harry's** (941/637-1177, 11am-10pm daily, $8-15).

In the town of Englewood, classy waterview dining can be had at **Gulf View Grill** (2095 N. Beach Rd., 941/475-3500, 11am-10pm daily, $12-32). Get the stone crab claws if they're in season.

fishing off of Punta Gorda

Undoubtedly the best restaurant in the area is **The Perfect Caper** (121 E. Marion Ave., Punta Gorda, 941/505-9009, 11:30am-10pm Wed.-Fri., 4pm-10pm Sat.-Tues., $20-45), where James and Jeanie Roland take a fresh approach to California-Asian fusion. Jeanie, a CIA grad, is strict about the ingredients. Her passion for the season's best can be seen in starters like fried jumbo prawns wrapped in phyllo and served with avocado relish and blood-orange vinaigrette, and entrées of grilled venison tenderloin with roasted purple potatoes.

★ PALM ISLAND

Almost everything on Palm Island revolves around **Palm Island Resort** (7092 Placida Rd., Cape Haze, 941/697-4800, www.palm-island.com, $400-1,200), one of the best places to stay on the entire Gulf Coast. Start by driving to Cape Haze, for which the directions are a little tricky: Take I-75 29 miles north from Sanibel. Take the County Road 768 West exit (exit 161) toward Punta Gorda. Almost immediately, turn right onto Taylor Road (County Road 765A), which then runs into the Tamiami Trial (U.S. 41 N). Follow this nine miles, then turn left onto El Jobean Road (Hwy. 776 W). Follow this eight miles, turn left onto Gasparilla Road (County Road 771), and drive another eight miles. Turn right onto Placida Road (County Road 775), go two miles, and you're there. Then you wait in line in your car for the car ferry. It comes, you drive on, and about 60 seconds later the ferry lands on Palm Island. Then you're in paradise. Nice young men in shorts greet you, take all your stuff, and tell you where to ditch your car; you get your own golf cart, and you motor over to your unit along gravel roads.

The island is due north of Boca Grande, with about 200 private homes, plus 15 more private homes within the resort. Resort guests stay in 154 one-, two- or three-bedroom villas right on the Gulf. In clusters of low-rise buildings, spacious units reflect a real range of tastes, from beachy casual to swanky contemporary—be specific about your tastes and needs when you call, or make sure and browse through the photos of each on the website before making reservations. There are several pools, tennis courts, a comfy restaurant called the Rum Bay, children's programs, and kayak rentals. Make sure to bring your own groceries from the mainland, as the prices at the little on-island market are exorbitant.

Beautiful beaches, clear green-blue waters, amazing sunsets, an abundance of sea oats—it's all worth the price of admission, making Palm Island a perfect getaway that everyone will appreciate.

GASPARILLA ISLAND

Named for the infamous pirate José Gaspar, who may have hidden out (and buried his treasure, never to be found) on this island in the 1700s with his band of adventurous men, Gasparilla Island has had a much more posh and refined recent history. Connected to the mainland by a short causeway near Punta Gorda, the island was founded as a vacation retreat and fishing spot by the DuPont family in the late 1800s. Its town of **Boca Grande,** at the mouth of Charlotte Harbor, is filled May-mid-July with tarpon fishers; the opening between Cayo Costa and Gasparilla Island has been called the "Tarpon Fishing Capital of the World." Tarpon are sparser in the pass and the estuarine waters of Pine Island Sound these days, but during peak season the dense cluster of fishing boats still pull into port to try their luck. There is driving access to the island via the Boca Grande Causeway, the causeway at County Road 775, and at Placida.

Boca Grande is on the southern tip of Gasparilla Island and has a quaint fishing village feel that appeals to anglers and is complemented by a number of upscale shops and restaurants (George W. Bush has been a regular guest). While there, walk around **Boca Grande Lighthouse Park** (Gasparilla Island State Park, 880 Belcher Rd., 941/964-0375, 8am-sunset, $3/car). The wooden Boca Grande Lighthouse was built in 1890 and is a maritime landmark. The lighthouse is open to the public 10am-4pm the last Saturday of the month, and there's a little lighthouse museum, gift shop, and the Armory Chapel. The waters in these parts have strong currents—not great for swimming, but you'll see people sailboarding.

The **Gasparilla Inn and Club, Boca Grande** (500 Palm Ave., 941/964-4500, www.gasparillainn.com, $245-2,000) completed renovations in 2007 and received designation as a Historic Hotel of America. Built in 1912 and opening to guests in 1913, the historic pale-yellow wooden frame, white-pillar entrance, and Victorian-style gable roofs define this grand resort, its main hotel surrounded by cute cottages. With a major Old Florida feel, it sits on 156 acres of well-manicured grounds with great views of the Gulf of Mexico and Charlotte Harbor. A Pete Dye-designed golf course, croquet lawn, two pools, fishing, spa, and 200-slip marina are some of the reasons it's been a Bush family favorite over the years. It's also pet-friendly.

USEPPA ISLAND

Across from Cabbage Key is Useppa Island. Pirate José Gaspar supposedly named the place for one of his more favored captives, a Mexican princess named Joseffa. Calusas may have lived here as far back as 5000 BC,

discarding their oyster and clam shells to create a greater amount of dry land. Barron Collier, for whom Collier County is named, bought the 100-acre island in 1912 and built a resort there in his own name that lured fishing enthusiasts from all over. The island is really a private residential club called the Useppa Island Club, with a couple of places on-island for visitors to stay. The **Collier Inn** (239/283-4443, $150-300) offers seven stylishly decorated suites, and there are also a number of cottages for rent. The **Useppa Marina** accommodates visitors' boats, and the **Tarpon Restaurant** is basically the only place to eat. The Useppa Island Historical Society's little **Useppa Museum** (239/283-9600, noon-2pm Tues.-Fri., 1pm-2pm Sat.-Mon., $5 suggested donation) is a worthwhile museum, full of an odd assortment of things. There are uniforms here from Cuban leaders who participated in the doomed invasion of the Bay of Pigs. These leaders were chosen in secrecy on Useppa by the CIA. And there's a forensic restoration of the "Useppa Man," taken from a skeleton unearthed during an archaeological dig in 1989. Other finds reflect the Paleo nomadic hunter-gatherer people who must have hung out here 10,000 years ago when the island was part of the mainland.

the Boca Grande Lighthouse

Useppa Island is only accessible by water taxi or private boat. Water taxis run every day from Pine Island, Captiva Island, and Punta Gorda. **Captiva Cruises** (239/472-5300, www.captivacruises.com, 10am-3pm Tues.-Sun., $40 adults, $25 children) has a luncheon cruise to Useppa that includes a visit to the museum.

CABBAGE KEY

The **Cabbage Key Inn** (Intracoastal Waterway, marker 60, Pineland, 239/283-2278, www.cabbagekey.com, $134-460, transient dockage available), built by writer Mary Roberts Rinehart and her son in 1938, has two tempting draws for the visitor. Apparently it was here that Jimmy Buffett drew his inspiration for "Cheeseburger in Paradise." And indeed, the inn serves a great burger. The second reason is the **Dollar Bill Bar,** located in the inn, which rides atop a 38-foot Calusa shell mound. The pub is lined with dollar bills, a custom that began in 1941 when a fisherman autographed and taped his last dollar to the wall for safekeeping (ensuring a beer on his return). Since then, people sign and date a buck, and tack them up—more than 30,000 $1 bills are taped to the walls, ceilings, and woodwork, providing a historical collage. (It's illegal to deface currency, but no one in this live-and-let-live bar will tell on you.)

Cabbage Key is accessible only by boat, helicopter, or seaplane, located directly across from mile marker 60 on the Intracoastal Waterway. It doesn't really have sandy beaches or many amenities, but it's a great day or overnight trip. **Captiva Cruises** (239/472-5300, www.captivacruises.com, 10am-3pm Tues.-Sun., $40 adults, $25 children) also offers a narrated cruise to Cabbage Key, and there are regularly scheduled water taxis every day from Pine Island, Captiva Island, and Punta Gorda.

CAYO COSTA

It's one of the quietest unbridged barrier islands in the chain, but one of the largest. Immediately to the west of Cabbage Key, stretching from Boca Grande Pass to Captiva Pass, it offers eight miles of pristine beach and unspoiled beauty. **Cayo Costa State Park** (4 nautical miles west off the coast of Pine Island, mail: P.O. Box 1150, Boca Grande, FL 33921, 941/964-0375, 8am-sunset, $2 honor system) is the least-visited state park in Florida, but it's because there are no cars, no electricity, and no hot water, not because it's not worthy.

Calusas occupied the island for hundreds of years, then in the early 1800s Cuban fishers landed here, and in 1848 the U.S. government started managing the land. There are 20 private homes on the island, only a couple of them lived in year-round. Really, it's a place to tent camp ($22/night) or overnight in one of 12 rustic cabins ($40), all on the northern end of the island. There are a small pioneer cemetery and a fair number of wild pigs—other than that it's sea creatures, birds, and swaths of sun-warmed sand.

Cayo Costa is accessible only by passenger ferry or private boat. Call **Tropic Star of Pine Island** (239/283-0015, $32 adults, $25 children) to make reservations.

NORTH CAPTIVA ISLAND

Once a part of Captiva Island, this island was severed during the hurricane of 1926. And then the right eye wall of Hurricane Charley in August 2004 passed over North Captiva Island and severed it into two parts (not surprisingly, folks call it Charley Pass).

The island has maintained a reputation as a remote retreat for the super wealthy. There are four miles of state-owned beaches—the state bought 350 acres, almost half of the island, in 1975. At the turn of the 20th century the island contained a vast tomato plantation; after that it was the processing plant for the Punta Gorda Fish Company. In recent years there have been about 50 year-round residents on the island, most of them on the northern part in an enclave known as the Island Club, with the rest of the island given over to affluent vacationers driving golf carts and strolling the sparsely populated beaches.

North Captiva Island is only accessible by

private boat, water taxi, or seaplane. Water taxis leave daily from Pine Island and Captiva Island.

PINE ISLAND

Pine Island is one of the largest islands off the Gulf Coast of Florida and consists of Matlacha (mat-la-SHAY), Pine Island Center, Bokeelia (bo-KEEL-ya), Pineland, and St. James City. Unlike many of the other barrier islands in this region, you don't need a boat to get to Pine Island. Just take Pine Island Road off U.S. 41 to find this great fishing retreat (the tarpon fishing craze started here in the 1880s) and lovely place from which to observe wildlife, such as the bald eagle nesting sites.

Matlacha is a funky fishing village, with a drawbridge over Matlacha Pass that has seen a lot of fishing action in its day. If you want to wet a line, there are plenty of bait and tackle shops and boat rentals at the **Olde Fish House Marina** and **Viking Marina. Pine Island Center** is the island's commercial district, where shopping, the school, fire station, ball fields, and community pool are located.

Bokeelia is the home port for many of the island's commercial fishing boats and the agricultural part of the island (you'll see mangoes and a whole bunch of only vaguely familiar-looking tropical fruits: carambola, longan, loquat). This part of the island contains a few historic buildings, including the **Museum of the Islands** (5728 Sesame Dr., 239/283-1525, www.museumoftheislands. com, 11am-3pm Tues.-Sat., 1pm-4pm Sun. Nov.-Apr., 11am-3pm Tues.-Thurs. May-Oct., $2 adults, $1 children 12 and under), with exhibitions on Pine Island pioneers.

Pineland is home to the **Randell Research Center** (13810 Waterfront Dr., 239/283-2157, www.flmnh.ufl.edu/RRC, $7 adults, $5 seniors, $4 children), one of the main historic sites of Calusa mounds. You can spend a day paddling the Calusa route and explore the Calusa Heritage Trail, a series of artistic signs interpreting the Calusa way of life and religious beliefs.

There are also guided tours out of **Pineland Marina** (13921 Waterfront Dr., Bokeelia, 239/283-3593) on Wednesday at 10am. Also in Pineland you'll find one of the country's smallest post offices and boat rentals and fishing charters out of Pineland Marina.

The Randell Research Center is within a stone's throw of celebrated Florida author Randy Wayne White's house; it also happens to be just across the street from the

Tarpon Lodge

Tarpon Lodge (13771 Waterfront Dr., Pineland, 239/283-3999, $110-350), where you can stay over in one of 12 rooms in the charming waterfront Island House. Ask for a water-view room with a private balcony overlooking the Gulf. There are also eight rooms in the on-site Historic Lodge, built in 1926. Throughout the lodge you'll find beautiful, original hardwood floors. For a little more privacy, stay in the one-bedroom cottage or two-bedroom boathouse. Both have a kitchenette. At the restaurant in the Historic Lodge, you can enjoy graciously served blue crab and roasted corn chowder, followed by fat Gulf shrimp scampi over linguini.

St. James City is Pine Island's residential community, with about two-thirds of the island's population living here. Most homes are located on canals with easy access to Pine Island Sound, San Carlos Bay, and the Gulf of Mexico.

Information and Services

Lee County is located within the **eastern time zone.** The area code is now **239,** but it used to be 941, which is now used farther north.

TOURIST INFORMATION

For visitor information, the **Lee County Visitors & Convention Bureau** (2201 2nd St., Ste. 600, Fort Myers, 239/338-3500 or 800/237-6444, www.fortmyers-sanibel.com) has a good website, with straightforward information and good media—an easy resource for planning a trip. Its office is less convenient for walk-ins. The **Sanibel & Captiva Islands Chamber of Commerce** (1159 Causeway Rd., Sanibel, 239/472-1080, www.sanibel-captiva.org, 9am-5pm daily) maintains a visitors center on Causeway Road as you drive onto Sanibel from Fort Myers. The chamber gives away an island guide and sells a detailed street map for $3.

This area has a fair number of small newspapers that serve Lee County, but no big metro paper. The *Fort Myers News-Press* (800/468-0233) is the daily in these parts. In Fort Myers Beach, look for the *Fort Myers Beach Observer* (239/263-4421), a weekly newspaper distributed every Wednesday. The *Island Reporter* (239/472-1587) is the newspaper of record for Sanibel and Captiva Islands, and there's also a magazine covering Sanibel called *Times of the Islands*

Magazine. On Boca Grande, look for the weekly *Boca Beacon.*

POLICE AND EMERGENCIES

As always, if you find yourself in a real emergency, pick up a phone and dial 911 or the local **Emergency Management Office** (239/533-3622). For a nonemergency police need, call the **Lee County Sheriff's Office** (239/477-1000), **Florida Highway Patrol** (239/278-7100), **U.S. Coast Guard** (239/463-5754), or **Florida Poison Information Center** (800/222-1222).

Sanibel and Captiva medical facilities serve the local community during business hours. For emergency medical needs, **HealthPark Care Center** (16131 Roserush Ct., Fort Myers, 239/343-7300) and **Lee Memorial Hospital** (2776 Cleveland Ave., Fort Myers, 239/343-2000) are full-service hospitals on the mainland with 24-hour emergency service. For your pharmacy needs on the islands, **CVS** (2331 Palm Ridge Rd., Sanibel, 239/472-1719) is convenient. If your pet has a medical problem, there's **Coral Veterinary Clinic** (1530 Periwinkle Way, Sanibel, 239/472-8387).

RADIO AND TELEVISION

If you're looking for NPR radio, turn to **WGCU 90.1 FM.** For local music programming, **WARO 94.5 FM** is classic rock; **WCKT**

107.1 FM is country music; **WINK 96.9 FM** offers adult contemporary programming; **WOLZ 95.3 FM** is, of course, oldies; **WRXK 98.1 FM** is classic rock; and **WXKB 103.9 FM** is Top 40 radio.

And on the television, **WBBH Channel 20** is the NBC affiliate, **WINK Channel 11** is the CBS affiliate, **WZVN Channel 26** is the ABC affiliate, **WGCU Channel 30** is the PBS affiliate, and **WFTX Channel 36** is the FOX affiliate out of Cape Coral.

LAUNDRY SERVICES

Large hotels and beach rentals often have laundry services of one sort or another. If you need to throw in a load of wash, launderettes are limited on the islands. Try an RV park along the route. In Fort Myers the laundry options are much broader. There are three **60 Minute Cleaners** locations (12842 S Cleveland Ave., 239/936-3616; Cypress Trace Shopping Center, 13300 S Cleveland Ave., 239/481-1900; and 16970 San Carlos Blvd.,

239/466-5115). In Fort Myers Beach, there's **Beach & Bubbles Coin Laundry & Dry Cleaners** (7205 Estero Blvd., 239/765-1771), a garden-variety coin-op laundry.

FISHING LICENSES

Fishing licenses are sold at all county tax collectors' offices and at many bait and tackle shops, or by phone (888/347-4356). On Sanibel, you can buy a license at the **Bait Box** (1041 Periwinkle Way, 239/472-1618); at **Bailey's** (2477 Periwinkle Way, Sanibel, 239/472-1516), at the corner of Tarpon Bay Road and Periwinkle Way; at **Tarpon Bay Explorers** (900 Tarpon Bay Rd., 239/472-8900, www.tarponbayexplorers.com, 8am-6pm daily); and at all the marinas. Also pick up the Florida Marine Fisheries Commission's publication about size and bag limits. You do not need a license if you are fishing from a boat that has a valid recreational vessel saltwater fishing license, if you are under 16, or if you are a Florida resident fishing from a pier, a bridge, or on shore.

Sarasota County

Highlights

★ **Spring Training at Ed Smith Stadium:** Visit the spring training home of the Baltimore Orioles, where all the Grapefruit League teams cycle through in preparation for the summer season. Tickets are cheap and the hot dogs are good (page 115).

★ **Marie Selby Botanical Gardens:** You don't have to be a master gardener or skilled horticulturalist to enjoy a day here. In 11 bayfront acres, the open-air and under-glass museum has more than 6,000 orchids and more than 20,000 other plants (page 119).

★ **John and Mable Ringling Museum of Art:** This museum is a must-see for fans of Flemish and Italian baroque art, with room after room of canvases, the most impressive of which is Peter Paul Rubens's *The Triumph of the Eucharist* (page 120).

★ **Film Festivals:** Time a trip to Sarasota to catch one of the city's two film festivals, the Sarasota Film Festival in April and the Cine-World Film Festival in November. Both are a citywide excuse for a party, in between two-hour popcorn-eating stints (page 128).

★ **Siesta Key Beach:** Beaches are a central draw of this area, with a couple of world-class

contenders. Siesta Key Beach, with its powdered-sugar sand, usually gets top honors (page 137).

Today, Sarasota is an undisputed cultural center, with theater, opera, symphony, ballet, art museums, and restaurants to rival those in much bigger cities. But it took a while for the city to get here.

In 1842, William Whittaker homesteaded in the area, planting some orange trees. Forty years later, as a means for drumming up some new residents, the Florida Mortgage and Investment Company went to Scotland and started talking up Sarasota (with a few serious exaggerations). Sixty Scottish families arrived in 1885 to find a waterlogged Main Street and a decided lack of amenities. Being Scottish, they promptly built a golf course (possibly the first in North America) and then got to work making it a real town.

Because there was no overland transportation, sailing ships and steamboats were the only connection to the outside world. In 1902 came the railroad, which connected Sarasota to Tampa; electricity and paved roads followed not too long after.

An influx of wealthy socialites settled the area starting around 1910. Among the early tourists to be smitten by the town was circus magnate John Ringling. He scooped up property all around Sarasota, moving the circus's winter home here and building himself a winter residence, art museum, circus museum, and college.

The population doubled in the Florida land boom of 1924-1927, with hotels, tourist attractions, and a causeway over the bay sprouting up to accommodate the surge in interest. Tourists gradually settled their sights on the keys, noticing the 35 miles of glistening white-sand beaches that fringe their Gulf side.

Each of the keys maintains its own identity, with abundant beach access being the central unifying theme. Lido and St. Armands are really just extensions of downtown Sarasota, connected by a causeway and fairly urban. Longboat Key is extremely upscale, with tall resort hotels and condominiums and an abundance of golf courses. Siesta Key is much more low-rise, with a personality to match. It's relaxed, laid-back, and definitely the most youthful spot on this part of the Gulf Coast.

Previous: the view of Sarasota from the city marina; Myakka River State Park. **Above:** Venice Beach.

Casey Key is less of a tourist draw, dotted with single-family homes. Anna Maria Island is a popular vacation spot, with an exceptional fishing pier and beach, a picturesque shopping district, plenty of lodging choices ranging from casual to upscale, and a surprising number of excellent restaurants for the island's size.

PLANNING YOUR TIME

A typical vacation in this area is about a week. This is partly because there's a week's worth of things to do, and partly because many of the beach houses and condos rent only by the week, especially in high season. Staying downtown in Sarasota is a little cheaper than staying beachside. Downtown streets and roads run east-west; avenues and boulevards run north-south.

The area's peak season begins in February and continues until Easter (average temperatures around 75°F). During that time, prices are hiked and reservations are necessary for accommodations. What travel agents call "the value season" is pretty much all summer in Sarasota, June-September. The Gulf waters are bathwater temperature during much of the summer—and as gentle and safe to swim in as your bathtub, too. On a hot day (in the summer this means about 90°F with a lot of humidity), the water temperatures aren't exactly refreshing, but that's the price to pay for a peaceful, sparsely populated day at the beach. Many of Sarasota's cultural institutions (symphony, ballet, opera, theaters) take a hiatus during the summer months, another drawback to visiting then.

Sarasota-Bradenton International Airport (SRQ) (6000 Airport Cir., at the intersection of U.S. 41 and University Pkwy., Sarasota, 941/359-2770) is the closest airport. Another option is to fly into **Tampa International Airport** (4100 George J. Bean Pkwy., 813/870-8700, www.tampaairport. com), which offers more arrival and departure choices and often better fares on flights and rental car prices. Tampa International Airport is just 53 miles north of Sarasota County via I-75 or I-275. Also check flights through **St. Petersburg-Clearwater International Airport** (although usually they aren't as frequent or as cheap as through Tampa). Private planes can use the **Venice Municipal Airport** in the city of Venice, just down U.S. 41 from Sarasota.

Sarasota

The circus built Sarasota. Sure, the 361 days of sun each year and the exotic subtropical plants and animals brought people to the area. But it was when circus impresario John Ringling snapped up real estate that others started giving this rural orange grove and celery farm another look. And in the 1920s, as Ringling began amassing huge numbers of baroque paintings in his new mansion, Cà d'Zan, so too did Ringling's cohorts begin assembling collections of their own for a little winter rest and relaxation. Soon the opera, theater, and symphony orchestras took root.

Beyond Ringling's generous gift of his house and museums to the city, the Circus King gave Sarasota a tradition of arts patronage. Sarasota's population of 54,000, with a little help from twice that number of winter visitors, supports a vast number of arts events along with an equally strong restaurant and shopping scene.

The striking thing is that it's all set in an incredible natural environment. Sarasota is home to world-class beaches and all the fun beach activities, with easy access to outstanding state parks and outdoor fun.

Sarasota

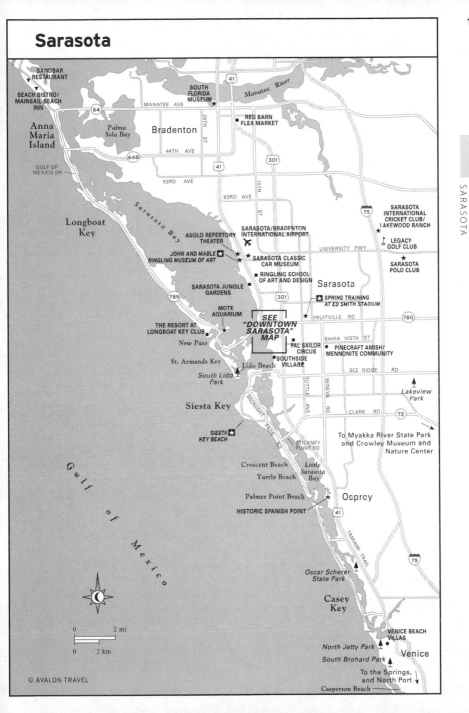

SANDBAR
RESTAURANT

BEACH BISTRO/
MAINSAIL BEACH
INN

Manatee River

SOUTH FLORIDA MUSEUM

MANATEE AVE

RED BARN
FLEA MARKET

64

Anna
Maria
Island

Palma
Sola Bay

Bradenton

26TH ST

44TH AVE

648

GULF OF
MEXICO DR

53RD AVE

41

63RD AVE

15TH ST

301

75

SARASOTA
INTERNATIONAL
CRICKET CLUB/
LAKEWOOD RANCH

Longboat
Key

Sarasota Bay

ASOLO REPERTORY
THEATER

SARASOTA/BRADENTON
INTERNATIONAL AIRPORT

LEGACY
GOLF CLUB

UNIVERSITY PWY

JOHN AND MABLE
RINGLING MUSEUM OF ART

SARASOTA CLASSIC
CAR MUSEUM

SARASOTA
POLO CLUB

RINGLING SCHOOL
OF ART AND DESIGN

Sarasota

SARASOTA JUNGLE
GARDENS

301

SPRING TRAINING
AT ED SMITH STADIUM

MOTE
AQUARIUM

SEE
"DOWNTOWN
SARASOTA"
MAP

FRUITVILLE RD

780

THE RESORT AT
LONGBOAT KEY CLUB

BAHIA VISTA ST

New Pass

St. Armands Key

PAL SAILOR
CIRCUS

PINECRAFT AMISH/
MENNONITE COMMUNITY

SOUTHSIDE
VILLAGE

Lido Beach

BEE RIDGE RD

South Lido
Park

Siesta Key

MIDNIGHT PASS RD

TUTTLE AVE

BENEVA RD

CLARK RD

72

Lakeview
Park

SIESTA
KEY BEACH

STICKNEY
POINT RD

To Myakka River State Park
and Crowley Museum and
Nature Center

Crescent Beach

Turtle Beach

Little
Sarasota
Bay

Gulf

of

Mexico

Palmer Point Beach

HISTORIC SPANISH POINT

41

Osprey

Oscar Scherer
State Park

TAMIAMI TRAIL

75

Casey
Key

0   2 mi

0   2 km

VENICE BEACH
VILLAS

North Jetty Park

South Brohard Park

Venice

To the Springs,
and North Port

Casperson Beach

114

SARASOTA COUNTY SARASOTA

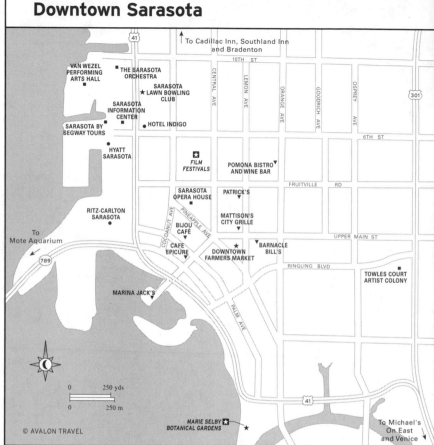

Downtown Sarasota

© AVALON TRAVEL

SPORTS AND RECREATION

Beaches

North Lido Beach is just northwest of St. Armands Circle, off of John Ringling Boulevard on Lido Key (which itself is just a 2.5-mile spit of beach from Big Sarasota Pass to New Pass). It's a short walk from shops or restaurants, and fairly secluded. There are no lifeguards, swift currents, nor real amenities. In the other direction from St. Armands Circle, southwest, you'll run into **Lido Beach,** which has parking for 400 cars, cabana beach rentals at the snack bar, playground

equipment, and bathrooms. It's a good hangout-all-afternoon family beach, but is more crowded than North Lido. The third beach on Lido Key is called **South Lido Park,** on Ben Franklin Drive at the southern tip of Lido Key. The park is bordered by four bodies of water: the Gulf, Big Pass, Sarasota Bay, and Brushy Bayou. It has a nature trail, and the beach offers a great view of the downtown Sarasota skyline. There's a nice picnic area with grills, as well as volleyball courts. Kayakers use this area to traverse the different waterways.

Golf

Sarasota is Florida's self-described "Cradle

A boardwalk leads to Lido Beach.

admission $8-14, parking $9) is the spring training home of the Baltimore Orioles (the Boston Red Sox now train a bit to the south in Fort Myers, and the Pittsburgh Pirates play in nearby Bradenton). To reach the stadium from I-75, take exit 210, Fruitville Road.

The little 8,500-seat stadium provides intimate access to big-league play in a small-time venue. In 2010 the stadium received a $31.2 million renovation that replaced all seats, moved bullpens, and added a Mediterranean-style facade. Cheap tickets and up-close seats make for a perfect outing on a warm Sarasota spring evening, even if baseball's not your sport. Day games start at 1:05pm and night games at 7:05pm; practices begin at 9am. Many spring training games sell out, so you might want to buy tickets in advance. For more information, visit www.baltimore.orioles.mlb.com.

of Golf," having been home to the state's first course, built in 1905 by Scottish colonist Sir John Hamilton Gillespie. The nine-hole course was located right at the center of what is now Sarasota's downtown. That first course is long gone, but there are more than 1,000 holes to play at public, semiprivate, and private courses in Sarasota, at all levels of play and most budgets. Of the top Southwest regional courses as voted by the readers of *Florida Golf News* (a nice resource, www.floridagolfmagazine.com), many are in the Sarasota area.

★ Spring Training at Ed Smith Stadium

Sarasota's Ed Smith Stadium has been an exciting part of the Grapefruit League's spring training program for years. The New York Giants arrived back in 1924, followed by the Red Sox and then the White Sox. These days, Sarasota's **Ed Smith Stadium** (2700 12th St., at the corner of Tuttle Ave., 941/954-4101, box seats $22-36, reserved $16-30, general

Polo

There are scads of spectator sporting opportunities in Sarasota, but polo trumps a fair number of them. Games are enormous fun, the horses racing around tearing up the lush sod of the polo grounds while their riders focus fiercely on that pesky little ball. Polo is amazingly physical and exciting to watch, whether you're in your fancy polo hats or your weekend jeans. **Sarasota Polo Club** (Lakewood Ranch, 8201 Polo Club Ln., 941/907-0000, www.sarasotapolo.com, 1pm Sun. mid-Dec.-early Apr., $12 adults, children 12 and under free) has been in operation since 1991, with professional-level players coming from around the world to play on the nine pristine fields. Bring a picnic or buy sandwiches and drinks once you're there. Gates open at 10am, and dogs on leashes are welcome. You can also take polo lessons at Lakewood Ranch.

Cricket

Polo's not the only game in town . . . cricket, anyone? The **Sarasota International Cricket Club** (Lakewood Ranch, 7401 University Pkwy., just east of Lorraine Rd., 941/726-6814, www.sarasotacricket.com)

was founded in 1983 and has around 40 active members who play about 35 matches a year with clubs from around the Southeast. The season runs weekends from late September through the end of May, and watching is free. Call for a game schedule.

Lawn Bowling

Are you starting to see a theme? Vast expanses of perfect grass, a ridiculous number of beautiful sunny days—people in Sarasota clearly love to spend their time outside. The **Sarasota Lawn Bowling Club** (809 N. Tamiami Trail at 10th St., 941/316-1123, beginning at 9am weekdays May-Nov., 12:50pm Nov.-Apr., $8/day to play) is the oldest sporting club in Sarasota, with three greens, $1 *boule* (ball) rentals, and free lessons. Wear flat shoes if you want to play.

Pétanque

Similar to lawn bowling but a little more obscure, pétanque is played at **Lakeview Park** (7150 Lago St., 941/861-9830, 9am Sun., free to watch). Players toss and roll a number of steel balls as close as possible to a small wooden ball called the *cochonet* (the piglet). Pronounced PAY-tonk, it's another great spectator sport, especially when accompanied by a wide blanket, a nice bottle of wine, and a tasty picnic. The Sarasota Club de Pétanque has 30 members of all skill levels, from beginners up to the national singles champion, and they bring extra *boules* and are happy to give instructions. Lakeview Park, which is adjacent to Lake Sarasota, also contains an enclosed dog park—even if Rover stayed at home, visitors find it fun to just watch all that canine enthusiasm. It's open 6am-dark daily.

State Parks and Nature Preserves

If you want to spend a day outdoors, the **Myakka River State Park** (9 miles east of Sarasota, 13208 Hwy. 72, 941/361-6511, 8am-sunset daily, $6/vehicle for up to 8 people, $4/vehicle single occupant, $2 for motorcycles, bicycles, and pedestrians) has a lot of activities to offer. The 28,875-acre park offers hiking, off-road biking, horseback riding, fishing, boating, canoeing, camping, and airboating. Both part of Florida Division of Forestry's Trailwalker Program, the North Loop (5.4 miles) and South Loop (7.4 miles) are fairly easy but scenic marked trails. Beyond these, there are 35 miles of unmarked trails open to hikers, mountain bikers (rentals $15 for 2 hours, or rent cool 4-person tandems for $30

Ed Smith Stadium is where the Orioles conduct their spring training.

for 1 hour, great for a family), and equestrians (BYOH—that's bring your own horse). If you just want to breeze in for a few hours, a ride on the **Myakka Wildlife Tours Tram Safari** (10151 Sommers Rd., Sarasota, 941/377-5797, Dec.-May only, $12 adults, $6 children 6-12, children 5 and under free if held in lap) takes visitors on a whirlwind tour of the park's backcountry, through shady hammocks, pine flatwoods, and lush marshes.

The 14-mile stretch of the scenic Myakka River has fairly easy-to-follow canoe trails (bring your own or rent at the Myakka Outpost; $20 for first hour, $5 each additional hour). Canoes and kayaks can be launched at the bridges, fishing area, other picnic areas, or at the boat ramp. During periods of low water (winter and spring), you'll have to portage around the weir at the south end of the Upper Lake. If you don't want to travel under your own paddle power, the park has a **boat tour** (941/365-0100, $12 adults, $6 children) that runs every 1.5 hours, and a couple of the world's largest airboats, the *Gator Gal* and the *Myakka Maiden*, are available for guided one-hour tours on the mile-wide and 2.5-mile-long Upper Myakka Lake (serious gator territory).

One unique park feature opened in 2004 in conjunction with Marie Selby Botanical Gardens; the Canopy Walkway, the first of its kind in North America, is an 85-foot-long observation deck suspension bridge that hangs 25 feet in the air in the midst of a subtropical forest canopy. Perched in the tops of live oaks, laurel oaks, and cabbage palms, your perspective on birdlife and animal life is unparalleled.

The park offers primitive camping ($5) and more equipped campsites ($26/night including water and electric), but the neatest option might be one of the five palm log cabins built in the 1930s. They're pretty comfortable, with two double beds, linens, blankets, and kitchen facilities. The fee is $70 per night for up to four people (call 800/326-3521 to reserve far in advance).

Adjacent to the state park you'll find the **Crowley Museum and Nature Center** (16405 Myakka Rd., 941/322-1000, www.crowleyfl.com, 10am-sundown Thurs.-Sun., $6.50 adults, $4.50 children 5-12, children under 5 free), a 190-acre wildlife sanctuary and education center. A couple of hours here dovetails nicely with time spent hiking or paddling in Myakka River State Park—there's a short nature trail, a boardwalk across Maple Branch Swamp, and an observation tower overlooking the Myakka River. To give more of a historical context to the area, the Crowley's real core is a

Myakka River State Park

Sarasota's Golf Courses

Call for tee times and greens fees, as they vary wildly by time of day and time of year.

Bobby Jones Golf Complex
1000 Circus Blvd., Sarasota, 941/365-4653
6,039 yards, par 71, course rating 68.4, slope 117

Heather Hills Golf Course
101 Cortez Rd. W., Bradenton, 941/755-8888
3,521 yards, par 61, course rating 58.6, slope 96

Imperial Lakes Golf Course
9680 Buffalo Rd., Palmetto, 941/747-4653
7,019 yards, par 72, course rating 73.9, slope 136

Legacy Golf Club at Lakewood Ranch
8255 Legacy Blvd., Bradenton, 941/907-7920
Semiprivate, 7,069 yards, par 72, course rating 73.8, slope 130

The Links at Green Field Plantation
10325 Greenfield Plantation Blvd., Bradenton, 941/747-9432
6,719 yards, par 72, course rating 72, slope 130

Manatee County Golf Course
6415 53rd Ave. W., Bradenton, 941/792-6773
6,747 yards, par 72, course rating 71.6, slope 122

Palmetto Pines Golf Course
14355 Golf Course Dr., Parrish, 941/776-1375
5,358 yards, par 72, course rating 68.4, slope 92

Peridia Golf & Country Club
4950 Peridia Blvd., Bradenton, 941/758-2582, www.peridiagcc.net
3,344 yards, par 60, course rating 55.0, slope 76

pioneer museum tricked out with a rustic one-room cabin, a restored 1892 Cracker house, a working blacksmith shop, and a little sugarcane mill. The museum sponsors Pioneer Days every December, an annual antiques fair, a folk music festival in October, and a yearly stargazing night with high-powered telescopes.

It won't knock your socks off with stunning topography or habitats, but **Oscar Scherer State Park** (1843 S. Tamiami Trail, Osprey, 941/483-5956, 8am-sundown daily, entrance $5/vehicle 2-8 occupants, $4/vehicle 1 occupant, $2 for pedestrians, bicycles, and motorcycles, $4 sunset entry) is a local hangout for birders and families who want to spend an afternoon in nature without a lot of hassle. Much of it is a classic Florida flatwoods (scrub pine and sawtooth palmetto populated with animals like scrub jays, gopher tortoises, and indigo snakes). The park has several marked trails open to hikers and bikers (it's sandy terrain, most suitable for mountain bikes), and kayakers paddle around South Creek (bring your own canoe or kayak or rent canoes from the ranger station for $10/hour, $40/day), launched from the South Creek Picnic Area. Birders may want to join the informal Thursday morning bird walks at 8am, the Friday morning ranger-led walks at 8:30am, or canoe tours on Wednesday at 9am. Check in at the park's nature center. The park also has a 104-site campground with tent and RV sites equipped with electricity and water ($32.70/night, 50 percent discount for seniors or disabled). The restrooms have hot showers, and the maximum RV length is 36 feet.

Pinebrook/Ironwood Golf Club
4260 Ironwood Cir., Bradenton, 941/792-3288
3,706 yards, par 61, course rating 59.9, slope 101

River Club
6600 River Club Blvd., Bradenton, 941/751-4211
7,026 yards, par 72, course rating 74.5, slope 135

River Run Golf Links
1801 27th St. E., Bradenton, 941/708-6331
5,825 yards, par 70, course rating 67.9, slope 115

Rosedale Golf and Country Club
5100 87th St. E., Bradenton, 941/753-6200
6,779 yards, par 72, course rating 72.9, slope 134

Terra Ceia
2802 Terra Ceia Bay Blvd., Palmetto, 941/729-1798
4,001 yards, par 62, course rating 67.9, slope 99

Timber Creek Golf Course
4550 Timber Ln., Bradenton, 941/794-8381
2,086 yards, par 27 (9 holes), course rating 35.1, slope 117

University Park Country Club
7671 Park Blvd., University Park, 941/355-3888
4,914-7,247 yards, par 72, course rating 67.8-74.4, slope 113-138

Waterlefe Golf & River Club
1022 Fish Hook Cove, Bradenton, 941/744-9881
6,908 yards, par 72, course rating 73.8, slope 145

SIGHTS
★ Marie Selby Botanical Gardens

Much has been written in recent years about the mystery of orchids, bromeliads, and other epiphytes: *The Orchid Thief, Orchid Fever* (an excellent read), and the more historical *The Orchid in Lore and Legend.*

The word *epiphyte* comes from the Greek roots *epi,* meaning "upon," and *phyton,* meaning "plant." Beginning their life in the canopy of trees, their seeds carried by birds or wind, epiphytes are air plants, growing stubbornly without the benefit of soil on the branches or trunks of trees. Orchids, cacti, bromeliads, aroids, lichens, mosses, and ferns can even grow on the same tree, a big inter-species jamboree.

And if you want to see some beautiful and alien epiphytes, spend a long afternoon at **Marie Selby Botanical Gardens** (811 S. Palm Ave., 941/366 5731, www.selby.org, 10am-5pm daily, $19 adults, $6 children 6-11, children under 6 free). The nine-acre gardens on the shores of Sarasota Bay are one of Sarasota's absolute jewels. Marie Selby donated her home and grounds "to provide enjoyment for all who visit the gardens." And there's a lot of enjoyment to be had meandering along the walking paths through the hibiscus garden, cycad garden, a banyan grove, a tropical fruit garden, and thousands of orchids. The botanical gardens also host lectures and gardening classes, and have a charming shop (beginners should opt for a training-wheels phalaenopsis—very hard to kill—or an easy-care bromeliad) with an exhaustive collection of gardening books (80 on orchids

Hope Springs Eternal

Nine million gallons of warm mineral water flow daily at the **Warm Mineral Springs** (12200 San Servando Ave., North Port, 941/426-1692, 9am-5pm daily, weather permitting, $20 adults, $15 students, $10 children 12 and under), with a higher mineral content than any other spring in the United States. Eighty-seven degrees year-round, it's thought to be Ponce de León's fabled Fountain of Youth.

North Port isn't exactly a tourist destination. It's a fairly rural town where the big draw is this natural wonder, an hourglass-shaped springhead, 1.4 acres around and 230 feet deep, filled with the heavily mineralized water believed by some to have healing powers.

You'll learn quickly upon exiting your car that heavily mineralized water has the sulfurous smell similar to a rotten egg. Also, the water's mineral content makes it somewhat slimy-feeling. Russians and other international visitors come from across the globe to splash around in this water. The snack bar is the proof: It's an all-Russian menu—goulash, something called Russian ravioli, pictured with descriptions beneath, written *in Russian*.

Because the spring contains no dissolved oxygen, organic matter that gets into the springs stays more or less intact. In 1973, a scientist named Wilburn A. Cockrell brought up a nearly complete skeleton of an adult Paleo-Indian male that was 11,000 years old. Dated to nearly the same time period, part of a saber-toothed cat was also found. If you enjoy mineral springs, a trip to this impressive site will keep you fulfilled for a half day. Who knows, maybe it will even heal whatever ails you and have you leaving feeling a bit younger. One can only hope.

alone). Spend an hour gazing at epiphytes in the tropical greenhouse and you'll become a fan, I promise. Kids get fairly bored here, with a brief flurry of interest around the koi pond and butterfly garden. I would recommend not bringing them unless they're really into plants or stroller-bound.

★ John and Mable Ringling Museum of Art

John Ringling's lasting influence on Sarasota is remarkable, but the **John and Mable Ringling Museum of Art** (5401 Bay Shore Rd., 941/359-5700, www.ringling.org, 10am-5pm daily, $25 adults, $23 seniors, $18 students, $10 active military and teachers, $5 children 6-17) makes it simply undeniable.

In 2007, the museum's six-year, $140 million master plan came to fruition, marking the completion of a most extraordinary transformation. It's now one of the 20 largest art museums in North America. Since 2006, the Ringling Museum has opened four new buildings: the Tibbals Learning Center, the John M. McKay Visitors Pavilion, the Ulla R. and

Arthur F. Searing Wing, and the Education/ Conservation Building, as well as the restored Historic Asolo Theatre.

The whole museum complex is spectacular, but the art museum is definitely worth its fairly hefty admission price. It was built in 1927 to house Ringling's nearly pathological accretion of 600 paintings, sculptures, and decorative arts including more than 25 tapestries. The Mediterranean-style palazzo contains a collection that includes a set of five extremely large paintings by Peter Paul Rubens, many other Spanish works of art, and the music room and dining room of Mrs. William B. Astor (Ringling bought all this in 1926 when the Astor mansion in New York was scheduled to be demolished). The permanent collection is spectacular, with Van Dycks, Poussins, and lots of other baroque masters, but there are shows such as a recent one on surrealism and another on the photos of Ansel Adams and Clyde Butcher that enter into at least the 20th century.

The complex also houses the **Museum of the Circus,** a peek into circus history. It achieves a certain level of overstatement in the interpretive signs when it parallels the ascendance of the circus with the growth of the country. Still, the museum's newspaper clippings, circus equipment, parade wagons, and colossal bail rings make one nostalgic for a time and place most people today probably never knew.

The single most impressive thing about the museum, the thing that causes rampant loitering and inspired commentary like "Whoa, cooool," is the Howard Bros. Circus model. It takes up vast space— the world's largest miniature circus, after all—and is a three-quarter-inch-to-the-foot scale replica of Ringling Bros. and Barnum & Bailey Circus at its largest. The model itself takes up 3,800 square feet, with eight main tents, 152 wagons, 1,300 circus performers and workers, more than 800 animals, a 57-car train, and a zillion wonderful details.

Fully restored and reopened in 2002, John Ringling's home on the bay, **Cà d'Zan** (House of John), is also open to the public, an ornate structure evocative of Ringling's two favorite Venetian hotels, the Danieli and the Bauer Grunwald. Completed in 1926, the house is 200 feet long with 32 rooms and 15 baths. It is truly a magnificent mansion.

Sarasota Classic Car Museum

What's your dream car? DeLorean? Ferrari? Mini Cooper? The **Sarasota Classic Car Museum** (5500 N. Tamiami Trail, 941/355-6228, www.sarasotacarmuseum.com, 9am-6pm daily, $9.85 adults, $8.50 seniors, $6.50 children 6-12, children 5 and under free) has examples of everyone's favorite wheels. A recent renovation has greatly improved the collection of more than 100 vehicles, from muscle to vintage to exotic cars. You'll see a rare Cadillac station wagon, one of only five ever made, and the gift shop has collectibles for most automotive preoccupations. The museum rents out some of its cars if you want to make a grand entrance somewhere, and the cars are also available for photo ops.

Historic Spanish Point

History buffs may want to visit **Historic Spanish Point** (337 N. Tamiami Trail, Osprey, 941/966-5214, www.historicspanishpoint.org, 9am-5pm Mon.-Sat., noon-5pm Sun., $12 adults, $10 seniors, $5 children 5-12), operated by the Gulf Coast Heritage Association. Bordered on its western edge by Little Sarasota Bay and by pine flatlands to the east, the 30-acre site tells the story of life in the greater Sarasota area going back

Cà d'Zan

many generations. Interpretive markers and an "Indian village" show how early Floridian natives fished and hunted here, building middens, or shell mounds, and a burial mound (an archaeology exhibit in the main hall gives you the background on this). Then there's a restored pioneer home and chapel, revealing the story of the early settlers here, the Webb family. After that, you'll stroll the gardens of heiress Bertha Matilde Honore Palmer's winter estate on Osprey Point. The site has a butterfly garden to add to the mix, showing the larval and nectar plants for monarch, zebra longwing, swallowtail, and other butterflies native to the area.

South Florida Museum

The **South Florida Museum** (201 10th St. W., Bradenton, 941/746-4131, 10am-5pm Tues.-Sat., noon-5pm Sun., $19 adults, $17 seniors, $14 children 4-12) is worth a short drive north to Bradenton for the history buff. There are ice age dioramas with animals and natural history exhibits that trace the state's ancient history. The Spanish explorers are covered with nice detail, and the museum houses the Tallant Collection of artifacts, an assemblage of loot from Floridian archaeological sites.

Downtown Farmers Market

Despite the fact that Florida is a huge agricultural state (citrus, sugarcane, tomatoes, strawberries), much of the Gulf Coast doesn't have serious farmers markets. Sarasota is an exception. Every Saturday morning year-round you'll find all the sights and smells unique to the local Florida farmers market: stacked produce; the cookie lady; a band of musicians passing the hat; babies in strollers, smiling around a mouthful of gummed peach; wind chimes and handicrafts; and bromeliads, orchids, and cut flowers filling the bulging bags of nearly every shopper. The **Downtown Farmers Market** has been going on for 30 years, the tents and tables of 50 or so vendors erected Saturday mornings by 7am and broken down around 1pm. It used to be located on South Pineapple Avenue, but now it sets up

each week on Lemon Avenue at the intersection of Main Street.

Tours

One of the more popular tours in the area is a 2-hour guided tour of downtown Sarasota on a Segway Human Transporter with **Sarasota by Segway Tours** (1370 Boulevard of the Arts, Ste. C, 941/312-2615, www.sarasotabysegway.com, tours 10am and 1pm, $65, no kids under 12), zipping along the bayfront and arts community. The two side-by-side wheels (as opposed to a bike or motorcycle, in which the two wheels are in a line) are self-balancing, and you stand above the wheels on a little platform and steer the electric-powered vehicle with the handlebars. With speeds of up to 12 mph, they can be used in pedestrian areas and are a perfect way to cover serious ground at a pace slow enough to really appreciate things. Tours are limited to 12 people, and there are weight limitations.

If your passion is architecture, you won't need to be told that Sarasota is the birthplace of a certain strain of American modernism. (If this is news to you, pick up a copy of the excellent *The Sarasota School of Architecture, 1941-1966*, by John Howey.) The **Sarasota Architectural Foundation** (P.O. Box 2911, Sarasota, FL 34230, 941/487-8728, www.sarasotaarchitecturalfoundation.org) hosts architectural tours, educational events, film screenings, exhibits, and parties for architecture lovers who travel to Sarasota to see its architecture up close and personal. A list of tours is posted on the website.

After indulging in several of Sarasota's cultural attractions, you need to clear your head and take a **Walk on the Wild Side** (3434 N. Tamiami Trail, Ste. 817, 941/351-6500, www.walkwild.com, $30-65). The friendly tour providers tailored trips, taking small groups kayaking, canoeing, day hiking, backpacking, camping, auto touring, bird-watching, or wildlife-viewing, according to people's interests and mobility. You don't need prior canoeing or kayaking experience (guides instruct you, but you still have to be fairly fit to work that paddle) to go out on the area's bays, estuaries, and rivers; guides point out birds, dolphins, gators, and manatees along the way. You can choose where you go and for how long (half day, full day, or overnight), but the most romantic is the sunset canoe outing with wine and cheese.

Several companies offer boat tours on Sarasota Bay and into the Gulf of Mexico. **Key Sailing** (2 Marina Jack, Bayfront Plaza, 941/346-7245, www.siestakeysailing.com, $55 for 2 hours, $75 for 3 hours) offers charters and sailing instruction aboard a sleek 41-foot Morgan Classic II. **LeBarge Tropical Cruises** (2 Marina Plaza, U.S. 41 at Marina Jack, 941/366-6116, www.lebargetropical-cruises.com, 9am-6pm daily, $25 adults, $20 children 4-12) offers two-hour cruises of Sarasota Bay. Choose from a dolphin watch narrated by a marine biologist, a narrated sightseeing cruise, or a tropical sunset cruise.

Family-Friendly Attractions

My favorite family attraction in Sarasota is **Sarasota Jungle Gardens** (3701 Bay Shore Rd., 941/355-5305, 10am-5pm daily, $15.99 adults, $14.99 seniors, $10.99 children 3-12, children under 3 free), but then I'm a sucker for quirky Old Florida attractions. Once part

boggy banana grove, part universally agreed-upon "impenetrable swamp," the subtropical jungle was purchased in the 1930s by newspaperman David Lindsay. He brought in tropical plants, trees, and bird species. It opened in 1940 as a tourist attraction, and it puttered along through a couple of ownership changes until it ended up in the hands of the Allyn family. Every elementary student within 100 miles has made the trek by school bus to sit and watch the short birds of prey show and then wander along the paths through the lush formal gardens, the farmyard exhibit, the tiki gardens, and the flamingo area. The zoological gardens are home to about 100 animals, many of them abandoned pets, so it's an odd assortment. Another section of the park, however, has nothing to do with plants or animals—in one back corner you'll find the Gardens of Christ. It's a series of eight two-dimensional dioramas by Italian-born sculptor Vincent Maldarelli depicting important events in the life of Jesus Christ.

The **Mote Marine Laboratory and Aquarium** (1600 Ken Thompson Pkwy., City Island, 941/388-4441, 10am-5pm daily, $19.75 adults, $18.75 seniors, $14.75 children 4-12, children under 3 free) is an enjoyable small aquarium that also serves as

Sarasota Jungle Gardens

a working marine laboratory. For kids, the coolest parts are the 135,000-gallon shark tank and the "immersion cinema" state-of-the-art theater with a 40-foot-wide, high-definition screen with Dolby Surround sound. Visitors get their own interactive consoles that change the outcome of the game or movie on the screen. Children will also like the underwater microphone in the Marine Mammal Center, which allows visitors to hear the resident manatees chirping at each other and methodically munching the heads of romaine lettuce that bob at the top of their tank. There's a touch tank, where you'll see parents cajoling their small ones to feel up a sea urchin, starfish, horseshoe crab, or stingless stingray, as well as nicely interpreted exhibits of eels, puffer fish, sea horses, and extraterrestrial-looking jellies.

The more impressive part of the Mote is not really open to the public—the Mote Marine Laboratory is known internationally for its shark research and more locally for its research on red tides, or algal blooms, which occasionally adversely affect Sarasota's summer beach season with fish kills.

Sarasota Bay Explorers (941/388-4200, www.sarasotabayexplorers.com) works in conjunction with Mote Marine Laboratory and runs their science boat trips out of the facility. They offer several wonderful styles of ecotours, all perfect for a fun yet educational family outing. There are narrated **Sea Life Encounter Cruises** ($27 adults, $23 children 4-12), backwater **guided kayak tours** ($55 adults, $45 children), and private charters aboard the 24-foot Sea Ray Sundeck *Miss Explorer* ($295 3-hour trip, $370 4-hour trip, $445 5-hour trip).

ENTERTAINMENT AND EVENTS

Sarasota describes itself as the "cultural coast" of Florida.

Theater

Celebrating over 50 years of professional theater in Sarasota, the **Asolo Repertory**

Theatre (5555 N. Tamiami Trail, 941/351-9010, www.asolorep.org, curtain times generally 2pm and 8pm Nov.-June, prices vary), until 2006 called the Asolo Theatre Company, is a professional company that performs primarily in the 500-seat Harold E. and Esther M. Mertz Theatre at the Florida State University Center for the Performing Arts, a theater originally built as an opera house in 1903 in Dunfermline, Scotland. There's a second, smaller 161-seat black-box Jane B. Cook Theatre on-site for performances of the conservatory season and smaller productions of the Asolo. Students also present a series of original works known as the LateNite series, and the FSU School of Theatre presents a variety of other special events and performances. Currently, the Asolo Rep and the Conservatory perform one show each in the Historic Asolo Theatre, located in the Ringling Museum's Visitors Pavilion. All of this means more shows and more variety for Sarasota's theatergoers.

Because the Florida State University Conservatory for Actor Training's graduate-level program yields so many newly minted thespians in Sarasota, the whole theatrical playing field has been elevated. Worthwhile community and professional theater troupe efforts include the contemporary dramas and comedies at **Florida Studio Theatre** (1241 N. Palm Ave., 941/366-9000). They perform mostly Broadway musicals at **Golden Apple Dinner Theatre** (25 N. Pineapple Ave., 941/366-2646). Enjoy six annual musical productions with **The Players of Sarasota** (838 N. Tamiami Trail, 941/365-2494, www.theplayers.org), dramas in the summer with **Banyan Theater Company** (at the Asolo's Jane B. Cook Theatre, 941/358-5330), and even the small community productions on two stages of the **Venice Little Theatre** (140 W. Tampa Ave., Venice, 941/488-1115).

Music and Dance

The oldest continuously running orchestra in the state of Florida, **The Sarasota Orchestra** (Beatrice Friedman Symphony Center, 709 N.

Tamiami Trail, box office 941/953-3434, www. sarasotaorchestra.org, prices and times vary) offers a wide array of more than 100 classical, pops, chamber, and family concerts per year. It also hosts the internationally recognized Sarasota Music Festival each June, an intense three-week event of chamber music, master classes, and concerts, with the coaching and performance of chamber music as its primary priority. Several Masterworks programs are presented by the symphony throughout the season, as well as a collection of Great Escapes programs of light classics and pops.

If you're not a huge symphonic music fan, you should try to catch a show at Sarasota's most distinctive landmark, the **Van Wezel Performing Arts Hall** (777 N. Tamiami Trail, 941/953-3368, www.vanwezel.org, times and prices vary). Designed by William Wesley Peters of the Frank Lloyd Wright Foundation, the building riffs on a seashell found by Frank Lloyd Wright's widow, Olgivanna, near the Sea of Japan. It has an eye-popping lavender/purple color scheme, and it looks accordion-folded, like a scallop shell (supposedly to maximize the space's acoustical possibilities). Love it or hate it, the Van Wezel presents a wonderful range of Broadway productions, world-class dance, music, comedy, and popular acts,

as well as being the home base for many of the local arts organizations.

For instance, the **Sarasota Ballet of Florida** (5555 N. Tamiami Trail, 941/359-0099, www.sarasotaballet.org, times and prices vary) splits its performances between the Van Wezel, the Asolo, and the FSU Center for the Performing Arts, offering a combination of treasured classical works and contemporary and modern dance. The ballet was founded as a presenting organization in 1987 by Jean Allenby-Weidner, former prima ballerina with the Stuttgart Ballet. Through community support, it became a resident company in 1990. The ballet often works collaboratively with other local arts organizations on productions—in 2005 it staged a ballet with Circus Sarasota that tells the story of John Ringling's life, complete with aerialists, clowns, and such. The Sarasota Ballet also runs the Sarasota Ballet Academy; The Next Generation, an award-winning scholarship program for youth at risk; and an international summer school.

The **Sarasota Opera** (61 N. Pineapple Ave., 941/328-1300, www.sarasotaopera.org) presents concerts year-round, but its much-anticipated (often sold out) repertory season is every February and March, housed in

the Asolo Repertory Theatre

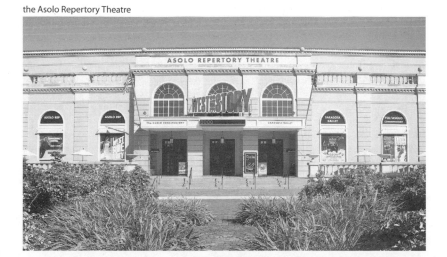

the beautifully restored 1926 Mediterranean Revival-style Edwards Theatre. The opera house underwent an extensive renovation in 2007. It also offers youth outreach, and Sarasota Youth Opera receives all kinds of recognition for its productions.

It's an endurance event, one that takes grit and a good pair of opera glasses: The Sarasota Opera's **Winter Opera Festival** draws opera buffs from all over the country for a compact season of four productions, which can be enjoyed nearly at one sitting for the especially enthusiastic. The festival provides a good program of obscure operas as well as the big crowd-pleasers. While you're hanging around in the striking art deco lobby during intermission, look up: The chandelier is from the movie *Gone with the Wind*.

Sarasota also has an annual chamber music festival each April, **La Musica International Chamber Music Festival** (rehearsals in Mildred Sainer Pavilion of New College of Florida, performances in the Edwards Theatre, 61 N. Pineapple Ave., 941/366-8450, ext. 7, www.lamusicafestival.org, 8pm, $40 single tickets, $60 pass to a rehearsal). Before the actual evening performances there are short lectures about the pieces.

Circuses

Five of the seven sons of August and Marie Salomé Ringling of Baraboo, Wisconsin, ran away and joined the circus. Or, rather, they invented their own. In 1870, they premiered their show and charged a penny admission, building it year by year from a modest wagon show (its first "ring" a strip of cloth staked out to form a circle) to a major national show that traveled via rail from town to town. Meanwhile, circus titans P. T. Barnum and James A. Bailey teamed up in 1888 to create "The Greatest Show on Earth," blowing away all the competition with their glitz, animals, and death-defying acts. It was Bailey's untimely death in 1906 that led the "Greatest Show" to be bought out by the Ringling brothers. The two circuses ran separately until 1919, when they were joined to form the mega-huge

the Van Wezel Performing Arts Hall

Ringling Bros. and Barnum & Bailey Circus, and the rest is history.

In the 1920s, John Ringling and his wife, Mable, built a spectacular Venetian-style estate on Sarasota Bay, called Cà d'Zan (House of John in Venetian dialect). They built an art museum to house their bursting-at-the-seams collection of 17th-century Italian paintings, Flemish art, and works by Peter Paul Rubens. But it was in 1927 when Sarasota became an official circus town—the Ringling Bros. and Barnum & Bailey Circus's winter quarters were moved here, giving the sedate Florida town a firsthand look at the oddity, eccentricity, and glamour that is the circus.

Many of the circus performers who acted in the *Wizard of Oz* and that ultimate non-PC film *Terror of Tiny Town* (a musical western starring all little people) called Sarasota home, with specially built homes in a section of town called, unsurprisingly, **Tiny Town** (you can visit this area on Ever-Glide guided tours).

Today visitors get a sense of Sarasota's circus history at the **Museum of the Circus,**

Clowning Around

Ringling Bros. and Barnum & Bailey Circus, the oldest—in addition to being the greatest—show on earth, reinvents itself every two years, with two totally different traveling units. The Red Unit and the Blue Unit each tour North America 11 months out of the year for two years before going back to winter quarters (now in Tampa, but historically here in Sarasota) and preparing a new edition. The Red Unit presents the odd-numbered editions, the Blue Unit presents the even-numbered editions (so, for instance, if you see the 140th edition Blue Unit this year, you'll see the 141st edition Red Unit next year).

So one year the show's centerpiece might be the Living Carousel, an assemblage of 105 people, 27 animals, and more gold lamé than a Liberace concert, with something like two million rhinestones and elephant blankets inset with 81,000 mirrors turning the whole arena into a disco-ball fantasy.

Or it's the Globe of Steel, a 16-foot steel globe, into which ride eight members of the Torres Family, riding a complicated routine of loops around the interior, reaching speeds of 65 mph, and then someone gets in and stands there, daring one of them to flub up. Talk about extreme sports.

Or maybe sixth-generation circus performer Taba (no last names please), the "tiger whisperer," who quietly persuades four different types of Bengal tigers to romp around the center ring. Then there are always the high-wire acts, the classic Clown Alley, and an incredible live band performing the zany circus music.

But the circus has its work cut out for it. It may be the greatest show on earth, but these days it's definitely not the only show in town. Ringling Bros. and Barnum & Bailey Circus comes to town in this new millennium with its usual pageantry and death-defying acts, and it has to lure audiences from other popular traveling shows like Cirque du Soleil and persuade them to choose the big top over the big screen—not an easy task.

To get a sense of how much the magic of the circus means today and meant in the past, you only need to visit the **Museum of the Circus** at the **John and Mable Ringling Museum of Art** (5401 Bay Shore Rd., 941/359-5700, 10am-5pm Fri.-Wed., 10am-8pm Thurs., $25 adults, $23 seniors, $10 military, $5 students and children 6-17). It was John Ringling who brought the circus to Sarasota, moving the winter quarters of the Ringling Bros. and Barnum & Bailey Circus from Bridgeport, Connecticut, in 1927—thus changing this part of Florida forever. The museum documents, preserves, and exhibits the history of the circus with props, rare handbills, parade wagons, tent poles, and memorabilia.

housed in the **John and Mable Ringling Museum of Art** (5401 Bay Shore Rd., 941/359-5700, 10am-5pm Fri.-Wed., 10am-8pm Thurs., $25 adults, $23 seniors, $10 military, $5 students and children 6-17) on the Ringling grounds, but during February and March the circus comes alive with **Circus Sarasota** (140 University Town Center Dr., 941/355-9335, $15-55). Founded in 1997 by Ringling Bros. alums Pedro Reis and aerialist Dolly Jacobs (she's a second-generation circus performer—her father was the famous clown Lou Jacobs), it's a single-ring, European-style circus that changes every year. Reis and Jacobs often perform an aerial pas de deux, and there are tightrope acts, trained horses,

aerial acrobats from China, clowns, tumbling, contortionists, and so forth, all performed in an intimate setting.

Despite the fact that Ringling Bros. circus now makes its winter home to the north in Tampa, Sarasota is still training the next generation of circus performers. **PAL Sailor Circus** (2075 Bahia Vista St., 941/361-6350, 11:45am and 7pm, $20 adults, $15 children) has been thrilling audiences for more than 50 years, educating kids 8-18 in the circus arts and then letting them put on a show. In 2004, the program was on the verge of closing. With the assistance of Sheriff William F. Balkwill, the Police Athletic League took over the Sailor Circus as one of its after-school programs.

About 90 students participate in the twice-annual training sessions, where they learn circus skills like clowning, tumbling, high-wire, flying trapeze, unicycling, juggling, rigging, and costuming. Then, in March and the end of December, the students perform for the public in an exciting four-ring circus.

★ Film Festivals

Sarasota supports not one, but two film festivals. By far the more famous of the two is the **Sarasota Film Festival** (multiple venues, box office at 332 Cocoanut Ave., 941/364-9514, www.sarasotafilmfestival.com), which happens every April. The fastest-growing film festival in the country, it showcases more than 180 independent feature, documentary, narrative, and short films. The event usually includes a Shorts Fest, a couple of family-oriented events, and lots of panel discussions with industry leaders and symposiums with guest stars. And every November there's the Sarasota Film Society's 10-day **Cine-World Film Festival** (Burns Court Cinemas, 506 Burns Ln., 941/955-3456), which showcases Florida film artists in addition to presenting the best of the preceding Toronto, Cannes, New York, and Telluride film festivals.

Festivals

February's not a bad month to visit, because you can catch the monthlong annual run of the European-style **Circus Sarasota.** Sarasota is the self-described "circus capital of the world," after all. Music lovers may want to come in February or March for the repertory season of the **Sarasota Opera,** although in April there's **La Musica International Chamber Music Festival.** April also brings the weeklong **Florida Wine Fest & Auction.**

If you're visiting the area strictly for the white, powdery sand, you might think of coming in May for the pro-am **Sand Sculpting Contest** on Siesta Key Beach. **Fourth of July** fireworks over the Gulf are wonderful from the vantage spot of Siesta Key Beach, too.

NIGHTLIFE
Bars

Downtown has a few nightspots that stand out. **Pomona Bistro and Wine Bar** (481 N. Orange Ave., 941/706-1677, 5pm-9pm Tues.-Thurs., 5pm-10pm Fri.-Sat., $15-30) has a vital bar scene with a remarkable by-the-glass wine list.

For a more rarefied experience, head to the **Cà d'Zan Lounge** at the Ritz-Carlton (1111 Ritz-Carlton Dr., 941/309-2000, 5pm-midnight Mon.-Thurs., 5pm-2am Fri.-Sat., 1pm-midnight Sun. $10-25). Overstuffed couches, clubby leather chairs, hickory wood walls, and an outstanding specialty drink menu define the place.

Beyond these, there are refreshing drinks and good times to be had many places here, including the **Beach Club** (5151 Ocean Blvd., Siesta Key, 941/349-6311, www.beachclubsiestakey.com, noon-2:30am daily) in Siesta Key Village and **Sharky's** (1600 Harbor Dr. S., Venice, 941/488-1456, www.sharkysonthepier.com, 11:30am-10pm Sun.-Thurs., 11:30am-midnight Fri.-Sat.), beachfront on the Pier in Venice. **Harry's** (6606 S. Tamiami Trail, 941/922-1110, 11am-10pm daily) is a local sports bar for watching the game, and go to **8 Ball Lounge** (3527 Webber St., 941/922-8314, noon-2am daily) when you feel like working on your own game.

Dance and Music Clubs

For when you're ready to get on the dance floor, the **Five O'Clock Club** (1930 Hillview St., 941/366-5555, www.5oclockclub.net for concert schedule, noon-2am Mon.-Fri., 3pm-2am Sat.-Sun., happy hour noon-8pm daily, small cover charges depend on band) in Southside Village has what the mechanic ordered. There's live music seven nights a week, with national and local rock/blues/pop bands taking the stage at 10pm. The 5-O draws a 30s and 40s crowd, and just a smattering of college kids. The **Gator Club** (1490 Main St., 941/366-5969) is another longtime nightlife haunt. There's live music every night, often of the Jimmy Buffett cover variety, plus pool tables upstairs and an impressive single-malt selection. Not recommended if you're a FSU fan. Go 'Noles.

For something totally different and un-booze-centric, track down the **Siesta Key Drum Circle** on Sunday evenings, a drop-in party in which everyone adds their own beat. It all gets under way about one hour before sunset, just south of the main pavilion between lifeguard stands 3 and 4.

SHOPPING

The shops of **St. Armands Circle** on Lido Key have been a primary retail draw in Sarasota for a long time, historically known for high-end boutiques. These days the shops cover familiar ground—chains like **Chico's** (443 St. Armands Cir., 941/388-1393), **Tommy Bahama** (300 John Ringling Blvd., 941/388-2888), **Fresh Produce** (1 N. Boulevard of the Presidents, 941/388-1883), and **White House/Black Market** (317 St. Armands Cir., 941/388-5033)—and a handful of upscale, independently owned boutiques. You can also explore the circle's novelty and giftware shops: **Fantasea Seashells** (345 St. Armands Cir., 941/388-3031), or **Kilwin's** (312 John Ringling Blvd., 941/388-3200), offering ice cream and fudge.

Towles Court Artist Colony (1938 Adams Ln., downtown Sarasota) is a collection of 16 quirky pastel-colored bungalows and cottages that contain artists working furiously and the art they've been working furiously on. You can buy their work and watch them in action 11am-4pm Tuesday-Saturday, or visit Towles Court on the third Friday evening of each month for Art by the Light of the Moon.

Palm Avenue and **Main Street** downtown are lined with galleries, restaurants, and cute shops, and historic **Herald Square** in the SoMa (south of Main Street) part of downtown on Pineapple Avenue has a fairly dense concentration of antiques shops and upscale housewares stores. Also on Pineapple you'll find the **Artisan's World Marketplace** (128 S. Pineapple Ave., 941/365-5994, 10am-5pm Mon.-Fri., 9am-2pm Sat.), which promotes self-employment for low-income artisans in developing countries worldwide by selling their baskets, clothing, and handicrafts.

Westfield Shopping Town, Southgate (3501 S. Tamiami Trail, 941/955-0900) is a pretty standard mall, with several anchor stores (Dillard's, Macy's) and many of the usual suspects (Ann Taylor, Talbots, Bare Minerals, Coach, Gymboree, and Chico's).

St. Armands Circle on Lido Key

For when you need to make those credit cards sizzle, you have to head north on I-75 to Ellenton to the **Prime Outlets** (5461 Factory Shops Blvd., Ellenton, 941/723-1150). There are more than 130 stores (Ralph Lauren, Gap, Guess, Tommy Hilfiger, Nike, Nautica) with deep, deep discounts.

And if your mantra is "reduce, reuse, and recycle," you'll find all kinds of used goods at the more than 400 covered booths of the **Red Barn Flea Market** (1707 1st St. E., Bradenton, 941/747-3794), in Manatee County to the north. Go on the weekend for the greatest number of vendors and the widest variety of things, from collectibles and antiques to out-and-out junk.

FOOD

Strips of chain restaurants pop up on the Gulf Coast of Florida like mushrooms after the wet season. In fact, many chains, such as Outback Steakhouse and Hooters, call the Gulf Coast home, and new chains are often market-tested first in the urban areas along this part of Florida. Why, I ask myself? It's demographics. In an area that still has a fairly dense concentration of retirees, the newest growth segment is young families. And what do the elderly and young families have in common? They like to eat out, but they want things to be familiar. They want to go to Chili's and eat the same thing they ate last time.

But even though Sarasota is awash with chain restaurants, the city still has a super-abundance of unique restaurants and the diners who love them.

Downtown

★ **Bijou Café** (1287 1st St., 941/366-8111, 11:30am-2pm Mon.-Fri., 5pm-9pm Mon.-Thurs., 5pm-10pm Fri.-Sat., $19-36) has been a local gem since 1986, making everyone's top 10 list and bringing praise from *Zagat, Bon Appetit,* and *Gourmet.* It's what you'd call continental-American fare, presided over by chef Jean-Pierre Knaggs and his wife, Shay. Located a couple of blocks from Ritz Carlton Sarasota in a 1920s gas

Bijou Café

station turned restaurant, the vibe is special-occasion or big-time-business dining. A 2004 renovation (after a fire) brought a bar, lounge, private room, and outdoor dining courtyards. The wine list features a number of South African wines (Knaggs is South African), and the menu contains dishes like shrimp and crab bisque, roast duck with orange-cognac sauce, and crab cakes with Louisiana rémoulade. And don't miss the crème brûlée.

Opened in 2003, **Mattison's City Grill** (1 N. Lemon Ave., 941/330-0440, www.mattisons.com 11am-11pm Tues.-Thurs., 11am-midnight Fri.-Sat., 9:30am-10pm Sun., 11am-10pm Mon., $17-25) is casual and hopping, with Italian-ish small plates and pizzas. It feels more urban than many of the other downtown restaurants, with great outdoor seating, cool wine events and cigar dinners, and live music nightly. It's been so successful that owner Paul Mattison has a virtual empire in the area now: Mattison's Riverside, Mattison's Forty One, Mattison's Bayside at

Table-Hopping

In the off-season, Sarasota's many culinary pearls are yours for the plucking—and during June that plucking gets all the more delicious with a 14-day **Savor Sarasota restaurant week.** In a city with one of the highest concentrations of *Zagat*-rated restaurants in Florida, dozens have banded together to offer the public value-priced, three-course, prix fixe menus.

It's definitely a bargain, but what's in it for the restaurants? According to Michael Klauber, proprietor of Michaels On East and one of the instigators of the restaurant week, "The original idea came from the local convention and visitors bureau. They got a few of us restaurateurs together to talk about it. We thought this would be a great way to showcase the restaurants, and it gives the restaurants an opportunity to explore something different with a special menu. I hope it can become a destination event, and that hotels and resorts will see an influx of people."

Some restaurants include interactive cooking demonstrations; others feature live music. Many of the restaurants offer several choices for appetizer, entrée, and dessert, some with suggested wine pairing flights. At the core, though, it's not complicated: Pick a participating restaurant, make a reservation, dine, pay ($15 for lunch, $29 for dinner). Repeat. For more information about participating restaurants, events, and pricing, visit www.savorsarasota.com.

Van Wezel, and a catering business—all fun, fresh dining experiences.

Marina Jack's (2 Marina Plaza, 941/365-4232, www.marinajacks.com, 11:15am-11pm daily, $10-35 depending on which dining room you choose) is a longtime downtown favorite with nightly live music. It's all about casual waterside dining, with a few different ways to eat with the water in view. Choose from the second-level Bayside Dining Room, the Blue Sunshine Patio, or a cocktail at the Deep Six Lounge and Piano Bar. If you still don't feel aquatic enough, there's the *Marina Jack II* yacht, which wines and dines you

in the bay. Back on land, the menu leans to crowd-pleasers like crab-stuffed mushrooms, conch fritters, and steaks.

In a similar style (fun, casual seafood joint) but with no water views, **Barnacle Bill's** (1526 Main St., 941/365-6800, 11:30am-9pm Mon.-Thurs., 11:30am-10pm Fri.-Sat., 4pm-9pm Sun., $15-25) renovated in its downtown location in 2005. This is the chain's white-tablecloth establishment, with choices like crab cakes, fried popcorn shrimp, or stuffed flounder. Its other location is at 5050 N. Tamiami Trail (941/355-7700).

It's not exactly downtown, but just slightly south. Still, any list of important downtown restaurants has to include ★ **Michaels On East** (1212 East Ave. S., 941/366-0007, 11:30am-2pm and 5pm-9pm Mon.-Thurs., 5pm-10pm Fri.-Sat., $15-30). It's won best-of-Florida accolades from nearly everyone since its opening at the beginning of the 1990s—and it's kept up with all the newcomers, consistently pushing the envelope and wowing diners with its "New American" take and lavish interior. During the day it's a power-lunching crowd; at night, romantic dinners include a grilled duck breast paired with Bermuda onion and shiitake fondue and fig and pecan risotto, all flavors showcased with a nice selection of wine.

For when you're tired of fish, ★ **Patrick's** (1481 Main St., 941/955-1481, 11am-11pm Sun.-Thurs., 11am-midnight Fri.-Sat., $10-20) gets top honors for Sarasota's best burger. It's a casual spot, with no reservations accepted, and the bar scene is fun. Patrick's has an extensive lunch and dinner menu with an exceptional variety of burgers, steaks, seafood, salads, and traditional bar-fare favorites like chicken wings and jalapeño poppers. The burger selection is creative and original—try the Bronx burger with grilled onions, swiss cheese, and barbecue sauce. The wine list contains around 20 well-selected wines, and the beer selection focuses on stout ales and Irish varieties.

Just want a quick, inexpensive bite? Head to downtown's **Cafe Epicure** (1298 N. Palm

Ave., 941/366-5648, 11am-10:30pm daily, $5-25). It's a cool bistro/deli/market, an easy place to hang out on the patio and write postcards while having a drink and enjoying a great sandwich, salad, or pizza.

Best breakfast? It's a chain, but this location is without a doubt the best of the breed. **First Watch Restaurant** (1395 Main St., 941/954-1395, 7:30am-2:30pm daily, $5-12) serves Sarasota's finest quick, no-fuss, inexpensive breakfasts with bottomless coffee and cheery service. Investigate the Inspired Italian omelet (roasted red peppers, tomatoes, mozzarella cheese, Italian sausage, topped with fresh herbs) or the carrot cake pancakes. Lines can be long, but they move quickly. If you just can't wait, walk south along Central Avenue and stop into one of the sidewalk coffeehouses.

St. Armands Circle and Lido Key

In 1893, a Frenchman named Charles St. Amand bought a little mangrove island off Sarasota, homesteading in the usual way with fishing, hunting, and growing a little produce. In the land deeds his name was misspelled, so it stuck when circus magnate John Ringling bought the property in 1917 (well, it's rumored he won it in a poker game). He planned for St. Armands Key to be a residential and shopping development laid out in a circle, bringing people over first by steamer and then via the John Ringling Causeway completed in 1926 (the major lifting done by circus elephants). The area has had a fairly consistent commitment to becoming as upscale as possible since Ringling wheedled it away from old Charles St. Amand. It's often compared to Rodeo Drive and other famous shopping districts.

There are a variety of shops, from upscale clothing stores to tourist souvenir types, and some of the city's best restaurants line up around the circle. So, explore the shops and go to dinner.

Two of the oldest on the stretch are **Café L'Europe** (431 St. Armands Cir., 941/388-4415, 11:30am-9pm Sun.-Thurs., until 10pm

Fri. and Sat., $25-40) and the **Columbia Restaurant** (411 St. Armands Cir., 941/388-3987, 11am-10pm daily, $10-25). Close together, both feature beautiful dining rooms and wonderful sidewalk dining. The Columbia opened in 1959, making it the oldest restaurant in Sarasota. (Its sister restaurant in Tampa goes one better, being the oldest restaurant in the state of Florida.) The Cuban food is authentic, and dishes include the red snapper Alicante and 1905 Salad with chopped cheese, olives, and a vinaigrette. The black bean soup and stuffed pompano in parchment are excellent choices. Columbia is also known for its fruity sangria. As for Café L'Europe, it's a broad collection of culinary influences that's hard to pin down: The kitchen does an equally good job with a New England lobster roll, wild mushroom ravioli, and herb crusted lamb with mint sauce.

15 South Ristorante Enoteca (15 S. Boulevard of the Presidents, 941/388-1555, 9am-2am Thurs.-Sun., 4:30-midnight Mon.-Wed., $15-35) seems to be the place to go in the area for northern Italian, and the upstairs nightclub features an excellent martini bar and diverse styles of music nightly (Latin acts, belly dancing, Caribbean tunes, a big band, you name it). The restaurant's menu will be familiar, but the dishes like grilled veal chop and garlic bruschetta are exceptional.

It's a chain, but **Tommy Bahama Tropical Café & Emporium** (300 John Ringling Blvd., 941/388-2888, 10am-11pm Mon.-Sat., 10am-10pm Sun., $20-30) is just plain fun, the food is excellent, and the drinks are too good for common sense to kick in. The store downstairs carries Tommy Bahama's signature mix of tropical leisurewear and cool housewares—you have to take a flight of stairs off to the side to reach the upstairs restaurant, which has huge windows that look out on the circle. Salads and drinks are fairly pricey, but good.

Cha Cha Coconuts (417 St. Armands Cir., 941/388-3300, 11am-11pm daily, $10-15) is a good place to go for a drink or to grab some island-inspired dishes like coconut shrimp or a burger topped with mango chutney. **Blue**

Dolphin Cafe (470 John Ringling Blvd., 941/388-3566, 7am-3pm daily, $7-15) is where to go for cheap, diner-style breakfasts with a twist (crab Benedict, raspberry blintzes). When you're ready for some great fudge, head to **Kilwin's** (312 John Ringling Blvd., 941/388-3200, 8am-11pm daily).

Southside Village

You may be driving through Southside Village and before you have time to ask, "Hey, why are all these beautiful young professional types drinking glasses of red wine at sidewalk tables in the middle of a Tuesday afternoon?" you've passed right through it on your way downtown. Visitors don't hit this little shopping/restaurant area with frequency, which is a shame. A few of Sarasota's most contemporary restaurants are right here. Southside Village is centered on South Osprey Avenue between Hyde Park and Hillview Streets, about 15 blocks south of downtown.

Perhaps the best place in Sarasota to pick up the ingredients for a picnic is in the same block. **Morton's Gourmet Market** (1924 S. Osprey Ave., 941/955-9856, www.mortonsmarket.com, 8am-8pm Mon.-Sat., 10am-7pm Sun.) has the kind of fresh salads, deli items, fancy specialty sandwiches, and cooked entrées that make you press your nose up against the glass case, leaving an embarrassing smudge. Most items are fairly cheap, and you can eat on the premises or take it all out.

Pacific Rim (1859 Hillview St., 941/330-8071, www.pacificrimsarasota.com, 11:30am-2pm and 4:30pm-9:30pm Mon.-Thurs., 11:30am-2pm and 4:30pm-10:30pm Fri., 5pm-10:30pm Sat., 5pm-9pm Sun., $7-15) takes you on a pleasant pan-Asian romp, from Thai basil curries to expertly rolled tekka maki sushi and beyond. You can play chef here and select your combinations of meats and veggies to be grilled or cooked in a wok.

Nearby **Hillview Grill** (1920 Hillview St., 941/952-0045, 11am-9pm Mon.-Tues., 11am-10pm Wed.-Fri., 4:30pm-10pm Sat., $15-30) traffics in another melding of cuisines, this time with a focus on steaks, seafood, burgers, salads, with several other dishes with a variety of ethnic influences. It's more of a neighborhood joint, with easier prices and a relaxed setting. Try the pan-seared chicken with rice and vegetables or the mahi fish tacos.

International District at Gulf Gate

Many of the better less-expensive restaurants can be found at the **Gulf Gate neighborhood,** a tiny international district that spans a three-block area from Gulf Gate Drive to Superior Avenue, and from Mall Drive around the block to Gateway Avenue. It's where to go to get a quick meal on the fly, takeout, or just something that won't break the bank. At Gateway Avenue you'll come upon **Pasta La Pizza** (6592 Superior Ave., 941/921-0990, 11am-9pm Tues.-Thurs., 11am-10pm Fri., noon-9pm Sat., 4pm-8pm Sun., $8-15) and **Rico's Pizzeria** (5131 N. Tamiami Trail, 941/358-9958, 11am-10pm Mon.-Sat., 4pm-10pm Sun., $6-15). And once you hit Gulf Gate Drive, there are a couple of Chinese and sushi takeout places, a Russian joint, and a British tearoom.

Pinecrest and Beyond

Amish cuisine. If that looks like a typo sitting there, you'll need to recall that Sarasota is a huge Amish and Mennonite winter resort. Both groups come down from Pennsylvania and the Midwest looking for sun and good Amish food, with luck on both counts. The locus of Amish activity here is in Pinecrest, where you'll see the bearded men in suspenders and wide straw hats, the women in long skirts and bonnets, all enjoying the Florida weather. While here, they eat at **Yoder's** (3434 Bahia Vista, 941/955-7771, 6am-8pm Mon.-Sat., $7-15). It's been a Sarasota institution since 1975, with wholesome, rib-sticking country ham and corn fritters, turkey and gravy, meat loaf and mashed potatoes, and pies, pies, pies. Note especially the peanut butter cream pie. **Troyer's Dutch Heritage** (3713 Bahia Vista, 941/955-8007, 7am-8pm Mon.-Thurs., 7am-9pm Fri.-Sat., $5-12) is even more venerable, dating back to 1969, with sturdy, accessible buffet-style meals and a gift shop on the second floor.

ACCOMMODATIONS

There are scads of condos and beachfront rentals in the greater Sarasota area, but most of these rent only by the week. If that's your time frame, the weeklong rentals often are a more financially prudent choice. If you're only in for a few days, hotels and motels run the gamut from moderately priced and no-frills to truly luxurious. Generally speaking, beachside places are pricier than mainland or downtown accommodations, and winter rates are highest, dropping down usually by a third in summer. Listed here are Sarasota and Lido Key accommodations—Longboat Key, Siesta Key, and Venice are covered in *The Keys* section of this chapter.

Under $100

The **Cadillac Motel** (4021 N. Tamiami Trail, 941/355-7108, $55-95) is a no-frills, clean, single-story motel. It's a bit away from all the action of downtown (about a mile), but there's a sweet little pool and shuffleboard to entertain you.

$100-200

Business travelers enjoy **Springhill Suites by Marriott** (1020 University Pkwy., 941/358-3385, $149-200), a moderately priced, all-suites hotel fairly close to the airport. All rooms have a king or two double beds with separate sleeping, eating, and working areas. There's also a pullout sofa bed, a pantry area with mini refrigerator, sink, and microwave, and a big desk with fancy chair and two-line telephones with data port. The free continental breakfast isn't an afterthought, offering items like sausage, eggs, oatmeal, and make-your-own waffles.

$200-300

The three-story **La Quinta Inn & Suites Sarasota** (1803 Tamiami Trail N., 941/366-5128, $145-300) is not far from the Ringling School of Art and Design, a few minutes' drive from downtown. Rooms are midsize, some with sofa beds, and those on interior hallways have desks. There's an outdoor pool, a pleasant complimentary breakfast, and free parking, and pets under 30 pounds are accepted.

Courtyard by Marriott (850 University Pkwy., 941/355-3337, $149-250) is a mostly business, recently renovated three-story hotel directly across from the airport. It's convenient to both Bradenton and Sarasota. This is a great hotel for business trips or family vacations. There's wireless high-speed Internet throughout the hotel and a hot breakfast buffet.

Over $300

It was controversial when it opened, but the **Ritz-Carlton Sarasota** (1111 Ritz-Carlton Dr., 941/309-2000, www.ritzcarlton.com, $500-1,000), a 266-room, 18-story luxury hotel right downtown, has managed to blend in beautifully, as if it has always been here. Ritz-Carlton's signature warm and efficient service, spacious rooms with balconies and marble baths, and great amenities make it the top choice among business and other travelers looking for upscale amenities. The downtown location is convenient to restaurants (although there are two laudable ones on-site) and attractions; there's a lovely pool, three lighted tennis courts, and the wood-paneled Cà d'Zan Bar & Cigar Lounge is always hopping.

The Ritz has a spa open to guests and members only, and the Members Golf Club, located 13 miles from the hotel, offers a Tom Fazio-designed 18-hole championship course. It is a par 72 and set on 315 acres of tropical landscape with no real estate development.

Lido Beach Resort (700 Benjamin Franklin Dr., 941/388-2161, www.lidobeachresort.com, $200-600) is a favorite among families vacationing in the area. The 12-story south tower is newer than the north and comprises one- and two-bedroom suites with kitchens. The hotel has two beautiful free-form pools and three hot tubs, all right on the beach, and one of Sarasota's few beachside tiki bars. It's a brief walk out the door to Lido Beach and St. Armands Circle shopping/dining area, 10 minutes to downtown, and 15-20 minutes to the airport. The hotel offers beach volleyball, a free shuttle to St. Armands, dry cleaning, and laundry. The resort has pet-friendly accommodations.

In 2008, the 12-story **Hyatt Sarasota** (1000 Boulevard of the Arts, 941/953-1234, $300-600) completed a $22 million transformation, with a full makeover of guest rooms, lobbies, corridors, meeting space, fitness center, business center, restaurants, and bars. It's a big convention hotel downtown with easy access to Van Wezel Performing Arts Hall, the Municipal Auditorium, and other attractions. It's right in the downtown business district, but waterside, with its own private marina, a floating dock, and a beautiful lagoon-style pool. The 294 guest rooms all have a view of the bay or marina, most with little balconies.

One of the trendiest and hippest hotels to open in recent years is the ★ **Hotel Indigo** (1223 Boulevard of the Arts, 941/487-3800, www.hotelindigo.com, $250-400). Guest rooms have wall-size murals and fabrics in bold blues and greens—altogether it's a fun, contemporary alternative, right in the thick of things. The on-site café and little wine bar is called H2O Bistro. They have a fitness center with recently updated equipment, and the two wading pools (one hot and one cool) are a nice, recent addition that will help you relax.

Vacation Rentals

Try giving **Argus Property Management** (941/951-4034) a call, or visit **Vacation Rentals by Owner** (www.vrbo.com). There are also golf resort condo communities, such as **Heritage Oaks Golf and Country Club** (4800 Chase Oaks Dr., 941/926-7602) and **Timberwoods Vacation Villas & Resort** (7964 Timberwood Cir., 941/312-5934), that rent by the week.

GETTING THERE AND AROUND

Car

Sarasota is along I-75, the major transportation corridor for the southeastern United States. Sarasota County is south of Tampa and north of Fort Myers, 223 miles from Miami (about 4 hours' drive time), 129 miles from Orlando (about 2 hours' drive time), and about 5-6 hours from the Florida-Georgia line. If you prefer I-95, take it to Daytona Beach, then follow I-4 to I-75 before heading south.

U.S. 301 and U.S. 41/Tamiami Trail are the major north-south arteries on the mainland; the Gulf-to-Mexico Drive (County Road 789) is the main island road. The largest east-west thoroughfares in Sarasota are Highway 72 (Clark Road); County Road 780; University Parkway; and (to the islands) Ringling Causeway, which takes you right to Lido Beach.

Air

Sarasota-Bradenton International Airport (SRQ) (6000 Airport Cir., at the intersection of U.S. 41 and University Pkwy., Sarasota, 941/359-2770) is certainly the closest, served by commuter flights and a half dozen major airlines or their partners, including Air Canada, American Airlines, Delta, JetBlue, United, and West Jet.

Alamo (800/327-9633), **Avis** (800/831-2847), **Budget** (800/527-0700), **Dollar** (800/800-4000 domestic, 800/800-6000 international), **Enterprise** (800/736-8222), **Hertz** (800/654-3131), and **National** (800/227-7368) provide rental cars from Sarasota-Bradenton International Airport. **Diplomat Taxi** (941/355-5155) is the taxi provider at the airport.

Bus and Train

Sarasota County Area Transit, or **SCAT** (941/861-5000), runs scheduled bus service 6am-7pm Monday-Saturday. A $1.25 fare will take you to stops in the city and St. Armands, Longboat, and Lido Keys. **Greyhound** (575

N. Washington Blvd., Sarasota, 941/342-1720) offers regular bus service to Sarasota from Fort Myers and points north, and Miami to the southeast; **Amtrak** (800/872-7245) provides shuttle buses between the Tampa station and Sarasota.

The Keys

These barrier islands off the Sarasota coast are where you'll find the best beaches in the area. They also offer the relaxed atmosphere that most vacationers desire. Go into Sarasota for a taste of the city and to listen to the symphony—then head to the keys to put your toes in the sand and listen to the waves of the Gulf of Mexico lapping ashore.

The northernmost of Sarasota's stretch of keys, **Longboat Key** is a 12-mile barrier island populated mostly by extremely upscale private residences. What you can see of the residences is showy enough, but I have a sneaking suspicion that the really incredible mansions are down all those long driveways and behind those tall hedgerows. There are only about 8,000 full-time residents, but in high season (Dec.-Mar.), Longboat Key is where the rich and/or famous come to play a little golf and get a little sun away from the prying eyes of the public. If you are interested in seeing celebrities, you can hang around at the Longboat Key Club or on the golf courses to catch a glimpse.

The island hasn't always been so swanky. It was the Arvida Company that laid the foundation in the late 1950s (literally, enabling construction to occur on previously loose, shifting soil) for the development of the island. Generally speaking, visitors stay in the high-rises that line the well-landscaped Gulf of Mexico Drive; residents live on the bayside in discreet, shielded estates.

Siesta Key is something else again. It's a similar eight-mile-long barrier island with beaches just as beautiful as those of Longboat Key. But Siesta is mostly casual and fun family-owned accommodations, none extremely upscale, with easy access to the beach from anywhere, fishing, boating, kayaking, snorkeling, scuba diving, and sailboarding. And at night, unlike on Longboat, these people like

Siesta Key Beach

to party. Siesta Key Village has the area's most lively nightlife.

Farther south, **Casey Key** is eight miles long, stretching from Siesta Key on the north to Venice at the southern tip. It is almost exclusively single-family homes with just a few low-rise Old Florida beach motels. Two bridges provide access to the key, including a cool, old "swing bridge" dating back to the 1920s. Parts of the key are only 300 yards wide.

The town of **Venice** is more like a real place than a tourist destination, in good and bad ways. The residents seem to be mostly retirees, very sociable and active. The downtown is quaint—a handful of upscale shops and galleries, a couple of restaurants, a place to get ice cream, a couple of coffee shops, and a good wine bar. There's a little community theater, of which the residents are extremely proud. But really, the biggest draw in Venice is teeth. Every August the Venice Area Chamber of Commerce holds the **Shark's Tooth Festival,** with arts, crafts, food stalls, and lots of little pointy black fossils. It seems that sharks of all species shed their teeth continually. They have 40 or so teeth in each jaw, with seven other rows of teeth behind that first one waiting in the wings to mature. The average tiger shark produces 24,000 teeth in 10 years. In order to find them when they wash up on Venice beaches, stop by one of the gift shops downtown and ask for a shark tooth shovel. And once you've found a few, visit www.veniceflorida.com/shark.htm to identify the species.

SPORTS AND RECREATION
★ Siesta Key Beach

We have a winner of the international whose-beach-is-better smackdown. In 1987, scientists from the Woods Hole Oceanographic Institution in Woods Hole, Massachusetts, convened to judge the Great International White Sand Beach Challenge, with more than 30 entries from beaches around the world. To this day, Siesta Key Beach remains the reigning world champ, with all other beaches too cowed, or too chicken, to demand a rematch. Its preeminence has long been known—supposedly in the 1950s a visitor from New York, Mr. Edward G. Curtis, sent a pickle jar of Siesta's sand to the Geology Department of Harvard University for analysis. The report came back: "The sand from Siesta Key is 99 percent pure quartz grains, the grains being somewhat angular in shape. The soft floury texture of the sand is due to its fine grain size. It contains no fragments of coral and no shell. The fineness of the sand, which gives it its powdery softness, is emphasized by the fact that the quartz is a very hard substance, graded at 7 in the hardness scale of 10."

The real test can't be done with sand in a pickle jar. You need to lie on the sloping strand, run the warmed granules through your fingers, sniff the salt air, and listen to a plaintive gull overhead. For those things, too, Siesta Key Beach wins—it's been named America's Best Sand Beach and ranked in Florida's Top Ten Beaches multiple years on the Travel Channel. Dr. Beach has named it in his top 10 beaches in America numerous times; *National Geographic Traveler* has also named Siesta One of America's Best Beaches. The list goes on.

Other Beaches

The greater Sarasota area has lots of beaches to recommend. The beaches described here run from north to south.

Longboat Key has 10 miles of white, powdery beach, but most of it is accessible only to those who live there or are staying in a resort or condo. **Longboat Key Beach** is accessible at several points—at Longview Drive, Westfield Street, Mayfield Street, and Neptune Street. It's mostly underpopulated and often offers incredible sand dollar collecting. **Beer Can Island Beach,** at the very north end of Longboat Key and accessible by boat or from North Shore Road off Gulf of Mexico Drive, attracts a fair number of anglers and sun worshippers.

Dickie Vitale's Local Favorites

Dick Vitale—Dickie V. to some—is the famous ESPN sports broadcaster who calls the greater Sarasota area home. If you don't believe it, take a trip to the Dick Vitale Health and Fitness Gym at the Boys and Girls Clubs of Sarasota County and see who stands outside in bronze.

Here's a list of his personal area favorites:

1. Siesta Key Beach
"I love walking that beach. I bring a lot of people there and it blows their mind—love the white sand!"

2. Sarasota Restaurants
"From Fleming's to Ruth's Chris Steakhouse to the Le Colonne Restaurant to the Café L'Europe," Vitale lists thoughtfully, splitting his favorites between tried-and-true chains and some of the area's independent eateries.

3. The Broken Egg in Siesta Key and Lakewood Ranch
Vitale notes, "It's my office away from home, five minutes from my house. I sit there for hours, doing all my work and just having a blast with all the people." Vitale is known to do radio shows and TV interviews from the hangout where he is, he jokes, "the mayor of The Broken Egg." And when he gets hungry? The Dickie V turkey burger, of course.

4. Lakewood Ranch Country Club
In 1994 ground was broken on a new upscale residential development set between Sarasota and Bradenton. It bears the distinction of being one of the largest master-planned communities in the state to achieve the Green Community designation by the Florida Green Building Coalition. "I live in the country club," says Vitale, "and I play tennis every day when I'm home."

5. Spring training at Ed Smith Stadium
"It's great to get up close," Vitale explains. The little 7,500-seat stadium provides intimate access to big-league play in a small-time venue.

6. Van Wezel Performing Arts Hall
"All the seats are great because it's so small, and it's got great sound," insists Vitale. The Van Wezel presents a wonderful range of Broadway productions, world-class dance, music, comedy, and popular acts, as well as being the home base for many of the local arts organizations.

7. Main Street in Sarasota and Lakewood Ranch
"Both are special places to walk around, with restaurants and shops and lots of activities and music on the weekends," says Vitale. Lakewood Ranch's version dates back only to 2005 but still has an appealing range of boutique-style stores and eateries. More established, Sarasota's is lined with galleries, restaurants, and cute shops.

8. St. Armands Circle
"A tourist's delight," notes Vitale. While it's often compared to Rodeo Drive and other famous shopping districts, Vitale's affection for it is a little less highbrow: "Kilwin's ice cream is just phenomenal. I take a lot of people there. It's romantic to walk to Lido Beach from there. Keeps your marriage going!"

9. The Ritz-Carlton Sarasota and the Beach Club
The 266-room, 18-story luxury hotel right downtown has Ritz-Carlton's signature warmth and personality which appeals to Vitale: "It's a great, great asset to the area. We love going there for dinner and going to listen to the great bands they have on the weekend."

10. Boys & Girls Club of Sarasota County
Vitale's commitment and enthusiasm on this topic are infectious: "My buddies and friends and I raised over $1 million to help build the Lee Wetherington Boys & Girls Clubs. It's always special to see young kids getting an opportunity in their lives."

shark teeth from Venice Beach

Then there's the aforementioned Siesta Key Beach, on the north side of Siesta Key (it is contiguous with another favorite beach called Crescent Beach—good snorkeling off this one), with white sand so reflective it feels cool on a hot day. Scientists estimate that the sand on this beach is millions of years old, starting in the Appalachians and eventually deposited on these shores. The water is shallow, the beach incline gradual, making it a perfect beach for young swimmers. There are 800 parking spots, which tend to fill up, and the lifeguard stands are painted different colors as points of reference, so you don't lose your way. The Siesta Key beaches south of a rock outcropping called Point of Rocks are not as white and soft, the sand being shellier and grayer. **Turtle Beach,** on Midnight Pass Road near the south end of Siesta Key, is another popular beach, prized for its more private feel, large picnic shelter, and good shelling opportunities.

There used to be a small inlet that separated Siesta Key from Casey Key, an inlet called Midnight Pass, which was filled in, amid great controversy, in 1983. There have been disruptive environmental consequences to this choice, but for the visitor it means you can walk all the way on **Palmer Point Beach** from Siesta Key to Casey Key. The northern part of the beach was the former home of Mote Marine Laboratory. These days it's a quiet dune-backed beach, usually with just a few people walking and relaxing in the sand. There are neither lifeguards nor facilities. Casey Key also has **Nokomis Beach,** directly west of the Albee Road Bridge, a nice average beach for the area, and **North Jetty Park** at its southernmost tip. North Jetty Park is one of the few Gulf Coast spots that draws surfers, and anglers seem to congregate here, too. Boats pass through the jetties from the Intracoastal Waterway to the Gulf.

South from here you enter into the beaches of Venice, rightfully known as the place to go when you're hunting sharks' teeth. Only now you might be worried that there are loads of sharks lurking offshore waiting to gum you to death. The sharks' teeth that wash up on the beach are fossilized, floating in from a shark burial ground a few miles offshore, a deep crevice where these cold-blooded predators once went to die. In addition to these gray/black teeth, fossilized bones of prehistoric animals like camels, bison, and tapirs sometimes wash up on this beach. In local shops you can rent or buy a shark-tooth scooper, a wire rake with a mesh box that sifts the sand and shell fragments at the water's edge, leaving the teeth behind in the basket. **Venice Beach** (so different from the beach of the same name in California) is at the west end of Venice Avenue not that far from town. **Brohard Park,** at the southernmost part of Venice, is the beach of choice among anglers, with a 740-foot fishing pier on the property for public use. Dogs are allowed at **Paw Park** at South Brohard Park, with a fenced area, a small dog beach, and dog showers. Farther south, near Venice's little airport, **Caspersen Beach** is really the locus of shark's tooth mania. Truth is, it's harder to find teeth than it used to be, partly because city boosters have replenished the sand on the beach with sand from an offshore sandbar. It's a pretty beach left in its natural state, with people surf casting and red-shouldered hawks swooping above the shorebirds.

Golf

In the early 1920s, John Ringling purchased major acreage on the south end of the Longboat Key. He constructed a golf course and planted Australian pine trees along Gulf of Mexico Drive; he eventually abandoned the construction of a luxurious Ritz-Carlton. With this legacy, the **Longboat Key Golf Club** (301 Gulf of Mexico Dr., 941/387-1632, resort courses, greens fees $45-116) offers several remarkable golfing experiences to guests (and their guests' guests). Opened in 1960, the Bill Mitchell-designed Islandside Course (par 72, 6,792 yards, course rating 73.8, slope 138) features 18 holes of crisp, up-and-down shot-making through a 112-acre bird sanctuary filled with more than 5,000 palm trees and flowering plants. Water appears on 16 of its 18 fairways. The resort also has three 9-hole courses with a more country-club feel (and where more of the private members play), played in three 18-hole combinations: blue/red (par 72, 6,709 yards, course rating 72.6, slope 130), red/white (par 72, 6,749 yards, course rating 72.7, slope 131), and white/blue (par 72, 6,812 yards, course rating 73.1, slope 132).

Fishing

Venice is a fairly well-known fishing destination—you'll see people wetting a line at the Venice jetties, Sharky's Pier, or Caspersen Beach. If you try your hand, expect to catch snook, redfish, Spanish mackerel, sheepshead, sea trout, and flounder, depending on the time of year. There are also lots of charter companies willing to take you deep-sea fishing out in the Gulf (grouper and snapper most of the year; kingfish, cobia, greater amberjack, and mahimahi seasonally). At the end of East Venice Avenue on the Myakka River, **Snook Haven Fish Camp** (5000 E. Venice Ave., 941/485-7221) has a fun riverside restaurant,

Venice Train Depot

boat rides, and fishing. **Reel Fast Charters** (941/650-4938, $75 sunset cruise, $425 for 4 hours, $600 for 6 hours, $725 for 8 hours) takes groups out fishing as well as on non-fishing sunset cruises. And **Triple Trouble Charters** (941/484-3225, rates vary) takes small groups out from the Dona Bay Marina in Nokomis, just minutes from the Venice Inlet, on a 25-foot custom-rigged Parker for inshore and offshore fishing.

Waterway Park

The **Venetian Waterway Park** (daylight hours, free) in Venice is a mixed-use linear park that features a recently completed 10-mile running trail that parallels the Intracoastal Waterway, ending on Caspersen Beach, one of the most beautiful on the Gulf. It's a long, winding, wheel-friendly park, good for in-line skaters, bikers, even jogging strollers.

While in Venice, visit the **Venice Train Depot** (303 Legacy Trail) downtown. The Mediterranean-style depot was constructed in 1927 and is listed on the National Register of Historic Places. The depot also serves as a trailhead for the Legacy Trail, more than 10 miles of paved paths that run from just south of the city of Sarasota to Venice following the former CSX railroad corridor.

SHOPPING

Shopping on Longboat Key is fairly limited: On the lush, tropically landscaped Avenue of the Flowers there's a little shopping center (525 Bay Isle Pkwy.) where you'll find a larger Publix grocery and a drugstore; at the **Centre Shops** (5370 Gulf of Mexico Dr., 941/387-3135) about mid-island, you'll find a small collection of shops selling T-shirts and resort wear, galleries, and little restaurants.

On Siesta Key there are two main shopping areas: **Siesta Key Village** on the northwest side of the key about one block from the Gulf, and **Siesta South shopping area** beginning at the Stickney Point Bridge and going south along Midnight Pass Road. Both have plenty of T-shirt-and-sunglasses shops, the shell-themed beachy giftware shops, and a few other stores not quite as touristy. Neither area boasts much in the way of high end merchandise—galleries, antiques, or clothing.

FOOD
Longboat Key

Sarasota's has a long-term love affair with **Euphemia Haye** (5540 Gulf of Mexico Dr., 941/383-3633, $22-43). Hours vary by dining locale here: 6pm-10pm Sunday-Friday, 5:30pm-10:30pm Saturday in the restaurant; 6pm-11pm daily in the dessert room; 5pm-midnight daily in the HayeLoft. Opened in 1975 on Longboat Key, the restaurant serves far-reaching food in a tropical setting. It's won top honors from national food magazines, and you need only try the smoked salmon on buckwheat crepes or pistachio-crusted Key West snapper to see why. The wine list is broad, with good selections at every price point. Food prices are high and dishes are rich in the restaurant; try the lighter/cheaper fare upstairs in the HayeLoft

if you feel inclined. Chef/owner Raymond Arpke also offers cooking classes at the restaurant ($65/person).

Located mid-key on the bay side of Longboat Key is a wonderful find, **Pattigeorge's** (4120 Gulf of Mexico Dr., 941/383-5111, 6pm-9:30pm daily, $16-28). Chef Tommy Klauber experiments with an East-West fusion style that somehow never seems contrived (he formerly owned a restaurant in Aspen called Gieusseppi Wong, serving Italian/Chinese food). Pattigeorge's has been around since 1998, making it another old-timer on the island. The dining room is comfortable but upscale, and the views are nice—still, the main attraction is dishes like five-spice calamari with orange blossom honey-mustard, or Thai green curry mussels, or maybe a chicken and shrimp pad Thai.

Siesta Key

Like everything else on Siesta Key, restaurants are mostly more casual here than on Longboat Key. Ocean Boulevard runs through Siesta Key Village, which is lined with loads of fun, laid-back, beachy bars and restaurants. Most places have outdoor seating, and many have live music at night.

When you're looking for that special romantic restaurant, only one place on Siesta Key will do. ★ **Ophelia's on the Bay** (9105 Midnight Pass Rd., 941/349-2212, 5pm-10pm Mon.-Sat., 11am-2pm and 5pm-10pm Sun., $20-40), at the southern tip of the key, has a waterfront terrace that I swear the moon favors with an extra luminous show over Sarasota Bay and the mainland. The interior of the restaurant is stylish and romantic, but you have to sit outside. The chef seems to prefer sweet-and-salty combinations that combine meats with fruits (coconut- and cashew-crusted mahimahi with papaya jam) and salty meats with fish (grouper with bacon braised spinach). It's a distinctive and memorable collection of dishes accompanied by a unique wine list. Try the maple pecan tarte or crème brûlée for dessert. (The oyster bar next door to Ophelia's is a wonderful place to kill a little time, and appetite, if you have to wait for a table at Ophelia's.)

Another great restaurant is **Siesta Key Oyster Bar** (5238 Ocean Blvd., 941/346-5443, 10am-midnight daily, $6-15), with the acronym SKOB on the sign out front. The sandwiches here are, in fact, called skobwiches, and the grouper or fried shrimp skobwich is mighty fine washed down with a house margarita while listening to a live rock band. Margaritas seem to find their foothold in Siesta Key, but if rum's more your drink, right down the way you'll enjoy the **Daiquiri Deck** (5250 Ocean Blvd., 941/349-8697, 11am-2am daily, $6-17). One of the better drinks is the Siesta Tea, a mix of raspberry liqueur, light rum, gin, vodka, raspberry juice, and melon mix—tangy yet sweet, and strong.

For a great beer batter-dipped hot dog, head to **The Old Salty Dog** (5023 Ocean Blvd., 941/349-0158, 11am-9:30pm Sun.-Thurs., 11am-10pm Fri.-Sat., $5-15). It's an institution among locals, who come for that particular treat or a bowl of clam chowder and a beer. It's open air, with great views, good burgers, and saucy waitresses. The beer bar is fashioned from the hull of an old boat, which adds a little nautical tilt to every drinker's voice. There's another location with the same hours at 1601 Ken Thompson Parkway (941/388-4311).

Best breakfast? That's the easiest call on Siesta Key. Anyone in town will promptly steer you to ★ **The Broken Egg** (140 Avenida Messina, 941/552-8320, 7am-2pm daily, $7-12), now one block down from its original location. The place is such a cheery and busy scene most mornings that they opened a second location in 2005 at Lakewood Ranch (6115 Exchange Way, 941/388-6898, 7am-2pm daily). Try the Floridian omelet (three eggs filled with cream cheese and topped with crabmeat, monterey jack, and onions) or cinnamon-roll French toast. The well-landscaped and shady patio is the place to sit.

Blasé Café (5263 Ocean Blvd., 941/349-9822, 3pm-1am Sun.-Thurs., 3pm-2am

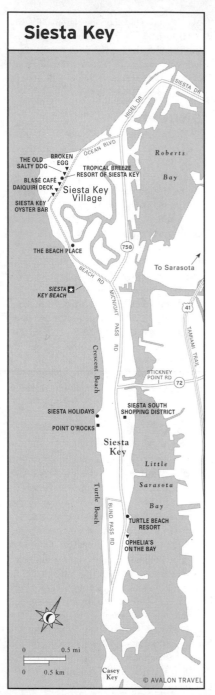

Siesta Key

Fri.-Sat., $7-23) recently reinvented itself from a well-loved breakfast spot to an even more well-loved lunch and dinner favorite with a martini bar that's hopping on most nights. They serve burgers, sandwiches, soups, salads, and a variety of entrées that feature steaks and seafood. Be sure to ask for outside seating on the wooden deck with the big palm tree in the middle (but if you're just stopping in for a drink, the bar is the seat of choice).

Casey Key

On Casey Key, the place to eat is **Casey Key Fish House** (801 Blackburn Point Rd., 941/966-1901, 11:30am-9pm daily, $5-15). This shambling restaurant and tiki bar does a brisk business, with diners navigating peel-and-eat shrimp while watching the sunset over picturesque Blackburn Point Marina. Casual seafood is the mainstay, and the fancier white wine-steamed mussels and almond snapper are brilliant.

Venice

Along Nokomis Avenue (the main drag downtown) you'll find shops, diners, coffeehouses, and lunch spots—the best of which is **Venice Wine and Coffee Co.** (201 W. Venice Ave., 941/484-3667, 8am-8pm Mon.-Thurs.,

8am-9pm Fri., 11am-5pm Sat.), a coffee shop by day and wine bar at night. To find Venice's Old Florida dining possibilities—all fun, all casual—you'll have to go farther afield. The **Crow's Nest, Marina Restaurant and Tavern** (1968 Tarpon Center Dr., 941/484-9551, 11:30am-10pm daily, $15-30) has been feeding locals since 1976, with a fun tavern and great views of the marina, Venice Inlet, and the Intracoastal Waterway. The wine list is extensive, and the fare is the fried oysters/fried shrimp/steamed clam kind. Happy hour in the tavern is 4pm-6pm. Marina hours are 8am-7pm daily.

The **Snook Haven Restaurant and Fish Camp** (5000 Venice Ave. E., past River Rd., 941/485-7221, 11am-8pm daily, $10-20) has a similar vibe, only more down-home and bayou-style, right on the Myakka River (rent a pontoon boat or kayak before you eat). The burgers are good, and you can count on some entertaining fellow customers and occasional live entertainment.

Sharky's on the Pier (1600 S. Harbor Dr., 941/488-1456, 11:30am-10pm Sun.-Thurs., 11:30am-midnight Fri.-Sat., $12-24) is closer to civilization, with beach views and the day's catch offered broiled, blackened, grilled, or fried. Sit outside on the veranda

a relaxing view at the Casey Key Fish House

and enjoy a margarita that's finished off with triple sec and blue curaçao for that dark-blue water look.

ACCOMMODATIONS
Longboat Key

Longboat Key is mostly dotted with expensive high-rise condos and resort hotels that loom over the beaches. If you like a more modest scale, the **Wicker Inn** (5581 Gulf of Mexico Dr., 941/387-8344, www.wickerinn.net, cottages $1,199-3,296/week) is more like it. There are 11 casual and fun Key West-style cottages set around an inviting pool and landscaped with purple hibiscus and oleander. There's a private beach just steps away and a 16-acre public park.

★ **The Resort at Longboat Key Club** (220 Sands Pointe Rd., 941/383-8821, www.longboatkeyclub.com, from $500) is where serious golfers come for the 45 holes of the private Longboat Key Golf Club, but there are lots of other reasons to settle into one of the 210 suites (with full kitchens) or one of 20 hotel rooms. There's a fine restaurant onsite, 38 tennis courts, bike and beach rentals, great pools, and a private stretch of whitesand beach with cabana rentals and beachside service. Despite the fact that this is an extremely upscale resort, the people who work here are friendly and personable.

Siesta Key

There are not too many chain hotels and no huge resorts on Siesta Key—which is fine, because you're more likely to have a memorable time in one of the modest mom-and-pop house rentals or small hotels. The warm, independent spirit of many of these hoteliers is apparent in the relaxed decor and easy beachside pleasures. Many accommodations on Siesta Key adopt an efficiency approach, with little kitchens, essential for keeping vacation costs down (have a bowl of cereal in the morning, then prepare yourself a great picnic lunch for the beach).

Rented by the week, the tropical garden beach cottages of **The Beach Place** (5605 Avenida Del Mare, 941/346-1745, www.siestakeybeachplace.com, $400-1,700/week) make a nice romantic or family beach getaway. There's a pool (but the beach is 30 seconds away), a tiki cabana with wet bar, beachside barbecue facilities, lounge chairs, beach cruiser bikes, and free laundry. The cottages themselves are modest but recently repainted and pleasant, whether it's the one-bedroom Coquina or Seahorse, the

Turtle Beach Resort on Siesta Key

two-twin-bed Starfish, the large one-bedroom Sand Dollar, or the huge studio cottage called the Dolphin.

★ **Siesta Holidays** (1015 Crescent St., 941/312-9882, $700-1,400/week, depending on the season and unit) is a similar place, with two options. It has the Siesta Sea Castle directly on Crescent Beach, consisting of a large two-bedroom, two-bath apartment, and four one-bedroom efficiency apartments. The ground-level units have patios directly on the beach. Then there's the Siesta Holiday House, a little farther from the beach, with two one-bedroom apartments on the ground floor (with a big private screened pool) and two two-bedroom, two-bath apartments on the second floor. Pets are allowed in the Holiday House.

The **Tropical Breeze Resort of Siesta Key** (140 Columbus Blvd., 941/349-1125, www.tropicalbreezeinn.com, $200-400) also offers a range of choices, spreading across four blocks of an attractive neighborhood between the village and the shoreline. There are one-, two-, and three-bedroom efficiencies and suites located directly on the beach as well as more privately located units in lush tropical gardens. Each building comes with its own pool, and the property has a centrally located

yoga deck. Everything is within walking distance of Siesta Key Village.

On the south end of the island, ★ **Turtle Beach Resort** (9049 Midnight Pass Rd., 941/349-4554, www.turtlebeachresort.com, from $300) is one of the area's best-kept secrets and without a doubt my favorite place to stay on Siesta Key. Reservations are harder to come by at this extremely relaxed and casual property, but the 10 clapboard cottages, each individually decorated with its own porch and featuring a private hot tub, are worth waiting for. There are views of Little Sarasota Bay, Turtle Beach is a short walk away, and guests have free use of bikes, hammocks, canoes, kayaks, paddleboats, and fishing poles. Paddle a kayak from the dock of the resort to the quiet and secluded beach at Midnight Pass to enjoy the sunset. Then paddle up an appetite on the way back and eat at Ophelia's next door for a real treat. Pets are welcome.

Just down the road a few blocks from the resort, you can pull up your RV or stake out your tent and camp at the wonderful **Turtle Beach Campground** (8862 Midnight Pass Rd., 941/349-3839, www.scgov.net/turtlebeachcampground, $32-60). The 14-acre park has 40 small, well-designed sites right on the Gulf. A short sandy path leads down

Venice Beach Villas

to the beach, and the campground offers a boat ramp, volleyball net, horseshoe pits, and a playground. The city center of Siesta Key is a short drive down the road and has plenty of fun shops, restaurants, and bars to keep you from having to rough it too much.

Venice

If you've come to the Sarasota area with the express purpose of collecting sharks' teeth, then it makes sense to stay in Venice. Otherwise, Venice lacks a lot of the amenities found in Sarasota, Lido Key, Longboat Key, or Siesta Key, and the downtown pretty much closes up at night. However, a bike ride or walk along the Venetian Waterway Park trails that lead to Caspersen Beach is fun, and exploring the park and beach is the perfect reason to spend a day or two in the area. There's the fairly inexpensive **Inn at the Beach** (725 W. Venice Ave., 941/484-8471, $150-250) and a **Best Western** (400 Commercial Ct., 941/480-9898, $175-250), both perfectly fine. My favorite place to stay in Venice is the **Venice Beach Villas** (501 W. Venice Ave., 941/488-1580, $75-250/night and $500-1,700/week). They offer charming efficiencies, studios, and one- and two-bedroom units equipped with full kitchens. Their two locations within blocks of one another let you choose from a variety of rooms that are all centered around beautiful pools and artfully landscaped tropical grounds.

Vacation Rentals

In the Siesta Key and Longboat Key area, contact **A Paradise Rentals** (5201 Gulf Dr., 800/237-2252, www.aparadiserentals.com); in Sanibel and Captiva, contact **Sanibel** **Holiday** (239/472-6565, www.sanibelholiday. com); and on Longboat Key, contact **Coast 2 Coast Vacation Rentals** (800/657-8966, www.longboatrentals.com).

GETTING THERE AND AROUND

Air

From downtown Sarasota, go east across the John Ringling Causeway to access St. Armands Circle and Lido Key, then continue north on Gulf of Mexico Drive (County Road 789) to Longboat Key. The drive from Sarasota to Longboat Key is a little over 12 miles and will take about 30 minutes in normal traffic.

To reach Siesta Key from Sarasota, head south on U.S. 41 (also called the Tamiami Trail), then take a right onto either Siesta Drive or Stickney Point Road—the former takes you to the northern, residential section of the key; Stickney takes you closer to the funky Siesta Key Village. The 6.6-mile drive will take about 20 minutes in normal traffic.

To reach Casey Key from Sarasota, drive south on U.S. 41, then take a right onto Blackburn Point Road. The 15-minute drive will take you about 40 minutes in normal traffic.

To reach Venice Beach from Sarasota, drive south on U.S. 41, then turn right onto West Venice Avenue. The 19-mile drive will take you about 40 minutes in normal traffic.

Bus and Train

Sarasota County Area Transit, or **SCAT** (941/861-5000), runs scheduled bus service 6am-7pm Monday-Saturday. A $1.25 fare will take you to stops in Sarasota and St. Armands, Longboat, and Lido Keys.

Anna Maria Island

Stand at the northern end of Longboat Key and look north. You'll see another long, seven-mile strip of sandy barrier island that couldn't be more different from Longboat. Manatee County's Anna Maria Island is an island both literally and metaphorically—it is far enough south of Tampa to be removed from the city's urban hustle and bustle, and it's far enough north of Sarasota to escape being just another feather in that city's cap. It's the northernmost of the string of barrier islands that extend down to the Florida Keys, with three distinct towns spread along its length. There's the town of **Anna Maria** at the northern end, **Holmes Beach** in the middle, and **Bradenton Beach** at the southern end—all of them linked by their sweet, laid-back atmosphere. Three drawbridges access the island, one from Longboat Key and two from the mainland (Hwy. 64 and Hwy. 684).

Really, the little island community owes its existence to the Fig Newton. The inventor of the "oo-ee, gooey, rich and chewy" Newton, Charles Roser, sold the recipe to Nabisco, made a fortune, and then bought up Anna Maria land and started building. (Actually, the island probably owes its existence to James Henry Mitchell, who invented the apparatus, a kind of funnel within a funnel, that supplies the necessary steady stream of fig jam inside a tubelike stream of dough. But, enough with the Newtons already.)

These days, there's an active year-round community as well as a robust tourist trade that has been reinvigorated by a major amount of impressive new development that has delivered a more upscale and charming atmosphere to Anna Maria Island while still retaining the Old Florida nostalgia of your dreams in the form of thoughtful architecture and brilliant city planning. Tourists mostly come to the island for the outstanding boating, sailing, scuba, snorkeling, and fishing. Parking is the only hassle on the island, so park your car

where you're staying and walk across to the beach—Holmes Beach, Anna Maria Beach, Coquina Beach, Cortez Beach, and Manatee Beach are all equally lovely stretches of white sand and blue-green water. (Manatee has the most parking and a nice picnic area.) None have lifeguards or restrooms.

Anna Maria is the kind of island on which it's easy to do nothing—not because there's nothing to do, but because the pace is such that you feel entitled to easy relaxation. If your work ethic forces you to do *something*, I recommend a sunset sailing cruise with **Spice Sailing Charters** (departures from next to Rotten Ralph's Restaurant on Anna Maria Island, 941/704-0773, $40/person). The captain has a wealth of information about Florida history, fishing, and the area's recent environmental challenges.

Also worth checking out is Bradenton Beach and its municipal pier complex, which includes a restaurant, 220-foot floating dock for free day docking, a bait house, and public bathing facilities. The 660-foot fishing pier and boater-related facilities sit at the bayside end of Historic Bridge Street in Bradenton Beach. Visitors can take advantage of watercraft transportation to the dock, but new bike lanes, sidewalks, a multiuse nature path along the beach, and a free trolley system add some other options for navigating the area.

FOOD

★ **Beach Bistro** (6600 Gulf Dr., Holmes Beach, 941/778-6444, www.beachbistro.com, $25-60) beats much fancier restaurants in Sarasota, Tampa, and beyond for best restaurant on the Gulf Coast, according to *Zagat*, *Wine Spectator*, and numerous other publications. The place is romantic and cozy, with the kind of charm that comes of an independent (noncorporate) culinary vision. In the main dining room, chef Sean Murphy serves up excellent food that lives up to his superstar-chef reputation. (If you just want to stop in for a less fancy bite to eat, a more casual bar/café on one side is a good pick for a tasty burger.) The more formal dining room is spectacular, with superb views of the Gulf and single long-stemmed roses adorning the center of each table. Although geared toward romantic dining, the Beach Bistro still extends real warmth and care to visiting children. For a restaurant of this caliber, it isn't outlandishly pricey if you opt for the "small plates," which are certainly adequate if you have an appetizer as well. It's the perfect spot for special occasions, and if you are a true foodie with a passion for culinary perfection, it is not to be missed. Start with the blue cheese and plum tomato soup or a side of fingerling potatoes roasted in duck fat and garlic. For the entrée, dive into their signature seafood bouillabaisse chock-full of mussels, jumbo shrimp, premium fish, and lobster tails, or enjoy an herb-rubbed rack of Colorado lamb finished with a demi-glace of port and rosemary. Make sure and ask about recommended pairings from their extensive and impressive wine list. For dessert, indulge in your darkest chocolate fantasies with their chocolate truffle terrine served with a selection of fruits and berries

and drizzled in a delectable, heavenly caramel sauce. Chef Murphy has said, "What we do must be done perfectly, and we must be relentless in the pursuit of that perfection"; you can taste that commitment to perfection in every bite at the Beach Bistro.

A favorite restaurant on the north end of the island is the **Sandbar Waterfront Restaurant** (100 Spring Ave., 941/778-0444, 11:30am-10pm Sun.-Thurs., 11am-10pm Sat., 10am-10pm Sun., $10-25), which recently underwent an enormous renovation. It's the place to go for a sunset cocktail, lunch, dinner, or Sunday brunch on the beach. The covered deck has unimpeded views of the Gulf, and their signature grouper sandwich is excellent. They also serve excellent grouper tacos and a variety of seafood, steak, and pasta dishes.

Oma's Pizza (201 N. Gulf Dr., Bradenton Beach, 941/778-0771, 11am-midnight daily, $8-15) serves seriously delicious, big, and cheesy pizza with a thin crust. The lasagna is good, too. For more everyday dining, it's hard to go wrong with the barbecue at **Mr. Bones** (3007 Gulf Dr., Holmes Beach, 941/778-6614, 11am-9pm Mon.-Sat., noon-9pm Sun., $7-15), and it also has good Indian and Greek food—go figure.

Mainsail Beach Inn

ACCOMMODATIONS

My favorite place to stay on Anna Maria is the **Mainsail Beach Inn** (101 66th St., Holmes Beach, 888/849-2642, www.mainsailbeachinn. com, $250-500), one of Anna Maria Island's newest and most upscale lodgings. The Gulf of Mexico is a stone's throw from the stunning, vaulted-ceiling lobby. The two- and three-bedroom condos have full kitchens, spectacular Gulf views from the private balconies, and spacious master bathrooms. Choose between spending the day on Holmes Beach or relaxing by the heated pool and hot tub. At night, just walk right across the street to the Beach Bistro, one of Florida's top-ranking restaurants. No detail is overlooked at this hidden gem.

For something a little more affordable, stay at **Palm Tree Villas** (207 66th St., Holmes Beach, 941/778-0910, www.palm-treevillas.com, $150-250), an inviting, warm haven, whether it's for honeymooning couples or families. The low-rise Old Florida-style motel has been nicely refurbished, the well-appointed units clustered around a central courtyard and swimming pool. There's a great packet of literature in each villa.

Another favorite on the island is **Harrington House Beachfront Bed & Breakfast** (5626 Gulf Dr., Holmes Beach, 941/778-5444, www.harringtonhouse.com, $199-749), a converted 1925 coquina-brick beachfront house. Most rooms feature French doors opening onto balconies that overlook the heated swimming pool, the beach beyond, and the Gulf beyond that. The breakfasts here are legendary, there's a sweet little beach gazebo from which you can watch the sunset, and the common living room is a surefire place to start lively conversations with total strangers.

INFORMATION

For more information about the island, contact **Anna Maria Island Chamber of Commerce** (5313 Gulf Dr. N., Holmes Beach, FL 34217, 941/778-1541), and they'll send you a great packet of information and maps.

GETTING THERE

To reach Anna Maria Island from Sarasota, drive north on U.S. 301, then turn left onto County Road 64 (Manatee Avenue West). The 22-mile drive will take you about 50 minutes in normal traffic.

Sandbar Waterfront Restaurant

Information and Services

Sarasota and vicinity are located within the **eastern time zone.** The area code is **941.**

TOURIST INFORMATION

The **Sarasota Convention & Visitors Bureau** (official Sarasota Visitor Information Center, 701 N. Tamiami Trail, aka U.S. 41, 941/957-1877, www.visitsarasota.org, 10am-5pm Mon.-Sat.) and the **Sarasota Chamber of Commerce** (1945 Fruitville Rd., 941/955-8187, www.sarasotachamber.com, 8:30am-5pm Mon.-Fri.) both offer heaping piles of reading material on the area. The former has more useful material and a more central location.

Sarasota has its own daily newspaper, the **Sarasota Herald-Tribune,** with multiple zoned editions serving the area, along with a 24-hour television news station, **SNN.** Local weekly publications include the **Longboat Observer,** Siesta Key's **Pelican Press,** and a business newspaper, the **Business Observer.** Nine magazines cover different aspects of Sarasota County, from business to the arts and the social scene.

POLICE AND EMERGENCIES

In any emergency, dial 911 for immediate assistance. If you need the police in a nonemergency, contact the **Sarasota Police Department** (headquarters 2099 Adams Ln., 941/366-8000). For medical emergencies, or problems that just won't wait until you get home, the nicest facilities are at the emergency care center at **Sarasota Memorial Hospital** (1700 S. Tamiami Trail, 941/917-9000).

RADIO AND TELEVISION

Ten radio stations are located within Sarasota County, with 40 more stations in neighboring counties, including all major affiliates. Tune to **WLSS 930 AM** for news and talk radio; **WLTQ 92.1 FM** is easy favorites. You'll find National Public Radio at **89.7 FM.**

On television, **WFLA Channel 8** is the NBC affiliate, **WTVT Channel 13** is the FOX affiliate, and **WWSB Channel 7** is the ABC affiliate. There are additional public television and local news channels.

LAUNDRY SERVICES

One of the perks of renting a beach house is the reliable presence of non-coin-op laundry facilities on-site. Big resort hotels in Sarasota and on Longboat Key invariably offer laundry services. If you absolutely need a launderette, there are several in Sarasota, such as **All Star Laundry & Dry Cleaning** (2241 Bee Ridge Rd., 941/907-6814).

Tampa

Highlights

★ Spring Training: Tampa Bay has both the boys of summer and the boys of spring. You can see Tampa's own Rays during the regular season and the Grapefruit League's spring training at the end of February and in March (page 160).

★ Bayshore Boulevard: These five miles of sidewalk are bordered on one side by the wide-open bay and on the other side by Tampa's fanciest historic homes. Runners, walkers, bikers, and skaters take advantage of the amazing views and carefully maintained expanse (page 161).

★ Ybor City: Once known as the Cigar Capital of the World, Tampa's Latin Quarter is one of only three National Historic Landmark Districts in Florida. Today, it offers visitors historic shops by day and the city's most vital nightlife and dining (Cubano sandwich, anyone?) when the sun goes down (page 162).

★ Busch Gardens Tampa: This park is an unusual mix of thrill rides, animal attractions, and entertainment (page 164).

★ Florida Aquarium: This 152,000-square-foot aquarium focuses on Florida's relationship to the Gulf, estuaries, rivers, and other waterways, with a strong environmental message (page 167).

★ Tampa Theatre: The theater, ornately decorated to resemble an open Mediterranean courtyard, features 1,446 seats, 99 stars in the auditorium ceiling, and nearly 1,000 pipes in its mighty Wurlitzer theater organ (page 169).

Tampa is a family-friendly town with plenty of upscale restaurants and shopping. The University of South Florida (USF), University of Tampa, and Hillsborough Community College lend a bit of youth and liveliness.

Tampa is centrally located on the Florida Gulf Coast, with an exceptional airport—an ideal city to fly into for trips to the region. It is home to Busch Gardens; a large cruise ship port; great zoo and aquarium; professional football, baseball, and hockey teams; and affordable accommodations and restaurants.

Since Tampa isn't that old, it's not the best place for history lovers. It wasn't until Henry B. Plant extended his railroad into Tampa in 1884 and started a steamship line from Tampa to Key West to Havana, Cuba, that the city really began to grow. In 1891, Plant built the Tampa Bay Hotel, which launched the city as a winter resort for the northern elite. Around the same time, O. H. Platt created Tampa's first residential suburb, Hyde Park, which is still the residential area of choice for many wealthy citizens. The Old Hyde Park Village collection of boutiques and restaurants is one of the city's biggest draws.

Don Vicente Martinez Ybor, an influential cigar manufacturer and Cuban exile, moved his cigar business from Key West to land east of Tampa in 1885. His first cigar factory drew others, and the area's more than 200 cigar factories created a vivacious Latin community known as Ybor City. The area is now a mix of historic buildings, artisan shops, restaurants, and nightclubs.

Another Tampa neighborhood, Davis Islands, developed during the Florida land boom. Two little islands off downtown Tampa, where the Hillsborough River empties into Hillsborough Bay, became booming real estate developments. Today the islands are home to an airport, Tampa General Hospital, and more than 100 of the original homes.

Rapid growth continued through the Roaring Twenties. Since then, Tampa hasn't been buoyed by the tourist dollar to the degree other Gulf Coast cities have, and so they've been less susceptible to the ups and downs of Florida travel.

Previous: Raymond James Stadium; park in front of the Henry B. Plant Museum. **Above:** the iconic sign of the Tampa Theatre.

Unlike other urban centers along the Gulf, in Tampa there are no beaches to speak of. For beaches, you need to drive over the causeway to St. Pete or Clearwater (about 30 minutes from downtown Tampa).

PLANNING YOUR TIME

How long you spend vacationing in Tampa largely depends on whether you have kids in tow. Tampa is a paradise for kids. Obviously, the big kahuna is Busch Gardens, but that's just Day One. There are at least four or five other attractions worthy of a day of family focus.

Many people choose to visit Orlando's Disney attractions and then tack on a day or two at Tampa's Busch Gardens. While this is a perfectly fine strategy (Orlando's only an hour away), it may be too much of a good thing. However, Busch Gardens is quite different from Disney, with more of a focus on thrill rides and wildlife excursions. If you love theme parks, then make sure to visit Busch Gardens while you're in the area. If you are already spending a few days at Disney, consider coming to Tampa and renting a canoe, going to the zoo, visiting the science museum, and then heading over to Clearwater for a day of leisurely beach time.

As with much of the Gulf Coast, the fall and early spring are the most enjoyable weatherwise, with days in the low 80s and very dry. The summer is unrelentingly hot and humid, right through each afternoon's huge thunderstorm. The best beaches are Clearwater Beach, Fort De Soto Park, Honeymoon Island and Caladesi Island, St. Pete Beach, Madeira Beach, Sand Key County Park, and Egmont Key State Wildlife Preserve.

The best way to see the greater Tampa area

downtown Tampa

is with a car, especially if you want to explore some of the surrounding barrier islands. The area is served by **Tampa International Airport** (5503 W. Spruce St., 813/870-8700, www.tampaairport.com). If you just want to fly into Tampa and plan on staying downtown with occasional trips out to Clearwater and Busch Gardens, you can manage just fine with community transportation and taxis. I-75 runs down to Tampa from the north, I-4 brings visitors over from Orlando, and I-275 and Gandy Boulevard North both lead over to St. Pete, while West Courtney Campbell Causeway is the primary thoroughfare to Clearwater.

Tampa

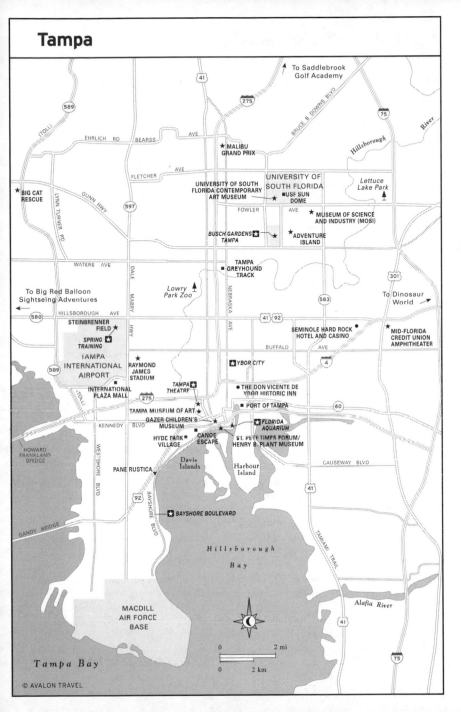

© AVALON TRAVEL

Sports and Recreation

LETTUCE LAKE PARK

If you're looking to get out in nature, head to **Lettuce Lake Park** (6920 E. Fletcher Ave., near the I-75 exit, 813/987-6204, 8am-8pm daily spring and summer, 8am-6pm daily fall and winter, $2/vehicle), just east of the University of South Florida. It's a stone's throw from urban sprawl, but don't hold that against it. The dense wilderness shelters a 3,500-foot-long raised boardwalk and a recently rebuilt tower overlooking the Hillsborough River, a perfect place from which to spy on tall wading birds, gators lurking among cypress knees in the swamp, or even delicate orchids and other epiphytes nestled in the trees' crooks. Rent a canoe for a closer look at the creatures that call this tannin-tinged water home, hike the fully accessible boardwalk or dirt trails (no dogs on the boardwalks), then settle in for a picnic at one of the waterfront shelters, equipped with barbecues. A kids' playground, restrooms, and water fountains make this wilderness park much more comfortable.

CANOEING

You want to see big gators? Great blue herons, river otters, turtles, and more fish than you can string on a lifetime of lines? Paddle down the gently flowing Hillsborough River in a 16,000-acre wildlife preserve called **Wilderness Park.** You can rent canoes or kayaks and head out on your own, choosing from six different self-guided day trips. All paddling adventures start at **Canoe Escape** (12702 U.S. 301, Thonotosassa, 4.5 miles east of I-75, 813/986-2067, www.canoeescape.com). Whether you go on a guided tour or on your own, call ahead. Staff will equip you, give you maps and paddling pointers, then take you over to your debarkation point (all paddles are downstream) and establish a pickup time.

The Sargeant Park to Morris Bridge Park trip is a two-hour paddle, 4.5 miles long, with 70 percent shade and alternating sun and shade. Morris Bridge Park to Trout Creek Park is a two-hour, 4-mile paddle, with 80 percent shade and a little full sun at the end. From Trout Creek Park to Rotary Park it's 5 miles of full-sun paddling, about two hours, whereas Sargeant Park to Trout Creek Park is a longer, 8.5-mile paddle with the first 75 percent in the shade. Morris Bridge Park to Rotary Park is a long, 9-mile route, and Sargeant Park to Rotary Park is for experienced paddlers only, with 14 miles of river to paddle.

Self-guided rentals are $49-69 per paddler for a tandem canoe or kayak depending on the trip (a child under 12 can usually fit as a center passenger). A solo kayak ranges $46-56. Prices include shuttle fee, paddles, and life vests. If solo paddling seems daunting, Canoe Escape offers a 4.5-mile interpreted guided tour for $75 per person for solo kayakers and $50 per person for tandem canoes. I'd recommend this for the newcomer to the area because the guides' vast knowledge of the local flora and fauna enrich the trip immeasurably.

GOLF

If you are thinking about picking up the sport, the **Saddlebrook Golf Academy** at the Saddlebrook Resort (5700 Saddlebrook Way, Wesley Chapel, 813/973-1111, www.saddlebrook.com) teaches golfers of all skill levels. Classes combine classroom and practice time with course play. The New Player Academy and all the other packages include accommodations, 18 holes of golf a day, instruction, meals, and use of resort facilities. There are two 18-hole Palmer-designed championship courses on the property, as well as 45 tennis courts in the four Grand Slam surfaces (the resort is also home to the **Hopman Tennis Program**).

SPECTATOR SPORTS

Tampa Bay sports fans are fanatical about their professional sporting franchises. And

Tampa Golfing

Tampa has a couple of dozen public and semiprivate courses for the visitor to try. Many of them are open to the public but located in Tampa's swankier northeast residential developments. Here are a handful of the area's top public courses:

Babe Zaharias Golf Club
11412 Forest Hills Dr., 813/631-4374, www.babezahariasgolf.net
18 holes, 6,244 yards, par 70, course rating 68.9, slope 121
Greens fees: $16-32

Heritage Isles Golf & Country Club
10630 Plantation Bay Dr., 813/907-7388, www.heritageislegolf.com
18 holes, 6,976 yards, par 72, course rating 73.2, slope 132
Greens fees: $18-35

Rocky Point Golf Course
4151 Dana Shores Dr., 813/673-4316, www.rockypointgolf.net
18 holes, 6,444 yards, par 71, course rating 71.7, slope 122
Greens fees: $16-21

Rogers Park Golf Course
7911 N. Willie Black Dr., 813/356-1670, www.rogersparkgolf.net
18 holes, 6,802 yards, par 71, course rating 72.3, slope 125
Greens fees: $16-40

TPC Tampa Bay
5300 W. Lutz Lake Fern Rd., Lutz, 813/949-0090, www.tpctampabay.com
18 holes, 6,898 yards, par 71, course rating 73.6, slope 135
Greens fees: $65-105, $20 for Juniors

University of South Florida Golf Course (also called "The Claw")
4202 E. Fowler Ave., 813/632-6893, www.theclawatusfgolf.com
18 holes, 6,863 yards, par 71, course rating 74.2, slope 132
Greens fees: $13-32

Westchase Golf Course
11602 Westchase Golf Dr., 813/854-2331, www.westchasegc.com
18 holes, par 72, 6,699 yards, course rating 72.6, slope 131
Greens fees: $17-54

why shouldn't they be? There are the Tampa Bay Buccaneers for football, Tampa Bay Lightning for hockey, Tampa Bay Rays for baseball (not to mention spring training for the New York Yankees, Philadelphia Phillies, Toronto Blue Jays, and their own Rays spread around the Bay Area), Tampa Bay Storm pro arena football (five-time world champs), and the gamut of University of South Florida Bulls athletics.

Tampa Bay Buccaneers
Raymond James Stadium (4201 N. Dale Mabry Hwy.) is a wonderful venue in which to see Tampa's beloved **Buccaneers** (813/350-6500, www.buccaneers.com) play. The stadium, completed in 1998, holds more than 66,000 fans—52,000 in general seating—but tickets sometimes sell out for the season opener and other big games. Tickets for individual games are sold in person at TicketMaster outlets, on the phone at 800/745-3000, and by visiting www.ticketmaster.com, or at the Raymond James Ticket Box three hours prior to kickoff on game days. Tickets for the 16 regular season games September-December are $55 for general admission; special seats range from $400 on down. The

$168.5 million stadium features Buccaneer Cove, a 20,000-square-foot replica of an early 1800s seaport village, complete with a 103-foot-long, 43-ton pirate ship that blasts its cannons (confetti and foam footballs) every time the Bucs score. Well, six times for a touchdown, once for an extra point, twice for a safety or two-point conversion, and three times for a field goal.

Raymond James also plays host every New Year's Day to football's **Outback Bowl** (Raymond James Stadium, 813/287-8844, 11am kickoff, $80). The game matches the third-pick team from the SEC and the third-pick team from the Big Ten Conference and is the culmination of a weeklong festival in Tampa.

USF Bulls

The University of South Florida **football team** (800/462-8557, game schedule varies, individual tickets $20-31), the USF Bulls have gone from nonexistence to Division I-AA Independent to I-A to Conference USA, and into the Big East Conference in 2005. For the spectator, this means real college football is played during the fall, at **Raymond James Stadium** (4201 N. Dale Mabry Hwy.).

Bulls' **basketball** (813/974-3002, tickets

$11-27) has also been notched up in recent years, resulting in the team moving to the Big East Conference. Home games are played at the **USF Sun Dome** (4202 E. Fowler Ave.).

Tampa Bay Storm

The local arena football team, the **Tampa Bay Storm** (813/301-6500, upper-level tickets $10-35, lower $35-150), five-time ArenaBowl champs, plays at the **St. Pete Times Forum** (401 Channelside Dr.). Arena football is played on an indoor padded surface 85 feet wide and 50 yards long, with eight-yard end zones. There are eight players on the field at a time, and everyone plays both offense and defense, with the exception of the kicker, quarterback, offensive specialist, and two defensive specialists. It's a dynamic game in a more intimate space, and the Storm provides a good introduction, having made it to the playoffs for 16 consecutive seasons.

Tampa Bay Lightning

The 21,000-seat, $153 million **Amalie Arena** (401 Channelside Dr.), on Tampa's downtown waterfront, is home to Tampa's professional hockey team, the **Tampa Bay Lightning** (813/301-6600, game times vary, tickets

Raymond James Stadium, home of the Tampa Bay Buccaneers

Lightning Strikes

Almost nobody is killed by alligators in Tampa. Hardly anyone is even roughed up by them. Lightning is much more deadly in Florida. In fact, about 50 people are struck by lightning each year in the state. Most of them are hospitalized and recover, but there are about 10 fatalities annually. The Tampa area is the Lightning Capital of the United States (Rwanda is the lightning capital of the world), with around 25 cloud-to-ground lightning bolt blasts on each square mile annually. The temperature of a single bolt can reach 50,000°F, about three times as hot as the sun's surface.

The problem is the tropical afternoon thunderstorms each summer, about 90 of them electrical storms. Short-lived but intense, the storms' clouds are charged like giant capacitors, the upper portion of the cloud positively charged and the lower portion negatively charged. Current flows between the negative cloud bottom and the top or, in the case of cloud-to-ground lightning, the positively charged earth's surface. This discharge of current substantiates the adage "opposites attract," and bolts, sheets, ribbons, and, rarely, balls of lightning hit the ground.

There's not much you can do to ward off lightning except to avoid being in the wrong place at the wrong time. The summer months of June, July, August, and September have the highest number of lightning-related injuries and deaths. Usually lightning occurs during daylight hours, with the highest concentration between 3pm and 4pm, when the afternoon storms peak. Lightning strikes usually occur either at the beginning or end of a storm and can strike up to 10 miles away from the center of the storm.

Still, 9 out of 10 people survive being struck. As long as the electrical surge is not to your brain, you are likely to be treatable. A lightning strike will often singe and burn a person's skin or clothes, but even when the electrical surge stops a victim's heart, emergency rooms have a high success rate of restarting the ticker.

TIPS

- Stay vigilant and go inside as soon as clouds darken and thunderstorms develop.

- If the time between seeing the lightning flash and hearing the thunder is less than 30 seconds, take shelter.

- Stay away from the Gulf, pools, lakes, or other bodies of water.

- Avoid using a tree or other tall object as shelter. Lightning usually strikes the tallest object in a given area.

- Stay away from metal objects (bikes, golf carts, and fencing are bad, but a car's rubber tires render the automobile's interior a safe retreat).

- The safest place to be during an electrical storm is inside and away from windows and electrical appliances.

$15-349), Stanley Cup champions in 2004. Its season runs October-April.

Tampa Bay Rays

Tampa is also home to Major League Baseball's **Tampa Bay Rays** (888/326-7297, game days vary, times usually 2:15pm or 7:15pm, tickets $18-80). Their first season was 1998. The Rays (formerly the Devil Rays) play at **Tropicana Field** in St. Petersburg (1 Tropicana Dr.). As a concession to summer temperatures and humidity in these parts, the ballpark has a dome roof (which is lit orange when the Rays win at home) and artificial turf.

There has been a great deal of dissatisfaction from Rays' fans with Tropicana Field over the years. The park is known for a heartbreakingly long list of lasts. It is the last park in Major League Baseball to have a retractable roof, the last of two parks to use artificial turf on their field instead of the fan-preferred natural grass. Tropicana Field is also consistently ranked last in stadium rankings by *USA Today* and ESPN, and the Rays' games had the worst attendance record for the 2015 season (they have never made it above rank 22 since 2001). However, the low attendance record can't be blamed on the team's poor performance. Since 2008 the Rays have been to the playoffs three times and made the trip to the World Series in 2008 but lost to the Phillies.

The devil of the problem for the Rays seems to be in the park's details. The ball field is more than 20 miles from Tampa where the majority of residents in the area live, and fans are separated from the park by often unbearable traffic over the bridge. The interior of the stadium is about as aesthetically unpleasing as ballparks come, from the dumpy-looking artificial turf field to the distracting metal rafters of the dome that occasionally obstruct high fly balls. The difficulty of finding decent parking is also a common complaint.

★ SPRING TRAINING

If you're in the area during spring training time, you can also catch the Rays at the **Charlotte Sports Park** (2300 El Jobean Rd., Port Charlotte, 941/206-4487, www.tampabayrays.com, $15-31), their spring training home. In the past for spring training the Rays

played at **Progress Energy Park, Home of Al Lang Field.** The stadium in Port Charlotte has a 7,000-person capacity and a natural grass field and received a $27.2 million renovation to bring it up to modern standards for the Rays.

Even with the departure of the Rays, the Grapefruit League's spring training remains a serious draw for sports fans each March. Since 1988 the **New York Yankees** have based their minor-league operation, spring training, and year-round headquarters for player development in Tampa. Modeled after the original Yankee Stadium in the Bronx, **Steinbrenner Field** (1 Steinbrenner Dr., off N. Dale Mabry Hwy., 813/875-7753, www.steinbrennerfield.com, $15-31) has been the Yankees' home since 1996. The complex houses a 10,000-seat stadium with 13 swanky luxury suites, a community-use field, and a major league practice field. It's also the home of the five-time **Florida State League Champion's Tampa Yankees** (New York Yankees-Florida State League Single "A" Affiliate) and the **Hillsborough Community College Hawks** baseball team.

Other spring training venues require only a short drive: the **Philadelphia Phillies** play at **Bright House Networks Field** in

Steinbrenner Field

Clearwater; the **Boston Red Sox** play in **Jetblue Park** and the **Minnesota Twins** play at **Hammond Stadium,** both in Fort Myers; the **Toronto Blue Jays** play at **Knology Park** in Dunedin; the **Baltimore Orioles** play at **Ed Smith Stadium** in Sarasota; and the **Pittsburgh Pirates** play at **McKechnie Field** in Bradenton.

Sights

MUSEUMS

The **Tampa Museum of Art** (120 W. Gasparilla Plaza, 813/274-8130, www.tampa-museum.org, 11am-7pm Mon.-Thurs., 11am-8pm Fri., 11am-5pm Sat.-Sun., $10 adults, $7.50 seniors, $5 students and children over 6, children under 6 free) moved to an impressive, new, 60,000-square-foot facility on February 6, 2010. It hosts changing exhibitions ranging from contemporary to classical, and showcases its permanent collection of Greek and Roman antiquities, 20th- and 21st-century sculpture, paintings, photography, and works on paper.

The **Henry B. Plant Museum** (401 W. Kennedy Blvd., 813/254-1891, www.ut.edu/plantmuseum, 10am-5pm Tues.-Sat., noon-5pm Sun. Jan.-Nov., $10 adults, $7 students and seniors, $5 children under 12) is housed in the dramatic hotel that railroad magnate Henry B. Plant built in 1891 at a cost of $2.5 million, with an additional $500,000 for furnishings. Its 511 rooms were the first in Florida to be outfitted with electricity. It operated as a hotel until 1930 and is now part of the University of Tampa. The museum consists of opulent restored rooms with original furnishings that provide a window on America's Gilded Age, Tampa's history, and the life and work of Henry Plant. The best time to see it is at Christmastime, when the rooms are bedecked for the season with elaborately trimmed trees, lush greenery, antique toys, and Victorian-era ornaments.

University of South Florida is an enormous institution, casting its imposing shadow on the cultural scene of Tampa. The visitor, however, may have little reason to walk around the less-than-picturesque campus.

A visit to the **University of South Florida Contemporary Art Museum** (3821 USF Holly Dr., 813/974-4133, 10am-5pm Mon.-Fri., 1pm-4pm Sat., free) is a good excuse to drive around the university before parking at the small gallery. USFCAM maintains the university's art collection, comprising more than 5,000 artworks. There are exceptional holdings in graphics and sculpture multiples by internationally acclaimed artists, such as Roy Lichtenstein, Robert Rauschenberg, and James Rosenquist, who have worked at USF's Graphicstudio. Contemporary photography and African art are also represented. The museum hosts USF student art shows and oversees public art projects on campus.

★ BAYSHORE BOULEVARD

Bayshore Boulevard may or may not be the world's longest continuous sidewalk, but it borders Tampa Bay for nearly five miles without a break in the gorgeousness. Joggers, walkers, skaters, and bikers dot its length, which goes from downtown through Hyde Park. Lined with the fanciest homes in Tampa, the boulevard was named one of AAA's Top Roads for its panoramic views. If you don't feel like walking it, it's Tampa's signature drive. (Also, Tampa Preservation has an excellent driving tour of Hyde Park and a walking tour of part of the neighborhood geared for younger travelers; for copies call 813/248-5437 or go to www.tampapreservation.org/heritage-education.)

BIG CAT RESCUE

The world's largest accredited sanctuary for big cats, **Big Cat Rescue** (12802 Easy St., across from Citrus Park Town Center down a dirt road next to McDonald's, 813/920-4130, www.bigcatrescue.org) provides a permanent retirement home to over 200 animals. For the visitor, the center offers tours, outreach presentations, animal interaction, and the opportunity to spend an evening in the heart of the sanctuary. Regular tours run at 3pm Monday-Wednesday and Friday-Sun., and 10am Saturday-Sunday; a children's tour is at noon Saturday and Sunday, feeding tours are 9am Friday-Sunday. Prices vary by tour: regular tours are $36 (for ages 10 and over), children's tours $19, feeding tours $65. On the last Friday of each month, register for the Wild Eyes at Night tour (at dark), in which guests roam the grounds equipped with flashlights that illuminate the hundreds of shining eyes in the cat enclosures.

BIG RED BALLOON SIGHTSEEING ADVENTURES

Big Red Balloon Sightseeing Adventures (8710 W. Hillsborough Ave., 813/969-1518, www.bigredballoon.com, 6am-10am daily, year-round by reservation only, weather permitting, $185 adults, $160 children) takes you up, up, and away in a beautiful hot-air balloon, and all you have to bring is a camera and your loved ones. Meet before dawn at a restaurant on the commerce strip of Dale Mabry (**Mimi's Café,** 11702 N. Dale Mabry Hwy.), where you are whisked into the Red Balloon van and taken to your agreed-upon launch site (there are more than 30 in the greater Tampa area from which to choose). Once inflated, the solid red balloon, the largest in the southeastern United States, is 8.5 stories tall and contains 210,000 cubic feet of air. The balloon, which comfortably accommodates eight passengers, takes a one-hour sunrise flight up to 1,000 feet, drifting over New Tampa, southeast Pasco County, Lutz, and Land O' Lakes. A champagne toast followed by a hearty breakfast back at Mimi's is included in the price.

After landing in a field, the pilot makes the champagne toast and recites a traditional

Henry B. Plant Museum

balloonist prayer, "The winds have welcomed you with softness, the sun has left you with warm hands, you have flown so high, and so well, that God has joined you in your laughter, and set you gently back again into the loving arms of Mother Earth." Feel free to join in.

★ YBOR CITY

Cigar makers Vicente Martinez Ybor and Ignacio Haya moved their cigar factories from Key West to Tampa in 1886, essentially settling 40 acres of uninviting scrubland northeast of the city. A railroad, a port, and a climate that acted as a natural humidor—Tampa had all the ingredients for cigar success. Soon other cigar factories joined suit until there were 140 cigar factories in the area producing 250 million cigars a year. The new Cigar Capital of the World became home to Cuban, Spanish, and Italian immigrants who worked the factories. These workers, both men and women, would hand-roll several kinds of tobacco into the signature shapes and sizes while listening to "lectors" read

Pasco County Excursion

Naked people. That got your attention. The sleepy, mostly residential county to Tampa's north, Pasco County, has at least a day's worth of a unique brand of fun, definitely worth a side trip, a couple of meals, and maybe even an overnight at one of the area's most upscale spa/golf/tennis resorts.

Lake Como Family Nudist Resort in the town of Land O' Lakes is the area's original nudist community, started in 1947. Since then, Pasco County has become a hotbed of naturist activity, with six all-ages nudist communities and recreational activities. These days the biggest player is the 120-acre **Caliente Club and Resort** (21240 Gran Via Blvd., Land O' Lakes, 813/996-3700).

Another Pasco original requiring a bit of courage is **Skydive City** (4241 Skydive Ln., off Chancey Rd., 813/783-9399, www.skydivecity.com, $199, plus $95 if you want the video documenting your experience) in Zephyrhills. The town has been a world-famous "drop zone" since the 1960s. Why here? According to owner T. K. Hayes, "It's in the middle of nowhere. It's really about the people—Zephyrhills is the largest skydiving place in the world." Tandem jumping (where a rookie jumps physically harnessed to an instructor) has opened skydiving up to people who never would have had the opportunity—the elderly, people with disabilities—really, anyone can do it.

If jumping out of an airplane sounds doable: It takes about an hour to prepare, with a 20-minute briefing. The whole experience is a three- to four-hour adventure, with free fall at 120 mph for about a minute from 13,500 feet, followed by up to six minutes of steering with the parachute open. Hayes says he's never had a student fatality or serious injury.

After that, take it down a notch and enjoy a walking tour of downtown **Dade City.** In the rolling hills of eastern Pasco County, the town has more than 50 antiques stores, gift shops, and boutiques. Stop into the historic 1909 Pasco County Courthouse and look at the sweet collection of artifacts from the turn of the 20th century. And then have a slice of pie at **Lunch on Limoges** (14139 7th St., 352/567-5685, www.lunchonlimoges.com, $12-18). It's a charming throwback to a former era of structured and unhurried lunching, with a daily-changing menu served on Limoges china by waitresses in nurses' uniforms.

Not far from downtown and usually taking about an hour, the **Pioneer Florida Museum** (15602 Pioneer Museum Rd., 352/567-0328, www.pioneerfloridamuseum.org, 10am-5pm Tues.-Sat., $8 adults, $6 seniors, $4 students and children 6-18, children under 6 and active-duty military free) consists of nine period buildings dating back to 1878. There's the John Overstreet House, the Lacoochee School, and the Enterprise Methodist Church, all displaying period furniture, clothing, toys, and tools.

If there's time, take a tour around **New Port Richey's Main Street** (walking tour maps at www.nprmainstreet.com) and then board a boat and ride the **Pithlachascottee River** to see historic homes once owned by Gloria Swanson, Thomas Meighan, and Babe Ruth. Then walk around **Centennial Park,** which contains the Pasco Fine Arts Council, the Centennial Library, and the 1882 Baker House, one of the oldest structures in Pasco County. If you're hungry, stop in at the waterside **Catches** (7811 Bayview St., 727/849-2121, $15-30).

If you're thinking about bedtime now, **Saddlebrook Resort & Spa** (5700 Saddlebrook Way, 813/973-1111, $200-500) is Tampa's nicest four-star resort hotel, only it's in the sleepy Pasco town of Wesley Chapel. It has 800 guest rooms, all beautiful, pools, tennis, the Palmer and the Saddlebrook golf courses (and the Saddlebrook Golf Academy), and a variety of dining options (if you eat on the Tropics Terrace you can see nesting wood storks).

For more information about Pasco County, visit www.visitpasco.net.

TAMPA SIGHTS

aloud great works of literature and the day's news. (For a window into this world, read Nilo Cruz's Pulitzer Prize-winning drama, *Anna in the Tropics*, which depicts a Cuban American family of cigar makers in Ybor City in 1930.)

The area flourished until the early 1960s, when embargos against Cuban tobacco and declining cigar consumption (coincident with the ascendance of the cigarette as the smoke of choice) caused the market to dry up.

Today Ybor City is one of only three National Historic Landmark Districts in Florida, with redbrick streets, wrought-iron balconies, and old-timey globe street lamps.

During the day visitors can still see cigars being hand-rolled and enjoy an authentic Cubano sandwich (invented here, some say), while at night Ybor is the city's nightlife district, drawing 40,000 visitors on weekends to dine at sidewalk cafés and drink and dance at nightclubs. Whether you explore during the day or at night, park your car in one of the many parking lots or garages (metered parking is strictly enforced 24 hours) and walk around or take the Ybor City trolley. You can still see little cigar shops and Latin social clubs mixed in with tattoo parlors and restaurants along La Setima (7th Ave.).

The **Ybor City Museum State Park** (1818 E. 9th Ave., 813/247-6323, www.ybormuseum.org, 9am-5pm daily, $4 adults, children under 5 free) contains photographs, cigar boxes, and other artifacts of the neighborhood's rich history. Another book, *The Immigrant World of Ybor City: Italians and Their Latin Neighbors in Tampa, 1885-1985* (Florida Sand Dollar Books) by Gary Mormino and George E. Pozzetta (University Press of Florida, 1998), is a wealth of information. Another good one is called *Urban Vigilantes in the New South: Tampa, Florida 1886-1936* (Florida Sand Dollar Books) by Robert P. Ingalls (University Press of Florida, reprint edition, 1993).

But still, you may get a more three-dimensional look at Ybor just by walking around: Walk by the **La Union Marti-Maceo mural** (226 7th Ave.), pick up a copy of *La Gaceta* (the neighborhood's Spanish-language weekly for the past 75 years), and walk by the restored former cigar workers' casitas on your way to get a Cubano sandwich, or buy a cigar at **Metropolitan Cigars** (2014 E. 7th Ave., 813/248-3304, 10am-8pm Mon.-Fri., 10am-4pm Sat.-Sun.), a 1,700-square-foot walk-in humidor.

Ybor City

FAMILY-FRIENDLY ATTRACTIONS

Of all the Gulf Coast cities, Tampa has the most lavish smorgasbord of kid-friendly attractions. This probably reflects the demographics of Tampa in recent years—it's a family town, wherein weekends are devoted, after Little League/soccer games/getting the car washed, to multigenerational outings to Busch Gardens, Adventure Island, the zoo, the aquarium, or the area's many sporting events.

★ Busch Gardens Tampa

How many people can say they rode on a Cheetah, a Tidal Wave, and a Congo River Rapid all in one day? You can join the ranks of the thrill-seeking elite with a quick trip to **Busch Gardens Tampa** (10165 N. Malcolm McKinley Dr., 888/800-5447, www.buschgardens.com). Busch Gardens is half high-energy amusement park and half first-class zoo. With somewhat of a personality disorder, this is the only park I know where you can alternate

Cigar Basics

handrolled cigars

Want to try a cigar but don't know the first thing? Tampa's a good place to begin. Even before you light up, a cigar's visual specifications can give clues to its character. The outer wrapper's color indicates a great deal about a cigar's flavor. A *maduro* wrapper is a rich, deep brown, imparting a cigar with deep, strong flavors. A *claro* wrapper, on the other hand, is a light tan and lends little additional flavor to a cigar. There are essentially six color grades. Roughly from lightest to darkest, these are *candela* (pale green), *claro, natural* (light brown), *colorado* (reddish brown), *maduro,* and *oscuro* (almost black).

Shape is another central factor in cigar selection. Among *parejos,* or straight sided cigars, there are three basic categories. A *corona* is classically six inches long, with an open foot (the end that is lighted) and a closed head (the end that is smoked). Within this category, Churchills are a bit longer and thicker, *robustos* are shorter and much thicker, and a *double corona* is significantly longer. *Panetelas,* the second category, are longer and much thinner than *coronas,* and the third category, *lonsdales,* are thicker than *panetelas* and thinner and longer than *coronas.*

Figurados comprise the other class of cigar, which spans all of the irregularly shaped types. This includes torpedo shapes, braided *culebras,* and pyramid shapes that have a closed, pointed head and an open foot.

A cigar band is generally wrapped around the closed head of a cigar. Its original function was to minimize finger staining, not to identify brands. Nonetheless, on the band you will find the name a manufacturer has designated for a particular line of cigars—names like Partagas, Macanudo, Punch, and Montecristo. Keep in mind that after 1959, many cigar manufacturers fled Cuba to open shop elsewhere, taking their brand names with them. Thus, a brand name does not always betray a cigar's country of origin.

For neophytes lighting up for the first time, a milder cigar may ease you in. The Macanudo Hyde Park is a mild smoke, as is the Don Diego Playboy Robusto or Lonsdale. For a fuller-bodied cigar, the Punch Diademas and the Partagas Number 10 are both popular. If you're looking for a robust, ultra full-bodied taste, you might try the Hoyo de Monterrey Double Corona. The best way to discover your own personal tastes is to stop into a tobacconist or cigar-friendly restaurant and have a chat.

between petting zoos and twisting, turning, high-speed roller coasters.

Rides for Little Kids: The amusement park has a huge section geared to children 2-7 years old (in a Sesame Street-centric part of the park to the far left when you're looking at the map, near **Stanleyville,** as well as in sections near the **Congo** and in **Timbuktu**).

Rides for Big Kids: Major coasters are the biggest draw for those over 48 inches tall (for the new Cheetah Hunt, Montu, SheiKra, and Kumba it's 54 inches) and with no serious health problems. The rides at Busch Gardens are either little-kiddie or pee-your-pants huge. The roller coasters, in descending order of excellence: The **Cheetah Hunt** is the newest coaster in the park and opened in May 2011 next to the new Cheetah exhibit that features large panels of glass where you can watch cheetahs sprinting across large fields. At the coaster's climax it reaches a top speed of 60 mph before climbing a nearly vertical 102-foot hill and then plunging down 130 feet for a bit of heart-in-your-throat fun. **Montu,** at the far right of the park, is one of the tallest and longest inverted roller coasters in the world. You are strapped in from above, so your feet dangle while you travel at 60 mph through 60-foot vertical loops. The **SheiKra** has got an incredible 90-degrees-straight-down thrill at the beginning, an underground tunnel, speeds of 70 mph, and water features late in the ride. The ride is a little short, so in 2007 it went floorless to add another level of thrill. **Kumba** is fourth best, with a full three seconds of weightlessness, an initial 135-foot drop, and cool 360-degree spirals. It offers good speed, a long ride, and one of the world's largest vertical loops. And the **Gwazi** is for purists—an old double wooden coaster, it's got that tooth-rattling charm as it barrels over the boards in 7,000 feet of track.

Beyond the coasters, the **Tidal Wave, Stanley Falls,** and **Congo River Rapids** boat ride are guaranteed to fully saturate you, so time them for the hottest part of the day.

Animal Attractions: Busch Gardens contains more than 2,700 animals. Colorful lorikeets will land on your shoulder in the aviary called **Lory Landing,** and there's a **Birds of Prey** show. The best animal attraction is the **Serengeti Plain,** which takes up the whole right half of the park—you see it all by getting on the Serengeti Express Railway (or the Skyride or a Serengeti Safari). Ostriches may race the train, and there are big cats and huffing rhinos. It's thrilling *and* a wonderful opportunity to sit down a spell and regroup.

In spring 2008, the park opened **Jungala.** Set in the Congo area, the four-acre attraction has guests mingling with exotic creatures, exploring a village hidden deep in the jungle, and connecting with the inhabitants of the lush landscape through up-close animal interactions, multistory family play areas, rides, and live entertainment.

The Details: Busch Gardens is expensive ($75 adults for one weekday, $89 for two days, children 2 and under free), so is it worth it? Definitely. It is a wonderful full-day extravaganza for people of any age (if you don't like rides, go to Beer School, where you can learn about the process of making beer and then get what you really came for—free samples). Busch Gardens can entertain you for a full two days, but if you do just one day, everyone will be clamoring for more. A 14-day, five-park **Orlando FlexTicket** ($355 adults, $335 kids) is a good deal if you have the stamina to hit SeaWorld Orlando, Universal Studios Florida, Islands of Adventure, and Wet 'n' Wild along with Busch Gardens.

Hours change seasonally: In the winter, it's generally open 9:30am-6pm daily; in the summer 9am-10pm daily. If you visit in the summer, count on heavy rains in the afternoon. Bathrooms are plentiful and clean, there are plenty of strollers to rent, the food is much better than it needs to be (Zambia Smokehouse serves good ribs and chicken), and there's even a dog kennel to watch your pet while you enjoy the park. The park is eight miles northeast of downtown Tampa. Parking is an irritating additional $10, with a free shuttle that takes you from the 5,000-spot parking lot to the park's entrance.

★ Florida Aquarium

The 152,000-square-foot **Florida Aquarium** (701 Channelside Dr., 813/273-4000, www.flaquarium.org, 9:30am-5pm daily, $23.95 adults, $20.95 seniors, $18.95 children under 12) is smart, focusing on the waters of Florida. It doesn't contain an exhaustive catalog of the world's aquatic creatures, but it tells a compelling story about Florida's relationship to the Gulf, estuaries, rivers, and other waterways. There are some exotic exhibits (the otherworldly sea dragons, like sea horses mated with philodendrons), but the best parts are the open freshwater tanks of otters, spoonbills, gators, Florida softshell turtles, and snakes. The aquarium manages to have a strong environmental message in its natives-versus-exotics exhibits, but it's all fun, never seeming heavy-handed. There's also a wonderful big shark tank, a colorful coral grotto, and a sea-urchin touch tank. It's a small enough aquarium that three hours is plenty of time, and not so crowded that kids can't do a little wandering on their own. Regularly scheduled shows involve native Florida birds and small mammals, as well as shark feeding (in fact, the aquarium offers "swim with the fishes" wetsuit dives into the shark tank for the stalwart). A cell phone audio tour may be the coolest thing yet.

After perusing the marinelife within the eye-catching, shell-shaped building, you can take your newfound knowledge out on the bay on an aquarium-run **Wild Dolphin Cruise** (813/273-4000, passes are offered as a combo ticket that includes admission, $49.90 adults, $44.90 seniors, $40.90 children 3-11, free for children 2 and under). Tampa Bay is home to more than 400 bottlenose dolphins. Tickets are available at the aquarium box office the day of the tour only, when you'll head out in a 64-foot, 49-passenger Caribbean catamaran, watching all the while for dolphins, manatees, and a huge number of migratory birds.

Museum of Science & Industry (MOSI)

You spent a day riding the rides at Busch Gardens, then a day with the fishes at the aquarium, what next? The third day is Tampa's **Museum of Science & Industry** (4801 E. Fowler Ave., 813/987-6000, www.mosi.org, 10am-5pm Mon.-Fri., 10am-6pm Sat.-Sun., $22.95 adults, $20.95 seniors, $18.95 children 2-12), a wonderful resource for local schools, family vacationers, or local parents. It's a sprawling modern

the Florida Aquarium in downtown Tampa

structure that contains 450 hands-on activities grouped into learning areas. There's some unique and fun stuff like the Gulf Coast Hurricane Chamber, which blows air at an incredible speed to simulate standing in the eye wall of a hurricane, and the High Wire Bicycle, the longest high-wire bike in a museum, which allows visitors to pedal while balanced on a one-inch steel cable suspended 30 feet above the ground. The Amazing You exhibit teaches all about the human body. The museum has an IMAX dome and—get this—the admission price to the museum includes one free viewing of an IMAX film. The museum hosts traveling exhibits as well. Through interactive exhibits, film, and immersion experiences, guests explore the principles of simple mechanics, optics, electromagnetism, math, and psychology.

If you time your visit to allow for some cooler temperatures, the free-flying butterfly garden is a treat, with microscope viewing, magnifying glasses, and chemistry stations.

Lowry Park Zoo

This zoo has recently made the overt decision to take it to the Big Time, going mano a mano with San Diego and the other big zoo kahunas. To this end, it imported four African elephants and created a huge habitat for them. (The previous elephant program was curtailed years ago when a trainer was killed by a panicked pachyderm.)

At the **Lowry Park Zoo** (1101 W. Sligh Ave., 813/935-8552, www.lowryparkzoo.com, 9:30am-5pm daily, $27.95 adults, $25.95 seniors, $20.95 children 3-11), habitats are naturalistic and nicely landscaped, but they are still designed for maximum viewing. All told there are around 2,000 native and exotic animals (white tiger cubs are a big draw), organized into reasonable housing developments, such as Wallaroo Station and Safari Africa. Lots of shade provided by big tropical plants seems to keep all the species comfortable, even in the fairly substantial summer heat. One of the zoo's highlights is its Manatee and Aquatic Center, one of only three hospitals and rehabilitation facilities in the state of Florida for sick sea cows.

Adventure Island

Adjacent to Busch Gardens but only open mid-March-October is **Adventure Island** (10001 N. McKinley Dr., 888/800-5447, www.adventureisland.com, $44 visitors 3 and up). Hours and days of operation vary here, and the park is closed during the winter. It's a 30-acre water park, with slides, corkscrews, waterfalls, and a monstrous 17,000-square-foot wave pool, and a children's play area. There are 50 lifeguards on duty, but it's still only appropriate for the truly water-safe. There's also a championship white-sand volleyball complex. If you buy a ticket to Busch Gardens, you can combine it with a ticket here for a discount.

Malibu Grand Prix

If they've been really, really good, take the kids to **Malibu Grand Prix** (14320 N. Nebraska Ave., 813/977-6272, www.grandprixtampa.com, 10am-9pm Sun.-Thurs., 10am-midnight Fri.-Sat., $6-50, depending on the activity). It's got killer miniature golf with lots of windmills, pagodas, and water play, Grand Prix-style go-cart racing, batting cages, and a frenetic game room with a wide variety of video games.

Glazer Children's Museum

Very young children (up to 10) will be more suited to an afternoon at the **Glazer Children's Museum** (110 W. Gasparilla Plaza, 813/443-3861, www.glazermuseum.org, 10am-5pm Mon.-Fri., 10am-6pm Sat., 1pm-6pm Sun., $15 adults, $12.50 seniors and military, $9.50 children). In kind of a miniature outdoor city, it has over 170 exhibits in 12 themed areas with hands-on exhibits about different kinds of work and play (a cruise ship, a mini-theater, a giant telescope, grocery store, etc.). Find out what you should be when you grow up.

Dinosaur World

If you or your kids are dinosaur-obsessed,

it is your duty to get in the car and drive about a half hour east of Tampa to an otherwise agricultural town called Plant City. It is known as the Winter Strawberry Capital of the World, but amid the strawberry fields lurks **Dinosaur World** (5145 Harvey Tew Rd., Plant City, 813/717-9865, www.dinosaurworld.com, 9am-5pm daily, $16.95 adults, $14.95 seniors, $11.95 children 3-12, children 2 and under free). There are 150 huge models (well, maybe 149, because one disappeared a while back—now, there's a trophy) of prehistoric beasts arrayed in a huge subtropical garden. Having recently spent time in the dinosaur exhibit at the Museum of Natural History in New York, I have a sneaking suspicion that Dinosaur World isn't preoccupied with strict accuracy (for instance, we don't really know about dinosaur coloring, but these ones all sport the mottled greeny-brown made popular in movies). In addition to the dinos, there are spooky fake caves to explore and an archaeological dig/sandbox area. This is best for kids under seven.

Entertainment and Events

MUSIC, THEATER, AND CINEMA
Straz Center for the Performing Arts

Tampa's heavy hitter for performing arts is the **Straz Center for the Performing Arts** (1010 N. W.C. MacInnes Pl., 1 block off Ashley St., 813/229-7827, www.strazcenter.org, times and ticket prices vary). It's a huge arts complex housing four distinct theaters, in which audiences can see Opera Tampa (the resident company), the Florida Orchestra, comedies, dramas, cabaret, dance, music, alternative theater, children's theater, and an annual Broadway series. Most local arts series and events find a home at the performing arts center—Tampa Bay's Festival of Latin American Art, Patel Conservatory's Tampa Bay Youth Orchestra Spring Concert—you name it, the curtain goes up here.

Mid-Florida Credit Union Amphitheater

In 2004, Tampa welcomed the **Mid-Florida Credit Union Amphitheater** (formerly known as the Ford Amphitheater and then the 1-800-ASK-GARY Amphitheater and then the Live Nation Amphitheater, 4802 U.S. 301 N., 813/740-2446, times and ticket prices vary), a state-of-the-art venue for 30-40 big-league music concerts a year. At an expense of $23 million, the outdoor open-air theater was constructed with huge video screens, a 7,200-square-foot stage, 9,900 reserved seats, and room for 10,500 more on the lawn; shortly afterward, big space-age sound shields were erected, to the relief of the neighbors. It's gorgeous, like a huge circus tent mated with the *Millennium Falcon*. There are enough bathrooms and lots of fairly tasty food options.

★ Tampa Theatre

Tampa has its share of multiplexes, but skip the 20-screeners in favor of two hours in the dark at the **Tampa Theatre** (711 Franklin St., 813/274-8981, www.tampatheatre.org, times vary, $11 adults, $9 children 2-11, seniors, and military). Built in 1926, it's a beloved downtown landmark with an acclaimed film series, concerts (Gordon Lightfoot, Keb Mo, Bright Eyes—it's a wide range), special events, and backstage tours. The motion picture palace's interior is vintage with statues and gargoyles and intricately carved doors. Many believe that the theater is haunted by the ghost of Foster Finley, who spent 20 years as the theater's projectionist. So if you feel a hand in your popcorn, it may not be your seatmate's. Sometimes the films shown are classics, complete with Wurlitzer, other times it's more indie; look online for the schedule. Theater concessions include excellent popcorn, sophisticated candies, and beer and wine. Interesting fact: It was the first public building in Tampa to be equipped with air-conditioning.

FESTIVALS

The biggest party in Tampa comes at the beginning of February with the **Gasparilla Pirate Fest** (www.gasparillapiratefest.com), a fun celebration over 100 years old in honor of legendary pirate José Gaspar, "last of the buccaneers," who terrorized the coastal waters of western Florida during the late 18th and early 19th centuries. The weekend festivities get under way when 1,000 people in pirate costume sail into downtown on a fully rigged pirate ship, a replica of an 18th-century craft that is 165 feet long by 35 feet across the beam, with three masts standing 100 feet tall. The ship is met by a flotilla of hundreds of pleasure crafts intent on "defending the city." The upshot is that pirates take over Tampa for a while, like Mardi Gras, only with more "argh, me matey" and eye patches accompanying the beads and buried treasure. The length of Bayshore Boulevard is lined with bleachers for the occasion, musical acts sprout on stages all over town, and there's general merriment and carousing.

The **Gasparilla International Film Festival** (813/693-2367, www.gasparillafilmfestival.com) began in 2006, and takes place mid-March at venues in and around Ybor City. Over five days, more than 40 films are screened in a variety of genres. It's spiced up with a handful of industry panel discussions, VIP parties, glamorous dinners, and celebrity sightings.

In mid-February is the **Florida State Fair** (813/740-2446, www.floridastatefair.com), a 12-day salute to the state's best in agriculture, industry, entertainment, and foods on a stick. Also in February there's a county fair, the **Florida Strawberry Festival** (813/752-9194, www.flstrawberryfestival.com), with a huge midway and lots of strawberry cookoffs. Plant City is known as the Winter Strawberry Capital of the World, and these sweet babies are delicious.

The second-biggest party is not unlike Gasparilla for its focus on wild costumes and wilder revelry. **Guavaween** is the city's Cuban-style Halloween celebration, held October 30. Riffing on the fact that Tampa was nicknamed The Big Guava, the celebration features the Mama Guava, who has sworn to take the "bore" out of Ybor City. Really, after the parade is over, it's just a big excuse to drink too much and wander the streets of Ybor City in preposterous attire.

Nightlife

YBOR CITY

Ybor City is where people come out to party in Tampa. During the week there are few bars with throbbing music drifting out onto the street—it's more about dining on the weekdays. But forget date night on the weekend; then it's a place you rove with buddies, looking for trouble.

Club Skye (1509 E. 8th Ave., 813/516-7593, 1pm-3am Mon.-Sat., cover varies, no cover before 11pm on Sat.) is a trendy spot for late-night partying that always draws a young crowd. The club mostly features hip-hop and DJs spinning dance music. Whether you're here for College Ladies' Night, International Night, or DJ nights, Skye is the party to beat in Ybor. Although only certain nights are technically Naughty School Girl Nights, every night has plenty of sexy post-collegiate girls, especially when the club runs costume nights or competitions.

Coyote Ugly (1722 E. 7th Ave., 813/241-8459, 5pm-3am Wed.-Sat., 7pm-3am Tues.) aims older, not more mature, and is often just about the biggest party in Ybor City, presided over by the most audacious bartenders to ever

Cruising into Tampa

a cruise ship in the Port of Tampa

The Port of Tampa is said to be the fastest-growing cruise port in North America, with a passenger count going from 200,000 in 1998 to more than a million in recent years. Cruise lines seem to beget cruise lines, with newer and larger vessels steaming into the downtown Channelside port all the time. It started with Carnival and Holland America cruise lines back in 1994, but these days a number of lines head out of Tampa on four-, five-, and seven-day itineraries.

Tampa now homeports five vessels from four cruise lines: Carnival Cruise Lines, Holland America, Royal Caribbean, and Norwegian Cruise Lines.

- Carnival has one ship in Tampa. The *Paradise* has four- and five-day cruises to the western Caribbean.

- Royal Caribbean International has two ships here. *Brilliance of the Seas* offers four- and five-day cruises to the western Caribbean, and the *Visions of the Seas* has seven-day cruises to Central America and the western Caribbean.

- Holland America Lines' *Veendam* offers passengers seven- and fourteen-day itineraries of the Caribbean and Mexico.

- Norwegian Cruise Lines' *Norwegian Star* has seven-day cruises to the western Caribbean.

The port's cruise terminals include customer-friendly information areas, superior security, full passenger amenities, and a covered on-terminal parking garage, at $15 per day (reservations are recommended). Valet services are also available. The port is in close proximity to the interstate highway system. For directions to cruise terminals, call 813/905-7678.

wield a shot glass. If you have to ask what a body shot is, you're ripe for a hard life lesson from one of Coyote's devilish (and usually gorgeous) bartenders. Just like in the movie (which in turn was based on a bar in New York City), all-female bartenders drag the unsuspecting up on the bar for some raunchy drinking, dancing, and whatever. The bare-bones room is festooned with discarded brassieres from exuberant all-ages patrons.

Czar Vodka Bar (1503 E. 7th Ave., 813/247-2664, www.myspace.com/czarvodkabar) is a nightclub where vodka drinks are de rigueur. This 14,000-square-foot cold war-themed club is located in the Ritz and features three different rooms with dance floors, video screens, nice booths, and a super swank chill-out room.

If music and drinking aren't your objective, stop into the **Tampa Improv** (1600 E. 8th Ave., 813/864-4000, www.improvtampa.com, hours and prices vary) for an evening of live stand-up with mostly local/regional acts.

The **Green Iguana** (4029 S. West Shore Blvd., 813/837-1234) is another bar for grown-ups: good drinks, perfectly acceptable food, and audible conversation.

HYDE PARK

There's lots of good nightlife to be had in this sophisticated South Tampa neighborhood. There's a lot of Irish zeal on and around Azeele. If you like your music—or your flirting—with a heavy brogue, head to everyone's favorite quaint Irish bar, **Dubliner Pub** (2307 W. Azeele St., 813/258-2257). **Four Green Fields** (205 W. Platt St., 813/254-4444) is another legendary Irish pub, with lots of regulars and lively conversation. The french fry basket is a bargain and could feed a small nation. **MacDinton's Irish Pub & Restaurant** (405 S. Howard Ave., 813/251-8999, 4pm-3am Mon.-Fri., 10am-3am Sat., 11am-3pm Sun., $7-12) is another Irish entry, with a killer black and tan, a warming Irish coffee, and a fair representation of Irish staples, from rib-sticking, mashed-potatoey shepherd's pie to corned beef and cabbage. They also serve sushi if you want a departure from the traditional Irish fare. This is absolutely the biggest scene in

Czar Vodka Bar

Tampa, with lines down and around the block on weekend nights.

VICINITY OF TAMPA

Bahama Breeze (3045 N. Rocky Point Dr. E., 813/289-7922, roughly 11am-midnight Sun.-Thurs., 11am-2am Fri.-Sat., $8-22) is a tropical-themed singles hangout with a huge waterside deck from which you can view a great sunset.

Shopping

HYDE PARK VILLAGE

Tampa's downtown doesn't really have a retail center. For that, you need to visit Hyde Park. It's not vast, but the outdoor shopping area along Hyde Park's West Swann Avenue, South Dakota Avenue, and Snow Avenue is the most appealing shopping destination in town, especially when the weather's nice. There's a large covered parking lot, free to shoppers, and a

nicely landscaped plaza at the center. Pottery Barn and Resoration Hardware are among the bigger stores, with Ann Taylor, Brooks Brothers, Anthropologie, Talbots, and Tommy Bahama. Top restaurants include the Cal-Ital Wine Exchange, the indoor-outdoor Sinatra-addled Timpano Italian Chophouse, and a French-inspired gem called Piquant. In the summer, **Hyde Park Village** (813/251-3500, store hours vary) hosts a free evening movie series, the classic films projected outside on a huge screen.

INDOOR MALLS

With anchor stores Neiman Marcus and Nordstrom, **International Plaza** (2223 N. Westshore Blvd., 813/342-3790, 10am-9pm Mon.-Sat., noon-6pm Sun.), opened in 2001, gets the nod for fanciest shopping. A handful of usual mall stores (J. Crew, Banana Republic, Ann Taylor) are spiffed up by their proximity to 200 other specialty shops, like Tiffany & Co., Jos. A. Bank, Louis Vuitton, Montblanc, Gucci, Apple, and Coach. Really, it's the most upscale assembly of stores in any shopping center on the Gulf Coast, served by an open-air village of restaurants called Bay Street, all in a location minutes from the airport and downtown. And during the Christmas season the Neiman Marcus store goes all out with decorations.

About a minute from International Plaza, **Westshore Plaza** (250 Westshore Plaza, 813/286-0790) features more than 100 similarly fancy specialty shops and four major department stores, including a Macy's. It contains a 14-screen AMC Theater and restaurants like Maggiano's Little Italy, PF Chang's, and Mitchell's Fish Market.

Located across the street from USF, **University Mall** (2200 E. Fowler Ave., 813/971-3465) is a typical indoor shopping center with mostly familiar mall stores, a 16-screen movie theater, and a standard food court.

Fairly far from where most visitors stay, **Westfield Shopping Town, Brandon** (459 Brandon Town Center Dr., 813/661-6255) and **Westfield Shopping Town, Citrus Park** (8021 Citrus Park Town Center Blvd., 813/926-4644) are both enjoyable malls with the full gamut of small shops and anchors, mostly serving the local community. Citrus Park is a little nicer, with a 20-screen Regal Cinema.

And if you want to get some great deals on name brands, you need to drive south on I-75 for 40 minutes until you reach the **Ellenton Premium Outlets** (5461 Factory Shops Blvd., 941/723-1150). There you'll find Perry Ellis, Ann Taylor, Nautica, Under Armour, Nike, and Polo Ralph Lauren—all offering deep discounts.

International Plaza

OTHER SHOPPING

Channelside Bay Plaza (615 Channelside Dr., 813/223-4250), the entertainment center on Tampa's downtown waterfront adjacent to the Florida Aquarium and the cruise terminal, has a few stores to investigate—a wine shop, Lit Premium Cigar Bar, Qachbal's Chocolatier, and a couple of galleries. And shopping along **7th Avenue in Ybor City,** Tampa's Latin Quarter, will yield some interesting finds. It's a little grittier, with a few vintage clothing shops and a fair amount of racy lingerie.

Food

Maybe it's Tampa residents' deep streak of loyalty, maybe their plodding constancy, but marketing geniuses have determined that Tampa is the perfect test market for new chain restaurant concepts. They are trotted out here, and if they fly, launched upon the rest of the country. For this reason, Tampa is the home base of numerous national and regional chains—Hooters, Durango Steakhouse, Beef O' Brady's, Checkers, Hops Restaurant Bar and Brewery, Shells' Seafood Restaurant, Carrabba's, and Outback Steakhouse. (Outback is also the mastermind behind chains Lee Roy Selmon's, Fleming's Prime Steakhouse, Bonefish Grill, and Roy's.)

You will find more Chili's, Macaroni Grills, T.G.I. Friday's, and Bennigans restaurants than you could possibly patronize. For this reason, only the unique, discrete, more-or-less independently owned restaurants that are the exception to the rule in Tampa are covered here.

HYDE PARK

This is the upscale part of town. It's a historical residential district, serviced by the Old Hyde Park Village of high-end shops and the long stretch of South Howard Avenue, or SoHo, where some great restaurants are located.

Asian

Picking out just a handful along Restaurant Row is difficult. For casual dining, ★ **Water Sushi** (1015 S. Howard Ave., 813/251-8406, 11:30am-9:30pm Mon., 11:30am-10pm Tues.-Wed., 11:30am-11pm Fri., 11am-11pm Sat., 11pm-9:30pm Sun., $8-12) is a Japanese-inspired seafood joint and a late-night hangout for the neighborhood. Water specializes in rice paper-rolled sushi (no nori) paired with punchy sauces and dynamic side dishes. A minimalist design aesthetic and a no-reservations policy cannot douse the enthusiasm for vibrant combos like unagi, banana, and avocado.

TC Choy Asian Bistro (301 S. Howard Ave., 813/251-1191, 11:30am-2:30pm and 5:30pm-10pm Mon.-Fri., 11am-3pm and 5:30pm-10:30pm Sat.-Sun., $10-20) serves authentic Cantonese cuisine and noonday dim sum (and an assortment of other pan-Asian dishes) in a stylish, open space with big tables perfect for large parties.

Mexican

From the same company who owns Water Sushi, **Green Lemon** (915 S. Howard Ave., 813/868-5463, 10am-10pm Sun. and Mon., 11am-midnight Tues. And Thurs., 11am-11pm Wed., 11am-1am Fri., 10am-1am Sat.., $6-12) is a super lively hangout for fresh Mex and good 'ritas.

Spanish

Not on the row, but off on the more upscale waterside Bayshore, the late-night **Ceviche Tapas Bar & Restaurant** (2500 W. Azeele St., 813/250-0203, 5pm-10pm Sun.-Mon., 5pm-11pm Tues.-Wed., 5pm-1am Fri.-Sat., $14-28) serves its namesake citrus-cured fish, sea scallops with manchego, and a variety of compact dishes with olives and almonds, all in a sleek nightclub atmosphere.

Casual

A thin-crust pizza hotshot by day, ★ **Pane Rustica** (3225 S. MacDill Ave., 813/902-8828, 8am-5pm Tues., 8am-10pm Wed.-Sat., 8am-3pm Sun., $8-25) hosts some of the fanciest Cal-Ital dinners around Wednesday-Saturday, with full table service and a well-selected short wine list. You can still opt for one of those delicious thin-crust pizzas (maybe one with gorgonzola and sweet caramelized shallot, or perhaps ricotta salata with olive tapenade and sun-dried tomatoes), or even a laid-back burger with brie and roasted red peppers. Don't miss Kevin and Karyn Kruszewski's awesome cookies, cakes, and other house-made desserts.

Fine Dining

After 15 years of being at the forefront of Tampa's restaurant scene, B. T. Nguyen may have reached her pinnacle in **Restaurant BT** (2507 S. MacDill Ave., 813/258-1916, 11:30am-2:30pm and 5:30-9:30pm Tues.-Sat., $10-30), located dead center in Old Hyde Park Village. Classic Vietnamese and French dishes are innovatively presented in the stylish, indoor-outdoor dining room. Trained as a sommelier, Nguyen has created an exceptional wine list and a short list of cocktails, which explains the locale's popularity as an evening gathering place.

The biggest gorilla on the Tampa dining scene is located on what is now a somewhat run-down stretch of South Howard, but fans of **Bern's Steak House** (1208 S. Howard Ave., 813/251-2421, 5pm-10pm Sun.-Thurs. 5pm-11pm Fri.-Sat., reservations recommended, $18-100) are undeterred. This world-famous, decades-old landmark has a wine list that could break a toe and a menu that so thoroughly explains dishes that it can sometimes seem a bit exaggerated. Waiters go through a grueling years-long apprenticeship, resulting in a staff that could, and does, quote verbatim from the offerings. What's offered is prime beef, aged and nurtured in Bern's own meat lockers. You, the customer, dictate the size, cut, cooking temperature, and many other details. After dinner, take the tour of the kitchen and wine cellar.

Then head upstairs to ★ **The Harry Waugh Dessert Room at Bern's Steak House** (1208 S. Howard Ave., 813/251-2421, 6pm-11pm Sun.-Thurs., 6pm-midnight Fri.-Sat., $10-20). Nothing prepares you for it. People tell you, "You dine in individual hollowed-out wine casks." Someone says, "There are individual wall-mounted radios to set the mood at your table." You hear a rumor about an accordionist, maybe something about flambéing waiters. The romantic date-night possibilities of this dessert-only upstairs of Bern's (named after a wine-writing crony of Bern himself) are endless. If that's not enough, there's Chocolate-Chocolate-Chocolate. That's actually the name of the chocolate-shellacked cylinder packing chocolate cheese pie, chocolate mousse, and chocolate cheesecake into one deadly package.

If Bern's doesn't sound like your cup of tea, try the more contemporary approach at the affiliated **Haven** (2208 W. Morrison Ave., 813/258-2233, 5:30pm-10pm Mon.-Wed., 5:30pm-11pm Thurs.-Sat., $18-32). The kitchen turns out great dim sum and world-beat small plates. The daily-changing selection of breads is absolutely knockout (curry sesame flatbread, kalamata and fig loaf).

Not among the 35 or so restaurants along South Howard, but still considered in Hyde Park, **Mise en Place** (442 W. Grand Central Ave., 813/254-5373, 11:30am-2:30pm and 5:30pm-10pm Tues.-Thurs., 11:30am-2:30pm and 5:30pm-11pm Fri., 5pm-11pm Sat., $15-32) is a romantic, intimate spot near the University of Tampa. The weekly changing menu ranges from pizza with chorizo, roast corn, chilies, and manchego to mole spice-rubbed seared tuna with purple potatoes, vanilla bean pineapple salad, and a prickly pear habanero vinaigrette. They also take great care to accommodate folks with special diets.

DAVIS ISLANDS

Nestled in the charming business district of Davis Islands, opinions on the best tables at

220 East (220 E. Davis Blvd., 813/259-1220, 11am-10pm Mon.-Thurs., 11am-11pm Fri.-Sat., $15-20) are divided—out front at one of the handful on the patio, or inside at one of the deep green booths. The restaurant stays pretty busy. The waitstaff is exceptionally friendly, serving fairly priced, casual meals that range through American, Asian, or even Cajun dishes.

YBOR CITY

Party central in Tampa, the century-old cigar-rolling center of town exhibits little of its Cuban heritage these days. The main drag is 7th Avenue, closed off to cars on the weekend, which is nice to be able to party and walk around without having to worry about traffic around you. It gets packed on the weekend with younger partiers looking to drink and enjoy dancing and live music in the clubs of the area. During the week, the area is calmer—a better time to try out one of the many restaurants that range all over the map.

Start your adventure at **Centro Ybor** (1600 E. 8th Ave., 813/242-4660, www.centroybor.com, 11am-11pm Sun.-Thurs., 11am-2am Fri.-Sat.), a shopping, dining, and entertainment complex right at the pulsing heart of the neighborhood. **Samurai Blue Sushi and Sake Bar** (813/242-6688, 11:30am-midnight Mon.-Fri., 5pm-1am Sat., 5pm-11pm Sun., $10-30) is another big, lively joint, but this one serves sake bombers, "spontaneous combustion rolls," and other unique spins on Japanese bar staples.

Tampa Bay Brewing Company (plaza level under Muvico, 813/247-1422, www.tampabaybrewingcompany.com, 11am-11pm Mon.-Thurs., 11am-midnight Fri.-Sat., noon-11pm Sun., $7-12) anchors Centro. There's good live music, excellent proprietary brews (try the Redeye Ale), and a fresh American bistro menu.

Centro Cantina (813/241-8588, 11am-9pm Mon., 11am-11pm Tues., 11am-1am Wed.-Sat., noon-1am Sun., $7-15) is more a drinking establishment. They have good margaritas and the usual Mexican dishes, so the

The Cubano

In Tampa, the Cubano is the king of sandwiches, or should I say the earl of sandwiches? It starts with the bread. If you've eaten anywhere in Ybor City, you've probably eaten Cuban bread. But why not go to the source? Rumor has it that **La Segunda Central Bakery** (2512 N. 15th St., 813/248-1531, www.lesugundabakery.com, 6:30am-5pm Mon.-Fri., 7am-3pm Sat., 7am-1pm Sun.) churns out up to 12,000 Cuban loaves daily.

You only need one loaf, in the form of the archetypal Cubano sandwich. The loaves themselves are about 36 inches long with a zipper-like seam down the top. The third-generation owners of La Segunda have reason to be proud of their bread's thin, flaky crust and soft, pillowy interior, even more so when piled high with roast pork and Genoa salami (a strictly Tampa twist), swiss cheese (some say emmentaler), sour pickles, and spicy mustard—the whole thing warmed and flattened in a special hot press. The outside is crisp, and the inside warm and a little gooey. It's perfection.

draw is the rustic indoor-outdoor space and abounding good cheer. After this, regroup at the Centro Ybor movie theater across the plaza.

Beyond Centro Ybor, the neighborhood's restaurants are spread along many blocks on **7th Avenue.** Nearly at the end of the strip of commerce you'll find the **Columbia Restaurant** (2025 E. 7th Ave., 813/248-4961, 11am-10pm Mon.-Thurs., 11am-11pm Fri.-Sat., noon-9pm Sun., $21-30), which bears the distinction of being the oldest restaurant in Florida (started in 1905) and the nation's largest Spanish/Cuban restaurant (13 rooms extending one city block). The ethnic food is authentic, and the experience is worth it. Some of these waiters have been here a lifetime, the many rooms manage to stay packed, and there are stirring flamenco shows Monday-Saturday nights.

People-watching is a popular pastime in

Ybor City. For the best sidewalk seat in town, pull up a chair at ★ **Bernini** (1702 E. 7th Ave., 813/248-0099, 11:30am-10pm Mon.-Thurs., 11:30am-11pm Fri.-Sat., 4pm-9pm Sun., $10-24). It's set in the historic Bank of Ybor City building and serves Cal-Ital cuisine—beef carpaccio and filet mignon with sweet corn puree. It generally attracts an older crowd than the bars and clubs around it.

CHANNELSIDE

Channelside is located dockside at the Port of Tampa, where all the cruise ships come in. The shopping/dining/entertainment complex has a big movie theater with IMAX; a fun, upscale bowling alley; small, mostly independently owned shops; and about a dozen restaurants.

Head first to the bowling alley-restaurant **Splitsville** (615 Channelside Dr., 813/514-2695, 4pm-1am Thurs.-Fri., noon-2am Sat., noon-8pm Sun., $7-18). Spares, strikes, whatever: It's good food, a whimsical environment, and the coolest bowling shoes ever. The decor sets you straight with oversized "bowling pin" columns, red velvet ropes, and 12 faultless lanes, and the food is excellent bar snacks.

Wet Willie's (615 Channelside Dr., 813/221-5650, 11am-midnight Sun.-Thurs., 11am-2pm Fri.-Sat., $7-12) is a fun place for daiquiris and live music. The restaurant serves tasty bar food; the wings, nachos, and piña colada shrimp are favorites.

INTERNATIONAL PLAZA

Tampa's fanciest mall (there's a Louis Vuitton store next to a Gucci store), **International Plaza** (all at 2223 N. Westshore Blvd., 813/490-5288), is also home to good restaurants. It contains **The Cheesecake Factory** (813/353-4200, 11am-11pm Mon.-Thurs., 11am-12:30am Fri.-Sat., 10am-11pm Sun., $12-20), **California Pizza Kitchen** (813/353-8155, 11am-9:30pm Mon.-Sat., 11am-7pm Sun., $8-15), **Earl of Sandwich** (813-879-1762, 8am-9pm Mon.-Thurs., 8am-9:30pm Fri.-Sat., 10am-7pm Sun., $6-12), and **The Capital Grille** (813/830-9433, 11:30am-10pm

Mon.-Thurs., 11:30am-11pm Fri., 5pm-11pm Sat., 5pm-9pm Sun., $30-60), for when you want to splurge on a $40 dry-aged steak. The mall's Bay Street is a Caribbean-themed pedestrian promenade lined with several good restaurants.

Best bets for a drink: **Bar Louie** (813/874-1919, 11am-2am daily, $12-20) has 40 beers on tap, cooks up excellent burgers, and offers a large variety of small plates from pan-seared pork potstickers to hand-battered calamari. **Blue Martini** (813/873-2583, 4pm-3am Mon.-Thurs., 1pm-3am Fri.-Sun., $10-20) is for when you aim to go the martini route, with a menu that leans to small plates (seared tuna, hummus and pita chips). There's also an elevated stage behind the bar to see live rock.

Another great restaurant is **Pelagia Trattoria** (4200 Jim Walter Blvd., 813/313-3235, 6:30am-10pm daily, $15-25), located on the main level in the Renaissance Tampa Hotel, Bay Street. Chef Brett Gardiner serves Mediterranean-inspired dishes: Breakfast brings special items like Godiva chocolate pancakes with a white chocolate mousse; at lunch, ricotta and asparagus ravioli served in a hot truffle butter sauce; and for dinner, lamb T-bone with juniper berry sauce. It's the most beautiful hotel restaurant in all of Tampa that also has an express lunch menu that gets people in and out lickety-split.

NEW TAMPA

New Tampa, as the name indicates, is all new. The upside is that things are clean, pristine, hygienic; the downside is that there's no sense of history, no gritty, timeworn ambience. If you are jonesing for something that seems older than a decade or so, ★ **Skipper's Smokehouse** (910 Skipper Rd., 813/971-0666, 11am-10:30pm Tues.-Fri., noon-11pm Sat., 1pm-9:30pm Sun., $7-15) has the ambience of a place 10 times its age. It's Tampa's best live music venue (blues, alt rock, Tuvan throat singers—the gamut), with concerts held outdoors under the canopy of a huge, moss-festooned live oak. It has a lively 30s-and-up bar scene (and a mighty fine mojito).

TAMPA
FOOD

A ramshackle restaurant serves a wonderful blackened grouper sandwich, gator nuggets, and black beans.

Everyone's favorite restaurant in New Tampa—the mostly residential area northeast of downtown—is **Ciccio Cali** (17004 Palm Pointe Dr., 813/975-1222, 11am-9:30pm Mon.-Thurs., 11am-10pm Fri., 10am-10pm Sat., 10am-9pm Sun.). Most nights it teems with families devoted to this health-conscious neighborhood favorite. Ciccio Cali serves thin, crunchy New York-style pizzas topped with interesting picks like caramelized eggplant and goat cheese, as well as a wide variety of sushi, sandwiches, and Asian-inspired entrees at lunch. Ciccio Cali is owned by the same company that owns Water Sushi and Green Lemon in Hyde Park.

The Greek **Acropolis Greek Tavern** (14947 Bruce B. Downs Blvd., 813/971-1787, 11am-midnight Sun.-Thurs., 11am-1am Fri.-Sat., $6-15) offers late hours, lively fun, and people yelling "opa" regularly.

VICINITY OF TAMPA

When you want to get a sense of Tampa's scale, distance, and scope, you have to dig deep into your wallet and head to **Armani's** (2900 Bayport Dr., 813/207-6800, 6pm-10pm Mon.-Sat., $25-40) atop the Grand Hyatt Tampa Bay. It's the undisputed top special-occasion restaurant in town, partly for the view, partly for the solicitous service, and partly for the scaloppine Armani (thin-pounded veal sautéed with wild mushrooms and cognac in a truffle sauce) or the grilled duck breast stuffed with liver pâté and dried cherries in a vanilla sauce. The wine list is extensive, with an emphasis on California and French wines.

Oystercatchers (2900 Bayport Dr., 813/207-6815, 11:30am-10pm daily, $18-35) is the hotel's No. 2 restaurant, a lovely seafood joint with water views and the town's best brunch. It offers exceptionally fresh seafood in a beautiful and upscale but still comfortably casual waterfront setting. The outdoor dining area features romantic fire pits right on the water that can be reserved upon request. For dinners, choose between dishes like wood-grilled Gulf snapper served with tuxedo orzo and baby vegetables or seared tuna drizzled with key lime and caper butter. And you have got to try the smoked sea salt. You'll never look at a dinner roll the same way again.

One of the innovative Hawaiian-fusion restaurants founded by acclaimed chef Roy Yamaguchi, **Roy's** (4342 W. Boy Scout Blvd., 813/873-7697, 5pm-10pm Mon.-Thurs., 5pm-11pm Fri.-Sat., 5pm-9pm Sun., $20-40) is another expense-account favorite in Tampa. An exceptionally good deal can be had with the three-course dinner for $35. It may start with grilled Hawaiian satay skewers, then segue to Thai lemongrass chicken with bok choy, finishing up with Roy's signature melting hot chocolate soufflé.

In the upscale neighborhood of Carrollwood, Andrea and Michael Reilly's little **Michael's Grill** (11720 N. Dale Mabry Hwy., 813/964-8334, 8am-9pm Mon.-Thurs., 8am-10pm Fri.-Sat., 8am-3pm Sun., $15-27) is an institution, as much for the warm and neighborly service as for the friendly patio and spare, brasserie-style dining room. You can eat your French onion soup or penne Bolognese at the bar and take in all the drama of the bustling open kitchen, but the out on the patio always seems to be having more fun. The daily breakfast and Sunday brunch are a treat with items like Belgium waffles and Sicilian omelets.

Also in Carrollwood, **Grille One Sixteen** (15405 N. Dale Mabry Hwy., 813/265-0216, 11am-10pm Sun.-Thurs., 11am-11pm Fri.-Sat., $20-40) has become a favorite with its hip-like-Miami design. Chef James Maita has a strong New American approach with a world-beat inspired menu.

For a great steak, head to **Malio's Prime** (400 N. Ashley Dr., 813/223-7746, 11:30am-9:30pm Mon.-Thurs., 11:30am-10:30pm Fri., 5pm-10:30pm Sat., $21-37). It opened downtown in Rivergate Tower, only in name similar to a historic restaurant that Malio Iavarone ran on Dale Mabry. It has prime steaks served in a soaring-ceilinged dining room with banks of riverside windows. In a similar vein, **Council Oak** (5223 N. Orient Rd., 813/627-7600, 5pm-10pm Sun.-Thurs., 5pm-midnight Fri.-Sat., $24-40) opened with much fanfare as part of the Seminole Hard Rock Hotel and Casino. Smack in the center of the gaming excitement, it mainly serves seafood and steaks, all well prepared and offered by an extremely knowledgeable waitstaff.

Some of the old guard are fairly far-flung: **Shula's Steak House** (InterContinental Tampa, 4860 W. Kennedy Blvd., 813/286-4366, 11:30am-2pm and 5:30pm-10pm Mon.-Thurs., 11:30am-2pm and 5:30pm-10:30pm Fri., 5:30pm-10:30pm Sat., 5:30pm-9:30pm Sun., $20-40), not surprisingly given coach Don Shula's hand in it, features decor that is all in tribute to the Miami Dolphins. It's the most elegant experience with football you are ever likely to have. They begin the meal with the menu hand-painted on a Miami Dolphins football, a fun, novel, and clever beginning to dinner that sparks conversation immediately. Everything at Shula's is large. The steaks are well-seasoned and perfectly prepared, and they're huge, up to a 48-ounce porterhouse. Even the salads are wonderfully oversized. The waitstaff is exceptional, and Shula's serves exemplary mixed drinks.

Charley's Steakhouse (4444 W. Cypress St., 813/353-9706, 5pm-10:30pm Sun.-Thurs., 5pm-11pm Fri.-Sat., $30-44) has more fat grilled steaks and California wines. Some of the selections include five-pepper-encrusted filet mignon with pesto, roast garlic mashed potatoes, and oak-grilled vegetables, or shrimp and scallop scampi with a side of grilled asparagus and a baked potato.

Accommodations

Tampa's hotel scene is stymied by one thing: Tampa has no beaches. Although it's on the water—with the active Port of Tampa and waterside residential communities like Davis and Harbour Islands—there is no possibility for a luxury resort hotel or charming bed-and-breakfast just steps from the waters of Hillsborough Bay. For that kind of experience you must head over the bay to St. Pete or Clearwater.

Still, Tampa has a preponderance of pleasant, fairly priced accommodations spread around the greater Bay Area, from the Latin Quarter of Ybor City to the Westshore business district or the Tampa Convention Center, to near Busch Gardens and the University of South Florida.

UNDER $100

For a wild experience at a tame price, **Gram's Place** (3109 N. Ola Ave., 813/221-0596, www.grams-inn-tampa.com, hostel room $25, private room $60) in Ybor City fits the bill. It's eccentric, with a different music theme (jazz, blues, rock) in each of the private suites and youth hostel-style bunks. All rooms come with a music menu of CDs. The hostel part looks like a railroad car fashioned around a 100-year-old train depot. The rooms are set in two circa-1945 cottages and share an oversize in-ground whirlpool tub, a BYOB bar in the courtyard, and a multitrack recording studio. The "Gram" in question is Gram Parsons, once a member of the Byrds and the Flying Burrito Brothers, the deceased musician responsible for that great song, "Grievous Angel," that Emmylou Harris made famous.

If you want to stay near USF or Busch Gardens and MOSI, there are a handful of reasonably priced chains. **La Quinta Inn Tampa Near Busch Gardens** (9202 N. 30th St., 813/930-6900, $70-120) is adjacent to Busch Gardens's entrance, with 144 nicely appointed rooms with roomy bathrooms, good lighting, large desks, and Wi-Fi. There's also a good-size pool.

$100-200

The **Bonita Casitas de Ybor** (1813 and 1815 E. 5th Ave., 813/334-1857, $100-200) offers two charming private guest cottages with full kitchens and two bedrooms each.

The **Tahitian Inn** (601 S. Dale Mabry Hwy., 813/877-6721, www.tahitianinn.com, $95-169) is a lovely, two-story, family-run motel yielding 60 Tahitian-themed (dark wood, tropical accessories), moderately priced rooms and 20 executive suites, a lovely pool with tiki huts and hammocks, and the Serenity Spa with massage and Tahitian hot stone treatments. There's also a lovely little on-site café with patio seating near a koi pond. The location is close to I-275 and lots of commerce.

For a different kind of experience in Ybor City, head to the historic ★ **Don Vicente de Ybor Historic Inn** (1915 Republica de Cuba, 813/241-4545, www.donvicenteinn.com, $159-169), constructed in 1895 by Cuban patriot Vicente Martinez Ybor. The boutique hotel's 16 guest rooms contain four-poster beds and also broadband, voicemail, and in-room desks. Even if you don't stay here, the magnificent grand salon is worth peeking at.

A little pricier, the **Grand Hyatt Tampa Bay** (2900 Bayport Dr., 813/874-1234, www.grandtampabay.hyatt.com, $170-400) is a big hotel near the airport that caters mainly to the corporate traveler. There are 445 deluxe guest rooms and suites, including 38 Spanish-style casita rooms and 7 casita suites in a secluded area at the south end of the property, which is set in a 35-acre wildlife preserve on the shores of Tampa Bay. The Hyatt contains two of the best restaurants in town, Armani's and Oystercatchers. Armani's underwent an impressive renovation in late 2012. The rooftop fire pit offers one of the best views of Tampa Bay in the city and is an excellent spot to watch the sunset.

$200-300

Numerous hotels cluster along Rocky Point Drive and Cypress Street, just a couple of minutes from the airport, Westshore business district, and Tampa Convention Center. These hotels have lots of business amenities and often offer significantly cheaper rates on the weekend. Of the chains, there's **DoubleTree Hotel Tampa Airport Westshore** (4500 W. Cypress St., 813/879-4800, www.doubletreetampawestshore.com, $170-310), **Courtyard by Marriott Tampa Westshore** (3805 W. Cypress St., 813/874-0555, $180-280), and the **Holiday Inn Express and Suites Rocky Point** (3025 N. Rocky Point Dr.,

the InterContinental Tampa

813/287-8585, $160-260), among many others, all with water views of the bay and pools and other amenities.

For a more independent approach in the same location, try **Sailport Waterfront Suites** (2506 N. Rocky Point Dr., 813/281-9599, $110-230), a four-story, all-suites hotel (all rooms have a queen-size sleeper sofa in the living room, convenient for families) with full-size kitchens, barbecue grills, outdoor heated pool, lighted tennis court, and fishing pier.

The USF hotel of choice is **Embassy Suites** (3705 Spectrum Blvd., 813/977-7066, $150-300), across the road from the university. It's a tall, suites-only hotel with a soaring atrium. Rooms are nice, with spacious living rooms, private bedrooms with either a king-size or two double beds, and two TVs in every room. Although the rooms cost a little more, included in the price is a nice daily cooked-to-order breakfast buffet and the manager's reception, where you get a free cocktail and some chips in the early evening.

The **Seminole Hard Rock Hotel and Casino** (5223 Orient Rd., 866/502-7529, www.seminolehardrockhoteltampa.com, $249-359) is the huge tower that rises up in the middle of nowhere off I-75. With an illuminated 12-story tower that shifts colors, the signature huge guitar at the entrance, a 90,000-square-foot casino, and popular restaurants like Kuro and Council Oak, it's like a little piece of Vegas right here in Tampa. The complex opened in 2004 and has been swamped with casino and overnight guests ever since. The 250 guest rooms and suites have a hipster art deco design. The most luxurious part is the pool area, with cascading fountains and private cabanas with televisions and refrigerators. In 2012 the Seminole tribe completed a $75 million expansion for the Hard Rock, which made the Hard Rock the sixth-largest casino in the world and larger than any casino in Las Vegas.

Over $300

One of Tampa's nicest luxury hotels is the **Renaissance Tampa Hotel International Plaza** (4200 Jim Walter Blvd., 813/877-9200, $339-389), near the Westshore business district at the International Plaza mall. The lavish decor is reminiscent of a Mediterranean villa. The hotel's not small, with 293 guest rooms on eight floors, but the service is personal and attentive, and it seems especially geared to the repeat-business, high-end business traveler.

The **InterContinental Tampa** (4860 W. Kennedy Blvd., 813/286-4400, www.intercontampa.com, $329-479) is a business traveler's dream. The 323 rooms, 17 junior suites, 4 business suites, and 2 presidential suites feature fresh decor, feather-top mattresses with luxurious linens, functional working areas, flat-screen TVs, and iPod docking stations. The hotel offers 21,000 square feet of flexible meeting space, wireless high-speed Internet throughout the entire hotel, fitness center, full-service concierge program, and a rooftop pool with views of the bay and city. The hotel has a Shula's Steak House, which offers the best steaks in town, and Shula's No Name Lounge. They also offer impressive sports packages for select games including transportation to and from the stadiums.

Information and Services

Tampa is located within the **eastern time zone.** All telephone listings are within the **813 area code** unless otherwise indicated. If you're trying to call the other side of the bay (Clearwater, Dunedin, St. Petersburg), the area code is **727.**

TOURIST INFORMATION

Tampa Bay and Company's **Visitor Information Center** is in the waterfront Channelside entertainment complex (401 E. Jackson St., 813/223-1111, www.visittampabay. com, 9:30am-5:30pm Mon.-Sat., 11am-5pm Sun.) at the Port of Tampa. It provides lots of brochures and information on attractions, events, and accommodations.

Tampa's daily newspaper is the *Tampa Tribune* (813/259-7711), with kiosks most places. The *Tampa Bay Times* (727/893-8111, www.tampabay.com) also covers the greater Tampa Bay area. *Creative Loafing* (813/739-4800, www.cltampa.com), the city's free alternative weekly, has great entertainment schedules, restaurant reviews, and a view into local politics. For quick and easy info on events, attractions, and restaurants, visit www.tampabay.citysearch.com. There are also numerous magazines: *Tampa Bay Magazine* covers the city of Tampa, *Tampa Style* covers only the northern suburbs of the city, and there are many glossy freebies in Hyde Park.

POLICE AND EMERGENCIES

In any emergency, dial 911 for immediate assistance. If you need police assistance in a nonemergency, visit or call the **Tampa Police Department** (411 N. Franklin St., 813/276-3200). The police department operates three districts that serve the greater Tampa Bay

area—they will assign your problem to the proper district. Tampa has several hospitals equipped with emergency rooms: If you have a medical emergency in the Hyde Park area, go to **Memorial Hospital of Tampa** (2901 Swann Ave., 813/873-6400). In Carrollwood, visit the **University Community Hospital Carrollwood** (7171 N. Dale Mabry Hwy., 813/932-2222). In the Westshore area, go to **University Community Health** (5101 E. Busch Blvd., 813/830-6236). In the downtown area, make your way to **Tampa General Hospital** (1 Tampa General Cir., 813/844-7000), near the causeway to Davis Islands.

RADIO AND TELEVISION

Of the local radio stations, my favorite is **WMNF 88.5 FM,** which has a huge following for its independent and eclectic programming—tune in and you'll hear salsa, or maybe Hawaiian slack-key guitar, or maybe a little alt-country. It has a snuggly relationship with Skipper's Smokehouse, and together they sponsor many of the city's best concerts. For a nonthreatening mix of pop, turn to **WMTX 100.7 FM,** for hits of the 1970s turn to **107.3 FM The Eagle,** and for sports talk turn to **WDAE 1250 AM.**

On the television, if you're looking for the FOX affiliate, turn to **Channel 13,** for NBC turn to **WFLA Channel 8,** for ABC turn to **WFTS Channel 28,** and for CBS turn to **WTSP Channel 10.**

LAUNDRY SERVICES

If you find yourself in need of coin-op laundry, head to **B & W Coin Laundry** (4810 E. Busch Blvd., 813/987-9847) or **Tampa Coin Laundry** (1613 E. Dr. Martin Luther King, 813/248-5588). Most big hotel chains offer laundry services.

Getting There and Around

CAR

Both I-75 and I-275 travel north-south, but I-75 skirts the edge of Tampa while I-275 travels through the city and over the bay. Both connect to I-4, which travels east-west, connecting Tampa Bay to Orlando and the east coast of Florida.

Once in town, from north to south, Bearrs, Fletcher, Fowler, and Busch Boulevards are the big east-west roads. Dale Mabry and Bruce B. Downs are the biggest north-south roads. This all sounds fairly simple, but once you get downtown in Tampa you need a map to find your way out. There are lots of one-way streets, and the highway on-ramps are a bit difficult to find. The Busch Gardens area and University of South Florida lie between I-75 and I-275 northeast of downtown. The airport is just southwest of downtown.

AIR

Tampa International Airport (4100 George J. Bean Pkwy., 813/870-8700, www.tampaairport.com) is perhaps the best midsize airport in the country—clean, easily traversed, with good signage and efficient staff. With one of the best on-time records around, it's Florida's fourth-busiest airport, located just seven miles southwest of downtown Tampa. It's serviced by Air Canada, Alaska Airlines, American Airlines, British Airways, Cayman Airways, Copa Airlines, Delta Airlines, Edelweiss Air, Frontier, JetBlue, Lufthansa, Silver Airlines, Southwest Airlines, Spirit Airlines, Sun Country, United, WestJet, and World Atlantic Airlines.

Located on the airport premises, **Avis** (800/831-2847), **Budget** (800/527-0700), **Dollar** (800/800-4000 domestic, 800/800-6000 international), **Enterprise** (800/736-8222), **Hertz** (800/654-3131), and **Thrifty** (800/847-4389) provide rental car service. Tampa has unbelievably good deals on rental cars from the airport—celebrate by upgrading to something stylish.

BUS AND TRAIN

Taxi service from the airport to downtown is about $18. Tampa is a call destination, not a flag destination. Most hotels offer shuttle service to the airport and major attractions.

Amtrak (800/872-7245) and **Greyhound** (813/229-2174) both service Tampa, with stations downtown. Amtrak operates out of historic Tampa Union Station, offering north-south connections as well as links to nationwide rail travel.

Within the city, **Hillsborough Area Regional Transit Authority** (813/623-5835, www.gohart.org, $4 unlimited ride all day) provides intercity bus service, with nearly 200 buses on 26 routes, nine trolleys, and eight electric streetcars. The In Town Trolley runs north and south through downtown and connects to the TECO Line Streetcar System, which runs from downtown to the Channel District/Port and Ybor City. Still, Tampa is so spread out that it's not a city in which to be without a car.

St. Petersburg and Pinellas County

I n some ways, Henry Ford's affordable $400 Model T foreshadowed the real estate boom in St. Petersburg in the early 1920s. It was the beginning of road-tripping—folks hopping in the car in search of sun, sand, and fun. They found the peninsula that hangs down Florida's west side like a thumb, the east side of it nestled against the placid Old Tampa Bay, its west side flanked by sandy beaches and the Gulf of Mexico. People liked what they saw. They bought up land, building big resort hotels, affordable motels, and homes.

Before the hordes of sun worshippers came, what is now Pinellas County had a diverse set of visitors-turned-residents. As was so common along the Gulf Coast, Spanish conquistadores ran off the original pre-Columbian Native Americans in the 1500s. Long after that, there came an intrepid Frenchman, Odet Philippe, who established a large orange grove near Safety Harbor in 1842; just after that came the Scottish merchants who settled Dunedin, the Russian immigrants who worked the Orange Belt Railroad and named St. Petersburg after their old-world hometown, and finally the Greeks, who came to harvest the area's rich sponge beds around 1900.

Today, St. Petersburg is Florida's fourth-largest city, the anchor of Pinellas County.

Combined with neighboring Tampa, it's the largest market in the state. It's had another boom period in recent years, an influx of tech businesses drawing younger families and driving down the median age. The city's downtown—on the bay, not the Gulf—has seen lots of growth, from pricey condos to the $40 million BayWalk shopping complex.

St. Pete Beach is not just the shortened name for St. Petersburg Beach. St. Petersburg is the big city adjacent to Old Tampa Bay, which looks out across at the big city of Tampa. St. Pete Beach, on the other hand, is an autonomous barrier-island town to the south and west of St. Petersburg. St. Pete Beach stretches seven miles from Pass-A-Grille on the south to Blind Pass on the north, before Treasure Island. Also, the city of Clearwater

---

Previous: A view of downtown St. Petersburg; Clearwater Beach. **Above:** Sunshine Skyway Bridge.

Highlights

★ **Fort De Soto Park:** More than just the site of a fort built during the Spanish-American War, the park features over seven miles and 1,136 acres of pristine coastal environment to explore (page 189).

★ **Honeymoon Island and Caladesi Island Beaches:** Why settle for just one beach when you can opt for the double whammy of Honeymoon and Caladesi, a pair of white-sand barrier islands flanking Dunedin north of Clearwater? Caladesi is accessible only by ferry from Honeymoon Island (page 190).

★ **Sunken Gardens:** It puttered along as a kitschy Old Florida attraction for years, until the city of St. Petersburg restored the four-acre tropical garden to its former glory (page 192).

★ **Sunshine Skyway Fishing Piers:** A local bridge has been repurposed as the world's longest fishing pier, with a tremendous concentration of sport fish lurking in the deep waters below (page 195).

★ **Salvador Dalí Museum:** The famous Spanish surrealist is honored in a sleek museum of his work and the work of those inspired by him (page 197).

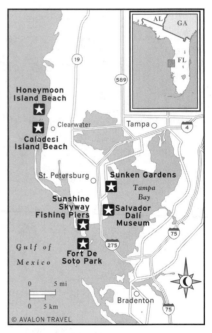

is on the mainland, but Clearwater Beach is on a barrier island connected by Memorial Causeway.

The Gulf beaches are 20 minutes from downtown St. Petersburg across the peninsula. More than 20 little towns dot the coastline in Pinellas County, St. Pete and Clearwater Beaches being perhaps the favorites for family vacations. Clearwater Beach offers a wide, inviting shore, serious beach volleyball, and lots of nightlife and casual seafood restaurants. The Jolley Trolley whisks visitors from their hotel through town and right to the beachside Pier 60, something like the center of town.

Clearwater and St. Pete Beaches aren't the only strands that draw accolades. Caladesi Island State Park, accessible only by boat to the north of Clearwater Beach, is often rated one of the top 10 beaches in the country, as is Honeymoon Island.

PLANNING YOUR TIME

Pinellas County is a peninsula, with Tampa Bay to the east and the Gulf of Mexico to the west. Its location, adjacent to Tampa, but with the benefit of long and wonderful beaches, makes it an ideal home base for a lengthy Gulf Coast stay, especially for families. Even Disney World is a fairly convenient 90 minutes to the east. The sights and attractions are more compelling on the Tampa side of the bay (Busch Gardens, lots of professional sports), and these are easily accessed by either the Howard Frankland Bridge (I-275) or the Courtney Campbell Causeway (Hwy. 60). In high-season traffic, the drive can be 45 minutes. The best way to explore the area is by car, especially if you want to drive the length of the barrier islands. The area is served by **Tampa International Airport** (4100 George J. Bean Pkwy., 813/870-8700) and **St. Petersburg-Clearwater International Airport** (14700 Terminal Blvd., Clearwater, 727/453-7800).

Where you stay depends on your priorities: The city of St. Petersburg lies on the bay side of the peninsula. It has more history, more of a sense of place and sophistication than the beach towns along the Gulf side. There are romantic bed-and-breakfasts, fine restaurants, and cultural attractions. Clearwater Beach and St. Pete Beach on the Gulf side have the densest concentrations of beachside accommodations—in Clearwater this often means tall resort hotels and condos right on the beach; in St. Pete Beach it's low-rise motels that date back a few decades. The communities in between these two—Belleair and Belleair Beach; Indian Rocks Beach and Indian Shores; Redington Shores, North Redington Beach, and Redington Beach; Madeira Beach; and Treasure Island—are fairly residential, but with pockets of beachside hotels/motels/rentals. The whole Gulf side is really composed of a series of tiny barrier islands connected to the mainland by causeways—it may not be totally clear to you when driving, but spend a little time with the map so you know whether you're looking at boats bobbing on the Intracoastal Waterway, Boca Ciega Bay, Clearwater Harbor, or the Gulf.

The peak season typically runs November-May. It's a little more spread out than elsewhere among the Gulf Coast's beach spots, partly because American families on spring break come in March and April, and lots of European travelers fill in the time around that. In the summer the waters here are so warm as to be slightly off-putting. September and October are great times to visit. In October, added enticements include the beloved annual **Clearwater Jazz Holiday** (727/461-5200, www.clearwaterjazz.com) during the third week of the month, with four days of free world-class jazz in Coachman Park. There's also the local **Stone Crab Festival** (www.stonecrabfestival.org) during that same time. In June, on the other hand, the **Taste of Pinellas** (www.tasteofpinellas.com) is a big bash catered by all the best local restaurants.

The best camping is at Fort De Soto Park, and the best beaches in the area are at Clearwater Beach, Fort De Soto Park, Honeymoon Island and Caladesi Island, St. Pete Beach, Madeira Beach, Sand Key County Park, and Egmont Key State Wildlife Preserve.

St. Petersburg and Pinellas County

© AVALON TRAVEL

Sports and Recreation

BEACHES

The beaches of Clearwater and St. Pete are textbook stretches of white sand and clear, warm Gulf water, with lots of comfy beachside hotels and waterside amenities for families. The area is home to a couple of world-class beach destinations, the kinds of places that often make Dr. Stephen Leatherman's (Dr. Beach has been ranking America's beaches for 12 years) annual top 10 list.

First, a fairly urban city beach, **Clearwater Beach** (west on Hwy. 60), the only Pinellas County beach with year-round lifeguards (9:30am-4:30pm daily), is a long, wide stretch offering showers, restrooms, concessions, cabanas, umbrella rentals, volleyball, and metered parking. **Pier 60,** where the beach meets the causeway, is the locus of lots of local revelry and activity—during the day it's a heavily trafficked fishing pier, while at night the focus is **Sunsets at Pier 60,** a festival that runs every evening two hours before sunset to two hours past sunset, with crafts, magicians, and musicians all vying with the showy sunset display over the Gulf of Mexico for your attention. Pier 60 contains a covered playground for the little ones, who will also like catching the bright red **Jolley Trolley** (727/445-1200, www.clearwaterjolleytrolley.com, $2.25 to ride, free for children 5 and under) from Clearwater Beach and heading back to your hotel, downtown, or to Sand Key.

Clearwater Beach has a few rules to follow: No alcohol on the beach. Swim within the "safe bathing limit" area, extending 300 feet west of the high water line and clearly marked by buoys or pilings. Personal watercraft and boats are not allowed within this line.

Clearwater Beach is just the warm-up, just to get your feet wet, so to speak. The area's other best beaches require more of a commitment and are more of a full-day adventure.

★ Fort De Soto Park

South of St. Petersburg, **Fort De Soto Park** (3500 Pinellas Bayway S., Tierra Verde, 727/582-2217, www.pinellascounty.org, open daylight hours, $5/vehicle parking, free for pedestrians and bicyclists) is 1,136 unspoiled acres with seven miles of beaches, two fishing piers, picnic and camping areas, a small history museum, and a 2,000-foot barrier-free nature trail for guests with disabilities, set on five little interconnected islands. The fort itself is in the southwest corner of Mullet Key, and there's a toll ($0.85) on the bridges leading into the park. The islands were once inhabited by the Tocobaga and visited by Spanish explorers. It was surveyed by Robert E. Lee before the Civil War, and during the war Union troops had a detachment on both Egmont and Mullet Keys. The fort was built in 1898 to protect Tampa Bay during the Spanish-American War and is listed on the National Register of Historic Places. And during World War II, the island was used for bombing practice by the pilot who dropped the bomb on Hiroshima. But you thought we were talking about beaches, right?

Well, exploring the old fort is part of what makes this experience special, drawing more than 2.7 million visitors annually. After checking out the four 12-inch seacoast rifled mortars (the only ones of their kind in the United States), head over to one of the two swim centers, the better of which is the North Beach Swim Center (it has concessions). At the beach you're likely to see laughing gulls, ibis, and ospreys, as well as beach sunflowers and beach morning glories peeking out from the sea oats. Fishing enthusiasts can choose between the 500-foot long pier on the Tampa Bay side or the 1,000-foot-long pier on the Gulf side. Each has a food and bait concession.

Once in the park, take a right at the stop sign, go one mile, and on the right look for **United Park Services** (3500 Pinellas Bayway

S., Tierra Verde, 727/864-1991, 10am-5pm daily, last rental at 3:30pm). It rents canoes and kayaks and issues maps of the area. Single kayaks rent for $23 for one hour, $29 for two hours; canoes cost $30 for one hour, $40 for two hours. Bike rentals are available inside the park at $8 an hour. Numbered signs along the shore mark a 2.25-mile kayak trail through Mullet Key Bayou.

Fort De Soto Park has the best camping in the area, with campsites directly on the Gulf. Camping is $33 per night (RV spots $40), but here's the rub for visitors: Most of the 236 campsites require reservations, which must be made *in person* far in advance. I figure it's a way to give locals the benefit of first pick. There are a handful of walk-in campsites available, but they are hot commodities. All sites have water and electrical hookups, and there are modern restrooms, dump stations, a camp store, washers/dryers, and grills. Primitive campsites are available at the Shell Key Preserve area of the park. Permits to camp at this primitive area are free and must be obtained from the park office in person. Pets are allowed in Area 2, and some of the spots are directly on the water. Be advised, the resident raccoons are more skillful than most, able to pick cooler locks and unwrap lunch meat with ease.

camping at Fort De Soto Park

★ Honeymoon Island and Caladesi Island Beaches

Honeymoon Island and Caladesi Island are a double whammy, perfectly suited to visiting back-to-back. In fact, the two islands were once part of a single larger barrier island, split in half during a savage hurricane in 1921. Together, they offer nearly 1,000 acres of mostly undeveloped land, not too changed from how it looked when Spanish explorers surveyed the coast in the mid-1500s.

The Tocobaga were the first known residents of Honeymoon Island, with ventures in more recent centuries having been quashed by deadly hurricanes. First known as Sand Island, then more inelegantly as Hog Island, it got its current name in the 1940s when

marketing people tried to pitch it as a retreat for newlyweds, with little palm-thatched bungalows and cottages. It didn't quite take, foiled also by World War II, and the island went through several changes of hands before becoming a state park.

After a huge beach re-nourishment project in 2007, **Honeymoon Island** (1 Causeway Blvd., at the extreme west end of Hwy. 586, Dunedin, 727/469-5942, 8am-sunset daily, admission $8/car for up to 8 people, $4/car single driver, $2 pedestrians and bicyclists) offers visitors all kinds of fun activities, but especially good is the fishing—you're likely to catch flounder, snook, trout, redfish, snapper, whiting, sheepshead, and, occasionally, tarpon. The island is home to 208 species of plants and a wealth of shore and wading birds, including a few endangered bird species. There is also a popular pet beach worth visiting for those traveling with their pets.

Directly to the south of Honeymoon and accessible only by boat, **Caladesi** (hourly ferry service available from Honeymoon,

727/469-5918, 8am-sunset daily, $14 adults, $7 children) is the wilder of the two islands. There's the state park marina and swim beach right near where the ferry lets you off, but the rest of the island remains undeveloped. The Gulf side of the island has three miles of white-sand beach (this is the part that always makes the top rankings of beaches), and the Tampa Bay side has a mangrove shoreline and sea grass flats. So, Gulf side for swimming and beach lolling, bay side for birding and wildlife-watching.

If you're a strong kayaker or sailor, you might take advantage of the kayak and sailboat rentals on the causeway near Honeymoon Island. Once on Caladesi, there's a 3.5-mile canoe trail starting and ending at the south end of the marina that leads paddlers through mangrove canals and tunnels and along sea grass flats on the bay side of the island.

Two cautions about Caladesi: Don't miss the last ferry or you'll be in a real pickle. And if you have brought a dog over to the dog beach at Honeymoon, it's a shame but Caladesi doesn't allow pets on the ferry (if you go by private boat, pets are invited on leash).

Other Beaches

St. Pete Beach has a lot of low-rise pastel motels and its fair share of high-rise hotel towers. For some reason you'll run into a lot of European travelers here; it has a livelier vibe than many Gulf Coast beaches, but not quite the spring break magnitude of Panama City Beach and other popular party spots. It is also a popular destination for families, and the resorts and hotels in the area commonly provide great children's amenities and entertainment to keep them occupied and having a good time.

The beach itself is long and wide, mostly as a result of sand restoration projects, with plenty of room to spread out and find a private patch of sand on the Gulf. There are concessions, picnic tables, lots of parking, showers, and restrooms. In all, you'll have a nice day at the beach.

There are a bunch of good beaches along **Sand Key,** which contains eight communities between John's Pass and Clearwater Pass. **John's Pass Beach** at the southern end of Sand Key and north for a couple of miles in **Madeira Beach** have beautiful sand and good fishing. Going north, the beaches in **Redington Beach** have limited public access but are pretty. Still farther north, **Indian Rocks Beach** has good public access and a party vibe, with lively beach bars. Bypass the

St. Pete Beach

beaches in **Belleair,** as access and amenities are limited, in favor of an afternoon at **Sand Key County Park** (north end of Gulf Blvd. at Clearwater Pass, 727/588-4852, $5/vehicle daily parking fee), which has lifeguards, playgrounds, cabana rentals, and lots of wide, white-sand beach.

GARDENS AND PARKS
★ Sunken Gardens

Sunken Gardens (1825 4th St. N., St. Petersburg, 727/551-3102, www.sunkengardens.org, 10am-4:30pm Mon.-Sat., noon-4:30pm Sun., $8 adults, $6 seniors, $4 children 2-11) was snatched from the jaws of death in 1999 and nursed back to health under the careful ministrations of the city of St. Petersburg. It was nothing a little nurturing and $3 million couldn't fix. It's a four-acre plot of land, much of it over 100 years old. There are 50,000 tropical plants and flowers, demonstration gardens, a 200-year-old oak tree, cascading waterfalls, and flamingos.

It's more than a garden—it's St. Petersburg's most beloved Old Florida attraction. In 1903, a plumber named George Turner Sr. bought the property, which contained a large sinkhole and a shallow lake. By dint of effort and a huge maze of clay tile, he drained the lake and prepared the soil for gardening. He sold the tropical fruit he grew here at a roadside stand, but folks liked walking through the tranquil greenery so much that he started charging admission. By 1935 the garden was officially opened as Turner's Sunken Gardens (because of the former lake and sinkhole, the whole thing sits down low in a basin), attracting approximately 300,000 visitors per year. It was followed by some other attractions: the World's Largest Gift Shop and the King of Kings Wax Museum.

But, as is common for these kinds of Florida attractions, business fell off as more upscale attractions became popular in this area among visitors. It poked along until the city felt compelled to help, also restoring the gift shop/wax museum space to its former glory (the children's museum **Great Explorations,** 1925 4th St. N., 727/821-8992, www.greatex.org, 10am-4:30pm Mon.-Sat., noon-4:30pm Sun., $10 general admission, $9 seniors, children 1 and under free, is housed here). If you're only able to visit one attraction here, make it Sunken Gardens. It is beautiful, and a definite slice of local history—a must if you can tear yourself away from the beach.

Other Gardens and Parks

For an outdoors experience, drive up to **Brooker Creek Preserve** (3940 Keystone Rd., Tarpon Springs, 727/453-6800, www.brookercreekpreserve.org, trail open sunrise-sunset daily). It's an 8,700-acre wilderness in the northern section of the county near Tarpon Springs. Currently, its environmental education center offers four miles of self-guided hiking trails at the southern end of Lora Lane off Keystone Road, about a half mile east of East Lake Road. The preserve also offers guided hikes every Saturday (reservation required, by phone or online) and hosts the annual **Music Jamboree** in December, a multi-genre acoustic jam session where musicians are encouraged to bring their instruments and join the fun.

Extending along the west side of Tampa Bay in Pinellas County, **Weedon Island Preserve Cultural and Natural History Center** (1800 Weedon Island Dr., St. Petersburg, 727/453-6500, www.weedonislandpreserve.org, preserve 7am-sunset daily, cultural center 9am-4pm Thurs.-Sat., free) is hard to classify exactly. Weedon Island Preserve is a group of low-lying islands in north St. Petersburg that as long as 10,000 years or so ago was home to Timucuans and Manasotas. The largest estuarine preserve in the county, it is also home to a large shell midden and burial mound complex. Visitors to the cultural center can see artifacts excavated from the site by the Smithsonian in the 1920s in exhibits designed collaboratively by anthropologists, historians, and Native Americans.

But you can't spend all your time at the cultural center watching videos about the art and history of the early peoples of Weedon

Island—the park has a four-mile canoe trail loop, a boardwalk and observation tower, three gentle miles of hiking trails, a fishing pier (snook, redfish, spotted trout), and waterfront picnic facilities. Weedon Island Preserve Center offers guided nature hikes every Saturday and regularly scheduled guided canoe excursions (registration 727/453-6506).

Accessible only by ferry or private boat, at the mouth of Tampa Bay, **Egmont Key State Park** (4905 34th St., St. Petersburg, 727/893-2627, www.floridastateparks.org, 8am-sunset daily, free) makes a great day trip. There aren't a lot of facilities on the island, which is wild except for the ruins of historic **Fort Dade** and brick paths that remain from when it was an active community with 300 residents. You'll see the 150-year-old working lighthouse (constructed in 1858 to "withstand any storm" after a first one was ravaged by two hurricanes in 1848 and 1852), gun batteries built in 1898, a pretty stretch of beach, and lots of gopher tortoises and hummingbirds. There is no camping on Egmont Key.

Owned by the state of Florida and maintained by the Manatee County Conservation Lands Management team, **Snead Island** (941/776-2295, 8am-sunset daily, free) is just east of Egmont Key, and another good opportunity to get out into the wilderness of this area—15 miles of it bordering shoreline along the Gulf and the lovely Manatee River. The park is favored by hikers because of its variety of trails and loops, with occasional boardwalks hugging the waterways. To get there, take Highway 41 into Palmetto, turn right onto 10th Street West, and follow signs to the island.

The west end of Snead Island is home to **Emerson Point Park** (5801 17th St. W., Palmetto, 941/748-4501, 8am-sunset daily, free), worth tacking on to your adventure—the park's 195 acres of salt marshes, beaches, mangrove swamp, lagoons, grass flats, hardwood hammocks, and semi-upland wooded areas are viewable from a well-maintained eight-foot-wide shell path, as well as more rustic walking and biking paths. Manatee County has poured money into this park in recent years such that master gardeners convene here regularly for guided walking tours of the varied plant and animal life. Call for the tour schedule.

Of special note to Native American historians, Emerson Point Park is home to the **Portavant Temple Mound** (east end of 17th St. W., Snead Island), an impressive mound complex. Walkways and boardwalks take you over and around a huge 150-foot flat-top temple mound and several horseshoe-shaped shell middens. Interpretive markers describe the site.

Anclote Key Preserve State Park (1 Causeway Blvd., Dunedin, 727/469-5943, 8am-sunset daily, free) is a similar island preserve accessible by boat, only this one offers primitive camping and is pet-friendly. During nesting season, rangers ask pet owners to keep their pets on the southeast end, as protected nesting birds take up residence in the north.

BIKING AND RUNNING

The best way to get oriented in the greater Tampa Bay area is to take a bike ride. **Northeast Cycles** (1114 4th St., St. Petersburg, 727/898-2453, $20/day, nice road bikes $50/day) will rent you bikes and a rack for an additional $10 so you can load them up and take them wherever you like, as will **Chainwheel Drive,** with two locations (1770 Drew St., Clearwater, 727/441-2444; and 32796 U.S. 19 N., in Palm Lake Plaza, Palm Harbor, 727/786-3883; 10am-7pm Mon.-Fri., 10am-5pm Sat., 11am-5pm Sun., $30 full day for hybrid, $40 full day for road bike).

Now that you've got the bikes, you may want to visit one of the most popular bike trails, the 34-mile-long **Pinellas Trail** (727/464-8400), one of the longest linear parks in the southeastern United States, running essentially from St. Petersburg up to the sponge docks of Tarpon Springs. A rails-to-trails kind of deal, the original rail track was home to the first Orange Belt Railroad train in 1888 and is now a well-maintained, 15-foot-wide trail through parks and coastal areas for bikers, in-line skaters, and joggers. There is a free guide to the Pinellas Trail available at the trail office, area libraries, and the Pinellas County Courthouse information desk (it can also be downloaded at www.pinellascounty. org—click on Overview Map of the Trail under Mileage Maps). It lists rest stops, service stations, restaurants, pay phones, bike shops, and park areas along the trail.

BIRDING

Every October Pinellas County hosts the annual **Florida Birding Festival & Nature Expo,** to which 3,000 avid birders flock. They come to hear a dynamic array of speakers and attend seminars, but mostly they come to tramp around on field trips to some of the region's top birding and wildlife areas. They come to look for some of the state's rarer bird species, like the reddish egret, little burrowing owls, and the Florida scrub jay, the only bird species unique to Florida.

If you're an avid birder or would like to learn more about birds, here's what you do: Go to the **Great Florida Birding Trail** website (www.floridabirdingtrail.com) and print out the *West Section* guide to the birding trail, which lists 117 sites in 21 counties. Many important birding sites are in Pinellas County. **Brooker Creek Preserve** and **East Beach** at Fort De Soto Park are both wonderful for birding. Beyond these, **Shell Key** (shuttle and charter boat access only, located at the southern end of Pass-A-Grille channel, just west of Tierre Verde), an undeveloped 180-acre barrier island in the area, is an important place for wintering and nesting seabirds and shorebirds, with more than 100 species sighted. **Boyd Hill Nature Preserve** (1101 Country Club Way S., St. Petersburg, 727/893-7326, 9am-7pm Tues.-Fri., 7am-6pm Sat., 9am-6pm Sun., $3 adults, $1.50 children) is 245 acres of pristine Florida wilderness, with five distinct ecosystems—hardwood hammocks, sand pine scrub, pine flatwoods, willow marsh, and the Lake Maggiore shoreline. This may be my favorite, as it is incredibly convenient,

an egret on St. Pete Beach

just minutes from downtown, but nonetheless feels far from the madding crowds. Precious green space in an urban landscape, it is an important stopover on the Atlantic Flyway—165 bird species have been observed here. You can camp at Boyd, and there's a small educational center with exhibits on five ecosystems.

Another spot on the Great Florida Birding Trail, also lauded by the National Audubon Society, is **Sawgrass Lake Park** (7400 25th St. N., immediately west of I-275 in Pinellas Park, St. Petersburg, 727/582-2100, 7am-sunset daily, free). Thousands of birds migrate through the park during the fall and spring. A one-mile elevated boardwalk winds through a maple swamp and oak hammock. There's an observation tower with views of the park's swamps, canals, and lake, where you're likely to see wood storks, herons, egrets, and ibis in addition to gators and turtles. The park has naturalist-led nature tours and field trips, and its Anderson Environmental Center contains a large

Smokin'

Here's a tricky scenario. You're on a great Gulf Coast vacation, the weather's perfect, you're feeling relaxed, so you decide to do a little charter fishing. You're out on the boat, you feel a yank, and there's a 40-pound greater amberjack on your line. You work for a while and haul in a couple more of those and a whole mess of 20-inch Spanish mackerel. What a great day. My question: Now what? Are you going to take that fish cooler back to the Radisson and stink up the joint?

Here's what to do: You go to **Ted Peters Famous Smoked Fish** (1350 Pasadena Ave., South Pasadena, 727/381-7931, www.tedpetersfish.com, 11:30am-7:30pm Wed.-Mon., $10-23, no credit cards) and they'll smoke them for you for $1.50 per pound. They can even make kingfish taste good, and that's saying something. They fillet them, throw them over a smoldering red oak fire in the smokehouse, then package them up for you to take. (The smoked fish keeps 4-5 days in the fridge.)

And if you don't have fish to smoke, still go to Ted Peters. It's been an institution for more than 50 years in Pinellas County, prized for its laid-back style and inviting picnic tables. The main attraction is obviously the smoked fish—the smoked fish spread with saltines is good, and the salmon and mullet are excellent. However, Ted Peters also produces some legendary cheeseburgers and potato salad (no fries here). This beer-drinking establishment gets busy in high season and closes early.

freshwater aquarium and exhibits on the area. My only caution is that during the wet months it can get a bit flooded in this park.

If you find an injured bird in your wandering, call **Suncoast Seabird Sanctuary** (18328 Gulf Blvd., Indian Shores, 727/391-6211), one of the country's largest nonprofit wild bird hospitals. With a new hospital facility, the sanctuary rescues and releases hundreds of birds each year into the wild. The sanctuary offers a free tour at 2pm Wednesday and Sunday, meeting at the beachfront deck.

FISHING
★ Sunshine Skyway Fishing Piers

It must have been a sight to see. In 1980, Hardaway Constructors of Tampa and a demolition team from Baltimore joined forces to perform the largest bridge demolition in Florida history. They were doing away with the 1954 Sunshine Skyway Bridge, a 15-mile crossing from St. Petersburg to Bradenton. From a long causeway on both sides, the steel bridge had a steep cantilever truss, 750 feet wide and with 150 feet of clearance above the water.

It wasn't enough clearance.

There had been some indication that this could happen—at least five freighters or barges were roughed up by this bridge, most of them with minor damage (the Coast Guard cutter USS *Blackthorn* met with disaster, but it was just west of the bridge and was weather-related). But it was during a violent storm on May 9, 1980, at 7:38am, when Captain John Lerro's visibility was nil, that the empty phosphate freighter *Summit Venture* slammed into the No. 2 south pier of the southbound span. It knocked 1,261 feet out of the center span, the cantilever, and part of the roadway into Tampa Bay. Thirty-five people on the bridge at the time perished, most of them in a Greyhound bus headed for Miami. The only survivor had his truck land by chance on the deck of the *Summit Venture.*

One of the worst bridge disasters in history, it prompted the design, funding, and building of a new **Sunshine Skyway Bridge.** At a cost of $245 million, it's the world's longest cable-stayed bridge, with a main span of 1,200 feet and a vertical clearance of 193 feet. The four-mile bridge opened for business in April 1987, equipped with a bridge protection system involving 36 large concrete bumpers (oddly called dolphins) built to withstand impact from rogue freighters and tankers up to 87,000 tons traveling at 10 knots.

So, you probably think I'm leading up to saying, "It's a gorgeous bridge, a real local landmark, you gotta drive over this thing." It's all true, but it's only part of the story. During the demolition of the old bridge spans, portions of it were preserved as fishing piers and the rubble piled alongside to form fish-friendly artificial reefs.

Since the original bridge span was built, fisherfolk have been bragging about the variety of game they catch: shark, tarpon, goliath grouper, kingfish, Spanish mackerel, grouper, sea bass. It's strange, because usually you have to be in a boat in order to have water deep enough for many of these species. Anglers have caught 1,000-pound tiger sharks from the bridge, traffic honking behind them. And now, with the artificial reefs adding extra enticement to the fish, the Sunshine Skyway Fishing Piers are killer fishing spots.

There's a 0.75-mile-long **North Pier** (727/865-0668) and a 1.5-mile-long **South Pier** (941/729-0117)—together said to be the world's longest fishing pier. You can drive your car onto the pier and park it right next to your fishing spot, parallel parking on the left lane, with room for cars to drive and walkways on either side of the span. There are restrooms on both piers, and bait shops sell live and frozen bait, tackle, drinks, and snacks. They also rent rods. The North Pier has a large picnic area next to the bait shop.

To get there, head south on I-275 toward Bradenton. The North Pier is about a mile past the toll ($1). To reach the South Pier, continue over the bridge and follow the signs. There is a $4 per vehicle charge, plus $4 general admission, $2 children 6-11, children under 6 free. *You don't need a fishing license to fish off the piers.*

So, yeah, drive over the new bridge, but, more importantly, wet a line on the remnants of the old one.

SPECTATOR SPORTS
Baseball

Tropicana Field (1 Tropicana Dr., St. Petersburg, 727/825-3250, game days vary, times usually 2:15pm or 7:15pm, tickets $5-32) is currently home to the Tampa Bay Rays. As a concession to summer temperatures and humidity in these parts, the ballpark has a dome roof (which is lit orange when the Rays win at home) and artificial turf. Out of season, Tropicana Field hosts other athletic events, conventions, trade shows, concerts, and other entertainment, with a seating capacity of 43,773.

For spring training, the Rays until 2008 played locally at **Progress Energy Park, Home of Al Lang Field.** Now the Rays relocate each spring to the **Charlotte County Sports Park,** a grass-surface park with a 7,000-person seating capacity located a couple of hours south in Port Charlotte. Don't fret, though, because there's other spring training action nearby. Spring training games are all month in March, and tickets usually go on sale January 15. The **Philadelphia Phillies** have been training at **Bright House Networks Field** (601 Old Coachman Rd., 727/712-4300, game days vary, times usually 1:05pm or 7:05pm, tickets $15-32) in Clearwater since 1948. It's a great venue, with a tiki-hut pavilion in left field, a kids' play area, group picnic areas, party suites, and club seats. The **Toronto Blue Jays** also have spring training in the area, playing at **Florida Auto Exchange Park** (373 Douglas Ave., Dunedin, 727/733-9302, game days vary, times usually 1:05pm, tickets $13-24), formerly Dunedin Stadium. Built in 1990, it's a smaller ballpark in a fairly residential area (you end up paying almost as much for parking as for your ticket). There are upper and lower sections, the upper section having a slight overhang, which can be cooling during warm day games.

Sights

ART MUSEUMS

The arts are booming in St. Petersburg, especially those visual. Opened in 2010, the **Chihuly Collection at the Morean Arts Center** is a beautiful showcase for the Seattle glassblower's eccentric work. **The Morean Arts Center** (719 Central Ave., 727/822-7872, 10am-5pm Mon.-Sat., noon-5pm Sun., $15 Chihuly collection, $20 full access, $9 glass studio) has a ton going on in its 5,000 square feet of gallery space, divided up into six small galleries, plus classroom space for ceramics, painting, drawing, digital imaging, photography, printmaking, jewelry making, metalworking, and sculpture classes.

In 2008, the **Museum of Fine Arts** (255 Beach Dr. NE, St. Petersburg, 727/896-2667, www.fine-arts.org, 10am-5pm Mon.-Sat., noon-5pm Sun., $17 adults, $15 seniors and students, $10 children 7-18, children 6 and under free) unveiled its much-anticipated Hazel Hough Wing. It started with a gangbuster exhibition of works that have been rarely on view or in some cases, never before displayed at the MFA. Featuring works by such noted artists as Renoir, Léger, Pissarro, Matisse, Fabergé, Chuck Close, and James Rosenquist, it showcased just how marvelous the museum's collection is. Right on the waterfront adjacent to Straub Park, the museum contains the full gamut of art from antiquity to the present day. The collection of 4,000 objects includes significant works by Cézanne, Monet, Gauguin, Renoir, Rodin, Henri, Bellows, and O'Keeffe. Its permanent collection's strength is 17th- and 18th-century European art, and the museum has a lovely garden as well.

Beach Art Center (1515 Bay Palm Blvd., Indian Rocks Beach, 727/596-4331, 8:45am-4pm Mon.-Thurs., 9am-noon Fri., class and exhibit fees vary) is another sweet nonprofit arts center with classes for locals in fine arts and crafts. It also has two small galleries set up in the old American Legion Hall. In a similar vein, the **Dunedin Fine Arts Center & Children's Art Museum** (1143 Michigan Blvd., Dunedin, 727/298-3322, www.dfac.org, 10am-5pm Mon.-Fri., 10am-2pm Sat., 1pm-4pm Sun., class and exhibit fees vary) has four galleries, studio classrooms, a children's museum, the Palm Cafe, and a gallery gift shop. The exhibits are often the work of students.

★ Salvador Dalí Museum

Perhaps the most popular art museum in Pinellas County is the **Salvador Dalí Museum** (1 Dali Blvd., St. Petersburg, 727/823-3767, www.thedali.org, 10am-5:30pm Fri.-Wed., 10am-8pm Thurs., $24 adults, $22 seniors, $17 students, $10 children 6-12, children 5 and under free), the world's most comprehensive collection of permanent works by the famous Spanish surrealist master, with other exhibits relating to Dalí. A new museum was constructed for the collection and opened in 2011 to worldwide acclaim. The architect Yann Weymouth designed an awe-inspiring building described as a "building that combines the rational with the fantastical: a simple rectangle with 18-inch thick hurricane-proof walls out of which erupts a large free-form geodesic glass bubble known as the enigma." The impressive helical staircase inside the building recalls Dali's own obsession with spirals and the double helix shape of the DNA molecule. The new Avante Garden outside the building extends this theme and provides a calming space to explore the relationship between math and nature. The new museum has quickly become nearly as popular as the collection housed inside. AOL Travel News listed the museum as one of the top 20 buildings to see in your lifetime, and the Florida Association of the American Institute of Architects named it as the top museum design in the state.

Dalí himself is as recognizable as his

St. Petersburg

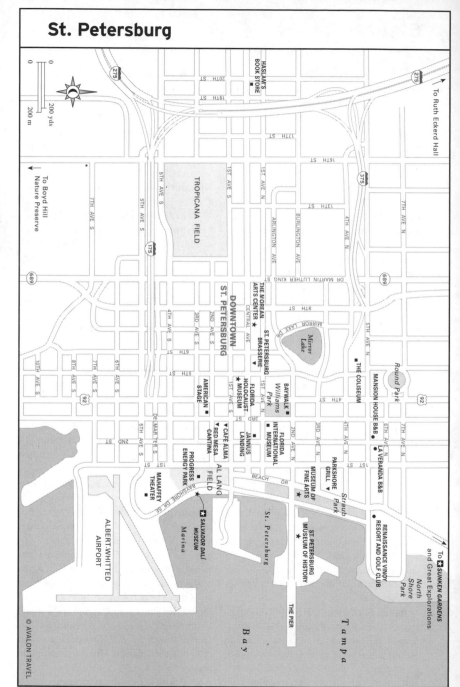

"paranoiac-critical" paintings. Maybe only Van Gogh in his post-ear-incident self-portrait is more reliably identified than Salvador Dalí, with his long, waxed mustache and extreme arched eyebrows. Upon moving to the United States in the 1940s, Dalí made himself the lovable eccentric who introduced the average American to surrealism—and the average American really liked it.

The Salvador Dalí Museum is a dense concentration of his surrealist works, what he described as a "spontaneous method of irrational knowledge based on the critical and systematic objectivation of delirious associations and interpretations."

The museum is wonderful—a great space where the work is described and presented well. Even if you don't care for what you have seen of his work in books and prints, it is an incredible experience to view the original works in their larger-than-life sizes. And if you have never experienced his works at all, the museum is almost sure to make you a fan.

HISTORY MUSEUMS

The **Florida Holocaust Museum** (55 5th St. S., St. Petersburg, 727/820-0100, www.flholocaustmuseum.org, 10am-5pm daily, $16 adults, $14 seniors, $10 college students, $8 students under 18) is the third largest of its kind in the United States. Some of the museum is devoted to the memory of millions of innocent people who suffered, struggled, and died in the Holocaust. It also showcases only loosely linked exhibits such as the work of Czech artist Charles Pachner (who lost his whole family during the war) or the mixed-media paintings, sculptures, and installations of contemporary French artist Marc Ash.

St. Petersburg Museum of History

(335 2nd Ave. NE, St. Petersburg, 727/894-1052, www.spmoh.org, 10am-5pm Mon.-Sat., noon-5pm Sun., $15 adults, $12 seniors and students, $9 children 6-17) is one of the oldest historical museums in the state, with family-friendly displays and exhibits depicting St. Petersburg's past. It was remodeled and enlarged in 2005, with a local history exhibit that contains a Native American dugout canoe, an exact replica of the world's first scheduled commercial airliner (it flew out of St. Petersburg), and lots of other interesting exhibits.

Beyond these, the history buff can visit the restored homes and buildings of the **Heritage Village** (11909 125th St. N., Largo, 727/582-2123, www.pinellascounty.org, 10am-4pm Wed.-Sat., 1pm-4pm Sun., free). It's a living

the Salvador Dalí Museum

history museum with people in period costume, spinning, weaving, and acting out other period activities. Most of the 25 structures date back to the late 19th century. If you go to Heritage Village, make a day of it and visit the **Florida Botanical Gardens** (12520 Ulmerton Rd., Largo, 727/582-2100, www.flbg.org, 7am-sunset daily, garden entry free), where you can take a tour through gardens led by a local master gardener. You walk 1.5 miles, it takes 1.5 hours, and you learn all about Florida gardening. The approaches can be vastly different—there's a rose garden, a beach garden, a tropical courtyard, a topiary garden, a bromeliad garden, and more. On a nice day, it's a wonderful spot.

AQUARIUMS

Just over the bay in Tampa, the Florida Aquarium usually gets most of the visitors. **Clearwater Marine Aquarium** (249 Windward Passage, Clearwater, 727/441-1790, www.seewinter.com, 10am-5pm daily, $22 adults, $17 seniors, $15 children 3-12) is a smaller, more modest facility. Reopened in 2008 after some major renovations, it's a working research facility and home to rescued and recuperating marine mammals (dolphins, whales, otters,

etc.) that include Winter, the dolphin that lost her tail and was made famous in the Disney movie *Dolphin Tales*. For the visitor, the thrust is education, with hourly animal care and training presentations and exhibits on animal rescue, rehabilitation, and release—and how the public can help to protect and conserve endangered marinelife. The aquarium offers on-site feeding and care programs for interested guests and operates a daily 90-minute-long **Sea Life Safari** (25 Causeway Blvd., Slip #58, Clearwater Beach, 727/462-2628, $26 adults, $23 seniors, $17 children) that takes visitors around the Clearwater estuary and Intracoastal Waterway, with commentary by a marine biologist.

Smaller, more like a really big pet store, the **Tarpon Springs Aquarium** (850 Dodecanese Blvd., Tarpon Springs, 727/938-5378, www.tarponspringsaquarium.com, 10am-5pm Mon.-Sat., noon-5pm Sun., $7.75 adults, $7 seniors, $5.75 children, children 3 and under free) has a 120,000-gallon main tank aquarium with more than 30 species of fish, including nurse sharks, bonnet head sharks, snook, tarpon, and protected goliath grouper. The best time to visit is shark or alligator feeding times: alligators at 12:30pm

a paved path through the Florida Botanical Gardens

Soaking up Greek Culture

Tarpon Springs, a coastal town 15 miles north of Clearwater, has quite the past. John Corcoris, a sponge diver from Greece, brought his capabilities along with his sponge-diving equipment (a rubber suit and a heavy copper helmet) to Tarpon Springs around 1900. Soon, he persuaded friends and family, sponge divers all, to relocate from Hydra and Aegena, Greece, to this little Florida backwater.

A booming town of Greek restaurants, Greek Orthodox churches, and Greek festivals was born, centering on the sponge industry. Tarpon Springs was the largest U.S. sponge-diving port in the 1930s. The town is still more than a third Greek, with a nice Old Florida charm and several fine restaurants. Sponges are still everywhere, but most of them are now imported from more sponge-rich lands.

Take an afternoon to see the museum **Spongeorama** (510 Dodecanese Blvd., 727/943-2164, 10:30am-6pm Mon.-Sat., 11:30am-6pm Sun., free) and the sponge docks, shop a little, and have dinner. A little down at the heels, the shop/attraction has mannequins

baskets of sponges for sale in Tarpon Springs

dressed as sponge divers and shows an old crackly movie called *Men and the Sea.*

If you're still angling for more sponge action, the **St. Nicholas Boat Line** (693 Dodecanese Blvd., 727/942-6425, $6 adults, $2 children 6-12, children under 6 free) offers a fun 30-minute narrated boat cruise through the sponge docks, with its own sponge-diving demonstration.

Out on the main drag, Dodecanese Boulevard, there are seven blocks of shops and restaurants. Before you settle on a place to eat, stop into nearby **St. Nicholas Church** (18 Hibiscus St., 727/944-3366), made of 60 tons of Greek marble. The church is a copy of the Byzantine Revival St. Sophia in Constantinople, with beautiful Czech chandeliers and stained glass.

If the weather's nice, stroll along one of the paths in nearby **Anclote River Park** (1119 Baileys Bluff Rd., Holiday, 727/938-2598, dawn-dusk daily, free). The park boasts an easy two-mile round-trip trail, as well as fishing access, a boat ramp, a playground for the kids, a swimming beach, and picnic facilities. It's also a notable destination for birders—favored for its resident reddish egrets and osprey nests. Actually, it's part of a cluster of parks on the Great Florida Birding Trail, along with the nearby **Key Vista Nature Park** (2700 Baileys Bluff Rd., Holiday, 727/938-2598, dawn-dusk daily, $2 parking), which has even more diverse natural habitats, from fresh- and saltwater marshes to pine uplands and tidal flats, all the better for observing species like loons and migratory warblers.

So now you're hungry. Everyone has a different favorite Greek restaurant here. One favorite is **Hellas Restaurant and Bakery** (785 Dodecanese Blvd., 727/943-2400, 11am-10pm daily, $10-20), a lively spot with a full bar and a wonderful Greek bakery attached to it. The best entrée is its slowly braised tomatoey lamb shanks. There are addictive garlic shrimp, gyros in warm Greek pita, and a delicious Greek salad. Others swear by **Mykonos** (628 Dodecanese Blvd., 727/934-4306, 11am-10pm daily, $10-20) for the lamb chops, Greek meat loaf, and slightly more upscale atmosphere. Still, **Mama's** (735 Dodecanese Blvd., 727/944-2888, 11am-10pm daily, $7-14) often gets the nod for casual, family-friendly booths and delicious but messy chicken souvlaki sandwiches. If you're visiting on a Saturday night, head over after dinner to the bouzouki club called **Zorba** (508 W. Athens, 727/934-8803), for some zesty belly-dancing and an ouzo.

For more information about Tarpon Springs, contact the **Tarpon Springs Cultural Center** (727/942-5605, www.tarponarts.com) or the **chamber of commerce** (111 E. Tarpon Ave., 727/937-6109, www.tarponspringschamber.com).

and 3:30pm; sharks at 11:30am, 1pm, 2:30pm, and 4pm.

NATIVE AMERICAN SITES

Pinellas County's rich Native American heritage is not very noticeable today—but there are a couple of sites that command quite a bit of enthusiasm among historical travelers. One is a platform mound set in a beautiful country park called both the **Safety Harbor Mound** and the **Philippe Park Temple Mound** (2525 Philippe Pkwy., Safety Harbor, 727/669-1947, 7am-sunset daily, free). The mound is behind shelter number two and is described with interpretive markers. The large mound complex is believed to be the village of Tocobaga, for which the Tocobaga are named. It is said that in 1567 Pedro Menéndez de Avilés, the founder of St. Augustine, visited this Tocobaga village. For a little more insight, two miles south of Philippe Park is the **Safety Harbor Museum of Regional History** (329 S. Bayshore Dr., 727/724-1562, 10am-4pm Tues.-Sat., 1pm-4pm Sun., free), which contains artifacts from the Weedon Island, Safety Harbor, and Mississippian periods.

Seeing more Tocobaga handiwork requires only a short drive to the **Pinellas Point**

Temple Mound (7am-sunset daily, free). The large flat mound, topped by a comfy bench, is all that remains of a sizable village. To get there, head east on 62nd Avenue South and turn south onto 20th Street, which ends at the mound.

FAMILY-FRIENDLY ATTRACTIONS

The No. 1 kids' draw is the beach, hands down. All the beaches of Pinellas County are enormously kid-centric, with amenities, snacks, bathrooms, and all the necessities for a day of seaside bliss. When you need a break from beachcombing and sand castle building, though, the area has lots of other lures.

Bilgewater Bill, Mad Dog Mike, Gangplank Gary, and the other pirates will greet you with an "argh, me matey" on the deck of **Captain Memo's Original Pirate Cruise** (25 Causeway Blvd., Dock 3, Clearwater Beach, 727/446-2587, www.captainmemo.com, 10am, 2pm, and sunset daily, $36 adults, $33 seniors, $28 children), a two-hour pirate cruise on a fancy, bright red pirate ship. In a similar vein, **John's Pass Village & Boardwalk** (12901 Gulf Blvd. E., just between Madeira Beach and Treasure Island, 727/394-0756, www.boattoursjohnspass.com, 11am, 2pm, and sunset

Clearwater Marine Aquarium

daily, $35 adults, $30 seniors, $25 children 2-20, $10 children under 2) offers a **Pirates at the Pass** cruise on a fully kitted-out pirate ship. You'll engage in water pistol battles and treasure hunts and listen to pirate stories.

John's Pass Village is home to a large commercial and charter fishing fleet, as well as art galleries, restaurants, and boutiques along a waterfront boardwalk. Families also seem to enjoy the dolphin tours out of John's Pass and into scenic Boca Ciega Bay. A couple of companies offer these—**Hubbard's Sea Adventures** (departs from John's Pass boardwalk, 727/398-6577, www.hubbardsmarina.com, 11am, 1pm, 3pm, and 5pm daily in summer, 1pm and 3pm daily in fall, $21 adults, $10 children 11 to 2) brings you face to face with the bay's abundance of wildlife.

Farther south, **Dolphin Landings** (4737 Gulf Blvd., behind the Dolphin Village Shopping Center, St. Pete Beach, 727/360-7411, www.charterboatescape.com, sailing times vary, $25-50) conducts two-hour dolphin-watch cruises and longer three- to four-hour trips to Shell Key, an undeveloped barrier island. The scheduled trips and private charters are conducted on one of 40 locally owned sailboats, pontoon boats, and deep-sea fishing yachts.

After spending time at Sunken Gardens, give the kids their due next door at **Great Explorations** (1925 4th St. N., St. Petersburg, 727/821-8992, www.greatex.org, 10am-4:30pm Mon.-Sat., noon-4:30pm Sun., $10 general admission, $9 seniors, children 1 and under free). The hands-on science center has lots of slick educational exhibits on things like the hydrologic cycle or ecosystem of the estuary. Many of the exhibits are best appreciated by late-elementary-aged kids (let's say kids up to about 11), but exhibits such as Gears and the Laser Harp have appeal even to little kids. If your family enjoys hands-on science museums, head over to Tampa's MOSI for a bigger dose. This makes a fun afternoon, though, especially when capped by an ice cream at Cold Stone Creamery, craftily located on the premises.

The artistically inclined kid might enjoy visiting Dunedin Fine Art Center, which contains the **David L. Mason Children's Art Museum** (1143 Michigan Blvd., Dunedin, 727/298-3322, www.dfac.org, 10am-5pm Mon.-Fri., 10am-2pm Sat., 1pm-4pm Sun., $4 general admission, $3 seniors, children 2 and under free), a gallery space for children. This smaller part of the museum provides hands-on activities that assist

John's Pass Village & Boardwalk

families in understanding and appreciating the work of Florida artists exhibited in the galleries. Even if you spend your time in the art center and not the children's museum, the scale is such that it's not intimidating or boring for kids.

If you're looking for something a little more exciting, **Celebration Station** (24546 U.S. 19 N., Clearwater, 727/791-1799, www.celebrationstation.com, 11am-9pm Sun.-Thurs., 11am-11pm Fri., 10am-11pm Sat., tokens $10/ roll, different prices for activities) brings you go-carts, bumper boats, games, miniature golf, batting cages, laser tag, and pizza.

Arts and Entertainment

MUSIC

A couple of big venues host a range of performances. **Ruth Eckerd Hall** (1111 McMullen Booth Rd. N., Clearwater, 727/791-7400, www. rutheckerdhall.com, times and prices vary) is the locus for much of the area's lively arts activity. The 2,200-seat space was designed by the Frank Lloyd Wright Foundation 25 years ago, and the space still looks fresh, the sound still full and lush (acoustically, it had a fairly recent overhaul). It's home to the **Florida Orchestra** (mail: 244 2nd Ave. N., #420, St. Petersburg, FL 33701, 727/892-3331, www.floridaorchestra.org), which is the top regional orchestra, performing more than 130 concerts annually here, at the Mahaffey Theater, and elsewhere. Beyond symphonic music, Ruth Eckerd hosts pop acts, visiting theater, and other performing arts. (Its educational wing, the **Marcia P. Hoffman School of the Arts,** features the 182-seat Murray Studio Theatre, three studio classrooms, four private teaching studios, a dance studio and rehearsal space, and an arts resource library.)

The **Mahaffey Theater at the Progress Energy Center** (400 1st St. S., St. Petersburg, 727/892-5798, www.themahaffey.com, times and prices vary) changed entirely in 2004 when it was determined that its Bayfront Center Arena was no longer viable in the marketplace. The arena was demolished at the end of that year, opening up space for the current Mahaffey Theater renovation. The $20 million project more than doubled lobby size, adding guest amenities and expanding ballroom capacity and versatility. The signature component of the renovated theater is a three-story glass-curtain wall and glass-enclosed atrium that overlooks the city's beautiful downtown waterfront. A lovely theater, it hosts the Broadway Across America series, many performances of the Florida Orchestra, jazz, ballet, opera, the circus, and contemporary performers as well. The Mahaffey is directly on the waterfront, within walking distance of shopping, some of the area's finest restaurants, and many of the downtown museums.

A smaller venue for rock and contemporary acts, **Jannus Landing** (220 1st Ave. N., St. Petersburg, 727/565-0550, www.jannuslive. com, times and prices vary) is supposedly the oldest outdoor concert venue in Florida. From jam bands like the Allman Brothers to Grizfolk to Lucinda Williams—it all sounds great from a spot in the outdoor courtyard. It's bigger than a nightclub, with bigger acts, but there's still a cool club vibe and usually a 30s-and-up crowd.

The historic **Coliseum** (535 4th Ave. N., 727/892-5202, parking area on the left $5, times and prices vary) was built in 1924 and purchased by the city of St. Petersburg in 1989. It has updated the beautiful space and reopened it as a multiuse facility, hosting a range of events from Florida Orchestra pops concerts to the Toronto All Star Big Band to an exotic bird show.

THEATER

At the top of the dramatic arts heap in Pinellas County, **American Stage Theatre**

Company at the Raymond James Theatre (163 3rd St. N., St. Petersburg, 727/823-7529, www.americanstage.org, curtain usually 7:30pm Tues.-Thurs., 8pm Fri.-Sat., weekend matinees 3pm, tickets $22-35) is Tampa Bay's oldest professional theater, with a six-play season on the main stage plus children's theater, educational outreach, and the annual Shakespeare in the Park festival.

In its 35nd year in 2013, American Stage entered into a partnership with St. Petersburg College and built a brand-new state-of-the-art building in the heart of downtown St. Petersburg, facing Williams Park only four blocks from the original location. The theater has expanded its audience capacity to 182 and added two large lobbies. There is free parking at the nearby Synovis Bank during performances.

The main-stage season shows breadth, reaching from Harling's *Steel Magnolias* to the classic musical *The Wiz*. The Family Series is a good deal, with single tickets $7.

For local community theater, several companies are worth checking out, all with reasonable ticket prices. Throughout its 83 years as Florida's oldest continuously operating community theater, **St. Petersburg City Theatre** (4025 31st St. S., St. Petersburg, 727/866-1973, www.spcitytheatre.org, curtain 8pm and 2pm matinees on Sun., $10-$22 nonmusicals) has presented up to six community productions per season, split fairly evenly between musicals, comedies, and dramas. It's usually crowd-pleasers like *Noises Off* or Neil Simon's *Brighton Beach Memoirs*.

Francis Wilson Playhouse (302 Seminole St., Clearwater, 727/446-1360, www.franciswilsonplayhouse.org, curtain 8pm and 2pm matinees, $26 adults, $15 children and students) is another venerable community playhouse, having opened in 1930. The intimate, 182-seat theater showcases eight comedies and musicals (*Sweet Charity, Auntie Mame*) per season and a family-oriented program in December.

In the little town of Gulfport on Boca Ciega Bay, the **Catherine Hickman Theater** (5501 27th Ave. S., 727/552-2222) hosts Gulfport Community Players community theater productions and Pinellas Park Civic Orchestra concerts.

the historic Coliseum

Shopping

The Pier (800 2nd Ave. NE, St. Petersburg, 727/895-7437) is the heart and soul of visitor activity in St. Petersburg, looking like an inverted pyramid, or the good guys' home base in a sci-fi movie. You can rent bikes, grab a rental rod and reel and fish off the end, depart from the Pier on a sightseeing boat charter, see a flick at the 20-screen movie theater, visit the little aquarium, dine in the family-friendly food court, or browse the complex's many shops. It's not high-end stuff—there's a pet accoutrement store, an entertainment-celebrity collectibles shop, a candle store, T-shirt stores, and that kind of thing.

Sundial St. Pete (153 2nd Ave. N., St. Petersburg, 727/800-3201, www.sundialstpete. com) underwent a significant redesign and remodeling in 2013. The shopping center, which formerly catered to more upscale chain shops like Ann Taylor and Chico's, has been transformed into an office park that centers around a gourmet market, a day spa, a Starbucks and a variety of mostly health care-related businesses. It still has a 20-screen movie theater that shows a mix of first-run films and independent movies and documentaries.

Florida's largest new and used bookstore merits a couple of hours of browsing, especially if the weather is inclement (a rarity). The independent **Haslam's Book Store** (2025 Central Ave., St. Petersburg, 727/822-8616, www.haslams.com, 10am-6:30pm Mon.-Sat., noon-5pm Sun.) is now owned by the third generation of the same family and has more than 300,000 volumes. The store has a large number of rare books, and they seem to be really into science fiction.

Food

Pinellas County is awash in restaurants, most of them fun and casual, many of them worthy of recommendation. Because the area is densely populated and traffic can get fairly impacted during high season, you're more likely to grab a bite near where you're staying or near the beach from which you're departing. For this reason, I'm listing the restaurants in the Clearwater-St. Petersburg area geographically, from north to south. There are, on the other hand, those restaurants that are worth a drive in traffic, what restaurateurs call "destination restaurants." I'll describe these first.

FINE DINING

In keeping with the glitz of the historic Vinoy, its restaurant, **Marchand's Grill** (The Vinoy Renaissance Resort, 501 5th Ave. NE, St. Petersburg, 727/824-8072, 6:30am-10pm daily, $18-35), features the central Vinoy Bar, velvet armchairs around all tables. A small wine cellar room provides an intimate dining space for four. The kitchen has a seafood focus, but dishes reflect a more Mediterranean approach. If you want to pull out all the stops at the Vinoy, **Fred's Steakhouse** is even more of a splurge, but you have to be a member or a resort guest to enjoy it.

The ★ **Cafe Ponte** (13505 Icot Blvd., Clearwater, 727/538-5768, www.cafeponte. com, 11:30am-2pm and 5:30pm-10pm Mon.-Thurs., 11:30am-2pm and 5:30pm-11pm Fri., 5:30pm-11pm Sat., $12-32) features Chef Christopher Ponte, who trained at Taillevent in Paris and studied at Johnson & Wales and the Cordon Bleu. His upscale restaurant in the Icot Center is located in a strip mall; the setting may confound would-be diners, but a single meal will set them straight. The kitchen prepares offerings such as a rich mushroom soup with a spoon of truffle cream and a potato encrusted sea bass.

Salt Rock Grill (19325 Gulf Blvd., Indian Shores, 727/593-7625, www.saltrockgrill.com, 4pm-10pm Mon.-Thurs., 4pm-11pm Fri.-Sat., noon-10pm Sun., $15-30) is fairly mobbed every night. The menu has enticing seafood like pan-seared scallops and mussels in white wine sauce, as well as expertly prepared steaks aged in-house and grilled over a super hot natural oak and citrus wood pit fire. It's more formal than most beachside spots around here, and the locals love it.

Maritana Grille at the Don CeSar (3400 Gulf Blvd., St. Pete Beach, 727/360-1882, www.loewshotels.com, 5:30pm-10pm daily, $18-40) has a great chef's table for groups up to eight, at which executive chef Kenny Hunsberger is put through his Floribbean-cuisine paces, from pan-seared scallops served with purple potatoes to grilled filet mignon with truffled mashed potatoes and candied shallots. The restaurant's interior is incredible, the patrons surrounded by 1,500 gallons of saltwater aquariums and indigenous Florida fish.

DUNEDIN

A fun place to start casually dining in Pinellas County is **Bon Appetit** (148 Marina Plaza, 727/733-2151, 7am-10pm daily, $12-35). It's in the Best Western Yacht Harbor Inn and Suites, and owners Peter Keuziger and Karl Heinz Riedl manage to add a definite style to the seafood-heavy menu, whether it's grilled sea scallops with a mango chutney or the season's freshest stone crabs with only a squeeze of lemon and butter. The thing is, you don't have to pay the big prices—guests can watch the dolphins play as the sun sets out on the water and not break the bank if they dine at the **Marine Café** adjacent to the restaurant. It's a different menu from the fancier sibling, but a single sheet of signature dishes from the main restaurant is available outside.

Downtown Dunedin has been reinvigorated with restaurants and cafés in recent years. For casual Mexican, go to **Casa Tina** (365 Main St., 727/734-9226, 11am-10pm Sun.-Thurs., 11am-11pm Fri.-Sat., $7-15). It's lively, with an eye-catching color scheme, and the food is a little less heavy than many local Mexican joints—that said, try the wild mushroom quesadilla.

About as family-friendly, **Kelly's Restaurant** (319 Main St., 727/736-0206, 8am-9:30pm Mon.-Thurs., 8am-10:30pm Fri.-Sat., 8am-9pm Sun., $8-20) has a comfort food menu that leaves no stone unturned, from baby back ribs to butternut squash ravioli. It's a kids' kind of joint, friendly and accommodating.

If you're looking to dine at a "nouvelle" restaurant, meaning a place that has high prices for small portions artistically arranged on the plates, **The Black Pearl** (315 Main St., 727/734-3463, 5pm-9pm Sun.-Mon., 5pm-10pm Tues.-Thurs., 5pm-11pm Fri.-Sat., $18-30) next door is perfect for you. Try the cedar-planked salmon or the crab imperial.

Around since 1993 in Dunedin, **Ivory Mandarin Bistro** (2192 Main St., 727/734-3998, 11am-9:30pm Mon.-Thurs., 11am-10pm Fri.-Sat., $8-25) has slowly accrued a wall's worth of accolades and "best of" awards along with its devoted clientele. Crisp linens and Chinese floral prints make the place feel more formal, but the menu reads like a greatest-hits list of Cantonese American dishes. That means hot and sour soup, juicy pork spareribs, sweet-tangy orange beef, and pan-fried chow fun noodles.

CLEARWATER

Clearwater has a fairly dense concentration of good restaurants. But really, you owe it to yourself to go to the original **Hooters** (2800 Gulf to Bay Blvd., 727/797-4008, 11am-11pm Sun.-Thurs., 11am-midnight Fri.-Sat., $8-20). Almost 25 years old, the original sports-oriented joint has spawned an international empire. It's a family restaurant, really, with good chicken wings offered in a variety of styles and sauces. Only it's a family restaurant in which all the waitresses are wearing flesh-colored pantyhose under orange nylon short-shorts.

By the way, a *cooter* is a red-bellied turtle that was historically serious eats for early Floridians. That's why **Cooters Raw Bar and Restaurant** (423 Poinsettia Ave., 727/462-2668, www.cooters.com, 11am-11pm Sun.-Thurs., 11am-midnight Fri.-Sat., $9-20) is called that. It's a fun place with good steamed crab legs and fried grouper.

Lenny's Restaurant (21220 U.S. 19 N., 727/799-0402, 6am-3pm daily, $5-12) is the hands-down winner for breakfast, for the Jewish staples of blintzes, knishes, and latkes.

Evening partying is to be found all around, in tiki huts and outdoor decks along the Gulf beaches. One bar, though, is worth mentioning: ★ **O'Keefe's Tavern and Restaurant** (1219 S. Fort Harrison Ave., 727/442-9034, 11am-2am Wed.-Sat., 11am-midnight Sun.-Tues., $7-14). It is the bar to beat for St. Patrick's Day. The Irish pub's history goes back to the 1960s when it was O'Keefe's Tap Room, a history still visible despite the many additions and remodelings. A white brick exterior gives way to a comfortable series of rooms decked out with lots of green accents and Irishobilia. The brogue-required bartenders are fast and furious with the beers (more than 100 offerings), and the all-ages crowd is unified by their affection for the place. Once known for its "seven-course Irish dinner" (that's six beers and a potato), O'Keefe actually serves good fare.

INDIAN ROCKS BEACH AND REDINGTON SHORES

Crabby Bill's (401 Gulf Blvd., Indian Rocks Beach, 727/595-4825, www.crabbybillsirb.com, 11am-11pm daily, $8-22) is a family-owned regional chain that has made a name for itself with family-style seating, group singing, seafood cookery, and flowing beverages.

Cafe Alma (111 Boardwalk Place, Madeira Beach, 727/502-5002, 11am-10pm Tues.-Thurs., 11am-midnight Fri., 9am-midnight Sat., 9am-9pm Sun., $16-25) has quickly become a favorite of Madeira Beach after it recently moved from downtown St. Petersburg

The menu underwent major changes and now features a wide variety of small tapas plates and large seafood-centric offerings. They also have wonderful tacos and a selection of tasty lunch sandwiches. If you're looking for a festive vibe, visit in the evening.

ST. PETERSBURG

Remember, downtown St. Petersburg is on the east side of the peninsula, not on the Gulf, but on Old Tampa Bay. There are several wonderful picks here—definitely the densest concentration of fine dining in Pinellas County.

The **Parkshore Grill** (300 Beach Dr. NE, 727/896-3463, 11am-10pm Mon.-Thurs., 11am-11pm Fri.-Sat., 10am-10pm Sun.), has a wonderful outside patio within sight of the Museum of Fine Arts. The menu leans to smart spins on contemporary American cuisine, with spice-seared tuna and roasted organic salmon fillet. The restaurant has received numerous accolades in recent years, the most remarkable being two Golden Spoon Awards in 2012 and 2013.

For some excellent Mexican food, try **Red Mesa Cantina** (128 3rd St. S., 727/896-8226, 11am-10pm Sun.-Wed., 11am-11pm Thurs.-Sat., bar closes at midnight Sun.-Wed. and 2am Thurs.-Sat.), which offers a hip menu of regional Mexican and ceviche.

For a simple burger, go to **El Cap** (3500 4th St. N., 727/521-1314, 11am-11pm Mon.-Sat., 11am-10pm Sun.).

GULFPORT

Gulfport has exploded on the dining scene in the past few years, with worthwhile restaurants lining several blocks. A local favorite is **Alesia Restaurant** (7204 Central Ave., 727/345-9701, 11:30am-2:30pm and 5:30pm-9pm Tues.-Fri., 10am-2:30pm and 5:30pm-9pm Sat., $16-24) that serves up an interesting mix of French and Vietnamese cuisine. It's definitely strange to see ratatouille and Vietnamese pho on the same menu, but the food is so good that the bizarre concept works like a charm. A local favorite for Italian food is **Pia's Trattoria** (3054 Beach Blvd. S.,

727/327-2190, 4pm-9pm Mon., 11am-9pm Tues.-Thurs. and Sun., 11am-10pm Fri.-Sat., $8-20). Try the chicken piccata cooked in a wonderful caper and butter sauce. The lasagna is a lunch specialty and is highly recommended. If the weather is nice, don't miss the charming outdoor patio area.

ST. PETE BEACH

If you can go to just one place in St. Pete Beach, get the blackened grouper sandwich at ★ **The Hurricane** (really on Pass-A-Grille Beach, 809 Gulf Way, 727/360-9558, 7am-10pm Sun.-Thurs, 7am-11pm Fri.-Sat., $8-24). I don't care if the place seems a little touristy; give me a grouper fillet, add some tomato and

lettuce on a bread roll, and that's as good as it gets in Pinellas County. There's a nice bar adjacent to the restaurant and a rooftop sundeck up top for watching the sunset.

On the other hand, if you go only to The Hurricane, then you'll miss out on the orange-pecan French toast or the creamed chipped beef on toast for breakfast at **Skyway Jack's Restaurant** (2795 34th St. S., 727/867-1907, 5am-3pm daily, $5-10). It's a classic around here, moved once because it was on the approach to the Sunshine Skyway Bridge and got pushed out to make room for more lanes. Stick with regular breakfast food or the smoked mullet and you won't be disappointed.

Accommodations

CLEARWATER
Over $300

The first new resort to be built on Clearwater Beach in 25 years, the **Sandpearl Resort** (500 Mandalay Ave., Clearwater, 727/441-2425, www.sandpearl.com, $250 700) is extremely impressive. The combined resort and condominium project features a 253-room

hotel, a full-service spa, upscale dining, state-of-the-art meeting and event space, 117 condominium units, and 700 feet of Gulf of Mexico beachfront. Rooms have an open, airy feel with balconies, high ceilings, and upscale, comfortable furnishings and fixtures. Fifty suites, located on the top two floors of the resort, offer one- and two-bedroom floor plans.

The Hurricane restaurant

ST. PETERSBURG
$100-200

Especially for romance seekers, **La Veranda Bed and Breakfast** (111 5th Ave. N., 727/224-1057, www.laverandabb.com, $99-250) is wonderful for couples as it's right near the heart of downtown St. Petersburg, but still quiet and romantic. It's set in a 1910 mansion surrounded by wide wraparound porches and beautiful tropical gardens, its suites including canopy beds, antiques, and Oriental rugs. Each suite opens directly onto the large veranda. Just up the block is a similar inn called **Mansion House Inn Bed and Breakfast** (105 5th Ave. NE, 727/289-2121, www.mymansioninn.com, $130-230). There are 12 rooms set in two Craftsman-style houses, one of which is thought to have been built between 1901 and 1904 by St. Petersburg's first mayor, David Mofett. A courtyard in between the houses is perfect for a little reading or downtime. And the pool on the property is a plus.

Over $300

The ★ **Renaissance Vinoy Resort & Golf Club** (501 5th Ave. NE, 727/894-1000, www.renaissancehotels.com, $250-600) was built by Pennsylvania oilman Aymer Vinoy Laughner in 1925. At $3.5 million, the Mediterranean Revival-style hotel was the largest construction project in Florida's history. Painstakingly restored in 1992 at a cost of $93 million, the resort is incredible. There are 360 guest rooms and 15 suites, many with views of the marina. The hotel also has a spa, a lovely pool with a waterfall, five restaurants, tennis courts, and an 18-hole golf course designed by Ron Garl. It hosts its own marina and is listed on the National Register of Historic Places.

ST. PETE BEACH
$100-200

For families, the **TradeWinds Island Resorts** (5500 Gulf Blvd., 727/367-6461, www.tradewindsresort.com) is the way to go. It offers a variety of accommodation choices, comprising the **TradeWinds Island Grand** ($150-450) and the new **Guy Harvey Outpost** (formerly the Sandpiper Hotel and Suites) ($125-200). Whichever one you choose includes playtime privileges at the other. The Island Grand is the fancier, a four-diamond property with soaring palms and a grand lobby. The whole complex offers multiple pools, a dozen places to eat and drink, multiple fitness centers, tennis courts, a pedal-boat canal, and a wide, private beach. Right out the back of the properties you can rent fishing or

Renaissance Vinoy Resort & Golf Club

snorkeling equipment, and try parasailing, waterskiing, and water scooters. The tremendous kids' program (KONK, Kids Only, No Kidding!) has with seasonal programs like the Swashbucklin' By the Sea pirate package, in which you get to meet Redbeard and walk the plank. For adults there is a lively nightlife to be found among the many bars and restaurants and an on-site Beef O'Brady's Sports Bar. To meet other people at the resort, join the fun TradeWinds pub crawl and visit all five of the on-site bars. Happily, the restaurants and bars are mostly affordable.

★ **Sirata Beach Resort** (5300 Gulf Blvd., 727/897-5200, www.sirata.com, $140-350) used to be connected to the TradeWinds but is now an independent, family-run midsize hotel, with a range of kids' programs and activities. It's the kind of place that locals in Tampa take their family for a weekend of R&R. Of the 382 rooms, 170 are one-bedroom suites, and most have excellent views of the Gulf. The kid-friendly suites with bunk beds and entertainment centers that include video game consoles are perfect for families, and suites with jet tubs are available for romantic visits. Enjoy the three beachfront pools and two hot tubs, as well as a relaxing beachside fire pit area.

Nearby is the ★ **Alden Beach Resort** (5900 Gulf Blvd., 727/360-7081, www.aldenbeachresort.com, $125-250), which is an attentively staffed, family-owned beach resort of 149 suites, especially favored by kids. It has tennis, volleyball, two heated pools (a little far from the beach, so the walk back and forth takes time for little ones), and a video game room. Rooms on the pool side are significantly cheaper than on the Gulf side. In 2013, the resort underwent a renovation that added high-speed Internet and flat-screen TVs to every room. Consider staying in one of their fully equipped one-bedroom suites with kitchenettes and water views. When you're ready to take a break from the beach, relax in their 12-person hot tub or grill up a catch of the day on their elevated deck with gas grills.

Over $300

For something more upscale, the huge, unmistakably pink **Don CeSar Beach Resort & Spa** (400 Gulf Blvd., 727/360-1881, www.loewshotels.com, $250-550) is a landmark in St. Pete and a longtime point of reference on maritime navigation charts. Named after a character in the opera *Maritana*, the Don CeSar hosted F. Scott Fitzgerald and wife Zelda, Clarence Darrow, Al Capone,

TradeWinds Island Resorts

Lou Gehrig, and countless other celebrities. Originally opened in 1928, the property was commandeered by the military during World War II and eventually abandoned. These days, it's a Loews hotel, with 340 lovely rooms, fishing, golfing, tennis, and the soothing Beach Club & Spa. Even if you don't stay here, make sure to take the tour and stop in for ice cream at its old-fashioned ice cream parlor.

SAFETY HARBOR
$100-200

Another piece of history, but I'm not sure if I'm buying this one, is claimed by **Safety Harbor Resort and Spa** (105 N. Bayshore Dr., 727/726-1161, www.safetyharborspa. com, $95-300). Many places along the Gulf Coast profess to be what Spanish explorer Hernando de Soto identified as the Fountain of Youth. Is it the mineral pools here at this 50,000-square-foot spa and tennis academy? The waters are mighty nice either way, filling three pools and used in the spa treatments. The resort is also home to a tennis academy, a fine-dining restaurant, and an upscale salon. The 174 guest rooms and suites are spacious and offer nice views of Tampa Bay.

PALM HARBOR
$200-300

For golfers, **Westin Innisbrook Golf Resort** (36750 U.S. 19 N., 727/942-2000, www.innisbrookgolfresort.com, $120-550) is a 900-acre property just north of Clearwater. It has four top-ranked golf courses, 11 tennis courts, six swimming pools (including the super kids-oriented Loch Ness Monster Pool), a children's recreation center, several restaurants, and 60 acres with a series of jogging and cycling trails. Rooms are all suites, with fully equipped kitchens. Its Copperhead Golf Course stretches more than 7,300 yards long and is home to the PGA Tour's PODS Championship.

VACATION RENTALS

Most of the vacation rentals are found around St. Pete Beach and Clearwater, with the offerings getting thinner the farther you venture away from those two main centers of action. Most rentals in this area are condos that range from the modest to the luxurious, but private homes are available in lesser numbers. Expect to pay $800-2,000 per week and $150-300 per night for most of the condos in the region. Homes are generally about 20 percent higher. Contact **Florida Beach Rentals** (516 Mandalay Ave., Clearwater, 727/288-2020, www.florida-beachrentals.com), which has extensive offerings throughout the region. For Clearwater rentals, contact **Beach Time Rentals** (800/691-8183, www. beachtimerentals.com).

Information and Services

Clearwater and St. Petersburg are located within the **eastern time zone.** The area code is **727,** but here's the annoying thing: Right over the causeway in Tampa the area code is 813. So you need to dial the area code, but you don't precede the phone number with a 1.

TOURIST INFORMATION

St. Petersburg/Clearwater Area Convention & Visitors Bureau (8200 Bryan Dairy Rd., Largo, 727/464-7200, www.visitstpeteclearwater.com) is not wildly convenient, but its website is tremendous. **St. Petersburg Area Chamber of Commerce** (100 2nd Ave. N., Ste. 150, 727/821-4069, www.stpete.com, 8am-5pm Mon.-Fri.) has a decent walk-in site with brochures and maps.

The various chambers of commerce have their own websites: **Tarpon Springs** (www. tarponspringschamber.com), **Clearwater** (www.clearwaterflorida.org) and **Clearwater**

Beach (www.beachchamber.com), and Dunedin (www.dunedin-fl.com), among others. For outdoors information, there's Clearwater Parks (www.clearwater-fl.com—drop down to Parks & Recreation under City Departments), Florida Parks (www.floridaparks.com), Pinellas County Parks (www.pinellascounty.org), and St. Petersburg Parks (www.stpeteparksrec.org).

St. Petersburg's largest newspaper is the *Tampa Bay Times* (490 1st Ave. S., 727/893-8111, www.tampabay.com). You'll see kiosks everywhere.

POLICE AND EMERGENCIES

In an emergency, dial 911. For a non-emergency police need, contact the St. Petersburg Police Department (1300 1st Ave. N., 727/893-7780). If you need medical assistance, the area has several large hospitals with good emergency care: St. Petersburg General Hospital (6500 38th Ave. N., St. Petersburg, 727/384-1414) and St. Anthony's Hospital (1200 7th Ave. N., St. Petersburg, 727/825-1100) in the south of the county, and Suncoast Hospital (2025 Indian Rocks Rd.,

Largo, 727/586-7178) in northern Pinellas County.

RADIO AND TELEVISION

Because it's a big metropolitan area, Tampa and St. Pete have an enormous number of radio stations between them. There's independent radio at WMNF 88.5 FM, variety at WMTX 100.7 FM, and NPR and classical at WUSF 89.7 FM.

For local television programming, Bay News 9 is Bright House Networks' 24-hour local news station, WFLA Channel 8 is the local NBC affiliate, WTSP Channel 10 is the CBS affiliate, WTVT Channel 13 is the FOX affiliate, and WFTS Channel 28 is the local ABC affiliate.

LAUNDRY SERVICES

Many of the larger hotels offer laundry service, as do most marinas in the area. If you find yourself in need of coin-operated laundry in St. Petersburg, try Wash N' Go Laundry (4154 Haines Rd. N, 727/522-3074) or The Gardens (3501 Central Ave., 727/323-0146). To the north in Clearwater, there's 24-hour laundry at Thompson's Dry Cleaners and Laundry (1713 Drew St., 727/461-2589).

Getting There and Around

CAR

Pinellas County is easily accessible from major interstates along the Midwest (I-75) and Northeast (I-95) corridors, as well as Orlando (I-4). I-275 serves the western portions of the Tampa-St. Petersburg area, including downtown Tampa, St. Petersburg, and Bradenton. It starts in the south at I-75 in Bradenton and extends up through St. Petersburg and Tampa, connected by two major bridges (Sunshine Skyway in the south and Howard Frankland to the north), before reuniting with I-75 at Lutz. I-75, by contrast, skirts both cities and acts as a bypass to southwest Florida and the Gulf Coast.

Once in Pinellas County, Clearwater is in the north along the Gulf, St. Petersburg is in the south along the bay. To reach St. Petersburg from Clearwater, head south on U.S. 19A, a slow, densely trafficked mess. Farther east, the regular U.S. 19 cuts down through the center of the peninsula to St. Petersburg.

In St. Petersburg, streets are set up in a grid pattern, with avenues running east-west and streets running north-south. Central Avenue divides north and south St. Petersburg, with the numbered avenues on either side—it's tricky, though, as to the left of Central there's 1st Avenue North, to the right it's 1st Avenue

South. There are some sections of town that are all one-way streets, so you may make a lot of little squares while driving.

From St. Pete Beach all the way up through Clearwater, all you need to know is that Gulf Boulevard (Hwy. 699) runs right up the coast and through each little town. The city of Clearwater is on the mainland, but Clearwater Beach is on a barrier island connected by Memorial Causeway.

AIR

The area is served by two midsize, easily traversed airports. **Tampa International Airport** (4100 George J. Bean Pkwy., 813/870-8700, www.tampaairport.com) is located just over the bridge and causeway from St. Petersburg and Clearwater and about 30-45 minutes from beachfront accommodations. Domestically, it is served by Air Canada, Alaska Airlines, American Airlines, British Airways, Cayman Airways, Copa Airlines, Delta Airlines, Edelweiss Air, Frontier, JetBlue, Lufthansa, Silver Airlines, Southwest Airlines, Spirit Airlines, Sun Country, United, WestJet, and World Atlantic Airlines.

You'll probably fly in and out of Tampa, unless you're coming from Canada. But there's also **St. Petersburg-Clearwater International Airport** (14700 Terminal Blvd., Clearwater, 727/453-7800), served by Allegiant, Sun Country Airlines, and Sunwing Airlines.

Alamo (800/327-9633), **Avis** (800/831-2847), **Budget** (800/527-0700), **Dollar** (800/800-4000 domestic, 800/800-6000 international), and **National** (800/227-7368) provide rental cars from both airports.

BUS AND TRAIN

Amtrak (800/872-7245, www.amtrak.com) offers service into nearby Tampa and other surrounding areas. Some services even allow you to bring your car with you. Also, **Greyhound Bus Line** (800/229-9424, www.greyhound.com) provides regular service into St. Petersburg (180 9th St. N., 727/898-1496). If you stay in Clearwater, it's easy to ditch your rental car and use the **Jolley Trolley** (727/445-1200, www.clearwaterjolleytrolley.com, $2.25) or the **Suncoast Beach Trolley** (727/540-1900, $2/ride, $4.50 all day) to get around. **Pinellas Suncoast Transit Authority** (727/540-1800, $2/ride, $4.50 all day) also has a fairly extensive busing system around the city.

The Nature Coast

Look for ★ to find recommended
sights, activities, dining, and lodging.

Highlights

★ **Nature Coast Canoe and Kayak Trail:** See this area as the Native Americans or early Spanish explorers did, from the seat of a canoe or kayak along the backwaters of this 20-mile paddling trail (page 222).

★ **Ellie Schiller Homosassa Springs Wildlife State Park:** Find out why Rodale's *Scuba Diving* awards this area the Best Place to See Large Animals title. The manatee is the goliath in question, and you can see it up close in the underwater "fishbowl" at this wildlife park (page 224).

★ **Cedar Key Scrub State Reserve:** Walk this rare ecosystem to catch a glimpse of the threatened Florida scrub jay and endangered burrowing owls (page 231).

★ **Dock Street:** Enjoy the shops, galleries, and restaurants along the wooden boardwalk. Join the pelicans on the pier to watch the sunset (page 236).

★ **Offshore Fishing:** With roughly 62 miles of Gulf Coast, 106 miles of rivers, and 19,111 acres of lakes—and that's just in Citrus County alone—you'll find lots of trophy fish in these waters, including tarpon, redfish, and bass (page 239).

The Nature Coast, known as "Mother Nature's theme park," is the rebuttal to Orlando's Disney World. If you're looking to fish, explore the outdoors, or just relax in a laid-back coastal town, the Nature Coast doesn't disappoint.

Nothing here is marketed, packaged, or sanitized by public relations specialists. It's rural, with the majority of the area set aside as parkland, preserves, reserves, and animal refuges.

In the weathered fishing villages along the coast and the quaint little inland towns, you're likely to see a spiffy fishing boat in every driveway. Residents stay for the affordable living, for the area's easy live-and-let-live tolerance, for the unhurried pace, and—for many, the most important reason—the fish. And that's pretty much why visitors come, too. People drive here to see manatees, black bears, and wading birds; to catch fish; and to dive, kayak, or simply contemplate the area's wealth of waterways. There are no white-sand beaches crowded with bikini-clad college kids, no swanky nightclubs with throbbing VIP rooms. From north of Clearwater all the way to the Big Bend (where the Florida peninsula tucks west into the Panhandle), there are precious few multiplexes, museums, or fancy cultural attractions. All that would get in the way of enjoying one of the least-developed stretches of Florida's Gulf Coast.

While traveling here, make sure to bring the fishing rods, bikes, and kayaks. Weeki Wachee, the southernmost town on the Nature Coast is known for its manatees, paddling, and real mermaids. (Okay, maybe they're just beautiful, young, divers in mermaid suits.) Farther north you can launch a boat, canoe, or kayak into the Chassahowitzka and Homosassa Rivers for access to spring-fed tributaries frequented by manatees. The fishing in these rivers is always outstanding. Cedar Key and Steinhatchee on the north end of the Nature Coast are small fishing villages known for their scallops, clams, and, yep, you guessed it—fish. Cedar Key is the larger of the two, with a historic downtown that might keep you interested for a day or two. However, it's not the towns themselves

Previous: Steinhatchee Landing Resort; kayaking on the Nature Coast. **Above:** snorkeling on Crystal River.

The Nature Coast

that matter most in this angler's paradise, because that's only where you're going to sleep. The rest of the time you'll be out on the water with a paddle or fishing rod in hand and a smile on your face.

PLANNING YOUR TIME

The Nature Coast has more than 700 square miles of scenic driving. The area is west of I-75 and accessible by the north-south corridor of U.S. 19, which is the main highway through the area. From south of Spring Hill, the long strip runs through small towns with a high number of boat dealers, fishing guides, and bait shops. North of Crystal River, U.S. 19 gets rural, with only the occasional mailbox and long driveway leading back to someone's private slice of heaven. Along the way you'll see osprey hunting overhead and cross an incredible number of waterways worth exploring. When you are traveling in this area, it is highly recommended to have a boat in tow or a canoe strapped to the roof of the car. It is one thing to see these amazing rivers, creeks, and bays from the shore, but the experience of getting into a boat and exploring them in depth is not to be missed. This is also the best way to fish.

Weeki Wachee Springs, Homosassa, and **Crystal River** are directly along U.S. 19. To get to any of the little towns perched along the Gulf's edge—**Yankeetown, Cedar Key, Suwannee,** and **Steinhatchee,** from south to north—you have to drive west on rural two-lane roads. None of these can be reached one from the other, except by boat or by driving back east, rejoining U.S. 19, and then more driving.

Weeki Wachee Springs is well worth a day trip, especially for families, either as an add-on to seeing Tarpon Springs farther south, or as an addition to a trip to elsewhere on the Nature Coast. Since manatee-viewing is best early in the morning, and fishing trips usually head out fairly early as well, it makes sense to stay over a night in Crystal River or Homosassa. Cedar Key and Steinhatchee, partly because they're harder to get to and partly because they're so charming, are each worth a couple of days of exploration.

Most of the Nature Coast is accessible by car or boat only. There is no public transportation to speak of besides two southbound and two northbound Greyhound buses that stop daily in Crystal River and Chiefland—but once you've arrived, you still need a car to get around.

Driving in Florida during the summer months can be especially challenging, with periods of heat and humidity and tremendous thunderstorms occurring almost every afternoon. It pays to have your car equipped with a first-aid kit, jumper cables, flashlight with new batteries, a jack, and cellular phone (although cell phone service can be spotty in the more rural communities).

If you happen to be piloting your own small plane, Cedar Key has a single 2,300-foot hard-surfaced runway, but this is uncontrolled airspace. The closest commercial airports are **Gainesville Regional Airport** (approximately one hour away, 3880 NE 39th St., 352/373-0249), with service provided by American Eagles Airlines, Delta, Silver Airlines, United Airlines, and US Airways Express, and **Tallahassee Regional Airport** (also one hour away, seven miles north of Tallahassee, 3300 Capital Cir. SW, 850/891-7800), with service provided by American Airlines, Delta, and Silver Airways. **Orlando International Airport** (1 Jeff Fuqua Blvd., 407/825-2001) and **Tampa International Airport** (4100 George J. Bean Pkwy., 813/870-8700, www.tampaairport.com) are both approximately 1.5 hours away by car, both offering many more commercial flights.

Alamo (800/327-9633), **Avis** (800/831-2847), **Budget** (800/527-0700), **Dollar** (800/800-4000 domestic, 800/800-6000 international), and **National** (800/227-7368) all provide rental cars from these airports.

Weeki Wachee to Crystal River

Florida is home to 700 freshwater springs, 33 of them first magnitude, meaning they discharge at least 100 cubic feet of water per second. Several of these first-magnitude springs are along the Nature Coast, a huge draw for swimmers, divers, and paddlers. It wasn't always such an easy sell, though. Weeki Wachee Springs languished as a tourist attraction until 1947, when a local entrepreneur figured out a way to lure the crowds: mermaids. Its underwater mermaid show is the kind of Old Florida attraction that makes people misty-eyed about the good old days. The town of Spring Hill owes its existence to the spring and its water park—not surprisingly, allies rallied as the park's commercial success waned and the mermaids beseeched Spring Hill to "Save Our Tails." At the end of 2007, its landlord, the Southwest Florida Water Management District, and the state of Florida agreed to make Weeki Wachee a state park. It was added to the state park system on November 1, 2008. Let's hope that saves those tails well into the future.

Farther north, the manatee is the 800-pound gorilla. But even bigger. Local cynics refer to these gentle mammals as "cash cows," and indeed the sea cows bring in a sizable revenue stream to the little towns of Homosassa and Crystal River. Upwards of 400 West Indian manatees make this their winter home, drawn by the warm waters of the seven spring-driven rivers that meet here at the Gulf of Mexico. Were it not for the manatees, both towns would still be on the map as fishing destinations. The area's anglers and manatee advocates make uneasy bedfellows, however: Many fisherfolk feel that overzealous Save the Manatee legislation has put unnecessary strictures on boating here.

Older than Crystal River by a good bit, Homosassa has more charm and the greater reputation as a fishing draw. The Calusa and Seminole tribes were the first to inhabit the area, but after the Civil War, families escaping the conflict and its aftermath settled many of the smaller islands, carving out a hardscrabble life of subsistence farming and fishing (often the little keys were named for the families who lived there). As real communities developed, commercial fishing became the mainstay, with the local catch transported north to Cedar Key by sailing sloop and, later, by railroad.

By the end of the 19th century, this rural area had developed a mighty reputation among sportsmen, and in 1886 a group of financiers bought up much of the swampy riverfront property on the Homosassa River. Extensive land filling, highway projects, and a major marketing blitz in the 1920s failed to draw many serious investors and residents. And it remains pretty much that way today: a few thousand people drawn by beautiful rivers, unmanicured wilderness, and fish.

SPORTS AND RECREATION
Buccaneer Bay
If you've been entranced by the lip-synching mermaids of Weeki Wachee Springs,

you'll be inspired to try some of your own aquatic tricks at the adjacent **Buccaneer Bay Waterpark** (6131 Commercial Way, Spring Hill, 352/592-5656, 9am-5:30pm daily, $13 adults, $8 children 6-12, children 5 and under free). The admission cost covers both the water park and Weeki Wachee Springs State Park. Pure, cold spring water laps against a tiny white-sand beach while families zoom down the flume rides and waterslides or hang out on the floating dock. It's a safe place to let kids roam free (lots of strict, eagle-eyed lifeguards make sure of that), and when they're exhausted, you can trot off to the riverboat cruise, petting zoo, and sweet animal show. Weeki Wachee Springs also hosts two-day **mermaid camps** (352/592-5656, ext. 30, $300), in which kids are taught the finer points of mermaidhood.

When you're ready to get away from the crowds, head for the rear of the water park parking lot and follow the arrows for **Paddling Adventures** (352/597-8484, $35 single-seat kayak, $40 two-seat kayak or canoe). It takes about three hours to paddle this serene stretch of the Weeki Wachee River, and when you've finished, they'll pick you up and bring you back upstream by van. Bring lunch or a beverage: There are spots along the

Manatees make their winter home in the Crystal River-Homosassa area.

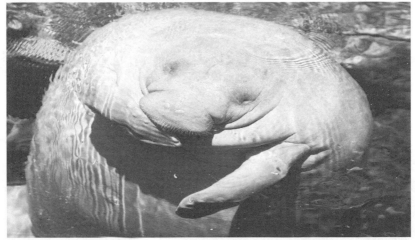

Fishing for the Silver King

Any fly fisher will tell you that Homosassa is the place to catch tarpon, or "the silver king." This little Old Florida town is where the big tarpon congregate, for no reason anyone can fathom. The current world record—202.8 pounds—was caught right here. But you won't find annual tarpon tournaments broadcast on ESPN. It's a low-key endeavor, with patience often yielding nothing but sunburn. On any given day, you'll see the river dotted with 25 or 30 flat boats navigated with push poles in a hushed silence of profound concentration, everyone waiting to see one roll along the surface in water depths of 5-25 feet. People come from all over the world to the Nature Coast to sight fish for these behemoths before releasing them gently into the warm, clear waters.

fishing on the Nature Coast

Regulations changed in 2013, and now only hook and line is allowed for tarpon fishing. Several other new rules have been adopted, and you can keep up to date by visiting the **Florida Fish and Wildlife website** (www.myfwc.com). Tarpon begin to run the last weeks of April and fade out in July. What many consider the Super Bowl of fishing, tarpon fishing requires a special $50 tag to keep one, and some serious know-how. The initial jumps and runs of that hooked fish are very exciting.

If you want to try your hand at chasing giant tarpon on the Gulf or in the backwaters from Homosassa to Cedar Key, try **Captain Rick LeFiles** (Osprey Guide Services, 6115 Riverside Dr., Yankeetown, 352/400-0133, $350 for a day of inshore fishing for reds and trout, $450 for tarpon) or fourth-generation Homosassa **Captain William Toney** (352/422-4141, www.homosassainshorefishing.com, half day $350, full day $400 for 1-2 people, $50 each additional person).

river where you can hop out on a sandy beach, swim, and relax.

Golf

Golfers will be sorely tempted to sneak away while their families visit Weeki Wachee Springs. The big kahuna of courses in these parts is the famous Tom Fazio-built **World Woods** (17590 Ponce de Leon Blvd., Brooksville, 352/796-5500, www.worldwoods.com, greens fees $28-170), just minutes away in Brooksville. It's a 45-hole complex with challenges for every golfer. Begin the day warming up on one of the hugest driving ranges you've ever laid eyes on (23 acres). From there you can bone up on the nine-hole short course featuring seven par 3s and two par 4s, and then attempt either the 18-hole Pine Barrens, modeled after the great Pine Valley, or the stately and refined Rolling Oaks parkland course, an homage to Augusta National.

Swimming with the Manatees

The West Indian manatee is still listed as an endangered species, but the population has rebounded tremendously in the past few years in this area. Manatee season is October 15-March 31, but you'll spot them all year long. Kings Bay in Crystal River has the densest concentration, but the Blue Waters area of the Homosassa River is a little less trafficked by boats, thus a bit quieter. Either way, you can swim with these gentle mammals from the distance that suits you (up close their size is unsettling—just remember they are herbivores, with blunt teeth so far back in their heads that you could, were it legal, hand-feed them with no worries). **Manatee Tour & Dive** (267 NW 3rd St., Crystal River, 352/795-1333, www.manateetouranddive.com, $24.50-39 for tour, $20-30 for gear) offers two-hour manatee swim and snorkeling trips suitable for the whole family in the waters of Crystal River, and scuba trips in Crystal Springs and Kings Spring, an underwater cavern praised for its excellent visibility, size, and potential for underwater photography (thousands of saltwater fish congregate at the cavern's two exits).

Sunshine River Tours (1 SW 1st Pl., 352/777-1796, www.swimmingwiththemanatees.com, $10-99) has a similar range of guided ecotourism escapades in Homosassa. If a manatee swim and snorkel tour doesn't sound like a good way to take to the waters, you can try your hand at scalloping (July 1-Sept. 25), or just enjoy a boat ride to follow the river out to the Gulf of Mexico.

canoes on the Nature Coast

Canoeing, Kayaking, and Boating

During the warm months when manatees are a little scarce elsewhere in Crystal River and Homosassa, head to **Chassahowitzka National Wildlife Refuge** (1502 Southeast Kings Bay, accessible from Rd. 480 off U.S. 19, south of Homosassa, 352/563-2088, 8am-sundown daily, free), where they seem to congregate. And during the colder months you're likely to spot endangered whooping cranes that make this their winter home. There are no walking trails at the refuge, but there is a small visitors center that will quickly connect you with a commercial boat tour or rental. The 30,500 acres of saltwater bays, estuaries, and brackish marshes are home to nearly 250 species of birds, 50 species of reptiles and amphibians, and at least 25 species of mammals. You can't camp here, but several miles east of the refuge you'll find **Chassahowitzka River Campground** (8600 W. Miss Maggie Rd., 352/382-2200, www.chassahowitzkaflorida.com, $23), which has a nice canoe and boat launch of its own. I highly recommend this campground for tent and RV camping in

this area. The sites are spacious and the campground gives you excellent access to fishing and paddling the river.

★ NATURE COAST CANOE AND KAYAK TRAIL

This trail is 17 miles long, beginning in the north on the Salt River, about one mile west of the town of Crystal River (near the Marine Science Station on Hwy. 44). Follow the markers on the Salt River south to the Homosassa River. From here, the trail goes east on the Homosassa River a few hundred feet to a little stretch of water called Battle Creek, and then it jags to the south through Seven Cabbage Cut to the mouth of the Chassahowitzka River. The calm, protected waters of this estuarine ecosystem, part of the Great Florida Birding Trail, are home to ospreys, cormorants, wood storks, and loads of other wading birds.

To rent kayaks and canoes, go to **Aardvark's Florida Kayak Company** (707 N. Citrus Ave., Crystal River, 352/795-5650, www.floridakayakcompany.com, $40 single, $50 tandem, closed Mon.-Tues., but will open by prior arrangement). But if paddling out on your own sounds daunting, **Riversport Kayaks** (5297 S. Cherokee Way, Homosassa, 352/621-4972, www.riversportkayaks.com) leads tours along this trail, as well as great paddling along the Halls River and even overnight camping trips with an experienced and knowledgeable guide. They also offer a lunch-and-paddle special that combines a kayak or canoe rental with a gift certificate to the Riverside Crab House good for dinner, lunch, or just drinks ($45 single-seat kayak, $55 two-seat kayak or canoe).

Birding

The area's salt marshes, hammocks, uplands, forest and prairie, freshwater marshes, swamps, lakes, and rivers provide a variety of habitats, which in turn draw a variety of birds. Hundreds of bird species call this area home, and birders can observe them via boating along waterways, driving trails, and walking trails all over Citrus County. Roseate spoonbills, great blue herons, ibis, and other wading birds; ospreys, bald eagles, and other birds of prey; shorebirds, wetland birds, and beach birds are all on view. March-May is a good time to see colorful mating plumage. One of the largest undeveloped river delta-estuarine systems in the United States, the **Lower Suwannee National Wildlife Refuge** (16 miles west of U.S. 19 on County Rd. 347, 352/493-0238) was established in 1979 in an effort to protect and maintain a rare ecosystem. The park is bisected by the Suwannee River, its tributary creeks fringed with majestic cypress (this part is best seen from the one-mile River Trail). Be sure to visit the upland area dotted with scrub oak and pine, and then explore some of the 26-mile stretch of tidal marshes along the Gulf.

Birders also gravitate to the **Withlacoochee Bay Trail** (from U.S. 19, turn east onto Sunset Parkway Rd., 352/236-7143), a five-mile walking trail from Felburn Park Trailhead to the Gulf. The child-friendly, two-mile looped **Eco Walk Trail** (5990 N. Tallahassee Rd., 352/563-0450) can be reached by taking U.S. 19 north to just before Seven Rivers Regional Medical Center, then turning left onto Curtis Tool Road for the Eco Walk Trailhead, which is at the intersection of Curtis Tool and Tallahassee Road. **Fort Island Trail** (5 miles west of U.S. 19 on Fort Island Trail) is a flat, paved, nine-mile trail that ends at Fort Island Trail Beach. All of

Pelicans are one of many bird species that call this area home.

these parks are open 8am-sunset, and admission is free.

Motorcycling

If you need a break from all that outdoor activity, you can hop on a hog and play *Easy Rider* at the **Harley-Davidson Shop of Crystal River** (1785 S. Suncoast Blvd., 352/563-9900). Sportsters, Big Twins, and V-Rods are all for rent for $150 a day for those over 21 with a valid driver's license.

SIGHTS
★ Ellie Schiller Homosassa Springs Wildlife State Park

Manatees, so famous in these parts, can weigh up to 2,000 pounds and are often seen feasting on algae and barnacles. You'll catch sight of them most often during cooler months, December-March, in the Suwannee River or at Manatee or Fanning Springs State Parks. From boat or shore, look for swirly "footprints" on the water's surface or torpedo-like shapes ambling across the shallow bottom. If you want a guaranteed viewing, stop into **Ellie Schiller Homosassa Springs Wildlife State Park** (4150 S. Suncoast Blvd., Homosassa, 352/628-5343, 9am-5:30pm daily, $13 adults, $5 children 6-12), where you can see these marine

mammals several ways. Visitors are loaded onto pontoon boats and shuttled through the canopied headwaters of the Homosassa River to a refuge for injured manatees and other animals. Alternatively, at 11:30am, 1:30pm, and 3:30pm, a manatee program allows you to watch guides wade out to feed stubby carrots to a slow-moving swarm of these creatures, many etched with outboard motor scars from run-ins with boats. Afterward you can walk down to the glass-fronted Fishbowl Underwater Observatory and see eye-to-eye with the gentle giants and the park's other indigenous aquatic creatures. (Mysteriously, the park hosts a hippo named Lu—a washed-up animal actor—that former governor Lawton Chiles declared an honorary Florida citizen.)

Yulee Sugar Mill Ruins and Vicinity

David Levy Yulee was the man responsible for bringing the Atlantic and Gulf Railroad to Cedar Key in 1860—putting Cedar Key on the map. When Florida became a state in 1845 he was the state's first U.S. senator, and he had another sweet business on the side: By 1851 his mill on the Homosassa River employed more than 1,000 people, producing sugar, syrup, and molasses. Yulee was imprisoned

Yulee Sugar Mill Ruins State Historical Site

Homosassa to Crystal River

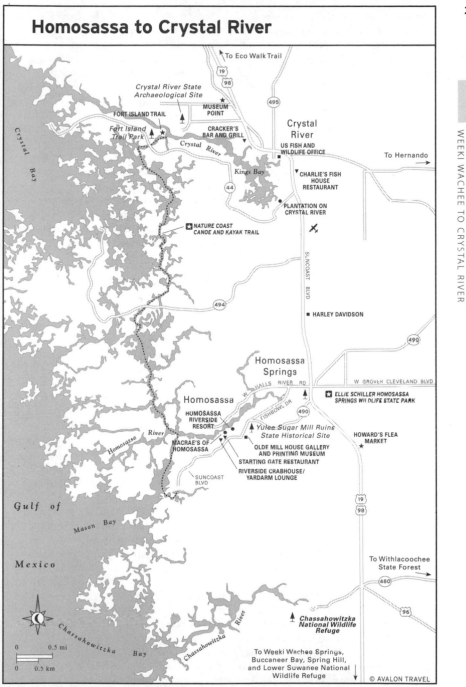

To Eco Walk Trail

19
98

495

Crystal River State
Archaeological Site

MUSEUM
POINT

FORT ISLAND TRAIL

Crystal
River

Fort Island
Trail Park

CRACKER'S
BAR AND GRILL

Crystal River

US FISH AND
WILDLIFE OFFICE

To Hernando

Crystal Bay

Kings Bay

CHARLIE'S FISH
HOUSE
RESTAURANT

44

PLANTATION ON
CRYSTAL RIVER

NATURE COAST
CANOE AND KAYAK TRAIL

SUNCOAST BLVD

494

HARLEY DAVIDSON

490

Homosassa
Springs

W HALLS RIVER RD

W GROVER CLEVELAND BLVD

Homosassa

ELLIE SCHILLER HOMOSASSA
SPRINGS WILDLIFE STATE PARK

FISHBOWL DR

HOMOSASSA
RIVERSIDE
RESORT

Yulee Sugar Mill Ruins
State Historical Site

490

HOWARD'S FLEA
MARKET

River

MACRAE'S OF
HOMOSASSA

OLDE MILL HOUSE GALLERY
AND PRINTING MUSEUM

STARTING GATE RESTAURANT

Homosassa

SUNCOAST
BLVD

RIVERSIDE CRABHOUSE/
YARDARM LOUNGE

19
98

Gulf of

Mason Bay

Mexico

To Withlacoochee
State Forest

480

Chassahowitzka
National Wildlife
Refuge

96

Chassahowitzka Bay

Chassahowitzka River

To Weeki Wachee Springs,
Buccaneer Bay, Spring Hill,
and Lower Suwanee National
Wildlife Refuge

0   0.5 mi
0   0.5 km

© AVALON TRAVEL

briefly for siding with the Confederacy during the Civil War, and his mill was permanently closed. Now the **Yulee Sugar Mill Ruins State Historical Site** (352/795-3817, 8am-sundown daily, free) is hardly more than a huge stone chimney and the bones of a partially restored 40-foot-long structure that houses steam boilers, crushing machinery, and large cooking kettles. Visitors walk on a short path through the six-acre site with interpretive plaques, and there is a small nearby picnic area with grills. To reach the site, take U.S. 19 to the town of Homosassa Springs, then turn west onto County Road 490 West (Yulee Drive). Proceed for approximately 2.5 miles to the park.

If the Yulee Sugar Mill doesn't sound like quite enough to make you detour from U.S. 19, right down the block is a nice museum/café called the **Olde Mill House Gallery & Printing Museum** (10466 W. Yulee Dr., 352/628-1081, 10am-3pm Tues.-Sat., free, tours by appointment). Presided over by Jim Anderson, the little museum explores the history of printing, focusing on the letterpress era. The café sells tasty authentic Cubano sandwiches and black beans and rice. And if you want to get even more return on your mileage investment, continue west on County Road 490 just a bit until you reach **Historic Old Homosassa,** a collection of craft and gift shops, restaurants, and one of the oldest residential communities on Florida's Gulf Coast.

Crystal River State Archaeological Site

In 200 BC, this was a happening spot. Florida's Native Americans came from all over to bury their dead and to participate in ceremonies and trade activities. People estimate that, for 1,600 years, roughly 7,500 Indians visited these 14 acres every year. Today, **Crystal River State Archaeological Site** (3400 N. Museum Point, Crystal River, 352/795-3817, park open 8am-sundown daily, visitors center 9am-5pm daily, admission $3/vehicle) is still hosting a fair number of visitors to the

banks of the Crystal River. They come to see the six mounds built by what are now referred to somewhat prosaically as the pre-Columbian mound builders. After viewing an eight-minute interpretive video and seeing the small museum's exhibit chronicling the archaeological excavations begun in 1903, you'll be better equipped to walk a paved, half-mile loop and marvel at the mounds, studded with shells, bones, jewelry, and pottery from early civilizations. The park also has an interesting dugout canoe exhibit and a Sifting for Technology interactive exhibit. With the latter, there are biweekly programs for the general public in which participants use sifting screens and other archaeological tools to recover artifacts from the spoils of a dredged boat slip.

ENTERTAINMENT AND EVENTS
Festivals

The average year-round temperature along the Nature Coast is 70°F, with an average of 294 days of sunshine. That means it's pretty all year, but you might want to schedule a visit to correspond to one of the local festivals.

In January, Crystal River hosts the three-day **Florida Manatee Festival** (call the Citrus County Chamber of Commerce at 352/795-3149) with free manatee-sightseeing boat tours, crafts, food, and entertainment. The **Cedar Key Arts and Crafts Festival** (www.cedarkeyartsfestival.com) in April is known as a hot place to find new talent. It's a big, fun arts show with lots of crafts for sale. The Homosassa River is home to a number of fishing tournaments worth watching: The annual **Cobia Tournament** (call MacRae's Bait and Tackle at 352/628-2602) is in mid-June, and the famous **Southern Redfish Tour** (www.redfishtour.com) comes a few weeks later in July. Cedar Key has a Fourth of July **Cedar Key Old Florida Clamfest** (352/543-5600, www.cedarkey.org) with live music, clam hunts, clam-shucking demonstrations, clam bag races, and so forth. On the third weekend in October, the **Cedar**

Mermaid Tales

The job requirements are tough: a winning smile, powerful athleticism, and a great body. Now add to that the ability to hold one's breath for 2.5 minutes. Florida is home to a variety of rare aquatic creatures, but perhaps none are so singular as the 20 mermaids and mermen who swim through their daily choreographed show at **Weeki Wachee Springs** (6131 Commercial Way, Spring Hill, 352/592-5656, 9am-5:30pm daily, $13 adults, $8 children 6-12, includes admission to Buccaneer Bay). Weeki Wachee is open year-round, but Buccaneer Bay is closed during the winter months and reopens in mid-March.

the mermaid show at Weeki Wachee Springs

In 1947, former U.S. Navy frogman Newton Perry thought of a way to bring added draw to one of the United States' most prolific freshwater springs. More than 170 million gallons of 72°F water pour dramatically into the Weeki Wachee River daily. Perry's notion was to make the springs more attractive by adding a school of beautiful mermaids—to this end, he taught a group of powerful swimmers to breathe through submerged air hoses supplied by an air compressor, the upshot being a remarkable 30- to 45-minute, entirely underwater extravaganza.

Conceived in the heyday of MGM's trademark aquatic musical spectaculars starring Esther Williams, the show at Weeki Wachee Springs is nonetheless a family affair. There are plenty of ogling opportunities, but these bathing beauties are put through their paces in a show that usually draws from past Disney movies such as, unsurprisingly, *The Little Mermaid* and *Pocahontas*.

The audience sits in a small underground amphitheater in front of a four-inch-thick plate-glass window, behind which the blue waters of the springs teem with fish, turtles, eels, and women in oversized, shimmering tails who twirl, undulate, and lip synch on cue. Many of the mermaids have been with the show for decades, a fact that can be ascertained with a quick look through photos and memorabilia in the small Mermaid Museum (a wall of fame includes early sea nymphs cavorting with Elvis and Don Knotts), opened to commemorate the show's 50th anniversary in 1997.

After getting your picture taken with a mermaid, it's off to the rest of the 200-acre family entertainment park, Florida's only natural spring water park. This includes a flume ride at Buccaneer Bay, a low-key Birds of Prey show, petting zoo, and jungle river cruise.

Past years had been hard for the attraction, with the mermaids and supporters launching Save Our Tail efforts. The upshot is that Weeki Wachee Springs became a Florida state park in 2008. For a truly wonderful record of the attraction's history, pick up a copy of Lu Vickers's *Weeki Wachee, City of Mermaids: A History of One of Florida's Oldest Roadside Attractions,* if only for the historic pictures.

Key Seafood Festival (352/543-5600, www.cedarkey.org) draws 30,000 people for two days of seafood gluttony (book a room far in advance for this one). And on the second weekend in November, the **Homosassa Arts, Crafts, and Seafood Festival** (www. homosassaseafoodfestival.com) whips up chowders and soft-shell crabs for the masses.

SHOPPING

Heavy shoppers will be a little left out by the Nature Coast's meager retail options. There is the **Crystal River Mall** (1801 NW U.S. 19, 352/795-2585) with stores such as Kmart, GNC, and Payless, and **Cedar Key's Dock Street** is host to the kinds of shell-themed giftware and handicrafts stores found in many little seaside towns. For a real local bit of excitement, sift through the 300 or so booths at **Howard's Flea Market** (6373 S. Suncoast Blvd., Homosassa Springs, 352/628-3532, 7am-2pm Fri., 6:30am-2pm Sat.-Sun.). To safeguard against rain and muggy weather, the market is enclosed, with vendors selling leather goods, antiques, tools, fishing gear, and even pets. A bird aviary and food vendors (good barbecue and excellent old-fashioned root beer) make it fun for the whole family.

FOOD
Weeki Wachee
The town of Spring Hill, where Weeki Wachee Springs is found, has a couple of fun, family-friendly places in which to refuel after a grueling day at the water park. **Richie Cheesesteak** (6191 Deltona Blvd., 352/600-7999, 10am-9pm Mon.-Thurs., 10am-10pm Fri.-Sat., $6-10) is the go-to place for lunch sandwiches, hamburgers, and cheesesteaks, of course. **Greek City Cafe** (3125 Commercial Way, 352/683-6606, 11am-9pm daily, $7-10) is a favorite for healthy lunches and dinners of Mediterranean-style salads, pizzas, wraps, and rice bowls.

For something a little nicer, **La Bella Napoli Italian Restaurant** (7386 Shoal Line Blvd., 352/556-5274, $12-25) serves up the best Italian food in town. The homemade meatballs, cannolis, and bread rolls are a favorite. The refined atmosphere is fitting for a romantic dinner.

Homosassa
The south shore of the Homosassa River, accessible from Halls River Road, is host to a memorable place. Dinner at **Riverside Crab House** (5297 S. Cherokee Way, 352/621-5080, 11am-9pm Mon.-Thurs., 11am-10pm Fri., 11am-10pm Sat.-Sun., $9-30) is a relaxed and casual joint specializing in two-foot platters heaped with sweet corn, hush puppies, scallops, soft-shell crab, steamed blue crab, clams, and catfish. The attached Yardarm Lounge and the outdoor Monkey Bar tiki lounge are great places from which to spy on the four

mostly tame monkeys who live on a tiny island a stone's throw away.

Dan's Clam Stand (7364 W. Grover Cleveland Blvd., 352/628-9588, 11am-9pm Mon.-Sat., $8-15) is no-frills but makes a mean clam chowder, a serviceable lobster roll, and a fine fried grouper sandwich. If you don't love seafood, the buffalo wings are hot and tasty. And **The Starting Gate Restaurant** (10605 W. Yulee Dr., 352/503-2076, 6:30am-1pm Fri.-Mon., $8-10) is the place to try the local breakfast: fried cornmeal-crusted mullet with cheese grits.

For nightlife in Homosassa, locals go to **The Freezer Tiki Bar** (5990 S. Boulevard Dr., 352/628-2452), attempt a little karaoke at the **Dunbar's Old Mill Tavern** (10465 W. Yulee Dr., 352/628-2669), or have a leisurely riverside beer at **The Shed at MacRae's** (5300 S. Cherokee Way, 352/628-2602).

Crystal River
In Crystal River, people tend to send visitors to **Charlie's Fish House Restaurant** (244 NW U.S. 19, 352/795-3949, 11am-9pm daily, $9-16) for the views of the river and the simply prepared local fish, as well as oysters and stone crab claws (you eat only the claws because fisherfolk haul 'em up, yank off one claw, and throw them back to grow another). The restaurant has a substantial boat dock for waterborne diners.

Cracker's Bar and Grill (502 NW 6th St., 352/795-3999, 11am-10pm Mon.-Fri., 11am-midnight Fri.-Sat., $6-13), just up the block, is a locals' hangout with a commitment to big portions and providing something for everyone. The menu is vast, with burgers, nachos, and such alongside sautéed scallops and shrimp. Live entertainment has things hopping in the tiki bar and deck on the weekend, with karaoke many nights. Tie your boat up to one of the restaurant's 14 slips, or hop on the restaurant's water taxi and see some of Kings Bay.

For nightlife, the young folks gather at **Castaway's Bar and Grill** (5430 N. Suncoast Blvd., 352/795-3653).

ACCOMMODATIONS

People are drawn to the Nature Coast for a raw view into the natural world. They come with rods and reels, their boats topped with gas and canoes packed to the brim with stocked coolers and camping gear. As a result, this swath of Florida is complete with RV parks, campgrounds, and fish camps that run from rough wooden cabins to affordable and simple motels. In nearly all the small towns that dot U.S. 19 or the little roads west to the Gulf, you can bet on finding a clean room in a casual and unique independently owned motel, where the amenities are whatever is happening out on the river, bay, or spring.

It in addition to these or the more upscale lodgings listed here, the area provides opportunities to indulge a lot of people's fantasy of endless, tranquil mobility: a stay on a houseboat. Go "way down upon the Suwannee River" with a 44-foot houseboat rented from **Miller's Marine & Suwannee Houseboats** (90 SE County Rd. 349, Suwannee, 352/542-7349, www.suwanneehouseboats.com, $599-899 for 2 days including weekends, $1,199-1,699/week). The houseboats sleep up to eight and are equipped with showers, bathroom facilities, linens, full kitchens, and cookware. The owners take renters on a warm-up cruise to teach them the basics, and then you're on your own with 70 miles of river, countless springs, and an up-close view of the area's wildlife. It's a great way to pretend you're Huckleberry Finn.

Under $100

For RV travelers, there are 398 picturesque sites set on 80 acres at **Rock Crusher Canyon RV Resort** (275 S. Rock Crusher Rd., Crystal River, 888/726-7805, www.sunrvresorts.com, $35). It contains a 7,000-seat outdoor amphitheater that has welcomed Willie Nelson, Three Dog Night, and Joan Jett, as well as some humongous RV rallies. Also in Crystal River, with lakeside and canalside spots that include your own boat dock space, **Crystal Isles Resort** (11419 W. Fort Island Trail, Crystal River, 352/795-3774, $41) is a 30-acre

RV resort not far from the Fort Island Trail Beach. For inexpensive and pleasant waterside accommodations in Cedar Key, try **Sunset Isle RV Park/Motel** (11850 Hwy. 24, 352/543-5375, www.cedarkeyrv.com, RV campsites from $39, motel rooms from $75).

In Crystal River you'll find many of the inexpensive chains, such as **Best Western Crystal River Resort** (614 NW U.S. 19, Crystal River, 352/795-3171, $90-140), with its own marina and excellent fish/dive shop; **Quality Inn** (4486 N. Suncoast Blvd., Crystal River, 352/563-1500, $65-90); **Days Inn** (2380 NW U.S. 19, Crystal River, 352/795-2111, $55-90); and **Econo Lodge** (2575 NW U.S. 19, Crystal River, 352/795-9447, $55-85). Most cater to visiting anglers and ring in somewhere around $75, many without a lot of bells and whistles beyond a computer in the lobby to check email. But for a more authentic experience, spend just a bit more and head for one of the independently owned places.

The area right around Weeki Wachee Springs has a lot of suburban sprawl, so it isn't the best vacation spot on the Nature Coast, but if you really want to be near this particular spring the **Quality Inn Weeki Wachee** (9373 Cortez Blvd., 352/596-9000, $80-99) is your best bet. It's right across the street from the spring and its water park, with 116 rooms in a nice two-story building.

$100-200

Homosassa Riverside Resort (5297 S. Cherokee Way, Homosassa, 352/628-2474, www.riversideresorts.com, $65-210) is the oldest resort along the Homosassa River. Many rooms have full kitchens, so you have dining flexibility, but the on-site restaurant and lounge are definitely worth a visit. From the hotel you can arrange a manatee-awareness tour, kayak and canoe rentals, airboat rides, and other adventures.

Presided over by Gator MacRae, **MacRae's of Homosassa** (5300 S. Cherokee Way, Homosassa, 352/628-2602, www.macraesofhomosassa.com, $100-150) is the rustic anglers' pick, with a series of log cabin-like squatty structures and old-fashioned rockers on the front porches. The 12 rooms and 10 efficiencies are equipped with kitchens, and there are laundry facilities on the premises. Its riverside marina offers boat rentals, a bait shop, and fishing charters.

Also in the "something different" category, **Nature's Resort Campground and Marina** (10359 W. Halls River Rd., Homosassa Springs, 352/628-9544, www.naturesresortfla.com, $120 cabins, $38-48 RV site, $38 campsite) has cabins; several hundred RV campsites; tent camping; canoe, kayak, and pontoon boat rentals; a marina; a country store; hiking trails; a pool; a restaurant; and a marina bar on 97 lush acres along the Halls River. Oh, and there's a band shell that hosts country and gospel acts when the weather accommodates.

If you want something nice in a romantic kind of way, **Pine Lodge Country Inn** (649 Hwy. 40 W., Follow That Dream Pkwy., Inglis, 352/447-7463, www.pinelodgefla.com, $110-160) is a bed-and-breakfast with four rooms, built in the 1940s and situated in the natural settings of Inglis. Located right at the Levy and Citrus county lines, it's along the picturesque Withlacoochee River.

The **Izaak Walton Lodge** (6301 Riverside Dr., Yankeetown, 352/447-4899, www.izaakwaltonlodge.com, call for rates) is one of the few reasons to get off U.S. 19 and amble down County Road 40 to Yankeetown. The small inn has a serene setting on the banks of the Withlacoochee River, with dock space where you can tie up your boat. The onsite restaurant, **The Riverside Inn,** includes a dining room and bar on the first floor and a multitiered dining terrace. The menu has excellent local seafood choices such as oysters Rockefeller and fried gator nuggets along with entrées like New York strip and lobster.

$200-300

The Nature Coast doesn't offer the abundance of golfing opportunities available elsewhere in Florida. If you're jonesing to tee off, the **Plantation on Crystal River** (9301 W. Fort Island Trail, Crystal River, 352/795-4211, www.plantationoncrystalriver.com, $154-350 including greens fees) boasts a par-72, 18-hole championship course and a 9-hole executive course for training and practice, in addition to manatee snorkeling tours, guided scuba diving, and 145 guest rooms (with 12 golf villas and six condos). Given all the amenities and glitz, room rates are a fairly reasonable.

GETTING THERE AND AROUND

From south to north, Spring Hill (the town of Weeki Wachee Springs), Homosassa, and Crystal River are lined up adjacent to each other right along U.S. 19. The 27-mile drive from Spring Hill to Homosassa will take you about 40 minutes. From Homosassa to Crystal River, the 10-mile drive takes about 20 minutes. Two northbound Greyhound buses stop daily in Crystal River, but once you arrive, you still need a car to get around.

Cedar Key

They say in Cedar Key it takes two hours to watch *60 Minutes.* There's only one road in and out of town; there's no movie theater, no Starbucks, and no fast food. In fact, there's no fast anything.

But it wasn't always that way. Back in the 1880s, Cedar Key was the busiest port in Florida, with a population of around 5,000.

It was founded in 1842 by Judge Augustus Steele as a seaside resort colony for prosperous plantation owners, but a wealth of local cedar trees quickly transformed the town into the foremost producer of pencils (Eberhard-Faber, Eagle, and others) in the country, and a relatively deep harbor made Cedar Key the natural choice as the first Gulf port and the terminus for David Yulee's cross-state Atlantic and Gulf Railroad in 1860.

A flattening 10-foot tidal surge from a hurricane in 1896, followed by other bad luck (fire, poor civic planning, reckless consumption of natural resources) crippled the little town, and when Henry Plant finished his own competing railroad, linking more cosmopolitan Tampa to Florida's east coast, it was the last nail in Cedar Key's cedar coffin.

Today, the constellation of tiny islands that juts three miles out into the Gulf of Mexico is inhabited by fewer than 900 year-round residents. Florida's 1995 net ban law ended the bustle of commercial fishing fleets. What that leaves are all the charms Judge Steele saw back in 1842: an abundance of birds, fish, and other wildlife; beautiful sunsets; and a profusion of dappled creeks and rivers that flow into the warm Gulf. Recently Cedar Key has become home to a substantial resident artist community, which has brought color to the town. It hasn't lost the rough-edged, casual environment that makes Cedar Key an easygoing pleasure, though. It is still the kind of place where the only locals who seem impatient are the pelicans on the Dock Street pier, hoping to steal some angler's unguarded bait stash.

SPORTS AND RECREATION
★ Cedar Key Scrub State Reserve

See some scrub before it vanishes. Okay, so scrub doesn't sound too sexy, but a scrub is an austere local plant community characterized by the dominance of shrubs (whereas forests are dominated by trees, prairies by grasses), and it is one of the fastest disappearing habitats in Florida. In the wet months, rainwater and wind rush through, cutting channels in the loose soil; when it's dry, fires sweep in and burn the scrub to the ground. And then those scrappy little shrubs grow again. Extremely hot in summer, the arid, sandy terrain is home to the Florida scrub jay and a bunch of other tough nuts of the animal world. **Cedar Key Scrub State Reserve** (6 miles northeast of Cedar Key on Hwy. 24, 352/543-5567, 8am-sundown daily, free) consists of 12 miles of beautiful, marked walking trails. It's dramatic in a quiet way. Pets are welcome on leash.

Fishing

Cedar Key has lots of ways to make you feel "reel" talented. Freshwater anglers can wet a line in the 3,657-acre **Lake Rousseau/Withlacoochee River** area to bag bluegill,

a fishing boat in Cedar Key

Cedar Key

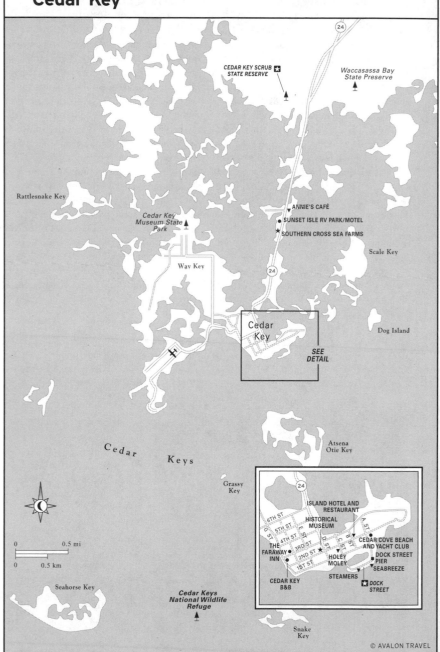

CEDAR KEY SCRUB STATE RESERVE

Waccasassa Bay State Preserve

Rattlesnake Key

ANNIE'S CAFÉ

SUNSET ISLE RV PARK/MOTEL

SOUTHERN CROSS SEA FARMS

Cedar Key Museum State Park

Scale Key

Way Key

Cedar Key

SEE DETAIL

Dog Island

C e d a r   K e y s

Atsena Otie Key

Grassy Key

0   0.5 mi

0   0.5 km

Seahorse Key

Cedar Keys National Wildlife Refuge

Snake Key

Cedar Key detail:

24

ISLAND HOTEL AND RESTAURANT

6TH ST

5TH ST

4TH ST

HISTORICAL MUSEUM

G ST

THE FARAWAY INN

3RD ST

2ND ST

1ST ST

D ST

C ST

B ST

A ST

CEDAR COVE BEACH AND YACHT CLUB

HOLEY MOLEY

DOCK STREET PIER

SEABREEZE

CEDAR KEY B&B

STEAMERS

DOCK STREET

© AVALON TRAVEL

redear sunfish, catfish, black crappie, or largemouth bass. For saltwater fishing, the waters of **Cedar Keys National Wildlife Refuge** and the **Lower Suwannee National Wildlife Refuge** teem with spotted sea trout, redfish, and sheepshead. And **Waccasassa Bay Preserve State Park** provides both freshwater and saltwater fishing opportunities.

Canoeing, Kayaking, and Boating

Designated a refuge by President Hoover way back in 1929, the **Cedar Keys National Wildlife Refuge** (at the end of Highway 24, most islands accessible only by boat, 352/493-0238) encompasses approximately 800 acres and is composed of 13 barrier islands in the Gulf of Mexico. The refuge is home to as many as 200,000 birds, making it a hot spot for bird-watchers. To protect the area's wildlife and fragile ecosystems, the refuge is accessible only by boat (time your trip for high tide, otherwise the shallow mud and grass flats can slow your progress), and all of the islands' interiors are closed to the public except Atsena Otie Key, the easiest island to access. You can paddle out from Cedar Key and collect shells, identify birds, picnic, and take pictures year-round. It's worth the effort of getting there—egrets, white ibis, cormorants, herons, pelicans, and anhingas make it a genuine avian convention.

Part of Seahorse Key, including the lighthouse, is leased by the University of Florida as a marine research laboratory and classroom and closed to the public. A few days each year, the refuge and university host an open house where the public is invited to visit the lighthouse. Formed as a giant kidney-shaped sand dune, Seahorse Key rises to a height of 52 feet, the highest point on the state's west coast. It was a military hospital and detention center for captured Indians during the Seminole Wars, with a decommissioned lighthouse built in 1855. Visitors, when they are allowed, are asked to pack out anything they take onto the islands and to refrain from removing any island animals, vegetables, or minerals.

If you don't think you can get out to view the islands under your own power, there are the **Cedar Key Boat Rentals and Island Tours** (east end of Dock St., 352/231-4435, $25 adults, $15 children). From the city marina, you can also rent pontoon boats, skiffs, kayaks, and canoes (for kayaks and canoes, call 352/949-0200). You can also rent canoes and kayaks from **Kayak Cedar Keys** (across from the Gulf Kart Company, 1st and A Sts. at the Cedar Key Beach and Park, next to the marina, 352/543-9447, www.kayakcedarkeys. com, $25-45).

If you don't want to go out on your own, **Brack Barker's Wild Florida Adventures** (Williston, FL 32696, 352/215-4396, tour lengths and prices vary) leads kayak tours from Shell Mound near Cedar Key to the estuaries and coastal islands of the Lower Suwannee National Wildlife Refuge, out to Atsena Otie, exploring the coastal marshes of Steinhatchee, and along the Waccasassa River.

Adjacent to Cedar Key Scrub State Reserve, the **Waccasassa Bay State Preserve** (352/543-5567, 8am-sundown daily, free) is also accessible only by boat. (Boats can be launched from County Rd. 40 in Yankeetown, County Rd. 326 in Gulf Hammock, and from Cedar Key.) This 32,777-acre coastal wilderness area consists of salt marsh scattered with wooded islands, themselves striated with more than 100 tidal creeks that flow into the estuary. Once here, visitors enjoy fresh- and saltwater fishing, canoeing, primitive camping, and checking out the local population of bald eagles, black bears, and manatees.

Biking

At the turn of the 20th century, steamships won out over the railroad as preferred freight and passenger carriers in this area. As in so many parts of the country, this left miles of abandoned track, which have slowly been repurposed to meet the needs of outdoor enthusiasts. The 32-mile paved **Nature Coast Trail State Park** (U.S. 19 just south of downtown

THE NATURE COAST

CEDAR KEY

Catch of the Day

AMBERJACK, GREATER
When: Caught year-round, this Atlantic species is often bagged way offshore.
Limit: 1 fish per person, minimum size requirement of 34 inches to the fork of the tail
Fun Factor: They're a big, strong fish, offering a wonderful pull and feisty runs to the bottom.

COBIA
When: They have a spring run and a late-fall run but are generally caught in spring.
Limit: 1 fish per person or 6 fish per vessel (whichever is less), 33-inch minimum
Fun Factor: Exceptional pullers, they will readily bite. They prefer to hang out near structures like pilings or channel markers.

FLOUNDER
When: Caught year-round
Limit: 10 fish per person, 12-inch minimum
Fun Factor: A smaller species than the Atlantic version (often under 10 inches), they are excellent table fare, but cleaning them is tricky.

GROUPER (BLACK OR GAG)
When: July 1-December 3 for most areas, but they swim way out in the summer. They move inshore fall and winter, in as little as 6 feet of water.
Limit: 2 gag per person (all other grouper species 4 total per day), 22-inch minimum (red, yellowfin, and yellowmouth species have a 20-inch minimum; scamp have a 16-inch minimum in Gulf waters; there is no size minimum for rock hind and red hind species).
Fun Factor: People love their fight and flavor so much that the big ones are mostly fished out. You'll find lots under 22 inches.

JACK CREVALLE
When: Caught year-round, they school in the summer months.
Limit: No limits
Fun Factor: The thuggish brute that hangs out in the dark alley, it's the toughest fighting fish in the Gulf. No good to eat.

KINGFISH
When: Caught year-round, but better in late winter
Limit: No limits
Fun Factor: With lots of fight, they are beautiful, long, silvery fish that taste terrible. They tend to hunt in schools.

MANGROVE SNAPPER
When: Caught year-round
Limit: 10 fish per person, 10-inch minimum
Fun Factor: One of the smaller snappers, it rarely exceeds five pounds. Find them around docks and piers. Watch out—they bite. Also called gray or mango snapper.

MULLET
When: Caught year-round
Limit: 50 per person, no size limit
Fun Factor: This fish jumps out of the water frequently and prefers vegetation; cast net or use cane poles and dough balls of white bread.

REDFISH
When: Caught year-round
Limit: 1 fish per person, 18-inch minimum, 27-inch maximum
Fun Factor: The bread-and-butter fish in this area, they are delicious table fare and good fighters. They have become the new inshore/shallow water tournament fish of choice. Also called red drum.

SEABASS, BLACK
When: Caught year-round
Limit: 100 pounds per person in the Gulf, 5 fish per person in the Atlantic; 10-inch minimum in Gulf, 13-inch minimum in Atlantic
Fun Factor: Extremely small in this area, they are generally too small to keep. More of an offshore and Atlantic species.

SHEEPSHEAD
When: Caught year-round, but easier to get in winter
Limit: 15 fish per person, 12-inch minimum
Fun Factor: With jailhouse stripes, it's not surprising they're bait thieves. They hang out near barnacle-crusted structures. Good table fare but a little on the bony side.

SPANISH MACKEREL
When: Caught spring through fall
Limit: 15 per person, 12-inch minimum
Fun Factor: Caught on light tackle, they are generally under five pounds, travel in large schools, and are easy to catch. Most locals smoke them.

SPOTTED SEA TROUT
When: Caught year-round, season closed Nov.-Dec. in southern areas, Feb. in northwest areas
Limit: Between 4 and 6 fish per person depending on your location, 15-inch minimum, 20 inch maximum (and you can keep one over 20 inches per day)
Fun Factor: One of the most abundant fish in the area, they like the grass flats. The commercial netting ban has increased their numbers.

TARPON
When: Caught April, May, and June
Limit: Catch-and-release only
Fun Factor: A protected species, they can only be caught and released using line and hook, and require a $50 tag to fish for them. They are the most explosive of inshore species.

Chiefland, 352/535-5181, 8am-sundown daily, free) links several wildlife and recreation areas together, including **Fanning Springs State Park** and **Andrews Wildlife Management Area.** The various trails wind along the Suwannee River, ranging in length from 4.3 miles up to 10 miles, with trailheads in the downtowns of five communities, including Cross City (along Hwy. 98), Old Town (adjacent to the Old Town Fire Station), Fanning Springs (near the Agricultural Inspection Station), Trenton (2 blocks off Main St. at the railroad depot), and Chiefland (near the railroad depot 2 blocks beyond downtown). This makes it easy to enjoy a ride and finish up with lunch or dinner in one of these sweet inland towns.

Bikes can be rented at **Suncoast Bicycles** (322 N. Pine Ave., Inverness, 352/637-5757, $15-80). There are also group rides that leave from the store most days, and the store's website, www.suncoastbicycles.com, contains great local cycling routes in pdf format. Or, right downtown in Cedar Key, the **Gulf Kart Company** (A St. at 1st St., across from City Park, 352/477-0041, www.gulfkart.com) rents golf carts that seat 2-6 people ($55 for 2 people all day, $75 for 4, $95 for 6, $35 for 4 hours for 2 people, $45 for 4—a fun way to move around the island).

SIGHTS
Southern Cross Sea Farms

You could call Cedar Key "Clamelot" if you wanted. It's a backbreaking, difficult business that requires the salty seadog's perseverance and grit combined with a huge amount of scientific knowledge. All you need to know is that the town is the nation's No. 1 producer of farm-raised littlenecks, available for your delight year-round. But if you want to learn more, sweet-talk your way into **Southern Cross Sea Farms** (12170 Hwy. 24, Cedar Key, 352/543-5980, www.clambiz.com). They don't give official tours, but if you show an interest, they'll walk you through the process, from the saltwater larvae tanks thick with silt (which, under

a microscope, is millions of perfect clams, each 60 microns in size) to the clam nursery and out to the clam bags sunk in the Gulf, where the bivalves spend 18 months maturing. Interesting clam tidbit: All are born male. It is at maturity that 50 percent become female.

★ Dock Street

Cedar Key might be lean on attractions, but that's part of the attraction. Cedar Key is made up of a series of small barrier islands, but the commercial and residential parts of town are clustered on Way Key. And on Way Key, the place to be is Dock Street.

The fishing pier is the center of the action, where anglers, pelicans, and onlookers enjoy the sunset over the wide wooden boardwalk. On the weekends a little live music wafts out from Seabreeze-Big Deck Raw Bar or Steamers, along with the aromas of just-caught seafood getting its culinary due. The couple of blocks of Dock Street that fan out on either side of the pier are crowded with gift shops, galleries, restaurants, and bars—a rewarding stroll at any time of the day.

Cedar Key Museums

St. Clair Whitman invented tools and gizmos for the Standard Manufacturing Company in the early 1900s, but more importantly, he was a persistent collector. He accumulated antique glassware, old bottles, photographs of Cedar Key, and an incredible number of seashells. The **Cedar Key Museum State Park** (12231 SW 166 Ct., 352/543-5350, 10am-5pm Thurs.-Mon., $2), in Whitman's house restored as it was in its 1920s heyday, proudly displays all his collections. But it's more than just a sweet little museum in which to see his treasures. Exhibits provide insight into the Timucuans who once inhabited this stretch of coast, as well as Cedar Key's 19th-century history as a center for pencil manufacturing and fiber broom and brush manufacturing. Docent-led tours are offered 1pm-4pm. Save this for an afternoon when the weather is gloomy or the fish aren't biting.

There are more opportunities to explore Cedar Key history at the **Cedar Key Historical Museum** (609 2nd St., 352/543-5549, 1pm-4pm Sun.-Fri., 11am-5pm Sat., $1 adults, $0.50 children) right downtown. Housed in one room of a former private residence circa 1871, the museum tells the story of Cedar Key through historic photos and a somewhat idiosyncratic assortment of memorabilia, as well as displays of Native American artifacts, minerals, and woodworking tools. It's worth checking out, especially if one of the guides is available to talk about the glory days of the local lumber, pencil, and fishing industries. Although it's a little pricey ($4.50), the brochure for a self-guided historical walking tour of downtown is a great short course on the area. Also, across the street from the museum is a quirky bookstore called **Curmudgeonalia** (2nd St. and D St., 352/543-6789, 9am-5pm daily) that offers a great collection of birding, naturalist, and offbeat Florida history books.

FOOD

Cedar Key has a handful of great restaurants, especially when it comes to fresh seafood. **Annie's Café** (just over the causeway on Hwy. 24, 352/543-6141, 6:30am-3.30pm

Thurs.-Tues., $4-8) is a local favorite for bird-watching over breakfasts of mullet, grits, sliced tomato, and a freshly made, steaming biscuit. Another breakfast joint is **Holey Moley** (510 2nd St., 352/477-5022, 7am-2pm daily, $8-10). Built in 1859, the **Island Hotel and Restaurant** (373 2nd St., 352/543-5111, 5pm-9pm Tues.-Sun., $15-25) is purportedly haunted by 13 ghosts, particularly during grisly weather. Even if you don't believe the story of the restless spirit of a murdered former owner, you'll enjoy the hearts of palm salad, the crab bisque, or just a stop at the friendly bar.

For more upscale waterside dining, head to the **Island Room Restaurant at Cedar Cove** (192 E. 2nd St., 352/543-6520, www.islandroom.com, 5pm-9pm Mon.-Thurs., 5pm-10pm Fri., 8am-10pm Sat.-Sun., $14-28) for Chef Peter Stefani's house-grown veggies and greens or bread pudding with bourbon sauce. After dinner, if you're not quite ready to turn in, head over to Dock Street for a drink with the locals at **Steamers** (420 Dock St., 352/543-5142, 11am-10pm daily) or **Seabreeze** (310 Dock St., 352/543-5738). And if you want something different, order Seabreeze's signature salad, a mix of lettuce, hearts of palm, peaches, pineapple, and

Dock Street

dates, topped with a scoop of peanut butter ice cream.

Opened in 2007 and owned by Peter Stefani of the Island Room, **Dock Street Depot** (490 Dock St., 352/543-0202, 11am-10pm daily, $8-15) serves great seafood jambalaya and shrimp Creole along with a menu of other seafood, fried or broiled.

ACCOMMODATIONS

★ **The Faraway Inn** (847 3rd St., 888/543-5330, www.farawayinn.com, $90-160) is set within a quiet, attractive residential area away from traffic and nightlife, but within a short five-minute walk past Victorian and traditional Cracker homes to restaurants, convenience stores, shops, boat launches, the public beach, and the city dock. The Faraway Inn was built in the early 1950s on the original site of the 19th-century Eagle Pencil Company Cedar Mill. The inn has little freestanding efficiencies and cottages as well as more motel-like accommodations. It's pet-friendly, too.

Cedar Cove Beach and Yacht Club (192 2nd St., 352/543-5332, www.cedarcoveflorida.com, $109-160) has more upscale amenities than most properties in this area. All rooms are fully equipped efficiencies with private balconies and access to a heated pool and an extensive fitness facility.

A stop on the town's historical district walking tour, the **Cedar Key Bed and Breakfast** (810 3rd St., 352/543-9000, www.cedarkeybedandbreakfast.com, $105-225) was built in 1880 as a home for Eagle Pencil Company employees. Today, it's a comfortable six-room inn with a nice breakfast.

GETTING THERE

To get to Cedar Key, take U.S. 19, then head 23 miles southwest on Highway 24, the only road in and out of town (much of which is a quite rural two-lane highway until you cross the causeway into town). Cedar Key is 55 miles (60 minutes) north of Crystal River.

If you happen to be piloting your own small plane, Cedar Key has a single 2,300-foot hard-surfaced runway, but this is uncontrolled airspace.

Steinhatchee

If you're really looking to get out into the wilderness of this region, you can get deeper into the backcountry in Steinhatchee (STEEN-hachee), pop. 1,500. The fishing and hunting are incredible. The trout, redfish, and wild game have kept things jumping around here since the mid-1800s. The mouth of the Steinhatchee River, called Deadman's Bay, was home to thousands of Native Americans who came for the exceptional fishing and beautiful environment. Hunters and fisherfolk have been following suit ever since. In recent years Steinhatchee's appeal has broadened, thanks in large measure to a Georgian entrepreneur named Dean Fowler.

Fowler's place, Steinhatchee Landing Resort, has drawn accolades from an array of travel magazines in recent years. This hasn't

picked up the pace around here—in fact, at his place the posted speed limit is 9 mph. Why, you ask? "If it was 10, no one would pay it any mind," says Fowler. It's that kind of folksy, down-home sensibility that makes Steinhatchee such a joy to explore.

The Steinhatchee River—along with the Suwannee, Wacissa, Econfina, Fenholloway, and St. Marks Rivers—has emptied its rich contents here into the Apalachee Bay of the Gulf of Mexico for centuries. The shallow bay's gentle, gradual slope and fertile grass flats have made it a world-class fishing destination and a summer scalloping hot spot. It's a place where everyone has a big fish story and the time to tell it right, a place where "live bait and cold beer" sound like two of the central ingredients in happiness.

SPORTS AND RECREATION

Scalloping

Beginning July 1 and ending September 10, the scalloping season brings thousands of visitors to the little town of Steinhatchee. You need a recreational **saltwater fishing license** (888/347-4356, www.myfwc.com, $17 for a 3-day license) before you can wade out into the grassy shallows to scoop up the sweet bay bivalves. Each harvester is limited to two gallons of whole scallops or one pint of shucked meat per day. Pack a snorkel, swim shoes, and a mesh bag for your catch.

★ Offshore Fishing

Folks visiting this area most often spend their time, and considerable money, on half-day or full-day charters out into the Gulf in search of amberjack, kingfish (not the best tasting, but a beautiful sport fish), redfish, cobia, and grouper. Black grouper limits are five per person per day, and they must be at least 22 inches long. **Big Bend Charters** (877/852-3474) takes groups of up to six far out on offshore ($750) or nearshore ($600) trips, or a "thrill" fishing trip that targets a range of species ($1,200).

Farther in, spotted sea trout, catfish, and redfish can be coaxed out of the grass flats of Deadman's Bay or the slow-moving Steinhatchee River. Kingfish travel through Steinhatchee spring and fall to stay in the perfect water temperature (72°F or so), and the town is a legendary trout and redfish fishery in the wintertime when the fish move up into the river. Freshwater fishing can be accomplished dockside or from a rented canoe, but it's more fun in a shallow-draft boat with a motor: A 24-foot deck boat with a 200-horsepower Yamaha motor with a bimini will run you $150 per half day plus fuel at the **River Haven Marina** (1110 Riverside Dr. SE, 352/498-0709, www.riverhavenmarine.com). First-timers should hire a guide (it's an eminent place to learn saltwater fly-fishing techniques), but if you're striking out on your own, head to one of the local marinas (Sea Hag, River Haven, or Gulf Stream) and listen carefully to suss out the latest hot spots and irresistible baits. (Tip: Wear sunglasses with polarized lenses so you can see into the water more effectively.)

Diving

Rodale's *Scuba Diving* magazine is always heaping kudos on the Nature Coast, and scuba devotees come from all over to try cave

Manatee Springs State Park

and freshwater diving in the crystal-clear waters. Many of the draws are north and east of Steinhatchee and Cedar Key.

Along the Santa Fe River in High Springs, **Ginnie Springs** (from U.S. 19 head northeast on Hwy. 47, 386/454-7188, www.ginniespringsoutdoors.com) may be one of the most popular freshwater dive sites in the world, a place Jacques Cousteau once characterized as "visibility forever." Certified cave divers will also have heard of its Devil's Eye/Ear cave system. If you're diving for the first time, Ginnie Springs is perfect—no waves or breaking surf, no boats to contend with. There's a noncertification guided Discover Scuba Diving program ($99/student), too.

There are also two first-magnitude springs, **Manatee Springs State Park** (on Hwy. 320 west of Chiefland, 352/493-6072) and **Fanning Springs State Park** (18020 U.S. 19, Fanning Springs, 352/463-3420), 10 minutes from each other and 30 minutes northeast from Cedar Key. Situated in a 2,075-acre park, Manatee Springs produces 117 million gallons of clear blue water daily, a haven for manatees, fish, wading birds, scuba divers, and swimmers alike. There are two spots for excellent cavern and cave diving, **Manatee Springs State Park** itself and **Catfish Hotel**

Sink. You can camp, fish, boat, and hike in the park as well, but for a quick day trip the boardwalk through cypress swamp to the Suwannee River is a must-see. At Fanning Springs, which releases about 50 million gallons of water a day, swimmers and snorkelers explore the 20-foot-deep spring basin fed by two springs, Big Fanning and Little Fanning. Fanning Springs also has a cool boardwalk to the river, a nature trail, volleyball, and picnic facilities.

And a little farther away on Highway 3 in the town of Williston, there are two diving draws: Visitors to **Devil's Den Resort & Springs** (5390 NE 180th Ave., 352/528-3344, www.devilsden.com, $5 general admission, $38 dive fee, $40 gear rental) descend wooden steps through a rock tunnel to a floating dock, and then the dive begins about 40 feet down with swim-throughs, nooks, and crannies to explore. One of the safest cavern dives in the state is the nearby **Blue Grotto** (3852 NE 172nd Ct., 352/528-5770, www.divebluegrotto. com, $40 dive fee), a limestone sink with heavy-duty guidelines and platforms down to the 100-foot depths.

Farther south, if you want to get a sense for the history of the Suwannee River steamboat era, you can dive to see

Fort Island Trail Beach

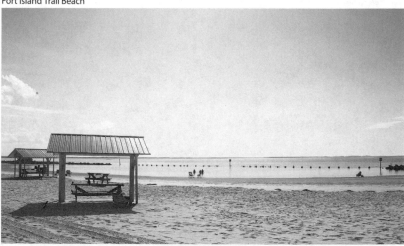

the **City of Hawkinsville Underwater Archaeological Preserve** (western bank of the Suwannee River, Old Town, accessible only by boat, 850/245-6444). Built in 1896 for the Hawkinsville Deep Water Boat Lines, the steamboat was used on the Suwannee River for the booming lumber industry before it ceased operation in 1922. Today, divers can explore the intact 141-foot hull of the sunken steamer, swimming along the long deck of the vessel to the stern paddlewheel alongside the area's more intrepid fish.

For diving equipment and services, options are plentiful. **American Pro Diving Center** (821 SE Hwy. 19, Crystal River, 352/563-0041), **Bird's Underwater** (320 NW Hwy. 19, Crystal River, 352/563-2763, www.birdsunderwater.com), and **Steve's Scuba & Snorkeling** (669 NE Hwy. 19, Crystal River, 352/795-1551) all have good reputations in the area.

Beaches

Of all the hundreds of miles of Florida's Gulf Coast, the Nature Coast offers the most limited beach access, much of it unsuitable for swimming. Tiny barrier islands and shallow grassy flats protect the coast from getting buffeted by Gulf winds and surf but also preclude the soft, white sand of elsewhere on the Gulf Coast. If you want to make a day of it, your best bet is **Keaton Beach,** a neat little beach town 17 miles north of Steinhatchee. Families and fisherfolk are drawn to the wide natural public beach, the 700-foot fishing pier, and the large boat ramp. The trick is getting there: Follow U.S. 19 north through Cross City, go approximately 11 miles, and turn left onto Highway 358. At the flashing light, stay to the right and once you go through Jena, turn right. Go over the bridge, turn left at the stop sign, and at next stop sign turn right. Go another 17 miles and turn left at the stop sign.

Beyond that, Cedar Key has a fair amount of private beach, but public access is limited to the downtown **city park** next to a colorful kids' playground on 2nd Street. The bay here is shallow and muddy, due to the outflow of numerous creeks and rivers, and the sand is rocky and hard on bare feet. A better bet is to head out to **Fort Island Trail Beach** (from U.S. 19, turn west onto Fort Island Trail and drive 10 miles). This Gulf-side beach is about 1,000 feet long, with a new fishing pier, concessions, and picnic facilities. A lifeguard is on duty Memorial Day-Labor Day, and the beach is open daylight-9:30pm.

FOOD

The dining scene is dominated by **Fiddler's Restaurant** (1306 Riverside Dr., 352/498-7427, www.fiddlersrestaurant.com, 6am-10pm daily, $10-20), a sprawling, lively spot populated by men swapping big fish stories and tucking into fried grouper (you can bring your own cleaned catch and have them cook it up). **Roy's** (100 1st Ave. SW, 352/498-5000, www.roys-restaurant.com, 11am-9pm daily, $13-16), a local favorite for 38 years, doesn't serve any booze but has an exhaustive salad bar, fried seafood, and fat burgers that keep people happy. **Lynn-Rich Restaurant** (202 15th St., 352/498-0605, 7am-4pm daily, $8-15) offers a familiar range of breakfast selections and sandwiches at lunch.

ACCOMMODATIONS

★ **Steinhatchee Landing Resort** (228 NE Hwy. 51, 352/498-3513, www.steinhatcheelanding.com, $140-500) is as upscale as it gets along the Nature Coast. Its 35 acres are dotted with dozens of individual one-, two-, and three-bedroom Victorian and Florida Cracker cottages, most equipped with French country furniture and oversize spa tubs. There's a new swimming pool and patio area, and it accepts pets up to 28 pounds.

The same folks own the nearby 17-room, budget-friendly **Steinhatchee River Inn** (1111 Riverside Dr., 352/498-4049, www.steinhatcheeriverinn.net, $79-129), where the rates range seasonally.

GETTING THERE

Steinhatchee is 33 miles north of Cedar Key on U.S. 19 and then 12 miles west on Highway 51.

Information and Services

The Nature Coast is located within the **eastern time zone.** The area code is **352.**

TOURIST INFORMATION

Citrus County Chamber of Commerce (915 N. Suncoast Blvd., Crystal River, 352/795-3149), stocks racks of local brochures and pamphlets. They are open 8:30am-4:30pm Monday-Friday, 8:30am-1pm Saturday. For more information about local events, pick up the *Citrus County Chronicle,* the largest daily in the county. There's also an easy-to-use online version at www.chronicleonline.com.

Cedar Key Chamber of Commerce (450 2nd St., 352/543-5600, 10am-3pm Thurs.-Mon.), right down the block from the city hall and library, has limited hours and limited offerings. Each Thursday you can pick up the *Cedar Key Beacon,* the little island newspaper that directs you to events and activities.

For other tourist information and maps of the area, contact **Florida's Pure Water Wilderness** (352/463-3467, www.purewaterwilderness.com). Birders will want to check out the award-winning website, www.citrusbirdingtrail.com, which catalogs birding opportunities on virtually every trail in the area.

POLICE AND EMERGENCIES

The **Crystal River Police Department,** the largest along the Nature Coast, is in back of city hall (123 NW U.S. 19, 352/795-4241).

In the event of a medical emergency, **Seven Rivers Regional Medical Center** (6201 N. Suncoast Blvd., Crystal River, 352/795-6560) has emergency services, as does **Nature Coast Regional Hospital** (125 SW 7th St., Williston, 352/528-2801). For anything major, you may want to head to **North Florida Regional Medical Center** in Gainesville.

RADIO AND TELEVISION

WXCV "Citrus" FM 95.3 broadcasts popular music and information about the Nature Coast; for news, tune in to **WFSU FM 88.9** out of Tallahassee; **WKTK FM 98.5** out of Gainesville pumps out easy 1970s, 1980s, and 1990s rock (and is the station to turn to for info on suspected flooding); **WJUF FM 90.1** sends out classical, jazz, and folk; and **WRGO FM 102.7** gives you oldies from Cedar Key.

On the television, **WCJB Channel 20** is the ABC affiliate out of Gainesville and Ocala. Also out of Gainesville and Ocala, **WOGX Channel 51** is the FOX affiliate.

LAUNDRY SERVICES

Catering to fisherfolk, many of the Nature Coast's motels, hotels, fish camps, and campgrounds offer laundry facilities. But if you need a coin laundry, try **Crystal Center Laundromat** (648 SE U.S. 19, Crystal River, 352/795-0979).

FISHING LICENSES

If you haven't planned ahead, fishing licenses can be purchased on the fly at the Kmart in Crystal River or the Walmart in Homosassa.

The Forgotten Coast

Look for ★ to find recommended
sights, activities, dining, and lodging.

Highlights

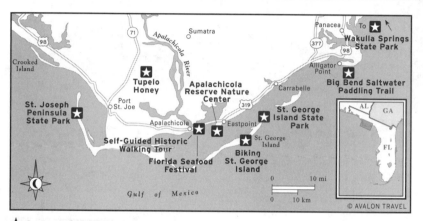

★ **St. Joseph Peninsula State Park:** This 2,500-acre park keeps showing up on Dr. Beach's top ten list due to its superior sand, surf, shells, and weather (page 252).

★ **Self-Guided Historic Walking Tour:** Go back in time to an era of antebellum grace and charm with a leisurely stroll in downtown Apalachicola. More than 200 of the buildings downtown made the National Register of Historic Places (page 256).

★ **Florida Seafood Festival:** You'll gain a robust appreciation for Apalachicola's beloved eastern oysters in November at this annual festival (page 257).

★ **Tupelo Honey:** Stop by one of the few operating tupelo honey apiaries in the world and sample the esteemed sweet treat (page 259).

★ **St. George Island State Park:** A nighttime beach walk on St. George reveals one of the darkest night skies in the United States (telescope optional) and possibly the marvel of baby

loggerhead turtles flapping their way back out to sea under a luminous moon (page 265).

★ **Biking St. George Island:** Start from the western side of the island, stop in town for a cool ice cream cone, and then continue along the roadside path until you reach the state park at the island's eastern end (page 267).

★ **Apalachicola Reserve Nature Center:** Learn more about fertile Apalachicola Bay's flora and fauna and check out aquariums of local fish and turtles (page 273).

★ **Big Bend Saltwater Paddling Trail:** Extending 60 miles along the Gulf Coast, this area is home to myriad bird species as well as a meandering, 105-mile mapped kayak and canoe trail (page 278).

★ **Wakulla Springs State Park:** What do *Airport '77* and *Tarzan's Secret Treasure* have in common? They were both filmed in the lush wilderness surrounding these crystal-clear springs, which pump 600,000 gallons of water per minute (page 278).

Despite its name, the area between Panama City and St. Marks is one of the most memorable regions on the Gulf Coast. The Forgotten Coast is best known for its protected lands (87 percent of the region is national or state park land), top-rated and underpopulated beaches, tasty oysters, affordable cost of living, and pristine waters. Apalachicola Bay is one of the most productive bays in the United States. It provides 90 percent of the oysters consumed in Florida and supports extensive shrimping, crabbing, and commercial fishing industries. The Apalachicola watershed has the greatest number of freshwater fish species in Florida and the highest density and diversity of amphibian species in North America.

In the early 1800s, the town of Apalachicola was founded by cotton and lumber magnates to provide an accessible port for the South's cotton plantations. Cotton warehouses were quickly erected, making it the third-largest cotton port on the Gulf Coast. More overlooked than forgotten, this region was disregarded by tourists for the greater part of the 1900s due to its unpalatable mix of industrial development and lack of infrastructure across large spans of wilderness.

The Forgotten Coast doesn't offer everything to everyone: There are no amusement parks, few malls, even fewer fast-food restaurants. Yet this is precisely the appeal for visitors who seek a more natural and adventurous Florida experience. The region reaches back to Florida's past, a time before most of the landscape became resorts and vacation homes—seemingly overnight.

Where you set up your base camp is a matter of preference. The historic port of Apalachicola is known for its restored Georgian and Victorian homes, cotton warehouses converted into antiques shops, and mouthwatering seafood restaurants. St. George Island, on the other hand, is an unparalleled barrier island retreat, with hundreds of beachfront rentals ranging in size and price. And Eastpoint on the mainland or St. Joseph Peninsula is where to go if you're here to fish, camp, paddle, boat, or otherwise

Previous: fishing boats in Apalachicola; the dunes at St. Joseph Peninsula State Park. **Above:** the lighthouse at Cape St. George State Reserve.

The Forgotten Coast

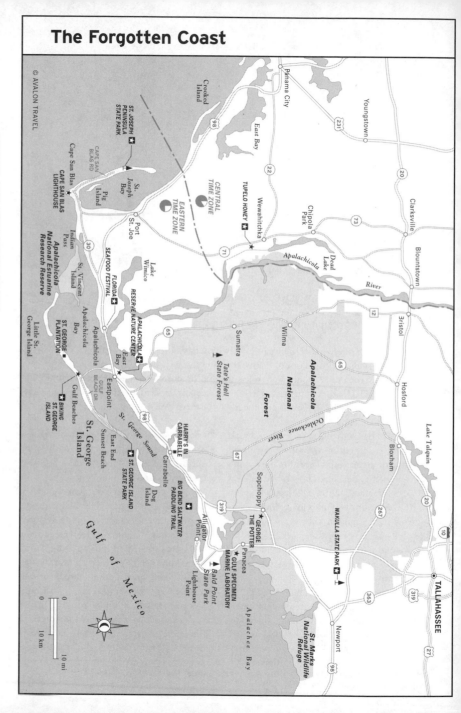

© AVALON TRAVEL

A network of trails offers excellent hiking and birding throughout the region.

A slower pace suits the area. The beaches of St. George Island, Cape San Blas, St. Vincent Island, and St. Joseph Peninsula State Park often make people's lists of top beaches in the United States. There are lighthouses, dunes towering up to 30 feet high anchored by sea oats and magnolia trees, miles of white sand dotted with perfect sand dollars, and hardly another person in sight.

High season here is very different from that in the rest of coastal Florida. It stays cooler here than elsewhere on the Gulf, making it a little chilly in the winter and more than tolerable in the summer. Summer is the peak, with rental prices jumping substantially on beach houses on St. George and hotel rooms in Apalachicola. Many beach houses book as far as a year in advance during summer. If you are more impulsive, try off-peak times to get a room on the fly. Spring and fall are gorgeous on this stretch of the coast, especially for camping and paddling trips (but watch out, Easter week tends to be a difficult reservation).

explore the unforgettable outdoor adventures of the Forgotten Coast.

PLANNING YOUR TIME

The Forgotten Coast, roughly speaking, is bounded on the west by Mexico Beach and on the east by St. Marks. From west to east, it includes the communities of St. Joe Beach and Port St. Joe, Simmons Bayou, Cape San Blas, Indian Pass, Apalachicola, St. George Island, Eastpoint, Carrabelle, Ochlockonee Bay, and Panacea. The communities worthy of most of your attention are Apalachicola and St. George Island. (Apalachicola will hold your interest for a minimum of a weekend, and St. George Island rentals, at least during high season, are mostly by the full week.) For tent camping, RV camping, and paddling, St. Joseph Peninsula State Park's Shady Pine campground sits right on the Gulf of Mexico and is one of the best on the Gulf Coast. Eastpoint, Carrabelle, and Apalachicola are the main hot spots for fishing guides and services in the surrounding bays, rivers, and offshore in the Gulf.

Transportation

To reach the Forgotten Coast by car, there are several routes worth considering. From the north, if your aim is to minimize back roads, take I-75 south to Tifton, then U.S. 319 to Tallahassee, then U.S. 98 to the St. George Island Bridge at Eastpoint, or continue west to Apalachicola. If you're coming west from, say, Orlando, find your way to I-75 heading north; exit on U.S. 441 west at Alachua, just before Lake City, quickly changing to U.S. 27, which intersects with U.S. 98 near Perry.

By boat, on the Gulf Intracoastal Waterway from Florida's west coast, enter at St. George Sound through East Pass, between Dog Island and St. George Island, or through Bob Sikes Cut (pretty shallow). From the west, take the Intracoastal Waterway through East Bay from Panama City, then on past White City. Continue east through Wimico to the Jackson River, which leads to the Apalachicola River. Follow markers past the Railroad Bridge to Apalachicola.

If you're piloting your own small plane, **Apalachicola Regional Airport** (8 Airport Rd., Apalachicola, 850/653-1366) is a former military base (serving B-17s in WWII), with three concrete runways and fuel available. The closest commercial airports are **Tallahassee Regional Airport** (service provided by Delta, US Airways, American Airlines, and Silver Airways, 3300 Capital Cir. SW, Tallahassee, 850/891-7802) and **Northwest Florida Beaches International Airport** (6300 West Bay Pkwy., Panama City, 850/763-6751), the first international airport built in the United States in a decade, 60 miles to the west. Northwest Florida Beaches Airport is served by Delta, United, Silver Airways, Southern Airways, and Southwest Airlines. **Alamo** (877/222-9075), **Avis** (800/230-4898), **Budget** (800/527-0700), **Dollar** (800/800-3665 domestic, 800/800-6000 international), and **National** (800/367-6767) provide rental cars from these airports.

Once you're in the region, the best way to explore is by car, as there is no real public transportation (no buses or trains) to speak of. The area is served by U.S. 98; while sometimes slow and congested, it is a picturesque roadway that stretches 300 miles along the northwest Florida coast. An easy way to explore the Apalachicola River Basin and Apalachicola National Forest is to take State Highway 12, also known as the Apalachee Savannahs National Scenic Byway. It begins in Bristol, Florida, and winds alongside the Apalachicola River for most of the way before veering into the heart of the national forest. Driving south from Alabama and Georgia, you can make time along east-west I-10, but it's about 65 miles to the north. Sooner or later you've got to hook up with U.S. 98 and slow down.

Port St. Joe

As you drive toward Apalachicola on Highway 98, consider making a stop in Port St. Joe. The once sleepy, coastal town of a little more than 3,000 people has experienced quite the renaissance in recent years. Sure, we all used to drive right through the former port town on St. Joseph Bay, but these days it's worth spending an evening or two exploring the new restaurants and shops in the historic downtown district, and perhaps booking a fishing charter or renting kayaks to explore the beautiful surrounding bay and waterways.

RECREATION AND SIGHTS

A good place to start exploring is at the **Port St. Joe Marina** (340 Marina Dr., 850/227-9393, www.psjmarina.com). The marina is one of the main gateways to the open water of the gulf in the area. If you're sailing into Port St. Joe, you'll be happy to find 109 wet slips, a gift shop, and a spacious bathhouse facility with laundry machines. Both landlubbers and salty sailors can get a break from the hardtack and sit down for a delicious meal at **Dockside Seafood and Rawbar.** Whether you eat at Dockside or not, the marina is an excellent place to watch the sunset.

Several fishing charters board at the Port St. Joe Marina, including the popular **Break-A-Way Charters** (850/340-1188, www.break-a-waycharters.com, $100/hour for up to 6 people). The father-son duo, Captains Bobby and Wade Guilford, offer inshore and offshore fishing trips, bottom fishing, trolling, tarpon trips, diving and scalloping trips, and sightseeing cruises. For diving trips they use a hookah rig system, which allows visitors to dive without a tank, and here's the best part—no special certification is needed.

More independent-minded anglers may want to rent a boat on their own. **Seahorse Water Safaris** (340 Marina Dr., Port St. Joe, 850/227-1099, www.seahorsewatersafaris.

com, $165-245 half day plus fuel costs) rents three different sized pontoon boats holding 6-10 people for you to take out on St. Joseph Bay.

If you'd like to take an ecotour with an experienced captain with a master's degree in marine biology, just call Captain Charlene Burke at **About Fun Charters** (130 Atlantic St., 850/340-1035, www.about-funcharters.com, $250-800). She'll take you out on the *Saint Misbehaving*, a 26-foot twin Vee that can hold up to six guests. She offers fishing trips ($250 for 2 hours, $400 for 4 hours, $600 for 6 hours, $800 for hours) to catch redfish, speckled trout, flounder, tripletail, black drum, pompano, cobia, mackerel, sharks, and bull-reds. From July to September 10, you can take a snorkel tour around St. Joseph Bay and she'll help you harvest scallops ($250 for 2 hours, $350 for 4 hours, $450 for 6 hours). Or you can search for wildlife and listen to the knowledgeable captain tell you all about the natural history and beautiful scenery that you'll see on one of her sightseeing ecotours, which can also be booked as a sunset cruise ($250 for 2 hours, $350 for 4 hours).

If you'd rather keep your feet on dry land, go explore the waterfront trails and other fun stuff at **Frank Pate Park** (502 Monument Ave.). The park is connected to the Port St. Joe Marina by the 0.7-mile Bay Walk Trail that leads to a pirate-themed playground, a boat launch, and a picturesque fishing pier with a nice viewing pavilion. From the park, you can take the short Pelican Run Trail to the historic downtown area of Port St. Joe, which is only 0.2-mile north of Frank Pate Park. After passing downtown, you can continue on the 0.75-mile Sandpiper Run Greenway that connects 10th Street Forrest Park and Buck Griffin Lake. It's a nice way to explore Port St. Joe on foot.

If you're looking for the best beaches in the area, you'll want to head north to one of the public access points near Mexico Beach, or drive south to Cape San Blas, St. Joseph Peninsula, or St. George Island.

ENTERTAINMENT AND EVENTS

If you're here on the first weekend in October, make sure to spend some time cracking shells and dancing at the **Florida Scallop and Music Festival** ($100 for both days). It's the largest annual festival in Gulf County and the celebration is all about the scallop, one of Florida's most delicious seafood delicacies. The gates open at 5pm on Friday and 10am on Saturday, and the headlining musical act takes the stage at 9pm. While vendors serve up the tasty saltwater clam prepared every way imaginable, the crowd dances the night away to music that can be heard clear across St. Joseph Bay.

FOOD

Dockside Seafood and Rawbar (340 Marina Dr., 850/229-5200, www.dockside-seafoodandrawbar.com, 11am-9pm Sun.-Thurs., 11am-10pm Fri.-Sat., $12-25) is on the Port St. Joe Marina. As the name implies, they feature seafood dishes, a variety of sandwiches, and raw oysters. The views of the marina are wonderful, and you can watch the charter boats sail in after a day of fishing and then gawk as they lay their catch on the docks.

While you're downtown, grab a pizza pie at **Joe Mama's Wood Fired Pizzas** (406 Reid Ave., 850/229-6262, 4:30pm-9pm Tues.-Sat., $7-15). They've kept the menu simple and offer salads, a wide variety of pizza, and a few starters like baked focaccia and grilled bruschetta. For dessert, you have two excellent options: a delicious cheesecake or something called a pot of chocolate, which is exactly what it sounds like and will make you wish you could take a pot of it home.

Another downtown favorite is **Provisions** (222 Reid Ave., 850/229-9200, 11am-9pm Tues.-Sat., $7-15). They offer a variety of international entrées that are all over the culinary map, from Southern comfort food to Italian pasta dishes and Asian-inspired noodle plates. The connecting factor is that all the food is delicious, no matter if you order the prime rib sandwich, the Thai stir-fry with peanut sauce, or the shrimp carbonara.

For something ultra-casual, stop by the **Mason-Dixon** (402 Reid Ave., 850/229-1999, 11:30am-2:30pm Tues.-Fri., $6-10). It's a permanent food truck that serves hot-pressed and cold cut sandwiches, salads, and some mighty fine sweet tea. They're pet-friendly with a relaxed outdoor eating space that's shaded by oversize umbrellas. Try the Garden State, a hot-pressed sandwich with shredded turkey, avocado, garlic-roasted asparagus, gouda cheese, roasted red bell peppers, and local tupelo-honey mustard.

Get your taco and margarita fix at **Pepper's Mexican Grill** (224 Reid Ave., 850/229-8540, 11:30am-2:30pm Tues.-Fri., $8-12). The atmosphere is fun and bright, as you would expect from the hippest Mexican joint in town. The cold margaritas and tasty sizzling fajitas may also get you in a festive mood.

ACCOMMODATIONS

After exploring the charming shops and restaurants downtown, you may want to stay the night. There are several small motels along Highway 98, but the best place to stay in town is the **Port Inn** (501 Monument Ave., 850/229-7678, www.portinnfl.com, $130-190). The historic, two-story inn built in 1909 has 21 rooms that were all recently renovated. Ask for a one of the ten rooms that have a view of the bay. In the morning, you can eat breakfast in the dining room downstairs, and at night you can enjoy drinks at the Thirsty Goat, a cozy lounge that's a popular spot for locals to gather and watch the sunset. The inn is in the heart of downtown, and it captures the charm and hospitality that this town along the Forgotten Coast is known for.

A few miles south off U.S. 98, **Mainstay Suites** (3951 East Hwy. 98, 855/849-1513, $100-160) is a little more of a bargain. It will get you closer to the beaches, but still keep you near enough to town to enjoy the restaurants and shopping there. Every room is equipped with a kitchen that includes a large refrigerator, which is nice if you want to cut down on dining costs. If you're fishing in the area, you're going to want somewhere to cook your catch. The hotel is clean and pet-friendly, with spacious rooms. A standard continental breakfast is offered.

GETTING THERE

From Apalachicola, drive west on U.S. 98 to reach Port St. Joe. This 23-mile route will take about 30 minutes in normal traffic. From Panama City, drive east on U.S. 98 for 36 miles, which will take about an hour in normal traffic.

Apalachicola

Say it with me: apa-LATCH-ee-CO-la. The locals shorten it to Apalach and, more so than many places along the Gulf Coast of Florida, they have strong Southern accents. The population here is roughly 3,000, but Apalachicola has the cultural opportunities of a much larger city and a coastal Southern charm only found in these smaller Gulf-front communities. Here you'll find Georgian and Victorian homes settled in along wide avenues, shaded by moss-covered live oaks, and a civic pride in the citizens that reflects the area's long and rich history.

You can't hold Apalachicola down. Even though the city has been pummeled by hurricanes and the BP oil spill in 2010, it continues to prove its resilience. The downtown historic district has been transformed from a crusty, dilapidated fishing town to a picturesque waterfront destination with a wide variety of shops and restaurants. This is a wonderful place to spend a day or two, exploring the historic homes, enjoying the bountiful seafood that is brought in daily aboard the local fishing fleet, and searching through

Apalachicola

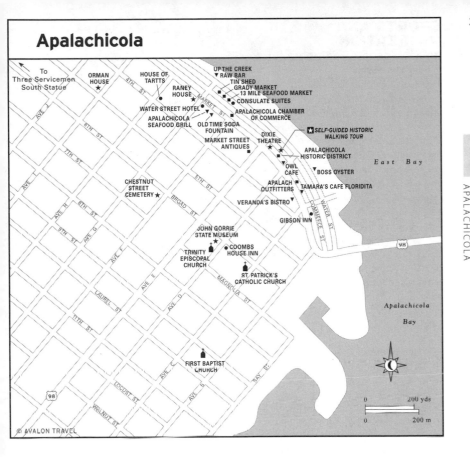

the plentiful antiques and maritime-themed boutiques. The hub of activity is found along Market and Water Streets, which border the Apalachicola River, and this is where your visit to Apalachicola should begin, preferably tucked into a plate of oysters and shrimp while you stare out into the Gulf of Mexico.

Locals will tell you that the oysters bring most people to Apalachicola. The plentiful and nutrient-rich mollusks are believed to have attracted the first Native American inhabitants, as evidenced by the ancient oyster shell mounds they left behind throughout the region. Today Apalachicola is the hub of an oyster industry that provides 90 percent of the oysters consumed in Florida and 10 per cent of the oysters consumed in the United States. While you're in town, consider hiring a local guide to take you oyster harvesting in Apalachicola Bay. Shuck the oyster on the bow of the boat. Throw it raw right on a cracker with a little horseradish, cocktail sauce, and a squeeze of fresh lemon juice and enjoy a culinary history dating back thousands of years. At the very least, buy some raw oysters at one of the restaurants that serve the popular seafood item. A raw oyster is a lot like the Forgotten Coast; it's not for everyone. But whether you love it or vow to never try it again, it's a Southern treat that you won't soon forget.

SPORTS AND RECREATION
★ St. Joseph Peninsula State Park

Dr. Beach, really a man named Stephen Leatherman, conducts an annual ranking of American beaches, rating them by water temperature, number of sunny days, color of sand, algae, smell, pests, and about 40 other criteria. No kidding around—this is serious. And one beach that keeps showing up on his top 10 list is **St. Joseph Peninsula State Park** (8899 Cape San Blas Rd., Port St. Joe, 850/227-1327)—it was No. 1 in 2002. Projecting seven miles out into the Gulf, this barrier peninsula is reachable from the mainland across Apalachicola Bay and via Cape San Blas. Sand blows up across the beach and lodges in sea oats to produce exceptionally tall dunes (30-40 feet), the water is a sparkling aquamarine and hovers around 84°F in summer, the surf is gentle, and the 2,500-acre beach park is never crowded.

And here's what Dr. Beach has to say about the local sand:

The sand is nearly pure quartz crystal. While most noncarbonated (noncoral) beaches are composed of 15 to 20 different types of sand, the Panhandle beaches are like a bar of Ivory soap—99.44 percent pure. The remarkable purity of the Florida Panhandle sand is related to its geologic history. Like most all beaches along the East and Gulf Coasts, the Panhandle sands came from the wearing down of the Appalachian Mountains, which brought an array of different minerals to the shore. But unlike other coastal areas, the rivers stopped bringing any new sand for tens of thousands of years. During this long period of time, wave action has ground the particles down to size. Quartz, being the most resistant mineral commonly available on the face of the earth, is the only type of sand grain left as the other minerals were ground down to dust.... What we find on the Panhandle beaches today is quartz sand crystal at its terminal size, meaning that all the grains are nearly the same size (well sorted in geologic terms).

It's not all beach, though. The park includes a large expanse of heavy pine forest that is home to bobcats, deer, raccoons, and rattlesnakes, as well as bald eagles, ospreys, and peregrine falcons. In the fall hawks and monarch butterflies perch for a while on

St. Joseph Peninsula State Park

their migration along the Yucatan Express to Mexico. And in July and August you'll find visitors searching the bayside for sweet scallops.

There are no hotels in the park, although there are eight loft-style, furnished cabins on the bay side of the park (they accommodate 5-7 people, $100/night) and 119 campsites with water and electricity available in two areas: Gulf Breeze sites are more open (better for RVs and big cars), and the Shady Pines area is more secluded and shaded ($24/night in either spot). You can also primitive camp on the peninsula ($4/person/night, reservations a must). A trail winds its way across the peninsula, and backpackers can hike to designated camp areas and also camp right on the beach. Fires are permitted in some areas, and the primitive campsites are great to use for overnight paddling and boating trips in the area. A marina with boat ramp ($5/day) is near the park entrance. Use of the ramp is free for overnight guests, who are permitted to leave their boat moored at the marina.

On your way to the park, visit the **Cape San Blas Lighthouse.** The picturesque iron tower was built on the site of two former brick lighthouses, which were removed due to beach erosion. In 2014, thanks to the tireless campaigning of local lighthouse preservationists, the Lighthouse along with the light-keeper's historic home and facilities were moved inland to Port St. Joe where they will be preserved and protected from the relentless forces of beach erosion. If you've never seen a lighthouse being pulled down the road on the back of a flatbed truck, then you haven't truly lived. It was a sight to behold, a beacon of modern marvels.

Barrier Islands

The Forgotten Coast's barrier islands serve to separate Apalachicola Bay from the Gulf of Mexico, acting as shock absorbers to protect the mainland from winds, storms, and waves. These little islands are also fabulous places to relax and explore.

Birding, shelling, surf fishing, beach relaxation—these are the offerings on **Dog Island** to the east of St. George Island, accessible only by water taxi from Carrabelle or by private watercraft. It's known as a refuge for loggerhead and leatherback turtles, and only a handful of people live on the island. There's a single funky hotel called the **Pelican Inn** (888/253-2971, $150 Mon.-Thurs., $200 Fri.-Sun., pets welcome for an additional $10/day, linens not provided), with eight studio units that each sleep up to four people. But be advised—there are no stores, no restaurants, really no other amenities on the island. The inn is more rustic Old Florida than a resort. If you have a zero-tolerance policy for lodgings that may need some minor repairs, then this probably isn't the place for you.

It used to be that St. George Island was 28 miles long. In 1954 the U.S. Army Corps of Engineers carved out an artificial channel to create two separate barrier islands (this was primarily to make it easier for the shrimpers to get out to the Gulf). The larger is still St. George Island, and the smaller, boomerang-shaped island is known locally as **Little St. George Island** and more formally as **Cape St. George State Reserve.**

Little St. George can be reached only by private boat—a worthwhile excursion. The nine-mile-long island was purchased by the state of Florida in 1977 under the Environmentally Endangered Lands program as part of the Apalachicola National Estuarine Research Reserve to protect it from development and to contribute to the protection of Apalachicola Bay. It's remote, wild, and populated only by an idiosyncratic assortment of creatures.

Originally established for waterfowl, the reserve's aim has broadened to protect a range of endangered species: Bald eagles nest in pines along the island's freshwater marshes; loggerhead sea turtles nest on the white-sand beaches; wood storks are frequent visitors; and indigo snakes burrow in the dunes.

Little St. George is open to the public for swimming, fishing, birding, and hiking. Primitive camping is permitted at designated sites at West Pass and Sike's Cut (at either end of the island; call the Apalachicola National Estuarine Reserve at 850/670-7700 with your dates and number of people). Fires are permitted at the campsites, but no live wood can be cut.

You have to book your own shuttle to get over to **St. Vincent Island,** to the west of Little St. George. **Captain Joey Romanelli** (850/229-1065, \$10 adults, \$7 children under 10, round-trip) will take you out on his 27-foot pontoon boat, departing from the end of Indian Pass Road. The whole island constitutes the **St. Vincent National Wildlife Refuge,** with 12,358 acres of dunes and woods.

In 1990 the island became a haven and breeding ground for endangered red wolves. These solitary animals once roamed the Southeast, but habitat loss reduced their numbers such that there were a mere 100 confined to a small area of coastal Louisiana and Texas. The wolves (bigger than a coyote, smaller than a gray wolf) now populate St. Vincent, and when pups are weaned they are taken to reintroduction facilities around the country.

Before becoming a refuge, the island was used as a private hunting and fishing preserve. Previous exotic-minded owners introduced Southeast Asian elk called sambar deer (big guys, they weigh up to 600 pounds, as opposed to the native white-tailed deer that weigh in at a modest 100 or so pounds) to the island, and they can be spotted to this day. There are native whitetails here too, and a fair number of other species (lots of rattlers, so beware) on what is one of the 500 refuges in the national system. You can bring a bike with you on the shuttle (\$10 extra/bike) or just hike the trails and beaches of the island.

Fishing

Apalachicola Bay, the Apalachicola River, and the Gulf of Mexico each provide stellar fishing experiences for the rookie or serious angler. There are dozens of charter providers in the area, but a handful of names come up time and again when you ask for locals' recommendations: **Captain Charlie's Charters**

the lighthouse at Cape St. George State Reserve

(850/653-6482, www.captcharlescharters. com, \$400-500 for bay area fishing trips, \$850-995 for offshore fishing) leads offshore fishing groups, sightseeing and shelling expeditions, oystering adventures, and, in season, tarpon trips; **Backwater Guide Service** (850/899-0063, www.backwaterguideservice. com, \$300-500) takes people bass fishing or fly-fishing on the river and in the bay on a 21-foot boat and offers sightseeing trips on the Apalachicola River, shelling trips to the barrier islands, and dolphin-watching tours; and the **Robinson Brothers Guide Service** (850/653-8896, \$400-900) gets the nod for flats fishing (that's shallow water, where anglers stand on the bow of a boat with their fly rod or spinning rod) as well as bay and offshore fishing with live bait in a bigger boat and deeper water. Tommy and Chris Robinson's knowledge of the area is impressive.

Diving

Scuba enthusiasts have a few excellent options in the area (including some nice artificial

the High Bluff Coastal Trail in Apalachicola National Forest

Here's how the story goes: A man named Cebe Tate once entered a vast swamp in search of a Florida panther that was killing his livestock. Gone for seven days and nights, when Tate emerged with his trusty hunting dog, shaken and thirsty, he announced, "My name is Cebe Tate, and I just came from Hell!" That's how **Tate's Hell State Forest** (access the forest from U.S. 98, County Road 67, or Hwy. 65, 850/697-3734, free entry, camping $10/day) got its ominous name. It's 185,000 acres between the Apalachicola and Ochlockonee Rivers, much of it suitable for hiking and biking. There's an observation tower at the **Ralph G. Kendrick Boardwalk** from which visitors can look out over a dense stand of rare dwarf, or hatrack, cypress, many of them 150 years old and only 15 feet tall. A number of endangered or threatened species call Hell home, including the bald eagle, red-cockaded woodpecker, gopher tortoise, and Florida black bear.

The forest contains 35 miles of rivers, streams, and creeks available for canoeing, boating, fishing (boat launch at Cash Creek and other sites), and primitive camping. The **High Bluff Coastal Trail** is a wonderful hiking path that's part of the Florida Division of Forestry's Trailwalker Program, its trailhead located on U.S. 98, four miles west of Carrabelle.

To the north, abutting Tate's Hell State Forest, is **Apalachicola National Forest** (850/643-2282, www.fs.fed.us/r8/florida), the largest national forest in Florida, spanning 632,890 acres. The area was largely destroyed at the turn of the 20th century by the timber and turpentine industries, but since 1936 it's been allowed to grow with much less environmental impact to the natural habitat and now has the largest red-cockaded woodpecker population in the world. Much of the forest is difficult to get to, but there are a few nice day hikes easily accessible: the 4.5-mile-long **Wright Lake Trail**, the 6-mile-long **Trail of Lakes,** and the 5.4-mile-long **Leon Sinks Geological Area Trail.** Mountain bikers

reef diving and clam-covered rock ledges in St. Joe), but the most celebrated wreck dive can be found 105 feet down, 20 miles south of Cape San Blas. Undulating with packs of curious amberjack, barracuda, snapper, and rays, the *Empire Mica* lies in disarray on the floor of the Gulf. A British oil tanker built in 1941, the ship was en route from Houston to England on June 29, 1942, when two German submarine torpedoes ignited the 12,000 tons of oil it was carrying. The ship went down in a series of fiery explosions, killing 33 men on board. Today, the bow section of the 479-foot-long ship is intact, as are 60-80 feet of deck, the metal getting lacy and thin. **Daly's Dock and Dive Center** (Port St. Joe, 850/229-6330, $150 includes air, weights, drinks, and snacks) provides wonderful all-day trips to the SS *Vamar,* which is one of Florida's Underwater Archaeological Preserves. **Seahorse Water Safaris** (850/227-1099) offers diving trips (prices vary by trip and duration) and guided snorkel tours, if scuba seems too hard core ($25 plus $10 gear rental).

Ice, Ice, Baby

Ice cube museum. Hmm. Are you imagining a cold room containing, maybe, a piece of the iceberg that sank the *Titanic*, a cube from Dean Martin's final cocktail, or the original "fly-in-the-ice cube" novelty gag?

Apalachicola luminary **John Gorrie** is known in the history books as the father of air-conditioning and ice manufacturing, recipient of the first patent for mechanical refrigeration in 1851. A charming museum in a little historic home tells the Gorrie story.

By the time the young doctor arrived in town in 1833, Apalachicola was bustling as the third-largest port on the Gulf, shipping cotton to Europe and New England. During his time in town, Gorrie served as mayor, postmaster, city council member, bank director, and founder of Trinity Church. But all that civic-mindedness pales when compared to his medical work. Yellow fever was a menace in those years, and no one had linked the terrifying sickness to those swarms of pesky mosquitoes that plagued these swampy, humid, low-lying floodplains. In addition to chills, headache, muscle aches, vomiting, and backache, the onset of the illness was marked by high fever. Gorrie posited that bringing the fever down was essential to prevent the shock, bleeding, and kidney and liver failure that often led to death.

As cold temperatures were hard to come by in these parts, he set about making some. His idea is one used in today's refrigeration: Cooling can be achieved through the rapid expansion of gases. He built a machine with two pumps that condensed and then rarefied air. He cooled the air all right, but the machine kept clogging with ice cubes. Unfortunately, Gorrie died before he was able to market his ingenious apparatus, but his contributions to our everyday lives can be seen and appreciated in so many ways, especially when you're visiting the Florida Gulf Coast in the middle of summer.

The **John Gorrie State Museum** (46 6th St., Apalachicola, 850/653-9347, 9am-5pm Thurs.-Mon., $2, free for children under 5) contains a replica of Gorrie's ice machine, built from his specs. There are also wonderful exhibits on the history of the area, from its days as a cotton port to sponge diving and oyster harvesting. The museum interpreters are a real wealth of knowledge and are willing to expound at length on Apalachicola lore.

will head to the **Munson Hills Off-Road Bicycle Trail,** in the eastern part of the forest, and the 16-mile paved **St. Marks Trail,** which is part of a rails-to-trails program that passes through the forest and terminates in the town of St. Marks. For serious backpackers and re-moter hiking, there's also a 68.7-mile section of the **Florida Trail** running through the forest that's a designated part of the Florida Statewide Greenways and Trails System. For a trail map and more information, visit www.florida-trail.org.

SIGHTS
★ Self-Guided Historic Walking Tour

Stop in at the **Apalachicola Chamber of Commerce** (122 Commerce St., 850/653-9419, www.apalachicolabay.org, 9am-5pm Mon.-Fri., 11am-4pm Sat.) for a copy of the self-guided historic walking tour map. More than 200 of the regal old homes in Apalachicola are listed on the National Register of Historic Places. Not all of them are in mint condition, but an hour or two of walking, gawking, and reading the brochure is a great way to get to know the downtown area.

There are a handful of little historic churches: **Trinity Episcopal Church** (79 6th St., 850/653-9550) dates all the way back to when Andrew Jackson was president and Florida was still a territory. It was actually built of white pine in New York and shipped down to Apalachicola—the white Greek Revival church is the sixth-oldest church in the state of Florida, the second-oldest church still holding services. Not far away, there's the **First Baptist Church** (46 9th St., 850/653-9540), originally built on

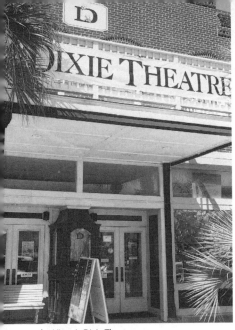

the Historic Dixie Theatre

Greenway Raney and family. The interior is now a small museum run by the Apalachicola Area Historical Society.

Chestnut Street Cemetery

Dating prior to 1831, historic **Chestnut Street Cemetery** (U.S. 98 between 6th St. and 8th St.) houses the remains of many Confederate soldiers, the world-famous botanist Dr. Alvin Wentworth Chapman, and many victims of yellow fever. The broad range of surnames speaks to the town's early diversity (Spanish and French settlers, shipwreck victims). To some spooky, to others just peaceful, the little urban cemetery contains beautifully carved funerary art tucked in the dappled shadows cast by gnarled old live oaks shrouded with Spanish moss.

Dixie Theatre

If you're looking to determine whether Apalachicola's on the wax or wane, the **Dixie Theatre** (21 Ave. E., 850/653-3200, performances usually 8pm Fri.-Sat., 3pm Wed. and Sun., tickets $25) is a pretty optimistic sign. Built in 1912, it was the locus of cultural activity—stage performances, then silent pictures, then the talkies—in the county for decades. It foundered in the late 1960s, but recent boosters have gotten it back up and running. The original building's decrepitude led to some ingenious restoration and re-creation. In 1998 the building was completed, with a facade that looks much like it did in 1912, and the original ticket booth painstakingly restored. There's now a winter repertory theater season, and it shows the occasional ragtime piano show or big town gala.

the corner of 6th Street and Avenue H, and the Romanesque **St. Patrick's Catholic Church** (27 6th St., 850/653-2100), built in 1929 (although the congregation goes back to 1845, the first structure was destroyed in a big fire that consumed 70 downtown buildings in 1846).

The historic homes are even more compelling, several of them tourable inside and out (and each May there's a fling-open-the-doors tour of historic homes, $25/guided tour). As part of a Florida state park, the **Orman House** (177 5th St., 850/653-1209, 9am-5pm Thurs.-Mon., $2), the original 1838 home of cotton merchant Thomas Orman, is open to the public. There is an hour-long narrated tour of the Federal and Greek Revival two-story house, the wood for which was cut and measured near Syracuse, New York, and shipped to Apalachicola by sailboat around the Florida Keys. The majestic, columned **Raney House** (128 Market St., 850/653-1700, 1pm-4pm Sun.-Thurs., 10am-4pm Fri.-Sat., free) dates to the same year, the home of David

ENTERTAINMENT AND EVENTS
★ Florida Seafood Festival

Apalachicola and surrounding towns are the undisputed eastern oyster capital of the world. The oyster industry began in the later part of the 19th century, and by 1896 there were three oyster-canning factories shipping something like 50,000 cans of oysters daily (the first time canning was attempted in Florida). The oyster industry in Apalachicola harvested 2.3 million pounds of oysters in 2011, worth an estimated $6.4 million, according to the Florida Fish and Wildlife Conservation Commission.

Naturally, oysters provide the foundation for the area's biggest annual party. The **Florida Seafood Festival** (850/653-4720, www.floridaseafoodfestival.com) is actually the oldest maritime festival in the state, drawing thousands each year during the first weekend in November. There are oyster-shucking and eating contests, parades, arts and crafts, musical entertainment, and a running race—but clearly the big draw is pot upon pot of just-caught seafood in a multitude of preparations.

Big Bend Saltwater Classic

The other big annual draw is the **Big Bend Saltwater Classic** (850/216-2272) fishing tournament in Carrabelle in June, an opportunity to see more than 700 serious anglers competing for big prizes in a weekend event that benefits the Organization for Artificial Reefs.

SHOPPING

The nine square blocks that make up downtown Apalachicola offer plenty of options for shopping. Retailers are spread among repurposed brick and tin cotton warehouses and early 1900s cottages. Located across from the docks, the **Grady Market** (76 Water St., 850/653-4099, 10am-5:30pm Mon.-Sat.) seems to be the locals' pride and joy, a 19th-century ship's chandlery made over to house about a dozen boutiques and galleries (including that of black-and-white photographer Richard Bickel). A block from there is a more eccentric spot called the **Tin Shed** (170 Water St., 850/653-3635, 10am-6pm Mon.-Sat.), specializing in antique nautical items like Japanese fishing floats, captains' telescopes, compasses, and ships' bells.

Market St. Antiques (115 Ave. B, 850/653-1006, 10am-5pm Thurs.-Mon., noon-5pm Sun.) is a fairly priced shop offering antiques and reproduction pieces, a small assortment of children's clothing, gifts, lamps, folk art, and marine-themed interior accessories.

If you're looking for crystal jewelry, lotions, gowns, wraps, and accessories, head to **Riverlily** (78 Commerce St., 850/653-2600, 10am-5:30pm Mon.-Sat.). Nearby, there's **The Oystercatcher** (79 Market St., 850/653-1616, 10am-6pm Mon.-Sat., 1pm-4pm Sun.), a rather funky boutique chock-full of denim, dresses, swimwear, and jewelry. Also an

Apalachicola has a variety of shops and restaurants along the waterfront.

interesting spot, **Petunia** (14 Ave. D, 850/653-9144, 10am-6pm Mon.-Sat., 10am-4pm Sun.) has a small collection of gifts and apparel for pets and their people.

For a large selection of rods, reels, fly-fishing tackle, and camping gear, you can head over to **Apalach Outfitters** (32 Ave. D, 850/653-3474, 10:30am-6pm Mon.-Sat., 12pm-5pm Sun. in the summer). It opened in the storefront that used to house Dolores' Sweet Shop and carries a full line of outdoor clothing and footwear with brands like North Face, Patagonia, and Prana. A couple of doors down is **Apalachicola Chocolate Factory** (75 Market St., 850/370-6937), for delicious handmade chocolates and homemade gelato.

★ Tupelo Honey

Just what was Van Morrison singing about in that song, anyway? He was comparing his sweetie to a rare honey, thought by connoisseurs to be among the world's finest. Prized for its flavor and for the fact that it never granulates, tupelo honey is produced by bees that cavort in the tupelo gum trees that grow with gusto along the Apalachicola River. Harvested for two short weeks in late April, tupelo honey was featured in the Peter Fonda vehicle *Ulee's Gold*.

The locus of tupelo production is in Wewahitchka, the only place in the world the honey is produced commercially. The process starts when bees are placed on elevated platforms along the river's edge. The bees then swarm the tupelo blossom-laden swamps and return with their treasure. The resulting honey is a pale amber color with a slight greenish cast, its flavor delicate and distinctive. Because it costs more to produce, tupelo is more expensive than many other honeys. But listen to Van the Man—this is the good stuff. The ongoing crisis in honeybees as a result of the colony collapse disorder, combined with Georgia's water shortage (resulting in less freshwater in Florida), means tupelo honey may be an endangered commodity. Get it while you can.

Regardless, every spring at Lake Alice Park in Wewahitchka, folks gather to celebrate the apian masterpiece. For years the **Tupelo Festival** (850/832-7006, www.tupelohoneyfestival.com) took place the third week in April during the tupelo pollinating time, but in recent years it's been moved to the third weekend in May to coincide with when the keepers scoop the honey from the hives. There's entertainment, arts and crafts, kids' activities, and a whole lot of things containing tupelo honey, from lotions to snacks.

If you're looking for some honey to take back home with you, many shops in the area usually stock it, but a heavy rain season in 2015 resulted in a complete tupelo honey crop failure. If the crop survives in 2016, you can expect to find quite a buzz surrounding the retailers of the product. To find out if there's any honey in the Wewahitchka hives you can call the ones who tutored Peter Fonda on beekeeping for the film, **L.L. Lanier & Son's Tupelo Honey** (850/639-2371, www.lltupelohoney.com), or stop by the extremely friendly **Smiley Apiaries** (163 Bozeman Clr., Wewahitchka, 850/639-5672, www.smileyhoney.com) and buy a bottle right from Donald Smiley's front porch.

FOOD
Oyster Bars

★ **Boss Oyster** (125 Water St., 850/653-9364, 11:30am-9pm daily, $10-25) seems to be the oyster palace to beat (tagline: Oysters All Ways 'n' Oysters Always). Topped with the sensible (a squeeze of lemon, and a dash of Tabasco) and the nearly obscene (envision a broiled oyster stacked with bacon, jalapeños, colby, and a splash of hot sauce), the local oysters are briny bliss. A lively family-oriented crowd, nightly drink specials, and a casual Apalachicola River-side setting keep it full. Try the heads-on shrimp; roll up your sleeves and don't be fussy. And if you advocate topping an oyster with something out of the ordinary, tell the staff and they just might name a dish after you.

Other staunch adherents of the slippery bivalves are at **Papa Joe's Oyster Bar and**

Grill (45 Ave. B, at Scipio Creek Marina, 850/653-1189, 11:30am-9pm Mon.-Thurs., 11:30am-10pm Fri.-Sat., $6-20). It's another waterside seafood-and-steak joint with a serious emphasis on local oysters, raw or broiled.

About 17 miles west of Apalachicola, the absolute must-eat destination is the ★ **Indian Pass Raw Bar** (8391 County Road C-30A, Indian Pass, 850/227-1670, noon-9pm Tues.-Sat., $5-10). It is always a party in this roadside shack (recently spruced up somewhat), every vinyl stool filled with someone vigilantly watching as the oyster shucker works his or her magic at the end of the bar. Raw on the half shell is best, but the garlic butter and parmesan baked version is a delicious spin on these briny beauties. Grab your own drink from the cooler and be sure to order the key lime pie.

Opened in 2013, rustic and casual **Up the Creek Raw Bar** (313 Water St., 850/653-2525, noon-9pm Mon.-Sun., $5-10) has become one of the most popular waterfront restaurants in Apalachicola. The large deck overlooking the bay and river is a relaxing spot to watch fishing boats come ashore. They serve oysters raw, steamed, and with toppings that feature regional ingredients, like oysters served "Southern fella" style, topped with collard greens, parmesan, and bacon. The menu includes Southern seafood classics, but also features a variety of healthy, creative fusion choices. Try the blackened shrimp basket with sweet potato fries if you're in the mood for seafood.

Fish Markets

If you're renting a house in the area or staying at a hotel with a kitchenette, consider buying fresh seafood from the local fish market and cooking it yourself. You'll find the best selection and service at **13 Mile Seafood Market** (227 Water St., 850/653-1399, 8am-4pm Mon.-Sat.) in downtown Apalachicola. They specialize in oysters and shrimp, but you can also pick up fresh grouper, sushi-grade tuna, mullet, flounder, crabs, and a nice selection of dips and smoked fish. Call ahead for big orders of steamed shrimp, or just stop in and pick up a delicious to-go box of steamed shrimp, corn, and potatoes for lunch. While they may have the only retail storefront in town, you're likely to find better prices at a small roadside stand, which are often operated by the fishing boat owners who are trying to make better profits by selling directly to consumers. Look for large coolers strapped down in the back of pickups for the chance to

The shrimp is tasty at Up the Creek Raw Bar in Apalachicola.

the 13 Mile Seafood Market sign

second floor, and an adjacent wine room. The high-ceilinged clapboard building is a replica of the original, lost to fire in 1911. Seafood is the strong suit, from the black grouper with garlic, capers, and artichokes to seafood pastas. The chicken Caesar salad is also not to be missed, and the wine list merits some perusal.

The **Old Time Soda Fountain** (93 Market St., 850/653-2606, 10am-5pm Mon.-Sat., $4-9) will satisfy your hankering for malts, floats, ice-cream sodas, and diner-style sandwiches. It's a 1950s-style, stools-at-the-counter relic that was once the town's drugstore. If you need a strong cup of organic Venezuelan coffee, a healthy sandwich, a wonderful salad, or a tasty pastry with a side of Wi-Fi, head to **Café Con Leche** (234 Water St., 850/653-2233, 8am-5pm daily). They are located in the Grady Market building and serve breakfast and lunch.

reel in the best seafood prices in the region, as well as the greatest opportunity to support local fisherfolk.

Lunch

Apalachicola Seafood Grill (100 Market St., 850/653-9510, 11am-9pm Mon.-Sat., $8-15) is the oldest seafood restaurant in town, and usually the first stop for many visitors. They've been open since 1903 and serve a wonderful fried fish sandwich—"largest in the world" they claim, although that may be a little culinary hyperbole. You'll find them under the town's only traffic light, and they offer a large selection of seafood and American diner food.

The Owl Café (15 Ave. D, 850/653-9888, 11am-3pm and 5:30pm-10pm Mon.-Sat., 10:30am-3pm Sun. brunch, $10-25), a long time lunch favorite, features black-and-white photos by local photographer Richard Bickel on the walls (if you like his work, local shops carry his latest book, *Apalachicola River: An American Treasure*), pretty wood floors, a

Fine Dining

Boss Oyster's sister restaurant, **Caroline's Dining on the River** (123 Water St., 850/653-8139, 7am-9pm daily, $16-24) combines a fine-dining atmosphere with a creative American seafood menu. Presided over by Caroline Madden, it's in the Apalachicola River Inn and the place to luxuriate in a lengthy Sunday brunch (opt for the oyster cakes or zingy shrimp Creole heaped over buttermilk biscuits). As with most places around here, the oysters and fresh finfish get the nod, and you can watch the shrimp and fish boats tooling by outside with the day's catch.

Latin

While seafood—oysters in particular—dominates this area, a few restaurants give their marine creatures a little twist.

★ **Tamara's Cafe Floridita** (71 Market St., 850/653-4111, 8am-10pm Tues.-Sun., $12-20) is where local seafood gets Caribbean and South American inflections, such as paella or a pecan-crusted grouper with a creamy jalapeño sauce, everything served with black beans and rice. Wednesday nights are the best times to take a group—it's tapas night, with

Eastern Oysters

Franklin County has historically harvested 90 percent of the state's oysters and around 10 percent of the nation's. More than 1,000 people in the county make their living in the oyster business. To give you a sense of quantity, in recent years the U.S. oyster haul has been roughly 30 million pounds of meat—about 75 percent of that eastern oysters, or *Crassostrea virginica,* the species that is shown off to finest effect in Apalachicola.

However, with a recent reduction in oyster production, Fish and Wildlife is calling for a possible halt in all oyster harvesting in the bay so that the bivalve population can have an opportunity to rebuild. The oyster beds in Apalachicola have been inundated by a perfect storm of human-instigated and natural impacts. A long-running drought in Georgia has been acerbated by the growing urban population of the city, and possible negative effects of the 2010 BP oil spill are impacting oyster health and production. As the amount of fresh water that flows down the Apalachicola River keeps dwindling, the saltwater from the gulf continues to encroach on the upriver estuaries, where all that tasty and economically vital Gulf seafood spawns. Some estimates put the Apalachicola oysters at half dead right now due to lack of freshwater, with the east and west ends of Apalachicola Bay the hardest hit. Some areas in the region saw an 85 percent reduction in oyster harvests in 2012. Let's hope this $200 million-a-year regional industry can bounce back, not just for the money, but for the health of the entire bay ecosystem—and to support my enduring raw oyster habit.

Found all around the Gulf of Mexico and up the eastern seaboard all the way to Canada, eastern oysters have historically flourished in the bay, which encompasses the waters of St. George Sound and St. Vincent Sound and is renewed constantly by the nutrient-rich freshwater of Apalachicola River. It's this balance of fresh- and saltwater that seems to act as some kind of magic growth serum. Oysters grow fast and sweet here, reaching marketable size in less than two years (in colder climates it can take as long as six years). The 210-square-mile estuary is shallow, 6-9 feet deep at low tide, with oyster harvesters skimming along in small boats to scoop up their mussels from the bottom with long-handled tongs.

Local oysters are carefully monitored. The Department of Health Services, the EPA, and other agencies test for water purity and natural threats such as red tide. In addition, the Department of Agriculture and Consumer Services has sponsored extensive efforts to restock oyster shell in the bay to create new oyster bars, and even to "plant" more than 100,000 bushels of adult and juvenile oysters on public oyster reefs in the bay. These transplanted oysters are taken from waters where harvesting is not allowed or where growth is poor and relocated to approved waters where conditions are more favorable for oysters to healthfully grow to market size. The ultimate aim: enhancing oyster production and ensuring oyster quality.

You know that expression, "What doesn't kill you makes you stronger"? A few bad oysters have given these bivalve mollusks a bum rap, but oysters are quite good for you. A dozen rings in at approximately 110 calories, rich in iron, copper, and iodine and high in calcium and vitamin A. Around here they are sold by the dozen, half bushel, peck, or bushel, graded according to size: The largest marketed are "selects" and the average are "standards." Look for oysters that close tightly when handled. They'll live in a cold fridge for more than a week (cover them loosely with a damp cloth, never in an airtight container). If you buy them already shucked, use them right away and don't freeze them.

While you're in Apalachicola, try them on the half shell. If you aren't in the mood to challenge fate by eating them raw, they are a treat eaten fried, baked, steamed, or broiled—that's paradise on the Forgotten Coast.

classics like shrimp sautéed with lots of garlic and a Spanish tortilla, all the little dishes affordable.

ACCOMMODATIONS
Under $100

Pretty much nothing in Apalachicola runs under $50, but the **Best Western Apalach Inn** (249 U.S. 98 W., 850/653-9131) and the **Rancho Inn** (240 U.S. 98 W., 850/653-9435, www.ranchoinn.com) both ring in around $85-130, right next to each other in a convenient location. The former offers complimentary hot breakfast and an outdoor pool, and children 17 and under stay free. The latter accepts pets for a $10 fee and still offers smoking rooms for a lower price.

$100-200

The Gibson Inn (51 Ave. C, 850/653-2191, www.gibsoninn.com, $120-270), on the National Register of Historic Places, had some major cosmetic surgery in 1985, but it still has the antebellum dignity that comes of wide wraparound porches, four-poster beds, antiques, and slowly revolving ceiling fans. This gracious tin-roofed Victorian right downtown (built in 1907 as a hotel, never a private residence) contains 30 rooms, each different. It's well-suited for romance-seekers and history buffs, and the inn does allow pets in certain rooms.

In a similarly Victorian vein, but even more spruce, is the sunny yellow **Coombs House Inn** (80 6th St., 850/653-9199, www.coombshouseinn.com, $125-275), built in 1905 by a lumber magnate. The three-story mansion has high ceilings, an ornate and creaky oak staircase, nine wide fireplaces, and a slew of historical photos. Guests in the 20 antique-bedecked rooms enjoy a pleasant breakfast, weekend evening wine receptions, and use of the inn's bikes, umbrellas, and beach chairs. If the quiet, chintz-and-doilies bed-and-breakfast experience isn't your idea of fun, you can still tour the Coombs House after checking out the Chestnut Street Cemetery across the street as part of a whirlwind local history lesson.

The **House of Tartts** (50 Ave. F, 850/653-4687, $120-135) is a restored guesthouse with three private rooms. A second-story carriage house is also available ($215) and includes two bedrooms, two baths, and kitchen.

The **Water Street Hotel & Marina** (329 Water St., 850/653-3700, www.waterstreethotel.com, $175-210) was opened in 2007 and offers 30 suites and a 20-slip marina (a

The Gibson Inn

floating dock servicing boats up to 55 feet), just blocks from the center of downtown Apalachicola. Despite a turn-of-the-20th-century vibe, it still boasts all the contemporary bells and whistles such as wireless Internet, and has enough space to make it family-friendly.

If you're looking for a little more privacy, the **Raney Guest Cottage** (46 Ave. F, 850/653-9749, $175) is a quaint house that dates back to around 1835, one of the oldest buildings in Apalachicola. Sit on a rocker or the handcrafted swing on the wraparound porch and sip a glass of ice-cold sweet tea, or walk the block into town (two to the river). It's definitely charming, and the historic house is all yours, with two cozy bedrooms, two baths, dining room, kitchen, screened back porch, two gas-burning fireplaces for the nippy north Florida winters, washer/dryer, and grill.

$200-300

Guests at the **Consulate Suites** (76 Water St., 850/635-1515, www.consulatesuites. com, $140-305) can pretend they're visiting

dignitaries. Prior to the Civil War, the French consulate was located in the second story of the bustling Grady Building, a ship's chandlery. The Grady Building has been renovated and transformed into a breezy shopping attraction of galleries and boutiques. Above it are four apartment-size luxury suites with 11-foot tin ceilings and lots of exposed brick. Three of the four suites overlook the river, and all have balconies and sleep four people (not a bad deal when compared to two rooms in an inn or hotel).

GETTING THERE

From Tallahassee, follow South Monroe Street to U.S. 61. Veer to the right onto U.S. 61 and follow for 4.2 miles. After U.S. 61 turns into U.S. 319, follow U.S. 319 for 71.7 miles until you reach Apalachicola. The drive 76-mile drive will take you about an hour and 35 minutes in normal traffic.

If you're piloting your own small plane, **Apalachicola Regional Airport** (8 Airport Rd., Apalachicola, 850/653-1366) is a former military base (serving B-17s in WWII), with three concrete runways and fuel available.

the Coombs House Inn

St. George Island

East of St. Vincent Island, St. George Island shelters Apalachicola Bay and St. George Sound, both productive bodies of water for commercial fishing and sportfishing. A 4.1-mile bridge connects the island to the mainland fishing village of Eastpoint. The whole eastern end of the island is taken up with the 1,900-acre St. George Island State Park, which contains some of the most pristine and under-populated white-sand beaches in Florida, as well as first-class fishing. St. George has got it all *right now,* and only a lucky few seem to know about it.

For much of its 5,000-year tenure, the island has been inhabited mostly by the avian, the reptilian, and a few small mammals. Humans arrived in the early 1900s to harvest the sap from the island's slash pines (used to make turpentine). The island's dunes were used for training exercises during World War II, but it's been mercifully underutilized since then.

In 1970, a Tallahassee real estate developer named John R. Stocks bought up much of the island, then sold Little St. George and the east end, now the state park, to the state of Florida. His company, Leisure Properties, then started selling five- and eight-acre tracts like hot-cakes. Growth was quick in what is now the Plantation area, but strict environmental rules keep the sight lines low and the water views spectacular. There are still only around 700 year-round residents, but thousands flock to the island for luxurious beachfront house and condo rentals during the summer months.

SPORTS AND RECREATION
★ St. George Island State Park

It's officially called the **Dr. Julian G. Bruce St. George Island State Park** (1900 E. Gulf Beach Dr., 850/927-2111, 8am-dusk daily, $6/vehicle), but most people around here just call it the state park. And what a state park it is. The land was acquired for the park in 1963, and the completed park facilities opened to the public in 1980. Imagine 1,900 acres of windswept, sea oat-fringed dunes, gorgeous enough and underpopulated enough to make

St. George Island State Park

most aficionados' lists of best beaches in the United States. The whole east end of the island is state park land, so officially it's the longest beach of any beachfront state park in Florida—nine miles of white sand.

The water is warm, shallow, and usually calm enough for hours of swimming. (Sorry, surfers, they don't call it the pond of Mexico for nothing.) The beaches seem to be stocked with perfect shells by the local chamber of commerce, and the abundant fish are often biting. Along the beach you'll see starfish and sand dollars, jellyfish, loggerhead sea turtle nests during the summer, and hardly another person. And when you get tired of all that perfect white sand, there are nature trails through the pine flatwood forest and live oak hammocks.

The park has no lifeguards or concessions, so bring your own picnic provisions and toys. There are, however, six sets of rustic wood-beamed pavilions with sheltered picnic tables, water fountains, outside showers, and bathrooms. It is illegal to walk through the sea oats along the high sand dunes—walk from the parking area out to the beach only along the weathered wooden boardwalks. Be on the lookout for the burrowing ghost crab, its semi-transparent carapace and huge eyes making it

a wild sight (they can also run up to 10 mph). In the woods you might glimpse raccoons and a fair number of snakes and diamond-back terrapins.

Anglers most often catch whiting, but you'll see them reeling in flounder, redfish, pompano, sea trout, and Spanish mackerel as well. (A saltwater fishing license is required.) Birders, on the other hand, train their sights on osprey, eagles, snowy plover, least tern, black skimmer, and willet.

RV and tent camping is permitted in the 60 pine-shaded campsites ($24) in the forests on the bay side, set behind the dunes. The campground features a dump station, flush toilets, and nature trails. The maximum stay is 14 nights; there are sites to camp with pets. There are also primitive campsites at Gap Point for those who wish to hike in along the 2.5-mile trail, which meanders from the bay through the pine flatwood forest to the campground. As with all Florida state parks, reserve campsites at www.reserveamerica.com. Boat ramps are located at the Youth Camp Area and East Slough, and kayaks are available for daily rental.

Loggerhead Turtles

St. George Island is said to have one of the

kayaks at St. George Island State Park

darkest night skies in the continental United States, making it a favorable place for stargazing. While a lot of this is merely a byproduct of low population density, some of it is by design. Franklin County adopted the Lighting Ordinance for Marine Turtle Protection in 1998, which restricts house lights, streetlights, and even flashlight use on the island.

Florida beaches are home to 90 percent of the loggerhead sea turtle nests in the southeastern United States, the largest population in the Western Hemisphere and one of the two largest in the world. St. George Island provides habitat for loggerhead, green, and leatherback turtles. Every year, starting around May 1, would-be mother loggerheads travel tremendous distances to come ashore here to nest (scientists think they return to the beach on which they were born). It's been shown that lights on and around beach homes can distract the mothers from their task and disorient the hatchlings enough to send them crawling inland instead of toward the sea, making them easy snacks for their many predators.

Currently, all seven sea turtle species are listed as either threatened or endangered. But finally there is some good news in the turtle world to report. Since 2009, the number of turtle nests has increased every year. Nest numbers spiked in 2012 for all five species that swim in the Gulf of Mexico and nest along the Florida Gulf Coast. There were close nearly five times the number of loggerhead nests recorded in 2012 when compared to 2009. Conservation efforts are still vital for this species, and it is important for visitors to help keep these species safe. If you've rented a beach house, keep outdoor house lights off as much as possible and pull your shades at night to minimize window light pollution on the beaches. Beyond that, you can call **Apalachicola Riverkeeper** (850/653 8936) or **Bruce Drye** (850/927-2103), the local permit holder for sea turtles, to report disoriented hatchlings or injured or stranded turtles.

If your visit to St. George Island coincides with nesting season (May-Oct.), you can take a night beach walk in the hopes of glimpsing mother sea turtles crawling ashore—they leave a distinctive, filigreed track in the sand—or the hatchlings clumsily flapping their way back out to sea. A single female loggerhead builds as many as three or four nests in a single season, laying about a hundred eggs in each one—it's quite a sight to see the little guys struggling to meet the sea, but resist the impulse to take flash photographs. And if you're compelled to help, you can a volunteer with St. George Island Volunteer Turtlers to find, mark, and protect turtle nests incubating in the warm sand. Call the Apalachicola National **Estuarine Research Reserve** (850/670-4783) to ask about volunteer efforts.

★ Biking St. George Island

If you enjoy a nice bike ride, then you'll probably love St. George Island, which has excellent bike accessibility and a remarkable number of paved bike paths. All the way from the Plantation side (west end) to the state park at the east end, there are straight, flat roadside paths for bicyclists, and miles of off-roading possibilities as well. Bikes can be rented from **Island Adventures** (105 E. Gulf Beach Dr., 850/927-3655, $12/day, $40/week). If you'd rather rent a golf cart, visit **Jolly Roger Beach Shop** (139 West Gorrie Dr., 850/927-2999, $175/day). To ride in style, rent their limo golf cart ($40/hour, $195/day, $550/week). They also rent surfboards ($45/day), kayaks ($48/day), fishing poles ($12/day, $38/week) and a long list of beach and fishing gear.

Birding

The shores and inland areas of St. George Island and the sheltered harbor of Eastpoint are rife with birding possibilities. In the latter, loons, gulls, and waterfowl play host to a number of vagrant bird species in the fall.

If you're attentive, from the bridge linking Eastpoint with St. George Island you'll see the nests of large colonies of least terns and black skimmers April-July. As its name implies, the least tern is the smallest of the terns, weighing about one ounce (don't confuse them with the medium-size gull-billed terns, with their heavy black bills and short forked tails, that also occasionally hang out here).

Florida birders also boast of the area's abundance of Sprague's pipit (although these little guys are hard to see, usually choosing to hang out in fields of short grass) in the late fall, and in the winter it's not uncommon to see the common goldeneye in nearby water.

Walking the shores of St. George Island, you'll view American oystercatchers, spotted sandpipers, ruddy turnstones, willets, sanderlings, several kinds of plovers, and loads of other shorebirds. And driving down the island's many wooded dirt roads yields a wealth of sightings in the spring and fall—bald eagles nest here, and in the fall you're likely to see sharp-shinned hawks, peregrine falcons, northern harriers, and American kestrels.

In the early spring, the youth campsite's oak hammock at St. George Island State Park is a good place to spot newly arrived migratory birds, possibly something as rare as a Connecticut warbler. If you go to the end of the park's paved road and walk out to the beach, you may find some snowy plovers. In winter, northern gannets are sometimes spotted in the park or in offshore waters.

One of the best ways to view many of the island's 200 species of birds is to arrange a bird-focused kayak trip with the guides at **Journeys of St. George Island** (850/927-3259, www.sgislandjourneys.com, $50/person). They'll take you on a relaxing paddle on the back side of St. George Island and identify the marine and birdlife while you explore one of the finest stretches of the Forgotten Coast.

Guided Tours

Journeys of St. George Island (850/927-3259, www.sgislandjourneys.com) offers a large variety of family ecotours and kids-only trips, including dolphin watches, shark fishing adventures, fly-fishing excursions, and bait-fishing trips both in the bay and offshore. The ecotours, fishing trips, guided paddling trips, and boat cruises range in price $30-450. The kayak tours on the Apalachicola River are a great deal at $50 for three hours (only $30 for children).

SHOPPING

St. George isn't famous for its shopping. On this island, the beach will heal almost any desire for retail therapy, but St. George does have a couple of gas stations, a handful of beach supply shops, and a plethora of ice-cream stands (most with prices that reflect some isolation inflation). If you want to shop and don't feel like driving to Apalachicola, visit **Island Outfitters** (235 E. Gulf Beach Dr., 850/927-2604, 10am-5pm daily), where you'll find resort wear and bathing suits along with saltwater fishing tackle, rods, reels, and other beach accessories. Island Outfitters offers inshore fishing charters for up to four people ($400 for 6 hours, $500 for 8 hours) in the bay and along the Apalachicola River. **Sometimes It's Hotter Seasoning Company** (37 E. Pine Ave., 850/927-5039, 10am-6pm daily) is a unique local institution and a nice place to pick up dried herbs and spicy sauces for grilling, blackening, and boiling seafood and meats.

If you arrived on-island without your beach essentials, the nearby **St. George Island Beach Chair Rentals** (137 E. Pine St., 850/670-4536, 9am-7pm daily) rents beach umbrellas ($15/day), kayaks ($15/hour for a two-seater), surfboards ($10/day, $60/week), a 28-foot Morgan sailboat ($250/half day), Hobie catamarans ($40/hour, $140/half day), and other beach necessities. They offer free delivery to any St. George Island rental unit.

FOOD

The majority of the island is given over to beach houses, many with impressive kitchens overlooking the bay or Gulf. Most vacationers come prepared to dine in with some regularity. Grocery stores include a **Piggly Wiggly** (130 U.S. 98, 850/653-8768) and an **IGA** (425 U.S. 98, 850/653-9695) in Apalachicola, the former a little nicer than the latter. Beyond that, you definitely need to patronize some of the local seafood retailers. On the island, look for **Doug's Fresh Seafood Market on Wheels** (at the intersection of Gulf Beach Dr. West and West Chili Dr.). He parks his trailer next to the lighthouse, and he's got exemplary shrimp, crabs, scallops, oysters, grouper, amberjack, and mahimahi.

Seafood

Restaurants on the island are more casual than those in Apalachicola, but that's fitting. On the beach side (the Gulf side, as opposed to the bay side of this long strip of an island), people gravitate toward the **Blue Parrot Oceanfront Café** (68 W. Gorrie Dr., 850/927-2987, 11am-9pm daily, $9-25), to relax on the wide deck or sidle up to the tiki bar, enjoying beer and cocktails over an excellent po'boy sandwich or burger. Opt for the local seafood (grouper and oysters) over the imports (conch fritters and Alaskan crab, for crying out loud) and you'll navigate the menu just fine.

As an aside, often in the month of June the Blue Parrot holds the annual **mullet toss.** They build a mullet-tossing range and you pay a small fee to try your hand at flinging these slippery raw fish as far as you can. Underhanded, overhanded, football-style—there are several competition divisions: men, women, children, and free form (in which you build a mechanical device to catapult your fish to victory).

On the bay side, **Eddy Teach's Raw Bar** (37 East Pine St., 850/927-5050, lunch and dinner daily, hours change seasonally) offers up cold beer, cheap oysters, peel-and-eat shrimp, steamed clams, and decent cheeseburgers, with music on the weekends.

American

The Beach Pit (49 W. Pine Ave., 850/799-1020, 7:30am-8:30pm Mon.-Thurs., 7:30am-9pm Fri.-Sun., $6-20) is one of the few options for standard American breakfast or a barbecue lunch. The food and the atmosphere aren't anything exceptional, but the prices are good and there are a few healthy options. Imagine a place with checkered tablecloths that serves biscuits and gravy and other heavy American-style selections at breakfast, as well as lunches of ribs and other barbecue delights that are smothered in sweet sauce and come with picnic-style sides. The dinner menu has steaks and a variety of seafood.

Mexican

For budget travelers who want something fast, visit **The Grub Hut** (123 W. Gorrie Dr.,

Doug's Fresh Seafood Market on Wheels

DOUG'S FRESH SEAFOOD MARKET LOCAL SEAFOOD FRESH DAILY

Oysters on the Forgotten Coast

Not long ago one out of every 10 residents in Franklin County had an oyster permit. There were oyster beds out in Apalachicola Bay that people swore by, magical spots with names like Cabbage Top, Catpoint, North Spur, and West Lump. With worn wooden poles, oystermen tap along, waiting for the thud to sharpen as the pole hits shell. Then the tongers, men with ropy arm muscles and profound tans, heave their tongs over the side of their small wooden flats boats and get to work. Like two metal rakes hinged together scissor-style, the long-handled tongs rake the bivalves off the shallow bottoms. Pulled aboard, the oysters are sorted with a practiced eye on a culling board, with only those three inches long kept as the morning's catch.

Things are changing, though. Franklin County's gorgeous setting has drawn luxury condos and other, more lucrative, beach development, inching out some of the career oysterers. Hurricane Dennis in 2005 ravaged the oyster docks and packing facilities. The BP oil spill in 2010 shut down oyster harvesting for nearly a year and has arguably had lasting negative impacts on the fisheries and oyster beds in the region. Then add to that the water wars that continue to rage between Florida and Georgia. To the north, Atlanta has a population of nearly 5.5 million people, and it's growing fast. They want to use as much of the fresh water flowing down the Chattahoochee River as they can, but that waterway becomes the Apalachicola River as it heads into Florida. The oysters need the fresh water and the nutrients that come with it to flourish, but instead they are getting more saltwater, which continues to encroach on the oyster beds as the saltwater increases.

Things have gotten so dicey in the oyster industry in Apalachicola Bay that in 2015, the Fish and Wildlife commission threatened to close down oyster harvesting in the region for eighteen months to allow the oyster beds enough time to replenish to a sustainable population. If you think this is a bit of oyster-hugging overreaction, consider the fact that in 2009 more than 173,000 oysters were recorded per acre at the East Hole, one of the most productive oyster beds in Apalachicola Bay. In 2012, that number had dropped more than 90 percent, down to around 11,000 oysters per acre. My guess is that if we keep treating our fisheries and water systems the same way that we've treated them in the past, filling them with oil and a multitude of pollutants and taking as much life-giving fresh water as we want from the ecosystems, then the world may be our oyster no longer.

770/403-6533, 8am-9pm daily, $4-8), a permanent food truck next to Jolly Roger Beach Shop. It's extremely popular and offers a tasty variety of American and Mexican breakfast and lunch choices. The fish tacos, Philly cheesesteak wraps, and quesadillas are local favorites.

Pizza and Ice Cream

BJ's Pizza & Subs (105 W. Gulf Beach Dr., 850/927-2805, 11am-10pm daily, $7-20) tosses good pizzas (also offered by the slice) and has a raucous game room in which to rapidly lose a pocketful of quarters. **Aunt Ebby's Island Deli & Ice Cream** (147 E. Gulf Beach Dr., 850/927-3229, 11am-5pm daily Mar.-Sept.) is the place to stop for a frozen treat after a long hot day at the beach.

Drinks

Harry A's (28 W. Bayshore Dr., 850/927-3400, 8am-midnight Sun.-Thurs., 9am-2am Fri.-Sat.) is just about the oldest building on the island, with the kind of wide, inviting front porch that's more and more difficult to leave after each successive beer. The tavern where locals meet visitors over a pint and some hot wings, Harry's A's brings in musical entertainment most nights and serves up straightforward bar fare like pizza, tacos, and fried seafood. If you're looking for a good steak or some seafood followed by a few drinks and a shot of live music, it's hard to beat **The Black Marlin Bar and Grill** (200 Gunn St., 850/927-4555, 4pm-8:30 Sun. and Tues.-Thurs., 4pm-9pm Fri.-Sat., $10-25). They have a full bar and a large deck out back to handle the large crowds that come in the summer for the live music. Pets are welcome on the back deck. The atmosphere inside is resort casual, and the high ceilings and multitude of windows give the dining room a breezy, open feel, which makes it a relaxing spot to enjoy their extensive menu of sandwiches, steaks, pastas, and seafood. The shrimp scampi, seafood gumbo, and grilled grouper sandwich are favorites. The music leans toward rock and blues.

ACCOMMODATIONS

On St. George Island, hotel or inn accommodations are only sensible if you are staying for less than two days and are traveling alone or as a couple. Families tend to rent one of 800 beach cottages or houses on the island, most offered by the week (and, off-season, by the weekend). Some of these houses are remarkably large (more than ten bedrooms), and provide a wonderful opportunity to convene several generations of your family or several families together under one roof. Pets are often allowed, and many homes have private pools, game rooms, and tremendous kitchens for preparing the daily catch.

Hotels

Affordable and geared toward families, the

Buccaneer Inn (160 W. Gorrie Dr., 850/847-2091, www.buccinn.com, $85-220) is a 1960s-style, low-rise beachfront motel. Rooms are clean and no-nonsense, with a lot of pale pastel coverlets and serviceable kitchenettes, and there's a courtyard swimming pool and a Gulf-side tiki hut.

A little fancier, the **St. George Inn** (135 Franklin Blvd., 850/927-2903, www.stgeorge-inn.com, $120-195) is two blocks from the beach with clean, modest rooms. The sprawling white house, with wraparound porches affording Gulf and bay views, has been recently remodeled to include a few two-room suites and a little conference room.

Vacation Rentals

★ **Resort Vacation Properties** (850/927-2322, www.resortvacationproperties.com) handles many of the upscale rental houses, with wonderfully detailed descriptions and photos of properties on their website. They deal with properties all over the island but seem to have a special lock on the large houses in the Plantation, the private community on the western end of the island. Other agents that traffic in properties all over the island include **Collins Vacation Rentals** (800/683-9776, www.collinsvacationrentals.com) and

The Beach Pit

Suncoast Realty (800/341-2021, www.uncommonflorida.com). Beyond picking your price range (they go from $1,000/week up to more than $5,000 for some of the more luxurious homes), there are lots of other factors to consider, such as whether to be on the Gulf or bay side, how close to town you want to be, and the kind of neighborhood in which you feel most comfortable.

ST. GEORGE PLANTATION

This is a gated community stretching from the Gulf to the bay on the island's west end, with slow, winding roads and lots of speed bumps to keep the pace leisurely. Homes are all distinctive in terms of architecture, amenities (many with spa or pool), and decor, but the general vibe is luxury. It's mostly large, three-story homes that sleep eight or more. Something to consider here is that the farther toward the west end of the island you settle, the longer the drive is to get a gallon of milk back in town.

Within the Plantation is an even more exclusive and secluded area called The Bluffs. It's two quiet cul-de-sacs of luxury homes, each with spectacular views of the Gulf and Apalachicola Bay beyond towering 25-foot dunes.

GULF BEACHES AND EAST END

The four miles in the center of the island are called the Gulf Beaches area. In this, the first populated area on the island, the architectural styles are all over the map, from little Cracker cottages to huge windswept wooden structures on stilts kitted out with widow walks. Not as fancy as those at the Plantation, the homes have the benefit of being a quick bike ride into town for ice cream or a video rental. Going east, the two miles before you get to the state park are called, not surprisingly, East End. This is less

densely populated, with comfortable-looking houses widely spaced, mostly up on high stilts, with great beach access. In the East End area, there are also town houses in a community called 300 Ocean Mile. It is close to the state park, and rentals, while not so fancy, are fairly affordable (around $800/week, $400 for 3 nights in the spring and fall, and $625/week in the winter).

SUNSET BEACH

This community on the Gulf is densely packed with Spanish tile-and-stucco villas and has a decidedly Mediterranean vibe. It has a pool and tennis courts and provides easy access to the state park, which makes it a great choice for birders, anglers, and anyone who is interested in exploring the park's miles of undeveloped beaches. There are a wide range of options for renters including a variety of homes, condos, and duplexes.

Camping

St. George Island State Park (1900 E. Gulf Beach Dr., 850/927-2111, $30.70/day) offers 60 campsites with electric and water hookups for RV and tent camping. Reserve far in advance with **ReserveAmerica** (800/326-3521, www.reserveamerica.com). Primitive campsites are available at Gap Point, a 2.5-mile backpacking hike-in site, which can be reserved by calling the park office. There is tents-only youth-group camping for organized groups of 6-25 campers.

GETTING THERE

From Apalachicola, drive east on U.S. 98 (South Bayshore Dr.) for 12 miles. Turn right to stay on South Bayshore Drive and continue for 1 mile. Veer right onto State Road 300 and continue for 4.8 miles until you reach St. George Island. The 12-mile drive will take you about 20 minutes in normal traffic.

Eastpoint and Carrabelle

In spite of the challenges facing Franklin County's oyster industry, the town of Eastpoint, traditionally populated by career oysterers, has managed to maintain its gruff, fishing-village beauty. Stop along the roadside waterfront to watch the remaining "housemen" at the wholesale seafood houses manhandle oysters, shrimp, and finfish, brusquely sorting and packing the catch into boxes or bags. It's a year-round venture, with the dwindling oyster harvest rotated seasonally from 10,000 acres of oyster beds in St. George Sound and environs. Virtually the whole length of Eastpoint's commercial district is perfumed with the briny waft of seafood docks and the sounds of WOYS FM, Oyster Radio, out of Apalachicola, competing with the boisterous calls of fourth-generation fisher-people getting off work for the day.

Visit soon, because all signs point to significant cultural changes in the future. Eastpoint has never had the kind of bells and whistles that would make it a big tourist draw, just a few restaurants, a couple of rustic bars, and more oysters than you could shake a tong at. However, like the rest of the Florida Gulf Coast, it is likely to be developed as soon as the rest of the surrounding shoreline is maxed-out with condos, resorts, and beach house rentals.

Carrabelle, 16.5 miles east of Eastpoint, is still an active fishing town with shrimpers and finfishers unloading their daily catch. For just this reason, it's been the filming location for a couple of Victor Nuñez movies, including *Ulee's Gold* starring Peter Fonda and *Coastlines* with Josh Brolin.

EASTPOINT
Apalachicola National Estuarine Research Reserve
Apalachicola Bay is one of the most productive estuarine systems in the Northern Hemisphere (an estuary is where a river meets the sea, where freshwater meets saltwater).

You might get a sense for this while touring the **Apalachicola National Estuarine Research Reserve** and its affiliated Nature Center. The reserve is said to house 1,162 subspecies of plants, 308 species of birds, 186 species of fish, and 57 species of mammals. Much of it is inaccessible unless you have a boat, and stomping around in some parts is discouraged except for those conducting long-term research, education, and stewardship programs.

★ APALACHICOLA RESERVE NATURE CENTER
The **Nature Center** (108 Island Dr., Eastpoint, 850/670-7700, 9am-4pm Tues.-Sat., free) is located on Apalachicola Bay at the foot of the St. George Island Bridge in Eastpoint, and it's an excellent outing for the whole family. The 4,800-square-foot visitors center that opened in 2010 offers educational exhibits and information, as well as aquariums of local fish and turtles, surrounded by a bayfront park complete with picnic pavilions and an outdoor amphitheater. You're likely to see dolphins, crabs, turtles, snakes, a variety of fish, ospreys, and eagles during a stroll around the visitors center and the surrounding Apalachicola Bay shore park.

ESTUARY TOUR
A remarkable way to explore the estuary is by taking a tour with **Apalach Tours** (850/899-5000, www.apalachtours.com, $35/person). The guides here will take you on an hour tour that explores the estuary while you wander upriver, through the marsh, and into the swamps.

For something a little more exciting, head out on an airboat and travel up to 40 miles per hour through the estuary with **Apalachicola Airboat Adventures** (850/653-5746, www.apalachicolaairboatadventures.com, $35/person). They offer tours that are one hour and more, with the longer ones exploring the interior of the St. Vincent Wildlife Preserve. They can get back to some spots that only airboats can get to, and you can take home a high-definition video of your adventure for an extra fee. The more adventurous should consider their stellar one-hour nighttime airboat excursions where you'll see the stars twinkling above as you race through the wetlands spotting alligators, raccoons, flying fish, and all sorts of other skittish nocturnes.

CARRABELLE

There are still fewer than 1,200 residents in Carrabelle, and the downtown has never been gentrified or prettied up for the tourists. It seems that terms like rustic, quaint, and even crusty were invented for places like this.

The town has historically had the world's smallest **police station** (a phone booth), but the force now works outside of that Superman-esque environment. The town had its five minutes (less actually) of fame when the phone booth police station was featured on the *Tonight Show with Johnny Carson* and *The Today Show.*

It doesn't take long to explore all the police station has to offer, so after you're done, visit the State Forestry Division's **Carrabelle Fire Tower** on the east side of town, which has

great views of the area, or the **Camp Gordon Johnston WWII Museum** (1001 Gray Ave., 850/697-8575) that pays tribute to the amphibious soldiers who trained here and served in World War II, Korea, and Vietnam. Camp Gordon Johnston actually covered 165,000 acres along the Big Bend, with 36 miles along the shores of the Gulf of Mexico. The area was left in its natural state for training purposes, where thousands of soldiers learned to land the crafts that would be used on the beaches of Normandy on D-Day.

Carrabelle also boasts the **Crooked River Lighthouse** (1975 W. U.S. 98), a rickety lighthouse constructed to replace the lighthouse on Dog Island that was destroyed by hurricane in 1873. The 103-foot iron tower was built in 1985, and at the end of 2007 the Carrabelle Lighthouse Association members restored and relit the structure. **Carrabelle Beach,** just west of town, is a popular spot for picnickers and beachcombers.

FOOD
Eastpoint

There are plenty of seafood markets in Eastpoint around the 300-500 blocks of U.S. 98: **Lynn's Quality Oysters** (402 U.S. 98, 850/670-8796), **Fred's Central Seafood**

Apalachicola National Estuarine Research Reserve

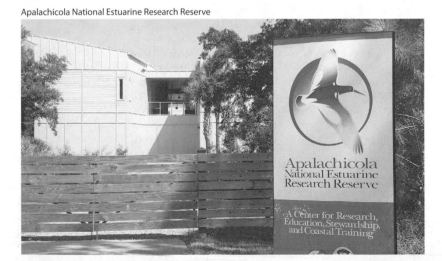

(322 Patton St., 850/670-8381), and **Barber Seafood** (510 U.S. 98, 850/670-8830) are top choices.

Carrabelle

Harry's in Carrabelle (306 Marine St., Carrabelle, 850/697-9982, 6am-9pm Mon.-Sat.), just behind the Georgian Motel, opens bright and early to serve the fisherfolk heading into the Gulf. It's mostly a drinking establishment. For food in Carrabelle, head for the ribs at **Hog Wild BBQ** (1593 U.S. 98 E., 850/697-2776, 11am-8pm Mon.-Thurs., 11am-9pm Fri., 7am-9pm Sat., 7am-8pm Sun., $6-12). They also have a popular all-you-care-to-eat breakfast buffet with unbeatable prices ($6 adults, $4 children under 12).

ACCOMMODATIONS

Eastpoint

Pretty much the only lodging in Easpoint is the **Sportsman Lodge Motel & Marina** (99 N. Bayshore Dr., 850/670-8423, $62-85), a rustic, fish camp-style motel and marina overlooking the East Bay. It's wooded and amenities include kitchenettes, a boat dock, ramp, and easy access to fishing guides and charters. It has an Old Florida vibe and is an option for budget travelers, but it may not be

well suited for families or those looking for quiet and well-maintained rooms. Even if you aim to explore the oyster-fishing charms of Eastpoint, you have a much greater range of hotel options in nearby Apalachicola, and you will find higher quality rooms at the **Buccaneer Inn** (160 W. Gorrie Dr., 850/847-2091, www.buccinn.com, $85-220) just over the bridge on St. George Island.

Campers can stay at the **Coastline RV Resort** (957 Hwy. 98, 850/799-1016, $32-60/day, $120-360/week, $850-1050/month) and enjoy their well-maintained, waterfront sites 3.4 miles east of Eastpoint. Features include a fishing pier, pool, bathhouse, and gift shop. You can rough it in luxury with access to their full kitchen, Wi-Fi, game room, and a small gym. Primitive campsites are available for tent campers ($20/day, $120/week), and the entire resort is pet-friendly.

Carrabelle

If you're exploring the Intracoastal Waterway in your own boat, or if you just enjoy being close to marina and sailing culture, you can stay at **Moorings of Carrabelle** (1000 Hwy. 98, 866/821-2248, hotel rooms $80/day and 490/week, $1.50/foot per night for boats 26 feet and up) located on the Carrabelle River.

Carrabelle Beach

They offer single hotel rooms, one- and two-bedroom condos efficiencies, as well as nightly, weekly, and monthly slip rates. They have a full service marina, and their marina store stocks bait, tackle, and boat supplies.

For something more historic and charming, stay at **The Old Carrabelle Hotel** (201 Tallahassee St., 850/528-3983, www.oldcarrabellehotel.com, $77-87). Opened in 2002, owners Kathy and Skip Frink revived the beautiful house that was built in the 1800s. You can choose from four rooms in the house, each with their own unique and tasteful decor, or rent the detached cottage ($350-400 for three nights, $500-700/week) with three bedrooms, two baths, full kitchen, living room, and an excellent screened porch.

GETTING THERE

To reach Eastpoint from Apalachicola, drive east on U.S. 98 for 6 miles. The drive will take you about 10 minutes in normal traffic.

the Crooked River Lighthouse

Apalachee Bay

The colorful little towns of **Panacea** and **Sopchoppy** are both in Wakulla County south of Tallahassee between Carrabelle and Crawfordville, along U.S. 98 near Apalachee Bay and the Gulf of Mexico, and tucked between Apalachicola National Forest and the St. Marks Wildlife Refuge. Sopchoppy is the nearest town to Alligator Point, and between those two towns there's a strange prevalence of white squirrels. There are many lyrical myths about how and why these creatures got here. A great many monarch butterflies also appear here in September and October in their migration south to Mexico. During the fall the beaches can be dotted with these beautiful butterflies. Panacea was developed as a tourist resort more than 100 years ago by residents looking to market the incredible local springs. These days it's a sweet town of about 1,000 people, with seafood shops along the main street.

More of a draw than the towns are the many parks in the area that draw outdoors enthusiasts from around the world. The birding here is exceptional, so make sure to pack binoculars. There also plenty of opportunities to paddle, hike, and camp in a diverse variety of landscapes. The most popular parks in the area are Ochlockonee River State Park and Wakulla Springs State Park, due to their developed campgrounds and amenities like hot showers and RV hookups. For something on the wilder side, consider exploring the less-visited areas, such as St. Marks National Wildlife Refuge or paddle around in the Big Bend Wildlife Management Area.

SPORTS AND RECREATION
Ochlockonee River State Park

Near Sopchoppy, on the northern border of Franklin County, you'll find **Ochlockonee**

River State Park (429 State Park Rd., Sopchoppy, 850/962-2771, 8am-sunset daily, $4/vehicle, $4 for boat launch). An extensive network of hiking and biking trails allow visitors to explore the pine flatwoods and oak thickets that border the Ochlockonee River. Bikes are available for rent at the park office ($10/day). Anglers, boaters, and paddlers can access the brackish water Ochlockonee River and the freshwater Dead River from several boat ramps in the park. Thirty campsites with electrical hookups ($24.70/night) are nestled in a beautiful oak forest and provide overnight campers with plenty of shade and access to hot showers in the bath house. A swimming area is located along the Dead River, and birders should bring their binoculars for viewing the healthy population of red-cockaded woodpeckers and ospreys found in the park.

Bald Point State Park

Another popular destination for birding and wildlife-viewing is **Bald Point State Park** (146 Box Cut Rd., Alligator Point Rd., 850/349-9146, 8am-sunset daily, $4/vehicle, $2 for pedestrians and bicyclists), located on Alligator Point, where Ochlockonee Bay meets Apalachee Bay. The park has two beaches, Sunrise and North End, which provide excellent habitat for coastal birds and nesting sea turtles, with picnic pavilions at Sunrise Beach. Paddlers can enjoy exploring the coast or venture into the interior of the park by launching their kayak at the boat ramp on the brackish water Tucker Lake, which feeds into Chaires Creek. Surf fishing is permitted at the beaches, and fishing is allowed by kayak or canoe in Tucker Lake and at the bridge over Chaires Creek on Range Road. This is an excellent spot to catch blue crabs, mullet, sea trout, redfish, flounder, and sheepshead. There is no camping allowed in the park, but hiking is available along more than eighteen miles of trails. If you're looking to view wildlife and birds, head to the observation deck and boardwalk that overlooks the marsh near North End beach.

St. Marks National Wildlife Refuge

St. Marks National Wildlife Refuge (1255 Lighthouse Rd., St. Marks, 850/925-6121, sunrise-sunset daily, $5/vehicle) is one of the oldest refuges in the National Wildlife Refuge System (established in 1931), with 68,000 acres of protected coastal land. The coastal marshes, islands, tidal creeks, and estuaries of seven north Florida rivers can be explored

Ochlockonee River State Park

by boat or by foot. Stop in first at the visitors center (8am-4pm Mon.-Fri., 10am-5pm Sat.-Sun.) to get an overview of what there is to do and see in the park.

The refuge has 75 miles of trails, including a 50-mile segment of the Florida National Scenic Trail, but there are wonderful short walking trails as well: the Plum Orchard Pond Trail (0.3 mile), Headquarters Pond Trail (0.25 mile), and Lighthouse Levee Trail (0.5 mile—the St. Marks Lighthouse is still in use today), and the Mounds Interpretive Trail (1 mile), which offers a diversity of habitats for bird-watching and wildlife-viewing. Hiking here is less pleasant in the summer months, when you might opt to explore via a driving tour with the air-conditioning on.

The park is a magnet for birders, who come for the myriad wading birds as well as the ospreys, red-cockaded woodpeckers, kestrels, red-shouldered hawks, and bald eagles. The refuge is open to fishing year-round and hunting in season. There are restrooms at the Refuge Visitor Center, Mounds Trail, and Otter Lake Recreation Area, and picnic facilities are next to Mounds Trail and at Otter Lake.

★ Big Bend Saltwater Paddling Trail

Birders enthuse about the **Big Bend Wildlife Management Area**'s Hickory Mound Impoundment (from Tallahassee, take U.S. 98 east, turn right on Cow Creek Grade, and go 6 miles to the check station, 850/488-5520). The list of birds that hang out here includes wading birds, ospreys, swallow-tailed and Mississippi kites, bald eagles, and a whole lot of birds I've never even heard of (buffleheads, gadwalls, American wigeons). This area is just one of the five, along with Spring Creek, Tide Swamp, Jena, and Snipe Island, that make up the Big Bend Wildlife Management Area. It extends about 60 miles along the Gulf Coast, with Tallahassee approximately 40 miles north of the northernmost part, all of it a gorgeous wilderness explored by bike, horse-back, foot, or—the best way—by kayak. The

Wakulla Springs State Park

105-mile **Big Bend Saltwater Paddling Trail** is open September-June. To order the $15, 40-page paddling guide for the trail, call 850/488-5520 or go online at www.myfwc.com. It details seven designated primitive campsites, exclusively for trail users, spaced 10-14 miles apart (permits required).

Canoes and kayaks can be rented in Tallahassee at **The Wilderness Way** (3152 Shadeville Rd., 850/877-7200, www.thewildernessway.net, single kayaks or canoes $30/day, $150/week; tandem kayaks or canoes $35/day, $175/week), which also leads nature-based canoe and kayak tours around the Panhandle, and **Blue Water Scuba and Travel Center** (2320 Apalachee Pkwy., 850/656-3483).

★ Wakulla Springs State Park

Wakulla Springs are said to be the world's largest and deepest freshwater springs, in which the water temperature remains a fairly constant 70°F. The springs have been the site of lots of Hollywood filming because of their wild, untouched jungle feel, just 15 miles south of Tallahassee. They were a tourist attraction long before Johnny Weismuller slipped into his loincloth to star as Tarzan or Ricou Browning donned the rubber suit for the film *Creature from the Black Lagoon.* In fact, as a teenager Browning was a lifeguard at Wakulla Springs and put on underwater shows for the glass-bottom boat tours (he helped develop the underwater hose-breathing that has made the mermaid show at Weeki Wachee Springs a hit for so long).

That same glass-bottom boat tour is a must-see today at **Wakulla Springs State Park** (465 Wakulla Park Dr., Wakulla Springs, 850/561-7276, 8am-sundown daily, $6/vehicle entrance to the park, $8 tour for adults, $5 children under 12). The 30-minute tours, offered only when the water is clear, provide a glimpse into the crystalline 125-foot depths, but more than that they offer a window into north Florida's past. The people who lead the tours give excellent narration as you explore the mysteries and history of this magical place. Oh, and a high-jumping fish named Henry is involved. The park offers a 60-minute riverboat tour that takes a different route, but I'd opt for the former if it's running.

In the past few years, Wakulla has also become home to numerous manatees that remain in park waters year-round. The park also contains a wonderful six-mile nature trail, picnic facilities, swimming (only in designated areas, as it's gator country), and the stately **Wakulla Lodge** (850/421-2000, $95-150) for overnight guests.

Flowing from Wakulla Springs nine miles to the St. Marks River are the crystal-clear waters of the **Wakulla River.** Along the Spanish moss-trimmed cypress lining the river's banks you'll see abundant wildlife, from manatees, otters, and eagles to numerous waterfowl. Several boat ramps provide access to the river, a perfect day's paddle by kayak or canoe. **TNT Hideaway** (6527 Coastal Hwy., Crawfordville, 850/925-6412) is a small, family-owned business with 20 canoes and 20 kayaks, offering guided tours on the Wakulla River (and also off-the-beaten-path tours to

St. Marks Lighthouse and National Wildlife Refuge, Spring Creek, the Aucilla River, the Sopchoppy River, and the Ochlockonee River). If your aim is to spot a manatee, the weekly *Wakulla News* carries a manatee-watch section that gives all the specifics of recent sightings.

SIGHTS
Gulf Specimen Marine Laboratory
You can visit Anne and Jack Rudloe's **Gulf Specimen Marine Laboratory** (222 Clark Dr., Panacea, 850/984-5297, 9am-5pm Mon.-Fri., 10am-4pm Sat., noon-4pm Sun., $9.50 adults, $8.50 seniors, $7.50 children 3-11). The Rudloes are both marine biologists and authors of well-known books on Florida natural history and marinelife. The independent nonprofit environmental center and aquarium is open to the public, enabling visitors to get a peek at green shrimp, scarlet sponges, comb jellyfish, and other local marine life in a sea grass meadow or on a limestone outcrop in a collection of seawater tanks and aquariums. It's a "small is beautiful" approach to aquatic creatures.

There's a tiny airport in Panacea, really just a grassy landing strip, out of which a few enterprising pilots take small charters. Show up and ask around and you might get a pilot to zip you over to Dog Island for the day.

George the Potter
George the Potter (110 Suncat Ridge, 850/962-9311) is a beloved local attraction, with a studio down a dirt road south off U.S. 319 just east of Sopchoppy. Look for his sign. He makes lovely bowls and mugs, and has a savvy self-promoting bumper sticker that says "Been to Sopchoppy met the Potter."

ENTERTAINMENT AND EVENTS
The first weekend in May draws more than 20,000 people to Panacea for the **Blue Crab Festival.** At night in the summer, the thing to do in these parts is to go swimming in the

Gulf when the water's **bioluminescence** lends an eerie shimmer to the dark water. Totally safe (after all, it's just the chemical-based light produced by a whole bunch of marine organisms), the gleam seems to echo the zillions of stars visible in the Panacea or Sopchoppy night sky.

In Sopchoppy the biggest industry is raising worms. Worm "grunters" pierce loose soil with a wooden stake called a stob. Once the stob is driven into the soil, it gets rubbed with a flat piece of metal called the bat. The vibrations in the ground drive the big earthworms up, where they are scooped, packaged, and sold for bait. If you want to see how it's done, there's an unbelievable nine-minute movie about it on YouTube. This is such a compelling calling that the town of about 500 holds a well-attended **Worm Gruntin' Festival** each April. The second-biggest festival comes in June with the **June Jam** of mostly local musicians performing in the square.

FOOD

For dinner in Panacea, the obvious choice is **Angelo's and Son's Seafood Restaurant** (on pilings over Ochlockonee Bay on U.S. 98 on the east side of the bridge, 850/984-5168, 4:30pm-10pm Wed.-Thurs., 4:30pm-11pm Fri.-Sat., noon-10pm Sun., $12-22). Destroyed in the storm surge from Hurricane Dennis, it's back with a vengeance in a sturdier structure, with just-caught fish and great views. Or else hit **Posey's Beyond the Bay** (1506 Coastal Hwy., 850/984-5799, $11-25) for topless oysters or smoked mullet, or enjoy the restorative comforts at the **Coastal Restaurant** (1305 Coastal Hwy., 850/984-2933, $7-15).

Also in Panacea, **Angelo's** (5 Mashers Sand Rd., 850/984-5168, 4:30pm-10pm Mon., Wed., and Thurs., 4:30pm-11pm Fri.-Sat., noon-10pm Sun., $12-22) is a long-standing and justifiably famous purveyor of the local blue crabmeat (try the seafood cakes). There are waterside tables, a wide wraparound porch, and friendly locals.

For great burgers, sandwiches, and the best pizza in Sopchoppy, head to **Sopchoppy Pizza Company** (106 Municipal Ave., 850/962-1155, 5pm-9pm Wed.-Fri., 11am-9pm Sat., $10-20), located in the historic district. Just look for the carved gorilla out front and you'll know you're in the right place.

ACCOMMODATIONS

If you're traveling to Wakulla Springs, you might want to stay at the **Magnuson Hotel Wildwood Inn** (3896 Coastal Hwy. 98,

historic Sopchoppy

Wakulla, 800/878-1546, $125-165). The nature and golf resort is one of the few lodges in the state to be designated a Certified Green Lodge by the Florida Department of Environmental Protection. The resort features an 18-hole golf course, 71 rooms and suites, a fitness center, a pool, and an indoor and outdoor meeting space that can accommodate up to 200 people, all near the St. Marks National Wildlife Refuge, the Apalachicola National Forest, and Wakulla Springs State Park.

The stately **Wakulla Lodge** (850/421-2000, $95-150) is located in **Wakulla Springs State Park.** The lodge was built in 1937, with 27 rooms, each individually decorated with antiques and period furniture. The lodge also has a nice restaurant called the Ball Room Restaurant—order the navy bean soup or the fried chicken. And make sure to check with the lodge during the slow season for incredible rates and specials, like the couples special usually offered September-February that includes dinner for two at the Ball Room Restaurant, a boat tour for two, and a night's stay at the lodge for $99

After a day at Wakulla Springs or along the Wakulla River, you can bunk down at the **Sweet Magnolia Bed & Breakfast** (803 Port Leon Dr., St. Marks, 850/925-7670, $135-155) or at one of the area's campgrounds: **Ochlockonee River State Park** (429 State Park Rd., 4 miles south of Sopchoppy on U.S. 319, 850/962-2771, $18) or **Holiday Campground** (14 Coastal Hwy., Ochlockonee Bay, 850/984-5757, around $30, depending on family size). You can also camp in Sopchoppy at the **Myron B. Hodge City Park** (Sheldon St. and Park Ave., 850/962-4611).

GETTING THERE

To reach Sopchoppy from Apalachicola, drive east on U.S. 98 for 32.4 miles, then veer left onto U.S. 319 and follow for 10.5 miles until you reach Sopchoppy. The 43-mile drive will take you about 55 minutes in normal traffic.

To reach Panacea from Sopchoppy, drive north on U.S. 319 for 6.3 miles, then turn left onto U.S. 98 and follow for 3.7 miles. The 11-mile drive will take you about 15 minutes in normal traffic.

To reach Panacea from Apalachicola, drive east on U.S. 98. The 47.8-mile drive will take you about 55 minutes in normal traffic.

Information and Services

The Forgotten Coast is located within the **eastern time zone.** The area code is **850.**

TOURIST INFORMATION

Forgotten Coastline is the local paper that you'll see being read all over. It gives you the inside track on the area's issues, gripes, and secret treasures. There's also an online version at http://forgottencoastline.com.

Beyond that, you'll find lots of useful information on the area by visiting www.apalachicolabay.org or www.visitgulf.com. Anita Grove at the **Apalachicola Chamber of Commerce** (122 Commerce St., 850/653-9419, www.apalachicolabay.org, 9am-5pm Mon.-Fri., 10am-4pm Sat.) is also a tremendous resource. Be sure to pick up the historic walking tour brochure while you're there.

POLICE AND EMERGENCIES

For any real emergency, dial 911. For nonemergencies, there's the **Apalachicola Police Department** (127 Ave. E, 850/653-9755), the **Franklin County Sheriff's Department** (270 Hwy. 65, Eastpoint, 850/670-8500), and the **Carrabelle Police Department** (1001 Gray Ave., 850/697-3691), which until recently was the smallest in the United States, being located inside the phone booth in town.

If you find yourself in need of a

doctor during your visit, you may choose from **Eastpoint Medical Center** (no emergency services, 35 Island Dr., Eastpoint, 850/670-8585, 8am-noon and 1pm-5pm Mon.-Fri.), **George E. Weems Memorial Hospital** (135 Ave. D, Apalachicola, 850/653-8853), and **Weems East Medical Center** (110 NE 5th St., Carrabelle, 850/697-2345).

For your pharmacy needs, try **Buy Rite Drugs** (45 Ave. D, Apalachicola, 850/653-8825) or **CVS** (139 Ave. E, Apalachicola, 850/653-8737). Pet emergencies are best handled at **Apalachicola Bay Animal Clinic** (187 U.S. 98, Eastpoint, 850/670-8306).

RADIO AND TELEVISION

When you're feeling musically nostalgic, tune in to **The Coast,** WFCT 105.5 FM out of St. Joe, with a mix of "favorites from yesterday and today." To seem like a real local, twist the dial to **Oyster Radio** at WOYS FM 100.5 out of Apalachicola, with daily local news, national news, hourly weather reports, and beach music (there's a sister station at 106.5 FM that broadcasts country). There are no local television stations, but out of Tallahassee, **WFSU Channel 11** is the PBS

affiliate, **WTXL Channel 27** is the ABC affiliate, and **WTLH Channel 49** is the FOX affiliate.

LAUNDRY SERVICES

Most rental houses on St. George Island have laundry facilities. If you're without access where you're staying (at an inn in Apalachicola, for instance), many of the marinas have self-serve laundries. There's also a nice little laundry in Eastpoint, **Pearl Wash** (191 U.S. 98, behind the car wash, 850/670-8703).

FISHING LICENSES

Fishing licenses are sold in the County Tax Collector's Office and in many local bait and tackle shops, or by calling 888/347-4356. It is free for Florida residents to obtain a saltwater license to fish from the shore or structures, but you still need to have a license. An annual saltwater license for Florida residents to fish from a boat is $17 and $32 for annual saltwater and freshwater combo. Saltwater annual license for nonresidents is $47; a nonresident three-day saltwater license is $17 and a seven-day annual saltwater license is $30.

Panama City Beach and the Emerald Coast

Look for ★ to find recommended sights, activities, dining, and lodging.

Highlights

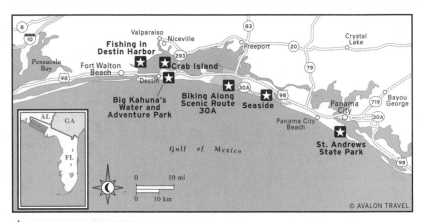

© AVALON TRAVEL

★ **St. Andrews State Park:** This state park in Panama City, at one point named "the world's best beach" by *Travel Magazine,* offers miles of Gulf-side beach as well as a broad, inviting Grand Lagoon and a 700-acre offshore barrier strip called Shell Island (page 289).

★ **Crab Island:** People congregate with their boats daily at this partially submerged island for some fun in the sun. Rent some form of watercraft and join the party (page 301).

★ **Fishing in Destin Harbor:** Offshore, inshore, cobia, sailfish, wahoo—Destin is a serious fishing destination. Arrange a fishing charter to find out why Destin is often called the "World's Luckiest Fishing Village" (page 302).

★ **Big Kahuna's Water and Adventure Park:** If the beach isn't enough to fully occupy the family, head for these 25 acres of waterslides, flumes, tubing, lagoons, wave pools, and more (page 308).

★ **Seaside:** Spend a day exploring this picturesque pastel beach town, featured in the Jim Carrey movie *The Truman Show* (page 314).

★ **Biking Along Scenic Route 30A:** Explore the Beaches of South Walton in your own time with a bike ride along the 19-mile paved path that follows Scenic 30A (page 317).

U nified by their eye-catching emerald water, the beaches of northwest Florida, from Pensacola to South Walton and Panama City, offer miles of unspoiled natural beauty. Some say the emerald color of the water in this area is the result of blue-green algae. Not true. It's just very clear water, layered over super-reflective white sand in the shallows that produces the green color—the deeper the water, the bluer it gets.

Each of the destinations in this region has its own distinct draws and a dramatically different character. Panama City Beach is known as the biggest draw along the Gulf Coast of Florida for college spring breakers. It's mostly about crowds of people partying and enjoying themselves at the beautiful beaches, miniature golf courses, and souvenir shops. It's bustling with personal watercraft and parasailers, girls in bikinis, restaurants heavily reliant on deep fryers, and partiers cruising the strip with their car windows down.

The Destin and Fort Walton Beach area is in the westernmost part, closest to Pensacola Beach. The fishing village of Destin has seen enormous growth as tourism has taken off, with lots of new construction, visitor attractions, and restaurants to lure ever more people. With one of the best locations for fishing on the Gulf Coast, Destin is only 30 miles inland from the 100 Fathom Curve where the best deep-sea fishing for tuna, wahoo, and blue marlin is found. It's getting built up, but most of the beachfront is still low-rise. Folks visit Destin, Fort Walton Beach, and Okaloosa Island to do some fishing, splash in the emerald-green water, and have a good time with the kids.

The Beaches of South Walton region, on the other hand, make up a 26-mile stretch of shoreline to the east of Destin, containing 14 beach communities. These pristine beaches offer pure, clear, emerald-green water; fine, sugar-white sand; and rare coastal dune lakes; together, these create a unique and varied landscape. Mostly it's private residences in newish, forward thinking, and ecofriendly planned communities. You won't find a lot of go-cart tracks, mini-marts, or T-shirt shops,

Previous: beachfront at the Destin Pass; miniature golf in Panama City. **Above:** lodging at Santa Rosa Beach.

and nearly all of the area's towns have an old-fashioned beach retreat style. None of this comes cheap, though. It's pricey to stay in the Beaches of South Walton, but the understated, upscale environment and back-to-basics feel are exceptionally memorable.

PLANNING YOUR TIME

The Emerald Coast region stretches from Destin in the west to Panama City in the east, a distance of roughly 56 miles. The best way to explore the area is by car. Ground travel is easy along several primary feeders: U.S. 98, U.S. 331, Highway 85, and I-10. If you have the luxury of owning a boat, you would gain a lot from exploring the Emerald Coast from the water and renting or bringing bikes along to explore each of the towns.

Where to spend most of your time largely depends on what you are interested in doing while in the area. There is a huge diversity in the type of attractions and the cost of accommodations and activities along this stretch of coast. But where to stay? Anglers: Go to Destin or Fort Walton Beach. If you're looking for upscale leisure with coastal beauty all around: Visit the Beaches of South Walton. Spring breakers: Get yourselves to Panama City Beach, and remember to have a designated driver. The latter is worth two days of intensive revelry, three if you have a long attention span.

High season along the Panhandle is summer, with rates dropping precipitously in the fall and winter. Spring break is a brief flurry around here in March and April, at its densest in Panama City Beach. Many of the rentals along the 14 communities of the Beaches of South Walton have a minimum stay, some as much as a week during high season. The area could certainly occupy you for that long, with a day trip to Pensacola, another one to visit the amusements in Panama City Beach, and a third to one of the wonderful state parks here. If you're interested in camping and hiking, the area to explore is just east of Destin, where you will find a whole string of great coastal state parks all within a few miles of each other, the

best being Topsail Hill Preserve State Park, Grayton Beach State Park, and Henderson State Park. There is an enormous amount of remarkable paddling in Choctawhatchee Bay north of Destin, the freshwater and saltwater lakes that dot the coastline, and in the collection of bays to the north of Panama City. The main road through the area is U.S. 98, which can become quite congested in the busy summer and spring months. Don't miss taking a drive along Highway 30A, which runs south from U.S. 98 through the smaller, upscale communities of Seaside, Blue Mountain Beach, WaterColor, and Rosemary Beach, to name just a few of the picturesque towns along this delightful stretch of coast. Many visitors prefer to rent a bike and pedal along the extensive bike path along Highway 30A. During the summer, spring, and early fall, accommodations along 30A tend to book farther in advance, with the most popular being the cottages at Seaside. Make plans as early as possible if you intend to visit one of these communities during high season. However, in the winter you can often find exceptional prices on some upscale rooms on this part of the Gulf Coast.

The nearest airports to Destin and Fort Walton Beach are the **Northwest Florida Regional Airport** (1701 Hwy. 85 N., on Eglin Air Force Base, 850/651-7160), a small airport serviced by Delta Airlines, American Eagle, United, and Allegiant, and the **Northwest Florida Beaches International Airport** (6300 West Bay Pkwy., Panama City, 850/763-6751), the first international airport built in the United States in a decade and served by Delta, Silver, Southwest Airlines, and United. A 50-minute drive to the west, the **Pensacola International Airport** (2430 Airport Blvd., Pensacola, 850/436-5000, www.flypensacola.com) is the biggest airport in northwest Florida.

As of this writing, the **Amtrak** (800/872-7245) Sunset Limited service was not operating in this area due to damage Hurricane Katrina caused to the tracks in New Orleans. You need wheels to get around locally.

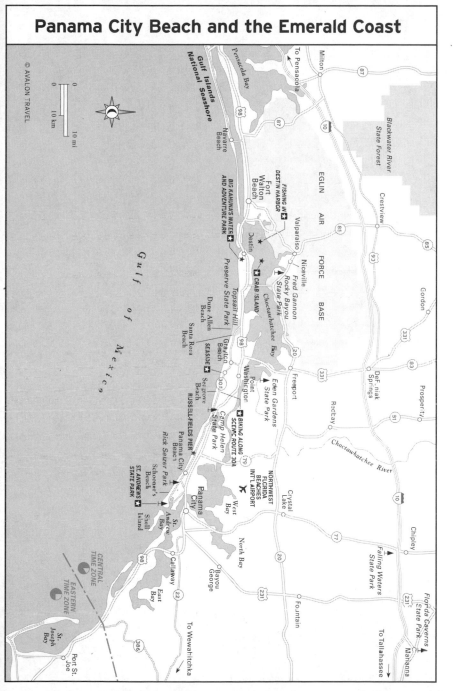

Panama City Beach and the Emerald Coast

© AVALON TRAVEL

0   10 mi
0   10 km

Gulf Islands National Seashore

To Pensacola

Milton

Pensacola Bay

Navarre Beach

Blackwater River State Forest

Fort Walton Beach

FISHING IN DESTIN HARBOR

BIG KAHUNA'S WATER AND ADVENTURE PARK

Destin

Valparaiso

Niceville

Fred Gannon Rocky Bayou State Park

CRAB ISLAND

Topsail Hill Preserve State Park

Dune Allen Beach

Santa Rosa Beach

Grayton Beach

SEASIDE

Seagrove Beach

RUSSELL-FIELDS PIER

Camp Helen State Park

Panama City Beach

Rick Seltzer Park

ST. ANDREWS STATE PARK

Schooner's Beach

Shell Island

Crestview

EGLIN   AIR   FORCE   BASE

Choctawhatchee Bay

Point Washington

Eden Gardens State Park

Freeport

DeFuniak Springs

Gordon

Prosperity

Ponce de Leon

Choctawhatchee River

BIKING ALONG SCENIC ROUTE 30A

NORTHWEST FLORIDA BEACHES INT'L AIRPORT

Panama City

West Bay

St. Andrew Bay

North Bay

Crystal Lake

Chipley

Falling Waters State Park

Florida Caverns State Park

Marianna

To Tallahassee

Callaway

East Bay

Bayou George

Fountain

CENTRAL TIME ZONE

EASTERN TIME ZONE

St. Joseph Bay

Port St. Joe

To Wewahitchka

Gulf of Mexico

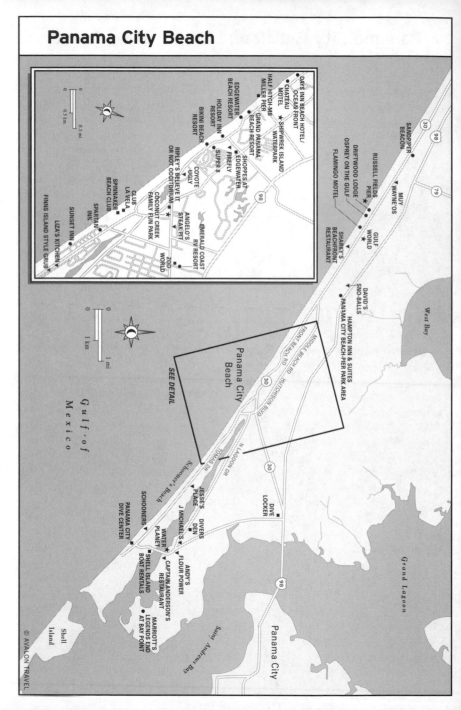

Panama City Beach

© AVALON TRAVEL

Panama City Beach

Panama City Beach gets billed as the No. 1 spring break beach in the country, attracting more than 300,000 people annually. It draws a young crowd ready to throw down for spring break and has a ton of attractions to keep them entertained. With the same green water and white sand found elsewhere on the Emerald Coast, these beaches are more action-oriented, with volleyball, Frisbee, skim boarding, Jet Skiing, and parasailing. Although the beach is wide with a lengthy expanse of shallows, there are hundreds of natural and artificial reefs offshore—Panama City Beach ranks with Key Largo in providing some of the best diving in the country. The fishing is also good, with mackerel, flounder, redfish, and other game fish swimming through the clear waters.

At the east end of the city, St. Andrews State Park is one of the most popular outdoor recreation spots in Florida. It contains verdant woods, sea oat-fringed sand dunes, fresh and saltwater marshes, a lagoon swimming area, fishing jetties, hiking trails, 2.5 miles of beach, and two campgrounds. From here, you can also take a pedestrian ferry to Shell Island,

an undisturbed 700-acre barrier island just across from the mainland, for sunning, shelling, birding, or watching the sunset. Outside of the beaches, the area is known for attractions like miniature golf, waterslide parks, go-cart tracks, and a marine park.

PCB is packed in March, April, and in summer, when tourists from Georgia and Alabama flock here. But in May and early fall, Panama City Beach makes for an entertaining beachside playground, with loads of modestly priced accommodations. It's at these times that you can understand why the area has been a popular beach vacation spot for more than 40 years.

SPORTS AND RECREATION

★ St. Andrews State Park

St. Andrews State Park (4607 State Park Ln., Panama City, 850/233-5140, 8am-sundown daily, $4/single driver, $8/vehicle 2-8 people, $2 pedestrians or bicyclists, $28 camping) has rolling, white-sand dunes separated by low swales of either pinewoods or

Panama City Beach

marshes. There are 2.5 miles of beach, with two different parking lots with access. You can rent bicycles during the summer at the park and explore the trails. There's a double-sided concrete boat launch for watercraft (if you don't own a boat, you can take a boat tour out to Shell Island in the spring and summer, tickets at the park concession), and they rent canoes at the boat ramp (paddle around Grand Lagoon or across the boat channel to Shell Island). If you want to fish, there are two fishing piers and jetties, from which you're likely to catch Spanish mackerel, redfish, flounder, sea trout, bonito, cobia, dolphin, and bluefish. The concession stores in the park sell bait and fishing licenses, along with other beachside necessities. For hikers, there's Heron Pond Trail (starting at a reconstructed Cracker turpentine still) and Gator Lake Trail (yep, you'll see gators), both easy and well marked. And if it's all too great to leave, there are 176 campsites in the park or on the barrier Shell Island.

Beaches

With more than 27 miles of beaches and countless beach access points in the Panama City Beach area, it's hard to make a list of the top stretches of coast. Paradise can be found on any beach when you have a sunny day, waves rolling on shore, and good company. If you're not staying at a beachfront hotel, all you have to do is drive down Front Beach Road and park at one of the many parking lots with beach access.

At the peak of summer, on holidays, and during spring break, it's nearly impossible to get away from the thousands of people that gather on at the beaches around Panama City. During these times your best bet to find solitude would be out at Camp Helen State Park, St. Andrews State Park, or by taking a ferry or your own personal boat to Shell Island.

SCHOONER'S BEACH

If you're looking for the hub of beach activity during spring break, head to **Schooner's Beach** (5121 Gulf Dr., 850/235-3555, behind Schooner's Beach Club) or to the beach behind **Club La Vela** (8813 Thomas Dr., 850/235-1061), where you can find the college crowd drinking, playing beach volleyball, and generally partying hard.

CAMP HELEN STATE PARK

For much quieter beaches where you can hear the surf and sand between your toes instead of loud music, park your beach chair at **Camp Helen State Park** (23937 Panama City Beach Pkwy., 850/233-5059, 8am-sunset daily, $4/vehicle, $2/pedestrian or bicyclist). It's a half mile walk to the beach, but it's worth the hike in your flip-flops to get to this secluded gem located just over the Phillips Inlet Bridge on the western side of Panama City Beach. While here, enjoy a hike on the Oak Canopy Trail through a mix of wetland and maritime forest or fish in the saltwater of the Gulf or the freshwater of Lake Powell.

RICK SELTZER PARK

Rick Seltzer Park (7419 Thomas Dr., open sunrise-sunset, free) is another less-visited beach. This park on the east end of Panama City Beach is known as one of the best spots for collecting shells and getting away from the crowds. Eat at Jesse's Place while you're here and then catch some rays on this quiet stretch of sand.

SHELL ISLAND

Shell Island (between the Gulf and St. Andrews Bay near St. Andrews State Park) isn't actually an island. It's a peninsula, but the locals call it Shell Island. It's nearly seven miles long, only accessible by boat, and as the name implies, it's a great place to for shelling. During spring break, the place can get crowded, with lots of boats anchoring offshore and pulling up on the beaches. If you don't own a boat, you can still get out here by taking the **Shell Island Shuttle** (4607 Thomas Dr., 850/233-0504, 9am-5pm, ferry departs every half hour during the summer, call for shuttle times during spring and fall, closed in winter, $16.95

adults, $8.95 children, infants free). If you want to go out on your own, they also rent snorkel gear and pontoon boats by the half and full day.

RUSSELL-FIELDS PIER

If you're looking to fish or go where the crowds tend hang out, a good place to plant your umbrella in the sand would be the **Russell-Fields Pier** (16101 Front Beach Rd., 850/233-5080, $3 to walk, $6 to fish), where crowds tend to gather during the spring and summer high season. Known as the City Pier and Beach, it was built in 2009 and extends 1,500 feet into the Gulf. Try your luck at reeling in a cobia, mackerel, redfish, pompano, flounder, and other types of fish. A small shop at the foot of the pier sells snacks, drinks, bait, and rents rods, tackle, and other fishing gear. It's also the best place to swim, especially for families, since this is the only beach in Panama City that has designated lifeguards (Apr. 1-Sept. 30, 10am-6pm). Built around the same time, the **M.B. Miller Pier** (12213 Front Beach Rd., 850/236-3035, $3 to walk, $6 to fish) is farther east. Nearly identical to the Russell-Fields Pier, this is a great spot to catch the sunset, people watch, or wet your fishing line.

Diving and Snorkeling

Panama City Beach was dubbed the Shipwreck Capital of the South by *Skin Diver* magazine. As such, this part of the warm Gulf of Mexico is an excellent home and breeding ground for all types of sealife. You'll see sea turtles, manta rays, puffer fish, sand dollars, blue marlin, horseshoe crabs, small coral, colorful sponges, and lots of other marinelife.

Of the "natural" wrecks in this area, you can investigate a 441-foot **World War II Liberty ship,** a 220-foot tug called *The Chippewa,* a 160-foot coastal freighter called the **S.S. Tarpon,** the 100-foot tug *Chickasaw,* another tug called *The Grey Ghost,* and the Gulf's most famous wreck, the 465-foot *Empire Mica.* A bunch of other artificial reef projects have sunk bridge spans, barges, and the City of Atlantis (a different one). Many of these dive sites are at depths of 80-100 feet and are just a few miles offshore; the best time for diving is April-September.

Experts say that the top five dives are the **USS *Strength,*** a naval mine sweeper; the **Blackbart,** a supply vessel; another supply vessel called the *B. J. Putnam;* the *Accokeek,* a 295-foot navy tug boat; and a huge aluminum hovercraft in 100 feet of water. If you want to rent diving equipment, **Dive Locker**

M.B. Miller Pier

(106 Thomas Dr., 850/230-8006), **Diver's Den** (3120 Thomas Dr., 850/234-8717), and the **Panama City Dive Center** (4823 Thomas Dr., 850/235-3390) will help you out.

Snorkelers will have a better time around the **St. Andrews Jetties,** an area with no boat traffic. Nineteen feet under the surface there is an old tar barge ideal for underwater exploration. If you want to snorkel with a guide, **Island Time** (Treasure Island Marina, 3605 Thomas Dr., 850/234-7377, adults $39 or $34 for spectators not getting in water, children 3-12 $29, infants and 2 and under $5) offers 3.5-hour catamaran excursions, wet suits available, and **Captain Ashley Gorman Shell Island Cruises** (5701 U.S. 98, east end of Hathaway Bridge, 850/785-4878, $40/person) does swim and snorkeling tours for the whole family.

Horseback Riding

You can ride to your heart's content at **Sunshine Riding Trails** (2273 Rolling Pines Rd., Chipley, 850/773-1900, 7am-9pm Mon.-Sat., $35 for 1 hour, $50 for 2 hours, $75 for 3 hours, $100 for 4 hours). Their Tennessee walking horses are friendly and easy to ride, and they have access to over 10,000 acres of rolling hills and forests. The facility is 30 miles north of Panama City Beach, but the drive is pleasant and scenic. It's a great way to get away from the crowds for a few hours and live your dream of being a cowboy or cowgirl in the wild west panhandle of Florida. They also offer incredible overnight horseback camping trips ($250/person for one night, $325/person for two nights). They include all the camping gear, breakfast, lunch, and dinner, and you get around 12 hours of horseback riding. Sit around the campfire at night and trot through the forest atop your trusty steed on this outdoor adventure of a lifetime.

Recreation Areas

All the other parks around here get overshadowed by St. Andrews, which is a shame. **Pine Log State Forest** (5583-A Longleaf Rd., Ebro, 850/535-2888) is a favorite locals' spot

for picnicking, hiking, off-road bicycling, horseback riding, fishing, and hunting. There are 23 miles of hiking trails winding through the forest. Nearby **Point Washington State Forest** (5865 U.S. 98 E., Santa Rosa Beach, 850/267-8325) is less developed but has 19 miles of trails for mountain biking, birding, and hunting.

Hike, bike, spot birds, or look for wildlife at the **Conservation Park** (100 Conservation Dr., Panama City Beach, 850/233-5045, sunrise-sunset daily, free). It's pet-friendly, so you can walk one of the 12 trails with your four-legged friend. Leashes are required. Trail lengths vary from 0.6 mile to 11 miles, and the headquarters has restrooms, maps, and water fountains. The trails and boardwalks are exceptionally maintained, and they have benches and picnic areas along the way to give you some rest on your outdoor adventure.

In general, the whole area has benefited from the completion of a U.S Army Corps of Engineers beach re-nourishment project, Florida's longest continuous beach restoration. The $23.5 million project elevated and widened a 16.5-mile stretch of beach by an average of 30 feet, with something like a billion cubic yards of new, white sand. Besides beautifying the shoreline, the re-nourishment provides critical storm protection.

SIGHTS
Gulf World

The best family attraction is **Gulf World** (15412 Front Beach Rd., 850/234-5271, 9am-7pm daily Mar.-Aug., 9:30am-5pm daily Sept.-Feb., $28 adults, $18 children 5-11, children 4 and under free), which got pumped up seriously around the millennium, with a $6.5 million expansion that netted it a state-of-the-art dolphin habitat, a new bird theater, and enclosed tropical gardens. It needed it. The marine mammal park opened in 1969 with animal shows and displays, but it also has a facility to rehabilitate stranded or injured marine animals from all over the Panhandle. As with so many of Florida's aquariums and water parks, there is a swim-with-the-dolphins option to the tune of $175 per person (also a trainer for a day program and a slumber-party option).

Coconut Creek Family Fun Park

Coconut Creek Family Fun Park (9807 Front Beach Rd., 850/234-2625, www.coconutcreekfun.com, 10am-6pm daily, $21 one price, $12 just for golf, 12 just for gran maze—why there's no "d" on that is a mystery) has two miniature golf courses in a kind of African safari/jungle motif. The maze is the better part, built in 1987 and completely rebuilt recently. It's a huge maze the size of a football field in which you will find disoriented children and lots of military personnel using their professional navigational skills to find the four checkpoints (for some reason, they are Fiji, Tahiti, Samoa, and Bali) essential to successfully navigating the maze. There's no shame in crawling under to get the heck out of here. Well, maybe a little shame.

Shipwreck Island Waterpark

Shipwreck Island Waterpark (12201 Hutchinson Blvd., 850/234-3333, www.shipwreckisland.com, 10:30am-5pm daily summer, $34.99 50 inches and above, $29.99 below 50 inches, under 35 inches free, $23.99 seniors) is the kind of water park with long slides and flumes, a wave pool, kiddie pools—in other words, what to do if the beach isn't holding the kids' interest for another warm summer day. There is a 48-inch height restriction on two of the more exciting rides (the Rapid River Run and Tree Top Drop), and you're not allowed to bring food in from outside, or flotation devices, goggles, or masks. Little ones not yet potty-trained are required to wear waterproof swim diapers.

Water Planet

For close encounters of the fin kind, visit **Water Planet** (5709 N. Lagoon Dr., 850/230-6030, www.waterplanetusa.com, 4-hour tour $98/person, 3-day program

$430/person, 1-week program $750/person) where you can swim with dolphins in their natural environment. They offer swim sessions for kids, adults, and therapy sessions for children with special needs. It's an incredible opportunity to get close to these amazing aquatic mammals. The folks at Water Planet have been giving dolphin tours and swimming with dolphins since 1997. The dolphin experience includes a boat ride across the St. Andrews Bay, the dolphin encounter, shelling on Shell Island, and an exploration of boat wrecks in the area. The dolphins are encountered in the wild in the bay or surrounding waters, so the experience is good for you and the dolphins.

Other Sights

Need more to do? There's a **Ripley's Believe It or Not! Museum** (9907 Front Beach Rd., 850/230-6113, 10am-6pm Sun.-Thurs. 10am-8pm Fri.-Sat., $17.99 adults, $12.99 children 6-12) with all the requisite shrunken heads and scale models of the *Lusitania* made out of ear wax. OK, I made that one up. Nearby you'll find **Zoo World Zoological and Botanical Park** (9008 Front Beach Rd., 850/230-1243, 9:30am-4pm Mon.-Sun., $16.95 adults, $15.95 seniors 65 and over, $12.95 children 4-11), a small and pleasant zoo. The best part is the interspecies interaction between Tonda the orangutan and T. K. the tabby cat. Little kids will enjoy **Sea Dragon Pirate Cruise** (departs from 5325 N. Lagoon Dr., 850/234-7400, times vary, $25 adults, $21 seniors 60 and older, $19 children 14 and under, reservations highly recommended), a cruise with Captain Phil on a totally kitted-out pirate ship, heavy on the "argh." **Museum of Man in the Sea** (17314 Panama City Beach Pkwy., 850/235-4101, 10am-5pm Wed.-Sat., $5 adults, $4.50 seniors, children under 7 free) is a small but interesting museum that delves into the history of deep-sea diving and ocean exploration.

SHOPPING
Pier Park

Shopping, dining, and entertainment

are all within easy reach at **Pier Park,** a 900,000-square-foot retail and entertainment complex sitting on 93 acres in the heart of downtown across from the City Pier. Target, Panera Bread, The Grand 16-Plex Theatres, and Longhorn Steakhouse were the first establishments to open in 2008. It is anchored by a 125,000-square-foot Dillard's, JCPenney, and Jimmy Buffett's Margaritaville restaurant and nightclub, with smaller stores including Ron Jon Surf Shop, Starbucks, Ann Taylor Loft, Ulta Cosmetics, Victoria's Secret, Bath & Body Works, and more. Its open-air eateries take best advantage of gorgeous Gulf views.

Beyond that, there are little pockets of shops all over, mostly of the sunglasses-and-suntan lotion variety. You may need to stock up on bathing suits at **Beach Scene Superstore** (10059 Hutchinson Blvd., 850/233-1662), which has something like 25,000 suits to try on. If you feel the need for more extensive browsing, the **Shoppes at Edgewater** (477 Richard Jackson Blvd., 850/249-6100) complex has a number of nice shops. Also, the Edgewater Movie Theater and Rock-It Lanes Family Entertainment Center are adjacent to the shopping center. **Panama City Mall** (at the intersection of U.S. 231, Hwy. 77, and 23rd St., 850/785-9587) is a standard enclosed mall anchored by Dillard's, JCPenney, and Sears, with stores like American Eagle Outfitters, Victoria's Secret, Kirkland's, Bath & Body Works, The Gap, and Express.

Spas

The spa industry makes up the fourth-largest leisure industry in the United States, something Panama City Beach has jumped on with a vengeance in recent years. The toniest might be the 12,025-square-foot **Serenity at Bay Point** (4114 Jan Cooley Dr., 850/236-6028), but there's also the **Spa at Majestic Beach Resort** (10901 Front Beach Rd., 866/494-3364), and the **Spa at the Edgewater Beach and Golf Resort** (11212 Front Beach Rd., 855/874-8686).

FOOD
Breakfast

For breakfast, try **Andy's Flour Power** (3123 Thomas Dr., 850/230-0014, 7am-2pm Mon.-Sat., 8am-2pm Sun., $6-10). Order their exceptional French toast covered in strawberries, an omelet, or one of their delicious pastries. They have a nice variety of traditional American and healthier European options, and the menu is full of vegetables and fruit, which can be hard to find at a breakfast spot in the South. The lunch menu features sandwiches and salads, including a great Reuben. The club sandwich and Caesar salad are also favorites. The atmosphere is colorful and fun, making this a great place to sip your morning coffee.

Near St. Andrews State Park, **Jesse's Place** (7008 Thomas Dr., 850/708-1356, 7am-2pm Tues.-Sat., $5-10) is a small breakfast and lunch café with healthy options. They serve a mix of home-cooking, soul food, and vegetarian dishes. The breakfast is wonderful and affordable. At lunch you can pick one meat like meat loaf or fried pork chops and three choices from their veggie-heavy sides for around $8, and that includes cornbread or roll. The food is delicious and the service is friendly. Grab a glass of sweet iced tea and all you'll need is a rocking chair and a front porch to call yourself an honorary southerner.

Casual

In Panama City Beach you mostly get fried seafood, wings, pizza, and burgers—the sort of food you would expect from a location mostly supported by college students. Yet there are some great restaurants for all tastes. One option is to keep it simple, heading for familiar offerings like **Bonefish Grill, Carrabba's Italian Grill,** or **Ruth's Chris Steakhouse.** For a great cheeseburger, go to **Flamingo Joe's** (2304 Thomas Dr., 850/233-0600, 11am-9pm Sun., 11am-10pm Mon.-Sat., $8-15). It also has an addictive salsa, served warm. **Sharky's Beachfront Seafood Restaurant** (15201 Front Beach Rd., 850/235-2420, 11am-10pm daily, $15-27) is a long-standing favorite for a good sunset, fine live entertainment in the world's largest tiki hut, and seafood-centric food.

Do you know what it means to miss New Orleans? If you do, head straight to **David's Sno-Balls** (13913 Panama City Beach Pkwy., 850/236-1998, 11am-9pm Mon., 9am-9pm Tues.-Sat., noon-9pm Sun., $3-8) and grab you a muffuletta, a tray of sugar-dusted beignets, a po'boy shrimp sandwich, or a classic shaved ice. On Mondays they have red beans and rice. For sides, grab a bag of Zapp's spicy Cajun potato chips and a Barq's root beer in a glass bottle to make you feel like you're back in The Big Easy, baby. This small eatery is packed on the weekends. They don't have the walk-up window like most sno-ball spots on the Gulf Coast, but you can go inside on a hot summer day to enjoy the air-conditioning. The bright, clean café has several tables and wrought-iron chairs that give it a decidedly New Orleans atmosphere.

Muy Wayne O's (303 S. Arnold Rd., 850/249-6830, 11am-7pm Tues.-Sat., $7-12) serves Tex-Mex food and margaritas to the tourist crowd. The specialty is a smoked briquette burrito that will keep your mouth watering for days after you try it. The place has become a must-stop for those staying or passing through Panama City Beach. The festive atmosphere that is the norm at Mexican restaurants keeps spirits high, and the thin, crunchy chips and spicy salsa help this south-of-the-border fusion spot stand out from the crowd.

Liza's Kitchen (7328 Thomas Dr., 850/233-9000, 11am-4pm Mon.-Fri., 9am-3pm Sat.-Sun., $5-9) is a small café on the eastern end of the beach near the Sunset Inn. The large menu includes hot and cold selections such as the Hippie Chick sandwich with chicken, goat cheese, spinach, red peppers, and spicy mayo on focaccia. Any sandwich can be ordered as a wrap or a salad, and you can build your own salad or sandwich from a long list of ingredients. Weekend brunch includes traditional items like eggs Benedict along with unique plates like Eggs Liza,

poached eggs with roast beef and pimento cheese on focaccia bread served with scallion hollandaise.

Finn's Island Style Grub (7220 Thomas Dr., 850/249-3466, 10am-3pm daily, $6-12) is a popular food truck across the road from Rick Seltzer Park. Their specialty is fish tacos, and they also offer a variety of Mexican favorites like nachos, tacos, and quesadillas. The fresh ceviche is spectacular, and the mahi quesadillas will bring you back to this little food cart on the beach time and again during your stay.

J' Michaels (3210 Thomas Dr., 850/233-2055, 11am-10pm daily, $8-15) is dockside of Grand Lagoon and the place to go for comfort food like red beans and rice. It's casual, with license plates and dollar bills all over the walls. They have an extensive seafood menu that includes oysters prepared all sorts of ways, and you can sit at the bar and watch them shuck the raw oysters right before you eat them.

Fine Dining

Firefly (535 Richard Jackson Blvd., 850/249-3359, 5pm-until closing, daily, $15-25) is the place to go for a romantic, or just generally fancy, seafood dinner. The she crab soup, crab cakes, and sesame-crusted tuna over a cucumber and radish salad are top picks. The wine list is extensive, but pricey for the area, so if you're on a tight budget, pick up drinks somewhere else before and after the fine meal.

You want to take it a little more upscale? **Angelo's Steak Pit** (9527 Front Beach Rd., 850/234-2351, 5pm-10pm daily, closed in winter, $14-26) always gets the nod for fat steaks grilled over aromatic hickory. It's been here since 1958, and the resident 20,000-pound steer, Big Gus, is practically a local celebrity.

Captain Anderson's Restaurant (5550 N. Lagoon Dr., 850/234-2225, 4:30pm-10pm Mon.-Fri., 4pm-10pm Sat., $12-35) is another serious locals' establishment, focusing on seafood. It's a waterfront favorite that's been here for years—go for the heads-on shrimp or the open-hearth whole fish.

NIGHTLIFE

Bars

Schooner's (5121 Gulf Dr., 850/235-3555, 11am-until closing, daily) is a favorite spring break hangout. They feature live bands on their large deck, and the views looking toward the nearby St. Andrews State Park are spectacular. They serve normal American pub grub like burgers and sandwiches, but most people come here for the libations and party atmosphere. This is a great place to catch sunset.

Coyote Ugly Saloon (10512 Front Beach Rd., 850/236-5965, 4pm-4am Tues.-Sat.) is a rowdy, western-themed bar made famous by the movie of the same name. There are bras hanging on the rafters, and the waitresses are scantily clad as if they are sorority girls dressing up as Annie Oakley in booty shorts. This is the kind of establishment where visitors can live out fantasies of taking body shots and dancing on the bar. Once you get nice and sauced, try riding the mechanical bull.

For something authentic to the local beach culture, wear your bikini (or board shorts) to the **Sandpiper Tiki Bar** (17403 Front Beach Rd., 850/234-2154, 10am-4am). This open-air poolside bar is a Gulf Coast gem hidden behind the Sandpiper Beacon Beach Resort. They have live music during the summer and

feature many of the area's top reggae bands. You can watch the game on the numerous televisions, or dance to the band, and then walk a few feet to the beach for swimming and great views. This small, casual place gets busy during the summer and spring break, but feeling the beach breeze while you dance to Bob Marley is hard to beat. This is the perfect spot if you want to avoid the intense club scene.

Clubs

Club La Vela (8813 Thomas Dr., 850/235-1061, 11am-4am daily in the summer, prices vary) calls itself the largest nightclub in America, and it is certainly the heart of nightlife activity during spring break in Panama City Beach. Made world famous by the MTV spring break specials hosted here, the club has eleven rooms, 48 bar stations, and can hold more than 6,000 people, which it regularly does during the summer and when it is hosting national music acts on one of its numerous stages. The place is one big party, with most fun being had in and around the massive pool.

You can continue the party right next door at **Spinnaker Beach Club** (8795 Thomas Dr., 850/234-7882, 11am-4am), where you can also get a decent seafood platter and burger at their

Captain Anderson's Restaurant is on the waterfront.

Paradise Grill. The menu has a mix of mostly seafood, Mexican, and New Orleans-style food. After the restaurant closes, the party ramps up at the connected club with two rooms: a dance room with a DJ and a rock room with a large stage and live bands.

Tootsie's Orchid Lounge (700 S. Pier Park Dr., 850/236-3459, 11am-until daily, under 21 permitted after 8pm only if accompanied by an adult, food served 11am-11pm, music in the summer from 2pm-3am) first opened in Nashville, Tennessee, and brought their country-themed party to the beach in 2008. The club was immediately a huge success, thanks to their focus on quality live music and their excellent location in Pier Park. It's a honky-tonk party with a live country band taking requests and a menu full of bar food to replenish the calories you'll burn while line dancing.

ACCOMMODATIONS

It seems that all of Panama City Beach has been under construction in the past few years, with condos, resorts, hotels, townhomes, and villas transforming the destination. Panama City Beach has recently completed over 30 resort and condominium projects, many big high-rises set right against the beach. Inventory has grown to an all-time high of more than 30,000 rooms. Due to the surplus of rooms in the off-season during the fall and winter months, you can find some of the best deals on the Gulf Coast right here in Panama City Beach.

Under $100

The **Sandpiper Beacon** (17403 Front Beach Rd., 850/234-2154, $59-119) is a comfortable, family-friendly place with lots of on-site amenities for the price. It has 1,000 feet of beachfront, with parasailing, personal watercraft, and the Big Banana Ride right out the back door. There are three pools (one indoor), a lazy river ride, and twin turbo waterslides, a game room, restaurant, children's playground, gift shop, and tiki bar. There are family units, with some suites sleeping up to 10 people.

Super 8 Panama City Beach (207 U.S. 231, between Hwy. 77 and U.S. 98, 850/784-1988, $39-80) is another no-frills home base close to the beach. It has clean rooms and basic amenities, but get this: During March and April a deposit of $200 is required, and you have to wear *wristbands* to prove you're actually staying here and aren't just crashing the joint.

Driftwood Lodge (15811 Front Beach Rd., 850/234-6601, $75-100) is a two-story motel with Old Florida charm. They have regular rooms, efficiencies with kitchens, and a suite with private sundeck. Off-season rates are exceptional, so visit during the winter for a low-priced stay just feet from the beach. The heated pool, sunroom, and beach volleyball courts make this a great choice for families on a budget.

Spartan Inn (8614 Surf Dr., 850/234-8482, $69-125) is a great choice if you plan on doing a lot of cooking during your vacation. With kitchens in every spacious room, this unassuming classic low-rise motel is not spartan at all. It's been popular with families since 1984 and features a large pool that is usually filled with kids having a blast in the summer months. The drawback is that it's not beachfront, but it can be a good choice and often a bargain when other properties are full.

$100-200

Flamingo Motel (15525 Front Beach Rd., 850/234-2232, $89-189) is across the street from Gulf World and a short walk from Pier Park shopping center. It's popular with families. The property is divided into a seven-story tower and a three-story building with a lush tropical garden courtyard. The owners of thirty-five years pride themselves on cleanliness and customer service. Parking is free. Wi-Fi and local calls are free, and they don't charge for extra people. The winter monthly rates ($390-990) are low if you want to stay long term on the beach during the warmer months.

Sunset Inn (8109 Surf Dr., 850/234-7374, $75-185) opened in 1981, and even though they're right down the street from Club La Vela, they're one of the more popular places to stay for families with young children, especially if you're looking for a bargain. The low-rise inn features a heated pool, balconies with Gulf views, a large deck with grills for barbecue and grilling the fresh fish you pull from the surf, and several rooms with kitchens to help you eat healthier, cutting back on your dining expenses. Queen sleepers are available in suites.

Chateau Motel (12525 Front Beach Rd., 888/842-3224, $100-200) is a favorite among young people, with 150 Gulf-view rooms 500 feet from the sand. It's right at the center of all the Miracle Strip excitement, with restaurants, attractions, shopping, and nightlife within walking distance. If you're under 25, they make you pay an extra $100 deposit until you pass checkout inspection.

Days Inn Beach Hotel (12818 Front Beach Rd., 850/233-3333, $115-180) is hopping, with 188 Gulf-front rooms and suites with private balconies. Room decor is tropical and breezy, but you'll spend most of your time outside at the seven-story volcano mountain waterfall. It's in the huge pool situated between the Days Inn and Ramada Limited. It's

a scene out there, with athletic young people sipping tropical drinks and flirting shamelessly in the whirlpool.

Osprey on the Gulf (15801 Front Beach Rd., 850/234-0303, $140-250) has 650 feet of beachfront, a heated pool and hot tub, Gulf-front balconies, and efficiency rooms with kitchens. Kids love the sand sculpture contests and other family-centric activities that the hotel plans. The hotel allows smoking on the balconies, which makes the place not so family-friendly for those who would like to keep their children away from cigarette smoke exposure. However, the rooms are clean, the view from the balconies is spectacular, and the price is a decent value for the amenities and location.

Bikini Beach Resort (11001 Front Beach Rd., 850/234-3392, $139-200) is a beachfront property located about 1.3-miles from Shipwreck Island Waterpark. The clean and fashionable interiors feature modern but tropical decor, and bright color schemes keep the rooms upbeat and fun. Dave's tiki bar by the pool makes this property a top choice for spring breakers and the younger party crowd. If you want to do a little of your own cooking, some rooms have kitchens.

Chateau Motel is popular with spring breakers.

$200-300

The upscale ★ **Grand Panama Beach Resort** (11800 and 11807 Front Beach Rd., 850/316-8964, www.grandpanama-beachresort.com, $149 and up) is a 35-acre resort cuddled against a 240-foot stretch of beach, the property featuring 299 units spread out over two beachfront towers, two pools and spas, a fitness center and two tiki bars, plus a playground, game room, and a jogging/bicycle path around the perimeter of the property. Besides its own on-site concert venue, the resort is also home to the Village of Grand Panama, a 55,000-square-foot retail center with an array of shops, services, and restaurants, including a spa and salon, a wine shop, and several clothing boutiques. Additionally, the property offers guests free high-speed Internet access, including Wi-Fi in designated outdoor and poolside areas. Guests staying at Grand Panama Beach Resort are granted exclusive access to the Sterling Club at Bay Point, featuring northwest Florida's only Nicklaus-designed golf course, the Serenity Spa at Bay Point, tennis, dining, and a water-sports marina.

Hampton Inn and Suites (13505 Panama City Beach Pkwy., 850/230-9084, $150-230) is about three miles north from Pier Park. The 95 spacious rooms have elegant furnishings, exceptionally comfy beds, and a large workstation. It's a classic hotel that is equipped for business travelers and families. The splash fountain and outdoor pool are fun for the kids, and the free hot breakfast will save time and money in the mornings.

A top pick for families is the ★ **Holiday Inn Resort** (11127 Front Beach Rd., 850/234-1111, $250-350), a modern hotel right on the Gulf. After you check in, head straight to the lagoon-style pool where you'll find a tropical oasis of palm trees, picnic tables with thatched-palm umbrellas, and a large splash playground for kids. You can see the Gulf from poolside, and adults can order drinks from the poolside bar. In the summer, you'll find live poolside entertainment that includes reenacted pirate invasions for the kids, a Polynesian dance troop, and live bands including local favorites The Rocklobsters. The rooms are clean, bright, and modern, with tropical furnishings. Choose from beachfront family rooms with a double bed and two sets of bunk beds (sleeps up to 6), kids suites with a double bed and two single beds in a portioned off area that gives couples more privacy, rooms with 2 queen beds, and suites with king beds. Each room has a full-sized fridge, ice maker, and microwave. There's a variety of on-site dining, including a poolside pizza place, the Oasis Bar, and The Bamboo Grill on the pool deck that serves lunch items like burgers, wraps, sandwiches, and salads. More formal dining can be found at The View Restaurant, featuring seafood dishes and tables close to the pool waterfall beneath the palms. The spot for evening cocktails is on the third floor at The Sunset Lounge where you can watch a Vegas-style show in the summer while you enjoy spectacular views of the Gulf. There's a store with snacks and beach accessories on the ground floor, a fully equipped and modern fitness center, and a Gulf-front spa. There's really not much reason to leave once you check in.

Edgewater Beach Resort (11212 Front Beach Rd., 850/235-4044, $81-516) is worth the splurge; it's Panama City Beach's premier resort and family-friendly. It's a great location on the beach, right across the street from Cinema 10 Theaters, Rock-It Lanes, miniature golf, and the Shoppes at Edgewater. On-site there are two restaurants, two bars, 11 heated outdoor pools, an executive 9-hole golf course, and the 27-hole Hombre Golf Club championship course just minutes away. The rooms themselves are spread throughout a vast property, from the Gulf Front Towers to the Golf and Tennis Villas to the Windward and Leeward Suites.

Over $300

An excellent place that's a bit removed from the fray is the **Marriott's Legends Edge at**

Bay Point (4000 Marriott Dr., 850/236-4200, $280-419). Each villa has a fully equipped kitchen, spacious living and dining areas, and well-appointed bedrooms. It's adjacent to the Marriott Bay Point Resort Village and situated in the midst of the Club Meadows and Lagoons Legends golf courses (designed by Bob von Hagge and Bruce Devlin in 1985, and a notoriously challenging course). The Gulf of Mexico is 10 minutes away, and the Grand Lagoon of St. Andrews Bay is within walking distance.

Camping

You can park your RV a mile from the beach at **Emerald Coast RV Resort** (1957 Allison Ave., 800/232-2478, www.rvresort.com, $69-225/night, weekly and monthly rates available). They have more than 150 sites set on more than 10 acres of expertly maintained grounds, and they are one of the few RV facilities to receive *Trailer Life*'s highest rating. A saltwater pool with waterfall and several ponds are centerpieces of the park, and the newly added volleyball and basketball courts are nice additions for families and active campers. The on-site dog run, pet baths, and pet-friendly policies will keep your dog's tail wagging.

GETTING THERE

Panama City Beach is on a barrier island. If you're visiting, note that Panama City Beach and Panama City are two separate cities and their names should not be used interchangeably. The Hathaway Bridge crosses St. Andrews Bay and connects the two of them. U.S. 98 splits at Panama City Beach and becomes U.S. 98 in the north (also called Panama City Beach Parkway) and U.S. 98A along the beach (also called Front Beach Road).

The **Northwest Florida Beaches International Airport** (6300 West Bay Pkwy., Panama City, 850/763-6751), the first international airport built in the United States in a decade, is served by Delta, Silver, Southwest Airlines, and United. **Greyhound** (800/231-2222) has a bus station in Panama City (917 Harrison Ave., 850/785-6111), but public transportation won't get you to most places along the Emerald Coast, unless you're just hanging out on the beach in Panama City Beach.

Fort Walton Beach and Destin

Spanish explorer Pánfilo de Narváez landed along the Emerald Coast in 1628 to find himself a drink of water. The Creeks chased him and his men back to the boat, thirst unquenched. There's no telling, really, why up until about 50 years ago a wide swath of the Emerald Coast, from Destin to Panama City, was unsettled sand dunes and quiet green waters. Most of the growth here dates back only a few decades.

Not so of Destin and Fort Walton Beach. Okaloosa County has got roots. In 1830, New England seafarer Leonard Destin fell for the place, the first settler in the area among several local Native American tribes. He lured other New England fishermen with big fish stories, and by 1845 there were 100 residents all employed in the fishing business. And Fort Walton Beach was a Civil War campsite, its location chosen because of its protection from the Gulf by the Santa Rosa Sound and Okaloosa Island.

During Prohibition the joint was jumping. "Entrepreneurs" like Al Capone came down to the area to hide out. Mobsters being mobsters, the area was soon dotted with hopping casinos filled with shady characters evading the law up north.

The casinos and mobsters are gone, but what's left is a beloved fishing destination, one that boasts five saltwater world records. It looks the part: Destin and Fort Walton

Beach were the shooting location for *Jaws II*, both admirably portraying charming seaside resort towns.

SPORTS AND RECREATION

Beaches

There are 24 miles of beach—the sand a shockingly fine, white quartz that somehow made its way here down 130 miles of the Appalachian River, the water a brilliant jewel green. Nearly 60 percent of the beach around here is preserved in perpetuity, or at least for a long, long time. There are five beachfront parks and 12 beach access ways along the Destin, Fort Walton Beach, and Okaloosa Island shoreline.

One of the best is the 208-acre **Henderson Beach State Park** (17000 Emerald Coast Pkwy., east of the city of Destin on U.S. 98, 850/837-7550, for camping call 800/326-3521 or visit www.reserveamerica.com, 8am-sundown daily, $4/vehicle with single occupant, $6/vehicle with up to 8 passengers, $2 pedestrian or cyclist, $30 camping), which has 6,000 feet of shoreline. There's urban sprawl off to the west in Destin; in fact, the beach's entrance is just across the street from a Walmart Supercenter. Once out on the coastal dunes you'd never know it—sea oats anchor the soft sand in the dunes, while the ocean's salt spray and wind cause the rosemary, magnolias, and scrub oak to grow low and horizontal, their limbs bent shoreward. During the fall the beach is dotted with colorful wildflowers— blanket flower and beach morning glory carpeting the clean sand.

At Henderson you can swim, surf fish, picnic, bike, in-line skate, walk the 0.75-mile nature trail, or camp (the campground has 60 full-facility campsites for tents or RVs). Colored flags indicate the wave and swimming conditions—red flag means "knee deep is too deep" as there is high potential for rip currents to form, and double red flag means the water is closed for swimming.

James Lee County Park (3510 Scenic U.S. 98, Destin, dawn to dusk daily, free parking) is another good beach, right at the Walton/ Okaloosa County line. This park has three pavilions, 41 picnic tables, nine dune walkovers, a playground, restrooms with changing rooms, and 166 parking spaces. It's a popular beach for families, with the water shallow and clear and the Crab Trap restaurant in the middle of the beach's parking lot.

Okaloosa Island has a series of beaches, really contiguous—first, the **John Beasley Wayside Park** (U.S. 98, Okaloosa Island, 1.2 miles east of Fort Walton Beach, 850-689-5772) is on the bay side of the barrier island just yards from the Okaloosa Boardwalk (an entertainment complex with clubs and restaurants). John Beasley has restrooms, picnic tables, showers, changing rooms, vending machines, and lifeguards. It has fishing for trout and reds, snorkeling activity, and even a little surfing. The same can be said of the adjacent **Brackin Wayside Park and Boardwalk** (U.S. 98, Okaloosa Island, 1 mile east of Fort Walton Beach, 850/651-7131), which has several pavilions, 41 picnic tables, restrooms with changing rooms, a children's playground, dune walkovers to the beach, lots of parking, and fierce beach volleyball during the warmer months.

★ Crab Island

North of the Destin Bridge, **Crab Island** used to be two islands in the middle of nowhere made of sand dredged by the U.S. Army Corps of Engineers from East Pass. It used to even be a real island with sea grass, shrubs, and seabirds. But now it's submerged a few feet and only surfaces at low tide. This is where people congregate with their boats for some fun in the sun. People are jumping off into the three-foot shallows, eating, chatting, and drinking. Sometimes there's even live music on the back of a boat or floating vendors serving food and drinks (often an ice cream guy) to all the folks gathered there.

To get there, you need something that floats—maybe a pontoon boat, or a glass-bottom boat, or a fishing boat, or even a WaveRunner. You can shop at **Boogies**

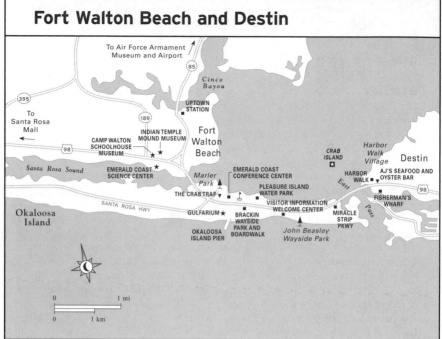

Fort Walton Beach and Destin

To Air Force Armament Museum and Airport

85

Cinco Bayou

395

To Santa Rosa Mall

189

UPTOWN STATION

CAMP WALTON SCHOOLHOUSE MUSEUM

98

INDIAN TEMPLE MOUND MUSEUM

Fort Walton Beach

EMERALD COAST SCIENCE CENTER

Santa Rosa Sound

Marler Park

THE CRAB TRAP

SANTA ROSA HWY

EMERALD COAST CONFERENCE CENTER

PLEASURE ISLAND WATER PARK

VISITOR INFORMATION WELCOME CENTER

CRAB ISLAND

Harbor Walk Village

Destin

HARBOR WALK

AJ'S SEAFOOD AND OYSTER BAR

98

East Pass

FISHERMAN'S WHARF

Okaloosa Island

GULFARIUM

BRACKIN WAYSIDE PARK AND BOARDWALK

OKALOOSA ISLAND PIER

John Beasley Wayside Park

MIRACLE STRIP PKWY

0   1 mi
0   1 km

Watersports (16 Harbor Blvd., www.boogieswatersports.com, 850/654-4497) to pick up a rental that suits your budget, skill level, and personal sense of style. Ask the rental place or any local for specific directions. The best time to go is at high tide, when the water is crystal clear. This place becomes a party zone during holidays and summer weekends, so plan on a different time if you want to beat the crowds.

★ Fishing in Destin Harbor

About 30 miles offshore (only 10 miles from Destin's East Pass), the Gulf of Mexico turns from emerald green to deep blue. It's at this point, called the 100-Fathom Curve, where you're in deep, deep water all of a sudden. This deep-water curve is closer to Destin than to any other spot in Florida, meaning a fishing charter from Destin is the quickest way out to deep water. And it's a lucky thing, because these waters are churning with fish. In the spring there's the migration of mighty

cobia (you can sight fish for these) and in May come the kingfish (inshore troll). People bottom fish for grouper, red snapper, triggerfish, and amberjack year-round. In summer, when the waters warm up, it's serious marlin and sailfish (offshore troll) and wahoo and tuna (inshore troll). Destin bills itself, so to speak, as the Billfish Capital of the World. The best I can figure, based on conversation with sometimes-taciturn fisher types, billfish is a tuna-like fish species similar to marlin, sailfish, and spearfish—those fish with the big, sword-like bill. Destin is also known by some as the "World's Luckiest Fishing Village," because its waters harbor four times more types of fresh fish per season than any other Florida destination except for Key West. Supposedly, during any given season there are 20 edible species of game fish to be found in local waters.

So you have to come here and fish. Offshore, bottom, inshore, or even surf-casting—there are lots of people around here with enormous experience willing to take you out

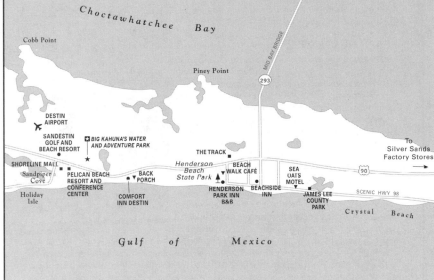

on a saltwater charter or just hook you up with gear. In addition, the area's rivers offer freshwater fishing for catfish, bass, and bream. And many restaurants in the area are willing to cook up your fresh catch.

The price of a private charter averages $150-165 per hour, for up to six people. Many boats only accommodate six people, so make clear how many people are in your party. You can also sign up for a group charter, pooling with other people who are looking to go out (prices are the same, you just split it between all the people on the boat). Obviously, you have to find others who are simpatico, in terms of what they're fishing for and how long they want to be out.

Destin Charter Service (Fisherman's Wharf, 850/837-1995) is one-stop shopping, with access to 40 of Destin's best charter boats (there are more than 100 vessels for hire around here). These boats offer year-round fishing trips for individuals or groups, from four-hour trips to overnights, either on the Gulf or the bay side. **Harborwalk Fishing Charters** (next to Lucky Snapper off U.S. 98, 10 Harbor Blvd., 850/837-2343, www.harborwalkfishing.com, $120/person for 4 hours, $175/person for 6 hours—it's customary to tip 15 percent) is another well-regarded local charter company. Staff will clean, fillet, and bag your catch at trip's end.

If you just feel like finding your own boat and giving it a go, **Gilligan's Water Sports** (Destin Harbor, 530 Harbor Blvd., 850/650-9000, www.gilligansofdestin.com) rents pontoon boats for reasonable prices ($275-450), good for snorkeling, fishing, or just tooling around. You can also head out into the Blackwater, Shoal, or Yellow Rivers in search of bass, bream, and catfish.

No boat is required to fish from the **Okaloosa Island Fishing Pier** (850/244-1023, 24 hours Apr.-Sept., 5am-9pm Oct.-Mar., $7.50 adults, $4.50 children 6-12, $6.50 seniors, no license necessary). It's a 1,261-foot pier, lighted at night, with rod holders and

Beach Basics

If you want your day at the beach to be, well, a day at the beach, keep a few things in mind.

BEACH HUSBANDRY

Bare coastal dunes are vulnerable to destruction by the same forces that form them: wind and waves. Dunes are built when sand blows up through beachside plantlife and is trapped, creating ever-taller mounds. These mounds in turn protect the shore during storms by washing back out to sea and decreasing the energy of the storm waves. For these reasons, do not trample, pick, spindle, or mutilate any beachside plantlife (like the sea oats). In fact, along public beach accesses, always use the **boardwalks and raised walkways** rather than tramping through the sand.

beach access in Seaside

Sea turtles nest on the Gulf beaches of Okaloosa County April-November. Recent hurricane seasons have wrought havoc on these already threatened and endangered species. Again, no spindling (it's illegal to disturb a nest or harm a turtle in any way) or even taunting. Never crowd around a turtle nest, don't impede a turtle's progress toward the water, and don't shine lights on the beaches at night if possible.

This area's beaches are all **clothing-required.** Navarre Beach used to have a lot of nude sunbathers, but federal agents have cracked down on the depravity and lawlessness that comes of lying nude on a beach towel. Be advised. Also, beaches in this area **prohibit pets,** and that goes double for nude pets. If you see animals on the beach, they probably belong to residents who have gotten special beach pet permits, available only to locals.

BEACH SAFETY

Jellyfish are common to Gulf beaches. Not the big, terrifying Man O' War types, but the local species' sting can still be pretty fierce. Shuffle your feet in the water to alert nearby jellyfish to your presence. In the event that you do get stung, the experts say ammonia poured on the sting relieves the pain, as does meat tenderizer and toothpaste. (Who figures these things out—is someone getting stung and then applying poultices of household products just in the name of science?)

Rip currents occur in any type of weather. If caught in a rip current, swim parallel to the shore until the current weakens and you can swim in.

And although shark attacks in these waters are infrequent, there are ways to further minimize your chances of a **shark encounter.** You're more vulnerable if you're swimming alone, and if you swim far from shore. Sharks are most active at dusk, when they have a competitive sensory advantage. They tend to hang out in areas between sandbars or steep drop-offs—use caution when swimming in these areas. As you know, sharks smell blood—if you have a wound, if you are menstruating, or if nearby fisherfolk are cleaning fish or throwing out bait, think about postponing a swim. And remove shiny jewelry before you go in—its reflective glinting looks like the sheen of fish scales to a hungry predator.

Use **sunscreen,** and lots of it. Experts say that an average-size person should use about two tablespoons per application.

benches built into it. You'll catch all kinds of things (including big mahimahi). You can also cast from the area's finger jetties, sandy shores, and the 3,000-foot **Destin Bridge Catwalk** to hook speckled trout, white snapper, and redfish. And there are stocked ponds in the area, such as the 350-acre **Hurricane Lake** in Blackwater River State Park, filled with channel catfish, largemouth bass, bluegill, and shellcracker.

When you want to find out what is biting and where, visit www.gulfcoastangling.com, then plan your fishing accordingly.

Shelling and Diving

The beaches are uniformly fine white sand, and compared to the beaches to the south there are few shells in sight. So how can the Emerald Coast be ranked as a top shelling destination? They're offshore—you have to dive for them. Giant sandbars about a mile from shore and a natural coral-encrusted limestone outcropping (the pre-ice age shoreline) three miles out act as natural shovels to collect perfectly formed shells—pastel lion's paws, true tulips, huge queen helmets, and Florida's signature shell, the horse conchs, are there for the picking.

The center of much of this shelling mania is **Sand Dollar City,** an artificial reef complex the county put together about a mile out. It's got six patch reefs placed in a hexagonal pattern around a single center point, the sunken 1941 tugboat called the *Mohawk Chief.* The whole area is a fish and shellfish haven, and by extension, a shelling bonanza. **Timber Hole** is another hot spot of shelling and intriguing marinelife observation (sea squirts, four-foot basket sponges, aqua and purple sea whips). It has a natural limestone reef 6-18 feet high and 110 feet deep, as well as sunken planes, ships, and a railroad car. There are loads of natural reefs in this area, for shelling, diving, and fishing; **Amberjack Rocks** is one of the area's largest reef systems, within three miles of Destin Pass. About 80 feet deep, it is known for shelling as well as spearfishing for black snapper and amberjack. **Long Reef** features staircase ledges and is known for lobsters and shells. The area also has intriguing wrecks to explore—an air force barge, a Liberty ship, *Butler's Barge,* and the rubble of the Destin Bridge. Divers here often enjoy 40-100 feet of visibility.

For safety reasons, all divers must display a free-flying, 12- by 12-inch flag with a white diagonal stripe on a red background—the diver-down flag—in the area in which the dive

Henderson Beach State Park

THE EMERALD COAST
FORT WALTON BEACH AND DESTIN

occurs. Divers should try to stay within 100 feet of the flag, and the flag and diver should never be in areas that might constitute a navigational hazard.

Emerald Coast Scuba (503-B Harbor Blvd., Destin, 850/837-0955, www.divedestin. com) provides scuba instruction and charters. Many other dive shops offer theme excursions like spearfishing, deep sea, shell, and lobster, with certification classes. They will also take you out snorkeling from their boats. If you just want to snorkel on your own, you can do so from the beach at **Destin jetties** or from the **Old Crystal Beach Pier.**

Golf

Emerald-green waters mirrored by emerald-green golf courses. There are 1,080 holes of golf in these parts, many of the courses designed by some of the world's best architects: Robert Cupp of Jack Nicklaus fame, or Finger, or Dye, or Fazio. Many of these courses utilize the area's lush natural beauty and surrounding waterways, with contrasts of woods and wetlands, for challenging and memorably beautiful play.

The 18-hole **Regatta Bay Golf Club** (465 Regatta Bay Blvd., Destin, 850/337-8080, www.regattabay.com, $59-129, par 72, 6,864 yards, course rating 73.8, slope 148) was designed by Robert Walker, winding along the shore of Choctawhatchee Bay and carved through wetlands and protected nature preserves. Another popular one, the creation of Fred Couples and Gene Bates, **Kelly Plantation Golf Club** (307 Kelly Plantation Dr., Destin, 850/650-7600, www.kellyplantationgolf.com, $69-145, par 72, 7,099 yards, course rating 74.2, slope 146) utilizes the Choctawhatchee Bay as well, nestled along its southern edge with rolling greens and beautiful fairways.

Acclaimed by *Golfweek* as one of the 50 Most Distinctive Development Courses in the Southeast, **Emerald Bay** (4781 Clubhouse Dr., Destin 888/465-3229, $49-125, par 72, 6,802 yards, course rating 73.1, slope 135) was designed by nationally recognized architect

East Pass

Originally, the Gulf of Mexico and the Destin Harbor did not connect to the Choctawhatchee Bay in this area, which posed some navigational challenges to the local fishing fleet and some flooding danger to the settlements as well. In 1926, three local, stalwart families took it upon themselves to change that. The Destins, the Marlers, and the Melvins grabbed a bunch of shovels and started digging by hand, making a two-foot-wide ditch across Okaloosa Island. Within two hours, supposedly, the trench was over 100 yards wide. A torrent of water rushed in, creating what is now East Pass. In 1935 the East Pass Bridge was built. To this day, the U.S. Army Corps of Engineers keeps close tabs on the pass, dredging it every two years or so (more in hurricane years) to ensure the water's deep enough for boats to move safely through it.

The East Pass is the only waterway connecting the Choctawhatchee Bay to the Gulf of Mexico for 60 miles in either direction (Pensacola to the west and Panama City to the east each have waterways that connect the bay with the Gulf). The East Pass is the lifeblood of the Destin fishing fleet—without it, the town would surely not be the angler's paradise that draws fisherfolk from around the world. All because of a few shovels.

Robert Cupp. He said of the course, "There is no signature hole, it is—instead—a signature golf course."

At **Indian Bayou Golf and Country Club** (1 Country Club Dr. E., Destin, 850/837-6191, www.indianbayougolf.com, $45-85, par 72, 7,000 yards, course rating 74, slope 132-142) there's an assortment of Earl Stone-designed nines, the Choctaw, Seminole, and Creek, which can be played in any 18-hole combination. The Creek course, the newest, has lots of water that comes into play; the Choctaw is heavily wooded; and the Seminole has wide fairways and large greens.

Also situated on the banks of Choctawhatchee Bay, **Shalimar Pointe**

Golf and Country Club (302 Country Club Rd., Shalimar, 850/651-1416, $20-45, par 72, 6,765 yards, course rating 72.9, slope 125) is a Finger/Dye-designed course that *Links* magazine accused of having "Two of the Hardest Holes on the Emerald Coast," the 11th and 17th. It is bordered by rolling white dunes and dense hammocks of pine, oak, and magnolia. Shalimar Pointe has been host to The Emerald Coast Tour.

Beyond these, there's **Shoal River Country Club, Fort Walton Beach Municipal Course,** the two courses at **Eglin Air Force Base** (available only with government ID), and the world-class courses at **Sandestin Golf & Beach Resort.**

SIGHTS
Museums
Located near Eglin Air Force Base's main gate, the **Air Force Armament Museum** (Hwy. 85 and Hwy. 189, seven miles north of Fort Walton Beach, 850/651-1808, 9am-5pm Mon.-Sat., free) is the only facility in the United States dedicated to the display of air force armament. You'll see thousands of weapons, an educational film called *Arming the Air Force,* and photography exhibits in addition to 25 cool reconnaissance planes, fighters, and bombers. There's a B-17 Flying Fortress, an F-4 Phantom II jet, and an SR-71 Blackbird Spy Plane. The museum spans four wars in its scope—World War II, Korea, Vietnam, and Persian Gulf. Kids love the fighter cockpit simulator.

The Fort Walton Beach community has a rich Native American past, having been settled by a number of prehistoric tribes as far back as 12,000 BC. The **Indian Temple Mound Museum and Park** (139 Miracle Strip Pkwy. SE, Fort Walton Beach, 850/833-9595, 10am-4:30pm Mon.-Sat. June-Labor Day, noon-4:30pm Mon.-Fri., 10am-4:30pm Sat. Sept.-May, $5.30 adults, $4.77 seniors, $3.18 children 4-17, children 3 and under free) provides a peek into the area's Native American history, with a thoughtfully assembled collection of southeastern Indian ceramic artifacts and an Indian Mound Temple that dates to AD 1400 and originally served as a religious and civic center.

It was the first schoolhouse constructed for the children of Camp Walton, later to be known as Fort Walton Beach. **Camp Walton Schoolhouse Museum** (127 Miracle Strip Pkwy. SE, Fort Walton Beach, 850/833-9595, noon-4pm Mon.-Sat., $5.30 adults, $4.77 seniors, $3.18 children 4-17, children 3 and under free) was built of native pine and oak, and when it opened in 1912, there were 15 students and one teacher. It was restored in the early 1970s and opened as an educational museum in 1976. These days, it's mostly for the benefit of local school groups, but it still makes a sweet nostalgic look at a past most of us never knew.

Family-Friendly Attractions
A good example of the compelling science museums for kids that seem to be popping up in every town these days is the **Emerald Coast Science Center** (31 SW Memorial Pkwy., Fort Walton Beach, 850/664-1261, www.ecscience.org, 9am-6pm Mon., 10am-2pm Tues. and Thurs., 10am-4pm Fri.-Sat., noon-4pm Sun., $9 adults, $8 seniors, $7 children 3-17, children 2 and under free), which has an interesting section devoted to color and light. You can fly and land a model airplane in a mini air tunnel or noodle with a laser spirograph or a Van de Graff generator (you know, that orb that makes your hair stand on end). There's also a nature part to the museum, with tarantulas and giant millipedes, and a human body section with presentations about the digestive system, the five senses, and the skeleton.

Opened in 1955, **Gulfarium** (1010 Miracle Strip Pkwy., Fort Walton Beach, 850/243-9046, 9am-4:30pm daily, closes earlier seasonally, $21.95 adults, $20.95 seniors, $13.95 children 3-12, children 2 and under free) was one of the country's original marine parks. Like a mini Sea World, it hosts Atlantic bottlenose dolphins, California sea lions, Peruvian penguins, Kemp's ridley turtles, and lots of

Eglin Air Force Base

Eglin Air Force Reservation in Fort Walton Beach is the largest air force base in the free world. It's the size of Rhode Island, covering 724 square miles of reservation and 97,963 square miles of water in the Gulf of Mexico. Eglin employs approximately 10,000 each of military personnel and civilians.

Unless you're in the military, much of it is off limits to you. Much of Eglin you wouldn't want to have access to if you could: The Mother of All Bombs (MOAB), the most powerful nonnuclear bomb ever created, was tested at Eglin. And for years Eglin Air Force Base has been testing depleted uranium (DU), with an estimated 220,000 pounds of DU penetrators expended there since 1973.

What is accessible to the public is much more fun. Eglin has **two 18-hole championship golf courses** (850/659-3080) open year-round. The Eglin Golf Course, host of a 2000 U.S. Open qualifier, has a hill on the seventh hole so steep that the course provides a towrope to golfers. Here's an interesting tidbit: Al Capone funded the layout of this course originally. In fact, Capone's private beach hideout house is now the officers' club at Eglin.

The **Air Force Armament Museum** (850/651-1808, 9am-5pm Mon.-Sat., free) is definitely a wonderful public part of Eglin, but it is just one of many opportunities for the visitor. The reservation covers 464,000 acres in Santa Rosa, Okaloosa, and Walton Counties. If you go to the **Jackson Guard** office (107 Hwy. 85 N., Niceville, 850/882-4164), you can get an outdoor recreation permit, a comprehensive map, and a list of regulations. This allows you to explore the area's many activities—hunting, fishing, primitive camping, canoeing, and hiking part of the **Florida National Scenic Trail** (www.floridatrail.org).

Hunting (which accounts for 4,200 of the 12,000 recreation permits granted annually) is for deer, turkey, wild hogs, and small game, seasonally. There's a huge managed quail area, another for "planted" doves, and two duck management units totaling 78,000 acres. There's even an annual hunt open to the mobility-impaired. Fishing in the reservation is on any of 17 stocked ponds (2 of them fully accessible).

Birders will enjoy the old-growth longleaf pine swath of Eglin reservation that is a designated part of the **Great Florida Birding Trail** (www.floridabirdingtrail.com). You may see the endangered Okaloosa darter, found in only six creek systems in the central portion of the air force base. It's also got the fourth-largest red-cockaded woodpecker population in the country. The area is home to more than 90 rare or listed plant and animal species.

Within the reservation there are seven miles of barrier island for swimming and canoeing, with lots of other creeks; enjoy open-water **kayaking** in the Choctawhatchee Bay, Santa Rosa Sound, or the Gulf.

The **Anderson Pond Recreation Area** (off Hwy. 85, 3 miles north of Niceville) is open to the public year-round, with an elevated boardwalk, a picnic shelter, a pier, and a camping area. All the facilities are fully accessible.

Gulf-focused educational marine exhibits. There are great dolphin shows with high jumps and soccer games, and a sweet sea lion show (they're not bad Frisbee players, considering the lack of opposable thumbs and all). For a fairly hefty fee ($150), guests can also have one-on-one interactions with the dolphins. The Gulfarium also sponsors the Dolphin Project, which focuses on interaction between dolphins and children with disabilities (like autism).

★ BIG KAHUNA'S WATER AND ADVENTURE PARK

Even adults get a little wide-eyed when they begin describing **Big Kahuna's Water and Adventure Park** (1007 U.S. 98 E., Destin, 850/837-8319, www.bigkahunas.com, 10am-6pm all summer, adventure park only with weekend hours in winter, $38 adults, $30 children and seniors, children 2 and under free), with more than 40 water attractions and an adventure park spread over 25 acres.

Clad in your bathing suit and a smile, you can wind through caves and waterfalls (the Tiagra Falls pumps 30,000 gallons of water per minute over 250 feet of mountain granite rock). There are three rivers, speed slides, body flumes, white-water tubing, leisurely lagoons, two wave pools, four children's areas with kid-size slides and variable-depth pools, and other exciting wet-and-wild attractions for kids of all ages. Then once you dry off, visit the attached Adventure Park attractions (be aware, it's a separate ticket price, and a steep one—it's cheaper if you get the combined all-day pass for, gulp, $57). There are 54 holes of miniature golf, a go-cart raceway, a bunch of other rides, and an arcade.

ENTERTAINMENT AND EVENTS
The Arts

The attractions on the Emerald Coast are mostly outdoors, where the sun, sand, and fish are. While art is not the largest draw for the Emerald Coast, it doesn't disappoint. The **Northwest Florida Ballet** (310 Perry Ave. SE, Fort Walton Beach, 850/664-7787) is the longest-running arts organization in northwest Florida, producing full-length semiprofessional ballets in a number of local venues, including summer ballet in the park and the requisite holiday performance of *The Nutcracker*. **Stage Crafters Community Theatre** (40 Robinwood Dr. SW, Fort Walton Beach, 850/243-1101, www.stagecrafters.com, 7:30pm, 2pm matinees, $20 musicals, $15 nonmusicals) is a small community troupe that puts on plays like the familiar *Godspell* and the unfamiliar *Meshuggah-Nuns*. The **Northwest Florida State College's Mattie Kelly Fine and Performing Arts Center** (100 College Blvd., Niceville, 850/729-6000, www.mattiekellyartscenter.org) stages community plays and hosts Broadway touring acts and other big ticket performers in its large 1,650-seat main theater, but also hosts dance, opera, the Northwest Florida Symphony Orchestra, and other arts events.

In visual arts, the **Arts & Design Society** (17 1st St. SE, Fort Walton Beach, 850/244-1271, www.artdesignsociety.org), founded in 1956 by a group of local artists, is more of a community art outreach, with classes, lectures, and children's programs, but it also hosts monthly local, regional, and national exhibits that are worth checking out.

Festivals

In the Destin area, there are annual events like the Spring Splash, the Billy Bowlegs Festival, the Sandestin Wine Festival, and the Christmas Boat Parade—but the biggest of them all is the monthlong **Destin Fishing Rodeo** (850/837-6734, www.destinfishingrodeo.org) in October. There are 30 different categories of prizes, with all saltwater game fish eligible—so you'll see people fishing all over the place with a vengeance. There's a more focused, single-species event in March and April with the annual Cobia Tournaments.

NIGHTLIFE

Destin and Fort Walton Beach can get lively, then it's quiet again to the east in the Beaches of South Walton area; still farther east in Panama City Beach it gets hopping again. Here, head dockside to **AJ's Club Bimini** (on the Destin Harbor, 0.25 mile east of the Destin Bridge, 116 Harbor Blvd., 850/837-1913, 11am-4am daily) for a Bimini Bash, a powerful concoction of cranberry, orange, and pineapple juices with a five-rum roundhouse punch. Then try out one of the theme nights at the sprawling **Nightown** (140 Palmetto St., Destin, 850/837-7625, www.nightown.com) and groove with the DJ. Or you could just stop in for a margarita at **Pepito's** (757 Harbor Blvd., Destin, 850/650-7734, until 4am daily), in front of the Destin Cinemas, or get crazy on the dance floor at **Harry T's** (46 Harbor Blvd., Destin, 850/654-4800, 11am-11pm Mon.-Fri.,10am-until closing Sat.-Sun.), which recently moved to the Harbor Walk village. Opened by a big-top trapeze artist, Harry T's is adorned with circus memorabilia, including a stuffed giraffe, and treasures from the sunken luxury liner *Thracia*. Then warm up with a few scales, because crowd participation is required at the dueling piano bar of **Howl at the Moon** (The Boardwalk, Okaloosa Island, 850/301-0111).

SHOPPING

Silver Sands Factory Stores (10562 Emerald Coast Pkwy. W, on U.S. 98, 8 miles east of Destin, near Sandestin Golf & Beach Resort, Destin, 850/654-9771, www.silversandsoutlet.com, 9am-9pm Mon.-Sat., 10am-7pm Sun.) is supposedly the nation's largest designer outlet center. And it keeps growing. Think Off Saks Fifth Avenue, Ann Taylor, Polo Ralph Lauren, Dooney & Bourke, Tommy Hilfiger, Ellen Tracy, Adrienne Vittadini, Banana Republic, Liz Claiborne, and the like. If shoes are your thing: Nine West Outlet, Famous Footwear, Liz Claiborne Shoes, Kenneth Cole, and Cole Haan. There are more than 100 designer outlet stores within 450,000 square feet of retail space, drawing something like six million shoppers annually.

FOOD

The restaurants of Destin, Fort Walton Beach, and Okaloosa Island tend to focus on fish, with lots of casual oyster bars and fish shacks.

There are upscale spots around, but the best places are the Southern-style casual seafood joints.

Breakfast

Start your day, and your visit, at the **Donut Hole** (635 U.S. 98 E., Destin, 850/837-8824, 6am-10pm daily, $4-12). It's breakfast all day, with sturdy baked goods and nice people.

Casual

The ★ **Back Porch** (1740 Scenic Hwy. 98 E., Destin, 850/837-2022, 11am-9pm daily, $10-25) is a fun, cedar-shingled seafood shack, an ideal place to try your first char-grilled amberjack. The view is great—you won't mind waiting because you can hang out right on the beach while they ready a table. Also, it's a notable surf spot, so you can watch surfers paddling out hopefully to the break.

AJ's Seafood and Oyster Bar (0.25 mile east of the Destin Bridge, Destin, 850/837-1913, 10am-11pm daily, 10am-9:30pm in the off-season, no reservations, $9-21) is another longtime waterfront favorite. Overlooking Destin Harbor, AJ's Club Bimini is the place to see the sunset over a plate of Oysters AJ (oysters baked with jalapeños, monterey jack, and bacon). AJ's charter fleet offers daily trips

AJ's Seafood and Oyster Bar overlooks Destin Harbor.

into shallow or deep waters to hunt for grouper, amberjack, and wahoo—the kitchen will cook your catch straight off the line. Try the fried fish sandwiches or the shrimp po'boy. Don't like fish? **Fudpucker's Beachside Bar & Grill** (20001 Emerald Coast Pkwy., Destin, 850/654-4200, 1318 Miracle Strip Pkwy., Okaloosa Island, Fort Walton Beach, 850/243-3833, www.fudpucker.com, 11am-10pm daily, $8-20) is the place for burgers, drinks on the deck, and some of the best bands on the beach.

In Fort Walton Beach, **The Crab Trap** (1450 Miracle Strip Pkwy., Okaloosa Island Boardwalk, Fort Walton Beach, 850/301-0959, 11am-9pm daily, $7-25), nestled in the beautiful James Lee County Park and overlooking the water, graciously accommodates the sand between your toes and your unmistakable whiff of suntan oil. Grouper, tuna, and amberjack are the freshest catches, with lots of fried seafood and all-you-can-eat snow-crab legs (they're not from around here, though). It's casual, but not as casual as the nearby **Angler's Beachside Grill and Sports Bar** (1030 Miracle Strip Pkwy., Okaloosa Island Boardwalk, Fort Walton Beach, 850/796-0260, 11am-9pm Mon.-Thurs., 11am-10pm Fri.-Sat., 10am-2pm Sun. for brunch, $7-20). You can eat right on the boardwalk or inside with all the games on big TVs.

Fine Dining

Some of the best food in the area is to be had from chef John Sallman at the ★ **Beach Walk Café** (Henderson Park Inn, 2700 U.S. 98 E., Destin, 850/650-7100, www.beachwalkcafe.com, 5: 30pm-11pm daily, $26-54). There is pecan-crusted grouper served over roasted and crisped potato cakes, and classic smoked-gouda shrimp and grits, just to name a few. It's one of the best fine-dining experiences in the area with a spectacular view of the Gulf of Mexico that just seems to make everything taste a little bit better.

Louisiana Lagniappe (775 Gulf Shore Dr., Holiday Isle, Destin, 850/837-0881, www.thelouisianalagniappe.com, 11am-9:30pm daily Mar.-Oct., no reservations, $15-26) overlooks Old Pass Lagoon and is a local favorite serving upscale Louisiana-style seafood, like pannéed fillet of grouper topped with lobster medallions, lightly covered with garlic beurre blanc. It traffics in live Maine lobsters and has a beautiful outdoor deck.

Marina Cafe (404 Harbor Blvd., Destin, 850/837-7960, www.marinacafe.com, 5pm-10pm daily, $17-28) is another special-occasion destination. It's owned by Harbor Restaurant Group, which also owns Destin Chops (a good steak and chop house not far away), with a second Chops location in Seacrest Beach. There's an outdoor dining deck overlooking the Destin Harbor, but inside seating is just as nice. The menu is all over the map, with Cajun/Creole dishes, a sushi bar, and Latin-inspired dishes like grilled Gulf fish tacos with tomató-cucumber salsa, and pan-seared grouper stuffed with lump crabmeat and served with a side of Creole succotash.

ACCOMMODATIONS
Under $100

Because of spring break maniacs, most of the hotels around here don't rent to people under 25 (unless they're with an "adult"). One of the good and bad things about the Destin area is that there aren't too many big hotels right on the beach. Most lodgings are just a bit of a drive. If you are looking for a quiet, independently owned place right at water's edge, try **Sea Oats Motel** (3420 Old U.S. 98 E., Destin, 850/837-6655, $85-160), which is a long, low-slung motel right on the sand, offering condo rentals as well.

If you're willing to hop in the car or on a bike to hit sand, there's the **Beachside Inn** (2931 Scenic U.S. 98, Destin, 888-232-2498, $85-180), with brightly colored rooms in a modest-size low-rise hotel. **Comfort Inn Destin** (19001 Emerald Coast Pkwy., Destin, 850/654-8611, $85-145) is fairly new and pretty deluxe for a Comfort Inn—no offense. It's got 100 rooms, nicely appointed, and two pools (one indoors).

$100-200

The **Best Western Summerplace Inn** (14047 Emerald Coast Pkwy., Destin, 850/650-8003, $110-150) is in the heart of Destin, a quick drive to public beach access. There's a decent complimentary continental breakfast, indoor and outdoor pools with a big whirlpool, and free high-speed Internet access.

$200-300

There are plenty of condos right on the beach, many only renting by the week in high season. The **Pelican Beach Resort and Conference Center** (1002 U.S. 98 E., Destin, 888/654-1425, $150-300, 2-night minimum much of the year) is a big, imposing cube. **Hidden Dunes Beach and Tennis Resort** (9815 U.S. 98 W., Destin, 850/654-1325, $130-600) has several ways to go, from a unit in a 20-story tower at water's edge, to luxurious three- and four-bedroom villas overlooking the private Hidden Dunes lake, to Carolina-style cottages with private screened porches, nestled in a wooded landscape. Farther east, into the Beaches of South Walton town of Seascape, the **Majestic Sun** (1160 Old U.S. 98, Miramar beach, 850/837-8264, $110-375) is a huge condo tower with beautiful pools, tennis, and golf, all just across the street from the

beach. **Sandpiper Cove** (775 Gulfshore Dr., Destin, 855/837-9121, www.sandpipercove. com, $170-320) is pretty much a Destin landmark, with a 43-acre landscaped property that has its own 1,100 feet of beach. These are individually owned (and decorated) condo units, so look at the pictures before deciding what's right for you. The property has five swimming pools and three outdoor hot tubs.

My favorite place to stay in the area is the **Henderson Park Inn Bed & Breakfast** (2700 Scenic U.S. 98, 866/398-4432, www. hendersonparkinn.com, $179-689), northwest Florida's only beachside bed-and-breakfast. Beyond the inn's lovely setting adjacent to the 208-acre Henderson Beach State Park, travelers are spoiled with tidbits like complimentary breakfast and lunch, nightly sunset glasses of wine and beer, an arrival wine and fruit assortment, evening turndown service with sweets, and a stocked kitchen pantry, all included in the room price. Guests also get complimentary use of water-sports equipment, high-speed Internet access, and beach service with chair and umbrella setup.

Vacation Rentals

If you want to rent a beach cottage or

Henderson Park Inn Bed & Breakfast

luxurious condominium, **Newman-Dailey Resort Properties** (12815 U.S. 98 W, Ste. 100, Destin, 850/837-1071 or 800/225-7652, www.destinvacation.com) is a well-regarded property management and vacation rental company that's been in the area for the past 22 years. The website offers virtual tours of properties.

GETTING THERE

U.S. 98 travels east-west along the Emerald Coast, edging the Gulf through Destin and Fort Walton Beach. Fort Walton Beach is 60 miles west of Panama City and 35 miles east of Pensacola. The beach of Fort Walton Beach is actually on Okaloosa Island, a barrier island at the southern end of Choctawhatchee Bay. Destin is about five miles east on U.S. 98 (sometimes called the Miracle Strip Parkway). To get to this area from the north, take U.S. 331 south, then take Highway 85 south at the Alabama/Florida line, straight into Destin and Fort Walton Beach. From I-10, exit onto Highway 85 south at the Fort Walton Beach exit.

The **Northwest Florida Regional Airport** (1701 Hwy. 85 N., on Eglin Air Force Base, 850/651-7160) is a small airport serviced by Delta Airlines, American Eagle, United, and Allegiant.

Beaches of South Walton

The Beaches of South Walton are fairly new. Obviously, the long expanses of white-sand beach have been here all along, but it's in the past 25 years that developers have set their sights on this area. Residents have kept a tight handle on growth—not out of a fear of change as much as a clear vision of how they'd like these communities to be. Some of it you may find contrived, like Disney for adults, but the idea of New Urbanism has taken hold with the creation and restoration of compact, mixed-use towns. Visitors have most of what they need within walking distance of where they're staying, and the Gulf of Mexico and Choctawhatchee Bay are soothing backdrops for a restful vacation.

Some of these 15 communities actually developed organically, while others were masterminded by architects and savvy developers. From west to east:

Seascape is the closest to Destin, with lakefront and golf villas in an upscale setting. **Miramar Beach** begins at the Gulf along Scenic Gulf Drive and then curves around to join Emerald Coast Parkway. It's mostly condos and private homes and is close to the Silver Sands Factory Stores. Next up is **Sandestin,** probably the most famous of these little communities, nearly overrun with enormous luxury golf/beach resorts, but all tasteful. The **Village of Baytowne Wharf** is here in the style of a wealthy but rustic Southern fishing village.

Dune Allen Beach is a quaint and quiet beach community two miles long with mostly classic wood-sided beach houses, homes on a lake, and smaller-size condo developments. This is where the area's eight-foot-wide, off-road bike path begins, winding all the way to Inlet Beach. Fairly developed, **Santa Rosa Beach** has a number of shops and commercial bits, with some golf and beachside amenities. There's a stylish outdoor mall here with boutiques, bike rentals, medical offices, antiques stores, a market, and a big handful of restaurants. Then there's **Blue Mountain Beach,** the highest point along the Gulf of Mexico; with wonderful views and beautiful sand, it has become attractive as an artists' retreat.

Grayton Beach is the oldest town between Pensacola and Apalachicola. Settled in the early 1900s, it is a tree-lined beach community of old cypress cottages and small narrow streets. There is a great bar called the Red Bar that you shouldn't miss, as well as many fine restaurants.

With Seaside to the east fully built out, builders turned not long ago to neighboring **WaterColor,** which is primarily a residential community. Many of the new stylized Cracker-style buildings are available for rent, and the town has a sleek hotel, the 60-room WaterColor Inn.

The next town over is **Seaside,** an upscale, planned beach community of pastel homes and cottages organized around a town square with an outdoor amphitheater, galleries, restaurants, and boutiques. You either love it, using words like "charming" and "picturesque," or you hate it and grumble words like "contrived" and "looks like a stage set" (which it technically was, as the shooting location for *The Truman Show*).

Seagrove Beach is next door to the newer and more fancy Seaside. This peaceful beach town is tucked between the coast's natural sand dunes and pine trees. Visitors can choose from rambling beach houses, cottages, or condos. The newest community, **WaterSound,** is one of the fanciest, with a resort that is plopped right against a pristine coastal dune lake. Then there's **Seacrest Beach,** a newish beach community made up of cottages and condominiums hidden behind natural dunes.

One of my more favorite communities is **Rosemary Beach.** Like Seaside, it's completely planned in a narrow architectural style, but this time it's all Caribbean-inspired homes connected to the shore by boardwalks and footpaths, with a town square and an exceptional eternity pool.

And finally, **Inlet Beach** is just west of Panama City Beach (over the bridge) and next to Rosemary Beach. Named for the large lagoon on its eastern shore, Phillips Inlet, the peaceful community is known for its secluded natural areas and minimal development.

SIGHTS
★ Seaside

It used to be that Americans retreated during the summers to simple beachside cottages for months at a time. Every day, after you got your sunburned hide up off the porch, you biked or walked into the little town center to take in a movie or get the local gossip and an ice cream. In 1946, J. S. Smolian bought 80 acres near Seagrove Beach on Florida's Panhandle with this vision floating in his mind—a utopian summer camp for his employees. His grandson, Robert Davis, was smitten by the same vision, growing up to become a fancy developer in Miami in the 1970s. Still, the sweet, multigenerational, seaside summer village eluded him. He infected Miami architects Andrés Duany and Elizabeth Plater-Zyberk with his gentle dream, and they built in their minds a fantasy town based on the northwest Florida architectural style of wood-frame cottages with peaked roofs, deep overhangs, and big windows for cross-ventilation. They traveled through Florida with sketchpads and eyes wide open.

Then they made it real in the early 1980s. They built a small town nestled against an idyllic curve along the Gulf Coast shoreline, against a wide swath of beach and mild emerald waters. There are 200 or so homes now, in a paradigm called New Urbanism, situated around a town square with an amphitheater, restaurants, elegant boutiques, a repertory theater, and the beach off at the edge of it all. There's also a much-lauded charter school, a chapel, and a medical arts building. It's a living laboratory—an experiment in harmonious beachside community life.

The kicker is that you can go to Seaside and visit. If you vacation here, you pull your car in, turn off the ignition, and that's the last you need of it for the duration. Everything is within walking distance in what *Time* magazine called "the most astounding design achievement of its era." Panama City is 40 miles to the east, Destin is 20 miles to the west—but Seaside seems miles and miles from anywhere.

SPORTS AND RECREATION
Beaches

Of the numerous beaches along the stretch, many have public beach access, with additional beach accesses located within the 14 beach communities if you're staying there. From west to east, most with access right along scenic Highway 30A, the beaches are Miramar Beach, Legion Park, Cessna Park (on the Choctawhatchee Bay side), Dune Allen Beach, Ed Walline, Gulfview Heights, Blue Mountain Beach, Grayton Dunes, Van Ness Butler Jr., Santa Clara, Inlet Beach, and Pier and Boat Ramp 331 (bay side). Which is the nicest is hard to say; most are sparsely populated, many have small, no-fee parking lots, and several have restrooms and showers. My favorite is probably **Santa Clara,** with a beautiful stretch of sand and picnic facilities, but the pristine windswept dunes of **Grayton Dunes** make a nice afternoon of exploration, too.

Parks and Recreation Areas

There's a large variety of outdoor activities, so bring your most comfortable hiking shoes. At the top of the list is **Grayton Beach State Park** (357 Main Park Rd., south of U.S. 98 halfway between Panama City Beach, near the intersection of Hwy. 30A and County Road 283, 850/267-8300, 8am-sundown daily, $5/vehicle, $2 pedestrian or bicyclist, $24-30 camping, cabin rental $110/day or $705/week), with sugar-white sand, emerald-green water, little development, and huge sea oat-covered sand dunes. Foot traffic is prohibited in the dunes and in bird-nesting areas. Despite its natural setting, there are great restaurants and accommodations in nearby Grayton Beach or Seaside. Camping is popular, with 37 campsites and 30 cabins. Make reservations early. Due to the number of endangered plants and animals found within the park (like the rare Choctawhatchee beach mouse), pets must be kept on a six-foot leash. If you visit in the fall, you may catch the thousands of monarch butterflies resting beachside during their southward migration to Mexico.

Identified as the most pristine piece of coastal property in the state, **Topsail Hill Preserve State Park** (7525 W. Hwy. 30A, in Santa Rosa Beach 10 miles east of Destin, 850/267-8330, 8am-sundown daily, honor $6/vehicle, $2 pedestrian or bicyclist, $42/night for RV camping, $24 tent camping, $100/night and $690/week for bungalows, $130/night for cabins) owes its existence to turpentine. More than a century ago, workers turpentined old-growth longleaf pine trees here for caulking the seams of wooden ships, a key mode of transport. Today, it features 1,600 acres of stunning Gulf-front pine forest, nature

the post office in Seaside

trails over mountainous sand dunes, and two freshwater dune lakes. It is one of only two remaining natural populations of the nocturnal, endangered Choctawhatchee beach mice. The park features a 140-acre RV resort as well as tent camping and nice bungalows to rent.

In the southernmost portion of Walton County, the 15,000-acre **Point Washington State Forest** (5865 E. U.S. 98, Santa Rosa Beach, 850/267-8325, 8am-sundown daily, $2/person, $20 reserved picnic space) is home to more than 19 miles of trails and boasts 10 different habitats with rare plant and wildlife species, from gopher tortoises to red-cockaded woodpeckers. For an easy day hike, try the Eastern Lake Trail System, the first trail established in this forest. It consists of three double-track loop trails. The hiker or bicyclist can travel the 3.5-, 5-, or 10-mile loops. Access to the trail system is at the parking lot and trailhead on County Road 395.

Nearby, and worth a stop to see, **Eden Gardens State Park** (181 Eden Gardens Rd., off U.S. 98 on County Road 395, just north of Seagrove Beach, 850/267-8320, 8am-sundown daily, honor $4/vehicle, guided tour $4 adults, $2 children), in historic Point Washington on the shore of Tucker Bayou, is a beautiful 1895 Greek Revival estate surrounded by gardens of azaleas, camellias, and large moss-draped live oak. This 12-acre sprawling park was once the home of lumber baron William Henry Wesley and his family. Find yourself a picnic spot on the wide, manicured lawn.

Just east of Seagrove Beach, **Deer Lake State Park** (6350 East County Rd. 30-A, Santa Rosa Beach, 850/267-8300, 8am-sundown daily, $3/vehicle, $2 pedestrian or bicyclist) is the newest park in these parts. It has an excellent beach with a dune walkover/boardwalk, from which there are great views of this dynamic dune ecosystem. North of here are acres of hiking trails worth exploring.

If you're interested in enjoying all this nature within the context of an ecotour or guided adventure, there are plenty of guides in the area. **Blue Sky Kayak Tours** (89 Lakeside Dr., Freeport, 850/368-3155)

Coastal Dune Lakes

Think about it for a second: When was the last time you saw a freshwater lake right up against a huge body of saltwater, just a little picturesque sea oat-fringed sand dune separating the two? It appears so gloriously natural that it's easy to overlook, but the Emerald Coast's coastal dune lakes are rare enough to be considered globally imperiled by the Florida Natural Areas Inventory. The 15 in Walton County have sister lakes in a few other spots along the Gulf Coast, then in New Zealand, Australia, and Madagascar. That's it.

These lakes were formed between 2,000 and 10,000 years ago. Coastal winds and flowing tides have kept these water havens safe, separated from the Gulf by ever-changing dune systems ranging 10-30 feet high. Intermittently, when they are swollen with rainwater, the lakes have little wandering fingers that empty out into the Gulf, meaning a canoe or kayak can paddle from freshwater to saltwater and back again without overland toting. These dune lake areas are also biologically diverse with fresh, estuarine, and marine all coexisting in this constant state of flux. Migrating birds are drawn to these coastal lakes as well.

Topsail Hill Preserve State Park has the densest concentration, with Morris, Campbell, and Stalworth Lakes as well as two minor unnamed coastal dune lakes on its property. For more information on the lakes at Topsail Hill Preserve State Park, contact Park Services specialist Leda C. Suydan at 850/267-0299 or Leda.Suydan@dep.state.fl.us.

offers guided tours in different local habitats. **Choctawhatchee Delta Tours** (710 Black Creek Rd., Freeport, 850/585-0445) also offers tours of this area, departing from the 331 Bridge. And **Big Daddy's Bike and Beach** (2217 Hwy. 30A, Santa Rosa Beach, 850/622-1165) offers bike rentals and ecotours on bike along Highway 30A and through a state forest area.

Seaside Swim & Tennis Club (394 Forest

St corner of Forest and Odessa Sts., 850/231-2284, 8am-4pm Mon.-Sat., 8am-2pm Sun.) is at the center of lots of the town's activities. It offers private tennis lessons and clinics for kids and adults, shuffleboard and horseshoes, bike rentals (including trikes), and three beautiful croquet courts. There are three pools—the West Side Pool is the largest, with an adult pool at the north end of Seaside Avenue and a family pool at the northeast corner of Seaside. **Camp Seaside** is a special program for kids 5-12, with half-day or full-day crafts, sports, swimming, and other activities. It also offers a kids' night out, with dinner and a movie, and regularly scheduled free storytime in the amphitheater.

Beyond that, Seaside has nearby golf, a long biking/walking path, deep-sea fishing, hiking, kayaking, and swimming in the Gulf to keep everyone occupied.

★ Biking Along Scenic Route 30A

The **Timpoochee Trail** is one of the longest and most widely used paths in Walton County. The 19-mile, paved trail winds through 9 of the 14 distinctive beach communities, traversing state recreational areas, state parks, dunes, and coastal dune lakes. Named after Timpoochee Kinnard, the most influential chief of the Euchee Indians, the path runs along Scenic Highway 30A parallel to the Gulf of Mexico. From migrating flocks of birds to blooming wildflowers and trees, the Timpoochee Trail is full of surprises all year long. Hop off the bike for an ice cream. Rent a bike with a basket and pick up some groceries for dinner along the way—a paperback from Sundog Books, maybe a bottle of wine for the sunset.

This is road or touring bike territory. For the mountain biker, there is also a 10-mile loop in the Point Washington State Forest called the **Eastern Lake Bike/Hike Trail,** which winds through natural vegetation and wildlife habitat. A newer stretch of trail goes to Seagrove, or go in the opposite direction for a scenic ride from Seaside to Blue Mountain Beach.

And then there's the **Longleaf Pine Greenway System** (850/231-5800), interlaced through several state parks and forests, with eight miles of trails through different terrain from the Gulf to Choctawhatchee Bay. Most bike shops will equip you with maps of the different cycling possibilities in the area.

Depending on where you're staying, there are several convenient bike rental

a coastal dune lake near Grayton Beach State Park

shops. From west to east: **Seaside Transit Authority Bike Rentals** (87 Central Sq., Seaside, 850/231-0035, $30/day, $65/5 days), **Butterfly Bike & Beach Rentals** (3657 E. Hwy. 30A, Seagrove Beach, 850/231-2826, with Caloi off-road bikes), and **Bamboo Beach & Bicycle Company** (50 N. Barrett Sq., Rosemary Beach, 850/231-0770, $15/day, $45/3 days, $65/week, children's bikes $10/day, $30/3 days, $50/week).

Fishing

Baytowne Marina at Sandestin is a good place to start. **Baytowne Bait and Tackle Store** (Sandestin, 850/267-7777) provides basic boating necessities, and it's a good place to hook up with a fishing guide. Similarly, **Old Florida Outfitters** (WaterColor, 850/534-4343), an Orvis-endorsed guide program, is a great source for specialized fishing charters, located in WaterColor's Town Center.

Not A Dog Charters (850/267-2514, www.notadogcharters.com) heads out from Grayton Beach; after a short boat ride you'll be bottom fishing for red snapper, grouper, and triggerfish, or trolling for king mackerel. In the spring, the target is cobia right along the beach. **Yellow Fin Ocean Sports** (850/231-9024) in Grayton will take you

fishing for redfish or trout in coastal bays or head out into the Gulf for grouper, snapper, dolphin, or marlin. **Dead Fish Charters** (174 WaterColor Way, #280, Seagrove Beach, 850/685-1092, www.deadfishcharters.com) specializes in Indian Pass half- or full-day trips, and inshore grouper and snapper trips in Grayton Beach.

SHOPPING

Shopping is clustered in a handful of tasteful centers along the Beaches of South Walton. The **Market Shops at Sandestin** (9375 U.S. 98 W. at Sandestin Golf & Beach Resort, 850/837-3077) complex has 30 shops, split between kitchenware, skin care, chocolates, housewares, and more. The **Shops of Grayton** (26 Logan Ln., Grayton Beach) are not as upscale, and here you'll find jewelry, clothing, and antiques. In Seaside there is **Ruskin Place Artist Colony** near the new Seaside Chapel and the rest of the 40 or so **Merchants of Seaside** (63 Central Sq., 850/231-5424) for cafés, galleries, clothing, books, and gifts. Head to the Beaches of South Walton, especially Seaside, if you're looking for art. This area is increasingly a hotbed of independent art galleries.

Ruskin Place, named after John Ruskin, the

the lake at Topsail Hill Preserve State Park

famous supporter of 19th-century art, is the town's center for galleries, with a good coffee shop and a few other diversions. There are plenty of shops worth a bit of exploration in Seaside, but definitely check out the vessels, chandeliers, sinks, and other blown-glass art of **Fusion Art Glass** (55 Central Sq., 850/231-5405, www.fusionartglass.com). **Sundog Books** (89 Central Sq., 850/231-5481) is a great place in the area to spend a few hours. The current fiction is always in stock, along with plenty of art and design books.

FOOD

All of the little communities of South Walton have their own cluster of restaurants, in a range of price points and culinary traditions. A few I would recommend include ★ **Bud and Alley's Restaurant** (2236 E. Hwy. 30A Santa Rosa Beach, 850/231-5900, lunch 11:30am-3pm daily, dinner 5:30pm-10pm daily, rooftop bar 11:30am-2am daily, $20-28), which opened in Seaside in 1986 and is actually named after a dog and a cat. It's an upscale yet casual and unpretentious place, with a cooking style that nods to the coastal Mediterranean, Basque country, Tuscany, and the American Deep South. Oysters Seaside are baked Apalachicola beauties with shrimp,

scallops, calamari, cilantro, garlic, and lime, and there are tempura-fried soft-shell crabs with rémoulade, or heads-on shrimp with garlic and shallots. The bar has an extensive wine list and is a great spot for conversation with the locals.

Chef Jim Shirley brings his brand of Southern cooking to Seaside at the **Great Southern Café** (83 Central Sq., Seaside, 850/231-7327, 8am-9:30pm daily, $10-28). The menu's regional flair includes Gulf shrimp, Apalachicola oysters, and traditional Southern vegetables. It seems like no one talks about the Great Southern Café without mentioning the Grits a Ya Ya, one of the most-ordered dishes, which offers seasoned shrimp in smoked gouda cheese grits topped with cream gravy, bacon, spinach, and mushrooms. **Dawson's Yogurt** (121 Central Sq., Seaside, 850/231-4770, 10am-9pm Sun.-Thurs., 10am-10pm Fri.-Sat.) is the place to indulge in your choice of over 20 flavors of yogurt. The Kahlua fudge is a favorite.

Cafe Thirty-A (3899 E. Hwy. 30A, Seagrove, 850/231-2166, 5pm-10pm daily, $12-34) is another upscale spot, with a large wine list, many selections by the glass. The menu has broad appeal, with dishes such as wood oven-roasted grouper served with baby

There are plenty of bike rental shops along Scenic 30A.

tiger shrimp and risotto in a sweet carrot sauce or maple barbecue pork chop with fried peaches and corn mashed potatoes on the side. I'm pretty content just to slice up one of the Hawaiian-style wood-fired pizzas.

Next there's **Basmati's Asian Cuisine** (3295 W. Hwy. 30A, Blue Mountain Beach, 850/267-3028, lunch 11am- 2:30pm Mon.-Fri., dinner 5pm-10pm daily, $9-28) with a full sushi bar and mostly Japanese fusion dishes served in a beautiful dining room and a nice sheltered deck.

In the Village of Baytowne Wharf, you've got **Graffiti's & The Funky Blues Shack** (109 Cannery Ln., Sandestin, 850/424-6650, 5pm-2am daily, dining 5pm-10pm, $12-23), a folk art-infused restaurant and live blues venue, or **New Orleans Creole Cookery** (Village of Baytowne Wharf, Sandestin, 850/351-1885, 11am-9pm Sun.-Thurs., 11am-10pm Fri.-Sat., $15-30)—if you've got the Nola jones, head here, especially for the barbecued shrimp and Creole bread pudding.

For breakfast, top honors go to Rosemary Beach's **Wild Olives Market** (104 N. Barrett Sq., Rosemary Beach, 850/231-0065, 11am-9pm Tues.-Sun.) or **Summer Kitchen** (60 N. Barrett Sq., Rosemary Beach, 850/231-6264, 7:30am-9pm daily) for pastries and egg dishes.

Locals have been flocking to **Wine World** (WaterColor Town Center, 850/231-1323, 10am-9pm daily), a low-key neighborhood wine, beer, and cheese shop that also serves a fine selection of coffees, pizzas, paninis, and tapas. It's right in WaterColor Market in the heart of Town Center, an easy place to hang out and enjoy the effects of a relaxing beach vacation.

ACCOMMODATIONS
Resorts and Vacation Rentals

The **Hilton Sandestin Beach Golf Resort & Spa** (4000 Sandestin Blvd. S., Destin, 850/267-9500, www.sandestinbeachhilton.com, $189-450) is a beautiful golf-and-spa resort of 598 rooms, the largest beachfront resort hotel in the northwest Florida region. There are 190 spacious standard guest rooms, 22 parlor suites, two presidential suites, and 385 junior suites that feature bunk beds with portholes in the sides for a nautical style and a private gaming system that kids will appreciate. The hotel has an award-winning program for children, with accessible on-site dining at Sandcastles Restaurant & Lounge, which has a great breakfast buffet. There's also a fancier restaurant called Seagar's Prime Steaks & Seafood that has a long sushi bar lining the

Sandestin offers a long stretch of accommodations along the coast.

Sandestin Golf & Beach Resort

for vacation rentals. All designed in a loose Caribbean style, there are family cottages, carriage houses, flats, and contemporary lofts, all connected to the shore by boardwalks and footpaths. It's a good location for families, because it's farther east than many of the communities, and thus closer to the liveliness of Panama City Beach but still out of the fray.

The **Sandestin Golf & Beach Resort** (9300 Emerald Coast Pkwy. W., Sandestin, 850/267-8000, $172-450) is the premier resort in this area, set on 2,400 beach- and bayfront acres. There are four championship golf courses, 15 world-class tennis courts, a full-service marina, water sports, charter sailing and fishing, fine and casual dining, a fancy fitness center, a professional salon and day spa, and fun children's programs. If you want to improve your game, professional golf and tennis trainers on-site use the most advanced swing analysis technology available. It's got 1,350 different rooms and accommodations, with a range of options—it's kind of like a little city unto itself, with leisure as the central preoccupation.

The **Village of Baytowne Wharf** (9300 Emerald Coast Pkwy. W., Sandestin, 850/267-8000, $180-800) is a sweeping pedestrian village right on the beach that rents its own accommodations. There are different choices on where to stay, grouped into five resort areas: Beachfront, Beachside, Village, Bayside, and Dockside. Each of the five Florida resorts offers a unique flavor, as well as a range of rates. Included with a stay at any of the resort accommodations options are free kayak, canoe, and bike rentals. The resort is also the host of many area festivals including the Sandestin Wine Festival and, my favorite, the Baytowne Beer Festival. They are also starting to host outdoor concerts with large nationally recognized acts. When I was there, Vince Gill was performing on the grounds of the resort, so make sure to check the events calendar on the website to see what's on the agenda.

To **rent a cottage at Seaside,** you need only to call 888/541-0801. The tricky part comes in figuring out what you want—people

back. The wine room located in the front of the restaurant is separated from the rest of the dining room and doubles as an intimate and private dining room. You can reserve the space for a small party or couple and hold your special occasion in a romantic setting surrounded by racks of the wine bottles.

So many of the nicer accommodations around here are private homes or condos. There are numerous property management companies—the **Beach Rental of South Walton** website (www.brswvacations.com) is a good place to start surfing for what you want. It's divided by community, specializing in the more affordable ones. Many of the swankier communities have their own websites with rental information and slide shows (www.rosemarybeach.com, www.seasidefl. com). My favorite is definitely ★ **Rosemary Beach** (on Hwy. 30A, in between Seacrest and Inlet Beach, 850/278-2030, www.rosemary-beach.com, roughly $200-500/night, but many rentals are by the week), with one- to five-bedroom Gulf-front and midtown cottages have built their dream homes in Seaside, and the prices, styles, and sizes are all over the map. There are more than 200 homes and cottages. It offers 400 individual accommodations, including private homes, cottages, luxury town houses, penthouses, and beachfront hideaways.

Camping

The only way to slide in under $50 around here is by camping—it's warm much of the year, with nice evening breezes, lots of beach, plenty of fresh air, and not so rural that you can't go out for dinner. One of the best places in the area to camp is located in the town of Grayton Beach near Seaside at **Grayton Beach State Park** (357 Main Park Rd., south of U.S. 98 halfway between Panama City Beach and Destin, near the intersection of Hwy. 30A and County Road 283, 850/267-8300, 8am-sundown daily, $5/vehicle, $2/pedestrian or bicyclist, $24-30 camping, cabin rental $110/day or $705/week). The campground has 34 sites accommodating tents and RVs and is located right on the Gulf of Mexico among trees and dunes. It has restrooms, electricity, and hot showers to rinse away those hours of swimming and wading in the salty warm waters of the Gulf of Mexico before you roast some marshmallows over an open fire with the waves of the Gulf lapping in the background.

In Sandestin you can camp on the Gulf at **CampGulf RV Park and Campground** (10005 W. Emerald Coast Pkwy., Destin, 850/226-7485, campsites $55-180, cabins $100-300), with an activity center, fishing, cable TV, and full hookups. **Destin RV Beach Resort** (362 Miramar Beach Dr., Destin, 850/837-3529) is hands-down the nicest RV campground I have come across. The owners call it a "luxury RV resort." It is right across from the beach, with a swimming pool and a free deep-sea fishing trip with a paid stay.

You can also camp at **Topsail Hill Preserve State Park** (7525 W. Hwy. 30A, in Santa Rosa Beach 10 miles east of Destin, 850/267-8330, 8am-sundown daily, $6/vehicle, $2 pedestrian or bicyclist, $42/night RVs and $24 tents, $100/night and $690/week for

the Village of Baytowne Wharf

bungalows, $130/night and $850/week for cabins) at the Topsail Hill Gregory E. Moore RV Resort, which has the highest possible rating from *Trailer Life* and Woodall's, placing it in the top 1 percent of RV campgrounds in the nation. The campground has a stunning 156 RV sites with electricity, sewer, water, and cable. It also offers 22 tent sites with electricity. The park has a swimming pool, bathrooms, hot showers, and a camp store with water, other drinks, snacks, and camping items. A tram will give you a lift to the beach. It's definitely more set up for RV enthusiasts, but it's a good place to tent camp as well if there aren't any sites left at Grayton Beach State Park.

GETTING THERE

The Beaches of South Walton communities are about 35 miles west of Panama City Beach, along Highway 30A (also called Scenic 30A and Scenic Gulf Coast Drive). Highway 30A splits off from U.S. 98 just before Highway 393 in the west and right after Panama City Beach in the east.

Information and Services

The Emerald Coast area is located within the **central time zone.** The area code is **850.**

TOURIST INFORMATION

The Panama City **News Herald** is the daily around here, but its parent company, Halifax Media Group, also operates the **Northwest Florida Daily News,** the **Destin Log,** the **Walton Sun,** and www.emeraldcoast.com.

To get tourist information, there are several different locations, depending on where your home base is. For Destin and Fort Walton Beach information, visit the **Emerald Coast Convention & Visitors Bureau** (1540 E. U.S. 98, Fort Walton Beach, 850/651-7131, www.emeraldcoastfl.com). There's also the **South Walton Tourist Development Center** (25771 U.S. 331 at U.S. 98, Santa Rosa Beach, 850/267-1216, 8am-5pm daily) and the **Destin Area Chamber of Commerce** (4484 Legendary Dr. at U.S. 98, 850/837-6241, 8:30am-5pm Tues.-Fri.).

For information about the Beaches of South Walton area in advance of your trip, contact the **Beaches of South Walton Tourist Development Council** (P.O. Box 1248, Santa Rosa Beach, FL 32459, 800/822-6877, www.visitsouthwalton.com).

In Panama City Beach, visit the **Panama City Beach Convention & Visitors Bureau** (17001 Panama City Beach Pkwy., 850/233-5070, www.visitpanamacitybeach. com, 8am-5pm daily) for brochures, maps, and information about attractions and accommodations.

POLICE AND EMERGENCIES

In an emergency, dial 911. For a nonemergency police need, call or visit the **Fort Walton Beach Police Department** (7 Hollywood Blvd., Fort Walton Beach, 850/833-9546) or the **Panama City Beach Police Department** (17110 Firenzo Ave., Panama City Beach, 850/233-5000).

In the event of a medical emergency, stop into **Sacred Heart Hospital on the Emerald Coast** (7800 U.S. 98 W., Miramar Beach, 850/278-3000) in the western part of the Emerald Coast; in the eastern part, go to **Bay Medical Center** (615 N. Bonita Ave., Panama City, 850/769-1511).

RADIO AND TELEVISION

There's lots of music radio in this area, heavy on rock and pop for all those spring breakers. **Beach 99.9 FM** is oldies, **94.5 FM** is talk radio, **92.5 FM** has country, **Sunny 98.5 FM** is soft rock, and **93.5 FM** is urban.

And on the television, there are two local ABC affiliates, **WMBB Channel 13** out of Panama City and **WEAR Channel 3** out of Pensacola. The CBS affiliate is **WCTV Channel 6** out of Tallahassee, the PBS affiliate is **WFSG Channel 56** out of Panama City, and the NBC affiliate is **WJHG Channel 7** out of Panama City.

LAUNDRY SERVICES

Laundry options are at their best in Panama City Beach. There's **Flamingo Beach Laundry** (7922 Front Beach Rd., 850/234-6186) or **EBR Laundry** (11309 Hutchinson Blvd., 850/235-4077).

Pensacola

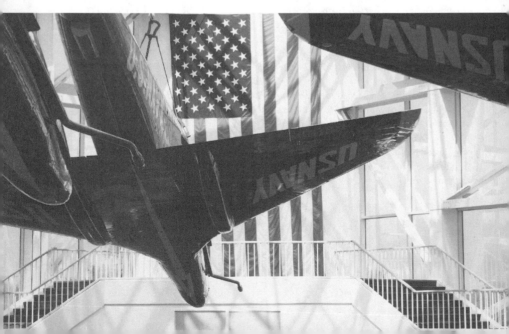

Pensacola is a picture-perfect beach retreat with deep turquoise waters and fine, white sand. Although it's more widely known as a summer vacation destination, the city is also rich in culture, having seen five flags—of Spain, France,

England, the Confederacy, and the United States of America—flown at different historic moments in the past four centuries.

The city and the popular beach that sits on the barrier island of Santa Rosa are both much more casual than most areas along the Gulf Coast. There are plenty of upscale resorts and restaurants, but they seem to find a common thread with a laid-back, informal style that leaves pretentiousness behind and has managed to retain much of the Old Florida charm that has been lost in many of the cities and beaches to the south. Pensacola is much more Southern in manner than most of the areas to the south.

In Pensacola you will find the hospitality that you often associate with the South and food that is a unique blend of flavors inspired by a convergence of coastal American, Spanish, and Cajun cultures. You're just as likely to find menus offering deep-fried mullet with coleslaw, hush puppies, and a tall glass of sweet tea as you are grilled grouper with a mango sauce served with a side of black beans and rice or a bowl of spicy New Orleans gumbo with a tray of raw oysters.

And then there are the beaches. Some are developed, fun, tourist spots such as Pensacola Beach; others are more uninhabited. The Gulf Islands National Seashore cuts through this area, a 150-mile-long, discontinuous string of undeveloped barrier islands that begins at Santa Rosa Island and extends into Mississippi. Santa Rosa Island contains seven beautiful, undeveloped miles of beach, with clear water, white sandy beaches, lots of fish and wildlife, and fewer people crowding the pristine shores.

Pensacola also has a strong military presence. It is the site of numerous important forts as well as Eglin Air Force Base and the Naval Air Station Pensacola, the launching point for the flight training of every American naval aviator, naval flight officer, and enlisted

---

Previous: Pensacola Beach; National Museum of Naval Aviation. **Above:** the historic Pensacola Beach sign.

Look for ★ to find recommended
sights, activities, dining, and lodging.

Highlights

★ **Pensacola Beach and Fishing Pier:**
With miles of beautiful coastline and the longest
pier on the Gulf of Mexico, the festive, action-
packed Pensacola Beach is a can't-miss. And you
don't need a fishing license to wet a line on the
pier (page 329).

★ **Gulf Islands National Seashore:**
This protected area has miles of delicate beach
habitat along Santa Rosa Island, as well as Fort
Pickens and other historic sights (page 330).

★ **Tubing on Coldwater Creek:** In the
warmer months, rent tubes and catch a bus
shuttle with Adventures Unlimited for a refreshing journey down Coldwater Creek (page 333).

★ **Historic Pensacola Village:** Stop off
for sustenance at the Seville Quarter's Rosie
O'Grady's before heading on to the cluster of
18th- and 19th-century museums and homes
(page 335).

★ **National Museum of Naval Aviation:**
Find out why Pensacola is called the Cradle
of Naval Aviation at this vast and spectacular
museum (page 339).

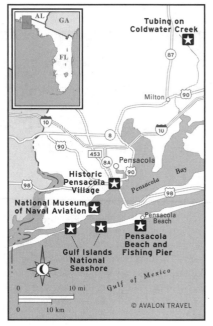

aircrew. Because of this, Pensacola is often called the Cradle of Naval Aviation. The free National Museum of Naval Aviation, the third largest in the world, showcases the history of aviation through indoor and outdoor exhibits.

HISTORY

Pensacola has a long history. Native Americans left pottery shards and artifacts in the gentle coastal dunes here centuries before Tristán de Luna arrived with his fellow Spaniards in 1559. Tristán de Luna was the first to attempt a settlement in Pensacola, but violent hurricanes uprooted his effort and sent the Spanish sailing around the peninsula to St. Augustine, where they established North America's first European settlement. Even after this first exploratory settlement didn't take, Pensacola was still settled by Europeans early on. It was one of a handful of colonial period communities in the southeastern United States, its Seville Historic District one of the oldest and most intact in all of Florida. Within this small neighborhood is Old Christ Church, Florida's oldest church still standing in one place (1832), and St. Michael's Cemetery, deeded to Pensacola by the king of Spain in 1822. A walk through Historic Pensacola Village will give you insight into the area's history.

PLANNING YOUR TIME

The best way to explore Pensacola is with a car, but you can get by with community transportation and taxis if you are planning on spending most of your time downtown and in the Pensacola Beach areas. If you want to use Pensacola as a home base and satellite out to the surrounding attractions, then you will want to rent a car. The Pensacola area is fairly spread out. The most popular area for accommodations is Pensacola Beach. Downtown Pensacola and the Perdido Key area come in a close second, with the downtown being more historical in nature with several excellent bed-and-breakfasts and hotels, and the beaches having mostly chains and high-rise condos to choose from. As on most of the Panhandle, high season is April-August. The value season runs roughly August-March. Regardless of when you'd like to visit, make reservations in advance. Visitors at the naval base tend to fill the hotels nearest it. The greater Pensacola area can easily occupy you for three or four days with its historical attractions, beaches, and nature parks. If you want to really explore all the great beaches in the area, then plan for a week, two if you want to spend an extensive amount of time fishing, paddling, or generally sightseeing in Perdido, Gulf Shores, and Dauphin Island to the west or the forests, creeks, and rivers to the north. If you fly into Pensacola and rent a car, think about tacking on a couple of extra days to explore the Emerald Coast area just to the east.

For camping, head to the Gulf Islands National Seashore at Fort Pickens just west of Pensacola Beach, north to the Blackwater area around Brewton, and west Big Lagoon State Park around Perdido. All of these areas offer excellent paddling, fishing, and hiking as well. The epicenter for fishing is in Pensacola Beach and the marinas surrounding the downtown areas, where most of the fishing charters run daily trips into offshore fishing spots. A favorite of serious anglers is a charter out to the *Oriskany*, an aircraft carrier that was sunk 24 miles offshore and is now utilized as an artificial reef and recreational dive spot.

I-10 is the main east-west interstate into the city with I-110 jutting out to the south and bringing visitors into the heart of downtown Pensacola. U.S. 98 primarily serves the beaches and connects the popular coastal areas of the region, while County Road 3999 or Via De Luna Drive serves as the main thoroughfare for Santa Rosa Island, the barrier island where Pensacola Beach, the Gulf Islands National Seashore, and Navarre Beach are located. The best beaches in the area include the stretch of Gulf Islands National Seashore between Pensacola Beach and Navarre, Casino Beach where you find the Pensacola Beach Gulf Fishing Pier, and the beaches at Big Lagoon State Park in Perdido.

Pensacola

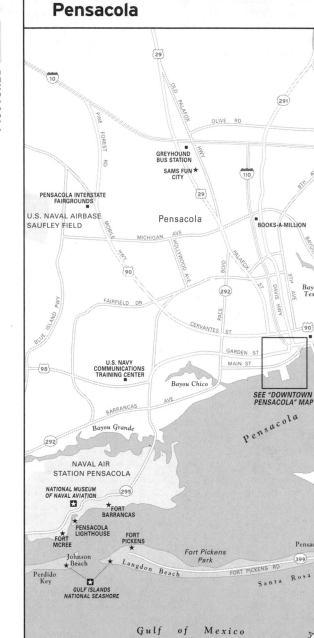

To Tallahassee

Escambia Bay

GREYHOUND BUS STATION
SAMS FUN CITY ★

PENSACOLA INTERSTATE FAIRGROUNDS

U.S. NAVAL AIRBASE SAUFLEY FIELD

Pensacola

BOOKS-A-MILLION

PENSACOLA REGIONAL AIRPORT

OLD PALAFOX HWY

OLIVE RD

PINE FOREST RD

MOBILE HWY

MICHIGAN AVE

HOLLYWOOD AVE

PALAFOX ST

BLVD

DAVIS HWY

9TH AVE

BAYOU BLVD

SCENIC HWY

9TH AVE

Bayou Texar

FAIRFIELD DR

CERVANTES ST

PACE

GARDEN ST

MAIN ST

PENSACOLA VISITORS INFORMATION CENTER

U.S. NAVY COMMUNICATIONS TRAINING CENTER

Bayou Chico

BLUE ISLAND PWY

BARRANCAS AVE

Bayou Grande

SEE "DOWNTOWN PENSACOLA" MAP

Pensacola

Bay

PENSACOLA BAY BRIDGE

NAVAL AIR STATION PENSACOLA

Naval Live Oaks Park

NAVAL LIVE OAKS VISITORS CENTER ■

NATIONAL MUSEUM OF NAVAL AVIATION

Gulf Breeze

To Panama City

BOB SIKES BRIDGE (TOLL)

★ FORT BARRANCAS

PENSACOLA LIGHTHOUSE

FORT MCREE ★

FORT PICKENS ★

Johnson Beach

Perdido Key

GULF ISLANDS NATIONAL SEASHORE

Fort Pickens Park

Langdon Beach

FORT PICKENS RD

Pensacola Beach

PEG LEG PETE'S

PARADISE INN

Santa Rosa Island

MARGARITAVILLE BEACH HOTEL

PENSACOLA BEACH AND FISHING PIER

Casino Beach

Gulf of Mexico

0   2 mi

0   2 km

© AVALON TRAVEL

Sports and Recreation

BEACHES

The long stretch of the **Gulf Islands National Seashore** and the **Naval Air Station Pensacola** and **Eglin Air Force Base** farther east have imposed restrictions on commercial growth. The communities in the area set quotas on density and height restrictions on new construction. Thus, the more urban beachfront areas around Pensacola aren't littered with high-rise condos and resort hotels, and there's another six miles of utterly preserved seashore in the park.

Perdido Key is the westernmost island in the long chain of barrier islands that line the Panhandle's edge, an island that Florida shares with the state of Alabama. The developed beach areas are called **Orange Beach** and **Johnson Beach,** and the more natural part is **Perdido Key State Park** (15301 Perdido Key Dr., 15 miles southwest of Pensacola, off Hwy. 292, 850/492-1595, 8am-sundown daily, $3 honor system for beach, $4 for main park). These beaches provide some of the best swimming in the state—warm, clear water, gentle surf, long stretches of shallows. **Big Lagoon State Park** (12301 Gulf Beach Hwy., 15 miles southwest of Pensacola, off Hwy. 292, 850/492-1595, 8am-sundown daily, $6/vehicle, $2 pedestrians and bicyclists, $10 boat launch fee for 1 person and 1 boat, $12 for 2-8 people with boat, $20 camping) is just across the bay from Perdido Key and offers tent, camp trailer, and RV sites. The secluded beaches at Big Lagoon State Park are excellent for fishing the flats or just relaxing on the shore of the lagoon's calm waters.

Santa Rosa Island, just to the east, is one of the longest barrier islands in the world, stretching 50 miles from Pensacola Bay on its western side to Choctawhatchee Bay to its east. All the beaches along this stretch of coast have exceptionally beautiful white quartz sand.

For beach sports gear rentals stop by

Innerlight Surf and Skate (655 Pensacola Beach Blvd., 850/934-9004). They rent surfboards and paddleboards ($15/hour, $30 for 3 hours, $45 for 10 hours, $60 per day), kayaks ($25/hour, $45 for 3 hours, $60 for 10 hours, $75 per day). If you're new to surfing, consider getting a lesson with an experienced wave rider ($55 1-hour private lesson, $45 1-hour semiprivate, $35 for an hour with a group of 10 or more) before shredding the surf in the Gulf.

★ Pensacola Beach and Fishing Pier

Pensacola Beach (Pensacola Beach Visitors Information Center, 800/635-4803) itself covers much of the island, with restaurants, shops, and entertainment at their highest density near the **Pensacola Beach Fishing Pier**—at 1,471 feet long and 30 feet above the water, the pier is second behind the new Gulf Pier at Gulf State Park measuring 1,540 feet long. Crossing the two bridges from Pensacola to Santa Rosa Island, you'll be on Pensacola Boulevard—it splits left and right, but directly in front of you is Pensacola Beach. The area is rich with water-sport possibilities: parasailing, sailboarding, deep-sea fishing, Jet Skiing, and scuba diving. Pensacola Beach is open to the public, accessible by car or by ECAT bus or trolley. The fishing pier is open to the public 24 hours a day and costs $1.25 to walk on, $7.50 for adults to fish, children under six are free; you're likely to catch flounder, bonita, Spanish and king mackerel, and cobia. From its end you're likely to spot dolphins, sea turtles, and the occasional manatee. If you've arrived unprepared, you can buy bait and rent fishing gear at the pier ($7 for rods, $6 for carts, coolers, nets, and gaffs).

At the corner of Pensacola Boulevard and Fort Pickens Road, which goes to the west, is **Casino Beach.** It is the heart of Pensacola Beach, named for an old beachside casino resort from 1933. The casino is long gone, but its beach ball water tank is still the beach's landmark. Casino Beach is home to the huge brick Gulfside Pavilion, site of numerous free concerts and events over the years. The beach has picnic tables, restrooms, restaurants, and souvenir shops. And just past the tollbooth onto the island, **Quietwater Beach,** on the Santa Rosa Sound side, is a gentle, shallow beach great for kids.

★ Gulf Islands National Seashore

The **Gulf Islands National Seashore** (850/934-2622, $7/person or $15/vehicle for 7-day pass) has numerous beaches along Santa Rosa Island. At its westernmost edge is **Fort Pickens Park,** maintained by the National Park Service. The road is located in a sensitive habitat for nesting sea turtles and colonial shorebirds, so be sure not to park along the sandy shoulder. This will also help you avoid getting your vehicle stuck and keep you from getting a park ranger-administered ticket.

Historic Fort Pickens is open for self-guided tours during daylight hours only. The fishing pier is open, and the Fort Pickens campground has 200 campsites equipped with water and electricity for $22 per night. Campers have access to running water,

grills, picnic tables, and bathrooms with cold showers. Boaters planning to camp can unload their passengers and gear near Battery Langdon on the bay side of the island and west of the Ranger Station dock and hike on the bike path or Fort Pickens Road to Loop A.

The J. Earle Bowden Way (Hwy. 399) on Santa Rosa Island connects Pensacola Beach with Navarre Beach.

Within the Fort Pickens area is another beach called **Langdon Beach,** which has picnic tables, restrooms, and outdoor showers. The scenic bike path, going from Langdon Beach all the way to the fort, has been restored, as have the Dune Nature Trail and the Blackbird Marsh Nature Trail.

Also part of Gulf Islands National Seashore, **Opal Beach** is three miles east of Pensacola Beach. It is generally less populated than Pensacola Beach, offering restrooms, showers, and picnic pavilions, and is a great stop for hikers and bikers taking in the beautiful dune landscape between Pensacola Beach and Navarre Beach on the Seashore Trail or the South Santa Rosa Loop Trail. The Opal Beach area can also be reached by motorists via Highway 399, which runs parallel to the multiuse trail through the national seashore. From Pensacola Beach, drive east toward

Pensacola Beach Fishing Pier

Fast Times

Addicted to speed? Pensacola has a couple of ways to scratch that itch. **Five Flags Speedway** (7451 Pine Forest Rd., on Hwy. 297 a mile south of exit 7 on I-10, 850/944-8400, www.5flagsspeedway.com, dates and times vary, $10-20) was built in 1956, one of the oldest established short track racetracks still in existence. A high-banked asphalt oval, it is the fastest half-mile track in the country and home to the annual Snowball Derby (usually the first few days of Dec.). The Snowball Derby is widely recognized as the country's premier short track Super Late Model event. The rest of the season features racing of different kinds, from the fire-breathing, fuel-injected, winged sprint cars of the United Sprint Car Series, to the Bombers, Spectators, Super Stocks, Vintage, and Pro Late Models. The track has attracted top drivers like Carl Yarborough and Rusty Wallace, and fans from all over.

Pensacola Greyhound Track and Poker Room (951 Dog Track Rd., off U.S. 98, 850/455-8595, www.pensacolagreyhoundtrack.com, 7pm Fri.-Sat., 1pm Sun., free) offers the thrill of high-speed greyhound racing and the equally thrilling attendant betting. You can watch the races from an air-conditioned restaurant/lounge called the Kennel Club or from rail-side seats. The facility also has live and instant replay televisions throughout the complex. Texas hold 'em, seven card stud, and Omaha poker are played in the newly added **Poker Room** (9am-3am Mon.-Thurs., 24 hours Fri.-Sun., free).

Navarre Beach on Highway 399. Opal Beach will be on the Gulf side (right). From Navarre Beach, drive west toward Pensacola Beach on Highway 399. Opal Beach will on the Gulf side (left).

Navarre Beach

Navarre Beach is the easternmost beach on Santa Rosa Island. It's a family-friendly beach, with bathrooms, picnic facilities, and a fishing pier. The Navarre Beach County Park is 130 acres of beach, wetlands, and scrub, a third of which is set aside for nondevelopment in perpetuity. After lolling on the beach, you can follow the multiuse Seashore Bicycle Trail alongside dunes, forests, and the Gulf for a nice array of picturesque scenery.

FISHING AND DIVING

The Three Mile Bridge over Pensacola Bay has in recent years carried traffic alongside the long-abandoned U.S. 98 bridge. That bridge, prior to Hurricane Ivan, was used by local anglers as their huge personal fishing pier. Now much of it lies on the bottom of Pensacola Bay. In 2010, the newly constructed fishing pier that runs alongside the Three Mile Bridge was completed, and anglers are back to reeling in their catches. In general, fishing in the area has taken a huge upswing. The decommissioned aircraft carrier **USS Oriskany** was sunk as an artificial reef in the Gulf of Mexico 22.5 miles southeast of Pensacola Pass in May 2006. The navy committed $2.8 million for its preparation and deployment as a reef, the first time a ship of this size had been sunk for this purpose. The decommissioned Mighty O (32,000 tons and 911 feet), which saw action in Korea and Vietnam, sits in 212 feet of water. The *Oriskany* is the first navy ship cleaned following the EPA's 2004 policies ensuring artificial reefs are environmentally safe.

Divers can reach the top of the *Oriskany*'s superstructure or "island" at 60 feet, while its flight deck sits in 130 feet of water, below the depth of recreational divers but well within reach of specialty divers trained in deepwater diving. With year-round warm water temperatures (mid-80s in summer and mid-60s in winter) and visibility of 60-100 feet, it's tempting.

Not surprising, then, that this has been used as the site of underwater weddings. Crystal and Cooper Labenske were the first to literally take the plunge here, in May 2006.

Pensacola Dive Company owner Captain Ron Beermünder officiated the underwater "I dos."

BOAT TOURS AND CHARTERS

If you're looking to take a dolphin and sightseeing cruise on Pensacola Beach, **Chase-N-Fins** (655 Pensacola Beach Blvd., 850/492-6337, 10am, 2pm, 5pm, $25 adults, $15 children 5-12, kids 4 and under free) is a good place to start. Climb aboard their 50 foot navy launch boat for a two-hour cruise. The boat can hold up to 49 passengers for a cruise around Pensacola Bay and the surrounding waters. For something less crowded, join **Jolly Sailing** (655 Pensacola Beach Blvd., 850/723-6142, $45-85) for a 2-hour dolphin, sunset, or sailing cruise on their 34-foot Pearson sailboat, their 27-foot covered powerboat, or aboard the *Jolly Roger*, a 26-foot fast cat powerboat that will take you farther and faster. Snorkeling and stand-up paddleboard tours are also available.

Captain Jeff Lacour pilots the **Dolphin Express** (701 Pensacola Beach Blvd., 850/619-8738, $25 adults, $15 children, 4 and under free), a 50-foot vessel with wraparound seating. If you plan on being in town for the Blue Angels Airshow, call ahead and reserve a seat for one great view. But if you want to catch some of the fish in Pensacola Bay, call **Hot Spot Charters** (655 Pensacola Beach Blvd., 850/449-5555, $450-800 inshore for up to 4 anglers, $800-1,600 offshore for up to 6 anglers, $1,300-2,300 offshore for up to 10 anglers), or **Bout Time Charters** (715 Pensacola Beach Blvd., 850/380-1671, $450-750 inshore for up to 4 anglers, $650-800 offshore for up to 6 anglers, $1,300-2,300 offshore for up to 10 anglers). The most common catches are speckled trout, redfish, red snapper, flounder, sheepshead, blue fish, Spanish and king mackerel, grouper, or amberjack.

Just across the bridge to Pensacola Beach, **Key Sailing** (400 Quietwater Beach Blvd., 850/932-5520) rents 22-foot pontoon boats that can hold 11 passengers ($190 for 2

hours, $275 for 3-4 hours, $450 all day), Jet Skis ($55-550), kayaks ($15-100 single, $25-135 double), paddleboards ($25-150), as well as 13-foot and 16-foot catamaran sailboats ($60-200). Or climb aboard their glass-bottomed 45-foot catamaran tour boat for a 2-hour dolphin cruise ($30 adults, $20 children). And if you want a bird's-eye view of Pensacola Beach, go parasailing ($90 for two people, $85 for one person). They take you out on a speedboat and then take you up 500-600 feet above the water for a 10-minute high-flying adventure.

In Navarre, **Navarre Family Watersports** (8671 Navarre Pkwy., 850/939-9923) offers dolphin tours on WaveRunners ($110/WaveRunner), WaveRunner rentals ($55/half hour, $90/hour), pontoon boat rentals ($250/half day, $425/full day), fishing kayak rentals ($10/hour, $30/4 hours, $50/day), a water park ($15/hour, $25/2 hours, $30/3 hours), mini golf ($6 adults, $3 kids 12 and under), and helicopter rides ($50 for 10 miles down the coast, $100 for 20-mile flight to a sunken ship, $200 for a 40-mile trip over the National Seashore from Navarre to Pensacola Beach, and $350 for a 60-mile flight to Fort Pickens). Military discounts are available.

In Perdido Key, you can chase fins with **Blue Dolphin Cruises** (29603 Perdido Beach Blvd., 251/981-2774) on their 51-foot covered pontoon boat. Their cruises are some of the most reasonably priced in the area ($18 adults, $15 children 3-10, free for kids 2 and under), and their tour boats have an enclosed area with heating and air-conditioning. The wraparound, open-air viewing deck lets you enjoy bay breezes with unobstructed views.

PADDLING

Paddlers can explore one of the finest waterways in the South along the **Coldwater Creek Paddling Trail**. The 19-mile paddling trail flows south from the Highway 4 bridge, which is just east of Berrydale (about 20 minutes north of Pensacola), and ends at the State Road 191 launch east of Whiting Field. The creek, which is spring fed and cold, offers the perfect retreat from the hot Florida summer. There are plenty of beaches to camp on along the way, and the swift current will require you to be vigilant for submerged logs. During low flow, paddling the creek may require some portaging.

You can rent a canoe or tube from one of the numerous local outfitters and paddle or float down the calm, sandy-bottomed river along the 31-mile designated **Blackwater River Canoe Trail** (maps found online at www.dep.state.fl.us.com). Blackwater is a winding and often wide river that's dotted with large beaches and high bluffs that are forested with pine and cedar groves. The canoe trail is divided into three sections, and outfitters provide shuttle trips between various launch points. The most popular section of the river for paddlers and tubers is a nearly six-mile section that traverses through Blackwater River State Park (about 40 minutes northeast of Pensacola). Paddlers and tubers begin at the Bryan Bridge Launch on Bryan Bridge Road and end at Deaton Bridge on Deaton Bridge Road, which is inside of the state park. This section can become crowded during the summer and holidays, so plan your trip accordingly.

★ TUBING ON COLDWATER CREEK

In the warmer months, April through September, hundreds of people float the Coldwater Creek in tubes every week. **Adventures Unlimited Outdoor Center** (8974 Tomahawk Landing Rd., Milton, about a 50-minute drive north of Pensacola, 850/623-6197) is the most popular outfitter in the area. They provide tubing trips (8am-3pm, 3.5-hour trip, 4 miles, $20/single tube, $10/cooler tube, includes shuttle). The float is a pleasant way to beat the heat and see one of the most beautiful waterways in northwest Florida. Make sure to pack a lunch to enjoy at one of the many sandbars along the creek. Also bring sunscreen and plenty of water.

In addition to tubing trips, Adventures Unlimited Outdoor Center provides canoe rentals ($60/canoe for day trips, choose between 4-, 7-, or 11-mile trips, children under 12 ride free, $70/canoe for overnight trip, $80-90/canoe for 2-day trips, $90-100/canoe for 3-day trips), kayak rentals ($35/kayak for day trips, choose between 4-, 7-, or 11-mile trips), campsites ($25/site up to 4 people, $5/additional person, water and 30-amp electrical hookups on-site), paddleboards ($45/board), a variety of private cabins ($49-309/night),

PENSACOLA

SPORTS AND RECREATION

Coldwater Creek

and an inn ($129/night). Want an invigorating adrenaline rush? Try soaring above the forest, beaches, and creeks on their network of ziplines and platforms ($89 for 3 hours, $129 for 5 hours). And if you're feeling adventurous, try one of their overnight paddling trips (1-3 nights available). Outdoor center employees will take you, your camping gear, and your canoes to the launch site and drop you off. After spending the day paddling, you'll stop for the night at a beautiful campsite on a beach alongside the rolling creek. On your last day, you'll arrive at the designated pickup site and then travel back to the outdoor center where your car and civilization awaits.

HORSEBACK RIDING

The **Coldwater Recreation Area** (south of Berrydale, off Hwy. 4 on Gordon Land Rd.) is popular with riding enthusiasts. The park has more than 50 miles of horse trails, horse stables, and a campground with electricity and water, as well as restrooms and showers. You'll need to call ahead to reserve stable space (850/957-6161).

SPECTATOR SPORTS

Pensacola Wahoos

Pensacola is embracing baseball with open arms at the **Pensacola Bayfront Stadium** (351 W. Cedar St.), their baseball and sports complex. It is primarily home to the **Pensacola Wahoos** (850/934-8444, www.milb.com, tickets $10-50), a Cincinnati Reds affiliate minor-league team, but the stadium occasionally hosts football games and concerts. Built right on Pensacola Bay just on the outskirts of downtown near the foot of the Three Mile Bridge, the new stadium quickly received accolades in the baseball community, including the Best Ballpark of 2012 award from baseballparks.com. The classic open-air stadium seats 5,038 fans and was designed by the same award-winning baseball stadium design firm that built the new Yankee Stadium, the Giants' AT&T Park, and completed the renovation of Wrigley Field for the Chicago Cubs. It's a beautiful ballpark in a stunning coastal setting and a great place to spend the evening after a fun day at Pensacola Beach just across the Three Mile Bridge. Starting in 2016, the stadium will host the Argos, the University of West Florida's football team.

Pensacola Ice Flyers

If you're into ice hockey, you're in luck: **The Pensacola Ice Flyers** (201 East Gregory

Pensacola Bayfront Stadium

St., 850/466-3111, $15-35) are the city's professional hockey team, part of the Southern Professional Hockey League. Games are held at the Pensacola Bay Center, and being close to all that ice feels great after a long, hot day in the sun at the beach. They won their first President's Cup in 2013 against the Huntsville Havoc in game three.

Sights

Downtown Pensacola has plenty of historical attractions, many of them clustered in one of several historic districts.

SEVILLE SQUARE

The survivors of an early, thwarted attempt to settle Santa Rosa Island hightailed it to more solid ground and established a permanent settlement in 1752. After the French and Indian War of 1763, the British took west Florida and occupied the area, laying out a clean grid of houses. The Spanish, upon capturing Pensacola after that, kept the old town square intact but renamed the streets to reflect the new Spanish presence. So about 20 blocks of historic 18th- to 19th-century residential and business streets have Spanish names. It's a beautiful area with a mixture of Victorian, Spanish-, and French-influenced Gulf Coast-style cottages (these are often 1.5-story houses with steeply pitched gabled roofs and a deep front porch) centered on shady Seville Square Park.

The Seville Historic District makes for a wonderful afternoon of walking. First, I encourage a stop at **Seville Quarter** (130 E. Government St., 850/434-6211, 11am-3am, late-night menus until 1am, $10-25, $3 Wed., $10 Thurs., $5 Fri.-Sat., free Sun.-Tues.) for live music, food, or a few cold drinks. Within this historic complex, down an east alleyway, stop into **Rosie O'Grady's** for some Dixieland jazz dueling pianos and the historic setting—it was built in 1871 as the Pensacola Cigar and Tobacco Company. Directly across from Rosie O'Grady's is the entrance to **Lili Marlene's World War I Aviators Pub,** once the Pensacola Printing Co., which for a long time was the oldest print shop in continuous operation in the country and the original home of the *Pensacola News Journal*. Beyond these, there are several other themed rooms in this entertainment and dining complex, outfitted with period antiques. The complex also has two inviting courtyards and a gift shop.

★ Historic Pensacola Village

Also part of the Seville Historic District, **Historic Pensacola Village** (850/595-5985, 10am-4pm Tues.-Sat., $8 adults, $7 seniors and active military, AAA members, $4 children 4-14, children 3 and under free, tickets half price on Sun.) is bounded by Government, Taragona, Adams, and Alcaniz Streets. The village consists of 20 properties in the Pensacola National Register Historic District. Ten of these properties are interpretive facilities open to the public: the Museum of Commerce, Museum of Industry, Julee Cottage, Lavalle House, Lear House, Dorr House, Old Christ Church, Weaver's Cottage, Tivoli House, and Colonial Archaeological Trail. Do them all if you've got the stamina—the guided house tour is the way to go. House tours are included in the admission price and leave from the Tivoli House at 11am, 1pm, and 2:30pm. Tickets are valid for seven days for the Historic Pensacola complex including the Historic Pensacola Village, the Pensacola Children's Museum, the **T. T. Wentworth Jr. Florida State Museum,** and the Hilton-Green Research Center.

T. T. Wentworth Jr. Florida State Museum (Plaza Ferdinand) is an elaborate Renaissance Revival building that houses rotating exhibits on west Florida's history, architecture, and archaeology (kids will go more willingly if you tell them there's also a

Downtown Pensacola

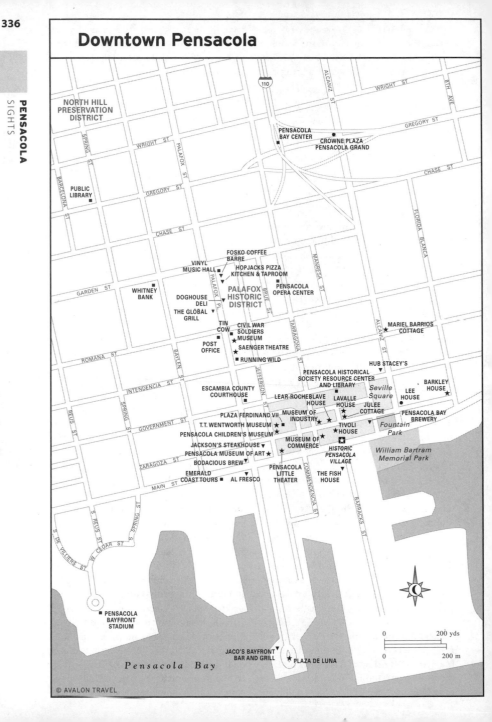

NORTH HILL
PRESERVATION
DISTRICT

PENSACOLA
BAY CENTER

CROWNE PLAZA
PENSACOLA GRAND

PUBLIC
LIBRARY

WRIGHT ST

GREGORY ST

CHASE ST

FOSKO COFFEE
BARRE

VINYL
MUSIC HALL

HOPJACKS PIZZA
KITCHEN & TAPROOM

PENSACOLA
OPERA CENTER

WHITNEY
BANK

DOGHOUSE
DELI

PALAFOX
HISTORIC
DISTRICT

THE GLOBAL
GRILL

TIN
COW

CIVIL WAR
SOLDIERS
MUSEUM

MARIEL BARRIOS
COTTAGE

POST
OFFICE

SAENGER THEATRE

RUNNING WILD

HUB STACEY'S

PENSACOLA HISTORICAL
SOCIETY RESOURCE CENTER
AND LIBRARY

ESCAMBIA COUNTY
COURTHOUSE

LEAR-ROCHEBLAVE
HOUSE

LAVALLE
HOUSE

Seville
Square

LEE
HOUSE

BARKLEY
HOUSE

JULEE
COTTAGE

PENSACOLA BAY
BREWERY

PLAZA FERDINAND VII

MUSEUM OF
INDUSTRY

TIVOLI
HOUSE

Fountain
Park

T.T. WENTWORTH MUSEUM

PENSACOLA CHILDREN'S MUSEUM

JACKSON'S STEAKHOUSE

MUSEUM OF
COMMERCE

HISTORIC
PENSACOLA
VILLAGE

William Bartram
Memorial Park

PENSACOLA MUSEUM OF ART

BODACIOUS BREW

EMERALD
COAST TOURS

AL FRESCO

PENSACOLA
LITTLE
THEATER

THE FISH
HOUSE

PENSACOLA
BAYFRONT
STADIUM

JACO'S BAYFRONT
BAR AND GRILL

PLAZA DE LUNA

Pensacola Bay

© AVALON TRAVEL

0   200 yds

0   200 m

WRIGHT ST

GREGORY ST

CHASE ST

GARDEN ST

ROMANA ST

INTENDENCIA ST

GOVERNMENT ST

ZARAGOZA ST

MAIN ST

SPRING ST

PALAFOX ST

BARCELONA ST

BAYLEN ST

REUS ST

SPRING ST

JEFFERSON ST

TARRAGONA ST

ALCANIZ ST

MANRESA ST

BRUE ST

FLORIDA BLANCA

8TH AVE

ALCANIZ ST

BARRACKS ST

COMMENDENCIA ST

S. REUS ST

S. DE VILLIERS ST

W. CEDAR ST

S. SPRING ST

shrunken head and a mummified cat on display). The **Museum of Commerce** (201 E. Zaragoza St.) is a brick turn-of-the-20th-century warehouse containing a reconstructed 1890s-era streetscape with a toy store; leather, hardware, music, and print shops; and horse-drawn buggies. The **Museum of Industry** (200 E. Zaragoza St.) houses an exhibit depicting several important 19th-century industries in west Florida: fishing, brick-making, railroad, and lumber. It was the most recent to reopen and features a variety of interactive displays teaching visitors about the area's natural resources and early industry.

The historic homes in the village include the **Lavalle House** (205 E. Church St.), an example of French Creole colonial architecture; the **Dorr House** (311 S. Adams St.), Greek Revival architecture furnished with fine antiques; and the **Lear-Rocheblave House** (214 E. Zaragoza St.), a two-story folk Victorian home with several furnished rooms. The **Barkley House** (410 S. Florida Blanca St.) is one of the oldest masonry houses in Florida, and the **Mariel Barrios Cottage** (204 S. Alcaniz St.) is owned and operated by the Pensacola Historic Preservation Society and exhibits household items and furnishings from Pensacola during the 1920s. The **Julee**

Cottage (210 E. Zaragoza St.) is a museum classroom once owned by Julee Panton, a free African American woman. The **Tivoli House** (205 E. Zaragoza St.) is a reconstructed version of an 1805 boarding- and gaming house and now home to the Historic Pensacola Village gift shop and ticket office.

After touring the homes, pick up the brochure for the **Colonial Archaeological Trail,** which was produced by the Archaeology Institute at the University of West Florida; it leads you through the ruins of the colonial commanding officer's house, the foundations of the officer-of-the-day's building, and the remains of what might have been a trader's home and warehouse just outside the western gate of the British fort built during the American Revolution.

Also, the **Pensacola Children's Museum** (115 E. Zaragoza St., 850/433-1559, 10am-4pm Tues.-Sat.) is in the midst of the historic village, operated by the Pensacola Historical Society. The museum is geared for children 13 and younger, with interactive exhibits that explore Pensacola history. An exhibit on the first floor recreates what it was like to live in Pensacola during colonial times. On the second floor, kids can interact with exhibits that further explore the area's rich history.

Seville Square

Currently, the exhibits focus on Pensacola's maritime, industrial, and Native American history. A store offers children's books and toys with historical themes.

PALAFOX HISTORIC DISTRICT

Palafox Historic District is another historic area downtown, contiguous with Seville Square, only just to the west of it. It runs up Palafox Street from Pensacola Bay in the south to about Wright Street in the north. Again, it's an area of beautiful homes and historic buildings with wide brick sidewalks. It's the commercial heart of Pensacola, and it houses a couple of the area's big cultural draws.

The **Pensacola Museum of Art** (407 S. Jefferson St., 850/432-6247, 10am-5pm Tues.-Sat., $7 adults, $5 military, seniors, and children 7-17, 6 and under free, last Tues. of each month free) is right at its center, with a wonderful space and intriguingly diverse visiting exhibits that range from the realistic sculptures of Duane Hanson to 20th-century Japanese printmaking. The permanent collection has minor works, most on paper, by some heavy hitters (largely 20th century) as well as lots of fine decorative glass. The museum is housed in what was

the city jail (1906-1954), so there are sturdy bars on the windows.

Just around the corner you will find the **Vinyl Music Hall** (5 E. Garden St., 850/607-6758, www.vinylmusichall.com, tickets $7-50), the newest music and entertainment venue in town. What was once a historic Masonic Lodge has been restored and remodeled into a hip music venue and bar. The intimate general admission venue is standing room only and draws large national acts mostly in the blues, rock, and alternative genres.

NORTH HILL PRESERVATION DISTRICT

Before you tire of all this history, another worthy walk is the **North Hill Preservation District,** which occupies 50 city blocks due north of the Palafox District, away from the water, bounded on the west by Reus and on the east by Palafox. On the National Register of Historic Places, the neighborhood is pretty much residential, with great examples of fully restored historic homes. You can't go inside unless you make friends, but some of the current owners are descendants of the original builders—Spanish nobility, lumber barons, French Creoles, and Civil War soldiers.

T.T. Wentworth Jr. Florida State Museum

Downtown Sightseeing Tours

A fun way to explore downtown Pensacola is to take a tour on **Pensacola Pedal Trolley** (225 East Zaragoza St., tours meet in front of the Pensacola Bay Brewery). They offer historic tours ($25/person), a 2-hour pub crawls ($19/person Sun.-Thurs., $25/person Fri.-Sat.), and will book private tours. This pedal-powered, ecofriendly trolley cruises through the historic district while the driver narrates the sights along the way.

To explore the history of this area, take a two-hour guided tour on a Segway with **Emerald Coast Tours** (5 West Main St., 850/417-9292, call to schedule tour, $65 adults, $60 students and military). Guide Nic Shuck offers a crash course on operating one of the two-wheeled Segways before you embark on a high-speed excursion that explores the best historical sights and landmarks in downtown Pensacola, including the Plaza De Luna where the Spanish officially handed over Florida to the United States. It's a great way to get yourself familiarized with the lay of the land when you first get into town and perfect for less mobile visitors who would rather not walk the long blocks of downtown. Along the way you'll learn the best spots for good eats and drinks. There are also night tours of the East Hill district (5:30pm and 7:30pm Sat. only, $55 adults, $50 students and military).

When you're walking to and from Pensacola Bayfront Stadium, or anytime you're downtown and need a quick lift, keep your eye out for **Gopher Carts.** They offer free rides in golf carts pretty much anywhere in the four-mile radius of downtown Pensacola. Their knowledgeable drivers who work off tips can usually give you the run down about what's happening in the city on any given night, and the carts are spacious, clean, and a lot of fun.

NAVAL AIR STATION PENSACOLA

Pensacola is known as the Cradle of Naval Aviation, a bold claim that can be authenticated through an exploration of one of the many sites open to the public at the **Naval Air Station Pensacola** and environs. To reach the historic mainland forts and the National Museum of Naval Aviation from the north, take exit 7 off I-10 (Pine Forest Rd., Hwy. 297), go about 1.5 miles, and take a right onto Blue Angel Parkway. Then drive 12 miles to the west gate of the Naval Air Station. (Visitors without military stickers can *depart* only from the main entrance on Navy Blvd.)

★ National Museum of Naval Aviation

If you're only going to devote time to one historic attraction in the greater Pensacola area, the **National Museum of Naval Aviation** (1750 Radford Blvd., NAS Pensacola, 850/453-2389 or 800-327-5002, 9am-5pm daily, free) is it. It's one of the largest air and space museums in the world, with 160 restored aircrafts representing Navy, Marine Corps, and Coast Guard aviation. There's a seven-story, glass-and-steel atrium in which four A-4 Skyhawks are suspended in formation. You can stand on the flight deck of the USS *Cabot* and fly an F/A-18 mission in Desert Storm in a motion-based flight simulator. There's an IMAX theater ($8.75) which hosts a rotation of films that are usually about aircraft, aviation, and military history, including the long running feature called *The Magic of Flight.*

If you're in town between March and November, don't miss the Blue Angels (55-minute practice sessions 11:30am Tues. and Wed., Mar.-Nov. at outside viewing stand north of museum on flight line). Watch the Navy's impressive acrobatic flight squadron of F-18 Hornets perform stunning barrel rolls, high-speed loops, their trademark diamond formation, and other daring flight maneuvers. After practice, spectators often have the opportunity to talk with the pilots and get their autographs.

Pensacola Lighthouse

Also on the grounds of the Naval Air Station Pensacola, you can climb the 177 steps to the top of the **Pensacola Lighthouse** (Hwy. 292 S., 850/393-1561, 10am-5:30pm daily, $6 adults, $4 senior, military, and children 12 and under), which follows on the heels of other lighthouses erected in this area. The construction of the first Pensacola lighthouse, the Aurora Borealis, was completed in 1824, also the first lighthouse on the Gulf Coast and the second lighthouse in Florida. It stood at the northern entrance of the bay near the present-day Lighthouse Point Restaurant. Unfortunately, trees on Santa Rosa Island obscured the light beam to ships. The present lighthouse was begun in 1856, and it was lit January 1, 1859. At night it still shines for sailors 27 miles out at sea, 171 feet tall and with a first-order Fresnel lens. In 1965, the lighthouse was automated, obviating the need for an on-site lighthouse keeper. The Keeper's Quarters now house the Navy's Command Display Center, with an exhibit on the lighthouse and the Naval Air Station.

The Forts

Accessed through Naval Air Station Pensacola, the historic forts in this area are actually part of the **Gulf Islands National Seashore** (mail: 1801 Gulf Breeze Pkwy., Gulf Breeze, FL 32563, 850/934-2600). The park spans 160 miles from Cat Island, Mississippi, east to the Okaloosa Day Use Area near Fort Walton Beach. The seashore was devastated by Hurricane Ivan, but recovery is now complete.

Fort Barrancas sits on a sandy bluff overlooking the entrance to Pensacola Bay. This site has seen three forts—first an earth-and-log Royal Navy Redoubt in 1763, then a Spanish two-part fort with Bateria de San Antonio at the foot of the bluff and Fort San Carlos de Barrancas above. The American brick-and-mortar Fort Barrancas was mostly completed in 1846, boasting 37 guns. During the Civil War, Confederate forces held Fort Barrancas until 1862. It was rearmed in 1890 and used as a training facility briefly during the Spanish-American War, after which it was disarmed again and used as an observation and communications post until 1930. Fort Barrancas was deactivated in 1947 and lay unused until it became part of the Gulf Islands National Seashore in 1971. It was entirely restored by 1980 at a cost of $1.2 million. Today, there's a visitors center with exhibits on the history

a view of downtown Pensacola

Pensacola Lighthouse

of Pensacola under five flags (1559-1971), with displays of Civil War and coastal artillery artifacts. The visitors center shows a 12-minute video on the fort and offers guided tours daily.

The **Fort Barrancas-Advanced Redoubt** (850/455-5167), 700 yards south, was built 1845-1859 to defend the Pensacola Navy Yard from overland infantry assault. It was only manned during the Civil War, after which it was deemed obsolete. Scheduled tours of Fort Barrancas are offered throughout the year. The 0.5-mile Trench Trail connects the Advanced Redoubt to the Fort Barrancas Visitor Center.

The largest of the four forts built to defend Pensacola Bay, **Fort Pickens** on Santa Rosa Island sustained serious damage during Hurricane Ivan but is now reopened to the public. All buildings in the historic area were flooded to a depth of several feet and the island experienced major erosion on its south side. The Florida Department of Transportation rebuilt sections of Fort Pickens Road, inland and north of where it used to be.

Construction of the fort was begun in 1829 and completed in 1834; the fort was used until the 1940s. It is said to be the only Southern fort not captured by the Confederacy in the Civil War, and that Geronimo surrendered here in 1886, marking the end of the Apache Wars. The park has a visitors center with a great self-guided tour map of the fort. There are also regularly scheduled ranger tours and a little museum with regular interpretive programs. There is year-round **camping** (850/934-2622, reservations 877/444-6777) in the area on the west end of Santa Rosa Island, as well as the Blackbird Marsh and Dune Nature Trails and a fully repaired fishing pier.

While Fort Pickens is on the western tip of Santa Rosa Island, **Fort McRee** is on a narrow bar of sand on the eastern tip of Perdido Key. Or maybe I should say it used to be there. Once used as the third point of the triangle (with Pickens and Barrancas) by the U.S. Army to defend Pensacola Bay, Fort McRee was built there 1834-1839. It was heavily damaged during the Civil War and then leveled by hurricanes over the years. It is a great day sailing trip to the fort, where you can usually have the beach and surrounding island all to yourself and wander through the remnants of the fort and Battery 233.

FAMILY-FRIENDLY ATTRACTIONS

There are only so many historic sites a kid can endure before reprehensible behavior sets in. Beyond the area's beaches, there are a couple of fun enticements for young ones. The **Gulf Breeze Zoo** (5701 Gulf Breeze Pkwy., 10 miles east of Gulf Breeze on U.S. 98, 850/932-2229, 9am-4pm Jan.-Feb., 9am-5pm Mar.-May 27, 9am-6pm May 28-Sept. 5, 9am-5pm Sept. 6-Sept. 30, 9am-4pm Oct.-Dec., $15.95 adults, $14.95 seniors, $11.95 children 2-12, children under 2 free) is home to something like 1,400 animals, spread across a 50-acre wildlife preserve. You can view the free-roaming animals from the boardwalk or from the cute red Safari Line train. The train ride is narrated by a guide who points out African wild dogs, giraffes, pygmy hippos, gorillas, and native wildlife. The zoo also has a tranquil Japanese garden, a gift shop, the Jungle Cafe, and Whistlestop Snack Bar.

If you happen to be in town during October, the **Pensacola Interstate Fair** (6655 W. Mobile Hwy., 850/944-4500, $11 12 and over, $5 children 4-11, $5 parking) is vast, with 147 acres of rides and exhibits. It usually takes place the last 11 days of the month. Along with the carnival rides and games, the fair always features headline music acts that have included names like Travis Tritt, Switchfoot, and Grand Funk Railroad. Other attractions include livestock, agriculture, and antique car exhibits.

It's fairly small-scale compared to Disney or Busch Gardens, but **Sam's Fun City** (6709 Pensacola Blvd., just south of I-10 on U.S. 29, 850/505-0800, www.samsfuncity.com, 11am-8pm Sun.-Thurs., 11am-10pm Fri.-Sat., weekend hours only during winter, $7-38) is Pensacola's amusement park. There are a bunch of midway-style rides along with go-carts, bumper boats, and miniature golf. It also has a 1,600-square-foot arena for laser tag and a huge game arcade. Sam's recently added **Surf City Water Park** with a wave pool, 15 waterslides, a 1,200-foot-long endless river, spray grounds, water play structures, and kiddie pools. The on-site Bullwinkle's Restaurant is a pleasant, something-for-everyone family restaurant.

Fort Pickens on Pensacola Beach

Food

DOWNTOWN
Breakfast

Bodacious Brew (407 S. Palafox Place, on the corner of Palafox and Main, 850/433-6505, breakfast menu served 7am-11am Mon.-Sat., until 8pm for coffee, tea, and pastries) offers an extensive espresso, coffee, and tea selection. For breakfast, try their jalapeño and cheddar scone or their bodacious gouda grits alongside a veggie quiche. At the long coffee bar, baristas get fancy and prepare java all kinds of ways, including pour overs, chemex, syphons, and French press preparations.

A good choice for coffee and pastries is **Fosko Coffee Barre** (8 Palafox Place, near the north end of the business district, 850/332-7737, 6:45am-10pm Mon.-Thurs., 7am-midnight Fri.-Sat., 9am-8pm Sun.). The brick and wood interior is cozy, clean, and historic, and their iced coffees and frappes are popular during the summer. A small selection of sandwiches and sweet treats has helped make this a popular spot to meet before catching a music show at the nearby Vinyl Music Hall.

Casual

In the same building as Bodacious Brew is the **Bodacious Olive** (10am-6pm Mon.-Fri., 9am-4pm Sat.) where you can shop fresh bread, seasonings, artisanal olive oils, and vinegars from around the world. For lunch, grab some healthy greens at their salad bar called **So Chopped** (11am-5pm Mon.-Fri., 11am-4pm Sat.) where you can build your own salad from their extensive fresh ingredients, or choose a wrap, soup, or salad on their menu. It's the best way to eat healthy while your downtown, and the prices are reasonable. And go upstairs to **The Wine Shop** (10am-6pm Mon.-Fri., 9am-4pm Sat.) for a wonderful selection of small production wines mostly from France, Italy, California, and New Zealand.

For pizza and beer, go to **HopJacks Pizza Kitchen & Taproom** (10 Palafox Place, 850/497-6073, www.hopjacks.com, $7-20). They have a stage for live music, and plush couches create a relaxing environment. Pizza is the house pride, along with 150 bottled and 36 tap beers. Take a seat inside or grab a slice and head out to the outdoor courtyard for an evening under the stars.

Before or after a Wahoos baseball game, slide in to the newly renovated **Doghouse Deli** (30 S. Palafox St., 850/432-3104, 11am-3pm Mon.-Thurs., 7:30am-5pm Fri.-Sun.) for a hotdog prepared nearly any way imaginable. This longtime Pensacola favorite originally opened in 1977, then reopened at their new, current location in December 2015. Favorites include the slaw hound with coleslaw, chili, and cheese, and the Chicago dog piled high with onions, relish, cucumbers, pickles, and tomatoes. Or pick your own toppings from an extensive list on the chalkboard. They also offer nachos, kielbasas, sandwiches, and a full breakfast menu.

Have you ever wanted a little rum or whiskey in your milkshake? Well, You can get it at the **Tin Cow** (102 S. Palafox Place, 850/466-2103, 11am-2am daily) along with hearty burgers and canned craft beer. The place is hipster at heart and features live music every Friday and Saturday 8:30pm to 11:30pm. Burgers are the staple, but they also have a wide array of appetizers, soups, salads, and sliders.

Popular with the lunch and budget-minded crowd, **Al Fresco** (501 S. Palafox Pl.) is a collection of stylish, clean, food carts around a classy, open-air courtyard with umbrella covered tables shaded by tall palm trees. It's right in the heart of the business district on Palafox and the perfect spot to get a quick bite when the weather cooperates. There's quite the selection: a taco spot called **Z Tacos** (11am-7pm Mon.-Thurs., 11am-8pm Fri.-Sat., and 11am-6pm Sun.), an oyster bar called

Shux (11am-9pm or later daily), **Gunshot BBQ** (11am-7pm Fri.-Sat., 11am-4pm Sun.), an Asian fusion spot with potstickers, popular Chinese dishes, and Thai favorites called **Fusion World** (11am-7pm Mon.-Thurs., 11am-8pm Sat., and 11am-6pm Sun.), and **Gouda Stuff** (11am-3pm Mon.-Thurs., 11am-7pm Fri.-Sat. 11am-6pm Sun.), which serves grilled cheese sandwiches, melts, soups, and sides. Several of the carts sell beer and wine if you want something to sip.

They don't serve food, but if you love craft beers you should open the taps and try one of the 15 seasonal varieties of local beer at **Pensacola Bay Brewery** (225 E. Zaragoza St., 850/434-3353, www.pbbrew.com, noon-9pm Mon.-Thurs., noon-11pm Fri.-Sat., noon-6pm Sun.). The brews range from light pilsners to dark oatmeal stouts, and all of them have names that harken back to Pensacola's past. Try a Desoto Berliner Weisse Ale or the Conquistador Dopple Bock, and for a virgin drink, stop in for a delicious Cannonball Rootbeer. For a behind-the-scenes glimpse into the world of brew mastery, embark on a brewery tour and taste a selection of their finest, chilled cold ones (3:30pm Fri. and Sat.).

Head to **Jacos Bayfront Bar and Grille** (997 S. Palafox Pl., 11am-10pm Thurs.-Sat., 10am-9pm Sun., 11am-9pm Mon.-Wed., $10-20) for a casual dinner or drinks overlooking the Palafox Pier Marina. Their eclectic menu features pizza, pastas, seafood, and steaks. It's American fare with Asian fusion selections and good vegetarian offerings. The wraparound outdoor seating makes this one of the best locations for sunset dining downtown, and the Sunday brunch is popular when the weather is nice. For lunch try their mahi tacos with mango salsa; for dinner dig into the ahi tuna with wasabi mashed potatoes. Brunch favorite include stuffed French toast.

Fine Dining

On the waterfront at the southern end of downtown, you'll find ★ **The Fish House** (600 S. Barracks St., 850/470-0003, www.fishhousepensacola.com, 11a.m. till close daily, 11am-2 pm Sun. brunch, 2pm-close Sun. dinner, $13-28). It's been seen on the Travel Channel, in *Food and Wine* magazine, and other leading media (*Wine Spectator* gave its wine list a nod). Just-off-the-docks seafood, sushi, an award-winning chef, and the Fish House Deck Bar—it's all a hit. From a fire pit conversation area and dining tables to an hors d'oeuvres menu and an outdoor bandstand and sprawling deck for dancing, this 3,500

Al Fresco

square feet of sun and Gulf breezes offers both local and regional bands serving up live music on Friday and Saturday nights.

Popular with locals, **The Global Grill** (27 S. Palafox Pl., 850/469-9966, www.globalgrill-pensacola.com, 5pm-9pm Tues.-Thurs., 5pm-10pm Fri.-Sat., $7-30) offers Pensacola some of its best tapas (actually, some of its only tapas). It's a world-beat approach that includes lamb lollipops with an Israeli couscous cake and sun-dried tomato au jus, or a crab West Indies and avocado martini.

The best fine dining in Pensacola is found at **Jackson's Steakhouse** (400 S. Palafox St., 850/469-9898, lunch 11am-2pm Tues.-Fri., dinner 5:30pm-10pm Tues.-Sat., $28-40), an upscale chophouse in an historic and elegant setting. They've won a long list of awards and accolades that include eight Golden Spoons, and eight *Wine Spectator*'s Awards of Excellence. Try the wood-fired filet with lump crab and fried green tomatoes or the beef brisket in sweet Florida barbecue sauce, and pair it with a glass of vino from their impressive wine list.

EAST HILL

To the north a bit and east of North Hill Preservation District, East Hill has a couple of my favorite restaurants. **Jerry's Drive-In** (2815 E. Cervantes St., 850/433-9910, 10am-10pm Mon.-Sat., 7am-10pm Sun. $5-9) offers killer cheeseburgers, onion rings, and fried okra in a comfy diner setting. It's been here since the 1940s, I'm told, and still has a line at lunch (but it's not really a drive-in, it's a walk-in).

J's Pastry (2014 N. 12th Ave., 850/432-4180, 6:30am-6pm Mon.-Fri., 7-6 Sat., 7am-2pm Sun., $2-10) is in the heart of East Hill. J's has been a local favorite for pastries, macaroons, peanut butter bars, and smiley-face cookies since 1946. The small bakery is also well loved for its fresh baked bread, birthday cakes, and tasty apple, cherry, and pecan pies. If you're in town during Mardi Gras, this is the place to get your colorful King's cake. Also along 12th Avenue is **Ozone's Pizza Pub** (1010 N. 12th Ave., 850/433-7336, 11am-midnight Mon.-Sat., 11am-10pm Sun., $10-20), the favorite neighborhood pizza joint. It's a family-friendly place during dinner hours that evolves into a college-aged hangout spot in the evenings. They serve thick-crusted pizza loaded with a generous amount of toppings. Their specialties include an extensive list of meat-centric and vegetarian pizza options, grinders, salads, and pasta dishes, along with a wide selection of beers.

★ **McGuire's Irish Pub** (600 E. Gregory St., 850/433-6789, 11am-2am daily, $10-30) is the Pensacola restaurant everyone knows about. "Irishmen of all nationalities" sign dollar bills and staple them to the ceiling, beer is brewed on the premises, the gorgeous wine cellar has a capacity of 8,000 bottles, and you can spend an ungodly sum on a burger (accompanied by caviar and champagne). It's a hard place to describe, really, set in Pensacola's original 1927 Old Firehouse. The steaks are good, and expensive (but it's fitting because all the beef is USDA-certified prime), but it still has a wild-and-woolly Irish pub feel to it. It's vast, with 400 seats and 200 employees, sprawling through a bunch of curio-packed theme rooms. Just go—it'll be fun.

GREATER PENSACOLA AREA

The **Tuscan Oven** (4801 N. 9th Ave., 850/484-6836, www.thetuscanoven.com, 11am-9pm Tues.-Thurs., 11am-10pm Fri.-Sat., $7-20) serves traditional southern Italian thin-crust pizzas prepared in a hardwood-fired oven shipped straight from Italy. The oven and counter bar that wraps around the kitchen are the centerpiece of the cozy dining room. You can chat with the friendly owners and staff while you watch your pizza get prepared. An outdoor patio is great for dining or drinking one of the wines from the selective list. The restaurant is close to Cordova Mall and a good choice on your way to or from the shopping center.

If you're staying in a condo or renting a house with a kitchen, you'll likely want to pick up some fresh seafood while you're in town. The best place to go is **Joe Patti's Seafood** (524 S. B St., 850/432-3315, 7:30am-6pm daily) located a few blocks west of the ballpark. It's a sprawling warehouse facility that has a large selection of seafood, shrimp, oysters, and crabs, as well as an impressive on-site sushi stand, seafood restaurant, and upscale deli.

Mariah's Fresh Seafood Market (621 E. Cervantes St., 850/432-4999, 8am-7pm Mon.-Sat., 8am-6pm Sun.) is more centrally located. They are smaller than Joe Pattis, but still offer all the seafood staples such as shrimp, snapper, grouper, mahi, oysters, crabs, scallops, and more.

PENSACOLA BEACH
Breakfast

Need coffee, breakfast, and the Internet? Go to the **Drowsy Poet** (655 Pensacola Beach Blvd., 850/203-1524, 6am-9pm Mon.-Sat., 6am-3pm Sun., $3-10), on the third floor above Innerlight Surf and Skate. Sip your coffee, cappuccino, or smoothie while you enjoy breakfast or lunch with an incredible waterfront view.

fish fillets

For breakfast and lunch, locals head to the **Native Cafe** (45 Via De Luna Dr., 850/934-4848, 7:30am-3pm daily, $5-12). At breakfast, they have the all-American fried eggs and pancakes sort of thing, but you can also get something special like crab cakes Benedict. They are located in the colorful row of businesses near the Gulf Islands National Seashore, so if you're renting a house on that side of the island, this is a nearby option. At lunch, fish tacos are the specialty, and New Orleans dishes like gumbo fill out the menu. The walnut-crusted key lime pie ($3.50) is a top pick for dessert.

Casual

Greatest oyster bar? ★ **Peg Leg Pete's** (1010 Fort Pickens Rd., 850/932-4139, 11am-10:30pm daily, $8-20), my personal favorite restaurant on Pensacola Beach, offers some of the best prices on the freshest seafood in Pensacola Beach. The little-known secret around town is that the owner also owns Maria's Seafood, the second-largest seafood distributor in town. The casual, pirate-themed atmosphere and the extensive playground make it a great place for families. The menu features local favorites and regional classics like grouper sandwiches, crab claws, and a perfect cup of seafood gumbo. Take the stairs down to the "under-where?" bar, where they serve cold drinks, raw oysters, and a full menu and feature live music on the weekends.

On the bay side, **Hemingway's** (400 Quietwater Beach Rd., 850/934-4747, www.hemingwaysislandgrill.com, 11am-9pm Mon.-Thurs., 11am-10pm Fri.-Sat., 10am-9pm Sun., $8-33) features an open kitchen and two levels of outdoor deck seating. The menu is island-inspired, with roasted corn and crab chowder, Key West ribs, and shrimp basted with dark rum sauce, and the drinks tend toward tropical cocktails and beach favorites.

Also on the bay, **Flounders Chowder House** (800 Quietwater Beach Rd., 850/932-2003, winter hours: 11am-10pm Mon.-Thurs.,

11am-midnight Fri.-Sat., 10:30am-10pm Sun., summer hours: 11am-midnight daily, $10-20) is a large, family-friendly restaurant with a bar. The first thing you notice is the impressive shrimp boat on the side of the building. An outdoor stage for live music has a sand pit in front for dancing. Inside, don't miss the confessional booths, taken from a New Orleans church. There's a lot of history in this sprawling Pensacola favorite, which opened in 1979. Steak and seafood are the main attraction, and you can get grouper, mahi, and tuna cooked on their wood-fired grill. The flagship dish is flounder stuffed with crabmeat. A new addition is their New Orleans-style snow cone stand ($3 and up a cone, $2 to add alcohol).

Sidelines (2 Via de Luna Dr., 850/934-3660, www.sidelinespensacola.com, 11am-11pm daily, $7-20) is a fun sports bar with an extensive beer selection and excellent chicken wings, burgers, ribs, and the like. The Caribbean chicken sandwich, smothered in honey barbecue sauce, and the Philly cheesesteak, with a hefty portion of thinly sliced beef, are favorites.

If you're a Jimmy Buffett fan and you're in town between March and October, stop by **Landshark Landing** (165 Fort Pickens Rd.,

4pm-10pm Mon.-Fri., noon-11pm Sat., noon-8pm Sun.), the casual bar and restaurant next door to the Margaritaville Beach Hotel. The wood and metal-roof building with open sides sits right on the Gulf, so the beach breeze rolls through. It's fun and lively, decorated with all sorts of Buffett memorabilia, and several televisions for watching the game. They have live music most weekends. The menu offers shrimp, nachos, and burgers, but most people come for the plentiful boat drinks and margaritas, of course.

Wild Roots (5 Via De Luna Dr., hours vary, $8-15) is the place to eat for the more health-conscious beach bum. Popular with the active crowd, the menu features organic wraps, soups, salads, pizzas, presses, sandwiches, and pastries. For a cold and healthy treat, pop in for a beach pop ($4 each), an organic frozen pop made from fruit juice, veggie juice, nut milks, or ice cream. They have 32 flavors to keep all the kids happy, and each pop has a paper cup attached at the bottom to keep the melting juice contained.

Cactus Flower Cafe (400 Quietwater Beach Rd., 850/934-5999, 11am-10pm daily, $8-15) will give you your Mexican food fix while you're out on the beach. Located at the Quietwater Boardwalk, this Pensacola

Flounders Chowder House

favorite has expanded to five locations on the Gulf Coast. Their success is a testament to their tasty California-style Mexican menu. They have all the mainstay tacos, burritos, and quesadillas, but their mahi tacos, enchiladas verdes, and traditional chicken posole soup stand out.

Fine Dining

Best sushi on the beach? It's fresh at **H2O Cajun Asian Grill** (12 Via De Luna Dr., 850/972-1700, 6:30am-11pm daily, $12-26). The views of the Gulf beach make this swanky, modern place a perfect spot for date night. The interior is colorful and fun. Choose from classic sushi rolls or build your own. The menu has a mix of seafood, Cajun dishes, Asian fusion, and Mediterranean-influenced selections, so it's likely to be a crowd-pleaser.

After dinner, relax around a conversation fire pit, listen to the waves roll in, and order cocktails from the poolside bar.

Look to the left when you cross the bridge to Pensacola Beach, and you'll see **The Grand Marlin** (400 Pensacola Beach Blvd., 850/677-9238, 11am-9pm Mon.-Thurs., 11am-10pm Fri.-Sat., 10am-9pm Sun., $15-30), where you can enjoy fine dining with views of Pensacola Bay and Santa Rosa Sound through the floor-to-ceiling windows. Steak and seafood dishes are the main features. You'll have a hard time picking between items such as grilled lobster tail drizzled in key lime butter sauce, oysters Rockefeller, or a sugar-cured pork shank with orange mustard glaze. Make sure to see the huge marlin that hangs in the dining room: It's a 1,228.5-pound behemoth that holds the North Carolina record.

Accommodations

UNDER $100

The **Ashton Inn & Suites Pensacola** (4 New Warrington Rd., 850/454-0280, and 910 N. Navy Blvd., 850/455-4561, $50 weekdays, $60 weekends) serves the Naval Air Station Pensacola and NTTC Corry Station, and is convenient to the National Museum of Naval Aviation.

A Pensacola Beach favorite is the ★ **Paradise Inn** (21 Via de Luna Dr., 850/932-2319, www.paradiseinn-pb.com, $70-160). The low-rise inn is tucked away among the newer, towering hotels and condos that have sprouted up like sand spurs along the shores of Pensacola Beach. It's on the sound side, but the Gulf is just a short walk away. The Paradise has Old Florida charm, and it offers some of the best waterfront rates in town. The inn's 55 renovated rooms are simple but stylish and come equipped with wireless Internet, cable, refrigerators, and microwaves. They surround a casual, fun bar and restaurant run by Renee Mack, who

serves a delicious mix of Southern seafood, American fare, and traditional New Orleans-inspired dishes. Renee runs a popular and successful catering business, and her food is found at many of the conventions, weddings, and parties around town. The food is affordable: most entrées are below $20. The atmosphere is also a big draw. Tables are set in the sugar-white sand under a covered pavilion with Santa Rosa Sound just a few feet away. At night, lit tiki torches add to the tropical setting. The inn and restaurant offer a private dock for boaters who want to sail in to dinner or take a break from touring the Intracoastal Waterway for a couple nights' rest. On weekends the Paradise brings in mostly blues, reggae, zydeco, and coastal country musicians for performances on its waterfront stage, and in recent years has gained a reputation as a favored entertainment venue among locals. They offer room specials on weekdays, so call and check the rates before you arrive.

$100-200

The **Crowne Plaza Pensacola Grand** (200 E. Gregory St., 850/433-3336, $125-145) experienced an extensive renovation in 2005. It has a fully equipped and updated gym on the second floor, an extensive library on the first floor, a heated pool, upscale dining in the 1912 Restaurant, and cocktails in the L&L lobby bar. The downtown location is convenient to the historic areas.

The **Courtyard by Marriott Downtown** (700 E. Chase St., 850/439-3330, www.courtyard-pensacoladowntown.com, $134-169) opened at the end of 2007, a boon to visitors who wish to enjoy the charm of the downtown area. The five-story hotel features 120 spacious rooms combining comfort and functionality, including high-speed Internet access, large desks, and ergonomic chairs. Amenities include a restaurant for breakfast, large fitness room, and swimming pool with hydrotherapy spa.

The **Hilton Pensacola Beach Gulf Front** (12 Via de Luna Dr., 850/916-2999, www.hiltonpensacolabeach.com, $109-259), previously known as the Hilton Garden Inn, is a large beachfront hotel within walking distance of water sports, shopping, dining, and nightlife. Many rooms are Gulf-front rooms and suites with private balconies. In 2007, it added on a tower with an additional 93 rooms. H2O, its signature restaurant featuring Cajun-Asian cuisine, has also nearly doubled in size and now offers a chef's table experience as well as private and semiprivate dining.

$200-300

On Pensacola Beach, it was a long time after Hurricane Ivan before hotels rebounded. They're back now, looking better than ever and with many new ones to experience.

You can now find out about the changes in attitudes at the Pensacola Beach latitude at Jimmy Buffett's **Margaritaville Beach Hotel** (165 Fort Pickens Rd., 850/916-9755, www.margaritavillehotel.com, $119-419). The most recent addition to the area, Margaritaville offers well designed tropical-themed rooms and suites decorated to capture the colors and natural environment of the Gulf of Mexico. All rooms have free high-speed wireless Internet and flat-screen televisions. The property features an airy lobby with high ceilings and slowly rotating fans that circulate above the Frank and Lola Love Pensacola Café. The café serves breakfast, lunch, and dinner with traditional American breakfast choices. For lunch it's Cheeseburgers in Paradise, along with seafood dishes. At

Margaritaville Beach Hotel

dinner it's mostly seafood and steaks in paradise and a great selection of less-expensive salads and sandwiches. Outside the hotel you will find a beautiful pool and a tiki bar. And when you want that Landshark beer and the namesake margarita, you can head over to the Gulf-front Landshark Landing, where you'll find nightly entertainment, volleyball nets, a playground, hammocks tied under palm trees, and a pared-down menu of mostly American food and lots of Jimmy Buffett's Landshark beer on tap.

Hampton Inn Pensacola Beach (2 Via de Luna Dr., 850/932-6800, www.hamptonpensacolabeach.com, $150-300) has 181 pleasantly outfitted rooms right on the Gulf. The property has a lively tiki bar on the west end of the hotel by the pool, with the waves of the Gulf of Mexico lapping in the background. Ring games and horseshoes are available to entertain visitors, and fun-loving bartenders can whip up any beverage you want, including specialty drinks like the Mojo, Voodoo Juice, or Island Ice Pick.

The historic **Lee House** (400 Bayfront Pkwy., downtown Pensacola, 850/912-8770, www.leehousepensacola.com, $150-245) was damaged by fire in 2001 and knocked down three years later by Hurricane Ivan. It has been resurrected as an upscale bed-and-breakfast, and the location can't be topped. Sitting across from Seville Square Park in the historic district of downtown Pensacola and less than a mile from the foot of the Three Mile Bridge that takes you over to Pensacola Beach, the inn is near everything you want to experience on your Pensacola visit. The owners, well known in the area for their local restaurants and catering services Norma's and Norma's-On-The-Go, prepare a wonderful breakfast for guests. The gathering room in the front of the inn is comfortably upscale with several plush couches and a grand piano, where musicians provide evening entertainment for guests. The private courtyard is a wonderful spot to break for coffee in the afternoon after exploring the historic homes and downtown waterfront surrounding the inn. Each of the eight suites has

a unique theme, from the elegant bridal suite with a private jetted tub to the eccentric purple and leopard print room and a classy nautical-themed suite. For something more private, consider staying in one of the two new cottages on the property. The smaller **Pi Cottage** ($210-245) sleeps up to two adults and two children and features a king-size bed, living area with pullout couch, flat-screen TV, galley kitchen, and bathroom. The **Sweet Shop Cottage** (424 East Zaragoza St., $630-735) is just down the street from the main bed-and-breakfast. The elegant historic home with two bedrooms and two-and-a-half baths was built in 1879 and has been painstakingly remodeled into one of the premier rental properties in all of downtown.

OVER $300

The **Portofino Island Resort** (10 Portofino Dr., Pensacola Beach, 850/916-5000, www.portofinoisland.com, $380-700) offers an upscale resort experience on Pensacola Beach. The property comprises five towers with over 300 suites available. Built right at the eastern end of the Gulf Islands National Seashore preserve, which extends seven miles from Pensacola Beach to Navarre Beach, the resort gives you convenient access to the large stretch of preserved beach with the most beautiful dunes in the area, as well as great flats fishing, kayaking, and boating on Santa Rosa Sound. The resort offers two- and three-bedroom suites, each equipped with kitchen, washer and dryer, and private balcony, offered with 2-, 2.5-, 3-, or 3.5-bathroom floor plans. The two-bedroom suites offer over 1,300 square feet of space; the three-bedroom suites offer over 2,000 square feet. Each tower has its own heated pool and spa. Luxurious options include having a private chef come to your suite or enjoying a massage on your private balcony with sweeping views of the white-sand beaches and Gulf of Mexico.

VACATION RENTALS

Most of the vacation rentals are out on Pensacola Beach. There are a large number

The Florida Scenic Trail winds through Blackwater River State Park.

of condos available for nightly, weekly, and monthly bookings. Many of the homes for rent that line the Gulf shoreline are large four- and five-bedroom homes. For a more afford-able stay, the condos and classic cinder-block homes that dot the residential areas of the beach are a great choice. For vacation rent-als on Pensacola Beach, contact **Vacation Rentals by Owner** (www.vrbo.com) and search in the Pensacola Beach and Perdido Key areas. If you're interested in staying in the more historic downtown or East Hill areas, check out the rental listings offered by **Pensacola Historic Dream Cottages** (850/232-1266, www.pensacoladreamcot-tages.com).

CAMPING

Near Pensacola Beach, you camp at one of 200 campsites in **Fort Pickens National Park** (1400 Fort Pickens Rd., 850/934-2600, camp-sites $26/night; entrance fees $15/vehicle, $10/motorcycle, $7/person on foot or bicycle). Tents and RVs are welcome, and each campsite

has water, electricity, fire rings, grills, and nearby restroom facilities. The Gulf, bay, and historic forts are just a short walk from the campground. This is the most affordable way to stay on the beach, and the campground's location near the island's tip makes it a great spot for fishing. The forts are fun to explore for a few hours. You can download a self-guided tour brochure from the National Park Service website. The fort held many prisoners when it was still operational, the most famous being Geronimo, the Apache warrior who was captured in the 1880s. Ghost stories around the campfire, anyone?

A fancier option for RV enthusiasts is the **Pensacola Beach RV Resort** (17 Via De Luna Dr., 850/932-4670, $65-125/day, $325-750/week, $750-1750/month) located in the heart of the business district, and near Casino Beach, the most popular beach on Santa Rosa Island. The sound-side campground resort features a large clubhouse with showers and an event space, a nice pool for hot summer days, two beaches with beautiful sound views, washers and dryers, and a small on-site shop. This is an exceptionally affordable option if you're looking for a week or month-long RV site that's on the beach and just a short drive from downtown Pensacola.

On the west side of town, some of the best campsites are found just north of Perdido Key at **Big Lagoon State Park** (12301 Gulf Beach Hwy., 850/492-1595, camping $20/night; en-trance fees $6/vehicle with 2-8 people, $4 single occupant vehicle, $2 pedestrians and bicyclists; $10-12 boat launch). The 655-acre park on Big Lagoon has 75 sites with water, electricity, a picnic table, fire ring, and grill. The campground has three bathhouses with showers. With more than five miles of hik-ing trails, excellent fishing, paddling around the lagoon and tributaries, boating in the surrounding waters, and close proximity to the Gulf, this park is a gem of the Florida Gulf Coast. Winter and fall are great times to camp here, as it's often quiet and tranquil. Numerous picnic pavilions make this a fine park to bring lunch and enjoy a day or more of outdoor activity. There are beaches along the Intracoastal Waterway, and birding is a popular activity along the forested trail or shorelines. Kayak, canoe, and paddleboards are available for rent at the ranger's station. Take a short drive up the road and hike the nature trails at **Tarkiln Bayou Preserve State Park** (2401 Bauer Rd., Pensacola, 850/492-1595, www.floridastateparks.org, 8am-sunset, $3 per vehicle, $2 for pedestrians, bicyclists, and motorcycles).

North of Pensacola, you'll discover a wealth of camping and outdoor recreation opportunities. The landscape changes dramatically to dense pine forests with a network of creeks and rivers running through them. There are thirty campsites at **Blackwater River State Park** (7720 Deaton Bridge Rd., 850/983-5363, camping $20/night; entrance fees $4/vehicle). Each campsite has water and electricity, and the bathhouse has hot showers. You can whistle the old Credence Clearwater Revival song as you watch old Blackwater River keep on rolling. Or better yet, rent a canoe or tube from one of the numerous local outfitters and paddle or float down the calm, sandy-bottomed river along the 31-mile designated **Blackwater River Canoe Trail** (maps found online at www.dep.state.fl.us.com).

There are several campgrounds, including all of the below, in Blackwater State Forest. Information on availability and reservations can be found by calling the **Florida Forest Service** (850/957-6140). The most popular is **Hurricane Lake** (Hurricane Lake Rd., off of Hwy. 4), which has two campgrounds, one on the north side of the 318-acre lake, and another on the south side. Bring your pole and tackle for the excellent bass fishing. The sites on the north side are a mix of primitive sites ($10/night) and sites with electricity and water ($25/night). The sites on the south end are all primitive. Both campgrounds have faucets, restrooms, and boat ramps to the lake.

Bear Lake Recreation Area (2.5 miles east of Munson off Hwy. 4, $25/night) has campsites with electricity and water, restrooms, showers, boat launch, and a pier. There are lots of hiking trail nearby, including the 1.3-mile Sweetwater Trail, and the 4-mile-long Bear Lake Loop Trail.

Karick Lake Recreation Area (7.5 miles north of Baker, east of County Road 189, $25/night) has two campgrounds with electricity and water on Karick Lake. Restrooms and showers are available, as well as a boat ramp, pier, and hiking trails nearby. The east end of the Jackson Red Ground Trail, a 21-mile hike that connects to the Red Rocks area of the state forest leaves from Karick Lake.

You'll find campsites on a small 6.5-acre lake at the **Krul Recreation Area** (half mile east of Munson, north of Hwy. 4, $25/night). The west end trailhead of the Sweetwater Trail connects to Bear Lake, which makes a nice overnight hike between campgrounds. The area also has a swimming area with net to keep the alligators away, restrooms with showers, and sites with electricity and water.

If you want something more rugged, you can backpack through the rolling forest along the Blackwater Forest segment of the **Florida Scenic Trail.** More than 43 miles of the scenic trail are found in the Blackwater State Forest. Three access points allow you to plan a backpacking trip along this section that traverses the Hutton Unit, Juniper Creek Trail, Jackson Red Ground Trail, and the Wiregrass Trail. The terrain is mostly flat and easy going, with plenty of shade. You will traverse paths alongside creeks and the Blackwater River, and navigate through pine, oak, cedar, and scrub forests. The bluffs at Red Rocks are one of the highlights. Designated campsites, campgrounds, and shelters along the way provide backpackers with plenty of options when the hiking day draws to a close.

Information and Services

Pensacola is located within the **central time zone.** It's that far west. The area code is **850.**

TOURIST INFORMATION

Begin a visit with a stop to the **Pensacola Bay Area Convention & Visitors Bureau information center** (1401 E. Gregory St., at the foot of the Pensacola Bay Bridge, 800/874-1234, www.visitpensacola.com, 8am-5pm Mon.-Fri., 8am-4pm Sat.-Sun.) to pick up maps, brochures, and a copy of the self-guided historic district tours. There's also a convenient **Pensacola Beach Visitors Information Center** (735 Pensacola Beach Blvd., Pensacola Beach, 850/932-1500, 9am-5pm daily).

The main daily newspaper is the **Pensacola News Journal,** and there's a free city magazine called **Pensacola Downtown Crowd** that covers local restaurants and the arts. **Family Sporting Network** is a free and popular paper that covers local sports and can be found on newsstands and business counters throughout the city.

POLICE AND EMERGENCIES

In an emergency, dial 911. If you need medical assistance, **Baptist Hospital** (1000 W. Moreno St., Pensacola, 850/434-4011) has full emergency services, as do **Sacred Heart Hospital** (5152 N. 9th Ave., Pensacola, 850/416-7000) and **Gulf Breeze Hospital** (1110 Gulf Breeze Pkwy., Gulf Breeze, 850/934-2000).

RADIO AND TELEVISION

On the radio, turn to **WUWF 88.1 FM** for NPR, **WTKX 101.5 FM** for straight-ahead rock, **WXBM 102.7** for country radio, and **WCOA 1370 AM** for local talk radio.

For local television programming, **WEAR Channel 3** is the local ABC affiliate, **WKRG Channel 5** is the CBS affiliate out of Mobile-Pensacola, **WALA Channel 10** is the FOX affiliate out of Mobile-Pensacola, **WPMI Channel 15** is the NBC affiliate out of Mobile-Pensacola, **WSRE Channel 23** is PBS, and **WBQP Channel 12** is a local independent.

LAUNDRY SERVICES

If you find yourself in need of coin-op laundry services, try **Dave's** (4124 Mobile Hwy., 850/455-6931) or **9th Avenue Coin Laundry** (6220 N. 9th Ave., 850/471-9224).

Getting There and Around

CAR

The major east-west roads in this area are I-10, U.S. 90, and U.S. 98. Running north-south are U.S. 29 and I-110. To get to Pensacola from I-10, you can travel south on Highway 85 into Fort Walton Beach, then west on U.S. 98 to Navarre, then west over Navarre Toll Bridge, and finally west on Highway 399 approximately 20 miles to Pensacola Beach. Or you can go south on I-110 (lots of chain motels along this stretch) or Highway 281, then east on U.S. 98, follow signs to the beaches, and finally drive over Pensacola Beach Toll Bridge into Pensacola Beach. To get to Perdido Key from Pensacola, go west on Highway 292 to Perdido and finally over Perdido Key Bridge onto Perdido Key.

In town, Palafox is the major north-south artery, and Garden Street, which becomes Navy Boulevard on the way to the naval station, runs east-west. The historic district to the waterfront is walkable; for most of the rest of the area you'll need a car. Naval Air

Station Pensacola is southwest of the city, and Pensacola Beach is southeast of the city on Santa Rosa Island. Pensacola is connected to Gulf Breeze by the Pensacola Bay Bridge (also called Three Mile Bridge), which in turn is connected to Pensacola Beach by the Bob Sikes Bridge.

AIR

Located in Escambia County approximately four miles northeast of downtown Pensacola, **Pensacola International Airport** (2430 Airport Blvd., 850/436-5000, www.flypensacola.com) is the biggest airport in northwest Florida, but that's not saying too much. It's not huge, serving more than 100 flights daily from AirTran Airways, American, American Eagle, Continental, Delta, Northwest, and US Airways. Delta has the largest number of direct flights.

Taxis queue up outside the main terminal entrance at baggage claim. Car rental agencies are inside the main terminal entrance across from baggage claim. **Alamo** (800/327-9633), **Avis** (800/831-2847), **Budget** (800/527-0700), **Dollar** (800/800-4000 domestic, 800/800-6000 international), **Hertz** (800/654-3131),

and **National** (800/227-7368) are all on the premises. Enterprise and Thrifty are off-site.

BUS AND TRAIN

Amtrak (980 E. Heinberg St., 800/872-7245, www.amtrak.com) has a train station in Pensacola that was still closed at the time of writing due to train tracks damaged by Hurricane Katrina in 2005. **Greyhound Bus Line** (505 W. Burgess Rd., 850/476-4800, www.greyhound.com), however, offers fairly extensive bus service. Such a large military presence usually ensures decent public transportation. There's even a local bus line run by **Escambia County Area Transit** (850/595-3228, www.goecat.com) that includes a University of West Florida (UWF) trolley service and a Pensacola Beach trolley. All in all, it is possible to get around here without a car, but difficult, with some of the more significant attractions inaccessible via public transportation. Pensacola Beach has a free seasonal **trolley** (May 22-Labor Day) that runs to all destinations on the beach. You can also use an online trolley tracker (www.visitpensacolabeach.com) to help schedule your ride.

Alabama Gulf Shores

Look for ★ to find recommended
sights, activities, dining, and lodging.

Highlights

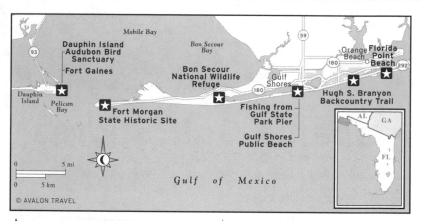

★ **Florida Point Beach:** There is ample, free parking for your car and more than 6,000 feet of sugar-white sand on which to park your beach chair. What more could you ask for (page 361)?

★ **Gulf Shores Public Beach:** With a cluster of entertainment and restaurants surrounding it, this is the perfect beach party (page 362).

★ **Hugh S. Branyon Backcountry Trail:** You can hike or bike through rare maritime forest habitat, past unique freshwater spring-fed lakes, and explore beautiful dune and coastal environments on this exceptionally maintained and mostly paved trail system (page 364).

★ **Bon Secour National Wildlife Refuge:** This preserve of more than 7,000 acres provides habitat for migrating birds, sea turtles, and other animals. There are miles of pristine beach and an exceptional network of hiking trails to discover (page 365).

★ **Fishing from Gulf State Park Pier:** The largest pier on the Gulf Coast extends more than 1,500 feet into emerald waters and is the best place in the area to reel in Spanish mackerel, bluegill, and more (page 369).

★ **Fort Morgan State Historic Site:** This fort, which played a vital role in the Civil War, hosts reenactments throughout the year—with cannon firings and all (page 370).

★ **Dauphin Island Audubon Bird Sanctuary:** Walk the boardwalks and trails at this sanctuary, which provides an important habitat for over 370 species of birds on their spring and fall migrations (page 383).

★ **Fort Gaines:** Walk back in time as you explore the intricate arched tunnels and high bastions of this fort, which played an integral role in the Battle of Mobile Bay during the Civil War (page 385).

The beaches in Gulf Shores and Orange Beach are just as beautiful and sugar-white as those in Pensacola and Destin. If the famous, ramshackle Flora-Bama (page 375) wasn't located right on the border crossing, you wouldn't even

know that you had just passed into Alabama. This stretch of coast is seen as a natural extension of the Florida Gulf Coast in both geography and culture.

From Orange Beach to Gulf Shores you have more than 32 miles of beautiful shoreline. Orange Beach and Gulf Shores are favored by younger travelers looking for a party as well as families who prefer plenty of entertainment, shopping, and dining options. Several new upscale developments have been built recently on the barrier island. On the western end of Gulf Shores, you'll find the larger and more expensive golf and beach resorts. However, there are still plenty of reasonably priced accommodations, and when compared to the Florida Gulf Coast to the east, these two cities are often a real bargain.

For something more laid-back and traditional, take the ferry from the western tip of Gulf Shores and cross Mobile Bay to Dauphin Island, a charming and culturally Southern

destination without the traffic jams and beach parties typical of Gulf Shores in the summer. The beaches aren't quite as nice as those to the east, and the offshore oil rigs are definitely an eyesore, but it's a wonderful place to rent a house for a weekend, a week, or more and spend every second with the family enjoying the slow pace of life, the quiet beaches, the surrounding wilderness and wildlife, and the welcoming people who live in this picturesque beach community.

This stretch of coast was settled in the late 1800s by anglers and farmers who were drawn to the undeveloped land and the easy access to a variety of freshwater and saltwater fishing environments. Early farmers grew a variety of crops, predominantly satsuma oranges, which is the explanation for the name Orange Beach. However, you won't see many orange trees around here today. In 1920 a salesperson peddling orange tree seedlings infected with blight wiped out most of the orange groves.

Previous: the famous Flora-Bama; Gulf State Park Pier. **Above:** the ferris wheel at The Wharf in Orange Beach.

Alabama Gulf Shores

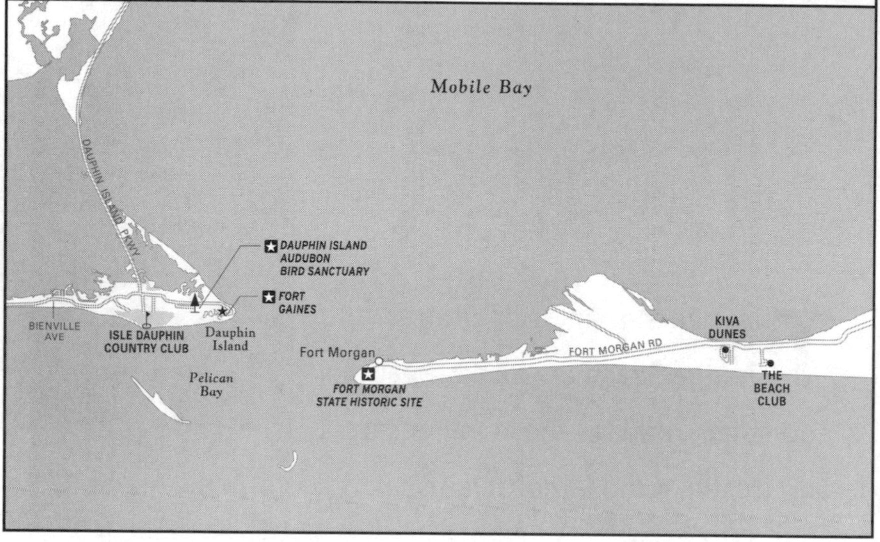

Mobile Bay

DAUPHIN ISLAND
AUDUBON
BIRD SANCTUARY

FORT
GAINES

BIENVILLE
AVE

ISLE DAUPHIN
COUNTRY CLUB

Dauphin
Island

*Pelican
Bay*

Fort Morgan

FORT MORGAN
STATE HISTORIC SITE

FORT MORGAN RD

KIVA
DUNES

THE
BEACH
CLUB

The building of the Intracoastal Waterway in the 1930s brought more commerce and development into the area and put the region on the map as a popular vacation spot for residents of the Southeast. Today the region is visited by more than one million travelers a year, most of them coming from the Birmingham, Alabama, and New Orleans area.

PLANNING YOUR TIME

Travelers typically come to the area for weekend-long vacations, with the number of tourists swelling during the summer holidays. However, there is plenty to keep you busy for a week or more. It's not difficult to find a condo or house that is rented by the day, week, or month. During the slow winter season, you can get exceptional deals on rentals by the month or for the entire season, which typically runs November-March, with prices going up slightly around the winter holidays. The busy season is during the hot summer months mid-May-late September. My favorite time to visit this area is in the late fall, October-November, or the late spring, mid-March-mid-April.

During the fall you have cooler weather, less crowded beaches, the fall bird migrations, and better prices on accommodations, activities, and food. However, June-November is considered hurricane season, and so the weather can be unpredictable. During this time of the year, I don't recommend booking week or month-long rentals too far in advance, but if you can escape for a weekend and know the coast is clear of hurricanes, then this is a great time to be here.

The spring is even better. The hurricane season is far away and the summer crowds haven't poured in yet. The weather is cool, and the hotels and rentals are less expensive. The result is beautiful, comfortable warm weather and the beaches and forests all to yourself. This is the best time to camp and enjoy outdoor activities like paddling and hiking. The bugs, particularly mosquitoes, have just started hatching but are far from intolerable. A main concern when pursuing outdoor activities during this time is the afternoon thundershowers. They often produce violent lightning storms that are beautiful and thrilling, yet extremely dangerous. The

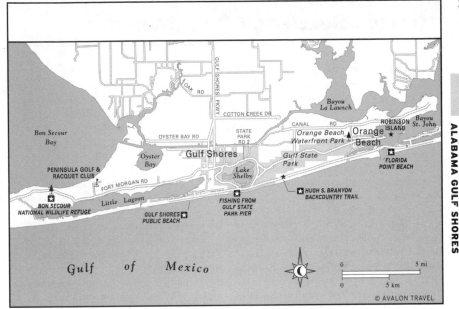

© AVALON TRAVEL

thunderstorms happen nearly every day, usually right around 2pm.

Transportation

Amtrak (800/872-7245, www.amtrak.com) offers train service as far south as the Hattiesburg, Mississippi, station, 100 miles west of Gulf Shores, but you'll have to drive from there. Amtrak has plans to repair the rail line that runs from New Orleans through the Panhandle. This route has been out of service since Hurricane Katrina badly damaged the tracks in 2005. Also, **Greyhound Bus Line** (239/774-5660, www.greyhound.com) provides regular service into Mobile, and the **Wave Transit System** (251/344-6600) operates a reliable network of city buses ($1.25 fare).

By air, the closest large airport is **Pensacola International Airport** (850/436-5000, www.flypensacola.com), one hour to the east in Pensacola. **Advantage Airport Shuttle** (850/420-7807, www.advantageairportshuttle.com, Pensacola to Orange Beach $60-70, Pensacola to Gulf Shores $75-90) provides service from Pensacola Airport to Orange Beach and Gulf Shores. There is a smaller regional airport in Mobile, the **Mobile Regional Airport** (800/357-5373, www.mobairport.com), which offers nonstop jet service on American Airlines, Delta, United, and US Airways to Atlanta, Charlotte, Houston, and Dallas. Private planes can also fly into Jack Edwards Airport in Gulf Shores, Foley Municipal, and Dauphin Island Airport.

Orange Beach and Gulf Shores

This stretch of Alabama's Gulf Coast is known as "Pleasure Island." It's not a natural island. In 1933 the Intracoastal Waterway was built, which cut the beaches off from the mainland of Alabama and left this 32-mile stretch of beach surrounded on four sides by water. If you visit, you'll understand the "pleasure" part. This has been the go-to destination for Alabamians wanting a beach vacation for generations.

The biggest draw of this area—apart from the miles of sugar-white beaches—is the abundant freshwater and saltwater fishing. An impressive collection of saltwater and freshwater spring-fed lakes dots the coast. Most of them are found within the 6,150 acres of Gulf State Park, which also features rare maritime forest, coastal beaches, and vital dune habitat. Most of the park is concentrated around the 900-acre Lake Shelby, and as you drive along the coast, you will discover large stretches of beach and dune habitat that are preserved as a part of the Gulf State Park complex. These preserved sections of beach are possibly the only thing that has kept this coastline from becoming entirely developed.

In more recent years the laid-back charm of the culture coupled with the exceptional bargains found along this stretch of coast have been drawing record-breaking crowds to the area from all over the country. A boom in development followed Hurricane Ivan in 2004, which expanded capacity for tourists and the development of new entertainment districts like the Wharf in Orange Beach, boasting the tallest Ferris wheel in the Southeast.

If you drive down from the north on Highway 59, you will literally dead-end at the emerald waters of the Gulf of Mexico. Right in front of you is The Hangout, a sprawling bar and restaurant favored by the party crowd, and more importantly the Gulf Shores Public Beach, which is the most popular and crowded beach on this stretch of coast. Turn right and you'll head toward the western tip of Gulf Shores, where you'll find several upscale resorts and much quieter beaches along the coast. All the way at the western tip of the island is Fort Morgan, a large fort used most

Florida Point Beach

Orange Beach

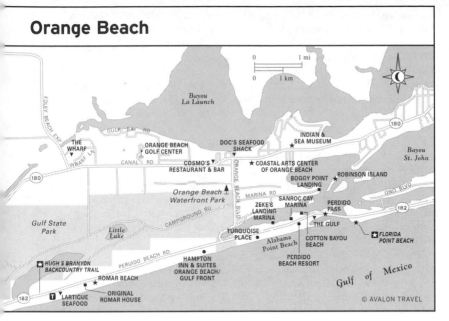

famously in the Civil War during the Battle of Mobile Bay. Also at the western tip is the ferry terminal that can transport you or your car over Mobile Bay to Dauphin Island. If you turn right at the end of Highway 59, you will drive toward Orange Beach and the Florida border and pass by several excellent beaches with ample parking.

BEACHES
Orange Beach

You can easily access the beach from many locations around Orange Beach. Often the difficult part is finding parking, especially in the busy summer months. The best place to start is at the large parking areas and popular beaches dotted along this stretch of coast that are a part of the Gulf State Park beach system.

★ FLORIDA POINT BEACH

Heading from east to west, the first beach you'll reach is the beach at **Florida Point,** just 0.3 mile east of the Perdido Pass Bridge. The beach is wide here, and there are more than 6,000 feet of Gulf shoreline to walk and find that perfect spot in the sugar-white sand.

Parking is free and so are the restrooms and showers. The beach sits on the eastern side of Perdido Pass, so it isn't the best spot for swimming due to the strong currents, heavy boat traffic, and higher presence of sharks in the pass. However, the beach does offer an excellent spot to watch incoming charter fishing boats at the end of the day.

ALABAMA POINT BEACH

Cross the Perdido Pass Bridge to reach the beach at **Alabama Point.** You can park along the west side of the bridge and walk down to the sand. This is the site of the ultra-hip Gulf Restaurant, built from two shipping containers. The owners of The Gulf have big plans for this stretch of beach. Alabama Point is slated for expansion. Plans call for a much larger boardwalk complex to be built that will include beach and bait shops. Alabama Point has historically been the most popular spot for surfing, but word on the beach is that the recent dredging by the U.S. Army Corps of Engineers has ruined the break. It's still one of the best spots on the Alabama coast to catch a wave, which isn't saying much—this area isn't particularly known for its sweet surfing.

COTTON BAYOU BEACH

Just two miles west of Alabama Point at the intersection of Highway 182 and Highway 161 is the Gulf State **Cotton Bayou Beach.** This small beach access point with parking lot is easy to miss. It's between two condo developments and a testament to Orange Beach's dedication to providing as much public access to the beach as possible. A small restroom is located in the parking lot. Like many of the beaches in this area, Cotton Bayou is an excellent spot for swimming.

ROMAR BEACH

Head two miles west of Cotton Bayou Beach to reach **Romar Beach.** There's only a small amount of free parking here and no restrooms or facilities. However, there are plans for development at this beach, so keep an eye out for new pavilions and restrooms in the years to come. Despite the lack of facilities at this beach, it's usually pretty busy in the summer and an excellent spot for swimming.

ORANGE BEACH WATERFRONT PARK

The **Orange Beach Waterfront Park** (26425 Canal Rd., 251/981-6039, www.obparksandrec.com, open daily, free) on Wolf Bay is a favorite for families. The beautifully maintained and landscaped park has plenty of outdoor activities to keep the kids entertained. The 400-foot fishing pier extends into Wolf Bay and features covered pavilions with seating at the beginning, middle, and end of the pier. The playground is lit at night, and it's so huge and impressive that it's officially called the "kid's park." There are enough slides, swings, and things to climb on in this castle-themed playground to make any kid feel like a princess or king for a day. You'll find grills and picnic tables underneath the covered pavilions and a paved walking path for riding bikes, jogging, or taking a leisurely stroll beside the picturesque Wolf Bay.

ROBINSON AND BIRD ISLANDS

Ever wanted to hang out on your own island? You can do that in Orange Beach, but you'll need your own boat to get there. In 2003 the city of Orange Beach purchased **Robinson and Bird Islands,** two small islands within a stone's throw of one another just north of Perdido Pass. The islands and their quartz-white beaches have been a popular destination of boaters for years. On a nice summer day, boats are often packed around the island as close as possible. The official line from the city is that the islands were preserved to protect them from development and to provide a refuge for wildlife, but the most common wildlife you'll see here are locals partying on the beaches.

Gulf Shores

You won't have a hard time finding a great beach in Gulf Shores. Like Orange Beach and Pensacola to the east, this area has plenty of public access points and parking lots that make getting your beach gear to the edge of the Gulf a breeze. Many of the beaches in Gulf Shores are also a part of the Gulf State Park complex, which boasts more than three miles of preserved beaches along this stretch of coast. In addition to the below, you'll also find miles of beaches within **Bon Secour National Wildlife Refuge.**

★ GULF SHORES PUBLIC BEACH

The most popular beach in the area is the **Gulf Shores Public Beach** (100 Gulf Shores Pkwy., 251/968-1420, www.gulfshoresal.gov, open daily, $5 parking). To find huge crowds of beachgoers, just drive to the end of Highway 59. The public beach is right where The Hangout is located, which is impossible to miss. There are volleyball courts, plenty of bars and restaurants in the area, three open-air pavilions, as well as restrooms with showers. It's where the young beachgoers hang out, and it usually draws more of the party crowd. This is a beautiful beach that is well maintained and regularly cleaned by the city of Gulf Shores. Lifeguards are here all day during

Gulf Shores

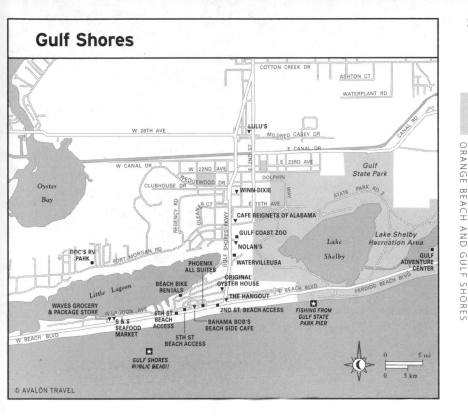

the summer, making this an excellent choice for families and those with little swimming experience looking to challenge the Gulf of Mexico riptides with a bit of summer swimming, surfing, or boogie boarding. The beach is wide, which makes it easy to find a spot to set up the beach chair for the day, even when huge crowds are packing the sand on summer weekends and holidays. However, you might not have as much luck with parking during these times. Get here early if you need a parking spot, otherwise ride a bike or walk from your hotel or condo.

Surrounding the main public beach is a cluster of smaller **public access points** (251/968-1420, www.gulfshoresal.gov): **2nd St. Beach Access** (240 W. Beach Blvd., open daily, $5 parking), **5th St.** (599 W. Beach Blvd., open daily, free parking), and the **6th St. Beach Access** (699 W. Beach Blvd., open

daily, $5 parking). If you're staying nearby, you can get to the beach via the crosswalks at 4th Street and 13th Street as well.

THE BEACH AT GULF STATE PARK PIER

If you want to get some fishing in with your beach-lounging, a good place to start is the **Gulf State Park Pier** (20800 E. Beach Blvd., 251/967-3474, www.alapark.com, open daily, free parking, fishing rates $9/day 12 and older, $5 under 11 or free with paid adult, fishing rod rentals $1.50/hour), located in Gulf State Park between Gulf Shores and Orange Beach. Hurricane Ivan destroyed the original pier in 2004, and five years later Gulf Shores opened the largest pier on the Gulf at 1,540 feet long. If you don't feel like fishing, you can walk the length of the pier or just enjoy the view for $3 per adult for one trip or $4 for all day access.

Newly added to the pier are indoor seating and air-conditioning to the concession area that sells snacks and drinks, an indoor shop with tackle and bait as well as souvenirs, restrooms at the midway point of the pier, and wheelchair-accessible rail fishing. Parking is free, and the parking lot can hold over 200 cars. At the base of the pier, you will find a restroom with showers and shaded picnic tables and benches. While the pier is extremely impressive, the beach is just as popular. The beach is wide around the pier, with plenty of room to spread out and enjoy the sand and surf with the family. The break on both sides of the pier pilings is popular with surfers and boogie boarders, while the rest of the beach area is excellent for swimming.

GULF STATE PARK PAVILION AREA
Another top spot to hit the beach is the **Gulf State Park Pavilion Area** (22250 E. Beach Blvd., 251/968-7296, www.alapark.com, open daily, $5 parking), located six miles east of Highway 59. This beach is usually a bit less crowded than the area around the pier, and it's a popular spot for surf fishing. Hurricane Ivan destroyed the original pavilion here, but the new pavilion is a major improvement, featuring restrooms with air-conditioning and private showers, a small snack bar, and a fireplace for cold days on the coast. It's $5 to park for the entire day, $12 for large vans. This is a great beach for families who don't mind the crowds on the weekends.

LAKE SHELBY RECREATION AREA
If you want a beach that is a little less crowded and don't mind leaving the Gulf, the beach at the **Lake Shelby Recreation Area** (20115 E. State Hwy. 135, 251/948-7275, www.alapark.com, 7am-sundown daily, free parking) is a good choice. Just one mile east from the junction of Highway 59 and Highway 182, the beach can be accessed from the Gulf State Park campground. The 900-acre freshwater lake is open to fishing, boating, kayaking, and swimming. At the beach you'll find restrooms, showers, picnic tables, and pavilions.

the Hugh S. Branyon Backcountry Trail

HIKING, BIKING, AND WILDLIFE-WATCHING
Orange Beach
★ HUGH S. BRANYON BACKCOUNTRY TRAIL
There are few coastal trail systems in the Southeast that are much better than the **Hugh S. Branyon Backcountry Trail** (trailheads on Hwy. 182 and Hwy. 161 in Orange Beach, 251/981-1180, www.backcountrytrail.com, daylight hours daily, free). This trail system has six different trails that total more than 11 miles. The Backcountry Trail is popular with hikers, bikers, and joggers. It's a great way to spend the afternoon exploring the unique maritime forest habitat of Orange Beach. Construction was completed on the trail complex in 2003, and it has been a huge hit with visitors and locals. Download the free app on the website to get an up-to-date map with virtual kiosks along the way that give details on the natural surroundings, local lore, Native American heritage, and historical significance of the areas that you'll hike or bike

through. Each of the six trails within the system traverses a unique habitat. The most popular trail is the Catman Road segment. This paved trail is perfect for biking or hiking. It takes you past a screened-in pavilion where you can have a picnic lunch before exploring the butterfly garden and ending at the northern edge of Little Lake. This is a great way to get some exercise and spend a little time in the shade if the beach has burned you out for a bit.

You can rent bikes for the trail at **Beach Bike Rentals** (22989 Perdido Beach Blvd., 251/968-1770, www.beachbikerentals.net, 9am-sunset daily, $20-25/day). They offer single three-speeds and cruisers as well as tandem cruisers and have daily and weekly rates. Locks and helmets are included with rentals—a huge plus that will keep the kids safe on the paved sections of the Backcountry Trail.

Gulf Shores
★ BON SECOUR NATIONAL WILDLIFE REFUGE

Some of the best hiking in the area is found at the **Bon Secour National Wildlife Refuge** (12295 Hwy. 180, 251/540-7720, www.fws.gov/bonsecour, 7am-sundown daily, park office 7am-3:30pm Mon.-Fri., free parking). This 7,000-acre preserve contains more than six miles of hiking trails through various coastal habitats that include beaches and sand dunes, fresh- and saltwater marshes, freshwater swamps, and upland forests. More than 370 different bird species have been seen inside the preserve boundaries including ospreys, great horned and eastern screech owls, yellow-billed cuckoos, and common loons. The refuge is one of the largest undeveloped stretches of land on the Alabama coast. It receives more than 100,000 visitors every year, but most of them get no farther into the refuge than the popular Gulf-side beach. Once you get out on the trails, you often have the backcountry to yourself. Bon Secour means "safe harbor" in French, and today the meaning couldn't be more appropriate. While hiking in the refuge, you're likely to encounter the many migrating and resident birds that live in and visit the preserve. You might even be lucky enough to spot a red fox or coyote on your hike.

All of the trails are located in the preserve's Perdue Unit, with one of the most popular hikes being the two-mile-long **Pine Beach Trail.** This trail provides the perfect overview of the preserve. The trailhead is near the entrance of the park on the left side of Mobile Street. The hiking is moderately strenuous, especially along the exceptionally sandy areas, where your ankles and calves will get a workout. Hikers traverse the maritime scrub forest and pass between two lakes on the way to the dunes ecosystem that leads to the beach and the Gulf. The most unique and impressive section of the trail is where you hike along a thin strip of land and have the freshwater Gator Lake and the saltwater Little Lagoon on either side of you. The trail usually takes about two hours, but there's so much of interest along the way that it is easy to spend three or four hours on this hike. It's also easy to make a day of the trip and spend hours sitting or walking on the beautiful beach at the Pine Beach Trail's southern end.

Another popular trail is the one-mile-long **Jeff Friend Trail** at the eastern end of the preserve's Perdue Unit. This trail is wheelchair accessible and loops around the northern edge of Little Lagoon. The hiking is easy, and along the way you'll explore sections of the maritime forest. The **Centennial Trail** connects the Jeff Friend Trail to the Pine Beach Trail and leads through the forest just north of Little Lagoon. Hike the **Gator Lake Trail** if you want to explore the shoreline of freshwater Gator Lake. During the winter this trail is favored by birdwatchers, who often spot yellow-rumped warblers and blue-gray gnatcatchers. And if you're lucky you might spot an endangered Alabama beach mouse. Look for them scurrying across the sand dunes. They play a vital role in the health of the sand dune ecosystem by distributing seeds for sea oats, grasses, and other vegetation.

The refuge has miles of beaches within the park, and they can be accessed by driving down the main park road, Mobile Street, until it ends at a parking lot on the Gulf, or you can hike the Pine Beach Trail to a more secluded and quiet beach to the east of the main beach area. Either way, once you are on the Gulf there are miles of beaches to walk and explore. You shouldn't have a hard time finding your own slice of paradise where you can sit and hear nothing but the waves crashing against the shore. And if you're walking the beaches on the Gulf side May-October, you may the loggerhead and Kemp's ridley sea turtles that use the beaches of the preserve as an important nesting ground.

ALABAMA COASTAL BIRDING TRAIL

If you're into bird-watching, you can find the flocks by following the **Alabama Coastal Birding Trail** (trailheads on Hwy. 182 just across Perdido Pass, 877/226-9089, www.alabamacoastalbirdingtrail.com, daylight hours daily, free). Detailed maps and information on all the best places to search for seabirds, sparrows, and other species can be found on the website. The site details exactly what birds you can expect to find during the different seasons in each location along the trail, which is especially helpful if you're checking off birds from your life list. The trail extends across much of Alabama, so if you want to just keep on birding, there's nothing stopping you. Much of the trail in this area is located in the Bon Secour National Wildlife Refuge and around Fort Morgan on the western end of the island. This region draws huge numbers of migrating birds during the spring and fall migrations. The birding around here is exceptional, but you can see even more birds by heading over to Dauphin Island to the west, which is considered to be one of the premier birding spots in the country.

GOLF
Orange Beach

Before you hit the course, you can practice your swing and get golf gear at the **Orange Beach Golf Center** (4700 Easy St., 251/981-1653, www.obparksandrec.com/golfcenter,

Both Orange Beach and Gulf Shores have great golfing.

7am-9pm daily, $3/bucket of 34 golf balls). This driving range and pro shop has 30 grass tees and 10 covered mat tees. The range is lighted for driving in the cooler nighttime hours during the summer.

Gulf Shores

The Peninsula Golf and Racquet Club (20 Peninsula Blvd., 251/968-8009, www.peninsulagolfclub.com, open at 7am daily, greens fee $59-79), a 27-hole championship course designed by Earl Stone, is tucked away beside Mobile Bay and the Bon Secour National Wildlife Refuge. Golfers of all skill levels can enjoy this extremely playable course with over 7,000 yards from the championship boxes. Winding through live oaks and native vegetation, the course attracts a wide variety of birds and wildlife that add a touch of nature to your golfing experience. The tennis courts, pools, activities at the clubhouse, and restaurant will keep the whole family occupied and happy during and after the game.

The **Gulf State Park Golf Course** (20115 Hwy. 135, 251/948-4653, www.alapark.com, open at 7am daily, 18-hole $27-13, 9-hole $16-11) is an exceptional value in a beautiful setting. PGA pro Harry Dwyer manages this course nestled right in the middle of a wildlife refuge. Alligators are often spotted on the lakes and water features of the 18-hole championship course designed by Earl Stone. Opened in 1972 the course has been a family tradition and a destination of golfers traveling to the area for over 40 years. The fairways are wide and there aren't too many water features, which makes playing a little easier than on some of the other courses in the area. This a great place to bring the kids for a few rounds with the folks.

An exceptionally manicured course with impressively low rates is found at **Kiva Dunes Golf Course** (815 Plantation Rd., #100, 888/833-5482, www.kivadunes.com/golf.php, open at 7am daily, rates from $69). Designed by Jerry Pate, the course was voted Best New Course by *Golf Digest* magazine in 1995, the year it opened. You can stay at the Kiva Dunes Resort and almost walk from your room right onto the course. They frequently offer specials at the resort like a three-night package that includes two days of unlimited golf, breakfast, and cart rentals at a deeply discounted rate, so you can get the most out of a golf vacation on one of the best courses in the area.

Formerly called the Gulf Shores Golf Club, **The Golf Club at the Wharf** (520 Clubhouse Dr., 251/968-7366, www.golf.gulfshores.com, open at 7am daily, rates from $59) underwent a major renovation in 2006 under the supervision of father and son team Jay and Carter Morrish. The par-71 course was lengthened by 300 yards, and many more bunkers, water features, and fairway enhancements were added. The ProLink Solutions GPS system allows golfers to quickly get familiarized with the course with five sets of tees that range from 4,866 to 6,919 yards.

The two courses at **Craft Farms Golf Club** (3840 Cotton Creek Cir., 251/968-7500, www.craftfarms.com, open at 7am daily, rates from $59) were designed by Arnold Palmer. The Cotton Creek Course is a traditional 18-hole 7,000-yard-long course with rolling fairways and forward tees. Surrounded by lakes and forest, the four-star course has been rated by *Golf Digest* as one of the best places to play. Bring your A game to this course and relish in the challenge of the sixth hole, which requires a well-placed tee shot over water. The Cypress Bend Course has staggered tees and is rated 4.5 stars by *Golf Digest*. The sprawling bunkers, wide fairways, and vast landing areas are punctuated with cordgrass lakes that come into play on almost every hole. The fourth hole is the one to watch out for on this Palmer course. The dress code is relaxed on both courses. Golfers can wear shorts, and collared shirts and spikes are required. Groups of five are welcomed if they keep up with the pace of play.

CANOEING AND KAYAKING
Orange Beach

The best place for paddlers to start in Orange Beach is to take a trip down the **Orange Beach Kayak and Canoe Trail.** You can download maps of the 10 official launch points along this trail at the Orange Beach Community Website at www.orangebeach. ws. The trail starts at the launch on Gulf Bay Road on Wolf Bay. Paddlers travel east past Waterfront Park and Harrison Park before reaching Arnica Bay and paddling into Bayou St. John, ending at the Boggy Point Boat Launch. There are launching and takeout points along the way if you want to paddle the trail in shorter sections.

If you need a kayak for your own self-guided tour, **Paddled By You Kayak Rentals** (26448 Cotton Bayou Dr., 251/752-9250, paddledbyyou.com, 9am-6pm Mon.-Sat., single kayak $45/day and $10/hour, double kayak $60/day and $15/hour) will rent you a kayak to take down the trail or to launch from wherever you like. They also rent paddleboards and special kayaks outfitted for kayak fishing.

Gulf Shores

A favorite paddling and kayak-fishing spot is the spring-fed freshwater **Lake Shelby,** which can be accessed from the Gulf State Park campground. During large storms and hurricanes, the Gulf will often breach the lake and deposit saltwater fish species. This gives kayak-anglers an opportunity to experience the best of freshwater and saltwater fishing and reel in largemouth bass, speckled trout, redfish, and bluegills from Lake Shelby. The mile-long **Little Lagoon** offers great paddling, as does nearby **Gator Lake.** Paddlers can launch their kayaks and canoes from the new Lagoon Park.

The legendary **"Ice Box" on the Bon Secour River** is a favorite of paddlers. This spring head stays nice and cold year-round and is the perfect retreat from the summer heat. You can rent a kayak and take an easy self-guided float down the slow river at **Beachnriver Kayak Rentals** (Foley, 251/971-8359, 7am-3pm Tues.-Sun. May-Aug., single kayak $35, double kayak $75, for 7 hours), which launches floats from the river's end just 15 miles north of Gulf Shores. Kayakers must return to the launch site by 3pm. The rental center only accepts cash, so don't drive all the way out there and ruin the chance to float down the river by only bringing credit cards.

For renting kayaks and paddleboards on the beach, just call **GoGo Kayaks** (921 Gulf Shores Pkwy., 251/752-5500, www.gogokayaks.com, 9am-5pm daily, single kayak $60/day and $115/week, double kayak $75/day and $145/week, paddleboard $165/week). You can pick up your rentals at their shop or they'll deliver to your rental house for an extra charge. They offer daily and weekly rentals and can accommodate rentals for groups of 50 plus. Another great place to rent kayaks, or anything else you may need for your beach vacation, is **Gulf Shores Beach Rentals** (3873 Gulf Shores Pkwy., 888/896-9854, www.gulfshoresalbeachrentals.com, open daily, single kayak $95/day, double kayak $125/day,

paddleboard $150/day, beach umbrella $40/day). They also rent beach chairs, cribs, bicycles, and more. They will even do your grocery shopping if you ask them to, and pay them of course.

FISHING

In addition to the Gulf State Park Pier, you can enjoy surf fishing all along the beaches on the Gulf side, freshwater fishing at the inland lakes, and saltwater light-tackle or flats fishing in the surrounding bays, bayous, and saltwater lakes.

Orange Beach

Distraction Charters (Orange Beach Marina, 251/975-8111, www.distractioncharters.com, 8am-6pm daily, $1,275 half day, $800 for 4 hours) specializes in deep-sea and inshore charters for up to six people. Charters can be tailored to catch specific fish. If it's running, Distraction Charters will help you get it.

A popular charter company geared for larger groups of seven or more is **Intimidator Charters** (Orange Beach Marina, 251/747-2872, www.gulfshoresdeepseafishing.com, 8am-6pm daily, $1,600 for 6 hours up to 10 people). Call **Brown's Inshore Guide Service** (Orange Beach Marina, 251/981-6246, www.brownsinshore.com, 8am-6pm daily, $350 for 4 hours and $500 for 6 hours for 2 people, $50 each additional passenger) if you want to do some light-tackle inshore fishing. The knowledgeable and experienced Captain David Brown will take groups on four- and six-hour fishing trips. All trips include bait, tackle, and fishing licenses.

If you have your own boat, you can launch at **Boggy Point Boat Launch** (end of Marina Road off Hwy. 161, 251/981-6039, www.obparksandrec.com, sunrise-sunset daily, free), near the Perdido Pass Bridge, or at the **Cotton Bayou Boat Launch** (Hwy. 182 just east of the Hwy. 161 intersection, 251/981-6039, www.obparksandrec.com, sunrise-sunset daily, free).

Gulf Shores

★ FISHING FROM GULF STATE PARK PIER

The **Gulf State Park Pier** (20800 E. Beach Blvd., 251/967-3474, www.alapark.com, open daily, free parking, fishing rates $9/day 12 and older, $5 under 11 or free with paid adult, fishing rod rentals $1.50/hour), located in Gulf State Park between Gulf Shores and Orange Beach, is the largest pier on the Gulf at 1,540 feet. That's more than a quarter-mile long. The pier can get crowded on weekends and holidays, but there is usually a spot available where you can wet your line and reel in a variety of fish species like ladyfish, king mackerel, Spanish mackerel, cobia, sheepshead, jack crevalle, speckled trout, flounder, redfish, bluefish, and black drum. The octagon-shaped end of the pier is more than 90 feet wide and offers lots of space for anglers to fish in the 26-foot-deep water of the Gulf. The snack bar, bait and tackle shop, and fish cleaning facilities that are scattered along the pier are nice additions to the new structure, which was rebuilt and reopened in 2009 after Hurricane Ivan destroyed the previous pier in 2004. A major improvement is the addition of restrooms at the midway point of the pier.

FISHING CHARTERS

The best choice if you're looking to charter a fishing boat that caters to families is **Miss Brianna Fishing Charters** (26619 Perdido Beach Blvd., 251/747-3126, www.gulfshoresfishingcharter.com, 8am-6pm daily, $750-2,000). They offer light-tackle and heavy rod fishing trips that last 4-36 hours. The 36-foot *Infinity* sleeps up to six for longer overnight charters, and the cockpit is comfortable and air-conditioned, with a flat-screen TV and marine satellite dish. On the deck you can grill up your catch or whatever else you want on the onboard Big Green Egg grill while you troll and search the Gulf for yellowfin tuna, swordfish, amberjack, snapper, and more. This charter is the top choice for families and serious anglers alike.

If you want to see the charter boats and meet the captains before you book your fishing trip, you can head down to **Zeke's Landing Marina** (26619 Perdido Beach Blvd., 251/981-4007, www.zekeslanding.com, open daily). Stop by in the morning or around sunset for the chance to look over one of the largest charter fleets on the Gulf Coast. The six-acre complex has several restaurants, apparel shops, and **Mo Fishin Bait and Tackle** (26641 Perdido Beach Blvd., Ste.

Many fishing charters board at Orange Beach Marina.

16A, 251/981-3811, www.topguntackle.com, open daily), where you can cover all your live bait, gear, and any other fishing needs. You can also get tackle and pick up your groceries, beer, and just about anything else you need for a day at the beach at **Waves Grocery and Package Store** (1154 W. Beach Blvd., 251/948-4010, 7am-11pm daily).

SIGHTS
Orange Beach
COASTAL ARTS CENTER OF ORANGE BEACH

You can explore and buy the work of local artists at the **Coastal Arts Center of Orange Beach** (26389 Canal Rd., 251/981-2787, www.coastalartscenter.com, 9am-4pm Mon.-Fri., free). Housed in an old homestead right on Mobile Bay and surrounded by beautiful low-hanging oak trees, this picturesque art center features paintings, crafts, pottery, and glasswork by the area's best local and regional artists. Hands-on workshops suitable for adults and children are offered in many art forms including glassblowing and are a great way to spend a rainy day when the beach isn't in the forecast.

the Coastal Arts Center of Orange Beach

INDIAN AND SEA MUSEUM

The small yet exceptionally interesting **Indian and Sea Museum** (25850 John M. Snook Dr., 251/981-8545, www.obparksandrec.com, 9am-4pm Tues. and Thurs., free) offers insight into the area's history with an emphasis on the role that Native Americans and anglers played in the rich past of Orange Beach and Gulf Shores. Housed in an old schoolhouse built in 1909, the museum opened in 1995 and quickly became a hit with locals and visitors. Make sure and allow some time to enjoy the wonderful collection of artifacts and memorabilia that fill the shelves and walls of this unique museum.

Gulf Shores
★ FORT MORGAN STATE HISTORIC SITE

One of the most important battles of the Civil War was fought at the **Fort Morgan**

State Historic Site (51 Hwy. 180, 251/540-5257, www.fortmorgan.org, 8am-5pm daily, $7 adults, $5 students and seniors, $4 children 6-12, children under 6 free). The fort can be explored on foot and is a must-see for anyone interested in the Civil War or history in general. Stop in at the visitors center and museum and pick up a self-guided tour brochure. Wonderful interpretive plaques along the route give detailed accounts of the construction of the fort and information about life here during various wartimes with an emphasis on the Battle of Mobile Bay. Located all the way on the western end of Gulf Shores, Fort Morgan was the site where Union admiral David Farragut spoke those famous words, "Damn the torpedoes, full speed ahead!" The fort contains more than 40 million bricks and was completed in 1834. The fort has seen its share of action during four wars: the Civil War, Spanish-American War, and World Wars I and II. It can get a little spooky walking around in the more enclosed sections of the fort, and young children may not enjoy those parts of the fort.

The star-like shape of the fort is interesting and unique. The design enabled soldiers to defend the main ship channel into Mobile Bay with a steady stream of artillery fire as attacking ships approached the entrance and then moved into the bay. You can also explore the old lighthouse keepers quarters onsite, which were built in 1872. Surrounding the fort are great opportunities for fishing, shell searching, or beach walking and relaxing. Also nearby is the ferry that takes you across the bay to Dauphin Island. The fort is a favorite spot to watch the sunset, and the boat launches at Fort Morgan are an excellent place to launch your watercraft into the bay or the Gulf.

ENTERTAINMENT AND EVENTS
Orange Beach

The central spot for entertainment in Orange Beach is unarguably **The Wharf** (4720 Main St., 251/224-1000, www.alwharf.com) Located on the Intracoastal Waterway, also known as Portage Creek, which feeds into Wolf Bay and the Gulf, you won't miss it if you drive down the Foley Beach Expressway. Just look out for the South's largest Ferris wheel, and you'll know that you've found the right place to do some shopping, catch a movie, see a concert, or eat a great meal. There are more than 10 different restaurants in the development, most of them catering to seafood lovers. From the expansive marina you can boat up and rent a slip for the night or catch a fishing charter and take a sightseeing cruise for dolphins. The Wharf is also home to the popular **Amphitheater at the Wharf,** which hosts world-class concerts. The 2013 lineup included Kenny Chesney, Kelly Clarkson, and The Fray, just to give you an idea of the caliber of musicians that perform at this picturesque outdoor amphitheater. If you're into music, make sure and check the listings at the Amphitheater while you're in town. You never know who will be coming through. You can catch a movie at the state-of-the-art **Rave at the Wharf Orange Beach.** The theater has 15 screens and matinees for those rainy days in paradise. Also at the Wharf is the indoor laser tag center called **Arena the Next Level.** You and the kids can run around more than 10,000 square feet of obstacles and structures playing laser tag or something called bazooka-ball, a game where players compete at shooting glow-in-the-dark soft foam balls from

Fort Morgan State Historic Site

adjustable-velocity guns. It's great fun and a high-energy game that will get your heart racing.

Over at the SanRoc shopping center, you can take the family on a dolphin sightseeing adventure with **Dolphins Down Under** (Sanroc Marina, 27267 Perdido Beach Blvd., 251/968-4386, www.dolphinsdownunder.net, 8am-6pm daily, $20 adults, $15 children 3-10, children under 3 free). They specialize in dolphin tours aboard their glass-bottom boats. The knowledgeable staff knows exactly where to go to find dolphins, and often you'll have the opportunity to see the playful mammals jumping out of the water.

If you just have to squeeze in a game of mini golf and go-carts into your beach vacation, bring the kids to **Adventure Island** (24559 Perdido Beach Blvd., 251/974-1500, www.adventure-island.com, 9:30am-midnight daily June-Labor Day), where you can see the live erupting volcano. OK, it's a fake volcano in a kitschy mini amusement park, but it's still neat. If that's not enough, they also have laser tag, bumper boats, and paddleboats.

Gulf Shores

Families will have a hard time running out of things to do in the Gulf Shores area. For some soaking-wet fun at a classic water park, bring the kids to **WatervilleUSA** (906 Gulf Shores Pkwy., 251/948-2106, www.watervilleusa.com, hours vary, $33.95 general admission, $26.95 military, $22.95 seniors and children under 42 inches). It's not a massive water park like you might find in a bigger city, but they have your typical waterslides that send you and your children careening down slides at phenomenal speeds, a lazy river, and other rides that are often found at county fairs, like a carousel and roller coaster. The indoor arcade offers relief from the heat on a summer day, and the food prices are extremely reasonable for an amusement park. You can make an entire day out of it, especially if you break it up with a trip to the beach or a nap for the younger kids, but a half day is just about right for most visitors. The water park is closed for much of

the winter and its hours change month-to-month. Make sure and check the website for the most up-to-date information on their operating hours.

A new addition to the Gulf Shores area is the **Gulf Adventure Center** (21101 Hwy. 135, 251/948-9494, www.gulfadventurecenter.com, $59-79). A series of high-elevation platforms connect six ziplines, two of which race over the edge of Lake Shelby. If you're not into the high adrenaline of zipping, you can take things a little slower and rent a kayak or paddleboard from their on-site outfitter. For a more classic adventure, take the family to the **Gulf Coast Zoo** (1204 Gulf Shores Pkwy., 251/968-5731, www.alabamagulfcoastzoo. org, 9am-4pm daily, $11 adults, $9 seniors, $8 children 3-12, children 2 and under free). This small zoo is just blocks from the beach and houses more than 290 animals. Opened in June 1989, the zoo has continually expanded and in 2013 added a pair of Bengal tiger cubs, which made this zoo the first in the country to have tigers from each of the species' four color variations. Along with the tigers you'll enjoy the lions, bears, monkeys, macaws, a petting zoo, reptile house, and aviary. In the summer, stop by and see their daily animal shows. This park makes a great half day of family fun.

If you're in town on the second weekend in October, make sure and stop by the **National Shrimp Festival** (along Hwy. 182, 251/968-7220, www.alagulfcoastchamber.com, $59-79). Widely considered one of the best seafood fests in the country, it attracts more than 250,000 people each year for a little peel-and-eat or deep-fried-decapod fun. It doesn't matter how you prefer to eat this area's most celebrated crustacean, you can find them served any way you like at this shrimp celebration that features over 250 vendors, local artists and musicians, and a 10k/5k run in the morning.

If you want to hold your own private film fest, you can spend the day watching movies at the **Cobb Theaters Pinnacle 14** (3780 Gulf Shores Pkwy., 251/923-0100, www.cobbtheatres.com/pinnacle14). And the best way to learn about the fascinating history of the area is to take some time for the **Gulf Shores Museum** (244 W. 19th Ave., 251/968-1473, www.gulfshoresal.gov, 10am-5pm Tues.-Fri., 10am-2pm Sat., free). Learn about the area's fishing history and how Gulf Shores has coped with intense and destructive hurricanes in the past at this small but interesting and informative museum.

SHOPPING
Orange Beach

Shopping is pretty limited to surf shops, beach-goods stores, and souvenir shops along most of the main drag, but you can find a nicer collection of mostly beach-themed boutiques at **The Wharf** (4720 Main St., 251/224-1000, www.alwharf.com). Another similar development built around a large marina is the **SanRoc Cay Marina Entertainment District** (27267 Perdido Beach Blvd., 251/981-5423, www.sanroccay.com). More of an extension of the Perdido Beach Resort, this shopping district features concerts by local musicians on weekends in the courtyard. The shops are all locally owned and mostly sell women's beach-themed apparel, art, and gifts. Four restaurants are on-site, and you can rent kayaks and Jet Skis, take fishing excursions, and enjoy dolphin cruises right from the marina docks.

To dig in deep to your desire for great deals, all you have to do is drive to the **Tanger Outlet Center** (2601 S. McKenzie St., Foley, 251/943-9303, www.tangeroutlet.com/foley) in Foley, Alabama. This enormous outlet mall features factory stores like Gap, Jos. A. Bank, J. Crew, and more, and is just 20 minutes or 18 miles from Orange Beach. For groceries, go to **Publix** (25771 W. Perdido Beach Blvd., 251/980-1400, www.publix.com, 6am-11pm daily).

Gulf Shores

All your surf gear and apparel needs can be met at **Blonde Johns Boardshop** (200 Gulf Shores Pkwy., 251/948-2182, www. blondejohns.com, 10am-7pm Sun.-Thurs., 10am-8pm Fri.-Sat.). A local favorite, Blonde Johns has a large inventory of surfboards, surf shorts, wax, and anything else you may need to catch a wave and hang 10—or at least appear as if you do. For the ultimate selection of bikinis and souvenirs, stop in at **Alvin's Island** (100 W. Beach Blvd., 251/948-3121, www.alvinsisland.com, 9am-midnight daily). This beach-goods megastore has an impressive inventory of everything you could possibly want for the perfect day at the beach. The best prices on groceries are usually found at **Winn-Dixie** (1720 Gulf Shores Pkwy., 251/968-7633, 7am-10pm daily). There's also a Publix in the area if you have a preference or just need one of those delicious Publix deli sandwiches to pack for a surfside picnic.

FOOD
Orange Beach

The Gulf (27500 Perdido Beach Blvd., www.thegulf.com, 11am-midnight daily, $7-12) is a good place to stop for a quick bite when you first roll into Orange Beach. The oceanfront restaurant, artfully built from stacked shipping containers, is a masterpiece of modern architectural design. Even if you're not hungry, stop by for a drink and enjoy the excellent view of the Gulf of Mexico. The menu is a welcomed departure from the "fry everything" edict that dominates Orange Beach culinary culture. Burgers and sandwiches keep the less-adventurous satisfied while specials like lobster spaghetti and mahi tacos bring fresh seafood flavors to this Gulf-side eatery.

Hot sauce and raw oyster aficionados will love **Doc's Seafood Shack** (26029 Canal Rd., 251/981-6999, www.docsseafoodshack.com, 11am-9pm daily, $7-16), where everything you need to mix your own custom cocktail sauce creation is sitting right on the table. Their specialty is oysters on the half shell. Doc's is as casual as a cracker barrel and a favorite of folks who love classic, Southern-style, fried seafood. If you're into sports, you can relax and watch the game with the family while you work your way through a pound of shrimp, a tray of raw oysters, and plenty of sweet iced tea.

★ **Cosmo's Restaurant and Bar** (25753 Canal Rd., 251/948-9663, www.cosmosrestaurantandbar.com, 11am-9:30pm Sun.-Thurs., 11am-10pm Fri.-Sat., $15-30) features steak, seafood, and classic New Orleans-style entrées. At lunch try the pecan-encrusted redfish, or keep it simple and savor a crab cake sandwich or shrimp po'boy. At dinner dig into the Chef Jack Baker's French influence with the chicken roulade, a chicken breast wrapped in bacon and then stuffed with asparagus and gruyère cheese, topped with a sage-and-leek cream sauce. The signature dish is banana-leaf-wrapped fish, and the sushi menu is extensive. Make dinner reservations on weekends during the summer. If the weather's cool and clear, sit on the outdoor patio. The lines can be long, but the experience is worth the wait.

For fresh and steamed carryout seafood, go to **Lartigue's Seafood Market** (23043 Perdido Beach Blvd., 251/948-2644, www. lartiguesseafood.com, 7am-9pm daily). The usual suspects such as raw oysters, fresh Gulf shrimp, snapper, and the like can be found on ice, ready for you to take home and cook up. The family-owned market has been open in Orange Beach since 1979, and they have some of the best prices in the area.

Gulf Shores

Restaurants are plentiful in Gulf Shores, and most of them are found along Highway 182 (Beach Boulevard) and Highway 59 (Gulf Shores Parkway). Choose wisely, as there are plenty of places that prey on the unsuspecting tourist with low-quality frozen seafood and subpar service. If you only visit one place in Gulf Shores, head to ★ **Lulu's** (200 E. 25th Ave., 251/967-5858, www.lulubuffett.com, 11am-9pm Sun.-Thurs., 11am-10pm Fri.-Sat., $10-25). It's owned by Jimmy Buffett's sister and is a venerable shrine to the Margaritaville lifestyle. It's colorful and tropical and everything you would imagine from a place run by the sister of the king of trop-rock. The main restaurant and bar is on Portage Creek and surrounded by a sprawling outdoor seating area complete with volleyball courts, a playground, and several smaller bars housed in Key West-style cottages. Drive in or sail your boat right up to the dock. The coconut shrimp coupled with a cheeseburger in paradise and a slice of key lime pie are the perfect pairing with a frozen concoction of your choice (available with or without alcohol).

The Gulf restaurant

Welcome to Flora-Bama!

Technically four inches over the Alabama line into Florida's Perdido Key, the **Flora-Bama** (17401 Perdido Key Dr., Perdido Key, 850/492-0611, www.florabama.com) is a ramshackle beachside roadhouse where fun flows as unchecked as the booze. The bartenders are famous—and there are 10 bars, along with three stages for bands, volleyball courts, an oyster bar, package store, and sprawling beachside patio.

But that's just the beginning. When it started in 1961, it was a little local bar. It's grown over the years into a huge local bar that looks as if it were built from driftwood and scraps of debris left behind by Hurricane Ivan. It also hosts the international spectacle, the annual **Interstate Mullet Toss,** whereby contestants grip deceased yet slippery fish and throw them as far as they can into the state of Alabama. It's a straight distance competition, but you definitely get style points. Football spiral, underhanded, shot put-style—practice at home with a trout or something to hone your craft.

Several hundred people compete, and nearly 30,000 people turn out to watch the third weekend in April. There's a Ms. Mullet contest, barbecue, crawfish, peel-and-eat shrimp, topless oysters, and a whole lot of cocktails to sweeten the deal. The Flora-Bama has a couple of other annual events of note, one of which is the **Polar Bear Dip** on the morning of January 1, an early morning bar-to-water mad scramble. After a bracing splash in the Gulf (many "bears" leave behind their clothing entirely), revelers go back to the Flora-Bama for some warming black-eyed peas—and if you find a dime in your peas, it's good luck for the whole year.

The Hangout (101 E. Beach Blvd., 251/948-3030, www.thehangoutal.com, 11am-9pm Mon.-Thurs. and Sun., 11am-10pm Fri.-Sat., $10-25), a sprawling, laid-back bar and restaurant right on the beach, features live music most nights in the summer. This is the place to go for a night of dancing or to watch the day game over wings, burgers, and fried shrimp. Before the party crowd arrives, it's an excellent choice for families—kids love playing in the large sand pit. Once the band starts up, the place draws a heavy-drinking college crowd. Expect rock, reggae, country, and alternative bands on the two stages. Enjoy the free foosball and table tennis, and, on winter nights, the outdoor fire pit.

For fine dining, locals go to **Nolan's** (1140 Gulf Shores Pkwy., 251/948-2111, www.nolansrestaurant.com, open at 6pm Tues.-Sat., $18-28). This upscale restaurant is a great choice for a romantic dinner. They specialize in steaks, seafood, and Greek-inspired cuisine with standout menu selections such as a Mediterranean-style grouper baked in olive oil and lemon and served with broiled tomatoes, onions, kalamata olives, and feta cheese. For something more adventurous, try the whole flounder stuffed with crabmeat and chestnut stuffing. After dinner head to the lounge and indulge in their extensive wine and martini list. They often have live music during the summer.

There are many options for oysters in Gulf Shores, but not many better than **The Original Oyster House** (701 Gulf Shores Pkwy., 251/948-2455, www.theoysterhouse.com, 11am-10pm Sun.-Thurs., 11am-11pm Fri.-Sat., $9-20). They've got oysters prepared every way you can imagine as well as the standard seafood options like fried flounder, gumbo, and one of those enormous platters of fried seafood that is ubiquitously known at Gulf Coast seafood restaurants as the fisherman's platter. This popular place is perfect spot for a large family dinner. The peanut butter pie is delicious.

If you didn't get enough of the Margaritaville lifestyle at Lulu's, continue your search for the perfect frozen concoction at **Bahama Bobs Beach Side Café** (601 W. Beach Blvd., 251/948-2100, www.bahamabobs.com, 11am-8pm daily, $10-20).

Well-loved for their fried shrimp and po'boys, this small tropical-style café is within walking distance from the beach. The outdoor seating is worth the wait and a better choice than the cramped indoor seating. A great pick from the menu is the shrimp and crab combo with boiled potatoes and corn. It's enough for two if you have a small- to medium-size appetite. Parking is limited.

For a sweet Southern-style treat, stop in at **Café Beignets of Alabama** (625 Gulf Shores Pkwy., 251/948-2311, 7am-2pm daily, $5-12), where like the name implies they serve those delectable, French-style, puffy, crispy donuts covered in a layer of delicious powdered sugar. The menu is simply beignets and coffee, which is sure to satisfy a café du monde craving without having to drive all the way to the French Quarter in New Orleans. My advice is to forgo your regular cup of joe and try the café au lait and chickory coffee that has that special Southern flavor that you don't want to miss. And if you're looking for a little more down-home Southern cookin', you can't go wrong with breakfast, lunch, or dinner at **Kitty's Kafe** (3800 Gulf Shores Pkwy., 251/943-5233, 6am-7pm Mon.-Sat., 7am-2pm Sun., $7-15), where owner Kitty Simpson will appease your craving for fried chicken and the like. They serve breakfast all day, so don't be shy coming into Kitty's at 1pm for pancakes and bacon after a late night at The Hangout or Flora-Bama.

Are you tired of paying those high prices for a small fillet of broiled snapper, but don't quite have the angler's knack? Then take the easy road and pick up your own fresh seafood to cook yourself or order take-out seafood at **S & S Seafood Market** (1154 W. Beach Blvd., 251/968-3474, 11am-8pm daily, $5-15). Their prices are better than most of the seafood restaurants in the area, and the spicy fried shrimp, fried grouper, and gumbo are some of the best in all of Gulf Shores. You can call ahead and place your order if you want to get back on the beach in a flash, and make sure to ask for a few hush puppies on the side.

ACCOMMODATIONS
Orange Beach
For a great value in the area, stay at the **Hampton Inn and Suites Orange Beach** (25518 Perdido Beach Blvd., 251/923-4400, www.hamptoninn3.hilton.com, $140-260). Breakfast and wireless Internet are included, and the suites have refrigerators and microwaves. The inn has easy access to a Gulf-front beach, and the views from some of the rooms

The Hangout

are excellent. The 160 guest rooms have modern decor and comfy signature beds. The over 3,750 square feet of meeting space, enough to accommodate more than 300 people, also makes this property a great choice for conventions, business meetings, and events.

Perdido Beach Resort (27200 Perdido Beach Blvd., 251/981-9811, www.perdidobeachresort.com, $150-249) is a classic resort. Choose between pool-view and Gulf-front rooms, some of which are set up more for business travelers, who may want to request a room with a desk when booking. The piano bar in the lobby area is a favorite with locals and visitors as a great place to bring a date for a classy cocktail over jazz. The tiki-style pool bar mixes good piña coladas with a wonderful poolside view of the Gulf. There is easy access to the beach and an excellent indoor heated pool. The resort has four lighted tennis courts and a spacious fitness center with a stellar view. And I love that there is absolutely no resort fee to stifle your fun.

Built in 2008 the ★ **Turquoise Place** (26302 Perdido Beach Blvd., 800/210-7914, www.turquoiseplacerental.com, $350 1,200) is architecturally stunning. The impressive glass condo tower is unarguably the focal point as you drive down this stretch of beach. The development was featured on the cover of *USArchitecture* magazine as one of the top projects of 2007/2008. The resort caters to both families and couples, and the Gulf of Mexico is just feet from the building. There are two heated indoor pools, an indoor children's pool, two seasonally heated outdoor pools (one of which is zero-entry), three indoor hot tubs, and—my favorite—the 450-foot-long lazy river that winds around the property. It's hard not to just swim and float your worries away at Turquoise. Stop in at the poolside tiki bar or spend the day at the full-service spa getting a massage or a luxurious body polish. The fitness center is top-notch with an excellent view of the Gulf to enjoy while you are getting your body back into summer shape. Every aspect of the resort is sleek, clean, and modern, yet without the sterility that some modern developments have unfortunately created at their high-end properties. The prices for rooms vary depending on the size, floor plan, and location, but all are definitely at the high end of the price spectrum for Orange Beach. If you are looking for luxury, pampering, and an inspiring modern environment in which to spend your beach vacation, you won't be disappointed with Turquoise.

For something casual and relaxing, choose the **Original Romar House** (23500 Perdido Beach Blvd., 251/974-1625, www.theoriginalromarhouse.com, $99-329), a six-room bed-and-breakfast. The spacious back deck overlooking the Gulf is the perfect spot to enjoy a cup of coffee. Each room has a theme and is decorated with antiques. The tropical-themed Parrot House Cottage has an entire kitchen and living room. The Captain's Quarters ($99), about as small as a room you would find on a ship, is perfect for solo budget travelers. Free wireless Internet, complimentary wine at happy hour, afternoon refreshments, and a hot tub make a stay at the Romar House a real treat. The best feature of this B&B, however, is the warm hospitality of the owners, Deborah and Greg Collard, and the wonderful breakfast served daily.

Gulf Shores

The Gulf Shores area has begun to lean toward more high-end development and for the most part outshines Orange Beach accommodations in this respect. However, there is still a wide variety of accommodation choices. Budget-minded travelers looking for a suitable efficiency can find a great deal at the **Staybridge Suites Gulf Shores** (3947 Gulf Shores Pkwy., 251/975-1030, www.ichotelsgroup.com, $95-160). The suites have fully equipped kitchens and are exceptionally spacious for the price. A complimentary hot breakfast is served every morning. The Internet is free, and many of the rooms have a work desk. There are not a lot of frills, but you can't beat the rates for these spacious and exceptionally clean rooms in a great location.

Enjoy a more upscale experience at the **Courtyard by Marriott Gulf Shores Craft Farms** (3750 Gulf Shores Pkwy., 251/968-1113, www.mariott.com, $110-180). Located on the front edge of the Craft Farms Golf Resort, this property is geared to golfers who want to mix business with playing one of the best courses in the Panhandle. Free Internet and desks are provided in all 87 rooms and three suites. The styling is sleek and modern, but warm, and there is an excellent pool. If you don't want to fight the traffic to the public beach four miles away, you can just enjoy the excellent pool.

For one of the best golf getaways on the Gulf Coast, stay at **Kiva Dunes** (815 Plantation Dr., 251/540-7003, www.kivadunes.com, $199-329). Surrounding an artfully designed course on the far west end of Gulf Shores is a collection of homes and condos that you can rent for a week, or for months. If golf isn't your thing, don't worry. Kiva Dunes has over 3,000 feet of quiet beach to explore. There are three outdoor pools, a fitness center, an on-site restaurant, tiki bar, golf pro shop, well-maintained tennis courts, and a spacious fitness center with modern exercise equipment. In short, they have everything you need; you can just park your car and never think about driving anywhere else during your stay. The size, price, style, and layout of the homes vary greatly. However, you can see photos, prices, and the exact location of every rental property in the resort on the detailed website.

The **Gulf Shores Plantation** (805 Plantation Rd., 251/540-5000, www.gulfshoresplantation.com, $200-500) offers a large variety of cottages and condos. This family-oriented resort should not be overlooked by deal seekers. Some of the smaller cottages are affordable. Staying at any of the condos and cottages here gives you access to the full amenities of the resort, which include one indoor pool and six outdoor pools as well as hot tubs, saunas, horseshoe pits, a putting green where you can sharpen your skills before hitting any of the 10 courses in the area, and thousands of feet of Gulf beaches. The resort has tennis courts, shuffleboard, and basketball courts as well as a fitness center for the more active ones in the family. All the cottages and condos are fully equipped with everything you need for cooking and relaxing, and all the units have either a patio or balcony. Free Internet service is included with the rentals, and there is a variety of floor plans and sizes to accommodate almost any budget.

Kiva Dunes

My personal favorite place to stay in the area is ★ **The Beach Club** (925 Beach Club Trail, 251/224-3200, www.thebeachclub.spectrumresorts.com, $230-600), located just to the east of Kiva Dunes on the west end of Gulf Shores. This is the perfect place for families. Each of the cottages and condos has a fully equipped kitchen, and all the condos have balconies with views of the Gulf. The condos range 1-5 bedrooms. They are all privately owned, but the website for the resort makes it easy to browse through the individual units and find a style, size, and price that fits your family. In the off-season (Nov.-Feb.), give the resort a call for help in finding a great deal on a condo. The cottages are a little more luxurious and give you the privacy of renting your own home while still allowing you access to the resort's amenities. Many of the cottages are situated around a lake, and some have expanded kitchens, hot tubs, and even private pools. The clubhouse has live music most nights, and there are several outdoor pools around the resort if you need a break from the beach. Organized kids' programs and activities including craft projects, scavenger hunts, and team sports games will keep the young ones busy throughout the day. A full-service spa and hot tubs will keep you relaxed, and you can grab a cold ice cream at the on-site ice cream shop. It is a classic beach resort that is geared toward families. Every corner of the resort has something entertaining and fun happening to keep those short attention spans engaged.

Vacation Rentals

The large majority of vacation rental companies in the area deal with properties in both Orange Beach and Gulf Shores. There is a wide range of homes and condos available for rent in the area, with most of the homes suitable for large or small families and running the gamut from simple, classic, modest beach cottages to impressively large and fancy beach homes big enough for several families to share. All along the coast are high-rise condo developments. The amount of offerings can be overwhelming, but a few of the expert rental companies in the area can help you get exactly what you are looking for, whether it is a small condo right on the Gulf or a large home tucked away on a wooded lot on Mobile Bay. The two most well-established and trusted rental companies in the area are **Meyer Vacation Rentals** (1585 Gulf Shores Pkwy., Gulf Shores, 866/382-9635, www.meyerre.com) and **Brett/Robinson Vacation Rentals** (3259 Gulf Shores Pkwy., Gulf Shores, 800/211-7892, www.brett-robinson.com), serving both Gulf Shores and Orange Beach. Either of these companies can get you headed in the right direction, and both have great websites with pictures and prices of all the homes available in the area.

An upscale selection of Caribbean-style cottages and condos can be found at **Martinique on the Gulf** (987 Boulevard Martinique, Gulf Shores, 855/858-6950, www.martinique-gulf.com, $250-575). This premier development is adjacent to the Bon Secour National Wildlife Refuge and offers a mix of two- and three-bedroom condos and two- to five-bedroom cottages. The idyllic resort environment is reminiscent of Seaside and WaterColor to the east and features a phenomenal pool area with a hot tub and kid's pool, a fitness center, professional tennis courts, and a private boardwalk that leads to the Gulf beaches. The two-story French colonial-style cottages will have you feeling as if you have been whisked away to the Caribbean.

Located in the middle of town are the **Phoenix All Suites Hotels** (201 E. Beach Blvd., Gulf Shores, 800/211-7892, www.phoenixallsuites.com, $150-300). The west and east towers feature one-bedroom suites with full kitchens. You can choose between the standard one-bedroom, one-bath floor plan or a unit with 1.5 baths. Each unit has a balcony with a view of the Gulf and a fully equipped kitchen. They're no-frills condos, but the price can make these clean yet somewhat utilitarian condos look much better. The nice outdoor pool and the fact that the condos are just 1,500 feet from the public beach make the Phoenix a great value.

Camping

The best camping in the Gulf Shores and Orange Beach area is at ★ **Gulf State Park** (22050 Campground Rd., Gulf Shores, 251/948-7275, www.alapark.com/gulfstate, 7am-sunset daily, $37-50 campsite, $115-300 cabins). This 496-site campsite is located along the north shore of Middle Lake and offers many lakefront campsites. The sites are close together, which makes the campground better suited for RV or pop-up camping. Some sites offer more privacy and shade for tent camping, but the size of the campground and the close proximity of sites can often lead to a loud camping experience. If you're tent camping and a light sleeper, make sure and bring some earplugs because during the hot summer months RV campers often run their air-conditioners at night, which can be quite loud. The campground offers direct access to miles of hiking trails, including the Rosemary Dunes Trail, which leads to the Gulf of Mexico and the Gulf State Park Pavilion Beach. If you don't want to hike the trail to get to the beach, it's just a 1.5-mile drive from the campground. And if you just don't think you can handle roughing it out on the beach for a few days, you're in luck. This campground offers more comforts than most. The swimming pool, wireless Internet, modern and clean bathhouse with hot showers, full laundry facility, and water, electric, and sewer hookups at every site will make you feel like you're staying at a nature-based eco-resort instead of a campground. The lake is open for swimming, fishing, and boating, and the campground is within walking distance of the Gulf State Park Golf Course.

If sleeping in a tent or RV just isn't your thing, the park offers even more comfort in their cabin and cottage rentals. The park has 20 cabins and cottages, which are mostly one- and two-room buildings that sleep 4-6 people. They are located along the lakeshore, near the golf course, and a few in a forested area of the campground. The cabins on the lakeshore are some of the best in the park. Each has a private dock, fish cleaning bench, and barbecue grills. Each cottage is fully equipped and linens are provided. The cabins are reserved far in advance, so make sure and book yours way ahead of time if you hope to enjoy some of the most comfortable camping you've ever experienced.

On the bay side in Gulf Shores, you can pull your RV into **Fort Morgan RV Park** (10397 2nd St., 251/540-2416, www.baybreezerv.com, $44-59/day, $565/month Oct.-Apr., $650/month May-Sept.), where 35 sites are spread over six acres right on Mobile Bay. Large oak trees provide ample shade at most of the campsites, and nearly every site has a water view of the bay. This park is favored by anglers, who can fish from the 200-foot pier. Beaches are just 1.5 miles from the park. A new bathhouse and free laundry facilities were added in 2013. Water, sewer, electric, cable, and wireless Internet are included with each site. A little more tucked away and on the northern side of Little Lagoon is **Doc's RV Park** (17595 State Rd. 180, Gulf Shores, 251/968-4511, www.docsrvpark.com, $35 daily, $225 weekly, $480-575/month). They have 75 RV sites and are only three miles from the beach. Each site has full electric and sewer hook-ups, wireless Internet, and cable. The campground features a swimming pool, playground, laundry, bathhouse, clubhouse, and 14 park-model cabins ($85/night, $595/week) you can rent if you don't own an RV. This campground is a favorite among long-term campers. And 25 more RV sites can be found in Gulf Shores at **Bay Breeze RV** (1901 Bay Breeze Pkwy., 251/540-2362, www.baybreezerv.com, $36-48 campsites, $89-109 RV sites, $110-135 cottages). Beach access on Mobile Bay is just a short walk from the campground. They also offer RV rentals and one cabin to rent. The fishing and boat dock make this campground the choice of boaters. The campground has a bathhouse and laundry facility, making it more comfortable to stay here for a longer period of time.

GETTING THERE

Car

The main driving access to the area from New Orleans in the west and Jacksonville and Tallahassee in the east is I-10. If you're coming from the north, you can take I-65 from Birmingham or I-85 from Atlanta. All these points lead to Mobile, Alabama. To get to the Gulf Shores area from Mobile, it's 49 miles, a one-hour drive. Just follow Highway 59 South to the Gulf Shores Public Beach and turn right to go toward the west end of Gulf Shores or left to go toward Orange Beach.

If you're coming from Pensacola, follow U.S. 98 to Highway 292, also known as Barrancas Avenue, Gulf Beach Highway, and Sorrento Road at different points along the route. Highway 292 goes through Perdido and right to the Florida/Alabama border, where it becomes Highway 182 once you cross into Alabama and reach Orange Beach.

Air

Advantage Airport Shuttle (850/420-7807, www.advantageairportshuttle.com) provides service from **Pensacola International Airport** (850/436-5000, www.flypensacola. com), which is about an hour east, to Orange Beach ($60-70) and Gulf Shores ($75-90).

Thrifty (877/238-0898), **Hertz** (850/432-2345), **Avis** (850/433-5614), **Budget** (850/432-5499), **Enterprise** (850/478-6730), and **Alamo** (888/826-6893) provide rental cars from Pensacola International Airport.

Dauphin Island

To escape the throngs of tourists often found around Gulf Shores and Orange Beach, load your car onto the ferry at the western tip of Gulf Shores and venture to Dauphin Island. The island is a favorite family destination for those living in and around Mobile, and is also coveted by anglers due to the easy access the island offers into Mobile Bay to the north, Bon Secour Bay to the east, and the Gulf of Mexico to the south. The fishing here is exceptional, which is why the island hosts the largest fishing tournament in the world, the Alabama Deep Sea Fishing Rodeo. Usually a relatively sleepy spot on the Gulf Coast, it's transformed every July into a bustling frenzy of anglers, fishing boats, and more than 75,000 spectators. If you don't want to deal with crowds, don't set foot on the island during rodeo time.

The pace of life is usually slow on Dauphin Island. It's an angler's and outdoor enthusiast's paradise; the kind of destination to visit if you're looking to avoid doing much more than working on your tan. There's hardly any shopping to speak of unless you're in the market for fresh oysters, shrimp, or blue crab, and the accommodation options are remarkably limited, with most visitors renting homes or condos on the island. Dauphin Island is genuinely Southern and a place where the influences of the French and Spanish express themselves in the cuisine, culture, and architecture in a wonderful way. To really experience the island, remember to do two things—first, take a boat out on the water, and then just relax. This is what the locals do, and they understand how to experience the best that this island has to offer.

If you love birds, grab your binoculars and visit in the spring to see some of the 347 species that have been reported on this 14-mile-long island. Dauphin Island is the first piece of land that birds often reach during their biannual migrations. The island is considered to be one of the top 10 most significant spots on the planet for birds and was named by *Wild Bird Magazine* as one of the top four locations to watch spring migrations in the United States. On the eastern tip of the island you'll find the Audubon Bird Sanctuary, a 164-acre parcel of land that is preserved and managed to support these massive migrations that occur every spring and fall.

Dauphin Island

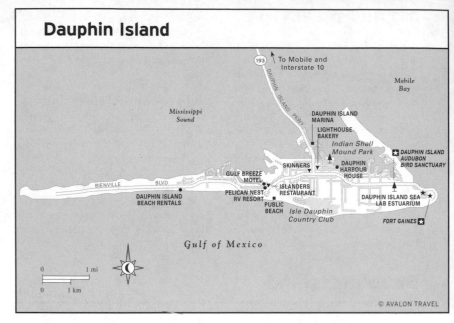

© AVALON TRAVEL

SPORTS AND RECREATION
Beaches

More impressive than the beaches on Dauphin Island is the island's laid-back atmosphere and culture. Now don't get me wrong, the beaches are worth going to and definitely enjoyable in their own way, but the beaches to the east in Gulf Shores and Orange Beach are nicer. On Dauphin Island the offshore oil rigs are close to shore, which can be clearly seen from the comfort of your beach chair. This might not bother many people, but when I look out across the Gulf, I prefer to see the clean, blue line of the horizon and not the blinking lights of an oil rig platform.

There are three main access points for the beaches on Dauphin Island. The largest and most popular beach is the **Dauphin Island Public Beach Access** (1509 Bienville Blvd., 251/861-3607, www.dauphinisland.org, $5/car or motorcycle, $2 for pedestrians or bicyclists, $20 for motor homes or buses), which is also the site of the Dauphin Island Fishing Pier. This is a beautiful spot with more than

two miles of undeveloped beaches, four large picnic pavilions, restrooms, outdoor showers, and a nice playground for children. When you first get to the beach, you'll notice two things. First, it is a long trek from your car to the edge of the Gulf where most people prefer to set up their beach chairs and umbrellas. Second, there is something extremely odd about the fishing pier. The pier never reaches the water. In fact, it doesn't even come close to reaching the Gulf. At one time this was a deep-water fishing pier. Over the course of 2007 and 2008, Pelican Island was slowly moved toward Dauphin Island by a series of harsh hurricanes and winter storms until Pelican Island connected with Dauphin Island. Now the beach is much larger, but the pier is sadly unfishable. Make sure and wear sandals for the long trek out to the water's edge. The beach is good for swimming, but be forewarned that there are no lifeguards, so keep your swimming close to shore, look for rip currents, and avoid the Gulf when it's rough if you're not accustomed to swimming in open waters.

On the east end of the island, you can use

Birding, Hiking, and Biking

★ DAUPHIN ISLAND AUDUBON BIRD SANCTUARY

The **Dauphin Island Audubon Bird Sanctuary** (211 Bienville Blvd., 251/861-3607, www.dauphinisland.org/audubon-bird-sanctuary, dawn-dusk daily, free) was created to accommodate the large number of migrating birds and butterflies that pass over Dauphin Island during their spring and fall migrations. Bring your binoculars and explore this 164-acre park on the eastern side of the island that features a wide variety of habitats. Explore freshwater lakes, swamp, beach, coastal dune, pine forest, and hardwood forest on six trails that cut through the park. The park can be accessed from the Dauphin Island Campground as well as from the main parking lot on Bienville Boulevard. Spring is the best time to come and spot birds on the island, and it is said that birds literally fall out of the sky when a cold front with rain is pushed over the island during the height of spring migrations. If you're into birding, the Audubon Bird Sanctuary should not be missed.

INDIAN SHELL MOUND PARK

For a more historical experience, hike the trail at the **Indian Shell Mound Park** (Iberville Rd., 251/861/2882, www.dauphinislandhistory.org, dawn-dusk daily, free). The short trail leads around an ancient shell mound left behind by early Indians that possibly used the island as a place to escape the cold winter weather. And if you want to burn off some of those extra calories from eating too much of the Southern seafood staples found all over the island, then lace up your boots or rent a bike and hike or ride the **Island-Long Bike Path.** The seven-mile paved path runs parallel to Bienville Boulevard and traverses most of the island. With such an excellent and accessible bike path, there's no reason why you can't see everything on the island and get a great workout at the same time. Besides, the more you hike or bike on the bike path, the more fried shrimp and daiquiris you're allowed to have.

Sea oats sprout in the sands on Dauphin Island.

the **Fort Gaines Public Beach Access.** It's not much of a beach, but the thin strip of sand around the fort area is a convenient place to get close to the water if you're visiting the fort. This beach is excellent for swimming, but again there is unfortunately no lifeguard on duty.

And with the pier now out of use at the main public beach, the island authority has decided to open the **West End Public Beach** (far west end of Dauphin Island, 251/861-5525, www.townofdauphinisland.org, 10am-6pm daily, $2 parking plus $3/person over 12). Opened in March 2013, this family-oriented beach has a waterslide, beach chair and umbrella rentals, food vendors, sno-cones, and cocktails. The waterslide and sno-cones are reminiscent of Pensacola Beach back in the 1970s and 1980s. The West End beach is nice and wide and known as a great place to find the best shells on the island. A lifeguard is on duty through the summer season, making this the best beach for swimming on the island.

Canoeing and Kayaking

If you want to further explore the rich aquatic environment around the island, you can rent a kayak from the **Dauphin Island Marina Kayak Shack** (650 LeMoyne Dr., 251/861-2201, dauphinislandmarina.com, 8am-5pm Wed.-Sun., single kayak $25 for 2 hours and $50/day, double or tandem kayak $40 for 2 hours and $80/day). If you want to do some kayak-fishing, you can buy your bait and tackle at the Dauphin Island Marina store. Guided ecotours that explore the open water of the Gulf as well as the bays are also available at the Kayak Shack.

If you want a kayak or bike brought to you, call Lynn at **Dauphin Island Kayak and Bicycle Rentals** (251/422-5285, 8am-5:30pm daily). She has been operating her bike and kayak delivery service for more than 10 years on the island. Single kayaks are $25 for two hours and $60 for a full day. She rents tandems and has the best prices on kayaks if you're looking at renting two or more boats for more than two days. Bicycles are $15 per day. Lynn offers tours of the island by boat or bike, and her tours can include lunches at one of the local restaurants or pre-packed picnics if you prefer.

Now that you've rented a boat, you can launch your watercraft at one of the many boat launches or beaches around the island. On the eastern side of the island you can launch at the Dauphin Island Campground or the boat launch at Fort Gaines. These are great launches to paddle out to Sand Island just south of Dauphin Island in the Gulf. The boat launch at the Dauphin Island Marina is centrally located and an excellent launch point into Mobile Bay. And it's easy to get into the Gulf from the main public beach that is centrally located on the south side of the island.

Fishing

Right before you get on the island, you can pick up all the fishing supplies you need and learn a little bit of the locals' secrets by stopping in at **Jemison's Bait & Tackle** (16871 Dauphin Island Pkwy., 251/873-4695, 5am-8pm daily). The ramshackle store might not look like much, but it offers a wealth of information if you ask the right people. Just past the store, you can put your newly purchased bait and tackle to the test at the **Cedar Point Fishing Pier** (18250 Dauphin Island Pkwy., 251/873-4476, www.fishingpier.net, 24 hours daily, $5). You can buy tackle and bait at the fishing pier's shop as well. A great place to fish late into the night, the pier is the

Explore the Dauphin Island Audubon Bird Sanctuary.

oldest privately owned fishing pier on the Gulf Coast, and it's been getting a lot more business since the Dauphin Island Fishing Pier has become unfishable. You can still walk out on the Dauphin Island Fishing Pier, but if you try and fish from this "pier," the only thing you'll be catching is sand crabs and the occasional tourist.

If you want a pro guide to take you out into Mobile Bay or any of the surrounding fishing hot spots, just call **Capt. Mike's Deep Sea Fishing** (650 LeMoyne Dr., 251/861-5302, www.captainmikeonline.com) to set up a fishing charter. He is based out of the Dauphin Island Marina and has three boats that range 40-65 feet. They can accommodate you whether you want to do some trolling and bottom fishing for red snapper, king mackerel, and grouper or just want to go after the big boys and try to reel in a blue marlin or record-setting tuna.

SIGHTS
Indian Shell Mound Park
Visit the **Indian Shell Mound Park** (Iberville Rd., 251/861-2882, www.dauphin-islandhistory.org, dawn-dusk daily, free) and walk the short trail through the 11-acre park that circles around a massive shell mound left

behind by early Native Americans who must have really loved oysters. They roasted boatloads of these yummy bivalves and threw the shells into a pile that over time grew to the highest point on the island. Almost as impressive as the mound are the enormous oak trees found in the park. Some of the larger ones are more than 800 years old and were mature trees when the Spaniards first visited Dauphin Island.

★ Fort Gaines
Arguably the most historically significant site on Dauphin Island is **Fort Gaines** (51 Bienville Blvd., 251/861-6992, www.dauphin-island.org/fort.htm, 9am-5pm daily, $8 adults, $4 children 5-12), located on the eastern tip of the island. Construction of the fort began in 1821 and was finally completed in 1861. The fort was used most notably in the Battle of Mobile Bay, one of the most significant clashes of the Civil War. During World War II, the fort became a station for an anti-submarine branch of the U.S. Coast Guard as well as the base for the Alabama National Guard.

After paying the entrance fee at the visitors center, you are free to explore the fort on your own. Constructed with brick and sand mortar, the fort's most notable features are the

the entrance to the historic Fort Gaines

tall arched tunnels and steep outer walls. In and around the fort are original cannons, a functioning blacksmith shop, kitchens, and an exhibit that includes the original anchor from the USS *Hartford,* where Admiral David Farragut spoke the famous words, "Damn the torpedoes, full speed ahead!" Even though the fort has received substantial damage from the ongoing tropical storms and intense hurricanes, it is still considered one of the best-preserved forts from the Civil War era, with excellent examples of early artillery.

To get here, drive east down Bienville Boulevard to the end of the road and you'll reach the fort. Take a self-guided tour or drive your vehicle around the fort's outer wall that runs parallel to the coastline of the island.

Dauphin Island Sea Lab Estuarium

To learn more about the Mobile Bay aquatic environment, visit the **Dauphin Island Sea Lab Estuarium** (101 Bienville Blvd., 919/861-2141, http://estuarium.disl.org, 9am-6pm Mon.-Sat., noon-6pm Sun., until 5pm Sept. 1-Feb., $10 adults, $8 seniors, $6 children 5-18). The primary focus of the estuarium is to facilitate Alabama's universities and grade schools with courses, workshops, and graduate programs in marine-science environmental education. However, the public can get a glimpse into what life is like below the waters of Mobile Bay, the Tensaw River Delta, and the northern Gulf of Mexico by visiting the estuarium and exploring the indoor visual exhibits as well as taking a walk on the boardwalk above the surrounding marsh. While exploring the estuarium, you will see alligators, turtles, snakes, gars, oysters, horseshoe crabs, blue crabs, stone crabs, shrimp, octopus, eels, starfish, sea horses, and jellyfish. The highlight of the facility is a touch tank that lets children touch sealife on display. The kid-centric aquarium and environmental education programs will get children of all ages interested in understanding what is happening in Mobile Bay, the fourth-largest estuary system in the United States.

EVENTS

The biggest festival on the island is the **Alabama Deep Sea Fishing Rodeo** (251/471-0025, www.adsfr.com). Held in mid-July, this fishing tournament has been active for more than 79 years and is the largest multispecies saltwater fishing tournament in the world, attracting more than 3,000 anglers and upward of 75,000 spectators every year. Even if you're not competing in the tournament, it's a ton of fun to watch the boats come in and unload their impressive catches onto the docks. The three-day event awards over $400,000 in prizes in 30 categories including a master junior angler award.

The **Art Fest in the Park** (Cadillac Sq., 251/861-5524, www.dauphinisland.org) is a juried art show featuring local and regional artists. In recent years the art festival has been combined with the Back to Nature Festival, which integrates a schedule of outdoor activities that promote environmental awareness. Spend the day strolling under the oaks enjoying displays of artwork in Cadillac Square and then join a boat tour, animal exhibition, or nature walk at this multithemed festival. The festival takes place in early June.

Ever wonder what life on Dauphin Island was like before Fort Gaines was built? You can find out at the **Colonies of the Gulf Coast** (Fort Gaines, 251/861-6992, www.dauphinisland.org/fort), which takes place in early March. This living-history day at the fort includes live reenactments by soldiers, pirates, and period craftsman, as well as some exciting live cannon firing.

Most people consider New Orleans to be synonymous with Mardi Gras, but the festival actually began in Mobile. You can experience Mardi Gras Dauphin Island-style at the **Island Mystics Parade** (Bienville Blvd., 251/861-5525, ext. 222, www.townofdauphinisland.org). Always the second parade of the season, which usually occurs sometime in mid- to late January, the parade is much more laid-back than the parades in Mobile or New Orleans. You won't find any barricades, but you will see families cooking out and partying along the parade route for the entire day, and usually into the late hours of the night. Crowds arrive early along the route to stake out and set up their camps for the day. So if you have dreams of catching piles of beads and stacks of MoonPies (those delectable, chocolate-covered, graham-cracker-and-marshmallow-stuffed treats that are tossed out at parades), you better get to the parade early in the morning before the first float rolls past.

SHOPPING

There's not much of a shopping scene on Dauphin Island, but there is plenty of island-themed clothing, jewelry, and other beach souvenirs at **Marti's Island Shoppe** (1606 Bienville Blvd., 251/861-8772, 10am-4:30pm daily). A nice collection of sealife-inspired art, gifts, and clothing can be found at the popular **Dauphin Island Sea Lab Estuarium Gift Shop** (101 Bienville Blvd., 251/861-2141, ext. 7545, http://giftshop.disl.org, 9am-6pm Mon.-Sat., 1pm-6pm Sun.). You don't have to pay the admission fee to get into the gift shop, and if you like Gulf-themed housewares, it is worth a stop.

You can find all the groceries and other beach supplies you need at the **Ship & Shore** (401 LeMoyne Dr., 251/861-2262, 5am-9pm daily), located just across the bridge on the right as you come onto the island. This grocery store doubles as the town's hardware store, too, so they should have just about everything you could ever need while you're in town. If you're in desperate need of retail therapy, you'll want to head over to Gulf Shores or Mobile.

FOOD

It's a small island, and the selection of restaurants is unfortunately limited. Most of them are located right across the Dauphin Island Bridge on LeMoyne Drive and along Bienville Boulevard, with a cluster of choice eateries around the intersection of these two roads.

For a delightful breakfast before you hit the beach, visit the ★ **Lighthouse Bakery** (919 Chaumont Ave., 251/861-2253, 7am-2pm Wed.-Sun., $4-10). This historic home has been turned into a wonderful bakery that serves large, flaky croissants and a wonderful selection of fresh-made sandwiches for breakfast or lunch. Eat outdoors at one of the tables that line the front porch or at the picnic tables on the front lawn if the weather is nice. If the bakery is busy, you can get effectively distracted by browsing the interesting and quirky

Lighthouse Bakery

collection of knickknacks and souvenirs they have for sale that line nearly every square inch of the restaurant walls.

A great place on the island for lunch, dinner, or a drink is **Islander's Restaurant** (1504 Bienville Blvd., 251/861-2225, 11am-9pm Thurs.-Mon., 11am-3pm Tues.-Wed., $12-20). Formerly the Oarhouse, the new management has turned things around and greatly improved the menu. There are fresh seafood dishes as well as some of the best shrimp po'boys on the island, with excellent, perfectly chewy rolls. The portions are large and the shrimp and grits and piña coladas are a perfect combo after spending the day on the beach.

For fresh seafood that you can cook at the beach house or condo, stop in at **Skinners Seafood** (703 LeMoyne Dr., 251/861-4221, www.skinnerseafood.com, 8am-6pm Wed.-Mon., 8am-5pm Sun., $7-15). They own their personal fishing boat, and as a result nearly everything in the store is brought in fresh daily from the Gulf and bay. Just don't go into the store hungry or you might leave with more raw oysters, shrimp, and red snapper than you can handle. They also sell a nice variety of hot sauces, spices, boils, and batters to accompany your effortless seafood catch.

ACCOMMODATIONS

Accommodations are extremely limited on Dauphin Island, and most visitors rent beach houses or condos during their stay.

Under $100

The best affordable choice on the island is the **Gulf Breeze Motel** (1512 Cadillac Ave., 251/861-7344, www.gulfinfo.com/gulfbreeze-motel, $69-129). Family owned and operated since 1982, this clean, no-frills motel with free Wi-Fi is located on the bay side and within walking distance to the public beach access. You can enjoy views of the bay from the balconies of most of 32 rooms. Two rooms include full kitchens. The dock behind the motel has boat slips if you want to sail up to your room. You can't see the Gulf of Mexico from your room, but it is such a short walk away that you can avoid fighting traffic and searching for a parking space and instead enjoy every minute possible out on the beach. Note that prices vary greatly from month to month.

$100-200

The **Dauphin Harbour House** (730 Cadillac Ave., 251/861-2119, www.dauphinhouse.com, $110-189) offers an enjoyable bed-and-breakfast experience. New owners Julie and Billy

Gulf Breeze Motel

Lindsey have made a lot of improvements on the property, including adding a large, second-story deck. They also cook up a wonderful breakfast. The 10 rooms vary greatly, some having larger bathrooms or better views of the bay than others. Let the owners know what you are looking for so they can get you the right room. The pier behind the house is a great place to hang out or fish for flounder and redfish. If you're sailing, boat slips are available ($50/night).

Vacation Rentals

The best way to set up a beach rental is to contact ★ **Dauphin Island Beach Rentals** (103 Treasure Ct., 251/455-1159, www.dauphinislandbeachrentals.com). They offer a wide variety of homes and condos to choose from, with most options being family-oriented beach houses that tend to be more modest in size and style than what you might find farther east. The homes and condos that are available for the most part reflect the island's laid-back and casual attitude and lifestyle. Most homes and condos on the island rent for $100-300 per night or $700-2,000 per week. Monthly and long-term rentals are available.

Camping

The only campground on the island is the **Pelican Nest RV Resort and Campground** (1510 Bienville Blvd., 251/861-2338, www.dauphinislandcampground.com, $35-80). The campground has 150 sites with access to power and water and 75 sites with RV hookups. In the bathhouse you'll find hot showers and restrooms. A boardwalk takes you from the campground to the beach, and a small store in the campground will keep your cooler stocked with all the camping and most of the beach supplies you need. It's free to use the boat launch, and when you're not on the water, you can explore the nearby Fort Gaines historical site. The campground is only a half mile from the where the ferry departs. This is great if you want to hitch a ride over to Gulf Shores for the day, but not the best situation if you are a light sleeper or a tent camper. The ferry arrives early in the morning, and when the ferry horn blows, there is little chance you'll be able to keep slumbering peacefully. For this reason, the campground is more accommodating for RV campers, but if you're set on tent camping, then just bring a good pair of earplugs.

GETTING THERE
Car

You can drive to Dauphin Island from Gulf Shores or Orange by heading north to Mobile and then driving back down south to the island, but the ferry is more fun and often faster. If you're coming from Gulf Shores or Orange Beach, the quickest way to Dauphin Island is to drive west on I-10 to Highway 193 South, which leads to the island.

Ferry

The **Mobile Bay Ferry** (101 Bienville Blvd., Dauphin Island, and 110 State Hwy. 180, Gulf Shores, 8am-6pm, departs every 45 minutes Mar.-Nov. and every hour and a half Nov.-Feb.; one-way tickets: $18 cars, $35 motor homes, $8 motorcycles, $10 boats with trailers, $4.50 additional passengers, children under 12 free) is more relaxing, and much more fun, than driving. It connects SR 193 at Dauphin Island on the west side with SR 180 at Mobile Point on the east. The ferry trip takes about 40 minutes each way.

Orange Beach, Gulf Shores, and Dauphin Island are located within the **central time zone.** The telephone area code is **251.**

TOURIST INFORMATION

The *Gulf Coast News* (251/943-2151, www.gulfcoastnewstoday.com) is the best way to find out about local events and entertainment. The same company also produces the *Baldwin Times,* the *Courier,* the *Robertsdale Independent,* the *Gulf Shores and Orange Beach Islander,* and the *Foley Onlooker.* You can find kiosks at many of the grocery stores, entertainment developments, and shopping centers around the area. For visitor information on Gulf Shores and Orange Beach, stop in at the **Alabama Gulf Coast Convention & Visitors Bureau** (23685 Perdido Beach Blvd., Orange Beach, 251/974-1510) to pick up brochures and maps as well as plenty of great coupons. They also maintain a website (www.gulfshores.com) with a tremendous amount of visitor information.

Dauphin Island events and information can be found easily online at www.dauphin-islandtimes.com. For more Dauphin Island information, call or visit the **Dauphin Island Chamber of Commerce** (1101 Bienville Blvd., 251/861-5524, www.dauphinislandtourism.com); they share a space with the community library and have free Wi-Fi, computers to use, and all the information and brochures you need to plan your Dauphin Island days.

POLICE AND EMERGENCIES

Of course, if you find yourself in a real emergency, pick up a phone and dial 911. For a nonemergency police need, call or visit the **Orange Beach Police Department** (4480 Orange Beach Blvd., 251/981-9777, www.obpd.

org). The **Gulf Shores Police Department** can be reached at 251/968-2431, and the **Dauphin Island Police Department** can be reached at 251/861-5523. In the event of a medical emergency, stop into the **Orange Beach Medical Center** (4223 Orange Beach Blvd., 251/974-3820) or **Gulf Shores Medical Center** (200 Office Park Dr., 251/968-7379). To fill a prescription there is a CVS pharmacy in Orange Beach (25761 Perdido Beach Blvd., 251/974-1590). The **Gulf Shores Pharmacy** (251 Clubhouse Dr., 251/968-3784) has an antique soda fountain and Wurlitzer jukebox to play while you wait.

RADIO AND TELEVISION

You can tune your radio station to **91.3 FM** for public radio, **94.9 FM** for country, **96.1 FM** for classic rock, **97.5 FM** for top 40 hits, or **99.9 FM** for a wide variety of adult contemporary music. Turn to **1350 AM** for sports talk, and either **870 AM** or **1400 AM** for news talk.

And on the television, **WPMI Channel 15** out of Mobile is the NBC affiliate, **WBPG Channel 55** out of Gulf Shores is the CW affiliate, **WKRG Channel 5** out of Mobile is the CBS affiliate, **WEAR Channel 3** out of Pensacola is the ABC affiliate, and **WEIQ Channel 42** out of Mobile is the PBS affiliate.

LAUNDRY SERVICES

Most of the hotels, condos, and resorts on Orange Beach or Gulf Shores offer their own laundry services to guests. There's also the **AAA Laundromat** (3645 Gulf Shores Pkwy., Gulf Shores, 251/948-9274) if you happen to be staying at a property without laundry machines. There's no Laundromat in Dauphin Island. However, most of the hotels and nearly all the homes and condos you can rent have access to laundry machines for a small fee.

Background

The Landscape

GEOGRAPHY

Florida is bounded on the north by Alabama and Georgia, to the east by the Atlantic, to the south by the Straits of Florida, and to the west by the Gulf of Mexico. The east coast of the state is comparatively straight, extending in a rough line 470 miles long. The Gulf side, on the other hand, has a more curving and complex coastline, measuring roughly 675 miles. In all, Florida's 2,276-mile coastline is longer than that of any other state in the continental United States and contains 663 miles of beaches and more than 11,000 miles of rivers, streams, and waterways.

It's nearly pancake flat, without notable change in elevation, and young by geological standards, having risen out of the ocean 300-400 million years ago. The state of Florida has six major geographical regions, several of which are represented along the Gulf Coast. First, the **coastal lowlands** encircle the state and extend along the shores inland 10-100 miles. The most recent to emerge from the ocean, the lowlands are covered with forests of saw palmetto and cypress. To the northwest, between the Perdido and Apalachicola Rivers, the **western highlands** are hilly uplands of pine forest. The highlands offer the highest elevation in Florida—345 feet above sea level in the northwestern part of Walton County. And farther east, between the Apalachicola and Withlacoochee Rivers, the **Tallahassee Hills** is a hilly region dotted with live oak and pine forests. It gradually slopes eastward to a plain until it hits the Suwannee River.

The Gulf side of the state has numerous deep-water bays: Tampa Bay, Apalachicola Bay, Charlotte Harbor, and Pensacola Bay. There is also an abundance of rivers (Caloosahatchee, Peace, Withlacoochee, Manatee, Suwannee, Ocilla, Ocklockonee, Apalachicola, Choctawhatchee, Yellow, Escambia, Perdido, and others) and harbors on the Gulf side, and a record-holding number of first-magnitude springs. Thus, the fishing, boating, and swimming along the Gulf Coast are legendary.

Starting in the south, the **Everglades** region consists mainly of submerged sawgrass plains. The water, about knee-deep and with a slight southward current, provides habitat to hundreds of fish species, birds, and small mammals. Some of the Everglades' water is overflow from **Lake Okeechobee**, the second-largest freshwater lake with boundaries entirely in the United States, 30 miles wide and 33 miles long.

North of the lake, extending through De Soto, Manatee, Osceola, and Brevard Counties, is a vast tract of prairie land with large swamp areas. This is where much of the state's cattle is raised. North of that, in Polk, Marion, Orange, Sumter, Lake, and Alachua Counties, there's a little rise along the central ridge (up to 300 feet above sea level), with large and small lakes dotting the fertile, gently rolling terrain. The **coastal plain** that runs along the length of the Gulf Coast is low-lying and sandy, skirted by a dense pine region and marshes in many parts.

Several geographical features and plant communities are common in Florida, such as barrier islands, mangrove islands, marshes, hardwood hammocks, pineland, and flatwoods.

Barrier Islands

Barrier islands are ridges of sand that usually run parallel to the main coast (Sanibel sticks out the other way), separated from the

---

Previous: a cannon at Fort Gaines; a seagull on the Apalachicola waterfront.

mainland by a bay or lagoon. They are sand deposits of recent geologic origin, in much of the Gulf Coast composed of almost pure milky quartz. Delivered to the Gulf by rivers, this sand is washed and well sorted, resulting in fine, even-grained sand along many Gulf beaches. Buffering the mainland from storms and heavy surf, they are constantly being contoured and molded by wave action and wind. **Sea oats** and other beachside plants provide a little structure and foundation for dunes to develop. They capture and hold the blowing sand—thus, they are to be preserved and nurtured (there's a steep fine for trampling or messing with the sea oats on Gulf Coast beaches). **Swales** are wetlands formed on these islands where the wind has scoured out the sand down to the water table or below, and often a **maritime forest** can be found on the back side of barrier islands behind the secondary dunes.

Mangrove Islands

Along Florida's south coast and halfway up the peninsula, mangrove swamps hug the shoreline. They create a fringing network around most islands, growing at the high-tide line and helping to stabilize the shore. In the maze of the **Ten Thousand Islands**

in between Marco Island and the Everglades, you can see entire island ecosystems created by saltwater-tolerant mangroves. These trees send their roots into the shallows, filtering pollution and providing a crucial habitat for fish and wading birds.

Marshes

Marshes make up a large area near the Gulf Coast—spaces that are partially or periodically submerged land, where the water table is near the surface of the soil. Water flows into marshes and swamps from rivers, creeks, and bayous, bringing with it rich organic debris that settles and accumulates in the marshes, compacting into peat. Trees in marshes, or in the larger category of **wetlands,** get used to living in standing water. Cypress and tupelo buttress their trunks by sending up "knees" for support (and for breathing air).

In **salt marshes** there is a clear line drawn between the wetland and upland, because the salt is detrimental to the growth of so many plant species. (From Apalachicola Bay south to Tampa Bay, salt marshes are the main coastal community.) In freshwater wetlands that line is more blurred, with the wetland plants shifting subtly into upland species. In the case of **tidal marshes,** affected by the

Santa Rosa Beach

ebb and flow of tides, the demarcation line is even more pronounced. Many tidal marshes along the Gulf Coast are dominated by stands of black needle rush and saltmarsh cordgrass.

Freshwater and saltwater marshes, as well as a similar community called a **seagrass meadow,** are enormously important to Florida's fish species, providing the shelter as a "nursery" for many species, a safe haven in which to mature among the marsh grasses before adult fish go out into the predator-dense Gulf.

Swamps, certainly a defining feature of Florida, are just forested wetlands. About 10 percent of Florida is covered by forested wetland bordering rivers or ponds, populated by plant species that tolerate periodic high water levels. For great examples of swamps, visit Fakahatchee Strand State Preserve or Big Cypress National Park.

Hardwood Hammocks

Hardwood hammocks may be the oldest natural community type in Florida, dating back more than 25 million years. There are **upland hardwoods** and **bottomland hardwoods,** the latter being the transition forest between a drier upland area and a wet river floodplain. Either way, the largest mature trees in a hardwood forest (laurel oak, sweetgum, Southern magnolia, and others) tend to hog all the light. The understory, the next level of stratification (trees like dogwood and shrubs like Elliott's blueberry or Florida anise), has to grab whatever light is left over. And then the forest floor (moss and ferns) lives in the low-light murk. Vines and epiphytes have to hoist themselves up on the canopy trees to gain access to light.

Pineland

Longleaf pineland used to cover 70 million acres in the South. Sadly, Florida pineland is an endangered plant community, a habitat that must be burned regularly to thrive. The small remaining pinelands in Florida are generally so close to residential and commercial areas that regular burning programs often aren't feasible. As if that's not bad enough, invading species like the Brazilian pepper are choking other species in these delicate habitats.

Long Pine Key in Everglades National Park is a great example of a pineland, much of it old-growth forest. And along the northwest Panhandle, **Blackwater River State Forest,** along with Conecuh National Forest and Eglin Air Force Base, contains the largest holding of longleaf pine trees in the world. Longleaf pine is a long-lived tree, between 350 and 500 years. A mature longleaf pine forest has an open canopy that allows sunlight to flood the forest floor, resulting in a forest floor with lots of plant species and grasses.

Flatwoods

Pine flatwoods (also called pine flats or pine barrens), on the other hand, are ubiquitous in Florida, historically covering almost half of the natural land area in the state. They are characterized by low, flat land, an open canopy of slash pine, and an understory dominated by palmetto prairie. Slash pine has historically been used to produce all kinds of commercial goods, from paper products to turpentine and household goods. Additionally, pine flatwoods provide important habitat for many wildlife species.

A **scrub** is a similar plant community—same pine up above with various shrubs and palmetto underneath—but scrubs are found in upland areas that are generally much harsher and drier, with no organic matter in the soil. It's an austere habitat, but home to the threatened **gopher tortoises** and the endangered Florida **scrub jay.**

CLIMATE
Heat and Humidity

Florida is closer to the equator than any other continental American state, located on the southeastern tip of North America, with a humid subtropical climate and heavy rainfall April-November. Its humidity is attributed to the fact that no point in the state is more than 60 miles from saltwater and no more

Gulf Coast Temperatures

City	Avg. Low (°F)	Avg. High (°F)
Apalachicola	59	79
Cedar Key	61	83
Fort Myers	64	84
Naples	64	85
Panama City Beach	53	81
Pensacola	59	77
Sarasota	62	83
St. Petersburg	66	82
Tallahassee	56	79
Tampa	63	82

than 345 feet above sea level. If this thick steamy breath on the back of your neck is new to you, know that humidity is a measure of the amount of water vapor in the air. Most often you'll hear the percentage described in "relative humidity," which is the amount of water vapor actually in the air divided by the amount of water vapor the air can hold. The warmer the air becomes, the more moisture it can hold.

When heat and humidity combine to slow evaporation of sweat from the body, outdoor activity becomes dangerous even for those in good physical shape. Drink plenty of water to avoid dehydration and slow down if you feel fatigued or notice a headache, a high pulse rate, or shallow breathing. Overheating can cause serious and even life-threatening conditions such as heatstroke. The elderly, small children, the overweight, and those on certain medications are particularly vulnerable to heat stress.

During the summer months, expect temperatures to hover around 90°F and humidity to be near 100 percent. The most pleasant times of the year along the length of the Florida peninsula fall between December and April—not surprisingly, the busiest time for tourism. Along the Panhandle, however, where temperatures are more moderate in the summer and chillier in the winter, the summer sees more tourist action.

The common wisdom is that the hard freeze line in Florida bisects the state from Ocala to Jacksonville. North of that, freezing temperatures rarely last long, and south of that it's just an hour here or there under the freezing point (with serious damage to tropical plants in years when the temperature dips low). The best approach for packing in preparation for a visit to Florida is layering—with a sweater for over-air-conditioned interiors or chilly winds, and lots of loose, wicking material for the heat.

Rain

It rains nearly every day in the summer along the Gulf Coast—and not just a sprinkle. Due to the abundance of warm, moist air from the Gulf of Mexico and the hot tropical sun, conditions are perfect for the formation of thunderstorms. There are 80-90 thunderstorms each summer, generally less than 15 miles in diameter—but vertically they can grow up to 10 miles high in the atmosphere. These are huge, localized thunderstorms that can drop four or more inches of rain in an hour, while just a few miles away it stays dry. The bulk of these tropical afternoon thunderstorms each summer are electrical storms.

Lightning

With sudden thunderstorms comes lightning, a serious threat along the Gulf Coast. About 50 people are struck by lightning each year in the state. Most of them are hospitalized and recover, but there are about 10 fatalities annually. Tampa is the "Lightning Capital" of the United States, with around 25 cloud-to-ground lightning bolt blasts on each square mile annually. The temperature of a single bolt can reach 50,000°F, about three times as hot as the sun's surface. There's not much you can do to ward off lightning except to avoid being in the wrong place at the wrong time. The summer months of June, July, August, and September have the highest number of lightning-related injuries and deaths. Usually lightning occurs during daylight hours, with the highest concentration between 3pm and 4pm, when the afternoon storms peak. Lightning strikes usually occur either at the beginning or end of a storm, and can strike up to 10 miles away from the center of the storm. Keep your eye on approaching storms and seek shelter when you see lightning.

Locals use the 30-30 rule: Count the seconds after a lightning flash until you hear thunder. If that number is under 30, the storm is within six miles of you. Seek shelter. Then, at storm's end, wait 30 minutes after the last thunderclap before resuming outdoor activity.

HURRICANES

Hurricanes are violent tropical storms with sustained winds of at least 74 mph. Massive low-pressure systems, they blow counterclockwise around a relatively calm central area called the eye. They form over warm ocean waters, often starting as storms in the Caribbean or off the west coast of Africa. As they move westward, they are fueled by the warm waters of the tropics. Warm, moist air moves toward the center of the storm and spirals upward, releasing driving rains. Updrafts suck up more water vapor, which further strengthens the storm until it can be stopped only when contact is made with land or cooler water. In the average hurricane, just 1 percent of the energy released could meet the energy needs of the United States for a full year.

In Florida, the hurricane season is July-November. These storms have been named since 1953. It used to be just female names, but now male names are also being used. Really powerful hurricanes' names are retired, kind of like sports greats' jerseys.

The 2004 hurricane season was the last really destructive year in Florida, with Charley, Frances, Ivan, and Jeanne wreaking havoc on the Gulf Coast in rapid succession. In areas like Pensacola, it was several years before insurance and FEMA monies had been entirely paid out and blue roof tarps weren't common any longer. In the Charlotte Harbor area, hit by Charley, the reconstruction efforts have yielded an even more attractive destination for visitors. Things are finally back to normal after Hurricane Katrina's devastating effects were felt in nearby Louisiana and Mississippi, and thankfully the past few years have been for the most part meteorologically uneventful in Florida.

Hurricane Safety

Monitor radio and TV broadcasts closely for directions. Gas up the car, and make sure you have batteries, a water supply, candles, and food that can be eaten without the use of electricity. Get cash, have your prescriptions filled, and put all essential documents in a large resealable bag. In the event of an evacuation, find the closest shelter by listening to the radio or TV broadcasts. Pets are not allowed in most shelters. There are designated pet shelters, but all animals must be up to date on shots. Alternatively, an increasing number of hotels and motels accept animals for a nominal daily fee.

ENVIRONMENTAL ISSUES
Oil Spills

The Deepwater Horizon well off the coast of Louisiana exploded on April 20, 2010. It killed 11 workers who were present on the rig at the time and, according to a *New York Times*

Hurricane Lingo

HURRICANE TERMS

- **Tropical Depression:** an organized system of clouds and thunderstorms with a defined circulation and maximum sustained winds of 38 mph (33 knots) or less

- **Severe Thunderstorm:** a thunderstorm with winds 58 mph (50 knots) or faster or hailstones 0.75 inch or larger in diameter

- **Tropical Storm:** an organized system of strong thunderstorms with a defined circulation and maximum sustained winds of 39-73 mph (34-63 knots)

- **Hurricane:** a warm-core tropical cyclone with maximum sustained winds of 74 mph (64 knots) or greater

- **Eye:** the "calm" center of a hurricane with light winds and partly cloudy to clear skies, usually around 20 miles in diameter (but the range is 5-60 miles)

- **Eye Wall:** the location within a hurricane where the most damaging winds and intense rainfall are found

- **Tornadoes:** violent rotating columns of air that touch the ground; they are spawned by large severe thunderstorms and can have winds estimated at 100-300 mph (87-261 knots). A **tornado watch** means they're possible; a **tornado warning** means they're in your area.

HURRICANE WARNINGS

- **Tropical Storm Watch:** issued when tropical storm conditions may threaten a particular coastal area within 36 hours, when the storm is not predicted to intensify to hurricane strength

- **Tropical Storm Warning:** winds ranging 39-73 mph that can be expected to affect specific areas of a coastline within the next 24 hours

- **Hurricane Watch:** a hurricane or hurricane conditions may threaten a specific coastal area within 36 hours

- **Hurricane Warning:** a warning that sustained winds of 74 mph or higher associated with a hurricane are expected in a specified coastal area in 24 hours or less

HURRICANE SCALE

- **Category I:** winds 74-95 mph with a storm surge of 4-5 feet and minimal damage

- **Category II:** winds 96-110 mph with a storm surge of 6-8 feet and moderate damage

- **Category III:** winds 111-130 mph with a storm surge of 9-12 feet and major damage

- **Category IV:** winds 131-155 mph with a storm surge of 13-18 feet and severe damage

- **Category V:** winds 156+ mph with more than an 18-foot storm surge and catastrophic damage

report, began releasing more than 60,000 barrels of oil a day into the Gulf of Mexico. When the well was finally plugged on July 15, 2010, it had released an estimated 53,000 barrels of oil a day into the Gulf. According to the Flow Rate Technical Group appointed by BP and the Coast Guard to estimate the extent of the spill, the total volume of oil released into the Gulf over the three months the well was leaking is believed to be at least 205.8 million gallons of crude oil. On September 19, 2010, the relief well was finally completed and the Coast Guard declared the well to be officially "dead."

What the oil spill has meant for the ecosystem in the Gulf of Mexico is still largely unknown, as the long-term effects of the largest oil spill to take place in the Gulf are still being studied and documented.

On April 23, 2010, the U.S. Coast Guard began receiving reports that oil was washing up in wildlife refuges and the seafood grounds on the Louisiana coast. By June 21, 36 percent of federal waters in the Gulf of Mexico were closed for fishing, totaling nearly 67,000 square miles and detrimentally impacting the fishing industry in the region. It is estimated that the impacts of the oil spill have cost the fishing industry along the Gulf Coast over $2.5 billion. More than 8,000 species that inhabit the area were impacted by the oil spill, including more than 1,200 fish, 200 bird, 1,400 mollusk, 1,500 crustacean, 4 sea turtle, and 29 marine mammal species. According to the U.S. Fish and Wildlife Deepwater Horizon Fish and Wildlife Collection Report released on April 20, 2011, 6,918 dead animals had been collected, including 6,147 birds, 613 sea turtles, and 157 dolphins and other mammals.

More than 1.8 million gallons of chemical dispersants were released into the Gulf of Mexico directly at the wellhead source in an effort to break up the oil before it reached the surface. Robert Diaz, a marine biologist at the College of William and Mary recently said on dispersants, "The dispersants definitely don't make oil disappear. They take it from one area in an ecosystem and put it in another." And University of South Florida researchers are finding that the dispersed oil is having a toxic effect on the phytoplankton and bacteria in the Gulf of Mexico—the microscopic plants that make up the basis of the food chain here. The EPA and NOAA have openly stated that they support the claim that dispersed oil is no less toxic than the oil alone. However, recently reports have contradicted this statement and claimed that the Corexit dispersants made the oil spill more than 52 times more toxic.

Other Environmental Issues

There are many complex and far-reaching

an oil rig on the Alabama Gulf Coast

environmental issues in Florida, from declining amphibian populations to an abundance of Superfund sites, paper mill water contamination, saltwater intrusion in the Everglades and other areas, and the quickly disappearing Florida panther population. Millions of acres have been bulldozed to make way for strip malls, condo developments, and all those beautiful golf courses and theme parks. It's the same story that is told of many recently developed natural settings.

Recent drought in Georgia has meant that the U.S. Army Corps of Engineers has repeatedly withheld water to accommodate the water needs of greater Atlanta; the Corps uses the Buford Dam to regulate water flow from Lake Lanier, which feeds freshwater into the Apalachicola River and eventually into Apalachicola Bay. Downstream along the Apalachicola River and Apalachicola Bay, the resulting salinity (less freshwater in

an estuary means a greater percentage of saltwater) may mean the end of the state's oyster industry, not to mention the destruction of endangered species like Florida sturgeon and several kinds of mussels.

Still, the state's commitment to the environment elevates the situation from hopeless. There's been an enormous grassroots effort in the past decade in Florida, which has largely moved into the mainstream after the BP oil spill, of regular people who have stood up against offshore drilling and supported the protection of the abundant and beautiful natural resources that are so directly tied to the quality of life and economy of everyone in the state. If their efforts are successful, the state's natural treasures, as well as its fishing and tourism industries that make up such a large portion of the Gulf Coast's economy, might be preserved, restored, and possibly even strengthened.

Plants and Animals

The abundance of sunlight and rain and the near absence of four traditional seasons allow for the successful growth of nearly 4,000 plant species and nearly that many animals in Florida. The lower Gulf Coast's palms, the great cypress swamps, mangroves, and on the Panhandle one of the greatest forested regions in the East—Florida's plantlife is richly diverse, providing a range of habitats. Even nonnative plants and animals flourish in these lush conditions, a fact that troubles Floridian scientists as more exotic species take hold. The trade in exotic pets and plants, as well as the movement of huge numbers of people and vehicles, can intentionally or unintentionally bring new species into Florida, devastating native species and invading natural areas.

PLANTS

On March 27, 1513 (Easter Day), Ponce de León landed on the coast of Florida and pronounced it a "land of flowers." And it's true,

mostly. The subtropical climate is warm, moist, and lush, with the kind of foliage in the summer for which you don't need a stop-action film in order to document growth. There are plants that grow like Audrey II in Little Shop of Horrors. Fast, loose, and weird. The even greater thing is that many native and even flourishing exotic Florida plants have huge advocates and devotees.

There are avid clubs devoted to carnivorous plants, to orchids, to bromeliads, to palms (which are really not trees—despite the fact that the state "tree" is the cabbage palm). It's a gardener's state, but there's a certain humility gardeners bring to the table. It's not generally a state for regimented topiary or manicured rose gardens. Serendipity, chance, and Mother Nature's whim play a part in Florida gardening. So much is given, but, as recent hurricane seasons have shown, so much can be taken away.

Trees

Palm trees are practically a Florida cliché. Also known as cabbage palm and palmetto, it's from the **sabal palm** that hearts of palm are harvested. Sabal palm grows in all conditions in the state—wet, dry, coastal, swampy—and it is from the fronds of the sabal that the Seminoles built watertight chickee roofs. In some parts of the Gulf Coast, you'll encounter **royal palm,** identified by its towering 80-foot pale gray trunk and bright, glossy crown shaft. Many of the other palm species usually associated with Florida are not native—the easily recognized **coconut palm,** the heavy-trunked **Canary Island date palm,** and the slim, statuesque **red latan palm.** You'll see them all along the Gulf Coast, but it's what they're in contrast to that gives this subtropical landscaping its own flavor.

Mangroves are often called walking trees because they hover above the water, their arching prop roots resembling so many spindly legs. Seeds sprout on the parent tree and drop off, bobbing in the water until they lodge on an oyster bar or a snag in the shallows. There, the seed begins to grow to a tree, the foundation of a new, tiny island. Around its roots sediment and debris build up to create a thick layer of peat upon which other plant species

begin to grow. This first tree drops more seed tubules, which get stuck in the mulchy ground and create more trees. This is how islands are often created off the Gulf Coast.

There are three types of mangrove along the Gulf: The red mangrove forms a wide band of trees on the outermost part of each mangrove island, facing the open sea. The red mangrove encircles the black mangrove, which in turn encircles the white mangrove at the highest, driest part of each mangrove island. Mangroves are protected by federal, state, and local laws.

Cypress is another oh-so-Florida tree. Forested wetlands in the state are often dominated by cypress trees, located along stream banks and riverbanks or in ponds with slow-moving water. Bald cypresses (they aren't always bald, they just lose their leaves in winter) are the largest trees in North America east of the Rockies. They can live for hundreds of years, quietly ruminating with their roots in water, their "knees" protruding above the soil and waterline. The function of these knees, part of the root system that projects out of the water, isn't totally known, other than that they provide stability and more air for the base of these flood-tolerant trees. The Gulf Coast offers several cypress swamps to explore.

an orchid

oak tree and spanish moss on Orange Beach

Live oaks are certainly not the sole custody of Florida. Throughout the South these huge semi-deciduous trees loom, gnarled and woebegone, draped with Spanish moss (which is neither Spanish nor a moss). The Tallahassee area is especially dense with live oak, but you'll see them all over.

The **gumbo limbo,** one of only three native tree species in North America, is common down toward the Everglades. They call it the sunburn tree, as its smooth bark peels off in sheets to reveal a red trunk color beneath. I love these trees, and I love saying their name even more.

Sawgrass

Also a defining feature of the Everglades, sawgrass looks like smooth, soft hay. It dominates wide swaths of marshland in this area, known as "The River of Grass," but sawgrass blades have little sawlike teeth along one side that make walking through it painful.

Epiphytes

Epi means "on" and *phyte* means "plant." Thus, an epiphyte is a plant that grows on another plant. They're sometimes called air plants because they grow above ground, in the air, roots wiggling in the breeze. Host plants support them high off the ground, where they don't need to compete for light and rainwater, and where they don't have to cope with floodwater and marauding animals. Epiphytes generally do no harm to the host plant and get their nutrients from their own photosynthesis and their own water from runoff on their host. Cardinal airplant and resurrection fern are wonderful plants to explore.

Within this category, **orchids** are probably the best known, with more genera than any other plant. They are among the most exotic and delicate flowers in the world, holding a special fascination for collectors, photographers, and hobbyists. Orchids abound in the Everglades' hardwood hammocks, marshes, pineland, and prairies. To see thousands of orchid species, visit the Marie Selby Botanical Gardens in Sarasota,

Bromeliads are another type of epiphyte, members of the pineapple family. They use shallow roots only to anchor themselves to a tree or the ground and absorb through their leaves the water and nutrients they need from the air and from the rain. These leathery, brightly colored tropical plants often collect water in little "tanks" or between their leaves. Of Florida's 16 species of native bromeliads, 13 are not found elsewhere in the United States.

Crops

The citrus fruit industry has been big business in the state since the 1890s when Chinese horticulturist Lue Gim Gong introduced a new variety of **orange** and a hardier **grapefruit.** Today, citrus is Florida's leading cash crop, with the state producing 90 percent of the country's orange juice (almost all Florida oranges are juiced, not sold whole). Florida is second only to Brazil in orange juice

Gators!

In his excellent memoir, *Totch, A Life in the Everglades,* Totch Brown describes a gator's sounds:

> Gators make three different sounds. One is the "grunt" used by young gators in distress to call their mothers. When you pick up a baby gator it'll start grunting every time. The mother will come to this sound right away. (With practice, you can imitate this "grunt" and often fool a grown gator into coming to you.)
>
> Then there's a blowing sound gators make when they're more or less hemmed up, or cornered and are good and mad.
>
> The third sound is the gator bellow—a bloodcurdling sound that can be heard for miles across the Everglades. When one gator bellows, usually another will answer.... When a 12-foot gator bellows, he raises his head up as high as possible, his mouth wide open, and with a full breath, lets out his air. It's a sight to be seen! The bellowing is generally in mating season, the late spring, when the rains are about to start. The gators seem to be asking Mother Nature for a drink of water.

I've seen a gator bellow with his head tipped way back. To me he didn't seem like he was asking anybody for anything other than to buzz off. It's a noise that has the same kind of effect as your first viewing of Jaws.

Alligators were first listed as an endangered species in 1967, their numbers threatened by hunting and habitat loss. Then the American alligator was removed from the endangered species list in 1987 after the U.S. Fish and Wildlife Service pronounced a complete recovery of the species. I'll say—conservative estimates put the population at over one million in Florida, Louisiana, Texas, and Georgia. Because they can tolerate brackish water as well as freshwater, they can be found in rivers, swamps, bogs, lakes, ponds, creeks, canals, swimming pools, and lots of Florida golf courses.

production, and it is the world leader in grapefruit production.

There are about 750,000 acres of citrus groves in the state and more than 100 million citrus trees, mostly in the lower two-thirds of the state. There are about 40 citrus packinghouses and 20 citrus processing plants in Florida. It is estimated that the growing, packing, processing, and selling of citrus generates a $9 billion per year impact on Florida's economy—not surprisingly, the orange blossom is the state flower.

Recent cold snaps that devastate the season's yield have posed a major threat to this Florida industry and the estimated 76,000 jobs in the citrus industry or related businesses.

Beyond citrus, though, Florida is the "winter salad bowl," providing 80 percent of the fresh vegetables grown in the United States during January, February, and March. The Gulf Coast is responsible for lots of tomatoes, peppers, and strawberries—Plant City near Tampa is the state's strawberry capital.

There are also exotic tropical fruits and vegetables grown along the Gulf Coast, from smooth-skinned avocados the size of softballs to mangoes (Lee County), guavas, lychees, sapotes, cherimoyas, and others.

ANIMALS
Fish

No other state in the United States and few other countries boast a more varied marine environment. Florida has hundreds of species of fish crowding its waters. There's the Atlantic and the fertile Gulf of Mexico with its hundreds of bays, sounds, inlets, and brackish marshes. But there are also freshwater rivers,

The American alligator is the largest reptile in North America (distinguished from the American crocodile by its short, rounded snout and black color). They can live 35-50 years in the wild, 60-80 years in captivity. The average adult male is 13 feet in length (half of the length taken up by the tail), although they can grow up to 18 feet long. Bulls are generally larger than females, weighing 450-600 pounds.

Alligators are cold-blooded (literally, maybe figuratively). It's a good survival tactic because they don't need to eat as much or as often as their warm-blooded counterparts. In fact, they can't eat unless their internal body temperature is 90 degrees. Thus, they don't eat all winter, and in the spring can be seen in the midmorning basking on the banks in a sunny spot. They're hungry and ready to mate in April and May—a good time to steer especially clear. In the summer the females lay their eggs in a nest (up to 70 eggs) and cover them, then the eggs incubate for 65 days. (As a cool aside, alligators lack sexual chromosomes, so that sex is determined by the temperature at which eggs incubate. Between 90 and 93 degrees they're all male; between 87 and 89 degrees they're female.) The mom stays close, carrying the freshly hatched babies to the water. Even after they're swimming around, mama is protective for up to the first two years (supposedly she can hear their cry for help up to a mile away). Still, it's said only 1 in 10 alligators lives through the first year.

Alligators are everywhere in Florida, and they eat just about anything. Usually that means lizards, fish, snakes, turtles, even little gators, but they'll also enjoy corgi and terrier if you don't keep your pup on a short leash.

a gator in the Everglades

lakes, estuaries, and numerous other marine environments.

The **Panhandle** has long stretches of white-sand beaches and ocean that quickly drops off to deep water—boaters in 70 feet of water can often see bathers on the beach. The area is also home to bountiful estuaries (where rivers meet the sea) tucked behind long, narrow barrier islands.

From **Apalachicola** to the **Big Bend,** estuaries are protected by oyster bars and rocky islands. Here the water depths drop off gradually. Off the Suwannee River and St. Marks Light, ordinary outboard motorboats can run aground more than three miles from shore. This area has few beaches and is dominated by marshes with vast sea grass beds. Farther south along the Gulf, anglers enjoy a number of exciting species, from huge **tarpon** to tasty **grouper, cobia,** and the fabled **snook.**

In much of this area, freshwater fishing is most productive in the spring, while sportfishing is good all year. But you need a license. An annual nonresident saltwater or freshwater fishing license is $47, a seven-day license is $30, and a three-day license is $17. You need to figure out what you're fishing for before you purchase your license, but either way the revenue generated by the sale goes to the Florida Fish and Wildlife Conservation Commission.

There are also numerous shellfish species: **scallops** in Steinhatchee, **oysters** in Apalachicola, **stone crabs** in Everglades City, **clams** in Cedar Key, and delicious **Florida blue crabs** all over the state.

Birds

With 500 bird species, both those native to the state and those that migrate here, the Gulf Coast is a bird lover's paradise in a range of habitats. Mangrove estuaries are home to many species of **egrets, herons,** and numerous other **wading birds. Waterbirds** occupy interior wetlands, and countless **shorebirds, terns,** and **gulls** populate the white-sand beaches. Unique to the state, the **Florida scrub jay** lives in a small patch of scrub-oak habitat; **ospreys** and **bald eagles** make their large nests all along the Gulf Coast. In the woods you can find **red-shouldered hawks** and endangered **red cockaded woodpeckers.** In backyard ponds you'll see the long, sinuous neck of the **anhinga**— what Native tribes called "snakebirds"—they stand in a confident-looking stance with their wings stretched out to dry them after a dive for fish. You'll spot **white pelicans,** the second-largest flying bird in North America, sailing low over the Gulf waters, while high above a **frigate** is barely a speck. Your hair might stand on end when you hear the nagging cry of a **little blue heron,** and you may be startled by the trilling call of the enormous **sandhill cranes** that stroll around in small family groups of three.

It's serious birding country, with loads of expert birders to lead you through the prime birding spots. There are numerous birding festivals along the Gulf Coast, and the **Great Florida Birding Trail** (www.floridabirdingtrail.com) for when you want to get out into the wilderness alone.

Large Mammals

After the alligator, the **West Indian manatee** is the Florida Gulf Coast's most famous animal. A manatee is a large, gray aquatic mammal with a body that tapers to a flat, paddle-shaped, beaver-like tail. Completely herbivorous, they are gentle and slow moving, found in shallow rivers, estuaries, saltwater bays, canals, and coastal areas. Manatees are migratory, meaning they move around and are concentrated in the warm Florida waterways in the winter. Most of their time is spent traveling, resting, and eating—they can consume 10-15 percent of their body weight daily in vegetation (and that's a lot, since adult males weigh 800-1,200 pounds). They have no known predators, but habitat destruction and collisions with watercraft propellers have kept this species on the endangered list (although at the end of 2007 the U.S. Fish and Wildlife Service discussed downgrading its status to threatened). There are an estimated 3,500 West Indian manatees left in the United States, many of them convened along the Nature Coast in Homosassa and Crystal River in the winter. Manatees are protected under federal law, and the Florida Manatee Sanctuary Act of 1978 states: "It is unlawful for any person, at any time, intentionally or negligently, to annoy, molest, harass, or disturb any manatee." It's a steep fine and imprisonment, so look but don't touch these guys. In many waterways on the Gulf Coast there are reduced boat speed zones for manatee protection.

Another locally protected animal is the **Florida panther.** They're called Florida panthers, but really they once roamed throughout the Southeast from east Texas to the Atlantic and north to parts of Tennessee. Overhunting, loss of habitat, and reduction of their primary prey reduced their population to just a handful living in southern Florida in pinelands and mixed swamp forests. Fewer than 100 remain in Florida, making them one of the rarest and most endangered mammals in the world. A subspecies of cougar that has adapted to the subtropical environment of Florida, they are still to be found occasionally in Fakahatchee Strand State Preserve and Big Cypress National Preserve, where there is a 26,605-acre **Florida Panther National Wildlife Refuge.** The Florida Fish and Wildlife Conservation Commission monitors panther activity using radio telemetry collars. Florida panthers are tawny and brown with cream or white undersides; adult males average 130-160 pounds with an average length of 6-8 feet.

Cattle were first introduced to North America in 1521, when Ponce de León landed on the Gulf Coast. He brought a small herd of Andalusian cattle, the descendants of which might be the foundation stock of Florida's **piney-woods cattle.** Spanish missions had herds of cattle, and the Native Americans learned to raise cattle from the Spanish. British and Creek invasions of Spanish Florida in 1702 and 1704 destroyed the Spanish herds, but the Seminoles kept their own herds intact. During the English occupation of Florida, the British brought their own longhorn and short-horn cattle, which eventually bred with the surviving Andalusians, resulting in a tough, compact cow weighing a scant 600 pounds. A speckled brindle pattern, sharp horns, and a cranky disposition still define the Florida piney-woods cow. Cows used to roam the state free, branded or earmarked for owner identification. In order to round them up, Florida ranch hands would crack long whips to get them moving. Some people say it is this that caused rural Floridians to be called Crackers.

Reptiles and Amphibians

There are so many sexy, exciting wild animals in Florida, from alligators to roseate spoonbills, that the little everyday animals often get short shrift. The Gulf Coast is Lizard Central, with several species duking it out for dominance. The **Cuban knight anole** was introduced into Florida in the 1950s. These guys and the **brown anole** are hardy and aggressive (although not in any way harmful to humans), and they have displaced the native **green anole** along the Gulf Coast. The green anole is still the top lizard species in the state's interior.

Turtles are also plentiful in Florida, with 26 different species. Of the species that prefer dry land, there is the **Florida box turtle** common to upland scrub and marshes. They can live up to 100 years but are now protected and fairly uncommon. The **gopher tortoise** you'll see in upland scrub areas. They are protected but occur throughout the state. **Florida snapping turtles** can get up to 70 pounds and are common throughout the state, whereas **alligator snapping turtles** are only found along the Panhandle. Both have powerful jaws and could snap a finger in half. The **Florida soft shell turtle** can be found throughout the state; it has a rubbery shell to allow it to bury itself in the sand as well as swim fast. The **Florida cooter** lives in large ponds, canals, slow-moving rivers, and lakes—it's historically a delicacy among Floridians, and occasionally you'll still find it on menus on the Gulf Coast.

Over 33 species of frogs inhabit the state of Florida, from the exotic **giant marine toad** once imported to control cane beetles to the ubiquitous **Cuban tree frog,** which has displaced many local frog species and has a pretty noxious skin toxin—as well as a fair number of snakes. The snake that seems to worry everyone is the **Florida cottonmouth**—almost always near water, reaching up to six feet, and highly venomous. You'll often encounter them sunning themselves on semi-submerged logs along southern Gulf Coast rivers, whereas Florida's **eastern diamondback,** the largest and most dangerous local snake, is more common in palmetto flatlands and pine woods. **Black racers** are much more common, most of them fairly small despite their potential to grow to six feet. Common in many Florida gardens, they're nonvenomous but can still bite if cornered.

Spiders and Insects

There are loads of big spiders in Florida, too. One of the coolest is the large **golden silk spider** common to wooded areas or groves, but there are also excellent brightly colored **jumping spiders** that don't build webs but instead hunt for their prey and pounce on the unsuspecting. The **black and yellow argiope spider** is another distinctive and fairly common Gulf Coast species—they build big webs with zipper-like zigzag bands of silk at the center.

There are two species of **fire ants** in

Florida, the red imported fire ant and the tropical or native fire ant. Either way, their sting is a nasty shock. They form loose, sandy mounds on the ground, and when perturbed, they swarm out of their house to bite you, leaving raised white or red welts that hurt and itch for days. Be aware of where you're standing while visiting Florida, and avoid mounds of loose dirt at all costs.

History

THE GULF COAST'S NATIVE AMERICANS

Twenty-five thousand years before the birth of Christ, small tribes of primitive hunters crossed the Bering Strait from Asia to the Americas. Generation after generation traveled southward until these hunters arrived in what is now Florida—perhaps one of the last places in continental North America to be inhabited by humans. A warm and mild climate, with waters teeming with fish, Florida was a hospitable home for early nomadic Paleo-Indians (circa 12,000-7500 BC). They built small huts of animal fur and lived off the land's bounty, fishing the bays and streams. Between 1000 BC and AD 1500, the tribes developed advanced tools and pottery-making skills. And by AD 1500, Florida's peoples were divided into large groupings, most ethnologically and linguistically related to the Creek family. Each grouping was divided further into small independent villages. Conservative estimates put the total numbers of Native Americans in Florida at 100,000 at that time.

In northwest Florida the **Apalachee** of the Tallahassee Hills, in between the Suwannee and Apalachicola Rivers, and the **Timucuans,** their dominion ranging more in the center of the Florida peninsula, between the Aucilla River and the Atlantic and as far south as Tampa Bay, brought farming skills to the area. They cultivated squash, beans, and corn, hunting to supplement their meals with meat. Highly organized and hierarchical tribes, they lived in great communal houses and had an absolute ruler (who was assisted by a shaman and a council of noblemen) and a delineated pecking order. They also built elaborate burial and temple mounds, the ruins of which can still be seen.

Along the southwest Gulf Coast the **Calusa** dominated, feared because of their fierceness. They were tall, with long flowing hair and simple garb consisting only of breechclouts of tanned deerskin. They were not farmers, living instead off the bounty of the local waters and the wealth of the nearby woods. Forty Calusa villages spread along the Florida Gulf Coast, with Mound Key near the mouth of the Caloosahatchee River the largest village. They had only primitive tools, but the Calusa built huge mounds of shell and deep moats to protect their villages of raised, thatch-roofed huts. They practiced sacrificial worship and exhibited little interest in the Spaniards' missionary overtures.

Franciscan friars fared better in bringing Catholicism to the Timucuans and the Apalachee, just as the Spanish soldiers were granted permission to steal from the native peoples. The missionaries taught the converts to read and write, and they became more like Spaniards, leaving their villages to build houses in St. Augustine or carrying corn along the Camino Real connecting St. Augustine with the Tallahassee area.

Both tribes lost numbers to diseases brought by the Spaniards, and then more to the British who tried to raid the Spanish missions and gain control of Florida. The British brought the Yamasee Indians from South Carolina, and together they destroyed the mission buildings and took many of the natives as slaves. In 1763, when the Spanish ceded Florida to the British, the Spanish departed the fort at St. Augustine and took the remaining Indians to Cuba. While the Calusa were less amenable to coexisting peacefully with the Spanish, they met the same fate, dying out in the late 1700s. Enemy tribes from Georgia and South Carolina began raiding the Calusa territory; some Calusas were captured and sold as slaves, and the rest seem to have died of diseases such as smallpox and measles.

The **Seminoles** were originally of Creek stock, hailing from Georgia and Alabama. They moved into Florida during the mid-1700s, occupying the spaces indigenous Florida Indians had left behind. They, too, ended up being annihilated by disease and the Spanish, British, and American settlers. Their refusal to withdraw to reservations resulted in the Seminole Wars of 1835-1842. By the end of the war, 4,420 Seminoles had surrendered and been deported to the West. Another 300, however, defied every effort of the U.S. government, retreating to the backwoods of the Everglades to hide out. Many of their descendants occupy the area to this day. According to 2000 census data, 581 tribes, bands, and groups are represented in the state's Native American population of 117,880.

In recent years the Seminole tribe, headquartered in Hollywood, Florida, has assumed a higher profile, with more noncontiguous reservations than any tribe in North America and lucrative gaming casinos getting more buff by the year.

SPANISH EXPLORATION

The southernmost state in the United States, Florida was named by **Ponce de León** upon his visit in 1513, clearly taken with the lush tropical wilderness. This expedition, the first documented presence of Europeans on the U.S. mainland, was ostensibly "to discover and people the island of Bimini." On the return voyage he rounded the Dry Tortugas to explore the Gulf of Mexico, entering Charlotte Harbor. He soon realized that Florida was more than a large island. Near Mound Key he encountered the Calusa, and while on Estero Island repairing his ship he narrowly escaped Calusa capture. Eight years later he returned

and headed to the Calusa territory with 500 of his men, aiming to establish a permanent colony in Florida. In an ensuing battle with the Calusa, Ponce de León was pierced in the thigh by an arrow and carried back to his ship. He never returned again.

Many of the subsequent explorers' missions were less high-profile. In 1516, **Diego Miruelo** mapped Pensacola Bay. In 1517, **Alonso Alvarez de Pineda** went the length of the Florida shore to the Mississippi River, confirming Ponce de León's assertion that Florida was not an island. In 1520, **Vasquez de Ayollon** mapped the Carolina coast (which at the time Spain claimed in the vast region they called "Florida").

Pánfilo de Narváez was a veteran Caribbean soldier, hired by Spanish authorities in 1520 to overthrow Hernán Cortés's tyrannical rule. After a lengthy imprisonment by Cortés, Narváez went back to Spain and obtained a grant to colonize the Gulf Coast from northern Mexico to Florida. Together with **Cabeza de Vaca,** an armada of five ships, and 400 soldiers, Narváez landed north of the mouth of Tampa Bay in 1527. Spanish-Native American relations deteriorated quickly during this period; the Spaniards' ruthless hunt for gold and riches met with violence on the part of the Indians.

Narváez ordered his ships back to Cuba, while a band of men headed northward to the Panhandle in search of gold. Empty-handed, Narváez finally returned to the Gulf at St. Marks. Assuming Mexico to be only a few days' journey to the west, Narváez had five long canoes constructed, which capsized in a storm off the coast of Texas. Narváez drowned, and only Cabeza de Vaca and four others survived. This little band traveled 6,000 miles and in 1536 reached Mexico City to report on their ill-fated mission.

SPANISH, FRENCH, AND ENGLISH COLONIZATION

Then came **Hernando de Soto.** In the spring of 1539 he sailed for Tampa Bay with seven vessels, 600 soldiers, three Jesuit

Famous Names in Florida History

- **Pedro Menéndez de Avilés:** founder of St. Augustine

- **William Pope du Val:** first territorial governor

- **Osceola:** Seminole leader

- **David Levy Yulee:** one of Florida's initial U.S. senators (first Jewish American senator)

- **Henry B. Plant:** famed Florida railroad baron of the late 19th century, on the Gulf Coast

- **Henry Flagler:** builder of the East Coast Railway, which connected the whole East Coast of Florida

- **Hamilton Disston:** bought four million acres in central Florida and created a canal system

- **Thomas Edison and Henry Ford:** inventors (well, they both just lived here part-time, but they left a big mark)

- **John Ringling:** circus entrepreneur

- **Barron Collier:** southwest Florida landowner and builder of Tamiami Trail

- **A. Philip Randolph:** labor leader

friars, and several dozen civilians with the intent of starting a settlement. Where he went exactly is a topic of much debate: Some say he landed in Manatee County; others believe it was in Charlotte Harbor. Like many of the conquistadores before him, de Soto was attracted to the stories of Indian riches to the north, so he sent his fleet back to Cuba, left only a rudimentary base camp on the Manatee River, and set off inland from the coast. He and his men never found what they sought, moving ever northward into Georgia, South Carolina, Tennessee, Alabama, Mississippi, and Arkansas, where he died of fever.

There were religious missions to the state during the same time—Dominican priest **Father Luis Cancer,** three additional missionaries, and a Christianized Indian named Magdalene arrived on the beaches outside Tampa Bay in 1549. Given the Native Americans' experience with outsiders, it's probably no wonder that Father Cancer was quickly surrounded and clubbed to death. The survivors in his party promptly sailed back to Mexico.

In 1559, the viceroy of Mexico decided a settlement on the Gulf was essential in helping shipwrecked sailors and to discourage French trading visits. He hired **Tristán de Luna** to establish this colony. With 1,500 soldiers and 13 ships, de Luna landed at Pensacola Bay. He sent a party to scout out the interior and decided to wait until they returned to unload the supplies from the ship. This proved to be a disastrous move for the explorers. The scouting party returned after three weeks, only finding one Native American village. But before de Luna and his men could unload the supplies from their ships, a powerful hurricane swept through on September 19, 1559, and destroyed five of their ships and most of their cargo. The party moved inland to an abandoned Native American village, but their dwindled supplies kept the settlers on the brink of starvation through the winter and spring. In the summer of 1560, the party moved upriver and into what is now North Georgia where they remained until returning to Pensacola Bay in November 1560. Eventually de Luna was replaced with a new governor in April 1561, but de Luna's impact and legacy as one of the early explorers of the Florida Panhandle remains to this day. (As an aside, in 1992 the Florida Bureau of Archaeological Research found the remains of a colonial Spanish ship in Pensacola Bay that might have been one of de Luna's sunken ships.) Shortly after de Luna's expedition, King Philip II of Spain announced that Spain was no longer interested in promoting colonial expeditions into Florida.

French Protestant Huguenots prepared to challenge Spain's sovereignty in Florida. Another failure, really. **Jean Ribault,** France's most lauded seafarer of the time, set sail for Florida on April 30, 1562, establishing a colony at Port Royal, South Carolina, that year. It didn't work out, and somehow on his return to Europe, England's Queen Elizabeth had him arrested for establishing a French colony in Spanish territory. Spaniard **Pedro Menéndez de Avilés,** a much-celebrated naval commander, took up where Ribault left off, establishing what is thought of as the first European settlement, in St. Augustine, Florida, in 1565.

The history of Florida during the first Spanish administration (1565-1763) centers along the east coast of the state, specifically around St. Augustine. The English neighbors to the north periodically attempted to capture the Florida territory (Governor Moore of South Carolina made an unsuccessful attempt in 1702, and Governor Oglethorpe of Georgia invaded Florida in 1740), and in 1763 Spain ceded Florida to England. They, in turn, did an equally incomplete job of populating the country and developing its resources, especially in light of the increasingly aggressive Native American tribes. The British controlled Florida 1763-1781, at which point the Spanish occupied it again 1783-1821. But in 1821 the Spanish government ratified a treaty turning over Florida to the United States.

STATEHOOD, CIVIL WAR, AND RECONSTRUCTION

After the signing of the Adams-Onis treaty ceding Florida to the United States in 1821, Andrew Jackson was appointed military governor of the territory. Florida's present boundaries were established, with Tallahassee as the new capital and William P. Duval as its first territorial governor. It was a plantation economy, with settlers expanding ever southward and crowding out the Seminoles. Florida was admitted to the Union in 1845, the 27th state. After Abraham Lincoln's election to the presidency in 1860, Florida's pro-slavery stance led to it seceding from the Union in 1861 and joining the Confederacy. Florida furnished salt, cattle, and other goods to the Confederate army. Relative to population size, Florida furnished more troops than any other Confederate state, participating in the campaigns of Tennessee and Virginia. Florida was represented in the higher ranks of the Confederate service by Major-Generals Loring, Anderson, and Smith, and Brigadier Generals Brevard, Bullock, Finegan, Miller, Davis, Finley, Perry, and Shoup. Florida was represented in the Confederate cabinet by Stephen H. Mallory, secretary of the navy. The most notable Civil War engagement fought in Florida was the Battle of Olustee (February 20, 1864), a Confederate victory.

After the war, a new constitution was adopted, the Fourteenth Amendment ratified, and Florida was readmitted into the Union in 1868. It took a decade or so for the state to establish social, educational, and industrial health. The state's general level of poverty led to four million acres of land being sold to speculative real-estate promoters in 1881. The discovery of rich phosphate deposits in 1889 improved the state's economy, as did its increasing popularity as a winter resort destination.

FLORIDA'S FIRST BOOM

Along with the phosphate mining in the southwestern part of the state, agriculture (especially citrus) and cattle ranching brought wealth to Florida, as did wealthy tourists who came to relax in the state's natural beauty and mild climate each winter. In the 1870s, steamboat tours on Florida's winding rivers were a popular attraction. Sponge diving around Tarpon Springs, cigar-making around Tampa—industry was booming in the later part of the 19th century even along the less-populated Gulf Coast.

The boom had its roots in the railroad and in road construction, industries that blossomed as a result of the state legislature's passage of the Internal Improvement Act in 1855. It offered cheap or free public land to investors, particularly those interested in transportation. On Florida's east coast, **Henry Flagler** was responsible for the Florida East Coast Railway, completed in 1912 and linking Key West all the way up the eastern coast of Florida. After making his money with Standard Oil, in retirement he realized that the key to developing the state of Florida was to establish an extensive transportation system. His biggest contribution might have been converting all of the small railroad lines he purchased to a standard gauge, allowing trains to travel the whole length without changing track.

On the Gulf Coast

Another Henry worked his magic on the other coast of Florida. **Henry B. Plant** was largely responsible for the first boom period along the Gulf, using his railroad to open vast but previously inaccessible parts of the state. Henry Plant's rails extended south from Jacksonville along the St. Johns River to Sanford then southwest through Orlando to Tampa. The Plant Investment Company bought up several small railroads with the aim of providing continuous service across the state, his holdings eventually including 2,100 miles of track, several steamship lines out of the port of Tampa, and a number of important hotels. The University of Tampa now occupies the lavish hotel Plant built at the terminus of his line. This new rail line not only provided passengers with easy access but also gave citrus growers quick routes to get their produce to market.

Around the same time, in 1911, **Barron Gift Collier** visited Useppa Island off the Fort Myers coast and fell in love with the subtropical landscape. Over the next decade he bought up more than a million acres of southwest Florida, making himself the largest landowner in the state. His holdings stretched from the Ten Thousand Islands northward to Useppa Island and inland from Naples into the Everglades and Big Cypress. He invested millions of dollars to convert this vast wilderness into agricultural land and a vacation paradise. His real gift, however, was his completion of the state's Tamiami Trail, a road that exists even today, linking Tampa with Miami. In gratitude, the state created Collier County in his honor in 1923, with Everglades City as the county seat.

The Roaring Twenties were good to Florida. With more Americans owning cars, it became the hip thing to visit the Sunshine State on vacation. Land speculators bought up everything, parcels being sold and resold for ever-increasing amounts of money. Great effort was expended to drain the Everglades and Florida swampland to create even more viable land for homes and agriculture. The land frenzy reached its peak after World War I in 1925, but a swift bust followed the next year due to a major hurricane, then another one in 1928, and then the Great Depression.

CUBAN REVOLUTION

Ninety miles south of Key West, Cuba has always been closely connected with the affairs of Florida, and vice versa. Under Spanish rule in the late 1800s, Cuban relations with Spain deteriorated, and in 1868 the two countries went to war, with 200,000 Cuban and Spanish casualties. In 1898, the Spanish-American War focused the country's attention on the Gulf Coast city of Tampa, the primary staging area for U.S. troops preparing for the war in Cuba.

During the war, many prominent Cubans fled to Key West, including Vicente Martinez

a modern building in downtown Sarasota

the freedoms of speech, press, and assembly and was forced to flee the country in 1933.

Colonel Fulgencio Batista y Zaldivar, who controlled the army, was elected president in 1940. During his term, Cuba entered World War II on the side of the Allies. Batista was defeated in 1944 by Grau San Martin, and then in 1948 Carlos Prio Socarras was elected president—but he was overthrown by Batista in 1952. Mayhem ensued, but Batista wasn't taking no for an answer. There continued to be strong anti-Batista resistance, and in 1959 Batista resigned and fled the country. Fidel Castro set up a provisional government with himself as premier. Political refugees from the Cuban revolution poured into Florida by the thousands.

Not long after came the Cuban Missile Crisis of October 1962, precipitated by the Soviets installing nuclear missiles in Cuba. Soviet field commanders in Cuba were authorized to use tactical nuclear weapons unless President John F. Kennedy and Premier Nikita Khrushchev could reach an understanding.

In 1980, more than 100,000 Cuban refugees came to the United States, mostly through Florida, when Castro briefly opened the port of Mariel to a flotilla of privately chartered U.S. ships, and in the early 1990s Florida received refugees from the military coup in Haiti and another wave of refugees from Cuba in 1994. Many of the Cuban expatriates live in Miami and environs, less so on the Gulf Coast. Still, the Cuban influence is robustly felt in areas such as Tampa's Ybor City.

Ybor, who opened a cigar factory, the El Principe de Gales, in Key West in 1869. (He eventually relocated the factory to a scrub area east of Tampa In 1886, once Henry B. Plant had completed rail service to aid in shipping and importation. This first factory begat a huge cigar industry in Tampa, with 200 factories at its peak.)

The war lasted only a few months after American involvement. Cuba was relinquished to the United States in trust for its inhabitants by the signing of the Treaty of Paris on December 20, 1898. Spanish rule ended January 1, 1899, and U.S. military rule ended May 20, 1902.

Cuban history after that continued to be fractious: Thomas Estrada Palma was the first president of the new republic, but he was ousted in 1906. Again, a provisional American government ruled, then withdrew in 1909. There was a period of prosperity, another revolt, and then General Gerardo Machado was elected president in 1925 and reelected in 1928. During his second term he suspended

MODERN FLORIDA

While it was the first state to be settled by Europeans, Florida might be the last state to have entered fully into modernity. It remained more or less a frontier until the 20th century, with the first paved road not until 1920. It was really World War II that changed things in the state, prompting a period of sustained growth that lasted more than 50 years. Immigration to the state has resulted in a real diversity of ethnic groups, with a dense concentration of Cubans in the Miami area and Mexicans throughout the state.

Tourism has been responsible for much of the growth in modern times, with a serious assist from Walt Disney World, the biggest tourist destination on the planet. There are more hotel rooms in Orlando than in New York City, I kid you not. The beaches have continued to draw multitudes of tourists, and the beaches of the northwestern part of the state have seen a recent surge of interest, with locations such as Seaside and Destin becoming increasingly popular vacation destinations.

Recently the state has seen a decrease in population, partly a result of the devastating hurricane seasons of the early 2000s, the recession, rising insurance costs, and the BP oil spill. For example, according to the *New York Times*, homeowner insurance rates in Florida have as much as tripled since the 2004 storm seasons.

In October 2010, Florida ranked second in states with highest number of foreclosures. It is estimated that in 2010, 1 in 167 homes in Florida were foreclosures. (The leader was Nevada where an astounding 1 in 69 homes were foreclosed.) In Florida, foreclosures made up more than 30 percent of home sales for 2010. On April 20, 2010, the Deepwater Horizon well exploded off the coast of Louisiana, killing 11 rig workers and releasing, over a three-month period, an estimated 185 million gallons of crude oil into the Gulf of Mexico. Eventually, some of the oil made its way onto the Gulf Coast of Florida. Most of the oil that impacted Florida washed onto the shores of northwestern beaches from Pensacola to just west of Port St. Joe. The well was capped on July 15, 2010, and slowly the areas most impacted by the spill have recovered, but not without environmental and health impacts.

Local Culture

DEMOGRAPHICS

Florida ranks third in the United States in population, only behind California and Texas. In 2015, the population was estimated to be 20,271,272 (up from 9,746,961 in 1980). According to the 2015 population estimates, Miami is the largest single metropolitan area with 5,929,819 residents. On the Gulf Coast, the other most populous areas are the Tampa Bay area (4,310,532), Fort Myers/Cape Coral (618,754), Sarasota/Bradenton MSA (702,281), Pensacola (52,703), and Naples (20,537). Nearly 1,000 people move to Florida every day, and the fastest-growing part of the state is in the central interior, particularly the corridor along I-4, which connects the Tampa Bay area through Orlando to Daytona Beach in the east.

Age

Florida's age distribution over the past several decades has changed very little regarding those 65 years and older. In 1990, there were 3,281,220 Floridians ages 65 and older (17.7 percent of the total population), whereas in 2015 the census counted 3,799,619 in this group (19.1 percent of the total). So the percentage and number of those over 65 has only slightly increased, yet this number is still the highest percentage of any other state in the country.

The Gulf Coast, especially the area around Tampa, has gotten younger in recent years. For instance, the youth population (those ages 0-19) has shown increasing growth rates over the last 30 years, from 15.5 percent in 1970-1980 to 22.6 percent in 2010.

The median age is at its lowest all along the northern border of the state where it meets Georgia and Alabama all the way out the Panhandle. There's another dense concentration of youth around Miami and Tampa (sister city St. Petersburg, famously a retirement destination, has also shifted younger,

Who You Calling a Florida Cracker?

That's a good question, really. Many Florida historians are devoted to the theory that the term Florida Cracker originated with the area's cow hunters. As Jesse Otis Beall describes it in the book *Cracker* by Dana Ste. Claire:

> Well, people didn't know what cracker meant and they thought it was just a slang word, you know, for a person. But it was named after the whip, I think, the crackin' whip, as the cowhunters come in. There wasn't cowboys in those days, there was cowhunters, and they used those whips and we'd say, 'Yep, here comes the Crackers.' That's where the word comes from. I'm always a callin' myself a Cracker.

Pretty convincing. This hypothesis goes back as early as 1810, with John Lambert's *Travels Through Lower Canada, and the United States of North America*. But a lot of historians aren't buying it, weighing in instead on the side of a different theory entirely. Even Florida cow hunter historian Joyce Peters believes that Florida Crackers were called such because of their diet—a poor, rural people, they had trouble rounding up enough calories. Cracked corn fit the bill, as it could be roughly stone ground and then made into a paste with water or fat, baked into a hard "cracker," and then either eaten as hardtack or reconstituted in a stew.

Still others say, yes, cracked corn is implicated, but in a more nefarious way. These Florida backwoodsmen were known to operate moonshine stills, stills that fermented cracked corn mash into a blisteringly alcoholic "white lightning."

Other theories that may or may not hold water: The people were named after the "crackerbox" shape of their simple log houses. Or, they were originally called *cuaqueros*, or Quakers, by the Spaniards who confused them for a colony of Quakers who settled early on in Florida. And the speculations go on.

The book *Cracker* wanders all over trying to figure out what one is exactly, but you have to wait until the glossary until it cuts to the chase: "Cracker—a self-reliant, independent, and tenacious settler of the Deep South, often of Celtic stock, who subsisted by farming or raising livestock and, as a general rule, valued personal independence and restraint-free life over material prosperity. Cracker settlers provided a spirited foundation for the peopling of the rural South and Florida."

These days Florida Cracker is still something a Floridian can call him- or herself, and with pride, but it's not a moniker to go slinging around lightly. There are still Florida Crackers along the Gulf Coast, and they carry the distinction with pride.

---

demographically). The oldest parts of the state, citizenry-wise, are Sarasota, Naples, and along the Nature Coast.

Race

The population of the Gulf Coast is still primarily white (22.2 percent nonwhite in 2015), with the greatest ethnic diversity in the Tampa Bay area. The African American population is twice that of the Latino population along the northern border of the state (along the Panhandle and the Alabama and Georgia borders), while in the southern part of the state, close to Miami, the correlation flip-flops.

Religion

In modern times the Gulf Coast is primarily Christian. Jewish retirees don't appear to settle along the Gulf Coast for whatever reason, with the exception of Sarasota (9 percent Jewish, as compared to the east coast of the state from Coral Gables up through Palm Beach, which is roughly 13-15 percent Jewish). The southernmost part of the state is predominantly Catholic, as is the area just north of Tampa up through the Nature Coast. Most Floridians are Protestant, with the number increasing the closer you get to the northern border of the state.

SNOWBIRDS

First, what's a snowbird? It's a temporary resident in Florida, someone who comes from a colder, less hospitable winter climate to bask in the Sunshine State all winter. Snowbirds are usually of retirement age, or nearing it. But let's get more specific: New Yorkers account for 13.1 percent of Florida's temporary residents, followed by Michiganders at 7.4 percent, Ohioans at 6.7 percent, Pennsylvanians at 5.8 percent, and Canadians at 5.5 percent. The average length of stay is five months. If Florida has roughly seven million households, there are an estimated 920,000 temporary residents during the peak winter months and another 170,000 during the late summer.

CIRCUS PERFORMERS

Most people connect Sarasota with the circus. It was in 1927 when Sarasota became an official circus town, with John Ringling bringing his Ringling Bros. and Barnum & Bailey Circus's winter quarters to Sarasota, giving the calm Florida town a bit of spectacle. Many of the little people who starred in the circus retired in Sarasota (in specially built small houses in an area known as "Tiny Town"). Still, Sarasota doesn't get the title "Showtown USA." That high honor goes to another Gulf Coast town.

Gibsonton, or Gibtown as it's often affectionately called, was made famous as a wintering town for sideshow and circus performers as well as garden-variety carnies. Many of them retired permanently to Gibtown and have, in recent years, died off, but they leave the town with a colorful history. It's in Hillsborough County, south of Tampa on U.S. 41 near the town of Riverview.

Gibsonton was home to Percilla "Monkey Girl" Bejano and her husband, Emmitt "The Alligator Skin Man" Bejano (billed as the "World's Strangest Married Couple" on sideshow midways all over). There was Jeanie the Half Girl, Al the Giant, and Grady "Lobster Boy" Stiles Jr. (from a long line of people with ectrodactyly, or "lobster claw" syndrome); Stiles committed murder but got off with

probation because prison wasn't equipped to handle him, only to be murdered himself some years later. The conjoined twin Hilton sisters (different Hilton sisters) ran a fruit stand here. Melvin "Rubber Face" Burkhart was the most recent to die, in 2001. His most famous routine was to shove an ice pick and a five-inch nail into his nose.

Gibtown has a post office counter that accommodates little people, and its zoning laws allow residents to keep elephants and circus animals in trailers on their front lawns. Still, it is home to the **International Independent Showmen's Association** (6915 Riverview Dr., 813/677-3590) and a bar called **Showtown USA Lounge** (10902 U.S. 41 S., 813/677-5443) that has rollicking karaoke on the weekend. A historic eatery called **Giants Camp Restaurant,** opened by Al Tomaini (8 feet, 4 inches tall) and his wife, Jeanie (2 feet, 6 inches tall), sadly, closed in 2006.

Even if you can't fit it into your trip, you can get a sense of Gibtown if you can get your hands on the "Humbug" episode of the *X-Files* (season two), in which Mulder and Scully travel to Gibsonton to investigate the death of Jerald Glazebrook, the Alligator Man. In the episode you'll meet Jim Jim, the Dog-Faced Boy, and the Enigma, who is covered in blue puzzle-piece tattoos and eats glass. Also, there is a 65-minute documentary called *Gibtown* that is hard to find, but worthwhile.

Gibsonton is also home to the largest tropical fish farm in the country, **Ekkwill Waterlife Resources** (813/677-5475, www.ekkwill.com).

MOVIES SET ON THE GULF COAST

Florida has been a film location just about as long as there've been movies. Today it is ranked third in the country for film production based on revenue generated. The climate, the scenery, the dense and tropical foliage—it has all sparked the imagination of countless directors, cinematographers, and actors, standing in for far-flung lands on several

Famous Floridians

It's an incomplete list, but these people were born and raised in the Sunshine State, or at least called it home for a long while.

- **Baseball players:** Buster Posey, Steve Carlton, Dwight Gooden, Barry Larkin, Sammy Sosa

- **Football players:** Emmitt Smith, Mike Ditka, Joe Namath, Daunte Culpepper, Mike Astott, Warrick Dunn, Tony Dungy, Chris Simms

- **Tennis players:** Jennifer Capriati, Martina Hingis, Anna Kournikova, Ivan Lendl, Martina Navratilova, Monica Seles, Andy Roddick, Serena and Venus Williams

- **Wrestlers:** Hulk Hogan, Rick Flair, Dwayne "The Rock" Johnson, Joannie "Chyna" Laurer, Randy "Macho Man" Savage

- **Actors:** Johnny Depp, Kelsey Grammer, Sidney Poitier, Butterfly McQueen, Burt Reynolds, Ben Vereen, Faye Dunaway, Buddy Ebsen, River Phoenix, John Travolta

- **Writers:** Harriet Beecher Stowe, Marjorie Kinnan Rawlings, Zora Neale Hurston, Ernest Hemingway, Carl Hiaasen, Stephen King

- **Artists:** John James Audubon, Winslow Homer

- **Singers:** Jim Morrison, Pat Boone, Jimmy Buffett, Frances Langford, Gloria Estefan, Enrique Iglesias, Lenny Kravitz, Tom Petty, Bo Diddley, Backstreet Boys, *and* some of 'N Sync, the brothers Gibb, Beyoncé Knowles, Jennifer Lopez, Scott Stapp

- **Military figures:** Joseph W. Stilwell (Army general), Daniel James (Air Force general)

continents. The earliest Florida films aren't anyone's flights of fancy, however, but the 1898 newsreels of U.S. troops in Tampa during the Spanish-American War.

The Museum of Florida History in Tallahassee has a collection of movie posters from films shot in the state. The following are some featured in this collection, and an idiosyncratic assortment of others, all shot along the Gulf Coast.

Hell Harbor (1930), the first full-length "talkie" to be made in the state, was shot in Tampa and depicts the story of the descendants of pirate Henry Morgan. *A Guy Named Joe* (1944), starring Spencer Tracy as a WWII pilot who dies and becomes the guardian angel of a young pilot in love with Tracy's girlfriend, was also shot in Tampa at Drew and MacDill air fields.

The Marx Brothers' *The Cocoanuts* (1929) may well be set in Miami, it's not totally clear, but it revolves around Florida's first land boom. *The Yearling* (1946) is also educational and an absolute classic starring Gregory Peck; it's based on the Newbery award-winning book by Marjorie Kinnan Rawlings and was nominated for seven Oscars. Parts of the film were shot at Rawlings's homestead in Cross Creek.

Then we get into some real camp faves, from *Mr. Peabody and the Mermaid* (1948), a William Powell film shot at Weeki Wachee Springs with local mermaids, to *Beneath the 12 Mile Reef* (1953), the story of a Greek sponge diver from Tarpon Springs who falls in love with a girl from the rival Key West sponge divers. The king of Gulf Coast films, *Creature from the Black Lagoon* (1954), was filmed in Wakulla Springs and Tarpon Springs and was followed by two sequels.

Directed by Cecil B. DeMille and starring Betty Hutton, James Stewart, and Charlton

Heston, *The Greatest Show on Earth* (1952) was filmed at the Barnum & Bailey headquarters in Sarasota and required all the actors to do their own stunts.

Elvis spent a little time on the Gulf Coast in Pasco County filming *Follow That Dream* (1962)—not a great film. And Christopher Plummer, Gypsy Rose Lee, and Burl Ives got to hang out in the Everglades for the making of Nicholas Ray's *Wind Across the Everglades* (1958), a story about the hardscrabble life in the wilds of south Florida.

Victor Nuñez has done a few excellent movies set along the Gulf Coast, from *A Flash of Green* (1988), based on the novel by J. D. MacDonald about corruption in Sarasota, to *Ruby in Paradise* (1993), a small film about a young woman, played by Ashley Judd, set on the Panhandle. Then he did the Peter Fonda pic *Ulee's Gold* (1997), a Panhandle family drama about beekeepers, and another not widely released Florida pic called *Coastlines.*

Peter Weir's *The Truman Show* (1998), starring Jim Carrey, is set in the scary-perfect Panhandle town of Seaside; Volker Schlondorff's crime drama *Palmetto* (1998) is set in and around Sarasota; and Spike Jonze's *Adaptation* (2002), a loose interpretation of Susan Orlean's book *The Orchid Thief,* takes place in the mangrove swamps of the Everglades.

John Sayles's *Sunshine State* (2002) is set in a fictional town in Florida, which might be the east coast, but it describes the conflicts of early Floridians and new developers so well that it's worth seeing. Kids will recognize Florida as the setting for *Hoot* (2006), Carl Hiaasen's environmental flick filmed in Boca Grande.

GULF COAST CULINARY SPECIALTIES

As you might expect, the Gulf of Mexico supplies most of the unique eats and culinary traditions for the region. When traveling the Gulf Coast, one of the most important questions to ask before you sit down for a meal is if the seafood is fresh. Next, consider what you have already tasted and then taste something new. Stretch the boundaries of what you are willing to eat, and stay away from things you have already tried. You won't know if you like raw oysters smothered in cocktail sauce and piled with horseradish and a squeeze of lemon until you try them, and chances are high that you will love them. Learn what seafood is harvested in the area and know what fish are typically running and fresh during the time of year that you are visiting a particular region. A good tip is to learn what type of seafood festivals occur in the towns you are visiting. This is an easy indicator of what variety of seafood is especially celebrated, eaten, and typically harvested in the region (there are exceptions such as the Fiddler Crab Festival in Steinhatchee!). Eating seafood along the Gulf Coast is as much a part of the culture and experience of the place as staking an umbrella in the sand and spending the day at the beach. You shouldn't miss out on either one.

Apalachicola Oysters

You won't get very far in Apalachicola without hearing about oysters. They are the favorite food of the area and also the source of an industry that brings in more than $6 million each year, which makes these mollusks the pearls of Apalachicola. Oysters grow many other places along the Gulf Coast, but the oysters here have become world famous as a result of the huge numbers that grow in the surrounding waterways, and because people say they taste better than any other oyster in the world. The nutrient-rich and spring-fed waters that flow primarily from the Apalachicola River have put this fishing town on the map as Florida's capital for oyster harvesting. While in town, buy a bag and shuck 'em yourself, try them raw, try them fried, steamed, or stuffed. It doesn't matter, just try them and you'll understand why so many are willing to travel so far to taste them.

Steinhatchee Scallops

Harvesting scallops is about as popular as

fresh-caught mullet

eating them in Steinhatchee. You should definitely try both if you're visiting the area. The harvesting season runs early July to late September, and each person can pull up to two gallons per day of scallops from the productive sea grass beds in the bay, and each vessel can have up to 10 gallons on board at a time. That's a lot of scallops. The epicenter of scalloping activity in the region seems to be at the picturesque Steinhatchee Landing Resort. Most of the seafood restaurants along the Gulf Coast offer them, so there's no excuse not to give them a taste. I like mine pan-fried and drizzled with fresh garlic and butter.

Cedar Key Clams

The clam industry has been thriving in Cedar Key for nearly a century now. The clean waters of the area have given rise to some of the largest clam canneries in the country. Stop in at the Island Hotel and Restaurant to get your Cedar Key Sweet's fix of littleneck clams. They come steamed, sautéed in butter, or in some truly delicious clam chowder ready for

all those northern snowbirds that flock down every winter.

Grouper Sandwich

It's a staple on the Gulf Coast for lunch or dinner after a day at the beach or out on the boat. The recipe is simple: Take a huge, flaky slab of grilled, blackened, or fried grouper and put it in between a chewy bun with some premium cheese, fresh tomato and lettuce, and maybe a slather of tartar sauce, and you've got one supreme sandwich sure to leave any coastal sightseer in a state of sublimity. The best I've found is at Peg Leg Pete's on Pensacola Beach or at the Sandbar Waterfront Restaurant on Anna Maria Island just off the coast of Sarasota.

Shrimp and Grits

What do you get when you combine fresh Gulf shrimp with a truly classic, Southern staple? Heaven in a bowl. If the idea of eating grits makes you cringe, then this is the perfect dish for you. One bite of this ultimate seafood fusion specialty is likely to convert even the most adamant opponent to the deep-South's take on porridge into a campaigning advocate with nearly pious zeal for the South's newest culinary classic. Usually served with a sprinkling or two (or three) of crumbled bacon and a few fresh green onion slices just to give it a little green, you can find the creative combo popping up on menus across the Gulf Coast. However, the farther south you go, the less likely you are to find this tasty treat. For the cream of the crop, cruise on over to The Fish House in Pensacola or the Beach Walk Café at Henderson Park Inn in Destin, or visit celebrity chef Jim Shirley for some Smoked Gouda Grits a Ya Ya at his Great Southern Café in the quiet and idyllic coastal town of Seaside on the Emerald Coast.

Fried Mullet

Don't be afraid. Mullet tastes good, especially when fried in a spicy and salty batter and then dipped in tartar sauce. Folks all across Florida have developed a taste for it, but you have seen less of it on menus in recent years due to the bad press that cornmeal's better half has unjustly received. For some major-league fried mullet, mosey on over to Posey's Beyond the Bay in Panacea or stop in and celebrate at the Interstate Mullet Toss held in late April every year at the Flora-Bama, a popular restaurant and bar right on the Florida and Alabama state line.

Seafood Bouillabaisse

The culinary traditions of the Gulf Coast are a reflection of the rich history of the place. The French never actually owned Florida, but they did have short-lived control over Pensacola and nearby Mobile. The French put their focus on Louisiana and New Orleans just to west, and as a result the Cajun and French culinary traditions have established themselves in the collective Gulf Coast cookbook. Seafood bouillabaisse is one of the favorite French dishes that can be found on the entrée lists of many restaurants in the region. Nearly everyone has a different take on this traditional French fish stew that is often served with a hodge-podge of fish, shrimp, and mussels. My favorite is the lobster tail, fish, mussels, and shrimp seafood bouillabaisse found at the Beach Bistro on Anna Maria Island.

Essentials

Transportation

GETTING THERE
Air

Tampa International Airport is the largest airport on the Gulf Coast, with 550 flights per day, and was ranked in 2013 by the U.S. Department of Transportation as eighth nationwide in on-time performance for arrivals and departures. Southwest Florida International Airport in Fort Myers has also experienced enormous expansion in the past few years. And the Northwest Florida Beaches International Airport outside of Panama City is the best way to fly into the popular beaches of South Walton County; opened on May 23, 2010, it is the first international airport to be built in the United States in over a decade. Generally, the most direct routes and cheapest fares can be found through these airports, but it's worth pricing flights through Orlando, which is an hour east of Tampa (mostly from Orlando International Airport, but there is a second airport that is increasingly popular for international travelers called Sanford International Airport). Gulf Coast airports are, from north and west to south:

- **Pensacola International Airport** (4 miles northeast of Pensacola, 850/436-5000)
- **Northwest Florida Regional Airport** (1 mile east of Destin, 850/651-7160)
- **Northwest Florida Beaches International Airport** (20 miles northwest of Panama City, 850/763-6751)
- **Brooksville Tampa Bay Regional Airport** (40 miles north of Tampa, 352/754-4061)
- **St. Petersburg-Clearwater International Airport** (7 miles southeast of Clearwater, 727/453-7800)

- **Tampa International Airport** (5 miles west of downtown Tampa, 813/870-8700)
- **Sarasota-Bradenton International Airport** (3 miles north of Sarasota, 941/359-2770)
- **Venice Municipal Airport** (0.5 mile south of Venice, 941/486-2711)
- **Punta Gorda Airport** (3 miles southeast of Punta Gorda, 941/639-1101)
- **Southwest Florida International Airport** (10 miles southeast of Fort Myers, 239/590-4800)
- **Naples Municipal Airport** (2 miles northeast of Naples, 239/643-0733)

FROM EUROPE

Most international flights on the Gulf Coast arrive and depart out of Tampa or Southwest Florida International in Fort Myers. Additional international flights arrive in Miami, Orlando, and Key West.

CHEAP FARES

All of the online travel resources (Hotwire, Kayak, Orbitz, Expedia, etc.) offer last-minute specials and weekend deals on travel. The way to get a good fare in advance on air travel or hotel rooms is by traveling outside of peak season. That period is different for different parts of the Gulf Coast (each chapter gives the approximate peak season dates in its introduction). For instance, peak season on St. George Island is the middle of the summer, while in Naples summer is the least desirable time to visit, thus the cheapest. Spring break in March and April seems to be the most expensive time to visit much of the Gulf Coast, but bear in mind that in the off-season, hours for restaurants and attractions are sometimes more limited.

Car

The main thoroughfares into Florida include I-95, which crosses the Florida-Georgia border just north of Jacksonville and hugs the east coast of the state all the way down, and I-75, which runs south from Georgia through the state's middle, then works its way west to the coast just south of Tampa. I-4 extends southwest across the state from Daytona through Orlando and then connects to I-75 in Tampa. On the Panhandle, I-10 is the big east-west road, which can be accessed from the north by U.S. 29, U.S. 231, or U.S. 19, and Highway 98 is a scenic route that hugs the coast along most of the Panhandle.

Boat

If you're traveling to Florida by boat, the **Gulf Intracoastal Waterway** is a 1,090-mile, toll-free East Coast channel that links Norfolk, Virginia, to Miami, Florida, and Carrabelle, Florida, to Brownsville, Texas, through gorgeous sheltered waters. (And there's a noncontiguous section of the waterway connecting Tampa Bay with the Okeechobee Waterway.) The Gulf Intracoastal Waterway follows a course of sheltered bays, rivers, and canals along the Gulf of Mexico, which makes it perfect for recreational cruising.

And the **Port of Tampa** is a huge home port for a variety of cruise lines (Carnival, Royal Caribbean, Celebrity, Holland America, and Crystal Cruises). Nearly a million passengers pass through its cruise terminals each year on their way to a vacation upon the sea, which is never complete without a little shuffleboard and cocktails on the Lido deck.

GETTING AROUND
Car

Florida's Gulf Coast is an ideal destination for those with a poor sense of direction. There are only a few major roads you have to master, and even the urban areas are mostly laid out in a grid. On the Panhandle, I-10 runs inland

east to west, while at the coast the major east-west road is U.S. 98. U.S. 98 curves all the way around the Big Bend of the Panhandle into the Florida peninsula, where it is also called U.S. 19. U.S. 19 extends along the coast all the way down to St. Pete. I-75 is the huge north-south artery on the Gulf Coast side of the Florida peninsula, stretching from where it enters the state at Valdosta, Georgia, all the way south to Naples, where it jogs across the state to the east along what is called Alligator Alley. One of the more famous north-south routes in Florida is U.S. 41, also known as the Tamiami Trail, which extends from Tampa down to Naples, where it, too, shoots east across the state (significantly south of I-75). The Tamiami Trail and I-75 run parallel, fairly close together—which you choose depends on your preference: I-75 has the speed; Tamiami Trail has the charm.

CAR RENTALS
Alamo (800/462-5266), **Avis** (800/831-2847), **Budget** (800/527-0700), **Dollar** (800/800-4000 domestic, 800/800-6000 international), **Enterprise** (800/736-8222), **Hertz** (800/654-3131), and **National** (800/227-7368) provide rental cars from most of the major airports on the Gulf Coast. You pay a small premium for the convenience of picking up and dropping off at the airport, and you pay significantly more if you pick up a car in one city and drop it off in another. Most rental car companies insist that the driver be at least 21 years old, some even older than that—be sure to have your driver's license and a major credit card (even if you aim to pay cash, the rental companies want a credit card for their own peace of mind) with you, or you're walking.

Whether to accept a rental agency's insurance coverage and waivers depends on your own car insurance—before leaving home, read your own car policy to determine if it covers you while renting a vehicle. Also, some credit cards cover damages to many basic types of rental cars, so it's worth checking into that as well. If you decline the insurance, rental car companies hold you totally responsible for your rental vehicle if damaged or stolen. The rental agency's insurance may add $15-35 per day to your bill.

HITCHHIKING

Florida is not a great hitchhiking state. The law reads: No person shall stand in a roadway for the purpose of soliciting a ride. Clearly, you can't stand *in the road* to thumb a ride, but there's nothing that says you can't stand on the shoulder. Still, police officers don't like it, and most people won't pick you up. Regardless, you will still see people thumbing on the highway, and in all the years I have lived in Florida I have never seen anyone get arrested for attempting to hitchhike or heard of anyone ending up in the slammer as a result of trying to do it. Still, I don't recommend it. Standing on the side of the highway is dangerous. Getting in a car with a stranger is dangerous. I don't recommend that you take the risk in Florida.

Bus

Greyhound (800/231-2222, www.greyhound.com) service has gotten spottier in recent years, but there are still regular routes that run from Naples up through Fort Myers, then up to Tampa and St. Petersburg, and all the way around the Big Bend of the Panhandle to Panama City and Pensacola. If traveling by Greyhound is new to you, here's some general information: There are no assigned seats (do not, under any circumstances, take the seats adjacent to the bathroom—it's olfactory suicide), no smoking, no pets, no meal service (but there are regular meal stops so you can jump out and buy something). Stopovers at any point along the route are permitted if you've paid a regular fare. The driver gives you a notation on your ticket, or a coupon, and you can get back on whenever you like.

Who rides the bus these days? The elderly, the military, the poor, and people who just don't fly. Regular patrons include children who wish they were somewhere else, and their parents, who also wish their children were somewhere else. There are better ways to see the state, but few that are cheaper, and the Greyhound buses have become much nicer in recent years.

Train

Train service is limited along the Gulf Coast. **Amtrak** (800/872-7245, www.amtrak.com) offers service exclusively up the eastern side of the Florida peninsula and Orlando, with the exception of the Gulf Coast city of Tampa and environs. To give some idea of price, the three-hour trip from Orlando to Jacksonville is usually about $40 one-way. Amtrak service has been greatly improved over the past few years. It now offers free Wi-Fi service on select trains, and there is always more legroom on the train than on a plane. Unfortunately, much of Amtrak's service that once existed throughout the length of the Panhandle has been out of commission since Hurricane Katrina destroyed the tracks in New Orleans in 2005. There are plans to restore this service, but the timeline remains unclear. Make sure to check with Amtrak about the availability of any route before you make your travel plans.

Visas and Officialdom

FOREIGN TRAVELERS

Visas

Unless you're coming from Canada, foreign travelers will need a valid passport and a tourist visa (a Non-Immigrant Visitors Visa B1, for business, or B2, for recreation). Keep your passport in a safe place, and make a copy of the passport number and other critical information and keep it elsewhere.

Money

Working with dollars is fairly simple—there's the $1, the $5, the $10, the $20, and, less common, the $50. The $100 bill is seldom used and seldom accepted without a lot of scrutiny. In coins, pennies ($0.01) are pretty much only good for wishing wells; then there's the nickel ($0.05), the dime ($0.10), the quarter ($0.25), the more rare 50-cent piece ($0.50) and golden dollar ($1) coins.

Money can be exchanged at a limited number of airports (Tampa, Orlando, Fort Myers) on the Gulf Coast. Exchange money before you arrive, or use U.S. travelers checks. For the most part, if you have a Visa or MasterCard, put all of your accommodations, restaurant meals, and attractions expenditures on that—an easy way to keep track of how you spent your money on vacation.

Electricity

The United States uses 110 to 120 volts AC, as opposed to Europe's 220 to 240 volts. For the most part, Gulf Coast hotels will have hair dryers for your use, so leave yours at home. If you have other electrical devices for which you need a converter, bring one from home.

Telephone Basics

Each urban area along the Gulf Coast has its own area code of three numbers that must be dialed if calling from outside. For example, the area code in Tampa is 813, but you needn't dial it if you're calling within the area code. If you're dialing another area code, you must first dial 1 (except on cell phones), then the three-digit area code, then the seven-digit phone number. Be aware that cell phones have rendered the pay phone an endangered species. If you don't have a cell phone that works in Florida, you're better off getting a prepaid international calling card. Hotels also charge by the call, so making calling-card calls is often more cost-effective.

If calling from abroad, the international code for the United States is 1. Within the United States, the 800, 888, 877, and 866 area codes are toll-free, meaning they cost you nothing to dial.

Tipping

Service-sector workers expect a tip. It's only in name a "gratuity," meaning an elective gift. In reality it's how they make the bulk of their money. Fifteen percent is pretty much the minimum, whether it's at a restaurant, a hair salon, or in a taxi. Tip bellhops about $1 per bag; tip the valet parking attendant $1-2 every time you get your car. Tip a good waiter or bartender 18-20 percent. But here's some tricky stuff: If the hairdresser or tour operator is the owner of the business, a tip can sometimes be seen as an insult. Crazy stuff. Keep lots of small bills at the ready for all these situations, but don't ever tip at the movies, a retail shop, the gas station, or at the theater, ballet, or opera.

Metric Conversions

The United States had a failed attempt at going metric in the 1970s. So, you need to know that one foot equals 0.305 meters; one mile equals 1.6 kilometers; and one pound equals 0.45 kilograms. Converting temperatures is a little trickier: To convert Fahrenheit to Celsius temperatures, subtract 32 and then multiply the result by 0.555. Got it?

Travel Tips

WHAT TO PACK

Florida is casual and what to pack is mostly about being comfortable.

If you're spending time in Naples, Sarasota, or Tampa's Hyde Park, bring something a little more formal, preferably in a tropical style, to wear in the evening. Elsewhere, the name of the game year-round is layering. For women, a twin set and slacks is a good dressy outfit, for men a polo shirt and khakis. You will need several pairs of shoes: something for dinner, sneakers for hiking (ones that can get wet and possibly muddy, repeatedly), and swim shoes or sandals.

Even if you're visiting the Gulf Coast in the summer, bring a sweater. Most places keep the air-conditioner going strong. You'll appreciate this when you first step inside from the relentless heat, but if you plan to spend any length of time indoors, you'll end up getting cold, especially when the cold air-conditioning is coupled with sweat on the skin. In the winter, a long-sleeved pullover with light slacks is usually fine unless you're up north on the Panhandle and in the Tallahassee area, where the temperatures can drop near and very occasionally below freezing during the winter months of January and February. During these times you will want to layer your tops, maybe bring a fleece or other good jacket and a pair of warm pants or jeans.

Bring sunscreen, binoculars, polarized sunglasses (for seeing depth when you fish and to better spot dolphins), a bird book, snorkel, swim flippers, a good novel, more bathing suits than you think you can use, bug spray, flip-flops or sandals, a digital camera, maybe a disposable waterproof camera, and your cell phone (it will work in almost every part of Florida these days, except a very few rural parts of the Nature Coast, especially with Verizon service).

A car is an essential tool in most of the area, but visitors can also rent bikes, scooters, skates, strollers, beach chairs, boogie boards, surfboards, skimboards, fishing equipment, motorboats, personal watercraft, kayaks, canoes, sailboards, and sailboats.

WHAT IT WILL COST

This information is hard to nail down: What it costs depends upon what you're willing to spend. If I averaged the prices at all the restaurants of the Gulf Coast, I'd say a restaurant dinner for one person costs $20. If I were to do the same thing for accommodations, I might find an average hotel room costs $100. But are those numbers really helpful? It's a range, with significant variation, on both counts.

Travel costs are at their most expensive during peak season, which for the Florida peninsula is December-April; for the Panhandle it's June-August. What's helpful to know is that the Gulf Coast is for the most part less expensive the farther north and west you go, and also in Tampa. However, some more rural coastal areas in the Big Bend region of the state such as Carrabelle and Sopchoppy tend to be some of the most affordable places to visit on the entire coast. Top-dollar honors go to **Naples,** where an average dinner for one is about $30 and an average room is about $150 per night mid-season. Then it gets cheaper and cheaper as you drive up I-75 and west along U.S. 98. Cheapest place on the Gulf Coast? **Panama City Beach,** where lots of bargain hotel rooms on the beach bottom out at $30. **Pensacola** is an affordable town and hands down the best value; **Sarasota,** not so affordable.

Beaches on the Gulf Coast are free, maybe a few dollars for parking and sunblock. What you do at them may cost more—a half-day offshore fishing trip will run at least $250, an ecotour kayak trip around $50, a brief WaveRunner rental $40. Of the attractions, everything pales financially by comparison to a day at Walt Disney World. Still, **Busch**

Gardens in Tampa, **Asolo Theatre** tickets in Sarasota, and **snorkel-with-the-manatees** charters in Homosassa are all pretty expensive.

If you can stay for a week, which I recommend, you can cut costs: A totally luxurious multibedroom beach house rental on **St. George Island** or even **North Captiva Island** will cost you less per night than a swanky single room in Naples. In a rental house, you can be even more fiscally prudent by preparing your own breakfasts and picnic lunches. Splurge on dinners.

With attractions, check their websites for free or reduced-rate days or nights. Museums tend to admit people free on Thursday nights or Sunday mornings, primarily to lure locals, but you can benefit. It's worth it to visit the local chambers of commerce or convention and visitors bureaus, not only for the information, but also for the coupons.

TOURIST INFORMATION

Maps

Visit Florida (www.visitflorida.com) sends a great map of the whole state with its Visit Florida literature. (And, as always, AAA members should raid the free-map smorgasbord that is their divine right.) The state's tourism office also has several welcome stations near Florida's border (one north of Pensacola on I-10, one off U.S. 231, one in Tallahassee, one in Jennings off I-75, and one on the state's east coast on I-95) that give out good state and regional maps. Some cities (Apalachicola, Naples) can be navigated with only the photocopied map the desk clerk at the hotel hands out; just follow the yellow highlighter marks. In other cities (Tampa), you need a real map. And if you're traveling alone, don't be chintzy—buy the laminated flip map to the area; its ease of use in the car may keep your wheels on the road.

A portable GPS is an absolute godsend for the frequent road-tripper. Unlike the built-ins, it can be stowed in luggage and plugged into every rental car. Garmin, TomTom, and Magellan all make affordable portable versions (some that have mp3 connectivity and fit in your purse or backpack).

Tourist Offices

Tourist office addresses are listed at the end of each chapter. Most convention and visitors bureaus have extremely helpful websites, and many will send you a vacation package of information, maps, and coupons free of charge.

ACCESS FOR TRAVELERS WITH DISABILITIES

The more developed parts of the Gulf Coast (Pensacola, Destin, Sarasota, Naples, Tampa) are very accessible to travelers with disabilities. As one would expect, the remoter and more rural areas may not have ramps, accessible bathrooms, and other amenities. You may want to consider buying a copy of **Wheelchairs on the Go: Accessible Fun in Florida,** an access guide for Florida visitors who use canes, walkers, or wheelchairs. The 424-page paperback covers wheelchair-accessible and barrier-free accommodations, tourist attractions, and activities across the state.

Society for Accessible Travel & Hospitality (212/447-7284, www.sath.org) provides recommendations and resources to help travelers with disabilities plan their vacations, and **Able Trust** (850/224-4493, www.abletrust.org) offers helpful links to disability resources throughout Florida.

Most major car-rental companies have hand-controlled cars in their fleets (give them 24-48 hours' notice to locate one). If you need to rent a scooter or wheelchair during your visit, **ScootAround** (888/441-7575, www.scootaround.com) is a mobility enhancement company with scooter and wheelchair rental service in a number of Gulf Coast cities.

Diabetic travelers can call the **American Diabetes Association** (800/342-2383, www.diabetes.org) to get a list of hospitals that provide services to diabetics, or log on to **Dialysis Finder** at www.dialysisfinder.com. The **American Foundation for the**

Vacation Rentals on the Gulf Coast

If you're planning on staying a week or more along the Gulf Coast, or just want more privacy than is usually found at resorts and hotels, you may want to consider renting a privately owned condo or a home. In most areas along the coast, there are companies that specialize in vacation rentals, and the offerings often run the gamut from mega-million-dollar mansions with Gulf-front views to bargain-priced studio efficiencies with tiny kitchenettes. Here are some tips to help you navigate the process of finding that perfect rental on the Gulf Coast.

USE ALL RESOURCES AVAILABLE

There are lots of options when it comes to searching and finding a vacation rental. Each chapter in this guide highlights some of the best local real estate companies in that specific area that help match up vacation-home owners with renters. Since these companies are tried-and-true, trustworthy sources for local vacation rentals, they are often the best sources for finding a vacation home or condo.

In recent years, however, much of the vacation rental market has moved out of the hands of these brick-and-mortar real estate companies and onto the Internet, where owners can cut out the middle man and market their vacation rentals directly to the renters. Currently, the top website online to search for vacation rentals is VRBO.com (VRBO stands for Vacation Rentals by Owner). The site is easy to use, and it has one of the largest inventories online. Tripadvisor.com has recently dipped its toes into the vacation rental market, and its offerings are growing rapidly. Make sure and check it out as well.

DECIDE WHAT YOU WANT BEFORE YOU START YOUR SEARCH

You can find almost any type of vacation rental you can imagine. Case in point: In Pensacola you can rent a dome-shaped home that claims to be able to withstand a Category V hurricane. Determine exactly what it is that you're looking before you call the vacation rental companies. And definitely don't dismiss the resorts, hotels, inns, and bed-and-breakfasts in the area that you are visiting. You might be able to find a great deal on a stay at one of these places, so check what kind

---

Blind (800/232-5463, www.afb.org) provides information on traveling with a dog guide.

TRAVELING WITH CHILDREN

The Gulf Coast is the kind of destination suited to a rambling family car trip. But how to face the open road with a carful of antsy travelers? As with a NASA launch, it's all about careful planning and precise execution. Consider yourself lucky that this doesn't mean devising zero-gravity suits and dehydrating food—you just have to keep your astronauts comfortable, fed, and entertained. To that end, consider carrying a master list of all that you've packed. Although it sounds pretty meticulous, it helps to see where your gaps are, it allows you to easily keep track of things from car to motel to final destination,

and if you generate this list on the computer, it can be used as the basis for future trip lists.

The list should be divided into categories: clothes and equipment (these are the things that go in the trunk, to be exhumed at your final destination), and the stuff that makes or breaks your travel time—food, entertainment, and car comfort. Older kids can each be put in charge of a category checklist as the car gets loaded.

For smaller kids, always take a change of underpants or diapers inside the car with you, rather than in the trunk with the luggage. For older kids, encourage a layered approach to dressing—when one child is chilly, donning another layer may be preferable to making everyone endure the car heater.

Think of packing foods that nature has already prepackaged—bananas, oranges, of specials they are running before you set your sights on a vacation rental.

Keep in mind that the closer you get to the water, the more the rental usually costs. Also, if you are going to be traveling with other families or friends, consider renting one large house that's big enough for everyone. It's a great way to save money on an extended trip. If you want to bring a pet along, you shouldn't have a problem finding pet-friendly rentals.

CLOSELY REVIEW ALL THE LISTINGS

Not all vacation rentals are created equal. While every condo in an entire development may have the exact same layout, the owners will leave their mark on their personal unit. Always look at the pictures of each rental that you're considering. This way you will find exactly what you are looking for.

KNOW WHEN TO WAIT AND WHEN TO BUY

a vacation rental in Homosassa

It's a tricky game to play, but sometimes if you time your purchase right, you can save some pretty big bucks, often 10-40 percent. Every area has its high season, and these months will be the most expensive time to stay at a vacation rental. However, there are often more rentals available than the market can fill. If you're flexible on what type of rental you want or on what dates you want to vacation, you will often save the most money if you wait until right before you want to rent. There are usually reduced prices being offered on vacation rentals if the available dates are just around the corner. It's a bit of risk versus reward, but if you really want a great deal, try rolling the dice and book at the last minute.

hard-boiled eggs. Avoid things with sauces or drip potential, chips coated with the dreaded nacho cheese orange goo, or things that crumb too easily. And for drinks, carry a large, plastic, spill-proof cup for each child. This way, you can get juices at convenience stores but you won't be at the mercy of those wide-mouthed, splash-prone glass bottles in the car. Alternatively, bring a bevy of frozen juice boxes. You won't have to wait in line for sodas, and the juice boxes will be nice and cold during the first leg of the trip.

The sight of the golden arches fills most kids with joy and most parents with dread. Fast food is the most common pitfall on long car trips, a wasteland of fat, salt, and sugar. To avoid the tortures of drive-through (it's everywhere, after all), you have to stand firm. Finding other food can be an adventure on

long trips. On the Gulf Coast, this is easy: Get off the highway and hunt down an old-fashioned diner, one with counter stools, a good jukebox, and a short-order cook who makes the perfect grilled cheese. In preparation for your trip, research the indigenous foods of the areas you'll be passing through. Use the Internet to print out pictures and histories of each city's culinary highlights.

When traveling in the car with small children, allow more time to reach your destination. Count on stopping every hour to stretch your legs and run around. Churches are good stopping spots if rest areas aren't available, as they often have open, grassy areas and playgrounds. Traveling at night or during nap times is a good way to make up time. Put blankets, pillows, and any necessary stuffed animals in the back seat at the ready.

Your local party goods and dollar stores are perfect places to find inexpensive new forms of amusement. Wrap each new toy as a gift, to make the excitement last. Caveat: Do not buy travel games with small pieces sure to get lost immediately under the back seat. Maze books, magic-pen books, stickers, a magnetic puzzle of the United States, even car bingo can keep everyone entertained. For long car trips, the book *Miles of Smiles* is filled with car games. Picture-puzzle books (like *I Spy* and *Where's Waldo*) can be made into games as well: One person names an object for the rest to find in the picture.

Even if you dislike the plugged-in feel of video games, iPods, or DVDs in the car, bringing a stereo headset for each child allows everyone to listen to their first choice, whether that's Taylor Swift or *Good Night Moon*. You can even make your own books on tape: Record your child's favorite stories on audiotape, and then they can have the stories "read" to them in the car.

Bring lap desks and art supplies for projects. Dated spiral-bound drawing pads can be a nice way to chronicle a trip, with each child keeping the finished pad (parents can annotate as instructed). Encourage older kids to journal with a cool pad and a set of gel pens.

TRAVELING WITH PETS

More and more hotel chains are accepting people's canine companions (other pets, from pot-bellied pigs to naked mole rats, are a harder sell). Best Western, Motel 6, Holiday Inn, and even swanky chains such as Four Seasons often accept pet guests for an additional fee. To get good information, visit www.petswelcome.com.

Flying with your pet to and from Florida can be problematic, as most major airlines have an embargo against pets as checked baggage during the summer months (any day in which the outdoor temperature might reach 90°F), and even for small pets that fit under an airplane seat, the airlines only allow one pet per cabin. The ASPCA strongly discourages pets as checked baggage.

Dogs are prohibited on many walking trails in Florida, as well as most beaches. There are designated dog parks and dog beaches all over the Gulf Coast. Pensacola, Panama City, Tampa, St. Petersburg, Sarasota, and Fort Myers all have designated dog beach parks with amenities such as fenced play areas, dog water fountains, and poop bags. Be aware that in much of the Gulf Coast's wilderness areas, poisonous snakes and alligators pose more of a threat to your dog than to you.

TRAVELING ALONE

Most activities on the Gulf Coast are well suited to traveling alone. The only exception to that is backwoods camping in the Everglades or deep wilderness, and traveling around high crime areas of the cities on the Gulf Coast. Consider giving rangers your schedule and detailed whereabouts when engaging in these activities. Be vigilant when traveling in urban areas. Look up crime data for the cities you are visiting and avoid the parts of town where most of the crime occurs. I wouldn't hesitate to recommend the Gulf Coast as a spot for quiet, solo travel—except, perhaps, during colleges' spring breaks, and then I would recommend it for loud, lively, socializing and partying.

GAY AND LESBIAN TRAVELERS

Miami's South Beach and Key West are the locus of lots of gay travel. Nowhere on the Gulf Coast is the nightlife as trendy, but that said, nothing on the Gulf Coast seems unsuitable for gay or lesbian travel. The Gulf Coast's wealth of outdoor activities seems suitable for any orientation, as do the restaurants and accommodations. It's a fairly nightlife-impoverished area regardless of your orientation, so you may spend your evenings curled up with a good book.

A good resource is the **Gay, Lesbian & Bisexual Community Services of Central Florida** (407/228-8272, www.thecenterorlando.org) for welcome packets and calendars of events, or the **International Gay &**

Alligators: Staying Safe

Florida residents have learned to be blasé about gators. They're an everyday part of living in this subtropical climate. But things are changing. Sanibel Island may be leading the way for a new stance on gators in the state. In the past six years, several people have died in alligator attacks across the state, with several in Sanibel. It's hard to be as sanguine about gator-human relations when women are getting chomped while pruning their gardens.

The problems are not just a function of large numbers—people feed the gators and thus they have gotten chummy and less fearful of humans, and vice versa.

So new policies are being put in place. In many spots along the Gulf Coast, if gators get large (over eight feet), they are taken away and "processed." Smaller ones get relocated. The jury is out on this interspecies relationship.

Here are a few safety tips to keep in mind:

· Don't feed the gators. And if you see others doing so, give them a hard time.

· Don't bug them during their cranky spring mating season.

· Don't bother the babies or come between a mother and her young.

· Closely supervise kids playing in or near fresh or brackish water. Never allow little kids to play by water unattended. The same goes for pets. In fact, just don't let your dog swim in fresh or brackish water in Florida, period.

· Alligators feed most actively at dusk and dawn, so schedule your lake or river swim for another time.

· They don't make good pets. They are not tamed in captivity, and it's illegal.

· If you are bitten, seek medical attention, even if it seems minor. Their mouths harbor very infectious bacteria.

· If you see a big one that seems especially interested in humans, call the local police nonemergency number.

· Don't throw your fish scraps and guts back into the water when fishing. This encourages gators to hang around boats and docks.

Lesbian Travel Association (954/630-1637, www.iglta.com, $99 annually to join) for a list of gay-friendly accommodations, tours, and attractions.

SPRING BREAK FEVER

Because school schedules vary across the country, spring breakers arrive in Florida at different times. Some come as early as late February, but March and April are the months most colleges and schools release for spring break. Students focus most of their attention on certain key cities along the eastern coast of the state (Daytona Beach, Miami Beach), but along the Gulf Coast, Panama City Beach and down by Key West are the big draws.

Health and Safety

Despite what it might look like in the backcountry of the Everglades, Florida is a modern, developed kind of place, with good emergency services and medical care pretty much all over the Gulf Coast. From Tampa to Sarasota you'll see more medical facilities, pharmacies, and billboards for MRI scanners than nearly anywhere else, a remnant of the area's recent past as a mostly retirement-age destination (as the Bob Dylan song says, "it's younger than that now").

Still, you want to do what you can to stay healthy during a visit here. The sun is probably the biggest underestimated foe. **Sunburn** can be wicked, so be sure to slather with at least an SPF of 30, and because you'll be in and out of water, and sweating in the steamy humidity, opt for waterproof or water-resistant cream such as Banana Boat Sport Sunblock Lotion (waterproof/sweatproof, SPF 30). Even better, one of my favorite finds on the Gulf Coast, Avon now makes an SPF 30 Skin So Soft cream with a DEET-free bug repellent in it to cope with the Gulf Coast's other big bully, the **mosquitoes.** DEET-based products are more effective in preventing mosquitoes from landing on you, but I hate to have that poison sitting on my skin all day. Lather up with the Avon product, then apply a DEET-based spray only if the mosquitoes are bad. Mosquitoes in Florida don't carry any diseases such as malaria, but their itching bites can certainly be preoccupying.

Another burning subject is **fire ants.** If you see loose, sandy mounds on the ground, do not stand in them. These little devils get incensed at the foot in their house and swarm up your shoe and beyond to bite, leaving raised white or red welts that really hurt and itch for days. There is no known treatment for their bites, but I have found that if you douse the bites with aftershave or just plain alcohol, it helps reduce the itching substantially, though maybe not the burning.

The Gulf Coast's water is perfectly safe to drink, although it tastes a little funky in some areas. A much safer bet is the food. On the Gulf Coast you'll find one great seafood restaurant after another. Make sure to try some of the most adventurous local foods when you're on the Gulf Coast, as they are usually the most memorable and tasty. Become the Sir Edmund Hillary of food. When asked "Why did you eat that?" answer back a gravelly "Because it was there." So, try the oysters, clams, whatever, raw on the half shell with a splash of Tabasco. For some, though, this is truly dangerous. Pregnant women, young children, the elderly, or anyone with an immune system problem should order all seafood baked, broiled, steamed, or fried. The bacteria *Vibrio vulnificus* can, at the very least, ruin your vacation. For a list of safe and sustainable flatfish, California's Monterey Bay Aquarium's website (www.montereybay-aquarium.org) has a useful seafood watch section.

Many travel articles suggest getting **medical travel insurance.** If you have medical insurance, though, that's probably all the coverage you'll need. The best emergency rooms are listed in each chapter, and you can always dial 911 (a number used nationwide to contact local emergency medical, fire, or police personnel) or the **Centers for Disease Control and Prevention** (800/232-4636, www.cdc.gov) for information on health hazards by region.

Resources

Suggested Reading

NAPLES, THE EVERGLADES, AND THE PARADISE COAST

Travel Guide

Molloy, Johnny. *A Paddler's Guide to Everglades National Park.* Gainesville: University Press of Florida, 2000. Paddling the Everglades is daunting, plain and simple. There are things in there that can kill you, others that can merely maim. This book well describes 53 designated paddling routes, camping spots, places to avoid, and wind and tide problems. Molloy is a serious outdoorsman who has written a handful of well-regarded paddling and camping books for Florida and Colorado.

Memoir

Brown, Loren G. "Totch." *Totch: A Life in the Everglades.* Gainesville: University Press of Florida, 1993. It's my favorite book about this area, told in glorious vernacular by the original Everglades renegade. A seasoned tall-tale teller, Totch harkens back to his days in the Ten Thousand Islands, moonshining, selling gator hides, fishing, smuggling dope, and any other thing he thought might be fun, or lucrative, or both. It's memoirs like this that clinch southwest Florida as this country's final frontier.

Nonfiction

Douglas, Marjory Stoneman. *The Everglades: River of Grass.* Sarasota, FL: Pineapple Press, 50th anniversary edition, 1997. Originally published in 1947, this was a book that actually changed the world. At the time, the Everglades were a worthless swamp that developers were scheming about draining, damming, etc. The publication of this straightforward natural history, heavy on the flora, fauna, and indigenous people, galvanized President Harry Truman to sign the controversial order protecting more than two million acres as Everglades National Park. Douglas has been called the Queen of the Everglades, and her descriptions of the Native Americans, pirates, runaways, and ne'er-do-wells who populated the 'Glades are as compelling as ever.

Orlean, Susan. *The Orchid Thief: A True Story of Beauty and Obsession.* New York: Ballantine Books, 2000. This was the book that the film *Adaptation* was loosely based on. *New Yorker* staffer Susan Orlean wrote an incredible piece on John Laroche, an orchid chaser who was arrested with three Seminoles in 1994 carrying contraband rare orchids and epiphytes from the Everglades. Orlean expanded upon the story, writing a book that reveals a whole world of eccentric and brilliant obsession. The Wild West feel of the Everglades and its swampy environs is clear, and the story is at times hilarious and moving. It is definitely one of my favorite books on the area, and you can also learn a lot about orchids. Be careful, though—you might just become obsessed.

Zimmerman, Stan. *A History of Smuggling in Florida: Rum Runners and Cocaine Cowboys.* Charleston, SC: The History Press, 2006. Wander through the Ten Thousand Islands and it becomes clear: This would be a good place to hide, or to get lost, or both. It's this geographic anomaly, plus Floridians' general sense of subversive fervor, that makes Florida a natural spot from which or to which to smuggle drugs, booze, or other contraband.

Fiction

Matthiessen, Peter. *Killing Mister Watson.* New York: Vintage, reprint edition, 1991. It's part of a trilogy, along with *Lostman's River* and *Bone by Bone,* that paints a vivid picture of the early settlers living at the edge of civilization in the Ten Thousand Islands and the Everglades. Drawn from bits of historical fact, Matthiessen creates a fictionalized oral history set in Chokoloskee and other little mangrove islands. Edgar J. Watson, who is said to have gunned down the outlaw Belle Starr, came here to elude the law but instead faced the rough frontier justice of his fellow fugitives. It's an absolute must-read if you plan to spend any time in Everglades City. At age 81, Matthiessen collapsed the three stories into one book (as he originally intended) and released the revision as an 890-page novel called *Shadow Country.* For this work he received his second National Book Award.

FORT MYERS, SANIBEL, AND CAPTIVA
Nonfiction

Smoot, Tom. *The Edisons of Fort Myers.* Sarasota, FL: Pineapple Press, 2004. Lots of biographies cover Edison's public life as a world-famous inventor, but this one explores the big loves of his life: Mina Miller and Fort Myers, Florida. It's an especially fun read preceded or followed by a visit to the Edison estate.

Turner, Gregg. *Railroads of Southwest Florida.* Charleston, SC: Arcadia Publishing, 2000. Turner's written a ton about Florida railroads, so he's something of an expert on the rails. This book covers Henry Plant, the Florida Southern Railway, and all the other railway endeavors that prompted accelerated growth in this part of Florida. The writing isn't super exciting, but there's a lot of good information here. He has a newer one called *Florida Railroads in the 1920s* (2006) about the "Big Three's" race in the state.

Witherington, Blair and Dawn. *Florida's Living Beaches: A Guide for the Curious Beachcomber.* Sarasota, FL: Pineapple Press, 2007. A handy paperback identification guide, it packs in 822 items, 983 color images, and 431 maps describing the state's plants, animals, minerals, and artificially created objects.

Fiction

Hiaasen, Carl. Where do you even put Carl Hiaasen in a guide about the Gulf Coast? He's everywhere in south Florida, bigger than a novelist, bigger than a *Miami Herald* columnist. He's like a rock star around here (he even owns a Fender Strat that Dave Barry helped him pick out), with so many titles it's hard to pick which ones to list. The most recent is *Star Island,* New York: Grand Central Publishing, 2010; before that *Scat, Downhill Life, Flush, Nature Girl, Skinny Dip, Basket Case, Sick Puppy, Lucky You, Stormy Weather, Strip Tease, Native Tongue, Skin Tight, Double Whammy,* and *Tourist Season.* He has a penchant for two-word titles and writes mostly about southern Florida. He likes to write about smart hookers with a heart of gold, finds tough-guy baldies especially amusing, and is a bulldoggish environmentalist. In addition to his novels, Hiaasen has also published two collections of his newspaper columns, *Kick Ass* and *Paradise Screwed,* and an anti-Disney book called *Team Rodent.*

White, Randy Wayne. *Sanibel Flats*. New York: St. Martin's Press, 1991. Randy Wayne White was a fishing guide at Tarpon Bay on Sanibel for 13 years. A prolific mystery novelist, he writes mostly about this part of southwest Florida, with numerous novels featuring super tough-guy Doc Ford solving various mysteries (*Black Widow, Hunter's Moon, The Deadlier Sex, Cuban Death-Lift, The Deep Six, The Heat Islands, The Man Who Invented Florida, Captiva, North of Havana, The Mangrove Coast, Ten Thousand Islands, Shark River, Twelve Mile Limit, Everglades, Tampa Burn*, and *Dead of Night*). In all his books, Florida is one of the main characters, described in all its glory. White is a columnist for *Outside Magazine* and *Men's Health*, and he's written lots of other books of essays and such, including *Batfishing in the Rain Forest* and a fish cookbook.

SARASOTA COUNTY
Photography
Evans, Walker. *Walker Evans: Florida*. Los Angeles: J. Paul Getty Trust Publications, 2000. Everyone knows Walker Evans's gutsy, gripping Depression-era photographs. But for six weeks in 1942, Evans focused his lens on Sarasota for *Mangrove Coast*, a book by Karl Bickel. These are some of the wonderful photos he took during that time of the circus's underbelly, old people, railroad cars, and decrepit Florida buildings. Text is by novelist Robert Plunket.

Nonfiction
Apps, Jerry. *Tents, Tigers, and the Ringling Brothers*. Madison: University of Wisconsin Press, 2006. Apps writes pretty much exclusively about Wisconsin. But this story started there, in Baraboo, Wisconsin, to be exact. It's a wonderful history of the Ringling Circus and the seven brothers who made "The Greatest Show on Earth" from scratch. It's got great photos of early circus life.

TAMPA
Travel Guide
Murphy, Bill. *Fox 13 Tampa Bay One Tank Trips With Bill Murphy*. St. Petersburg, FL: Seaside Publishing, 2004. An offshoot of a television segment Murphy does, the books showcase 52 Florida-based adventures that are all within a full tank of Tampa. It's got lots of off-the-beaten-path attractions, all worthy of your time, from Pioneer Florida Museum in Dade City to the excellent camping at Fort De Soto Park in Pinellas County.

Drama
Cruz, Nilo. *Anna in the Tropics*. New York: Theatre Communications Group, 2003. This play won Cruz the Pulitzer Prize for drama in 2003. It is a romantic drama, loosely a retelling of Tolstoy's *Anna Karenina*, that depicts a Cuban-American family of cigar makers in Ybor City (Tampa) in 1930. It tells the story of the factory's new lector, a person hired to read aloud great works of literature and the day's news to the cigar workers. A beautiful stage play—keep your eyes open for any performances of it during your visit to Florida.

ST. PETERSBURG AND PINELLAS COUNTY
Nonfiction
Klinkenberg, Jeff. *Seasons of Real Florida*. Gainesville: University Press of Florida, 2004. *St. Petersburg Times* writer Klinkenberg may have invented the term "Real Florida," which means the Old Florida, without Disney, fancy golf courses, or really anything glamorous. This book is an assemblage of largely humorous essays he's written for the paper that tell great stories about the people, flora, and fauna in west-central Florida. Another collection of essays entitled *Pilgrim in the Land of Alligators* was published in 2008 by the University Press of Florida.

Fiction

MacDonald, John. *Condominium*. New York: Fawcett, reissue edition, 1985. For most of his life MacDonald was considered a pulp fiction writer, and prolific, who spent more than half his life in west-central Florida, first in Clearwater, then in Sarasota and Siesta Key. This book still seems fresh, especially in light of 2004's hurricane season. The setting is Golden Sands, a Sunbelt condo in the path of Hurricane Ella. It's a multicharacter disaster book—think *The Towering Inferno* or something like that. (*Cape Fear*, by the way, was based on a MacDonald book.)

THE NATURE COAST
Nonfiction

Warner, David T. *Vanishing Florida: A Personal Guide to Sights Rarely Seen*. Montgomery, AL: River City Publishing, 2001. I love this book, written by a guy who sounds like a dead ringer for Ernest Hemingway (Papa features occasionally in the book, so maybe Warner fancies a resemblance himself). Some of this book appeared as features in *Sarasota* magazine—mostly it's chapter-long ruminations and odes to small towns along the Gulf Coast (especially good chapters on Cedar Key and other parts of the Nature Coast), with lots of drinking and womanizing thrown into the mix.

Fiction

Cook, Ann. *Trace Their Shadows*. San Jose, New York, Lincoln, and Shanghai: Mystery and Suspense Press, 2001, and *Shadow Over Cedar Key*. San Jose, New York, Lincoln, and Shanghai: Mystery and Suspense Press, 2003. As a baby the author was the model for the original Gerber baby (daughter of cartoonist Leslie Turner, who drew the famous baby head in 1928), but as an adult she has turned to mystery writing. The cool thing about these books is the setting—they are easy, beachy reads with plucky reporter Brandy O'Bannon having exciting adventures all over charming Cedar Key.

THE FORGOTTEN COAST
Nonfiction

Cerulean, Susan, ed. *Between Two Rivers*. Tallahassee, FL: Red Hills Writers Project, 2004. If you can find it—give it a serious college try—you'll be mesmerized by this anthology of 29 writers telling stories about the rich cultural and environmental landscapes of the Red Hills and northern Gulf Coast. (The two rivers in question are the Aucilla to the east and the Apalachicola to the west.) The Red Hills Writers Project is a group of mostly Florida writers with a serious nature and ecological bent to their writing. Editors include Susan Cerulean (biologist, activist, and writer of *Book of the Everglades* and *Wild Heart of Florida*), Southern author Janisse Ray (*Ecology of a Cracker Childhood, Wild Card Quilt*), and Tallahassee poet Laura Newton (poetry editor of the *Apalachee Review*).

Rudloe, Jack. *The Living Dock of Panacea*. New York: Alfred A. Knopf, 1977. Rudloe is one of the contributors to *Between Two Rivers*. He's a longtime Florida naturalist, director of Gulf Specimen Marine Laboratory, and author of nine or so books on the area. He's big into turtles (*Time of the Turtle, Search for the Great Turtle Mother*), but this older book (recently reprinted with a new introduction and called just *The Living Dock*) is a great rumination on the Gulf Coast's marinelife, told from the author's floating dock in the tiny fishing community of Panacea.

THE EMERALD COAST
Travel Guide

Hollis, Tim. *Florida's Miracle Strip: From Redneck Riviera to Emerald Coast*. Jackson: University Press of Mississippi, 2004. This is a nostalgic look at the area that is now the fairly glamorous Panama City Beach, Fort

Walton Beach, Destin, and Pensacola Beach, with lots of fun descriptions of the campy Old Florida attractions that used to bring people here—like Castle Dracula and the Snake-A-Torium. It's got lots of cool vintage photos and postcards.

Fishing

Dew, Gregory. *The Barefoot Fisherman's Guide to the Emerald Coast: From Gulf Shores, Alabama, to Apalachicola, Florida.* Birmingham, AL: Crane Hill Publishers, 1999. It's a little techie, with lots of talk about tackle and rigs, so the beginning angler might just be interested in chapter three, which enumerates 40 or so fabulous fishing spots on this gorgeous stretch of coast. Dew also gives great information on all of the species you're likely to catch here, and then what to do with them if you aim to eat 'em.

Hoskins, Jim. *Fishing the Local Waters: Gulf Shores to Panama City.* Gulf Breeze, FL: Maximum Press, 2006. A guide to angling in Florida's Gulf Coast waters, written by two local anglers, includes LORAN coordinates for 50 tried-and-true spots. Even for the rookie it's a valuable book because it gives a listing of guides and services in the area.

PENSACOLA
Nonfiction

Pensacola Historical Society. *Pensacola in Vintage Postcards.* Charleston, SC: Arcadia Publishing, 2004. It's just a packet of postcards, but a riffle through will give you a sense of the way Pensacola used to be.

ALABAMA GULF SHORES
Nonfiction

Jackson, Harvey. *The Rise and Decline of the Redneck Riviera: An Insider's History to the Florida-Alabama Coast.* Athens: The University of Georgia Press, 2013.

Rogers, William, et al. *Alabama: The History of the Deep South State.* Tuscaloosa: University Alabama Press, 2010. A comprehensive history of the state. The book is divided into three main sections; the first concludes in 1865, the second in 1920, and the third brings the story to the present.

CHILDREN'S BOOKS ABOUT THE GULF COAST
Travel Guides

DeWire, Elinor. *Florida Lighthouses for Kids.* Sarasota, FL: Pineapple Press, 2004. Great pictures and fun stories about Florida's 33 lighthouses (many on the Gulf Coast)—it gives kids something to read in the car and a way to participate in the process of planning a trip.

Lantz, Peggy, and Wendy Hale. *The Young Naturalist's Guide to Florida.* Sarasota, FL: Pineapple Press, 2006. Again, this gives kids a fun window through which to see the kooky plants and animals of the state, with information on careers in the environmental field.

Fiction

DiCamillo, Kate. *Because of Winn-Dixie.* Cambridge, MA: Candlewick Press, 2001. Now a major motion picture, this book about 10-year-old India Opal Buloni and her ugly dog Winn-Dixie (named for where she found him) has captured the attention of lots of families. It's a great story, set in a fictional town of Naomi, Florida (I like to think it's modeled on someplace down toward Port Charlotte). Opal's had kind of a hard life, so it might be too much for a sensitive kid.

George, Jean Craighead. *Everglades.* New York: HarperTrophy, reprint edition, 1997. Geared toward littler kids (maybe 5-8), it tells the story of a man poling through the Everglades and teaching his five young passengers about the 'Glades' sawgrass, hundreds of species of animals, and fragile ecosystem. It's not as preachy as it sounds—the environmental message is light, and Wendell Minor's illustrations are wonderful. Newbery medalist Jean Craighead George has written lots of wonderful children's books with the Florida wilderness at their centers—older kids might like the eco-mystery *The Missing 'Gator of Gumbo Limbo,* New York: HarperTrophy, 1993.

Hiaasen, Carl. *Hoot.* New York: Knopf Books for Young Readers, 2002. Geared for readers 9-12, this Newbery-honor book by Florida great Carl Hiaasen does double duty. As with many of Hiaasen's novels there's a heavy environmental message (this one about protecting rare burrowing owls and their habitat), but it also tells an exciting tale of new kid Roy Eberhardt, who moves to Coconut Grove and gets mixed up in a crazy ecological adventure with Mullet Fingers and bully-beater Beatrice in a fight against Mother Paula's All-American Pancake House. A middle-school mystery, the language and plot are edgy. A second book, *Flush,* New York: Knopf Books for Young Readers, 2005, follows a similar formula: Misunderstood teen iconoclast takes a stand and helps preserve the environment in the face of adults' scheming machinations.

Hogan, Linda. *Power.* New York: W.W. Norton & Company, 1999. In an area that was once populated exclusively by Native American tribes, it's exciting to read about what life must have been like before all the development. This is a coming-of-age story about a 16-year-old Native American girl named Omishito, who witnesses the killing of a sacred animal, the Florida panther. It is based on a true story.

Konigsburg, E. L. *T-backs, T-shirts, Coat and Suit.* New York: Aladdin, 2003. A more contemporary book from the author of the classic Newbery winner *From the Mixed Up Files of Mrs. Basil E. Frankweiler,* this one tells the story of 12-year-old Chloe, who spends the summer in Florida with her wild aunt Bernadette, who drives a commissary van and sells junk food at roadsides. For ages 9-12.

Rawlings, Marjorie Kinnan. *The Yearling.* New York: Simon Pulse, 50th edition, 1988. Rawlings wrote 10 books while a resident in Cross Creek, Florida, the most popular of which was *The Yearling,* which won a Pulitzer Prize in fiction in 1939. It tells the story of scrappy young Jody Baxter and his pet fawn Flag, who together roam the Florida scrublands wrestling big swamp gators and cavorting with bear cubs. Rawlings's second-best book is called, simply, *Cross Creek,* also with the same earthy Florida Cracker dialect.

Smith, Patrick D. *A Land Remembered.* Sarasota, FL: Pineapple Press, 1998. Beginning with Tobias MacIvey's arrival in Florida in 1858, this young-adult historical novel tells the story of three generations of Floridians carving out a hardscrabble life for themselves in the wilds of central Florida. This sweeping story is rich in Florida history.

GUIDES TO FLORIDA WILDLIFE
Birds

Maehr, David. *Florida's Birds: A Field Guide and Reference.* Sarasota, FL: Pineapple Press, 2005. For birders and rookies alike, birds can be quickly identified in this book via picture (pretty ones with birds grouped by similar species), text, or index. Maps indicate when migratory birds are present or breeding, and where.

Tekiela, Stan. *Birds of Florida Field Guide.* Cambridge, MN: Adventure Publications, 2005. It's a great small-sized book organized by bird color. This makes it easy to narrow things down when you've just spotted a flash of wing color in your binoculars.

Even better than these books, though, is the sand- and waterproof *Florida's Gulf Coast Birds* flip map illustrated by Ernest C. Simmons (visit www.floridabooks.com if you can't find it in area bookstores). It puts birds into rough groups—wading birds, shorebirds, wetland birds, birds of prey, etc. And another great resource is the spring and fall bird migration tables at www.birdnature.com.

Fish

Arnov, Boris. *Fish Florida: Saltwater/Better than Luck—The Foolproof Guide to Florida Saltwater Fishing.* Houston: Gulf Publishing, 2002. This is a fairly good beginner book: It describes a kind of fish, let's say amberjack, then tells you how it fights (fiercely); appropriate tackle, whether you're spinning or plug casting or fly-fishing; and technique for live bait or light tackle casting. It also gives catch and size limits and other regulations.

Dew, Gregory. *The Barefoot Fisherman's Guide to the Emerald Coast: From Gulf Shore, Alabama, to Apalachicola, Florida.* Birmingham, AL: Crane Hill Publishers, 1999. Flip to chapter three, which enumerates 40 or so fabulous fishing spots on this gorgeous stretch of coast, and what you're likely to catch there.

Mammals

Adams, Alto. *A Florida Cattle Ranch.* Sarasota, FL: Pineapple Press, 1998. You'll learn about Cracker cows, scrub, and the hardscrabble world of Florida ranching.

Maehr, David. *The Florida Panther: Life and Death of a Vanishing Carnivore.* Washington DC: Island Press, 1997. The author makes these endangered cougars spring to life in their last frontier in the Big Cypress National Preserve and around the Okaloacoochee Slough.

Sobczak, Charles. *Alligators, Sharks & Panthers: Deadly Encounters with Florida's Top Predator—Man.* Sanibel, FL: Indigo Press, 2006. It chronicles grisly attacks, but with an underlying environmentalist's message about humans mucking about in creatures' natural habitats.

Butterflies

Daniels, Jaret. *Butterflies of Florida Field Guide (Our Nature Field Guides).* Cambridge, MN: Adventure Publications, 2003. It's a lovely field guide with great pictures and not-too-Latin text.

Shells

Witherington, Blair and Dawn. *Florida's Seashells.* Sarasota, FL: Pineapple Press, 2007. It's light enough to pack in your beach bag, with good color photos and interesting text about the marine animals.

Where to Find Good Florida Wildlife Books

Haslam's Book Store (www.haslams.com) is a St. Petersburg institution and one of the best bookstores in Florida, while in Tampa **Inkwood Books** (http://inkwoodbooks.com) has a broad Florida nature, wildlife, and gardening section.

Pineapple Press (www.pineapplepress.com) is the best local small press, producing a handful of books on Florida each year, all of high caliber and many with an environmental bent.

The **University Press of Florida** (www.upf.com), the consolidated publishing efforts of all the Florida state universities, groups Florida books by helpful categories (environment, people, arts, and artifacts).

Florida Plants Online Bookstore (www.floridaplants.com) indeed lists lots of excellent books on local flora, but its reach also extends to fauna, highbrow literature, and books for young readers.

438

RESOURCES
INTERNET RESOURCES

For rare or out-of-print books, **Grove Antiquarian** (www.abebooks.com) traffics in preowned books, specializing in south Florida and the Caribbean.

The bookstore at **Everglades National Park** (www.nps.gov) features a long reading list of Everglades-centric books. And way up in Cedar Key, there's **Curmudgeonalia** (2nd St. and D St., Cedar Key, 352/543-6789), which proffers a discerning collection of birding, naturalist, and offbeat Florida history books.

Internet Resources

GENERAL GULF COAST

Visit Florida
www.visitflorida.com
For a good introduction to the Gulf Coast, contact the state's official tourist information organization, Visit Florida (or call 888/7-FLA-USA), for a copy of its excellent annual *Visit Florida* guide, the *Florida Events Calendar,* or *Florida Trails.* Online resources include a number of electronic travel guides (for which you can order printed versions if you prefer). Visit Florida also has a 24-hour multilingual tourist assistance hotline at 800/656-8777.

Florida Secrets, The Insider's Guide to Unique Destinations
www.floridasecrets.com
The graphics have a cheese factor and it's heavy on the advertising, but the site is a treasure trove of little-known destinations in Florida, divided up on the Gulf Coast by southwest, west-central, eastern, and western Panhandle.

FISHING

Florida Fishing
www.floridafishing.com
It's a clearinghouse of fishing guides, fishing charters, and fishing captains in the state, divided by region.

CAMPING

Florida Association of RV Parks & Campgrounds
www.campflorida.com
It's an easy-to-use comprehensive database of Florida campgrounds, including amenities information for each site. You can also go on this website and order a print version of the guide. To make reservations at a Florida state campground (or in any state), however, you must utilize www.reserveamerica.com.

PARKS AND FORESTS

Florida State Parks Department
www.floridastateparks.org
Find a park, its affiliated camping and lodging, or get a bead on what events are coming up along the Gulf Coast. The site also has maps and directions to Florida's state parks, and it runs an amateur photo contest of state park photography.

Florida Trail Association
www.floridatrail.org
The Florida Trail Association is a nonprofit that builds, maintains, promotes, and protects hiking trails across the state of Florida, especially the 1,400-mile Florida Trail. From this site you can download all kinds of trail maps and park brochures.

SPORTS

Florida Sports Foundation
www.flasports.com
The foundation usually posts the "Grapefruit League" Florida spring-training baseball schedules on its website late in January. Another way to find out about spring training for your favorite team is by visiting the website of Major League Baseball (www.mlb.com).

NAPLES, THE EVERGLADES, AND THE PARADISE COAST

Naples, Marco Island and Everglades Convention & Visitors Bureau

www.paradisecoast.com

A slick website for the area, it features convenient charts for local accommodations, a round-up of attractions and recreation, and well-written background on the area. The only thing that's missing here is detailed restaurant info.

Guide to Southwest Florida

www.florida-southwest.com

Naples and Marco Island enticements are laid out in categories, and the restaurant write-ups here are fairly reliable.

FORT MYERS, SANIBEL, AND CAPTIVA

Lee County Visitor and Convention Bureau

www.fortmyers-sanibel.com
www.leevcb.com

One of the most professional-looking sites around from a convention bureau, its information is helpful, current, and entertainingly written.

Charlotte Harbor and the Gulf Islands

www.charlotteharbortravel.com

This area gets short shrift due to its proximity to more well-known vacation destinations. Still, as the website shows, Charlotte Harbor has loads to do and abundant natural beauty. It has an easily downloadable list of local accommodations.

SARASOTA COUNTY

Sarasota Convention & Visitors Bureau

www.visitsarasota.org

The convention and visitors bureau's award-winning site is about as user-friendly as they come, with easily sortable menus of restaurants, accommodations, outdoor attractions, and more. The excellent feature stories on the area's lures are written by local travel writers.

The site is offered in English, Spanish, and German. A second site, www.discovernaturalsarasota.org, focuses exclusively on the natural draws of the area, including beaches, parks, gardens, and historic sites.

Anna Maria Island Chamber of Commerce

www.annamariaislandchamber.org

Too far from Tampa in the north and too far from Sarasota to its south, Anna Maria Island doesn't really get covered in other, bigger regional websites. This one doesn't have as many bells and whistles as other sites, but it's got all the basics of where to stay, what to do, and where to eat.

TAMPA

Tampa Bay Convention & Visitors Bureau

www.visittampabay.com

This is a good site for background on the Bay Area as well as travel strategies and accommodations.

Creative Loafing

www.cltampa.com

The local alternative weekly newspaper has a great website. The writing is provocative and witty and covers politics, arts and entertainment, local events, and regional news.

ST. PETERSBURG AND PINELLAS COUNTY

St. Petersburg/Clearwater Area Convention & Visitors Bureau

www.visitstpeteclearwater.com

Similar to the Tampa Bay Convention and Visitors Bureau site, this one focuses, not surprisingly, on the beaches. It's easy to book a room from this site, and it features excellent downloadable maps.

Tampa Bay Times

www.tampabay.com

The daily metro paper covers local as well as national news. It has a great website, and the paper's movie, book, and pop music reviews are notable. The paper's food-critic column by Laura Reiley is also worth the read for her outstanding, mouthwatering descriptions of the area's best eats.

THE NATURE COAST

Citrus County Tourist Development Council

www.visitcitrus.com

This is an interactive site with a wealth of information on Homosassa, Crystal River, and environs. It's a good site from which to choose a manatee snorkeling trip or fishing charter.

Cedar Key Chamber of Commerce

www.cedarkey.org

The chamber's site is a fine resource for information specifically about Cedar Key, especially good for local events.

Steinhatchee Landing Resort

www.steinhatcheelanding.com

Steinhatchee is one of the Gulf Coast's least-known destinations, and generally the web doesn't help much to illuminate. This is the best site about the area, a site brought to you from the most popular upscale resort on the Nature Coast. The recreation section is helpful in planning a trip.

THE FORGOTTEN COAST

Forgotten CoastLine Online

www.forgottencoastline.com

My favorite resource for Forgotten Coastobilia, it's the website for a monthly tabloid of the same name, heavily impacted by local Chuck Spicer. It's quirky and opinionated, like a good little local paper should be.

Apalachicola Bay Chamber of Commerce

www.apalachicolabay.org

It's a little more straightforward and no-nonsense than the Forgotten CoastLine site, but it has good background information on the area and a list of chamber members that actually provides guidance when you're choosing a fishing charter or beach house rental.

THE EMERALD COAST

Beaches of South Walton

www.beachesofsouthwalton.com

About as nice as a site like this can be, this resource well describes the dozen-plus little communities that make up the area, providing useful insight into where to eat, what to do, and where to stay. (Seaside has its own website, www.seasidefl.com, that is even more impressively stylish.)

Emerald Coast Convention & Visitors Bureau

www.emeraldcoastfl.com

This is a fairly serviceable site that explores the areas of Destin, Fort Walton Beach, and Okaloosa Island. The best feature is the lodging locator, in which you can sort by a long list of amenities.

Panama City Beach Convention & Visitors Bureau

www.visitpanamacitybeach.com

For information specifically on Panama City Beach, this is the best resource. It offers lots of spring break-specific material during the months of March and April. From the site you can also order a 96-page vacation guide that provides helpful and accurate information about activities, entertainment, accommodations, and dining.

PENSACOLA

Pensacola Bay Area Convention & Visitors Bureau

www.visitpensacola.com

All there is to do in Pensacola, Pensacola Beach, and Perdido Key is outlined in an organized fashion, with a special emphasis on the beaches as well as the historical and military attractions.

ALABAMA GULF SHORES

Gulf Shores and Orange Beach Tourism

www.gulfshores.com

This site is a great resource for planning

your trip to Gulf Shores and Orange Beach. A daily updated entertainment and event calendar gives you the scoop on what's happening in the area, and a section that features deals and packages is a great place to find specials on lodging, restaurants, and activities here.

South Mobile County Tourism Authority
www.dauphinislandtourism.com

This site provides extensive listings for area restaurants, events, attractions, and lodging. A nice feature is the section on birding, where you'll find an overview of the area's best birding destinations.

Index

List of Maps

Acknowledgments

I'd like to thank everyone at Avalon Travel for all their help in making this project possible, as well as Laura Reiley, author of the first and second editions of *Moon Florida Gulf Coast*.

I'd also like to thank the following people for their time and expertise during the researching of this guide: Sarah Brazwell at Sandestin Golf and Beach Resort; Kelly Grass Prieto at Hayworth Creative; Anita Grove of the Apalachicola Bay Chamber of Commerce; Lee Rose of Lee County Visitor and Convention Bureau; Hue Reynolds at the Florida Department of Education; Bob Thomas at Florida State University; Katie Kole at Visit Tallahassee; Michelle Moran at Sunstream Resorts; Shannon Hagen of the Beaches of South Walton Tourist Development Council; Sandee Harraden at North American Canoe Tours and the Ivey House in Everglades City; Laura A. Lee of the Pensacola Bay Area Convention & Visitors Bureau; Alissa Hopkins at the Morean Arts Center; Josh Hall at the St. Pete and Clearwater Convention & Visitors Bureau; Jamie Veronica at the Big Cat Rescue in Tampa; JoNell Modys of the Greater Naples, Marco Island & Everglades City CVB; Lindsay Bennett at the Panama City CVB; Kelly Robinson of Visit Florida; Shawn Collier and Angie Hester; and all the wonderful people I've met while traveling across the Gulf Coast of Florida.

Also Available

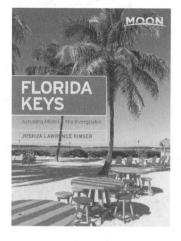

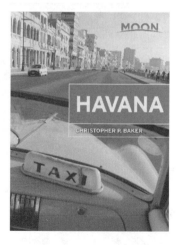

MAP SYMBOLS

▨▨▨	Expressway	★	Highlight	✗	Airfield	⚲	Golf Course
———	Primary Road	○	City/Town	✈	Airport	🅿	Parking Area
———	Secondary Road	◉	State Capital	▲	Mountain	▟	Archaeological Site
▪ ▪ ▪	Unpaved Road	⊛	National Capital	✦	Unique Natural Feature	🍶	Church
- - - -	Trail	★	Point of Interest			⛽	Gas Station
··········	Ferry	•	Accommodation	🐚	Waterfall	⬭	Glacier
▬·▬·▬	Railroad	▼	Restaurant/Bar	▲	Park		Mangrove
▨▨▨	Pedestrian Walkway	▪	Other Location	🚩	Trailhead		Reef
▥▥▥▥	Stairs	⋀	Campground	⛷	Skiing Area		Swamp

CONVERSION TABLES

°C = (°F – 32) / 1.8
°F = (°C x 1.8) + 32
1 inch = 2.54 centimeters (cm)
1 foot = 0.304 meters (m)
1 yard = 0.914 meters
1 mile = 1.6093 kilometers (km)
1 km = 0.6214 miles
1 fathom = 1.8288 m
1 chain = 20.1168 m
1 furlong = 201.168 m
1 acre = 0.4047 hectares
1 sq km = 100 hectares
1 sq mile = 2.59 square km
1 ounce = 28.35 grams
1 pound = 0.4536 kilograms
1 short ton = 0.90718 metric ton
1 short ton = 2,000 pounds
1 long ton = 1.016 metric tons
1 long ton = 2,240 pounds
1 metric ton = 1,000 kilograms
1 quart = 0.94635 liters
1 US gallon = 3.7854 liters
1 Imperial gallon = 4.5459 liters
1 nautical mile = 1.852 km

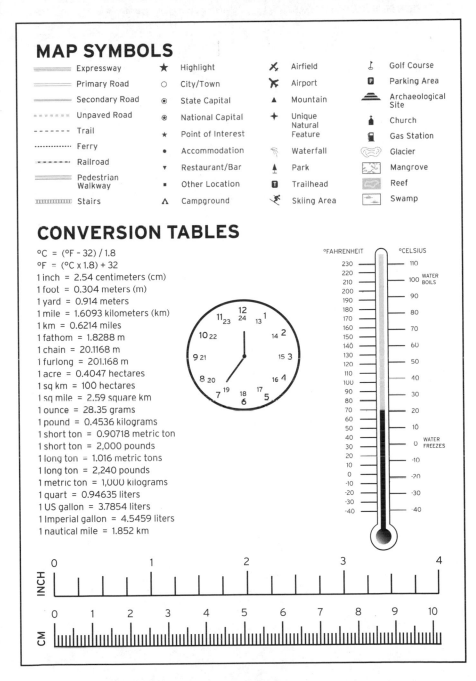

°FAHRENHEIT   °CELSIUS

230 — 110
220
210 — 100 WATER BOILS
200
190 — 90
180 — 80
170
160 — 70
150
140 — 60
130
120 — 50
110
100 — 40
90
80 — 30
70
60 — 20
50
40 — 10
30
20 — 0 WATER FREEZES
10
0 — -10
-10
-20 — -30
-30
-40 — -40

INCH 0 1 2 3 4

CM 0 1 2 3 4 5 6 7 8 9 10

MOON FLORIDA GULF COAST

Avalon Travel
An imprint of Perseus Books
A Hachette Book Group company
1700 Fourth Street
Berkeley, CA 94710, USA
www.moon.com

Editor: Rachel Feldman
Series Manager: Kathryn Ettinger
Copy Editor: Ashley Benning
Graphics Coordinator: Darren Alessi
Production Coordinator: Darren Alessi
Cover Design: Faceout Studios, Charles Brock
Interior Design: Domini Dragoone
Moon Logo: Tim McGrath
Map Editor: Kat Bennett
Cartographers: Karin Dahl, Brian Shotwell
Indexer: Greg Jewett

ISBN-13: 978-1-63121-399-1
ISSN: 1556-0309

Printing History
1st Edition — 2005
5th Edition — October 2016
5 4 3 2

Front cover photo: Naples, Florida © Brian Jannsen / Alamy Stock Photo
Back cover photo: © Sdbower | Dreamstime.com
Interior photos: © Joshua Kinser except page 24 © Stephen Meese/123RF.com; page 136 © Todd Arena /123RF.com; page 220 © Lloyd Luecke/123RF.com

Printed in Canada by Friesens

All recommendations, including those for sights, activities, hotels, restaurants, and shops, are based on each author's individual judgment. We do not accept payment for inclusion in our travel guides, and our authors don't accept free goods or services in exchange for positive coverage.

Although every effort was made to ensure that the information was correct at the time of going to press, the author and publisher do not assume and hereby disclaim any liability to any party for any loss or damage caused by errors, omissions, or any potential travel disruption due to labor or financial difficulty, whether such errors or omissions result from negligence, accident, or any other cause.